Mission to the World

MISSION
TO
THE WORLD

A History of Missions in the Church of the Nazarene Through 1985

by
J. FRED PARKER

Nazarene Publishing House
Kansas City, Missouri

Unless otherwise indicated, all Scripture quotations are from *The Holy Bible, New International Version,* copyright © 1973, 1978, 1984 by the International Bible Society, and are used by permission.
KJV—King James Version.

10   9   8   7   6   5   4   3   2

Contents

PART THREE
Appendixes

Foreword

"We are debtors to every man to give him the gospel in the same measure we have received it."
—P. F. Bresee

"The Full Gospel to the Whole World by the Printed Page."
—Motto, Nazarene Publishing House

"That the World May Know."
—Theme, Church of the Nazarene, 1985-89

"Go ye into all the world, and preach the gospel to every creature."
—Jesus Christ

From its beginning the Church of the Nazarene has taken its missionary mandate very seriously. At the same time the infant denomination was starting new churches and expanding its frontiers across the United States, Canada, and the British Isles, missionaries were climbing on trains, boarding oceangoing steamers, riding oxcarts, lacing up hiking boots, paddling canoes, using every means to make their way into the world's unexplored interiors. There they found people who otherwise would have been overlooked, and took them the good news of Jesus Christ.

By the time modern transportation had dramatically shortened the distances, these missionaries had already planted congregations, built clinics and hospitals, put up school buildings, and significantly impacted cultures and societies with the gospel's life-changing message. New advances in science and technology increased the effectiveness of missionary outreach, and the worldwide church grew even faster. The tempo increased because sacrificial service never diminished.

Now commitment of a different nature, just as demanding and requiring every bit as much labor and faith, recognizes the place these Christian brothers and sisters have in the continuing growth of the church. A new word, *internationalization*, has entered our vocabulary.

General church gatherings have become scenes of rainbow-type mixtures of browns, blacks, yellows, and whites, all sharing in debate and concern for the church's future. Missionary zeal now characterizes the entire church from Canada's most northern reaches to the tip of Argentina in the far south, from the U.S.A. in the west to the Far East, and in many, many countries in between.

Nazarenes are a diverse group. Language, culture, history, and racial background all divide us. As the sun circles the globe, from the time the day begins at the international date line in the mid-Pacific, it shines on a wide variety of worship structures. Nazarenes gather in thatch-roofed churches, makeshift tabernacles, and beautiful brick edifices to declare a common faith that unites us in love and service. This is summed up in what is considered unofficially to be the theme song of Nazarenes everywhere:

> *"Holiness unto the Lord" is our watchword and song,*
> *"Holiness unto the Lord" as we're marching along.*
> *Sing it, shout it, loud and long,*
> *"Holiness unto the Lord," now and forever.*

—LELIA N. MORRIS

The updated and official history of this global enterprise could properly be called "Acts, Chapter 29." Dr. Fred Parker, while being technically accurate and giving attention to important historical details, has written in a style that is reminiscent of Dr. Luke's own writing of the Acts of the Apostles. Students in the classroom following this text as a guide for study, as well as ministers and laymen throughout the church, will be equally inspired with the historical document that follows. All of us are indebted to Dr. Parker, a writer of great skill as well as a lifelong student of church development and structure, for the legacy he leaves his denomination. His love and loyalty to the Church of the Nazarene, especially to the missionaries who have given lifetimes of service, is clearly seen in these pages. Yet his bias does not restrain him from authentically reporting the facts. For that reason, the contents of this book will never be outdated but will continue to serve as a reference for generations of missiological students, both now and in the challenging years to come.

—JERALD D. JOHNSON
General Superintendent

Preface

"Missionary activity is always a sign of vitality in the Church," says noted historian Stephen Neill, and the Church of the Nazarene is a splendid illustration of this fact. Recognized as among the fastest-growing denominations in its first 77 years, it also stands in the vanguard of missionary advancement. Over one-third of its members are now products of that missionary effort.

This volume seeks to capture the intriguing story of the church's outreach around the world. It is a study in contrasts—dramatic, explosive growth and disappointing retrenchment; exciting opportunities and discouraging reverses; high hopes and lonely struggle. But the overall picture is one of almost uninterrupted expansion.

The story of over 75 years of work in which over 75 countries have been reached cannot be adequately told within the confines of one volume. However, here is at least a distillation of what has gone on in the missionary program of the church around the world. To God be the glory for all that He has enabled the church to accomplish.

The book is in three parts, the first having to do with the organizational phase, principally the evolvement of the General Board and its strategic World Mission Department or Division. Included also are the developments in missionary program and strategy under each of the executive secretaries/directors of World Mission. Incidentally, distinction must be made between the Department of World Mission as a part of the governing General Board of the church, and the World Mission Division of Headquarters, which directs the day-by-day operation of the far-reaching, multimillion-dollar missionary enterprise.

The second part of the book is the story of each of the 75 fields in which the church is operating in world mission areas. This section is essentially a greatly revised and extended version of the author's earlier volume, *Into All the World*. The cutoff date of 1985 was arbitrarily chosen simply because the line had to be drawn somewhere. A General Assembly year and the conclusion of the term of Dr. L. Guy Nees as general director seemed a logical break point. But exciting developments are constantly taking place, and it has been difficult to put a period. In fact, there is some spillover into 1986. It will remain for others in later years to chronicle these succeeding developments.

Part Three includes two extensive appendixes of statistical and personnel information, including a complete roster of the 1,700 or so missionaries who have served the church during the 77 years covered by this volume. These are the true heroes of this narrative, and the church owes to them a great debt of gratitude.

Part Two was put together with the special assistance of a group of knowledgeable researchers intimately acquainted with the areas assigned to them. Their basic manuscripts were the core around which the various accounts were put together. Augmenting information came from many other sources, principally the missionaries themselves, plus considerable personal research. I am indebted to the dozens of missionaries and church leaders, particularly the regional directors, whose careful reading of the material provided helpful correction and added insights. These greatly improved both the accuracy and the quality of the original presentation. But special recognition is due those who were the pilot researchers:

Ted P. Esselstyn—Africa to 1960
Rose Handloser—Africa after 1960
Mary L. Scott—China, Taiwan, Hong Kong, the Philippines
Donald Owens—Japan, Korea
George E. Rench—Indonesia
Carol Anne Eby—Papua New Guinea
John E. Riley—Italy, the Middle East, Cape Verde Islands, Portugal
Honorato T. Reza—Mexico, Central America
Ruth O. Saxon—the Caribbean and the Bahamas
W. Howard Conrad—South America
John C. Oster—Middle Europe, Australia, New Zealand

Invaluable assistance has been generously given by John Smee, assistant to the general director in the World Mission office; by Helen Temple, for many years editor of *World Mission (Other Sheep)* magazine; by Steve Cooley and Stan Ingersoll in Nazarene Archives; by Franklin Cook, current editor of *World Mission,* who provided much helpful material on India; and by Mary Scott, who in the process of doing research for the World Mission office, jotted down numerous notes she thought might be of use to me. My special thanks is due the two most recent directors of the World Mission Division, Jerald D. Johnson and L. Guy Nees, with whom I have worked closely.

And while credits are being handed out, allow me the privilege of acknowledging the support and help of my wife, Neva, who has "sweat out" with me this seemingly endless task. She has typed the manuscript from my much-worked-over original handwritten material, many parts of it more than once, and offered helpful suggestions for improvement along the way.

This book stops short of being classified as the "official" missionary history of the church, yet a concerted effort has been made to achieve factual accuracy and consensual commentary. I regret the necessity, because of the restrictions of space, to omit innumerable stories of heroic missionary effort and achievement. There have been, and are, unsung heroes and heroines of the faith out there in the front lines to whom we owe great praise for their sacrificial efforts. May God bless them all.

—J. FRED PARKER

October 1986

PART ONE

**The Structure and Development
of the World Mission Enterprise**

Chapter 1

The Worldwide Mission
of the Church

"Go and make disciples of all nations" was Jesus' parting command to His disciples (Matt. 28:19). To the Jewish mind this was a revolutionary idea. Historically they had seen themselves as a "chosen people," the selected custodians of divine revelation. It was an ingrown, walled-in mentality that excluded all other peoples. Alien nations were to be shunned, not shared with.

Now these disciples were to become apostles—sent ones—emissaries of the risen Lord to all the world. Jerusalem was only the beginning point, for the message was to be carried "to the ends of the earth" (Acts 1:8). That arena of action was limitless, not confined to their Palestinian enclave.

The Messiah of the Jews was really the Savior of the world. Had not the announcement been made at Jesus' baptism that He would take away "the sin of the world" (John 1:29)? And had not the charter of the Kingdom been enunciated in Jesus' own words: "God so loved *the world* that he gave his one and only Son, that *whoever* believes in him shall not perish but have eternal life" (3:16, italics added)?

Confirmation came at Pentecost when the gift of languages made the testimony of the exuberant, Spirit-filled disciples intelligible to those of many nations. Subsequently, Thomas took the message eastward, possibly as far as India, to establish the gospel in Asia. The apostle Paul championed the Gentile cause and rooted the gospel in Europe, while Mark is reported to have first preached the gospel in Egypt and founded the church in Alexandria for a toehold in Africa. Other apostles and their followers went in different directions, and by the middle of the fourth century Christianity had won the support of the Roman emperor, Constantine.

In the chaos that followed the collapse of the Roman Empire, and as Europe fell into the period of the Dark Ages (500-1500), the gospel candle flickered low but was never fully extinguished. Out of the darkness shone such bright lights as Gregory the Great, bishop of Rome 590-604, who possessed great missionary zeal. It was he who sent Augustine to England in 596. Not long before, in 563, Columba had taken the gospel to Scotland; and over a century before, Patrick had gone to Ireland, thus making the British Isles a stronghold of the faith.

Then came Boniface (ca. 675-755), the Apostle of Germany, whom Stephen Neill has characterized as "the greatest of all the missionaries of the Dark Ages."[1]

Early in the sixth century, the Nestorians of Asia Minor began their great missionary movement eastward that ultimately reached China, Japan, Korea, and Southeast Asia.

In the midst of these advances a new threat to Christianity came from the Muslims, the followers of Muhammad. They marched steadily across the southern shores of the Mediterranean and thence across into Europe's Iberian Peninsula. It was as much a military operation as a missionary one, which eventuated in the confrontation with Christian forces at Tours in the heart of France in 732. There it was soundly repelled.

By the time Charlemagne (742-814) came on the scene, the church in Europe was ready for explosive advance. This great military leader and statesman "brought nominal Christianity to vast portions of Europe and was the prime mover in the Carolingian Renaissance that fostered learning and a wide variety of Christian activity."[2]

A disastrous interlude in the story of Christianity's advance was the period of the Crusades (1095-1291). This costly, misguided effort to drive the Muslims by military force from the Holy Land resulted in more than mere military defeat. Of greater consequence was the diversion of much fervor and energy from the true mission of the church. Ralph Winter, in *The Kingdom Strikes Back*, appraises the Crusades as "the most massive, tragic misconstrual of Christian mission in all history."[3]

The next threat came from the invading Vikings from the north. These fearsome warriors plundered the monastery outposts of the church and even penetrated into the heart of Europe. Their incursions were particularly damaging in the British Isles, where Christianity was well nigh stamped out.

Devastating as these attacks and attempted conquests were, however, they could have been withstood more effectively had it not been for the corruption within the church itself. A degenerate papacy brought discredit on the church and virtually destroyed its effectiveness as an evangelizing force.

But "God has always had a people," and in this dark hour great spiritual leaders arose. Bernard of Clairvaux (1090-1153) was a true evangelist who caught the wave of monastery reform begun at Cluny a century before and began a widespread revival movement throughout Europe. He was followed by the revered Francis of Assisi (1181[2?]-1226). The friars (preaching monks) were the evangelists of the day.

The Waldensians were the first "Protestants" who sought to restore the fervor of New Testament Christianity to the church. Their influence from the 12th to the 15th centuries was significant. Other reformers followed in their train until the 16th-century Protestant Reformation burst upon the scene, dispelling much of the darkness of the previous millennium. Luther, Calvin, Melanchthon, Zwingli, and Knox were the most influential of the Reformers. But the emergence of the Protestant church was not the boon to evangelism that might have been anticipated. It revitalized the people within the immediate orbit of the church, but outreach was not a vital concern.

The Pietists and their successors, the Moravians, however, did catch the spirit of the Great Commission and developed a network of mission stations around the world. As Stephen Neill observes, they "tended to go to the most remote, unfavorable, and neglected part of the surface of the earth."[4] It was the Moravians who had such a profound spiritual influence on John Wesley during his voyage to America. This eventuated in his life-changing experience that propelled him into the leadership of the great 18th-century evangelical revival in England.

The age of exploration and colonization of the 18th and 19th centuries spawned still another missionary movement. The earliest colonizers were from the Roman Catholic countries of Spain, France, Portugal, and Italy, and in each new establishment a priest became a prominent figure. In many cases also the most dominant building erected in the settlements was the cathedral. Unfortunately the religion that developed among many of the native peoples was a sort of syncretism in which tribal customs were incorporated into the traditional worship. With warlike zeal the intrusion of any other religious group was violently opposed.

Where English and Dutch colonists went, Protestant missions were established. In the 13 American colonies there was a lively interest in reaching the native Indians, and missionaries like John Eliot, David Brainerd, and the Whitmans became leaders in this endeavor.

The Modern Missionary Movement

Though in the post-Reformation era the spread of the gospel gained some momentum, it was not until the 19th century that organized missionary activity really took hold. Latourette calls it "The Great Century."

The evangelical fervor created by the Great Awakening of the 18th century became the springboard. By this time, rationalism had peaked and people were becoming more receptive to traditional values and "things of the heart." Non-Christian religions such as Hinduism, Buddhism, and Islam (Mohammedanism) were also in semi-eclipse, and even Roman Catholicism was suffering reverses. The field was wide open to the true gospel.

Great Britain and North America became the centers of evangelistic activity. Not only was the church revived internally, there was a new awareness of its worldwide mission. This awareness broke beyond the bounds of the organized church, however, and the major vehicle for this outreach activity became the missionary society. Some of these societies were denominationally oriented, but most were independent. It was strongly a lay movement, particularly from the support side. Latourette writes in his monumental *History of the Expansion of Christianity:* "Never before had Christianity or any other religion had so many individuals giving full time to the propagation of their faith. Never had so many hundreds of thousands contributed voluntarily of their means to assist the spread of Christianity or any other religion."[5]

The first of these missionary organizations was the Baptist Missionary Society, launched in 1792. It was followed three years later by the London Missionary Society and in 1797 by the Netherlands Missionary Society. The first United States group was the American Board of Commissioners for Foreign Missions (later abbreviated to American Board). It was organized in 1810 by Samuel Mills as a spin-off from the historic "haystack prayer meeting" a year or so before, when a group of young college students committed themselves to missionary service.

Dozens more such societies were to follow. Perhaps the most significant was the China Inland Mission, founded by J. Hudson Taylor, which by the turn of the 20th century had over 600 missionaries and at its peak just before World War I was the largest missionary organization in the world.

By 1861 there were 51 known missionary societies—22 in Great Britain, 15 on the Continent, and 14 in North America. About 2,000 missionaries were being supported in 1,200 mission stations. By 1900, however, the number of sending agencies had jumped to 600 with 62,000 missionaries at work around the world.

Tucker points out that the missionary enterprise was greatly facilitated by colonialism and imperialism. Inadvertently these outpost settlements and trading posts often afforded a comparatively safe haven for missionaries who went out into the surrounding territory to preach the gospel. Sometimes the misionaries went out solely to serve the colonists, but this could not be classified as truly missionary work.

The British government was particularly supportive of missionary efforts; and since at one time a quarter of the earth's land surface was under the British flag, this was a considerable factor in the expansion of the gospel. The trading companies were far less cordial, however, particularly the East India Company, which considered missionaries and missionary work to be contrary to their interests.

It was important that the work of the church not be too closely associated with either colonialism, which tended to be patronizing, or imperialism, which was exploitive. Nor should Western culture be imposed. For this reason some missionaries, such as Hudson Taylor, adopted the way of life of the people, including dress, food, and dwellings. Too often, however, Christianizing was identified with Westernizing.

Great Missionary Pioneers

The 19th-century missionary movement brought to the fore a great list of pioneers whose names became legend. These were the trailblazers who fueled the fires of missionary interest in the homeland by their heroic exploits.

One of the first of these, and generally recognized as the father of modern missions, was **William Carey,** English cobbler-turned-missionary, who went to India under the Baptist Missionary Society in 1793. His Serampore mission station near Calcutta became a model that others followed. There he spent 34 years chiefly in translating the Bible into Bengali, Sanskrit, and Marathi.

Following in Carey's footsteps was **Adoniram Judson,** who with his wife, Anne, were the first United States missionaries. They arrived at Serampore in 1812 but soon went on to Burma to become its most famous missionary pioneers.

The London Missionary Society took a great interest in Africa, and its most renowned pioneer there was a Scotsman, **Robert Moffat,** who began his work in 1816. He won a wide reputation as evangelist, translator, educator, diplomat, and explorer, and his Kuruman station 600 miles northeast of Cape Town was the scene of 29 years' work among the Africans. The last 15 years of his life were spent in England as an effective promoter of missions.

Moffat's considerable achievements were somewhat dimmed by the glamor surrounding his son-in-law, **David Livingstone,** who was more explorer than missionary. With the support of the London Missionary Society and inspired by the words of Moffat, who told of having seen "the smoke of a thousand villages where no missionary has ever been," he landed in Africa in 1841. His explorations won him great acclaim, including burial among history's greats in Westminster Abbey; but more importantly, he is credited with opening up the continent to missionary endeavor.

The Far East, first touched by the Nestorians in the sixth century and influenced by them long after, became strongly isolationist and resistant to Western influence. As a result it was long closed to the gospel. But in 1807, English-born **Robert Morrison** was sent out by the London Missionary Society to establish a work in Canton, China. This was the only city outside of the tiny Portuguese colony of Macao where foreigners were allowed to reside. After over 25 years of labor he had won but 12 converts, but his translation work, in particular, paved the way for missionary work when the country became open to the gospel after the Opium Wars of the late 1830s and early 1840s.

The one who made the most of this opening up of China was **Hudson Taylor,** another English missionary who left for China in 1853. He had a great vision for planting the gospel in every Chinese province. His crowning achievement was the organization of the earlier-mentioned China Inland Mission.

Jonathan Goforth, a Canadian, sailed to China in 1888 and became that country's greatest missionary evangelist. He kept up an exhausting schedule that included ministry also in Korea and Manchuria until at age 73 he was stricken with blindness.

The missionary trail went also to the South Pacific where **John Williams** became the Apostle of the South Seas. Beginning in Tahiti in 1818, he evangelized by boat, going from island to island. By 1834 it was said that "no single island of importance within 2,000 miles of Tahiti had been left unvisited." But it was on a missionary safari to yet another island that he lost his life to cannibals in 1839.

John G. Paton, a Scotch Presbyterian, also left his indelible mark in the New Hebrides beginning in 1858. After a rough beginning, he became enormously successful and in his latter years was somewhat of a missionary statesman.

James Chalmers will ever be remembered as the great missionary to New Guinea. After 10 years on the Christianized island of Rarotonga, in 1877 he went to New Guinea where Stone Age cannibals lived. He was known as a peacemaker, and in five years cannibalism had been abolished in the region where he worked. But in seeking to reach a new tribe, he was murdered in 1901.

One other name should be mentioned: that of **C. T. Studd,** the famed cricket player converted under D. L. Moody. He served as a missionary in China for almost 10 years, returned to England in 1894 for 6 years of speaking tours, and then went to India in 1900 to minister to an English-speaking congregation. In 1910, after an exploratory trip to Africa, he established the Heart of Africa Mission, whose name later was changed to the more inclusive Worldwide Evangelization Crusade. He personally served as a missionary in the Congo for 18 years.

The Shift to North America

It was during the 19th century that the center of missionary interest gradually shifted from the British Isles and continental Europe to America. Samuel J. Mills is considered the father of American missions. At Williams College in Massachusetts, he gathered together a group of six students who shared his interest in spreading the gospel to other lands. Caught in a thunderstorm one day, they sought refuge under a haystack where, as mentioned above, they held their now-historic prayer meeting in which each pledged himself to missionary service. Mills transferred to the newly established college in Andover, Mass., where he had a great influence on a fellow student, Adoniram

Judson. Similar missionary fervor there resulted in the formation, in 1810, of the American Board of Commissioners for Foreign Missions (American Board), the first such organization on that side of the Atlantic. Other societies were organized until by midcentury there were more than a dozen of them in the United States.

Other missionary-oriented movements added fuel to the fire of overseas evangelism. The Student Volunteer Movement, which was launched at Mount Hermon, Mass., in 1886, was responsible for influencing some 20,000 students to go to the mission field before it began to wane after World War I. Still another force was the establishment across the United States of many training centers for future missionaries. One of the first of these was the Union Missionary Training Institute of Brooklyn, N.Y., founded by William B. Osborn in 1882. "A score of self-supporting missionary training schools [were] founded during the next 30 years."[6]

It was amid this mission-charged milieu that the Church of the Nazarene came into being. Several of those who became members of the new denomination were among the estimated 17,000 serving on mission fields. Some were under the auspices of independent societies, while others were being supported by various holiness associations that united to form the Church of the Nazarene in 1908. Among them were the Schmelzenbachs in Africa, the Kiehns in China, the Tracys in India, and John Diaz in the Cape Verde Islands. The uniting of the Pentecostal Mission in 1915 brought in others in both Latin America and India, notably the R. S. Andersons of Guatemala.

A strong, pervasive interest in missions, particularly in the East, characterized the Church of the Nazarene from its inception. Nor did that interest ever wane. The key leader who set this course for more than two decades was Dr. H. F. Reynolds. In 1932, in an address before the General Assembly in Wichita, Kans., General Superintendent J. B. Chapman said of him: "We as a church and people owe more to the early vision, enthusiasm, and zeal of H. F. Reynolds for the success of our missionary enterprise than to any other man."

The following chapters in this volume outline the unfolding missionary saga of the Church of the Nazarene. From its faltering beginnings it has emerged as one of the great world outreach programs of its time.

Chapter **2**

The Development of Nazarene World Mission Administration

No emerging organization comes into being with its operational structure fully in place. In its beginning phases the infrastructure is simple and minimal. But with growth comes the need for ever-increasing organizational machinery to provide coordination and control, along with continuity and development. Astute, long-range planning may anticipate such expansion need, but more often than not modifications are of necessity injected as the need arises and in the direction called for at the moment. Like Topsy, who explained her existence by saying that she "just growed," management structures usually follow a need-response pattern. It is a "build your wagon as you go" procedure.

When the pioneers of the Church of the Nazarene were putting the pieces together to form the denomination that officially came into being at Pilot Point, Tex., on October 13, 1908, they had high hopes and ambitions for the future. But they had no inkling of what phenomenal expansion was in store for this fledgling group of 228 churches. Consequently the organizational structure developed as the denomination grew, with several major restructuring periods along the way.

The missionary phase of the church was of critical concern. "No area of the church's activity," writes Timothy L. Smith, "needed central direction as much as foreign missions."[1] Each of the three parent bodies that came together at Pilot Point were already involved to some degree in foreign mission activity. Each also had its missionary committee or board to direct the work. True, the support structure was shaky and the missionaries abroad were largely "living by faith," but the commitment of the new denomination to world evangelism was firm. This was enunciated in its first (1908) *Manual:* "We seek holy Christian fellowship, the conversion of sinners, the entire sanctification of believers and their upbuilding in holiness, together with *the preaching of the gospel to every creature*" (p. 22, italics added). This last phrase has been retained in every subsequent edition of the *Manual.*

Dr. Bresee's oft-repeated statement: "We are debtors to every man to give him the gospel in the same measure as we have received it," became the clarion call of the denomination. Out of it grew a flourishing world mission enterprise that has been a hallmark of the Church of the Nazarene since its inception.

MISSION STRUCTURES PRIOR TO PILOT POINT, 1908

The Association of Pentecostal Churches of America

The eastern branch of the Church of the Nazarene, the Association of Pentecostal Churches of America, came into being in the New York area on December 12, 1895. In its original resolutions were the words: "We will cheerfully contribute of our earthly means as God has prospered us, for the support of a faithful ministry among us, for the relief of the poor, and for the spread of the gospel over the earth."[2]

When the administrative structure of their three-church association was set up, a Missionary Committee of six persons was selected to include the three pastors and three laymen. Chosen were Rev. William H. Hoople, Rev. John Norberry, Rev. F. W. Sloat, O. J. Copeland, Henry Elsner, and A. M. Owens. In addition, it was voted to add "a sister from each church . . . to act as Auxiliary to the Missionary Committee." The three selected were Mrs. Willis, Mrs. Rowe, and Mrs. Sandford. The seeds of an eventual women's missionary organization were thus sown.

The broad power of this one committee was evidenced when a year later it was given responsibility to effect a union with the Central Evangelical Holiness Association of New England, which had begun in March 1890. The union was consummated in April 1897 and brought to 17 the number of churches in the enlarged APCA.

The Missionary Committee of this new body was to consist of 12 members to be elected at the annual meeting. The group elected constituted a who's who of the eastern church: William H. Hoople, Hiram F. Reynolds, A. B. Riggs, H. N. Brown, E. E. Angell, F. L. Sprague, C. BeVier, J. C. Bearse, F. A. Hillery, D. Rand Pierce, H. B. Hosley, and J. N. Short. William H. Hoople was its first chairman.

A full-time secretary was considered necessary to develop the missionary program, and in October 1897 H. F. Reynolds was selected for the task. Thus began a long and distinguished career in this capacity. As Dr. Mendell Taylor put it: "Dr. Reynolds was destined to become the embodiment of missionary fervor and passion which has characterized the church. From this moment until his death [in 1938] Dr. Reynolds never ceased to radiate an influence in behalf of missionary interests."[3]

Specific foreign missionary endeavor did not actually begin until December 1897, when a group of five missionaries was sent to India. In that number were Lillian Sprague, Carrie Taylor, Rev. and Mrs. M. D. Wood, and F. P. Wiley. This was followed in 1901 by the sending of John Diaz back to his native Cape Verde Islands as a missionary.

The Church of the Nazarene

In the West, the Church of the Nazarene, organized in Los Angeles by Phineas F. Bresee in October 1895, was initially absorbed in a church-by-church buildup of its organization. There were no groups or associations of congregations to bring together, such as was the case in the East or was taking place in the South. Bresee considered this development of new congregations as missionary work. "Perhaps no missionary work needs more to be done than the planting of centers of fire in this country," he wrote in the November 12, 1903, issue of the *Nazarene Messenger.* However, he went on to add: "Yet, Christian hearts long to find immediate access to the lands and people who have never heard the blessed, glad tidings of the Christ of Calvary. . . . It seems as if the time has come when we should take up the missionary work both at home and abroad, in a more systematic way. To this I call your prayerful attention" (p. 2).

This flicker of interest was perhaps prompted by Mary A. Hill, who the previous year had recruited a group from Bresee's church to go to China to reopen an abandoned mission in Shantung Province. This project was never officially adopted by the church, however.

A positive response did come at the following annual assembly when for the first time in the eight-year history of the Church of the Nazarene, a Committee on Missions was set up. This committee, made up of Leslie F. Gay, a Mrs. Armour, C. W. Ruth, and Mrs. DeLance Wallace, brought in two major recommendations:

1. That this Assembly do proceed to organize a Missionary Society to be known and designated as the Home and Foreign Missionary Society of the Church of the Nazarene. . . .

2. That a board of fifteen shall be elected by the Assembly to act as a General Missionary Board of the Church of the Nazarene; to be nominated in this first instance by our General Superintendent and elected one by one by this Assembly.[4]

The board was duly elected with the following officers chosen from their number: president, P. F. Bresee; vice presidents, Leslie F. Gay, C. W. Ruth, Mrs. DeLance Wallace; secretary, Mrs. Lillie D. Bothwell; treasurer and recording secretary, Leora Maris. Later J. W. Goodwin became recording secretary and Leslie F. Gay, treasurer.

The first project of the Missionary Board was the opening in 1904 of a Spanish mission in Los Angeles under the leadership of Mrs. May McReynolds. Converting "heathen immigrants" did not satisfy Leslie Gay's concept of missions, however, and so he persuaded the 1905 Assembly to pass a resolution urging each congregation to give a tithe of its total income for foreign endeavors. This concept of "10 percent giving" was picked up many years later as an official norm for missionary support.

In the spring of 1906 came the opportunity to sponsor the Hope School for orphans and widows in Calcutta, India. The Missionary Board accepted the challenge and promised $1,800 a year plus $25.00 for each widow and child.

The Holiness Church of Christ

In the South, where congregational autonomy was the pervading spirit, any missionary endeavor was carried on under local sponsorship. Furthermore, the "faith missions" idea was strongly emphasized, which, in effect, absolved the church itself of direct responsibility in the missionary enterprise. Nevertheless, missionary interest ran high. Some even felt that this and rescue mission work absorbed so much attention as to be detrimental to church growth.[5]

When in 1903 Samuel M. Stafford established a pioneer mission in Tonala, Chiapas, southern Mexico, he did so with the firm support of Pastor R. M. Guy and his congregation in Pilot Point, Tex. Then, when the various holiness groups of the South united under the banner of the Holiness Church of Christ in November 1905, this Mexico project became a common interest.

The need for supervision as well as support for this work was apparent, for Stafford was of an entrepreneurial stripe and inclined to take things into his own hands. As a result, J. D. Scott was appointed missionary secretary and treasurer. "All our churches are kindly advised to send their missionary offerings [to him]" was the rather pointed directive.

In 1906 the Pilot Point church listed 17 missionaries on its roll, but there is no indication that this one church supported them all. Besides the ones in Mexico, these missionaries were reported to be at work in Japan and India as well.

Perhaps prompted by Stafford, C. B. Jernigan, editor of the *Holiness Evangel*, published a plea for missionary support and involvement in his October 1, 1906, issue. "The door of Mexico stands wide open," he wrote. "The hands of the brown man, our nearest neighbor, are stretched out to us calling for help." Under the impetus of this article, the work in southern Mexico expanded rapidly. But there was little evidence of control from the homeland, and matters were in disarray at the time of the 1908 union.

It was during this time that a young student at Texas Holiness University in Peniel, Tex., Harmon Schmelzenbach, was wrestling with a pent-up desire to fulfill his call as a missionary to Africa. He could not wait to finish his training. With the blessing and promised support of both the college and the Peniel church he set sail from New York on May 5, 1907. He was destined to carve a legend in the annals of missionary history in Swaziland. The following spring, months before the Pilot Point union, his supporting church and college joined Bresee's Church of the Nazarene.

The Pentecostal Mission

A center of powerful missionary interest that was to become a few years later a part of the Church of the Nazarene was the Pentecostal Mission of Nashville. This group, brought together by J. O. McClurkan about the turn of the century, had an early association with the missionary-minded Christian and Missionary Alliance. This along with the turn of international events at that time incited an unusual zest for missions. Though the CMA affiliation was short-lived, the vision for world evangelization did not wane. A 25-member local board of missions was elected to "foster, direct, and finance" this part of the work. They lost no time in launching an overseas project.

In 1902 a group of perhaps 10 persons set out to found a mission in Colombia. They stopped off in Cuba on the way, where they learned that, owing to a war situation that had developed in Colombia, they would not be allowed to proceed to their desired destination. Undaunted, most of the group elected to stay in Cuba and attempt to establish a mission work there. More details of this venture will be found in the Cuba section of Part Two of this volume.

In 1903 Mr. and Mrs. C. G. Anderson were sent to Guatemala. Then, in 1904, work was begun at Igatpuri, India, northeast of Bombay, where four missionaries under the leadership of R. G. Codding established a work that spread to Khardi and Vasind. (Also see Part Two under India.)

Although the missionary effort was to be a "strictly undenominational and faith work," monthly contributions were solicited and duly recorded by the treasurer. They averaged between $200 and $400. Large special offerings were also received at camp meetings and other gatherings. It was noted, however, that "only $4,000 of the $9,000 annual cost of the foreign missionary venture regularly came from the Nashville membership."[6]

Tentative agreements as early as 1911 concerning the union of the Pentecostal Mission with the Church of the Nazarene would have made Nashville the missionary headquarters of the church. The 1911 General Assembly was held in Nashville at the invitation of the Pentecostal Mission, and even though the hoped-for union failed to materialize at that time, there was talk of at least combining the missionary work of the two groups.

When the union was finally consummated on February 13, 1915, it was agreed that the Nazarene General Missionary Board would "assume financial responsibility for the missionary work of the Pentecostal Mission." Though certain conditions were attached, the work in India with nine missionaries, Cuba with five, and Central America with four, were specifically mentioned. The Articles of Agreement continued: "It is expressly understood that the former members of the Pentecostal Mission will use their best endeavors through all the avenues that they have to contribute to the support, not only of the missionaries which are being transferred but all the missionary work under the board of the Pentecostal Church of the Nazarene."[7]

The diverse nature of the organization, supervision, and financial support in each of the above missionary programs presented a challenge to the framers of the constitution of the newly formed denomination. The evolvement of the administrative and promotional structure is an interesting study in itself.

THE DEVELOPMENT OF THE GENERAL BOARD AND THE DEPARTMENT OF WORLD MISSION

When East and West united in 1907 at Chicago to form the Pentecostal Church of the Nazarene, two outstanding leaders, one from each constituency, became the architects of missionary strategy for the new denomination. They were Leslie F. Gay, a Los Angeles layman, and H. F. Reynolds, already missionary secretary of the eastern group.

Among Gay's recommendations to the Chicago assembly, painstakingly detailed, was the proposal that there be separate mission boards at each administrative level: general, district, and local. At the general level, the existing two missionary boards would be replaced by a General Missionary Board with headquarters in Chicago. This board would consist of 16 members, 2 from each district (of which there were four in the East and four in the West).

All documents, deeds, bequests, money, pledges, contracts, and so forth would be turned over to the new board "immediately." This board would be authorized to employ an executive secretary to be paid from missionary funds.

The rather elaborate structure Gay had devised was adopted, and the 16-member board was duly elected. H. F. Reynolds, even though voted to be one of the two general superintendents (along with P. F. Bresee), was elected chairman of the board and general missionary secretary. He continued to serve in this dual role until 1915.

When the Holiness Church of Christ united with the Pentecostal Church of the Nazarene at Pilot Point, Tex., in October 1908, a new dimension was added to the foreign missionary enterprise. A principal change was the addition to the Missionary Board of 2 representatives from each of the new group's seven districts, plus 2 each from three new eastern districts that had been formed. This brought the total to a cumbersome 36 plus 1 additional person from Chicago, which, the previous year, had been established as the headquarters of the board.

But integrating the three missionary programs was not a simple task. Particularly at issue was the Mexico program, which there was great reluctance to accept. Perhaps Stafford's usual high-powered presentation at the Pilot Point assembly had turned people off. The commercial overtones were also a stumbling block. There was no question, however, that he had substantial supporters in the South who were ready to stand with him.

To help solve the problem, Bresee proposed that the elected 37-member board be divided into three separate boards according to the geographical areas from which they had been chosen. In effect, this meant a perpetuation of the three divisions of the church—East, West, and South—at least for missionary purposes. Leslie F. Gay, writing in the November 19, 1908, issue of the *Nazarene Messenger,* explained it this way: "For one more year it was considered best for each of these divisions to carry on their own work and seek to perfect and adjust all work in foreign fields for greater efficiency, hoping that by another year all fields can be taken up under one management" (p. 14). Among other advantages this would leave the southern group alone to wrestle with the thorny "Mexico problem."

But Reynolds was not pleased with the arrangement. Not only was it contrary to the spirit of the union that had been consummated, but it would deny him, as general missionary secretary, access to the whole church for promotion and fund raising. His agitation no doubt speeded up the integrating process, and the 1909 meeting was of a united board.

To further consolidate the situation, E. H. Sheeks of the South group was elected treasurer in place of Leslie Gay. The generally improved financial picture also inspired optimism. During that year of separate operation, a total of $16,472 had been raised for missions—$8,023 by the West, $5,287 by the East, but only $3,162 by the South. Suspicion was strong that substantial private contributions sent directly to Stafford had affected the South's reported total.

By the time of the convening of the 1911 General Assembly, there were 24 districts. According to the established formula this would have created an unwieldy Foreign Missions Board of 48 members plus the ex officio personnel. To avoid this, legislation was introduced to divide the United States constituency into six missionary divisions, cutting across both district boundaries and the old East/West/South sectional lines. A minister and a layman from each division was to be elected to the Board of Foreign Missions. The three general superintendents and the missionary secretary would be ex officio members.[8]

Up to this time, the only standing board in the general church was the Board of Foreign Missions. However, it had responsibility for both foreign missions and home missions, plus some marginal interests such as rest homes and orphanages. In a significant move, the 1911 General Assembly ordered the creation of a separate Board of Church Extension to care for the home missions work and other adjunct items. This left the Board of Foreign Missions with a clear and exclusive area of responsibility. Two other general boards were also created: the General Board of Publication and the General Board of Education.

Since the 1911 General Assembly was being held at Nashville at the invitation of J. O. McClurkan's Pentecostal Mission, there was strong hope that this group would choose to unite with the Church of the Nazarene. When this did not materialize, as previously noted, the suggestion was made that at least the missionary programs of the two could be combined. But although some helpful liaison was achieved, no workable organizational structure could be devised. When the union was finally consummated following the death of McClurkan, the addition of its considerable missionary program to that of the Nazarenes gave added stature to the Board of Foreign Missions.

In 1912 Bresee proposed opening a work in Japan. There had been an incipient beginning some years before by two of the Pilot Point-supported missionaries mentioned above, Misses Lillian Poole and Lulu Williams. Though reinforcements had been sent out in 1910 by the "southern" board, health problems decimated the group, and the work collapsed. With experienced missionaries available and groundwork already laid, it was a logical choice for the first new overseas venture of the Board of Foreign Missions.

At this time also, Reynolds tightened the administrative reins by inaugurating a highly detailed field report system. He also worked out basic procedures for the recruitment and appointment of missionaries.

The 1915 General Assembly reduced the membership of the General Board of Foreign Missions to one member per geographical division. Those elected under this formula were the stalwarts, H. F. Reynolds (president and general secretary), John T. Benson (vice president), Herbert Hunt (recording secretary), E. G. Anderson (treasurer), C. A. McConnell, and Leslie F. Gay. Shortly afterward Dr. Reynolds relinquished the direct leadership of the missionary work, and E. G.

Anderson was elected to the combined office of secretary-treasurer of foreign missions.

In 1919 the general president of the newly formed Women's Foreign Missionary Society, Mrs. S. N. Fitkin, was added to the board. At this same General Assembly, J. E. L. Moore was elected in place of Herbert Hunt.

A Unified General Board

Beginning with the creation of the 4 general boards in 1911, new ones were added along the way until by 1923 there were 10 such boards. Each had its own elected members and, at first, separate times of meeting. Most confusing of all was that each had its own treasurer, its own budget, and its own field representative, which meant a plethora of fund-raising activities throughout the church.

Although as early as 1916 steps were taken to have all the general boards meet simultaneously in Kansas City each year, the system became increasingly cumbersome and confusing. Finally, the 1923 General Assembly approved a sweeping restructure of the corporate framework of the denomination. In essence, it called for the creation of a single General Board to administer all phases of the church's program. This involved also the setting up of a unified budget.

Elective procedures adopted called for a 14-member board. There were to be 12 elected members equally divided between ministers and laymen plus 1 general superintendent and the general treasurer. The latter was to be "custodian of all the funds belonging to the general interests of the church." The elective members were to be chosen by ballot from a list of 12 nominees in each category (ministers and laymen), the 6 highest in each group being declared elected.

The General Board, in turn, was divided into four departments—Foreign Missions, Publication, Church Extension, and Home Missions. Some members served on more than one department. All actions of the individual departments had to be ratified by the total board.

Assignments to the various departments were made by the board itself subject to ratification by the General Assembly prior to its final adjournment. The resulting Department of Foreign Missions consisted of John T. Benson (chairman), E. G. Anderson (secretary), C. A. McConnell, J. E. Bates, and J. T. Little.

In 1928 still further changes were made in the composition of the General Board. The six geographical (educational) zones that had been set up in 1923 now became the basis of representation on the board. The General Assembly delegates from each zone, meeting in caucus, presented one nominee from their respective zones for each of the four departments. This list of nominees was officially voted on by the General Assembly. The result was a 24-member General Board with 6 members preassigned to each of the four departments. There were thus no duplications from any zone on a department.

The resulting Department of Foreign Missions consisted of C. A. McConnell (chairman), C. Warren Jones (vice-chairman), C. W. Davis, R. B. Mitchum, Edwin Burke, and J. E. Bates. Allowance was also made for the Women's Foreign Missionary Society council to nominate two to the department to be elected by the General Assembly. Thus Mrs. Paul Bresee and Mrs. Bertha Lillenas were added.

In 1932 further modifications were introduced in an effort to cut down on the size of the General Board. To compensate, each member would have to serve on two departments. The new plan called for each zone caucus to submit the names of 4 ministers and 4 laymen as nominees to the General Board. From these the General Assembly would elect only 1 from each category. In addition, four auxiliaries (the Women's Foreign Missionary Society, the Nazarene Young People's Society, the Committee on Church Schools, and the Committee on Education) were each allowed to nominate 2 persons to the General Board, from which the General Assembly would elect 1. A Canadian-British Isles Zone was also created, which was allowed 1 ministerial member. The end result was a board of 17 members, each of whom had the privilege of selecting the two departments he wished to serve on.

The most popular choice proved to be the Department of Foreign Missions. The 1932-36 membership consisted of C. A. McConnell (chairman), J. W. Short (vice-chairman), C. Warren Jones, J. T. Little, J. E. Bates, R. B. Mitchum, George Sharpe, C. E. Thomson (the latter two from the Canadian-British Isles Zone to serve in alternate years), and Mrs. S. N. Fitkin—over half the members of the total board.

Subsequent General Assemblies added further modifications to the General Board structure. The 1936 assembly introduced the factor of numerical strength as well as geography in determining representation from each zone. There was the accompanying limitation that no zone caucus could nominate more than one person from a particular district on that zone until all districts had a nominee. This meant that only in rare cases would any district have more than one member on the General Board.

With this numerical formula adopted, the result was a general "upsetting of the fruit basket" with many new names appearing on the roster of the General Board. The Department of Foreign Missions likewise experienced considerable turnover. Those elected were: A. K. Bracken (chairman), Hardy C. Powers (vice-chairman), Samuel Young, R. V. DeLong, M. Kimber Moulton, A. E. Sanner, E. O. Chalfant, and Mrs. S. N. Fitkin.

The 1944 General Assembly made no basic change in General Board structure, but the increasing popularity of the Department of Foreign Missions resulted in the addition of 2 more members for a total of 10. The problem of imbalance was not addressed until 1948 when legislation passed to restrict membership in any department to one-third of the total board, whose membership now stood at 24. The 8 elected to the Department of Foreign Missions were: A. K. Bracken (chairman), Roy Cantrell (vice-chairman), L. M. Spangenberg, A. E. Sanner, Selden D. Kelley, Paul Updike, A. E. Ramquist, and Mrs. Louise R. Chapman.

By this time some semblance of routine had been established in the conduct of General Board business. For the Department of Foreign Missions it meant meeting for several days ahead of the General Board session to take care of all its business. Chief items on the agenda were hearing personal reports from missionaries on furlough, interviewing prospective missionaries including making assignments to the various fields, and drawing up the annual budget. The budget requests from the fields, as might be expected, totaled much more than available funds, and determining the allocations to each one was a long and painful process. By now the foreign missionary program had become a multimillion-dollar business and was experiencing explosive growth, particularly in the years immediately following World War II.

In 1964 the name of the Department of Foreign Missions was changed to the Department of World Missions, and further modified in 1976 to Department of World Mission. Also in 1976 the title of the operational head of the department was changed to executive director instead of executive secretary, and later was amended to simply director.

In the major restructuring of the General Board in 1980, the World Mission Department was the least affected of all. In line with the new terminology, however, it was renamed the Division of World Mission, further modified in 1982 to World Mission Division.

Perhaps the most significant change affecting the General Board from 1976 on was the inclusion of representatives from world mission areas in its membership. By 1985, there were 18 such members, constituting 31 percent of the total elected board. What is more, 2 of these were on its World Mission Department.

Chapter 3

The Executive Secretary of the Department of World Missions

The oversight of the worldwide missionary program of the church is in the hands of a director, in earlier years called an executive secretary. Although he is amenable to the World Mission Department of the General Board, to which he gives an annual accounting, the day-by-day operation of the program is his responsibility. Administration of the far-flung enterprise, including personnel and finance, is exceedingly and increasingly complex.

In the beginning of the movement, the demands were not so overwhelming. The faith-mission concept was still in vogue, and those who in answer to God's call went to the "foreign field" did so with, at best, only local congregational support. The profession of a call was all the credentials one needed to become a missionary.

At the time of the Chicago union of East and West in October 1907, each of the regions had its champion of the missionary cause: H. F. Reynolds in the East and Leslie F. Gay in the West. (J. D. Scott was to play a similar role later for the South.)

It was Leslie Gay who framed the initial constitution of the Foreign Missions Board, but it was H. F. Reynolds who provided the dynamic to make the machinery work. It was Reynolds who was elected foreign missionary secretary, a responsibility he carried along with the general superintendency. It was but a continuation of the kind of work he had been doing with the Association of Pentecostal Churches of America before its union with the Church of the Nazarene.

The demands of the general superintendency were not as large in those days, with a total of only eight districts. This gave him much freedom to travel the length and breadth of the United States and Canada, urging upon all the need of a world vision for the church.

The 1911 General Assembly reelected Dr. Reynolds to the dual posts, but in 1915 he withdrew from active leadership of this phase of the work. He did, however, become chairman of the General Board of Foreign Missions, which office he held until the unified General Board was organized in 1923. He also served from 1926-28 as interim secretary following the resignation of E. G. Anderson.

The highlight of Dr. Reynolds' administration was his storied round-the-world missionary safari in 1913-14. Accompanying him on the first part of his journey were 10 missionaries headed for Japan, China, and India. The group embarked at San Francisco on December 16, 1913, landing first in Japan. While the China- and India-bound missionaries continued to their destinations, Dr. Reynolds spent a month in Japan helping the four missionaries, two of them veterans there, to set the work in order.

Dr. Reynolds then went on to China, which was a new field where the church's territory needed to be "staked out" and the program launched. The Peter Kiehns knew the country from previous service with another mission board, so Dr. Reynolds left for India with firm confidence in their ability to carry on.

The India situation was more complicated, with three separate areas to visit. Each of them had been started under the auspices of one of the three branches of the church that had united at Pilot Point in 1908, one in the Calcutta area, one near Bombay, and one in Central India. A semblance of integration needed to be worked out.

Then it was on to Africa and a historic trip inland to visit Harmon Schmelzenbach in Swaziland. The next stop was with John Diaz in the Cape Verde Islands. By this time, World War I was under way, which thwarted a planned visit to the British Isles and forced a hazardous Atlantic crossing. When he arrived back in Kansas City on November 1, 1914, he had been gone almost 11 months.

When Dr. Reynolds released the duties of executive secretary in 1915, the offices of secretary and treasurer of the Board of Foreign Missions were combined, and the incumbent treasurer, E. G. Anderson, assumed leadership. He was also elected to the newly created office of general church treasurer. He carried on in the dual role until he submitted his resignation in 1925 from the latter office and subsequently from the leadership of the Foreign Missions Department, both taking effect in early 1926. The campaign to raise a "million for missions" during the 1919-23 quadrennium was perhaps his most significant contribution.

When E. G. Anderson resigned, H. F. Reynolds again assumed the leadership of the missionary program in the interim until the General Assembly of 1928. By that time, the need for a full-time administrator was apparent. Accordingly, a separate office of foreign missions secretary was set up, the person to be elected by ballot by the General Board upon nomination jointly by the Department of Foreign Missions and the Board of General Superintendents.

THE OFFICE OF EXECUTIVE SECRETARY

J. G. Morrison, 1928-36

The first person to be elected to the office of executive secretary of the Department of Foreign Missions was J. G. Morrison, who served two quadrenniums until he was elected to the general superintendency in 1936. In his earlier ministry he had been the leader of the Laymen's Holiness Association in the Dakotas, Minnesota, and Montana, of which more than 1,000 members followed him into the Church of the Nazarene in 1922. When, that year, the Central Northwest District was created, Morrison was appointed superintendent.

In 1926 Dr. Morrison was elected president of Northwest Nazarene College in Nampa, Idaho. It was a task to which he soon realized he was ill-suited; and when in 1927 the General Board elected him to the newly created office of executive field secretary of the denomination ("to promote and direct the raising of the General Budget"), he accepted. He had been at Headquarters only a few months when, in October 1927, Dr. Reynolds appointed him as his assistant in the Department of Foreign Missions. His election to the office of executive secretary of the department the following year was therefore not unexpected.

Morrison's fervency in espousing the cause of missions had a powerful effect on the church. During the difficult depression years his storied appeal, "Can't you do a little bit more?" doubtless saved the missionary program from even more drastic curtailment than was experienced.

C. Warren Jones, 1936-48

The successor to Dr. Morrison, elected at the 1936 General Assembly, was C. Warren Jones, a member of the Department of Foreign Missions of the General Board since 1928. He had been a missionary himself in Japan for a brief period and had visited Central and South America. A native of eastern Washington State, he had had varied experiences of service in the church, including pastorates in Chicago and Spokane, Wash., a teaching stint at Pasadena College, superintendency of the Northwest District, and the previously mentioned missionary experience in Japan, aborted by a physical breakdown.

A highly successful pastorate from 1921 to 1928 at Cleveland First Church, followed by an equally effective superintendency of the Pittsburgh District, brought him into the leadership echelons of the general church. Election to the General Board and the Department of Foreign Missions in 1928 were natural entrees into the office to which he was elected in 1936.

Dr. Jones's 12 years of service spanned the traumatic World War II era and subsequent period of adjustment. Yet it was during the latter years of the war that the first "million for missions" year was achieved.

The necessary concentration on missionary expansion close to the United States during the time of international upheaval resulted in significant growth there. During the Jones era the number of mission fields expanded from 17 to 24, the corps of missionaries increased from 69 to 204, and giving for missions more than tripled.

Remiss Rehfeldt, 1948-60

Upon the retirement of C. Warren Jones in 1948, the General Board elected as foreign missions secretary a young 33-year-old, rising leader in the church, Remiss Rehfeldt. He had just been elected a regional representative on the General Council of the Nazarene Young People's Society and also a zone representative on the General Board. It was a rare occurrence for one to be elected to the dual roles, but it was indicative of his recognized leadership talents.

Dr. Rehfeldt's active ministry had begun only 11 years before when, soon after his marriage to Frances Phillips in September 1937, he assumed the pastorate of a home mission church in Burlington, Iowa. After six successful years there, he moved to Council Bluffs First Church. A year later he became district superintendent when his predecessor, Dr. Hardy C. Powers, was elevated to the general superintendency at the 1944 General Assembly. He served effectively until he resigned the post in 1948 to assume the missions office assignment.

It was during the Rehfeldt period that substantial development began to take place in national leadership. The three districts in Mexico, which were set up in 1952, each had national superintendents because missionaries had been barred from the country since 1917. India had pioneered the idea of indigenous leadership in 1937 when Samuel J. Bhujbal was elected their first national superintendent. In Guatemala, as early as 1954 Federico Guillermo had served as an assistant leader but in 1960 became the national superintendent. In his report to the General Board in January 1954, Dr. Rehfeldt made note of the fact that "other mission districts have a large measure of self-government." It was a trend he eagerly espoused.

Another area of distinct progress was in missionary giving. In 1949, when a crisis arose in financing the missionary program, an all-night prayer meeting of members of the Department of Foreign Missions was held. Out of that emerged the concept of the general church giving a tithe of its income for missions. Ever since, the "10% Plan" has been a keystone of the foreign mission support program. It was not an entirely new concept, however. It will be recalled that the "tithe of a church's income" for the support of foreign missions had been a proposal back in 1905 by Leslie F. Gay, secretary-treasurer of Bresee's Church of the Nazarene.

By 1952 there were three 10 percent districts and four 9 percent, with an overall average of 7.02 percent. In 1954 a slight decline was reported, which prompted setting a goal of having all districts at the 10 percent level by 1958. Although the church fell far short of the goal, the concept was established and became the basis of outstanding missionary giving in the years ahead.

The Rehfeldt term also saw significant numerical gains as the missionary program entered a new era of expansion. Fifteen new fields were opened to bring the total to 39, and the missionary force was increased from 204 to 410.

George Coulter, 1960-64

The successor to Remiss Rehfeldt was George Coulter, a native of Ireland who grew up in western Canada. At the time of his election in 1960, he was superintendent of the Northern California District. A graduate of Northwest Nazarene College, he had begun his ministerial career in Alberta and held subsequent pastorates in California and Oregon before his 12-year term as district superintendent.

Although he was in the missionary office for only four years, being elected to the general superintendency in 1964, significant strides were made in developing a comprehensive missionary program. Of particular note was the involvement of the executive secretary in foreign visitation. Heretofore the general superintendents had conducted supervisory journeys to all areas of the world, and individual reports of their travels were a highlight of the annual meetings of the General Board. But only occasionally were they accompanied by the foreign missions secretary. Although he was thoroughly briefed by the general superintendents concerning their findings, nothing could take the place of firsthand contact by the secretary himself if he were to truly understand the work. The emergence of jet airplanes that reduced travel time from days to hours further accelerated the process. During his term in office, Dr. Coulter visited Mexico, Guatemala, Italy, Trinidad, Haiti, Puerto Rico, Brazil, Japan, Okinawa, Taiwan, and Korea. The journey to the Orient was in company with General Superintendent Young.

In 1961 a significant program of annual workshops for missionaries on furlough was begun. Twenty-seven were in attendance at the first one. Then in June 1962 the first Missionary Institute was held. This was a two-week orientation training period for 37 newly appointed missionaries. They were drilled in all phases of missionary work—language, customs, culture adaptation, and methods, along with the minutiae of missionary policy. For the final four days the group was joined by 36 missionaries on furlough who were holding their second annual workshop. In subsequent years the two phases were separated, the institute (for new misionaries) usually being held in the spring and the workshop (for furloughed missionaries) in late summer.

Further supporting missionary preparation was the introduction in 1961 of a quarterly publication, the *Missionary Beam.* Designed as a recruitment tool, it was sent to a mailing list of 900 who had expressed an interest in missionary service and/or were members of the missionary societies on the various Nazarene college campuses. In 1963 the monthly newsletter, *Link,* was launched. Published by and for the missionary family, it was sent by air to all the fields. It did much to develop esprit de corps.

Another innovation was the program of cross-country missionary conventions featuring a traveling group of prominent missionaries. Nine of these two-day extravaganzas were held in 1961 in strategic cities throughout the United States. In all, 38 services were conducted and over 500 young people registered commitment to respond should God call them to missionary service. Similar conventions were held in subsequent years, though not on an annual basis.

Still another project was a major revision of the missionary policy, which brought the extensive document in line with the contemporary situation. Of particular significance during those years had been the rapid expansion of national leadership. Among other things, this forced a redefining of the missionary's role, which was increasingly advisory and supportive rather than directive.

Concurrently, a new emphasis on self-support on the mission fields was being made. The result was a doubling of offerings on the mission fields during that quadrennium. Perceptibly, the foundations were being laid for the sweeping changes that took place in the succeeding decade in matters of mission policy and methodology.

By the close of the Coulter term, the church was at work in 40 world areas. The missionary staff had increased to 467, 126 of whom had been appointed during that quadrennium.

Everette S. Phillips, 1964-73

When the 1964 General Assembly elected Dr. Coulter to the general superintendency, the General Board chose Everette S. Phillips, pastor for 15 years of Bethany, Okla., First Church, as his successor. He had earlier pastored for 6 years at Baltimore First Church and before that had held two pastorates in New England. He was also for 2 years vice president of Eastern Nazarene College, Wollaston, Mass. He was a longtime member of the General Board, and having served on the Department of Foreign Missions for 9 years, he had an excellent grasp of the program. He brought both leadership expertise and personal concern to his new task.

A significant change at the outset of Dr. Phillips' term was the renaming of the Department of Foreign Missions to the Department of World Missions. This action, taken by the General Assembly in 1964, removed the "us-them" onus that the word "foreign" implied.

One of the earliest involvements the new executive secretary had was with the Nazarene Evangelistic Ambassadors. Those were the years of foment and rebellion on college campuses across the United States. As early as 1962 Dr. Coulter and Paul Skiles, executive secretary of the Nazarene Young People's Society, had begun to discuss methods for involving college youth in the missionary program. The result was the formation of two seven-man teams of talented college men under the direction of Dr. H. T. Reza and Dr. Paul Orjala, respectively. On each team was one student from each of the six United States liberal arts colleges, while Canadian Nazarene College had a member on one of the teams, and Nazarene Theological Seminary a member on the other. Each team had an accompanying evangelist (Lester Johnston, William Fisher, or Kimber Moulton) and a music director (Ray Moore for the Reza team and Jim Bohi for the Orjala team). Each group went to one English-speaking country and two Spanish-speaking ones. Accordingly, the Reza team was scheduled to go to Trinidad, Mexico, and Guatemala, while the Orjala team went to British Guiana (now Guyana), Nicaragua, and Puerto Rico. The teams left for their assignments immediately following the 1964 General Assembly and spent almost two weeks in each place.

So successful was the program that it was repeated in 1966 and again in 1969. The leaders were the same in 1966 and the team structure similar. However, a shorter time was spent in each place, making a more extensive itinerary possible. Team I with H. T. Reza went to British Honduras (now Belize), Panama, Argentina, Chile, Peru, and Mexico. Team II with Paul Orjala worked in Barbados, Brazil, Uruguay, Bolivia, Haiti, and Jamaica. In 15 evangelistic campaigns in 49 days the teams conducted 234 public services, ministered to 130,000 people, prayed with almost 5,000 seekers, and logged 30 hours of prime time on radio and television.

The 1969 trip was to the British Isles and the European continent. The format was similar to the previous tours. Time alone will reveal the full impact of these campaigns upon the fields that they visited. Some of the results are revealed in the stories of these respective fields recorded in Part Two of this volume.[1]

Early in Dr. Phillips' term, the first missionary film was released, titled *From Darkness to Light.* This was followed in 1967 by *The Spreading Flame* and another on the translation program. This was the beginning of a very successful filming program that saw the more elaborately filmed subjects shot on location. These included *They Cry in the Night* (Africa), *To Wipe the Tear* (India), *Mission: Europe,* and *To Make a Miracle.*

These films augmented a long-standing program of missionary slide sets on almost every country in which the Church of the Nazarene was at work. From meager beginnings in the 1960s this program mushroomed with dozens of new sets being added and old ones periodically replaced. In 1985 there were 22 different sets available free of charge for local church use. "Rental" charges were a freewill offering to the missionary program.

At the January 1965 meeting of the Department of World Missions a policy study was ordered of the growing use of short-term missionaries on the various fields. This had been a boon to beleaguered missionaries who were grateful for the temporary lift. It was particularly true of the doctors in the mission hospitals. These gifted persons had taken time out and gone to the fields at their own expense to serve for periods of several months to a year (and sometimes longer). Out of the study came a policy document to clarify the bounds of the program that came to be known as "Specialized Service," and ultimately "Specialized Assignment" (1976).

As a counterpart of the Nazarene Evangelistic Ambassadors program and to broaden the challenge to the youth of the church, in 1967 the Youth Assistance Missionary Corps (YAMC) was begun, soon after called Student Mission Corps (SMC). The program was launched by a series of youth and missions conventions held on college campuses across the country, which drew a total of 15,000 in attendance. At these conventions, opportunity was given for upper-division students to volunteer to serve on selected mission fields for the summer. The program, directed for the first seven years by Franklin Cook, was a joint project of the Department of World Missions and the Nazarene Young People's Society.

The first year, 16 students were selected and were divided into five teams going to Puerto Rico, Guyana, Trinidad, Barbados, and British Honduras. The following year, Guatemala and Nicaragua were added to the list, and 30 students participated. The program gathered momentum until in 1973, 74 students went to 18 nations in the Western Hemisphere plus the Philippines. At that point, 344 had participated in the program (counting duplications for those who served more than one year).[2] In 1974 the entire group of 50, divided into teams led by veteran missionaries, invaded the Dominican Republic as the work was being opened up there.

The students served in various capacities on the field as determined by the missionaries, including manual labor, office work, conducting Vacation Bible Schools, and so forth. "Send us two singing carpenters and some secretaries," wrote William Porter from Puerto Rico. The cost of the program was borne by the students themselves, and by parents and home churches.

Dr. Phillips also continued the policy of personal field visitation.

In 1967 he went to Mexico to participate in the All-Mexico Pastors Conference. In 1969 he was in Africa with General Superintendent Lewis. He also visited the Central America and Caribbean fields. A trip to the Middle East was made part of an extensive visit to Africa. In 1971 he accompanied General Superintendent Jenkins on a tour of the Orient. Declining health hindered further journeys abroad.

Indigenization

In line with the dictum expressed by the veteran missionary C. S. Jenkins, "We are going to reach the Africans only by the African," Dr. Phillips, following the lead of his predecessor, placed a strong emphasis on indigenization. In the late 1960s he published, with General Board endorsement, a *National Church Policy*. It stated flatly, "It is the purpose and intent of the Church of the Nazarene to place leadership of its developing districts in the hands of the national church." By 1970, as the program began to take hold, there were 15 national district superintendents. Within a decade this number had increased to 75 or almost 75 percent of world mission district leadership.

A giant step in the direction of indigenization and the crowning achievement of the Phillips administration was the landmark change in the governing structure of the mission fields, passed by the 1972 General Assembly. This legislation outlined four levels or categories of self-government achievement for each district:

1. *Pioneer District* (beginning level, with a missionary appointed by the general superintendent as its superintendent)
2. *National-Mission District* (a measure of growth and self-support, with an appointed or elected national district superintendent)
3. *Mission District* (a minimum of 50 percent self-support and an elected national superintendent)
4. *Regular District* (fully self-supporting [exclusive of institutions], stable situation, and a minimum of 1,000 full members)

Election to regular status was to be subject to approval by the General Board upon recommendation by the Board of General Superintendents.

Shortly afterward, a fifth, entry-level category was added, called the *Pioneer Area*. This was often part of an established district set apart for development into a self-supporting district of its own. When a pioneer area had at least two organized churches, it became a pioneer district.

This structuring of the mission fields was built around the well-known "three self" concept of indigenous development enunciated by Rufus Anderson and Henry Venn: (1) self-government, (2) self-support, and (3) self-propagation.

At the same time, involvement on the councils of the general church such as representation at the General Assembly and on the General Board were defined. The above four categories later were designated by the term "phase" (for example, "pioneer district" became "Phase 1," etc.).

In 1973, when the plan was implemented, the 67 organized world mission districts were cataloged as follows:

Pioneer—32
National-Mission—29
Mission—5
Regular—1 (though not officially approved until January 1974)

The national church rapidly responded to the challenge this new plan presented. Not only was there a marked increase in self-support but redoubled outreach as well (see growth charts in Appendix A). By the 1980 General Assembly there were 89 districts reported, divided as follows: pioneer—21; national-mission—25; mission—40; regular—3 (Guatemala Northeast, Peru North, and Japan). In addition there were 12 pioneer areas.

By 1985 there were 146 districts, 27 of them at Phase 1 (pioneer) level, 63 at Phase 2 (national-mission), 34 at Phase 3 (mission), and 22 at Phase 4 (regular). There were also 13 pioneer areas.

The profound effect this structuring had on world mission strategy was readily seen. One area in which it made an impact was in the makeup of the delegation at the General Assembly. The representatives from the world mission areas, once made up entirely of missionaries, began to see the addition of nationals in increasing numbers. This made it necessary to provide simultaneous, closed-circuit translation of the proceedings and the use of personal interpreters for the non-English-speaking delegates. At the 1985 General Assembly one-third of the 861 delegates were from world mission regions.

Dr. Phillips had a number of bouts with cancer in the later years of his administration, but he continued his duties with determination and fortitude. His acceptance of reelection to office in 1972 was a reflection of that resoluteness and courage. Little more than a year later, however, he was forced to relinquish the task. Wisely he suggested that his successor be named while he was still physically able to assist in the transition. He passed away on October 12, 1973, barely a month after Jerald D. Johnson had been elected.

By the close of the nine-year Phillips era significant numerical gains had been recorded. The church was now at work in 52 world areas, 5 of them having been entered that year (1973). Membership in mission areas stood at 107,245. The process of indigenization had advanced to the point that the first world mission district (Guatemala Northeast) was ready to be elected to regular status.

Chapter 4

The Director of the
World Mission Division

An outcome of the reorganization of the General Board and its Head-quarters operation in the 1970s and 1980s was a change in terminology used to designate the leaders and their areas of responsibility. Initial steps in 1976 introduced the title of executive director in place of executive secretary, later amended to simply director. This was followed by the change from Department to Division with reference to the Headquarters operation of the church. ("Department" now referred only to an organizational unit of the General Board.)

Since the change of title took place during the tenure of Jerald Johnson, the accounts of his administration and that of his successor, L. Guy Nees, have been placed together under this separate chapter heading.

Jerald D. Johnson, 1973-80

Though the somewhat revolutionary new mission field structure outlined in the previous chapter had been worked out by E. S. Phillips, the implementation was left largely to his successor, Jerald D. Johnson. The coming to office of this new leader marked a watershed in world mission activity in the church. Ahead lay a period of innovative change and marked expansion of the missionary program that caught the wave of internationalization launched by E. S. Phillips. New concepts, new structures, and new methods were introduced, and new fields were opened with increasing speed. It was a time of dramatic and exciting activity.

Dr. Johnson, a native Nebraskan and graduate of Northwest Nazarene College, had highly successful early pastorates in Coeur d'Alene, Idaho, and Eugene, Oreg. In 1958 he was called to pioneer the work of the Church of the Nazarene in West Germany. He became the first superintendent of the European District (later Middle European). In that role, he was a leader in the establishment in 1965 of the European Nazarene Bible College near Schaffhausen, Switzerland.

After national leadership had been well established in Europe, Dr. Johnson returned to the United States in 1969 and after a brief pastorate in San Jose, Calif., was called to the College Church in Nampa, Idaho. He was soon elected to fill a vacancy on the General Board from the Northwest Zone and thus became a member of the Department of World Missions. It was a providential turn of events that helped in a measure to prepare him for the office to which he was later elevated.

Although officially elected in September 1973, Dr. Johnson did not take office until October 15, three days after the death of his predecessor. In the four-week interim he commuted to Kansas City between Sundays to talk with Dr. Phillips concerning the various aspects of the task he was about to assume. Though Dr. Phillips was physically weak he did all he could to orient him to the complex details of the office.

In line with the department's change of name from Foreign Missions to World Missions, consummated in 1964, an early move by Dr. Johnson was to have the name of the missionary magazine, *Other Sheep,* changed to *World Mission.* This took place with the September 1974 issue.

Another early action was to appoint assistants in two vital areas: (1) someone to provide a pastoral ministry to the missionary family; (2) a public relations person to handle deputation schedules, tours, information, and so on. Two former missionaries, William Vaughters and James Hudson, respectively, were selected for these new posts.

To an even greater degree than his predecessors, Dr. Johnson felt that personal visits to the fields were essential to an adequate understanding of his responsibility. He mounted a large world map on his office wall and began inserting pins at the places he visited. By the end of 1974 there were 26 pins on the map. Before his seven-year term was over, he had visited every world mission field at least once.

The Student Mission Corps received Dr. Johnson's full support, and 72 young people were sent out in the summer of 1974.

As was expected, a dramatic upturn was taking place in the status of world mission districts. In one year, 14 districts moved up from national-mission to full mission status, and there were now 38 national superintendents.

A new publication, *Inter-Mission,* was introduced, which was geared specifically to missionary families. Also, some significant additions were made to mission policy, particularly with respect to short-term missionaries who were offering themselves in increasing numbers for limited service.

Another significant development in 1975 was the establishing of specific formulas for the disbursement of General Budget funds. Although a strict proportionate division of money received for the General Budget had not heretofore been established, a rule of thumb that had developed over the years was that 80 percent of the General Budget should go to world evangelism (basically World Missions and Home Missions). The remaining 20 percent was to cover all other general interests including administration and Headquarters operations.

Now an additional formula was emerging whereby the 80 percent going to world evangelism, plus Alabaster giving, would be divided roughly 80/20 between World Missions and Home Missions.

In 1976 still another dimension was added to mission financing when field budgets were divided into two parts: (1) national, and (2) missionary. This was an important step in the process of indigenization and self-support.

Lay Involvement

In 1975 a famine crisis in Haiti was met by the creation of a Hunger Fund, which financed a planeload of food and vitamins to that stricken nation. When on February 4, 1976, a devastating earthquake struck Guatemala, two airplanes were dispatched carrying not only 1,000 pounds of medical supplies but also medical personnel (three doctors and a nurse) to put them to use. Tents and 2,500 blankets were also flown in. This occasioned a broadening of the name to Hunger and Disaster Fund. Response to other needs as they were made known was immediate and generous churchwide.

Supporting further the compassion phase of missions, in 1975 the Nazarene Medical Action Fellowship was formed (later called the Nazarene Medical-Dental Fellowship). This was a formalization of a movement already active whereby doctors were giving blocks of time to serve, at their own expense, in mission hospitals. This organization of medical people (potentially 500 in number) set about to expand its effectiveness, not only donating their time and expertise but also supplying equipment and medicines needed in the hospitals and clinics overseas.

Not unrelated was the emergence of another lay-involvement program known as Work and Witness. It was an outgrowth of the Men in Missions assignment of Dr. Paul Gamertsfelder, the first man to be elected to the NWMS General Council (1972). In spontaneous response to emergency situations such as the Guatemala earthquake in 1976, and the growing awareness of the need for places of worship in the rapidly expanding mission fields, more and more teams were going out at their own expense to build churches, schools, and parsonages. In 1980 it was reported that 765 teams had gone out the previous year, investing close to $1 million in travel expense and construction materials. (See Chapter 6 for a more extensive report on both Work and Witness and Compassionate Ministries.)

Steps in Internationalization

To facilitate jurisdiction and development of the spreading missionary work, Dr. Johnson proposed at the General Board session in January 1976 the creation of three Intercontinental Zones:

Zone I: Europe, the Middle East, and Africa (including the Cape Verde Islands)

Zone II: Australia, New Zealand, Asia, and the islands of the Pacific (Japan, Taiwan, the Philippines)

Zone III: Mexico, Central America, the Caribbean, South America

These divisions were not unlike those set up for similar reasons back in 1924, though at that time India and the Near East were included with Africa. There were of course comparatively few fields then. This earlier plan had had to be abandoned in 1926, chiefly because of a financial shortage, but the logic of the supervision arrangement was still valid.

The concept of Intercontinental Zones was approved, and Rev. Darrell Teare, then superintendent of the work in New Zealand, was placed in charge of Zone I plus the South Pacific, and Rev. James Hudson, longtime missonary to Guatemala, was assigned to Zone III plus Asia.

Each zone was to have two representatives on the General Board. This was the first time that there was official representation on this august body from mission areas.

At the same time, representation at the General Assembly was worked out for all mission and regular districts. Since there were already 31 mission districts and 2 regular ones on world mission fields, this portended a significant alteration in the balance of delegates from home and world mission districts. As a result, of the total of 701 elected delegates at the 1976 General Assembly, 128 were from world mission areas, or 18 percent. Such representation was not out of line with the membership on world mission fields, which in 1976 stood at 130,892. This was 21.6 percent of the total world membership at that time of 605,185.

"Internationalization" was becoming a catchword as the concept of a worldwide church evolved. The general superintendents, in their report to the General Board in February 1976, wrote: "We are definitely committed to the idea of greater and faster movement toward internationalization in the Church of the Nazarene, and it is our plan to bring a proposal that there be a Commission to Study Total Internationalization of the Church."[1]

Such a Commission on Internationalization was indeed ordered by the General Assembly in June 1976. This representative group of ministers and laymen was instructed to explore all areas of the subject, including government, theology, finance, and ethical standards, and to report back to the 1980 General Assembly. The challenge before them was to create a worldwide fellowship that would encompass the whole spectrum of cultural settings yet retain the key Nazarene distinctives of holiness doctrine and practice.

There were parallel moves in other areas that reflected the spirit of the day. In 1975 the Latin Publications Division, which had been working largely in the Spanish and Portuguese languages, was renamed the International Publications Board to coordinate the many different translation and printing programs throughout the world.

At the General Assembly in 1976, as noted earlier, the name of the department was modified from Department of World Missions to Department of World Mission to more precisely define the unified task of the church. At the same time there was a reassignment of some of the fields between Home Mission and World Mission responsibility. The Latin American districts in the United States and the North American Indian work, once under the Department of World Mission, were transferred to Home Missions jurisdiction. At the same time, the South African European District, Samoa, Australia, New Zealand, and the entire European work were placed under World

Mission. This, in effect, anticipated the restructuring presaged by the creation of the Intercontinental Zones and the more extensive restructuring the Internationalization Commission was working on.

One more step in the integrating process was the first International District Superintendents Conference held in Kansas City, January 3-7, 1978. Fifty-eight superintendents from World Mission districts attended this historic meeting.

In his report to the General Board in February 1977, Dr. Johnson enunciated an evolving concept concerning the deployment of missionary personnel. Flexibility was the keynote.

> The established pattern of entering a country and settling in for a timeless period of missionary-guided development is no longer assured us. Missionaries must go, not knowing whether they will stay a lifetime or two or three years. . . .
>
> We are developing a fluid missionary program, geared to planting the church, developing national leadership, and transferring responsibility for reproduction and growth to them as rapidly as possible.[2]

The basic premise of this policy, that a call to missionary service was a call to serve anywhere, referred not only to the place of initial assignment but to the possibility of reassignment as needs arose. Usually this meant movement within a language group so the missionary was not having to constantly master a new tongue. A clear example was the moving of the Earl Mostellers from Cape Verde to Brazil, to Portugal, and then to the Azores, all Portuguese-speaking. But this was not always the case, as with the Jack Rileys, who served among four different language groups in Africa.

Another development of 1976, which was a significant year in world mission strategy, was the establishment of an Advisory Council on Education (ACE). Its purpose was to coordinate all mission school programs, establishing uniform standards and curricula. This group was constituted as a permanent council of the department with Dr. John E. Riley as its professional consultant. Under the council's jurisdiction were 35 ministerial training schools, 4 high schools, and 136 elementary schools.

Four levels of ministerial training schools were established: (1) G-level (graduate); (2) U-level (college or university—beyond high school); (3) A-level (advanced or high school); (4) M-level (middle or elementary). Although achievement levels in various cultural settings were difficult to standardize, the attempt was made to establish minimal requirements. A *Basic Accreditation Manual* was prepared to give guidance in this area. To further assist the schools, a second manual, *A Guide to Self-Evaluation,* was provided as a preparation for some sort of accreditation policy.

The missionary policy book needed extensive revision to keep up with the many innovations and adjustments being instituted. A major move was to place all items subject to frequent change, such as salary matters and medical coverages, in separate booklets. Sections were added concerning such new activities as the International Publications Board and the Work and Witness program.

In 1978, 17 Mission to the World conferences were held on 11 United States districts in which Alabaster giving received special emphasis. Such building funds were needed particularly in areas not reachable by Work and Witness teams. In fact, a secondary result of the conferences was the redoubling of interest in the Work and Witness program. The following year, 76 teams were involved with 1,500 people participating.

The REAP Program

In December 1979 the Department of World Mission took a radically new step in outreach to new areas. An international training team called REAP (Resource for Evangelism And Projects) met in Kansas City December 6-12 "to develop a strategy for evangelizing new areas when resident missionaries are not possible."[3] The purpose was to train and indoctrinate new groups who expressed a desire to unite with the Church of the Nazarene.

Members of the team were Wilfredo Manaois of the Philippines; Farrell Chapman of Trinidad/Tobago; Neville Bartle, New Zealand missionary to New Guinea; and Donald Owens and Paul Orjala, both at that time on the faculty of Nazarene Theological Seminary. John Riley, retired president of Northwest Nazarene College, served as convener. Since the first assignment had to do with preparing training programs for Nigeria and South India, Samson Udokpan of Nigeria and Rev. and Mrs. Bronell Greer of India were called in as resource persons.

Since visas could not be obtained for missionaries to enter these countries, the plan was to send in a REAP team on visitors' visas to provide up to three weeks of intensive training programs for pastors and key laypeople in Nazarene doctrine, organization, and administration. This would be repeated two or three times a year. The first such training program was conducted in South India in February

1980, with 120 attending. This was followed by a similar training session in Nigeria where a group of about 10 churches under the leadership of Rev. Udokpan's brother, Rev. Udoh, had already assumed the Nazarene name for their group.

Similar sessions with churches in other world areas were projected, and pilot investigations were conducted. But for all its promise and idealism, the REAP program failed to gain momentum and did not survive as a viable missionary strategy.

By the time of the 1980 General Assembly when Dr. Johnson was elected to the Board of General Superintendents, membership in world mission areas had grown to 173,491, a 24.5 percent gain during the quadrennium. Eight districts had met the qualifications for regular or Phase 4 status, 36 had reached Phase 3, 31 Phase 2, while 22 were at Phase 1 level. In addition there were 13 pioneer areas. There were now 70 national superintendents.

In what proved to be his farewell report as executive director of the Department of World Mission, Dr. Johnson quoted excerpts from an analysis prepared by the director of the U.S. Center for World Mission in Pasadena, Calif. It stated that though a quarter of the world's 4 billion population were Christians (in name at least), over half (2.4 billion) lived outside of direct contact with Christians. More disturbing was the fact that 91 percent of the missionary force was involved in maintaining and strengthening the established churches with only 9 percent engaged in cross-cultural evangelism. It was both a warning and a challenge lest Nazarene missionary endeavor become equally ingrown.[4]

The almost seven years in which Dr. Johnson served saw a number of significant changes take place under his innovative leadership. But above all he will be remembered as the architect of internationalization. He had introduced the earlier concept of Intercontinental Zones, which led to the formation of the Commission on Internationalization in 1976 on which he was a leading voice. The basic structure of regional administration that this commission devised was ready for submission and ratification by the time of the 1980 General Assembly. The implementation of its provisions was the task of his successor.

L. Guy Nees, 1980-86

In August 1980 Dr. L. Guy Nees, then president of Mount Vernon Nazarene College, was elected director of the Division of World Mission. He was a man of broad experience in the church both in pastoral and administrative posts. He had served some of its most prestigious churches including the "mother church," Los Angeles First. He had served as president of two of its colleges—Canadian Nazarene College and Mount Vernon Nazarene College—and was chairman of the board of Pasadena College at the time of its historic move to San Diego. For 11 years he had been superintendent of the Los Angeles District.

He had served several terms on the General Board but, uniquely, had not been a member of its Department of World Mission. In all his assignments he had showed himself a man of "steady strength and caring spirit."[5]

The immediate and pressing task that Dr. Nees faced was to put into place the administrative structure ordered by the Commission on Internationalization. But there were three other goals that he set for himself to accomplish during his term of service: To refine the educational policy, particularly as related to the training of ministers on world mission fields; to clarify the missionary policy book, which over the years had become somewhat cluttered and confusing; and to set up a viable pension program for retiring missionaries.

1. *Internationalization*

The starting point for the restructuring of the World Mission program was the monumental report of the Commission on Internationalization to the 20th General Assembly with its recommendations and its cautions. It addressed not only the administrative aspects but also theological and cultural implications. Excerpts of its major provisions were as follows:

> The Commission affirms the biblically sound and historically expressed theological position of the Church of the Nazarene in the "Agreed Statement of Belief" (*Manual* 25-25.8), and in the Articles of Faith (*Manual* 1-21), with specific emphasis on the church's distinctive doctrine of entire sanctification in Article X (*Manual* 13-14). The Commission expresses concern that this stated position be clearly articulated as non-negotiable in all doctrinal statements pertaining to the process of internationalization. . . .
>
> The Church of the Nazarene as an international expression of the body of Christ, acknowledges its responsibility to seek ways to particularize the Christian life so as to lead to a holiness ethic. The historical ethical standards of the church . . . should be followed carefully and conscientiously as guides and helps to holy living.

... Culturally conditioned adaptations shall be referred to and approved by the Board of General Superintendents" (*Manual* 32.2). ... The Commission recommends the continuing study of the emerging needs for cultural adaptations. ...

We urge every district to strive toward full financial support at the earliest possible time. ...

The organizational structure through which internationalization of the Church of the Nazarene is to be realized is ... by means of division into world regions which will have final amenability to the General Assembly.

The Commission therefore recomends: The creation of the following six church regions out of the existing three intercontinental zones:

Africa
Asia
Europe and the Middle East
Mexico, Central America, and the Caribbean
South America
South Pacific . . .

That the General Assembly delegates from each church region nominate by majority vote in caucus the exact number of representatives for election to the General Board by the General Assembly which would then vote an electing ballot on the slate presented by the regions. Nominees shall be from mission and regular districts. . . .

Our final goal shall be to involve all in the total program of the church with rights, privileges, and responsibilities without limitation or stigma because of culture, color, or area of origin.[6]

The implementation of this statement of policy and the working out of the administrative details was no simple procedure. Not only was there the selection of directors and the establishment of regional offices, but the task of communicating to the missionary staffs and national leaders the implications of the new format and securing their cooperation.

Some of the elements of restructure were already in place. James Hudson had been serving as a coordinator for Dr. Johnson, principally in Latin America. In July 1981 he was officially assigned the directorship of the combined regions of Mexico, Central America, and the Caribbean (which came to be known as the MAC Region) and the South America Region. Richard Zanner, who in July 1980 had been named coordinator for the African work and in addition had recently become superintendent of the South Africa European District, was named director of the Africa Region.

The Asian and South Pacific regions were combined under Donald Owens in June 1981. He was a former missionary to Korea and at the time a missions professor at Nazarene Theological Seminary in Kansas City. He moved to Manila in the summer of 1981. To his assignment was added the responsibility of launching the proposed Asia-Pacific graduate seminary. Property for this institution had already been purchased in Manila.

Initially, Dr. Nees himself assumed responsibility for the Europe and Middle East Region.

Statistically, in 1981, the six regions presented the following membership profile:

Africa	35,840
Asian	42,550
Europe/Middle East	6,219
Mexico/Central America/Caribbean	80,554
South America	16,780
South Pacific	3,536
Total	185,479

By 1982 the establishment of the Asia-Pacific Seminary had become such a demanding task that Dr. Owens asked to be relieved of some of his other duties. Thus, in January 1983 the South Pacific Region was assigned to Darrell Teare, who combined this with his role as superintendent of the Hawaii Pacific District, to which he had been elected in 1979.

Also in 1982 Thomas Schofield, district superintendent of the British Isles South District, took on the added duty of assistant to Dr. Nees for the Europe/Middle East Region. The following year, May 1983, he became the full-time director.

In July 1983 the original format that called for making South America a separate region was carried out, and Louie Bustle, who a few years before had been transferred from the Dominican Republic to Lima, Peru, was appointed director. Then, in November 1985, after Dr. Owens became president of Mid-America Nazarene College in Olathe, Kans., George Rench, mission director in Indonesia and former missionary to Taiwan, became Asian regional director.

Dr. Nees felt strongly that the regional leaders should live in the areas to which they were assigned, and establish regional offices there. Accordingly, the Africa office was set up in Florida, Transvaal; the Asian office in Manila; the Europe/Middle East office in Bolton, England; the MAC office in Guatemala City; the South America off' in Quito, Ecuador; and the South Pacific office in Honolulu.

The stated intent of the original commission was that p'

ically the geographical structure of the regions should be reexamined and alterations be made if it seemed appropriate. In line with this, a realignment of the regions was worked out and officially ratified by the General Board in February 1986, as follows:

Region	Director	Territory
Africa	Richard Zanner	Countries of the African continent except those bordering the Mediterranean, plus the Republic of Cape Verde
Asia-Pacific	George Rench	Australia, New Zealand, Papua New Guinea, Indonesia, islands of the Pacific, continental Asia as far west as and including Burma
Eurasia	Thomas Schofield	British Isles, continental Europe, countries of Africa bordering the Mediterranean, Middle East, subcontinent of Asia east to and including India
Caribbean	James Hudson	Countries of the Caribbean plus Belize, Guyana, Suriname, French Guiana, and Bermuda
Mexico-Central America	Jerry Porter (April 1, 1986)	Mexico, all of Central America except Belize
South America	Louie Bustle	All of South America except Guyana, Suriname, French Guiana

Regional Conferences

In connection with the adoption of the report of the Commission on Internationalization, the 1980 General Assembly adopted the following resolution:

> That as early as is practicable following the General Assembly, the general superintendent in jurisdiction shall call for a meeting of the General Board members, district superintendents, and college presidents (or equivalent) of the following six church regions to give suggestions for study of the involvement and service of the departments of the General Board in world areas, and that the results of these studies be forwarded to the General Board. The role of the General Board members on their regions shall be included on the agenda.[7]

This somewhat vague recommendation became the seed idea for what developed into six regional conferences conducted during 1983-84. To the originally suggested delegate group were added the mission directors and leaders of the auxiliaries (NWMS, NYI, and CL/SS). The general directors of these three divisions (Mrs. Phyllis Brown, Larry Leonard, and Phil Riley) were invited to participate, as was Bennett Dudney of the International Publications Board and Ray Hendrix of International Radio.

The format was to consist of two days of study and discussion on topics of mutual concern, addressing the need for cooperation and understanding. Each night, including the opening session, was to be an inspirational rally open to the public. In his introductory letter to the regional leaders, Dr. Nees pleaded for openness and freedom of expression. He suggested an unstructured program with a minimum of formal presentations. "Let's just talk to one another," he said.

At the opening session of each conference Dr. Nees read a statement of purpose. Among other things he said: "It is not our intent to develop the Church of the Nazarene into a federation of national churches [as some other denominations have done]. . . . The purpose of these regional conferences and any others that follow is intended to knit us closer together rather than separate us."

Coming as they did in the 75th anniversary year of the denomination, they were billed as Diamond Jubilee Regional Conferences. A feature of several rallies was the ordination of a large group of elders. For example, in Africa there were 34 and in South America a number of Aguaruna Indian pastors. The conference locations and dates were as follows:

Region	Location	Date
Asian	Seoul, Korea	Apr. 12-14, 1983
Europe/Middle East	Hanau, W. Germany	Oct. 31—Nov. 2, 1983
Africa	Manzini, Swaziland	Dec. 13-15, 1983
South Pacific	Brisbane, Australia	Jan. 11-13, 1984
MAC	Monterrey, Mexico	Jan. 17-19, 1984
South America	Lima, Peru	Jan. 31—Feb. 2, 1984

The conferences proved to be of immense value for both the Headquarters personnel and the district leaders. Bridges of understanding were built, and a sense of unity of purpose was developed.

2. *Educational Policy*

In 1976 under Dr. Johnson's leadership an Advisory Council on Education (ACE) had been established, and under the guidance of Dr. John Riley, educational consultant, excellent groundwork was laid in terms of policy and standardization.

Building on this foundation, on Feburary 15, 1983, a new Committee on Theological Education was called together to explore more deeply the ministerial training programs in World Mission areas. The members of the committee were L. Guy Nees, chairman; Phyllis H. Brown, secretary; Mark R. Moore, Donald S. Metz, Charles R. Gailey, and Charles W. Gates. At the May 14, 1984, quarterly meeting, the name of the committee was expanded to World Mission Committee on Theological Education, which was in turn reduced to the acronym WOMEC.

There were 35 theological institutions under WOMEC's purview (see list in Appendix A). These schools represented a wide range of academic levels, size, and facilities, but all were strategic in the on-going of the work. The steady increase in the number of churches required a supply of trained pastors to serve them. In fact, it was roughly estimated that already 500 churches were without pastors. An accelerated education program was needed.

It was also important that this training be received in the national setting and under national auspices so that the language and cultural barriers would be minimized. Administratively, the goal set by WOMEC was to have a minimum of 50 percent of the governing boards to be nonmissionary. Only 16 of the presidents/directors of the 35 institutions were nationals, but the intent was to increase this number as quickly as possible.

Three manuals were developed by the committee: (1) *Handbook for Accreditation: Curriculum and Degree Granting Processes for Nazarene World Area Theological Education Institutions;* (2) *A Basic Accreditation Manual;* and (3) *A Guide to Self Evaluation.* Manuals 2 and 3 were extensions of earlier manuals prepared by ACE. WOMEC was, in effect, the accrediting agency for Nazarene international theological institutions. But it also provided motivation and resources for the schools in addition to monitoring their progress. Its function was basically advisory as it sought to achieve the broad goal stated by Dr. Nees: "To upgrade and standardize the educational program in world mission areas."

The establishment of the Asia-Pacific Nazarene Theological

Seminary in Manila, the first graduate-level seminary for the denomination outside of the United States, along with the promotion of various extension programs, the development of the Africa Nazarene Theological College by combining three campuses under one administration, and the establishment of Seminario Nazareno Mexicano, A.C., in Mexico City were major achievements in the area of theological education during the quinquennium.

A unique project of WOMEC, sponsored by Dr. Mark Moore, was the "Books for Enrichment" campaign in which North American colleges were encouraged to "adopt" a G- or U-level institution abroad and augment its library holdings by sending duplicate volumes from their own libraries.

Using the "GUAM" formula, in 1985, the 35 theological training schools under WOMEC were classified as follows:

G-level (graduate)	1
U-level (university/college)	15
A-level (advanced/high school)	16
M-level (middle/grade school)	3

Not included was the U-level Africa Nazarene Theological College, which was actually a combination of the three colleges (all U-level) in southern Africa: at Florida, R.S.A.; Siteki, Swaziland; and Port Elizabeth, R.S.A. Nor was the South India Biblical Seminary on the list. The Church of the Nazarene had an excellent affiliate relationship with the World Gospel Mission in the administration of this school. (See the South India story in Part Two of this volume.)

Resident students in these 35 schools totaled 1,408. In addition, a number of the schools conducted extension programs that enrolled 2,233 students. The Seminario Nazareno de las Americas in Costa Rica was a leader in its extension program (CENETA) that blanketed Latin America. These concentrated short courses conducted by faculty members in strategic centers allowed pastors to continue serving their churches with minimal disruption as they continued their education.

For the granting of degrees, the Caribbean Nazarene Theological College in Trinidad affiliated with Canadian Nazarene College, while European Nazarene Bible College and Africa Nazarene Theological College (after March 11, 1983) affiliated with Mid-America Nazarene College.

3. *Missionary Policy*

The third goal Dr. Nees set for himself was to restructure the missionary policy book into a more useful and understandable format. The policy statements themselves were not so much at issue as was their presentation. Over the years, as new matters were written into the policy, they tended to become appendages rather than being incorporated into the whole.

Various methods had been tried to solve the problem, including the most recent supplementary booklet approach. Dr. Nees felt that everything should be under one cover, but because of frequent changes and additions there would need to be a loose-leaf format. This would make possible the insertion of new material at the appropriate places and facilitate the removal of old material where such was being replaced. Color coding of the pages in each section and the dating of each page were two other ways of keeping tab on the material.

The total mission policy book as eventually put together consisted of a 76-page section covering the World Mission Division, the Mission Field, and the Missionary; a 19-page section on National Church Policy; and a 23-page Health Care Plan Document. A 2-page supplement on current salaries and benefits was also included. Each of these was in a different color. The heart of the document was the 45-page section having to do with the person of the missionary.

4. *Missionary Pensions*

Dr. Nees's fourth area of concern was the retirement plan for missionaries. Heretofore, the major source of income for emergency medical assistance and pensions for retired missionaries had been through the Nazarene World Mission Society plus some designated gifts. It was obvious that as the needs of a larger missionary force increased and the number of retirees correspondingly grew, the available funds were falling farther and farther behind, and increasing subsidies were needed from general funds. Permanent funding was essential.

The first step was to separate the medical and the retirement accounts, leaving the medical phase to the NWMS and making the pension part a department responsibility. Several basic actions were taken:

1. All available funds were brought together for this pension fund pool.

2. The General Board made an initial special contribution of $800,000 and subsequently made annual appropriations.

3. Interest from reserve accounts such as the one to cover catastrophic events was channeled into the pension fund.

By 1984 the turnaround point had been reached, and the actuarial fund was beginning to grow, reaching $3.5 million by 1985. Projections at that time indicated that it would take $8 million to fully fund the retirement program, but excellent progress had been made.

The scale of retirement benefits for missionaries was set at essentially the same levels as that for U.S. ministers except that additional amounts were provided missionaries with more than 20 years of service.

Lay Involvement

While all these basic administrative developments were taking place, the ongoing missionary program was experiencing a great wave of homeland interest and support. Giving to the World Mission cause was escalating, as demonstrated especially in the Easter and Thanksgiving offerings, now reaching a combined total annually of more than $17 million. Mission specials brought in another $6 million each year.

But there was also significantly increased involvement in lay-participation projects such as Work and Witness and Compassionate Ministries programs. The former had emerged in the late 1970s but during the Nees era came into full flower.

Carpenters, masons, plumbers, electricians, painters, contractors, and just plain laborers were becoming involved directly in missions. Whereas in the beginning days of Work and Witness these construction crews worked in countries near at hand, such as in Central America and the Caribbean, they were reaching out farther and farther to Europe, Africa, the Orient, the South Pacific, and even India.

No mission program ever caught on so quickly or was so universally adopted. But it became a victim of its own success. Its cherished spontaneous character eventually had to yield to the imposition of rules and regulations. With over 100 teams a year, some guidelines had to be laid down. Ultimately it meant the appointment of a central coordinator. Thus in November 1984 David Hayse joined the staff in Kansas City to direct this program. He had been serving as project coordinator for Mexico and Latin America.

During the 1980-85 quinquennium, approximately 400 Work and Witness teams, made up of some 8,000 people, were involved in this program. The total investment in labor, travel, and materials was estimated at $12 million.[8] (See chapter 6 for an extensive study of the Work and Witness program.)

Compassionate Ministries also came to the fore during the Nees administration. There was a new awareness across the church of the need to address the physical needs of a suffering world in the name of Christ. As crises of hunger, natural catastrophe, revolution, and refugee displacement mounted, the demands on the Hunger and Disaster Fund ballooned. But just as readily the church responded. In 1982, $160,000 was contributed to the fund, and in 1983 giving jumped to $285,000. In 1984 a major famine in Africa called for a special added appropriation of $100,000 from general funds. During the 1980-85 period, $1.25 million was contributed to the Hunger and Disaster Fund, and 23 countries were recipients of this aid.

Not all this money went out in the form of direct relief, however, for there was growing interest in long-range preventive measures as well. The improvement of agricultural methods to increase food supplies, and the development of self-help projects to lift the people out of poverty were examples. Haiti and South India were in the vanguard of this effort.

In his report to the General Board in February 1984, Dr. Nees recommended that a full-time person be hired to coordinate the total Compassionate Ministries program. He turned to Dr. Steve Weber, 10-year veteran missionary to Haiti who had done significant work there in both relief and development programs. He, along with Dr. Al Truesdale of Nazarene Theological Seminary, organized the phenomenally successful Compassionate Ministries Conference held in Kansas City on November 8-10, 1985, at which 500 were registered. "What started as an idea with modest expectations," wrote Franklin Cook, editor of *World Mission,* "developed into a conference of monumental significance and proportions."[9] (See chapter 6 for an elaboration of this and other phases of Compassionate Ministries.)

Not unrelated to this was the creation of an organization called Nazarenes In Volunteer Service (NIVS). Heretofore, noncareer missionary work had been largely confined to medical personnel and some builders. The plan was to involve persons of other skills and professions in short-term service on mission fields. Teachers, nurses, clerical workers, computer programmers, architects, and the like were inspired to offer themselves for periods of two months to a year wherever the need arose—all at their own expense.

In July 1985 a group of 25 of these dedicated people gathered in Pasadena, Calif., for a 14-day orientation with 15 well-qualified instructors. After the conference several went immediately to assignments in various parts of the world, while others remained on a stand-by basis should a call for their specific skills arise.

Field Visitation

Dr. Nees was as convinced as his predecessors that nothing could take the place of personal contact with the mission field to adequately understand his assignment. His 1981 journeys took him to Haiti, the Dominican Republic, Papua New Guinea, the Philippines, Europe, and Africa. Eight days of this last trip were spent in Nigeria, where a promising opening for the church was being explored.

In 1982 Dr. Nees visited 21 fields, including a trip into mainland China in October. (The story of this attempt to reach the former Nazarene field in North China is told in Part Two of this volume under "China.") In 1983, 20 fields were visited, and in 1984, 12 more. His last trip was to Cyprus for the dedication of the new training center there.

The Goal of 75 Fields

As the 75th anniversary of the denomination in 1983 approached, the idea was conceived of bringing the total number of world mission fields to 75 by the anniversary year 1983-84. This would necessitate opening five new fields. The plan had dramatic appeal and interest was high as the five targeted areas were announced: the Azores (in the mid-Atlantic), Botswana (in the heart of southern Africa), Kenya (in east central Africa), Suriname (on the northeast coast of South America), and Burma (in southern Asia).

Preliminary contacts to some degree had been made with each of these countries, which gave some assurance of success, but more intensive exploratory work remained to be done. It was well into 1984 before work had begun in all five, and some were not officially organized until even later. (See Part Two of this volume for the detailed stories of how each of these fields was developed.)

Prospective fields continued to open. Significantly, there were two in the Middle East—Egypt and Cyprus. Two different groups in Egypt had expressed interest in aligning themselves with the Church of the Nazarene, and both consisted of several churches. By the end of 1985 negotiations were still pending but showed great promise.

When the California group, Investments Eternal, was given options from Dr. Nees concerning another missionary project, they chose Cyprus. The church needed some neutral place to establish a ministerial training center for the Middle East, and this nearby island offered an excellent base. The building purchased provided a missionary home with adequate basement space for an education center. This was not planned to be an organized church, though that was a possibility. Rev. and Mrs. Jamil Qandah, graduates of European Nazarene Bible College, were placed in charge.

An interesting comparison of the missionary statistics since 1908 appeared in the minutes of the General Board for February 1983, the 75th anniversary year. The figures for each 25-year span were given as follows:

Year	Countries	Missionaries
1908	6	19
1933	16	85
1958	34	329
1983	69	553

By 1985 these figures had climbed to 74 and 620 respectively, still one short of the anniversary goal of 75 countries because not all the new fields had been officially organized.

As Dr. Nees's term of service drew to a close (officially at the General Board meeting in February 1986), there was no slackening of vision or perspective. Goals for decadal growth were proposed as follows:

20 new countries
72 new districts
2,200 new churches
224 new missionaries
400,000 new members

With such projections, the membership in world mission areas, which already constituted 30 percent of the denomination's total, could well be in the majority by the turn of the century. At present rates of growth, this was not an unrealistic expectation.

The 1980-85 quinquennium had indeed been an active one on the World Mission scene. Work had been established in 13 new areas.

There were now 3,106 organized churches with a total membership of 247,244. This represented a 45.5 percent increase for the five years.

A New Director

Elected to fill the office of director of the World Mission Division upon Dr. Nees's retirement was Dr. Robert H. Scott, most recently superintendent of the Southern California District, where he had served since 1975. He had pastored churches earlier at Santa Ana, Sacramento, and Fresno, all in California. For over seven years he had been a member of the Department of World Mission of the General Board and since 1983 its chairman. He assumed his new office on March 1, 1986.

Chapter 5

The Nazarene
World Mission Society

The missionary program of the Church of the Nazarene has had. strong support from the outset. In the early days its leading champion was Dr. H. F. Reynolds. But over the years it has been the foreign missionary society that has provided the principal dynamic to sustain and expand that initial interest. The story of its faltering beginnings and its subsequent vigorous development forms an important chapter in the annals of Nazarene world mission.

The story begins in the East, where missionary interest had become a special province of women. In 1861 the Women's Union Missionary Society had been organized in New York to bring the "organized womanhood of the churches of all denominations into the work of missions." As a logical spin-off from that, in 1899 a women's missionary auxiliary was organized among the 20 churches of the Association of Pentecostal Churches of America.

The sequence of events concerning the missionary society leading up to the 1907 union of the APCA with the Church of the Nazarene is summarized in a statement presented to that first General Assembly:

> On April 16, 1899, while the annual meeting was in session in Providence, Rhode Island, a few sisters met and organized a society to be known as the Women's Foreign Missionary Society of the Pentecostal Churches of America with eight charter members. . . . The first year there were two auxiliaries organized and $6.05 raised. . . . Since that time we have been steadily growing until now we number 18 auxiliaries and a membership of about 400.[1]

The $600-700 these societies had raised had been used to assist the missionaries in India and to erect a chapel for John Diaz in the Cape Verde Islands.

The obvious hope in presenting the above report was that such an organization would be made a part of the new Pentecostal Church of the Nazarene. But this was not to be. The only response was a brief, noncommittal statement by the Committee on Missions that read: "That the Women's Foreign Missionary Auxiliary, as far as possible or practicable, continue their most noble and successful efforts."[2]

An even more cryptic statement appeared in the minutes of the 1908 General Assembly: "That the Women's Foreign Missionary Society, as far as is practicable, continue their most helpful work." But still there was no definitive action to effect an organization. Local societies continued, particularly in the East where the tradition was strong. But the 1911 General Assembly ignored the matter completely.

By 1915, however, the climate had changed. The missionary-minded Pentecostal Mission of Nashville had joined forces with Nazarenes, and interest in the "regions beyond" was greatly increased thereby. There was also the persistent, behind-the-scenes effort of the existing local missionary societies who would not let the matter die.

Seventeen of the 51 members of the Committee on Foreign Missions at the 1915 General Assembly were women, and these were doubtless back of the presentation of a memorial to the General Assembly that read, in part, as follows:

> That, inasmuch as, from the peculiar character of the work, and woman's unique adaptability to, and grasp of the same, she has been most efficient on these lines in years that have passed— they do sanction the organization of a Women's Missionary Auxiliary. . . .
>
> Its purpose is to work in conjunction with, or as an auxiliary to said [Church Missionary] Board, in order to increase missionary interest—both of the home and foreign field—in ways and means best devised by themselves—such as holding prayer meetings, obtaining special speakers, keeping in touch with missionaries on the field, and to cooperate with the Church Board in raising its apportionment.[3]

The memorial was referred to the Committee on Foreign Missions, which drafted a recommendation adopted by the Assembly "that Women's Missionary Auxiliaries be organized in all our churches, where practical, to increase missionary intelligence and assist in raising funds to carry on the missionary work of the church."[4]

Implementation was left in the hands of the General Board of Foreign Missions, which, at its meeting on October 18, 1916, appointed a committee of three to prepare a constitution and bylaws for the organization. Named to this pilot committee were Mrs. Susan N.

Fitkin of New York, one of the eight charter members of the original WFMS organized in the East in 1899; Mrs. Ada E. (Paul) Bresee of Los Angeles, daughter-in-law of P. F. Bresee; and Mrs. Eva G. (John T.) Benson of Nashville.

As requested, these three drafted a proposed constitution and bylaws to govern the organizational structure at all three levels—local, district, and general. They recommended the appointment of a 14-member General Missionary Committee with representatives from all the geographical zones, including Canada and the British Isles, to elect officers and set the organization in motion.

Although the proposals of this three-member initiating committee would not be acted upon until the 1919 General Assembly, the creation of the missionary society was considered to have taken place at the time of the originating General Assembly action. Thus the natal date of the organization was set at 1915.

The 1919 General Assembly voted to adopt the recommendations of the committee, and the General Board of Foreign Missions accordingly appointed the 14-member committee as follows: Rev. Susan N. Fitkin and Dr. Julia R. Gibson (Northeast); Mrs. E. G. Roberts, Mrs. R. G. Codding, and Mrs. D. W. Thorne (Midwest); Mrs. John T. Benson and Miss Fannie Claypool (Southeast); Mrs. E. J. Harrell (South Central); Mrs. H. T. Wilson (North Central); Mrs. Edith Whitesides, Mrs. Paul Bresee, and Mrs. S. P. Richards (Far West); Mrs. F. Toppin (Canada); and Mrs. James Jack (British Isles).

The committee held its first meeting on October 7, 1919, in Kansas City and elected Mrs. Susan Fitkin as general president; Mrs. Paul Bresee, vice president; Mrs. J. T. Benson, treasurer; and Dr. Julia Gibson, secretary. (When Dr. Gibson found it necessary to resign shortly thereafter, Mrs. R. G. Codding, recently returned missionary from India, was elected in her place.) The General Missionary Committee was to meet only in connection with the General Assembly, while the elected officers, as an executive committee, were to meet at least annually. Organizations spread rapidly across the country, and by the next General Assembly, in 1923, there were 68 societies with a total membership of 5,329 (1922 statistics).

At the General Assembly in 1923 there was a major restructuring of general church organization, which included the absorption of the General Board of Foreign Missions into the General Board. As part of the change, the members of the Women's General Missionary Council (note change from "Committee") were now to be elected by the General Assembly from a list of nominees submitted by a special nominating committee of five appointed by the chairman of the General Assembly (the general superintendent). There were no geographical stipulations this time, except that of the 16 to be elected there must be 1 each from Canada and the British Isles.

At the same General Assembly, the constitution of the Women's Missionary Society was officially adopted and placed in the *Manual.* Henceforth, also, the General Council was to meet annually.

The first General Convention was held in Columbus, Ohio, in June 1928, just prior to the General Assembly. At this time the logical change was made to have the General Council elected by the convention delegates rather than by the General Assembly. However, it was not until the following convention in 1932 that the election of the general president was placed in the hands of the delegates, not the General Council. Whatever the method of election, Mrs. S. N. Fitkin continued to be returned to office until she ultimately retired in 1948 after having served for 29 years.

As years passed, the organizational structure of the missionary society altered little, with members of the General Council being elected from geographical areas and assigned specific phases of responsibility in the general program. It was at the 1936 General Convention that the word "Foreign" was added to the name to distinguish its area of interest from home missions.

A significant change took place in 1940 with the election of Miss Emma B. Word as the first full-time general secretary of the WFMS. She had already worked a number of years in the general missionary office. She served until 1949, to be followed by Miss Mary Scott, newly returned from China, who served for 25 years, 1950-75. During that time, in 1964, the title was changed to executive secretary.

Mrs. Wanda Knox, former missionary to New Guinea, held the office from 1975 to 1980, to be followed by Mrs. Phyllis Hartley Brown (Perkins), 1980-85, who had had missionary experience in Japan. By this time, in line with the General Board restructure of 1980, the office was called "general director," which technically was now a staff position in the World Mission Division.

In early 1986, Mrs. Nina Gunter, longtime General Council member and district president in South Carolina, was elected general director.

The 1952 General Convention voted to change the name of the organization to Nazarene Foreign Missionary Society (deleting

"Women's"), which opened the door for the inclusion of men in the active membership. Over the years there had been much talk about how to involve men in the missionary program of the church, and a "Men's Missionary Movement" became a rallying call in the 1930s. For some reason, promotion of this abruptly ceased in 1938. Some said it was because of the mounting pressure to form a rival men's missionary society. The other alternative was to allow men to become full members of the WFMS with voting and office-holding privileges. Many felt, however, that this would destroy the genius of the organization.

Even though in 1952 men were admitted to full membership, it was not until 20 years later that the first man was elected to the General Council. He was Dr. Paul Gamertsfelder, whose assignment was to develop ways in which men could be involved in the program. It took the title of Men in Mission.

Though over the years some local presidents and other officers both local and district were men, the missionary organization remained firmly in control of the women. As far back as 1947, Dr. G. B. Williamson, speaking on behalf of admitting men as full members, stated, "It is our belief that for many years the women will be the leaders in the missionary program of the church, and therefore, we do not believe that great changes will take place."[5] The situation almost 40 years later had proved him correct, nor had there been any agitation to alter the status quo.

In 1964, because of the undesirable connotations of the word "foreign," it was removed from both the name of that department of the General Board and that of the missionary organization, whose title became Nazarene World Missionary Society. Then in 1980, to align the name with the General Board restructure, it was further modified to Nazarene World Mission Society.

Some outstanding women have served in the office of general president of the organization. Following Mrs. Fitkin was Mrs. Louise Robinson Chapman, whose dynamic "If you don't like it, change it!" philosophy characterized her 16 years of leadership (1948-64). From then on, terms of office were limited to two. Mrs. Rhoda Olsen served from 1964 to 1972, and Mrs. Bea Oliver from 1972 to 1980. Mrs. Lela Jackson began her first term in 1980 and was reelected in 1985.

The Program of the NWMS

While the organizational structure of the society was going through its metamorphosis, its program was also being developed and expanded. In this the stated purpose of the organization was the guiding factor. The fourfold purpose as stated in the 1985-89 *Constitution* is as follows:

1. To encourage our people to pray for all the activities of world evangelism through the missionary arm of the Church of the Nazarene.
2. To provide an informative program to increase the knowledge and understanding of the needs of the world and the efforts of our church to reach all with the gospel.
3. To inspire and challenge our youth to keep their lives available to God's will for their lives.
4. To help raise funds to support the missionary outreach of the Church of the Nazarene.[6]

In all these areas, the NWMS diligently sought to give both motivation and direction. Prayer was a pervasive theme, epitomized best perhaps in the Prayer and Fasting program, which continued to be one of the most enduring of its emphases. In 1953 a prayer chart, provided for each society, was designed to encourage "definite prayer for specific needs." A star was to be placed beside every request when a prayer was answered. Although each month of the year had its special emphasis (Bible study, Alabaster, Medical Plan, etc.), Prayer and Fasting was highlighted all year long.

Likewise, concern for children and youth was an early emphasis. A children's page in the missionary magazine (*Other Sheep/World Mission*) first appeared in the 1940s and was continued thereafter. Missionary stories and pictures were published for a time in a leaflet titled *Junior Light Bearers*. Children's chapters for ages 4 to 11 years were part of the local structure. The first reading books written specifically for children were published in 1957, and special study packets for this age-group became available in 1977.

For the teenage level, beginning in 1950, three of the adult reading books were designated each year as of particular interest to youth. This replaced an earlier program that listed a large number of missionary books for young people and encouraged teenagers to read 16 of those recommended during a quadrennium. In 1978 study packets for teens became a regular production item.

In 1932 a Young Women's Foreign Missionary Society (YWFMS) was attempted but met with limited success and was eventually abandoned in 1948. It was replaced by the youth chapters sponsored by the parent organization.

Financial Projects

The NWMS has been historically project oriented, and almost all of the projects have included financial goals. One of the earliest was the Relief and Retirement Fund, which was begun in 1919. The first constitution of the organization stated that this was to be a "vested fund, the interest to be used for the relief of our sick and super-annuated missionaries." Contributions for this fund were to come from three sources: (1) an annual 10¢-per-member assessment, (2) the Memorial Roll, and (3) Life Memberships.

The Memorial Roll was a listing of deceased members of the organization whose names could be added by the payment of $25.00 to the Relief and Retirement Fund (later increased to $30.00). By 1923 there were 21 names on this list. By 1985 the total was 4,307 for that year alone.

The Life Membership idea was somewhat less successful. Originally the plan was that "anyone may become a life member of the society by the payment of twenty-five dollars ($25.00) and an honorary life member by the payment of one hundred dollars ($100.00) to the Relief and Retirement Fund." The leaders apparently had difficulty explaining that such payments did not absolve the person from future financial obligations. The Life Membership concept became somewhat of an anachronism and was dropped in 1948 but not before 17,464 names had been placed on the roll.

In 1948 the 10¢-per-member annual assessment was also dropped, and in its place $1.00-per-member annual general dues were introduced. Sixty cents of this was to go to Relief and Retirement and 40¢ to general office expense including materials furnished free to the local societies, such as Prayer and Fasting envelopes, posters, membership cards, and (later) Alabaster boxes.

In 1976 the general dues item was itself dropped. To bolster contributions to the newly renamed Medical Plan and Retirement Fund, the Distinguished Service Award was introduced. By the payment of $100 a church could honor a person in its membership for some special type of service not necessarily related to missions. This was a highly successful program and annually increased until in 1985 alone, 1,404 individuals were so honored.

In the meantime, however, the fund was failing to match the astronomical rise in medical costs or meet the demands of caring for a mounting number of aging missionaries joining the retirement roll. The time came when interest and offerings could no longer keep pace with the needs, and slowly even the once substantial capital fund was depleted.

When in 1982 an adequately funded pension program for missionaries was established by the World Mission Division, the retirement phase of the original NWMS program was detached. Special offerings for the remaining medical phase were used to augment income from the Distinguished Service Awards and Memorial Roll. In 1984-85 the total from the three sources amounted to $312,438 ($38,493, $137,348, and $136,596 respectively).

Another source of income that continued to be a mainstay of the society's program was Prayer and Fasting. It strongly addressed the No. 1 goal of the society, that of enlisting prayer support, but also proved to be a major financial source.

The idea of prayer and fasting first surfaced in California when in 1917, at the suggestion of E. I. Ames, Pasadena College adopted the plan to gain prayer and financial support. When in 1923 talk of retrenchment in the foreign missionary program surfaced, Mr. Ames and others, including Bud Robinson, presented a resolution to the General Assembly calling for a churchwide adoption of prayer and fasting as a means of financing the missionary work.

It was not, however, until the General Board took action the following October that the idea was, in principle, adopted unanimously. The wording of the resolution was published in the *Herald of Holiness*, and interest began to grow. Early in 1924 Rev. R. J. Kunze, a New York pastor, shared with General Superintendent Reynolds a specific plan that had been successfully used in his own church. He was urged to write it up and send it in to the *Other Sheep*. The article, which appeared in the April 1924 issue, contained a twofold plan:

> First, in every local church let a prayer and fasting league (or any other name you want to give it) be organized, each member to do without one meal each week and put into the missionary treasury what the meal would cost. We would think the minimum would be about 25¢.
>
> Second, let each member also pledge to spend in prayer for the missionaries and their work, the time it would take to consume the meal.[7]

The Board of General Superintendents proposed that the Prayer and Fasting program be strictly for missions with the missionary society as sponsor. The response churchwide was immediate and the results phenomenal. Whereas giving through the WFMS in the 1919-23 quadrennium had been $60,602, for 1928-32 it rose almost eightfold to $466,245. "The roots of the NWMS were put down firmly in prayer and fasting," declared Mary Scott in her recollections recorded on tape on November 1, 1983.

In another financial crisis in 1949, after an all night of prayer during the General Board meeting in January, the inspiration came to challenge the churches to give 10 percent, or a tithe, of their income to missions. The concept was not entirely new, for it had first been proposed by Leslie F. Gay at the 1905 assembly of the Church of the Nazarene in Los Angeles. The idea was now, however, to be given concrete implementation. Although it was to be a total church emphasis, all NWMS giving except local, district, and general expense was to be applied to the 10 percent. As the years passed, more and more churches achieved this goal until by 1985 there were 1,929, or about 40 percent of the churches in Canada and the United States, who were at or above that level of missionary giving. By then the 10 percent concept was beginning to take hold on world mission fields as well.

Alabaster Giving

At the time the NFMS Life Memberships were dropped, Mrs. Elizabeth Vennum, the General Council member who had had charge of this program, was asked to devise some challenging project to take its place. Accordingly, at the January 1949 meeting of the council, she presented the historic Alabaster Box program. It was based on the Gospel story of Mary breaking the "alabaster box" of perfume on Jesus—an extravagant gift of love. Mrs. Vennum's plan was to provide each member with an Alabaster box in which money would be placed from time to time. Twice a year these would be brought to the church on a designated Sunday in February and September for an "Alabaster Opening." All funds so collected would be used exclusively for the construction of buildings on mission fields and for the purchase of building sites.

No program was ever adopted more enthusiastically, and in the first full year (1949-50) $63,998 was brought in. By the end of 1985, however, the annual offering was topping $2 million. Over the years, almost $30 million had come in, which paid in whole or in part for about 3,000 buildings and/or properties.

In 1953 a challenge of a different nature was presented. A Spanish version of the "Showers of Blessing" radio broadcast was proposed, to be called "La Hora Nazarena." The missionary society was asked to raise the necessary $10,000 for the project on an annual basis. As years passed, more stations and more languages were added, and the offering name was changed to World Mission Radio. Giving to this cause likewise increased until in 1985, $398,000 came in. Broadcasts were now going out in 38 different languages around the world.

There had been other fund-raising ideas adopted over the years, such as the selling of Scripture text calendars, which began in 1922 and by 1948 was bringing in about $10,000 per year. There was also the Indian Head Penny Fund, which was first proposed in 1918 to support work among American Indians. It was not until 1928 that the program was officially adopted, however. Indian head nickels were added, and the name was changed to Indian Fund. At its height, the project netted over $30,000 a year.

The missionary society began to be involved in specific overseas projects as early as 1926. That year the WFMS undertook to raise $10,000 to add to the substantial amount being given by the Fitkins to erect the Raleigh Fitkin Memorial Hospital in Swaziland. The following year, $10,000 was raised for the Bresee Memorial Hospital in China, and in 1932, $5,000 for the Reynolds Memorial Hospital in India.

In 1940, to commemorate the 25th anniversary of the organization, the members were challenged to raise $25,000 for the Reynolds Memorial Bible Training School Fund, to be used where needed. Then in 1948, upon the retirement of Mrs. Fitkin as general president, an offering was taken in her honor to build a Bible training school in the new field in South China. The goal was $50,000, but over $74,000 actually came in. Unfortunately the political situation in China was such that it was unwise to proceed with building the school, though property had been purchased and a wall built around it. The money was therefore parceled out to other school projects, including $24,000 to Japan and $9,000 each to British Honduras (Belize) and the Philippines.

In 1954, in celebration of the 40th anniversary of the NWMS coming up the following year, the society sponsored a $100,000 offering to open the work in New Guinea. Ten years later, on the 50th anniversary, $150,000 was raised to build a hospital on that same field. At the 1960 General Convention, $15,000 was spontaneously raised for the work in Panama.

A special Literature Fund offering for Africa in honor of Mrs.

Louise Robinson Chapman, who retired in 1964, brought in $50,000. Then in 1982 an offering for the opening of work in Venezuela more than doubled its goal when $592,000 came in.

Over the years the NWMS had proved its ability to inspire support for missions, and by 1985 its annual income had reached $2,993,262. This did not include its considerable contributions to the General Budget and missionary specials not channeled through the NWMS.

Missionary Education

The other major area of challenge for the NWMS besides finance was that of disseminating missionary information: "to increase the knowledge and understanding of the needs of the world and the efforts of our church to reach all with the gospel."[8] In this phase, the society also had an excellent record. The keystone was its monthly chapter meetings, which had been a basic part of the program from the beginning.

The denomination's main communication channel for missionary information has been the *Other Sheep/World Mission* magazine, which began publication in July 1913. Although at the time there was not yet a missionary society, the organization became its most ardent supporter. When the original "committee of three" met in 1915 to set up the missionary society, Mrs. John T. Benson was asked to prepare a small leaflet recommending the reading of the *Other Sheep* as a source of information and study.

Beginning in October 1920, the *Other Sheep* carried a two-page section titled "Women's Missionary Society News," which informed the readers of what the organization was doing on behalf of missions.

In 1922 a committee of three was set up "to prepare as early as possible outline studies for this year, also examine and recommend certain books on the various countries for a study course." Miss Mary E. Cove of Lowell, Mass., Mrs. S. P. Richards of Los Angeles, and Miss Fannie Claypool of Nashville were appointed.

In 1923 this pioneer "study committee" reported that leaflets had been prepared on China and India, and a leaflet for children. Also outline studies were being published in the *Other Sheep*. This aggressive beginning prompted the Women's General Missionary Committee to elect Miss Claypool as the first superintendent of study, which office she held until her death on June 2, 1925. She was succeeded by Miss Mary E. Cove, also a member of the original committee.

The first full-fledged study book, titled *Latin Americans, Our Southern Neighbors,* was prepared for the 1927-28 assembly year. Members were urged to read "missionary books published by the Nazarene Publishing House," though Amy Hinshaw's *Messengers of the Cross in Latin America* was the only Nazarene book among the six recommended for that year. Amy Hinshaw was to become one of the most prolific writers of missionary books in those early years.

In 1932 Mrs. Olive M. Gould became superintendent of study. Under her leadership, in 1934 a Missionary Training Course was launched, and by 1936 some 321 persons had completed it. The course of study included the study book (until 1936 a biennial volume and thereafter an annual) and a biography of some outstanding missionary on which a series of questions were to be answered, plus brief reviews of two others books selected from a recommended list. Completion of these assignments was rewarded with a certificate with a gold seal to be attached for each year in which the work was completed. For the first full quadrennium of the plan, 1936-40, 638 earned all four seals.

Teenagers were urged to read 16 of 25 books listed during the quadrennium, and certificates were issued to those who did. Missionary stories and pictures were published for children in a leaflet titled *Junior Light Bearers.*

In 1952 a correlated Missionary Study Committee was ordered on which there was representation from the Department of Foreign Missions, the missionary society, the NYPS, Christian Service Training, and Nazarene Publishing House, later to be joined by the Spanish Department (International Publications Board). The chairman was usually the executive secretary of the Department of Foreign Missions (World Mission Division). A study cycle was established whereby all areas of missionary work would be covered over a certain span of years, and an annual study book covering the year's area of emphasis was prepared. A set of reading books mostly related to the fields under study was also published. Each member of the missionary society was urged to read at least three of these and thus become a "reader." The total number of such readers became part of the achievement record of the local society.

In 1957 books especially prepared for children began to be published, to be followed by study materials for leaders of junior societies. Selected books from the adult reading list were recommended for teen reading, and missionary program material was for a time published in the *Young People's Journal* and *Teen Topics*. Finally, separate study packets for teens appeared in 1978.

By 1980 the study cycle had gone through several revisions as new countries were added. It was now taking nine years to go through the complete list of countries. In 1983 an attempt was made to have an overview study of the entire mission enterprise based on the book *Into All the World*. The following year an updating study was added. This set the stage for major revision of the study curriculum, which was now to be largely theme oriented (missionary methods, organization, policy, etc.). Some studies of individual fields, particularly new ones, would also be included. There would be the usual list of reading books available.

Star Societies

From the earliest days of the NWMS achievement standards were set for both local societies and districts. "Standard Society" certificates were first issued in 1924 to those societies that reached the designated goals. At the first General Convention in 1928, 70 Standard societies were reported. Each quadrennium the goals were modified and expanded until in 1936 an elaborate 15-point system was instituted with achievement levels of Superior and Standard societies. Each item was given a valuation of 5 or 10 points, which totaled 105. For example, 5 points were earned if 12 regular meetings were held; 10 points if dues were paid in full; 10 points for having an *Other Sheep* agent (no matter the number of subscriptions); 5 points for having 75 percent of the membership in the Prayer and Fasting League; and so on. A Superior society was one that achieved 100 of the possible 105 points; a Standard society one that reached 85 points.

In 1940 the number of categories was increased to 20 with some having two parts. The system was beginning to smother under its own complexity, so in 1944 the number of categories was reduced to 10; however, half of these had two parts. Further simplification was needed.

Finally, in 1956 the "Star Society" program was instituted. The five points of the star were:

1. Membership (increase of 7 percent up to 60 percent of church membership)

2. *Other Sheep* subscriptions (equal to 60 percent of church membership)
3. Missionary book readers (60 percent reading at least three)
4. Prayer and Fasting League members (equal to 75 percent of membership)
5. Completion of study book lessons

By 1963 not only were there 3,262 Star societies, but the five-star goal was reached denominationwide. By the 1970s, however, the Star society incentive also began to wane. Thus in 1976 the "Mission Award" concept was introduced, which set achievement goals in three basic areas: membership, reading, and General Budget giving. This was later expanded to include a prayer ministry and youth program. Thus to qualify to receive a Mission Award, a local society needed (1) to develop a mission prayer ministry; (2) to have a minimum of 1½ times church membership in number of missionary books read including regular reading of *World Mission* magazine (English-speaking areas only); (3) to involve youth and children in specific mission activity; (4) to pay the General Budget in full. Because of the difficulty in establishing worldwide norms, guidelines for achievement were left to regional leaders to decide. An entire district could also earn the Mission Award if 90 percent of these goals were achieved districtwide.

Box Work and LINKS

Another phase of NWMS activity was its direct ministry to the missionaries themselves. This began as part of the "Box Work" program, the forerunner of which was a project promoted in California by Mrs. Paul Bresee as early as 1913. This original plan was to send clothing, boxed foods, and other supplies to the missionaries.

When Mrs. Bresee was elected to the first General Council (committee) in 1919, she presented the plan as a worthy project for the new missionary society to consider. It was officially adopted by the Executive Committee of the General Council in February 1921. As might be expected, the responsibility for the program was delegated to Mrs. Bresee, who continued the work until her death in 1946.

To the personal items for missionaries were added boxes of used clothing for distribution to the people, bandages (rolled from discarded sheets), books, and equipment items. The value of these boxes mounted into the hundreds of thousands of dollars per year. But as time passed, problems developed in receiving countries. Import restrictions, theft, high duty charges, confiscation by "authorities," and rising mailing costs all created confusion and disillusionment.

But the desire to help the missionaries was still strong, and the basic concept could not be allowed to die. Thus in 1976 the LINKS program was devised—Loving, Interested Nazarenes Knowing and Sharing. The purpose was to help the churches become more intimately involved with the missionaries. Each church was assigned by the district LINKS secretary a missionary (or missionaries) for whom they were to be responsible. The missionaries were asked to send a list of their needs to the general office, and this information was relayed to the specific churches involved. In some countries it was better to send money than goods. Detailed instructions concerning packaging were provided, and estimated duty money was to be deposited with the general treasurer ahead of time.

In addition to personal gifts sent during the year and especially at Christmas, the societies were encouraged to send letters, cards, and cash gifts. The missionaries were also asked to send lists of needs for schools, hospitals, and clinics with which they were connected. The sharing of prayer requests was likewise an important part of LINKS.

This program provided a direct link from the local church to the mission field and to specific missionaries. Every church was involved, and no missionary was forgotten.

Information Lines

The communication of ideas and suggestions from the Headquarters offices to the local societies was maintained on a regular basis through a quarterly publication first called *Bulletin.* In 1946 it was enlarged and given the title *General Council Tidings.* In January 1982 the name was again changed to *Focus* with even broader content and larger format. The channels of *World Mission* magazine were also open to the NWMS, and a monthly two-page NWMS news feature was part of every issue beginning in October 1920.

Another communication line between individual societies and Headquarters was the Prayer Mobilization Line, which was begun in 1980. Prayer requests received from the fields were compiled in the NWMS office and recorded on tape each Wednesday and Friday. By calling the specified telephone number at any time, the recorded information could be heard.

The NWMS continued to be the key to missionary information and inspiration in the church. By the end of 1985 its worldwide membership had reached 498,825, of which just over 100,000 were in world mission areas.

Chapter 6

Support Programs of World Mission

I. WORK AND WITNESS

Work and Witness has been described as "one of the great missionary success stories of the Church of the Nazarene."[1] It exploded on the scene in the mid-1970s and within a decade had become the most dynamic lay-oriented program ever to develop in the denomination. Its genius was its spontaneity. As James Hudson put it, "It just seemed to happen." Basically, Work and Witness is the sending out of teams to build buildings on the mission fields—churches, parsonages, schools, clinics, and so on.

Though almost all of the structures were new, sometimes the workers were involved in adding to or refurbishing existing buildings. Many times it meant continuing the work of a previous team. Not always have the teams gone outside their own countries, either. Many United States teams, for example, were involved in the building of the Nazarene Indian Bible School in Albuquerque, N.Mex.

By 1985 nearly 200 teams a year were going out on various projects around the world. Up to that time, 8,000 people had been involved in the program, and an estimated $12 million in labor, travel, and material had been invested. And the program was continuing to escalate.

How It Began

In 1952 the Women's Foreign Missionary Society decided to expand its active membership to include men, who had heretofore been allowed only associate status. Predictably this did add to the membership rolls, but it was still very much a women's organization.

Twenty years later, however, when the first man, Dr. Paul Gamertsfelder, was elected to the General Council, the situation markedly changed.

Dr. Gamertsfelder's assignment was "to develop programs in the local church for prayer and fasting for missions, study groups, and *programs for men*" (italics added). A year and a half later, January 15-25, 1974, he put together a group of five Ohioans—himself and two lay couples—to go to Panama and hold meetings among the Choco and Guyami Indians. They paid their own expenses both for travel and for board while there.

Out of this experience evolved the idea of doing building projects while on the field. They saw the inadequate shelters into which the people crowded for worship, and the need for parsonages and missionary homes.

By 1976 work teams were beginning to go out. A catalyst to initiate this was the devastating Guatemala earthquake that destroyed or damaged many churches. A. L. Braswell and his wife spent seven months there in 1976, helping to rebuild seven churches. They returned several times afterward to build new churches.

Another catalyst was the explosive growth of the new work in the Dominican Republic, which called for new buildings in rapid order. James L. Jensen, a team leader, worked on 16 churches there over a period of 2 years. He was a member of Indianapolis First Church, which congregation sent teams out every year for 10 years to build churches in that country. Raymond C. McGuire of Arlington, Va., also led several projects in the Dominican Republic, as well as elsewhere.

Neighboring Haiti was an area of concentration for Ken Key of Jasper, Ala., who directed more than 20 teams there. Jerome Richardson of Indiana recruited and organized 17 teams to help build the Caribbean Nazarene Theological College in Trinidad. As a coordinator for the Work and Witness program, he made over 40 trips abroad (nearly all at his own expense) to evaluate needs and set up projects.

Though the nearby Caribbean, Mexican, and Central American fields attracted the most participation at first because of lower travel costs, Work and Witness teams were soon going as far away as southern Africa, Europe, the South Pacific, the Philippines, and even India. A number of team leaders returned to the fields for months and even years of additional service, completing projects and building other churches, schools, clinics, and parsonages.

Not all the members of the teams were men. Out of an average-sized team of 20, there were usually 3-5 ladies. Their most common role was preparing meals for the team, but many worked on the projects as well. Some 10 percent of the teams were teenagers, for whom lighter projects were devised. An increasing number of retirees were also being involved.

Work and Witness Policy

By its very nature, the Work and Witness program was a free-wheeling kind of operation. Yet as the projects proliferated, certain guidelines had to be laid down. Because of an aura of glamour surrounding these trips, it was easy for a church to raise money for a Work and Witness project to the neglect of their lifeline budget responsibilities. Also, visiting teams sometimes consumed much of the time of busy missionaries who at that particular time had other responsibilities that needed their attention. In addition, the various projects needed to be prioritized so that the more pressing situations would not be neglected. Thus the following principles were laid down:

1. Work and Witness projects in World Mission areas are to be assigned by the World Mission Division. [Usually three or four options were offered for a team requesting a project assignment.]
2. Projects in the United States and Canada are assigned by the Division of Church Growth.
3. Districts and local churches having paid their General Budget are eligible to request a Work and Witness project.
4. Work and Witness projects shall be funded by a combination of one or more Work and Witness teams and participation by the local congregations on the field in keeping with World Mission and Church Growth policy. . . .
5. Purchases of land, materials, and equipment with Work and Witness funds shall be considered an Approved Special with 10 percent credit for World Evangelism.
6. Travel cost of working members of the team shall also be eligible for 10 percent credit. . . .
7. Recommendations as to maximum size of team and minimum funding are as follows:

Team size	Minimum funding
10-12	$ 7,500
13-18	10,000
19-25	12,000[2]

Each team member was, in effect, responsible for a minimum of $500 toward the cost of materials (usually paid for by the sponsoring church) plus transportation to the field and housing and food while there. Project funds were to reach the field three months ahead to allow time to purchase necessary materials and have them on the site when the team arrived. This meant that each project was completely self-supporting.

On multiple-team projects only one team per month was scheduled, which meant about a two-week break between each. Usually on a small church building (say, 30 x 60 ft.) foundations would be poured by the local people ahead of time, which made it feasible to erect the walls and roof in the normal two-week work span.

As the Work and Witness program mushroomed in the early 1980s, the need for a full-time coordinator at the World Mission office in Kansas City became imperative. As a result Rev. David Hayse, missionary to Central America and most recently coordinator of development in Mexico and Latin America, moved to Kansas City on November 1, 1984.

Matching field requests with applications from local churches and districts for project assignments was a major task. An instruction handbook was prepared to guide the groups in their preparations and in their activities on the field. Detailed advice concerning special local situations was also provided when appropriate. Insurance for participants was arranged through the Work and Witness office.

A book of basic, standardized plans was prepared along with starter ideas. Where customs duties were not prohibitive, prefabricated buildings were sometimes sent in for assembly by the teams. "Skill banks" were organized for special phases. For example, steel fabricators could be sent in ahead of the team to prepare roof trusses. Also these specialists provided instruction in building techniques for outgoing teams when requested.

Because of numerous construction projects going on simultaneously on certain fields, it was sometimes necessary to assign a missionary on the field to coordinate all the activity. Paul Say directed the work in the Dominican Republic, where over 50 buildings were erected in six years. Freddy Williams took charge in Haiti, where self-help programs were part of the work projects. David Hayse himself had served as a building coordinator in Mexico.

The impact of the program on the missionary vision of the local churches was phenomenal. Seeing missions firsthand, investing their own sweat and money in tangible ways, and being part of the fulfillment of the Great Commission had a transforming effect on the lives of thousands of laymen who participated. By 1985 over 40 countries had been visited by Work and Witness teams, and 1,000 buildings had been erected, enlarged, or renovated.

Because of the success of the program, Alabaster funds could now be concentrated in the more distant fields not readily reached by Work and Witness teams. Having more adequate facilities provided great impetus to the work on the various mission fields. An important by-product was the intensified interest in missions generated by the returning workers who had seen the gospel at work in other lands.

II. COMPASSIONATE MINISTRIES

The concept of compassion has been a motivational factor in missionary endeavor from the earliest days. The physical suffering of the people that the missionaries encountered as they moved among them could not go unanswered. Consequently as much a part of their equipment as their Bibles was their satchel of simple medical tools and potions. These caring ministrations were an expression of Christian love and concern, but they also provided a significant entrée to the hearts of the people.

Another compassionate ministry was the establishment of orphanages, which were common on mission stations, particularly in earlier days. The distribution of clothing was also a prominent phase of missionary work until the complications of distribution (customs duties, government restrictions, theft, etc.) made this difficult and in some cases impossible.

As mission work developed, medical dispensaries and clinics were built to minister to the people who came for help. Some were operated full-time, while others were manned on stated days, by missionary nurses going out from main stations. Mobile clinics were a natural outgrowth of this.

The next step was the building of full-fledged hospitals, most of which grew out of earlier clinics. The first of these was the Bresee Memorial Hospital in China, which was officially opened in October 1925. The second was the Raleigh Fitkin Memorial Hospital in Bremersdorp (Manzini), Swaziland, which was dedicated in July 1927. (It should be noted that an earlier small hospital had been launched at Piggs Peak, 50 miles north, in 1920 but never reached full operating status.) The third was the Reynolds Memorial Hospital in India, which was opened in June 1938. Meanwhile a clinic established by the International Holiness Mission at Acornhoek in the Transvaal, R.S.A., had by 1939 blossomed into a 66-bed hospital but had no resident doctor until 10 years later. This became a Nazarene hospital when the IHM joined forces in 1952. The fifth hospital was in Papua New Guinea, which was dedicated in March 1967.

The Bresee Hospital in China ceased operation when the Japanese overran the country in December 1941. In 1975 the Ethel Lucas Memorial Hospital in Acornhoek was taken over by the government and renamed Tintswalo (meaning "Mercy"). But the remaining three continued a strong and effective ministry.

With substantial financial assistance from agencies of the West German and Netherlands governments, in the mid-1970s the Raleigh Fitkin Memorial Hospital was almost completely rebuilt and enlarged in a million-dollar project that made it the second-largest hospital in the country. It had the largest patient load, however, with 55,000 being treated there in 1985. A related ministry was the nearby government leprosy hospital at Umbuluzi whose operation for many years was placed in the hands of the Church of the Nazarene.

By 1985 there were 15 clinics operating out of the Swaziland hospital, which served 120,000 patients that year. The hospital in India ministered to 36,018 patients in 1985, while the Papua New Guinea hospital treated 57,071. Eighteen satellite clinics of the latter served over 10,000 additional patients.

Each of these three hospitals had nurses' training colleges in connection with them with 121 enrolled in Swaziland, 21 in India, and 60 in Papua New Guinea in 1985. Countless stories could be told of how over the years these medical institutions ministered with great compassion in times of personal and national crises. (See Part Two of this volume under the countries named for further information on these hospitals.)

Samaritan Hospital, Nampa, Idaho

Another hospital that in its heyday played a significant role in the missionary program of the church was located in the United States at Nampa, Idaho. At the time of its official incorporation on February 27, 1929, it was called Nazarene Missionary Sanitarium and Institute but became more popularly known as Samaritan Hospital and School of Nursing.

The hospital was the product of the concern and determination of Dr. Thomas E. Mangum, who envisioned the establishment of a hospital to serve two purposes: (1) to provide medical help for ailing missionaries on furlough, and (2) to provide a training center for future missionary nurses. Seeking a friendly environment for his project, he found warm supporters in H. Orton Wiley, president of Northwest Nazarene College, and District Superintendent N. B. Herrell of the Idaho-Oregon District. He thus moved from Texas to Nampa, Idaho, in 1918 to pursue his project. The previous year the college had instituted a Department of Medical Missions and First Aid Instruction for outgoing missionaries.

A modest start was made in a remodeled house in early 1920. The following year the hospital program was separated from the college, and its own board of directors was set up. In October 1921, in a remodeled home the Mangums had originally built for themselves across the corner from the NNC campus, the Reynolds Memorial Home, a small 17-bed hospital, was dedicated.

Obtaining official recognition and support from the denomination proved to be quite illusive, however. At the 1923 General Assembly, a Sanitarium and Hospital Committee was appointed. This group recommended only that the nurses' training phase be referred to the Committee on Education and that the hospital be made "a special interest of the Women's General Missionary Council." The 1928 General Assembly, once again addressing the issue, went so far as to classify it as "an institution of the general church," but specifically forbade the solicitation of funds from across the church.

The General Board in January 1929, however, did authorize a contribution of $5,000 to the hospital's building program and specifically stated that "the Department of Foreign Missions shall have supervision of the sanitarium and hospital"—but only in an advisory capacity. More importantly it stated: "The Department of Foreign Missions shall in no-wise be obligated for the financial support of any sanitarium or hospital."

By this time a building program begun in 1924 and laboriously carried out on a pay-as-you-go basis had resulted in the completion of the shell of a 50-bed hospital. In subsequent years portions were completed until by 1933 the complete building was in operation. In 1930 the nurses' training school had been accredited, and the first class graduated in 1931. Over the following 20 years many of its graduates went abroad to serve with dedication and distinction on mission fields around the world.

To maintain the accreditation of the nursing school, it became necessary to substantially enlarge the hospital; and in 1950 an ambitious expansion program was launched that would double the capacity and incorporate new treatment programs. But the support base was inadequate, and when at the 1952 General Assembly a memorial to include the hospital in the General Budget in the amount of $18,000 was rejected, the death knell was sounded. A token gift from the general church of $5,000, followed by another for $10,000 in 1953, though appreciated, were not sufficient to turn the tide. The expansion project had to be abandoned in a partially completed state.

The college took possession of the new wing and completed it for its science department, while the nurses' home became a men's dormitory. The original hospital was operated for a few years as a private institution until it, too, folded, and the building was taken over by the college.

Dr. Mangum's dream was never fully realized, but eternity alone will reveal the profound influence this institution had on the missionary program of the church through the outstanding group of nurses it sent forth. Also, scores of furloughing missionaries would testify to the loving care provided for them in the hospital.

Emergency Relief Involvement

Although this extensive medical work was the flagship of Nazarene compassionate ministries, famines, war, and natural disasters provided other opportunities for service to the suffering. The first recorded instance of such aid was in China when in 1920 a drought-caused famine left 20 million people starving. In response to a cabled plea from Rev. Peter Kiehn, $1,000 was sent immediately, and a China Famine Relief Fund was set up that received contributions totalling $25,000. In addition, Nazarene missionaries there were placed in charge of many relief projects and the distribution of thousands of dollars worth of food provided by the International Relief Commission. (See the China story in Part Two of this volume.)

This scenario was repeated in subsequent years in a number of countries when our missionaries were entrusted with the handling of relief programs after national crises. For example, in 1961 in Belize it was a hurricane and accompanying tidal wave that put Prescott Beals in the center of a government rehabilitation program. It was a logical procedure, for missionaries formed a natural bridge between the sending countries and the recipients. They also had the necessary administrative machinery in place and knew the people and their needs. Most importantly, they could be trusted not to use the aid for personal gain.

Organized Compassionate Ministries

Even though compassion lay at the heart of Christ's ministry and certainly was, as Dr. W. M. Greathouse put it, "an authentic expression of holiness," the church seemed reluctant to embrace this ministry as a basic element in its mission. There was a lingering apprehension that such activity might dilute the primary emphasis on evangelism. The two were somehow perceived as being mutually exclusive. "Social gospel" implications were inherent in such activity.

The net result was a less-than-ardent response to humanitarian concerns and in some quarters outright resistance. True, there was box work for the sending of used clothing to the mission fields. Orphanages continued as important adjuncts on many stations. Special appropriations were made from time to time to meet emergencies overseas occasioned by floods, famine, earthquakes, and so on. In fact, an informal survey revealed that 30-40 percent of all missionaries were involved in some way with compassionate ministries, though mostly in medical missions.[3]

As the concept of world community grew, however, and the news media, particularly television, shattered the complacency of favored nations by depicting the multiplying human tragedies around the world every day, the call could not be ignored. The church had to respond, not to the detriment of its evangelistic mission but to augment and reinforce it.

It was a multifaceted challenge. Not only did food need to be sent to avert famine, but long-range solutions had to be found with improved agricultural practices and nutritional improvements. Self-help projects needed to be launched to lift the 800 million people living in abject poverty out of their miserable existence. Sixteen million refugees needed to be rehabilitated.

In the 1970s the Church of the Nazarene began to enter the arena of compassionate ministries as part of its planned agenda. It began in Haiti when in 1975 a famine called for response, and a planeload of food and vitamins was sent in. This prompted the establishment of a Hunger Fund to help meet such crises.

Then on February 4, 1976, a violent earthquake devastated a large area of Guatemala, and the church responded with supplies, medical aid, and personnel for reconstruction and to aid the rehabilitation of displaced families. This new dimension to the humanitarian cause prompted a change of name to Hunger and Disaster Fund.

Appeals to the church for contributions to this fund found ready response as new calamities struck around the world. By 1980 not only Haiti and Guatemala, but Peru, Nicaragua, Ecuador, Cape Verde, India, Chile, Cambodia, the Philippines, Mozambique, and South Africa had been recipients of aid. Contributions went from $104,243 in 1980 to $285,000 in 1983. By the close of the quinquennium $1.25 million had been sent in, and 23 countries had received help.

Famine relief, particularly in Central Africa and Mozambique, brought forth a great outpouring of support. In addition to a special grant of $100,000 from general funds, over half a million dollars came in to purchase, ship, and deliver grain, dried milk, and other food items to these countries. In Kenya, one of the prominent directors of the food distribution program was a Nazarene layman, Leo Mpoke. Relief was also sent to sufferers of numerous natural disasters—typhoons in the Philippines and Fiji, an earthquake in Chile, floods in Argentina and Portugal, drought in the Cape Verde Islands, to name a few.

Long-range Programs

Haiti was also in the vanguard of development of long-range projects of humanitarian nature. In 1973 Charles Morrow introduced modern agricultural methods there that improved both the quantity and nutritional quality of their food. Steve Weber came in 1975 to launch various cooperative self-help projects that eventually numbered about 20. South India, under the leadership of Bronell Greer, established similar programs.

The term *agmissions* was coined to cover farm projects to improve soil productivity and the quality of herds. Well-drilling projects in Haiti, Swaziland, and India sought to provide safe drinking water as well as irrigation for the fields. By 1985 some 7 percent of the Compassionate Ministries budget was being invested in the various agmissions projects. The agriculture department of Mid-America Nazarene College provided principal support for this program.

Health clinics in India, Haiti, Guatemala, and Brazil were also given assistance, and nutrition centers were set up in several countries. Grain mills in Malawi aided a self-support program there.

An unusual opportunity for the Church of the Nazarene came when missionary Dr. Glenn Fell, an expert in soil science, became a high-ranking government official in the area of development in the Christian-controlled South African Black Republic of Ciskei. Other missionaries were similarly involved.

So rapid was the expansion in this area that in 1984 an office of Compassionate Ministries was created in the World Mission Division. Dr. Steve Weber was named full-time missionary coordinator. His decade of missionary service in Haiti in this phase of activity fitted him well for the task.

Volunteerism

Long before Work and Witness teams began to shuttle to the mission fields, numbers of medical doctors had been offering themselves for temporary service in mission hospitals. This was a great boon to the weary doctors whose caseloads were staggering.

This activity led to the organization of the Nazarene Medical Fellowship in the early 1970s. Its purpose was to encourage such participation and provide some central coordinating agency. It also encouraged sending needed equipment and supplies to the overseas hospitals and clinics. The doctors also made themselves available for consultation by long-distance telephone or shortwave radio when unusual case situations arose in the mission hospitals. Still another service was to invite furloughing doctors to join their staffs to learn the new medical techniques and to sharpen their skills.

When dentists asked to join the program, the name was changed to Nazarene Medical-Dental Fellowship.

In the fall of 1985 Dr. Paul Wardlaw, formerly medical superintendent of the Raleigh Fitkin Memorial Hospital in Swaziland, was named executive secretary of the NMDF, which was now a unit of Nazarene Compassionate Ministries.

In the early 1980s Rev. H. B. London, Jr., a missionary enthusiast and pastor then at Salem, Oreg., conceived the idea of a "Great Commission School of Missions" for the purpose of instructing those in various skills and professions who wished to volunteer a few months of service on World Mission fields. The plan had the endorsement of the World Mission Division, for there was need from time to time for teachers, nurses, clerical workers, computer programmers, architects, and so forth in various fields.

When Dr. London moved to the pastorate of Pasadena, Calif., First Church in late 1984, the program was picked up by the World Mission office in Kansas City under the name Nazarenes In Volunteer

Service (NIVS). It was placed under the jurisdiction of Compassionate Ministries.

An intense, two-week, cross-cultural orientation session was required for assignments of three months or more. Volunteers paid their own travel costs and served without remuneration. As earlier mentioned, the first of these orientation sessions was held in Pasadena in July 1985. Twenty-five persons were involved in the 14-day workshop, at the close of which several left for immediate assignments in Brazil, Swaziland, Guatemala, and Venezuela. The others remained on standby.

A spin-off of NIVS was Nazarene Agmission Volunteers (NAV). The organization's stated purpose was "to provide leadership in the battle to provide essential food supplies to the poorest of the poor through appropriate agricultural methods." Among other things it proposed to work in conjunction with preventive medical programs to provide pure drinking water through capping springs, digging wells, and constructing closed water systems.

In November 1985 a Compassionate Ministries Conference in Kansas City drew 500 registrants from across the United States and Canada and even from abroad. The blue-ribbon list of speakers represented nearly all the major Christian relief agencies. Out of the conference came a renewed awareness of the place of compassion in the church's mission to the world. The assembled Nazarenes, over half of whom were college and seminary students, were made aware of the denomination's roots of social concern. It remained for them to find the balance between that and the basic mandate of the gospel, to preach "Jesus Christ and him crucified" (1 Cor. 2:2).

III. World Mission Radio

The phenomenal communications explosion of the 1980s with its paramount emphasis on the visual through television and the videocassette recorder has obscured the fact that radio is still the most powerful of all communication mediums. In fact, as Merritt Nielson points out in his book, *A Sower Went Forth to Sow*, "It is the *only* mass communications medium for the billions who live in the Third World." The place that radio holds in missionary endeavor is therefore extremely significant. This includes three areas, all of which have been part of the Nazarene radio ministry:

1. Radio has been an effective instrument to introduce the

church and its message to new areas about to be entered. Venezuela is a prime example of this strategy. "The best identification for the Church of the Nazarene," noted William Porter, who launched the work there, "is to be known as the church that sponsors 'La Hora Nazarena.'"

2. Radio has been a channel by which the gospel has reached many who live outside of areas of missionary activity.

3. Radio has been a means of Christian nurture through follow-up programs such as Bible studies and correspondence courses.

World Mission Radio began when in March 25, 1945, the first program of "Showers of Blessing" was aired. Among the 40 stations that carried the program was HCJB (Heralding Christ Jesus' Blessings) of Quito, Ecuador, whose powerful shortwave transmitters even then reached a major portion of the world. (The station presently [1985] carries Nazarene programs in six different languages over transmitters that now blanket the world.) As time passed, scores of other local stations were added. But of great importance for missionary outreach, two powerful shortwave outlets began to carry the program, namely, the Far East Broadcasting Corporation and Trans World Radio. The FEBC, based in Manila (Philippines), had transmitters also in Korea (Orient), Saipan (western Pacific), Seychelles (Indian Ocean), and San Francisco; while TWR, headquartered in New Jersey, operated 10 large transmitters located in such strategic places as Swaziland (Africa), Bonaire (South America), Guam (Pacific Ocean), Sri Lanka (south of India), Argentina (South America), Monte Carlo (Europe), and Cyprus (eastern Mediterranean).

"Showers of Blessing," however, was reaching only the English-speaking world. A great, latent potential lay in the multitude of other languages spoken throughout the world. The first move in that direction came in 1954 when the first Spanish program, "La Hora Nazarena," was produced in Kansas City with Honorato T. Reza, head of the Spanish Department of the Nazarene Publishing House, as director and speaker.

Mexico was a key target for this broadcast, but religious broadcasting was forbidden there, so the program had to be beamed in from border stations and HCJB. Little by little, however, ways were found to get the program on local stations, principally through commercial sponsorships, until 75 outlets were being used. Then in the late 1970s the laws were tightened, and overnight the program was cut off. Again, gradually the roster of stations was built back up with

5- to 15-minute local "tags" being added to the regular broadcast.

At one time 800 local Latin American stations of all sizes were listed as carrying "La Hora Nazarena." In return for airing the program, the stations were allowed to keep the tapes and reuse them for their own purposes. A survey revealed, however, that many of them had not been running the program at all. They had signed up merely to receive the free tapes, which were valued anywhere from $15.00 to $50.00, depending on the country. It was necessary to make up a selected list of 350 stations, each of which were put under contract. There was no loss of total coverage as "La Hora Nazarena" blanketed the entire Hispanic world.

The lack of indigenous flavor in the music became an increasing problem, so tapes of locally recorded singers and instrumentalists were obtained and dubbed in at the Kansas City studios.

Finally, in 1980-81 the so-called Costa Rica Experiment made the Spanish broadcast truly indigenous. Juan Vazquez Pla of Puerto Rico, who had joined the faculty of the Seminario Nazareno de las Americas in Costa Rica in 1978, was a specialist in radio communications. To capitalize on his expertise, his contract was modified to allow him time to travel throughout Latin America, training, advising, and encouraging local groups in the use of radio and other media. He gathered tapes of musical groups and messages by local pastors and church leaders. From these he put together programs for use throughout the area. In 1981 production was shifted from Kansas City to Costa Rica, and the program took on a distinctively Latin flavor. In addition to "La Hora Nazarena," 175 spots of 30 to 90 seconds each were produced and two daily 5-minute programs developed, one beamed to youth and the other addressing family concerns. Also 16 subjects covering the entire ministerial course of study were being put on videotape for home study, the entire series scheduled for completion by 1988.

In 1968 another Latin language was added when the Portuguese program, "A Hora Nazarena," was launched. Its target was the 100 million people around the world who spoke that language, not only in Portugal itself but also the Cape Verde Islands, the Azores, Brazil, Mozambique, Angola, and other former Portuguese colonies. All were covered by TWR's transmitters, but many local stations also carried the program.

Missionary radio played an ever-increasing role in the church's world outreach. Missionary personnel began to be specifically assigned to this phase. In Africa, for example, programs were developed in six principal languages or vernaculars—Zulu, Afrikaans, Sotho-Pedi, Shangaan, Tswana, and simplified English. The regular English "Showers of Blessing" and Portuguese "A Hora Nazarena" were also used.

The key leaders in this African development were missionaries Bill and Sherrill Wagner. When they went to the field in 1977, they took with them excellent equipment, including portable recorders with which much local material, both music and speaking, could be taped on location. Besides the powerful TWR transmitters in Swaziland and other major outlets, many local stations aired the programs. In 1981 a well-equipped permanent studio was completed near the Africa regional headquarters in Florida, Transvaal. From there the extensive Bible studies and other follow-up programs were also directed.

In Japan, under the leadership of Bart McKay, a 15-minute radio program was developed as early as 1956 and received wide acceptance. In 1982, however, new government regulations forced a change in format in which the Nazarene program became a 10-minute segment of a five-hour-long regular national broadcast.

In India a Marathi program, "Tilak and Christ," was begun in the mid-1960s. This capitalized on the popularity of the famous Indian poet/philosopher Tilak. It was broadcast principally from Sri Lanka. A radio correspondence course of 24 lessons was developed, with between 5,000 and 6,000 participants. M. V. Ingle was the leader in this diverse ministry. With the opening of work in South India, a Tamil language broadcast was begun. In 1981 two special Tamil programs were added, one for adults and one for children. Heading up this radio work was Ezekiel George.

The Philippines presented a difficult challenge because of the 47 dialects spoken there besides the official English and Tagalog. In the late 1970s and early 1980s radio programs were produced in 7 of these dialects. In conjunction with these, a 15-lesson correspondence course was developed in which over 5,000 listeners participated. The Far East Broadcasting Corporation was very cooperative, granting the use of its studios as well as its transmitters.

The Italian broadcast, "L'Hora Nazarena," began in 1973 with programs being produced in Rome. Radio Monte Carlo (TWR) was the principal broadcast outlet, but a number of local FM stations throughout the country carried the program as well.

Indonesia, with its 13,000 islands, 300 tribal languages, and 85 percent Muslim population, was a special challenge. In 1978 a beginning was made in Java with the program "Pancaran Berkat" ("Showers of Blessing") going out over the FEBC in Manila and a number of local stations.

The French program, "L'Heure du Nazaréen," begun in 1974 and produced in Montreal, was beamed to French Canada (Quebec), the French Antilles in the Caribbean, and Haiti. Its effectiveness in France itself was hampered by the different accent of the speakers from that in the "homeland."

On September 4, 1977, a Mandarin (Chinese) broadcast was begun, principally to reach the 5 million people in Hong Kong and to publicize the newly established work there. In the 1980s it began to be targeted three times a week into mainland China. Though it was impossible to determine the measure of response there, indications were that the program was being received warmly.

Other examples of how radio has been used on the mission field include half-hour daily broadcasts in both Kekchi and Pocomchi Indian dialects in Guatemala, Creole programs in Haiti and the Bahamas, and twice-weekly 15-minute programs in Korea supplemented by five dramatic spot messages, six days a week, on national prime time. By 1985 the church was broadcasting the gospel message in 38 different languages and dialects around the world.

The central figure in the coordination and development of World Mission Radio has been Ray Hendrix, son of veteran Latin American missionaries Spurgeon and Fae Hendrix. He came to the Department of Communications in 1973 and has tirelessly sought to explore every avenue of electronic outreach. This included not only radio but television, videotape, and other modern media.

It was Hendrix who originally coordinated the Nazarene Amateur Radio Fellowship into a highly useful communication link with missionaries in many parts of the world. Although later restrictions on conducting business transactions over amateur radio bands limited its earlier usefulness, regularly scheduled "meetings" over the airwaves have continued. Also the advent of vastly improved telephone connections, the use of telex machines, and satellite communications have largely obviated the earlier need for amateur shortwave assistance.

All this varied activity has since 1976 been supported principally through the annual NWMS-sponsored World Mission Radio Offering. In 1985 contributions reached an all-time high of $398,000, almost double what it was in 1980. Each year, however, requests for financial assistance were running 50 percent higher than what was received. The medium of radio still held tremendous challenge and opportunity.

IV. CASA ROBLES: MISSIONARY RETIREMENT CENTER

On a five-acre campus in Temple City, Calif., 12 miles east of downtown Los Angeles, live 46 retired missionaries of the Church of the Nazarene who have given an aggregate of 1,400 years of service on the field. This is Casa Robles (House of Oaks), a retirement center consisting of a large, two-story central residence and 32 cottages. First established in 1946, it has been home for varying lengths of time to 81 veterans of missionary labor.

The idea of providing a home for retired missionaries was first presented at the 1940 General Assembly in Oklahoma City. But no official action was taken on the resolution, which had been presented by the Southern California District. When the matter was again presented at the 1944 General Assembly, a commission was set up to explore the matter and find a suitable location. Dr. A. E. Sanner, Dr. H. Orton Wiley, Mrs. S. N. Fitkin, and Mrs. Paul Bresee were named for the task.

At the January 1945 meeting of the General Board a Missionary Home Committee was set up, and Dr. A. E. Sanner, Dr. H. Orton Wiley, and Rev. M. Kimber Moulton were appointed. The names of Mrs. Bresee and Foreign Missions Secretary C. Warren Jones were later added. The fact that all appointees except Dr. Jones were from Southern California was a rather clear indication of where the major support lay and the likely ultimate location. This was confirmed when on March 14, 1946, a large, two-story, nine-room dwelling on a 150 x 337-foot tract of land was purchased in Temple City. It had been built in 1911 and was currently owned by the Harold Barricks, members of Los Angeles First Church.

At the first official meeting of the Missionary Home Committee on May 14, 1946, Rev. V. P. Drake was appointed superintendent. At a following meeting in June, the name Casa Robles was chosen because of the beautiful oak trees on the property. In January 1947 an adjacent property, including a commodious two-bedroom home, was added.

Dedication day was February 16, 1947, attended by over 250 guests. Considerable renovation had taken place, and contributions of linens, drapes, and furnishings had come in from several states.

A one-room cottage at the back of the "Big House" was remodeled for the use of the first resident missionary, Catherine Flagler of China, who moved in on April 16. Building permits were obtained and construction began in the fall of 1947 on the first two new cottages, and by September 1948 three others had been completed. Five more cottages were built during 1949-52.

In January 1952 purchase of a tract on the east side of the original land was authorized. A former stable there was remodeled into a home for the newly appointed superintendent, A. E. Sanner, who took over in October of that year. By that time there were 13 residents. Construction continued as funds came in, including several memorial contributions. The purchase of additional property to the south in 1955 made further expansion possible, and in 1959 another property purchase brought the total to 4½ acres. The five plots, including a house on each, had been purchased for a total of $113,520. The final half acre, purchased in November 1979, included four houses.

Superintendents of Casa Robles have been as follows: Rev. and Mrs. V. P. Drake (1946-52), Dr. and Mrs. A. E. Sanner (1952-66), Rev. and Mrs. James Young (1966-71), Dr. and Mrs. Everette Howard (1971-75), Rev. and Mrs. G. H. Pearson (1975-83), and their successors, Mr. and Mrs. Robert Ashley (1983—).

A number of professional nurses, many of them former missionaries, watched over the physical needs of the residents. Taking care of such a large group of aging persons was a heavy task. Doctors too, notably Dr. Glenn Julien in the earlier years, gave generously of their services. Also a succession of efficient and dedicated maintenance engineers kept the grounds and equipment in order as well as doing much of the actual building of cottages.

Numerous activities keep the missionaries occupied, including a regular Thursday morning prayer meeting. A 1,700-volume library in the Big House, renamed the Sanner House, provides reading materials. Many are still involved in speaking at missionary rallies and Faith Promise conventions. A number are avid gardeners, and the flowers around their cottages are tended with pride and care. Some even have small vegetable gardens. No cats or dogs are allowed, but several have pet birds. Hobbies pursued are many and varied. An official Casa Robles Fellowship was organized in October 1952, which plans and coordinates many special activities and celebrations (birthdays, anniversaries, etc.). It is an active, happy community with much to occupy the attention of the residents.

The requirement for admission is a minimum of 25 years of service and age 65. Availability of space has also been a consideration, for there is always a waiting list. When residents can no longer take care of themselves, they have to be transferred to a nursing home or elsewhere, because facilities for custodial or nursing care are not available there. Despite this limitation, however, the ministry of Casa Robles is filling a large need in the church's responsibility to its veteran missionaries.

PART TWO

The Histories of the Individual Fields

This section of the book is structured according to the regional divisions as they were up to the 1985 General Assembly. The order of presentation of the separate fields or countries is generally according to the years in which they were opened.

Contents

I. AFRICA REGION

II. ASIAN REGION

III. EUROPE/MIDDLE EAST REGION

IV. MEXICO, CENTRAL AMERICA, AND CARIBBEAN REGION

V. SOUTH AMERICA REGION

VI. SOUTH PACIFIC REGION

I

AFRICA REGION

- Swaziland
- Eastern Transvaal
- Witwatersrand Mines and Mozambique
- The International Holiness Mission
- The Republic of South Africa
- Trans South Africa
- Central Africa
- European South Africa
- The Republic of Cape Verde
- Namibia, Nigeria, Botswana, Kenya,
  Ciskei/Transkei

Researchers:

Ted P. Esselstyn—Africa to 1960
Rose Handloser—Africa after 1960
John E. Riley—Cape Verde Islands

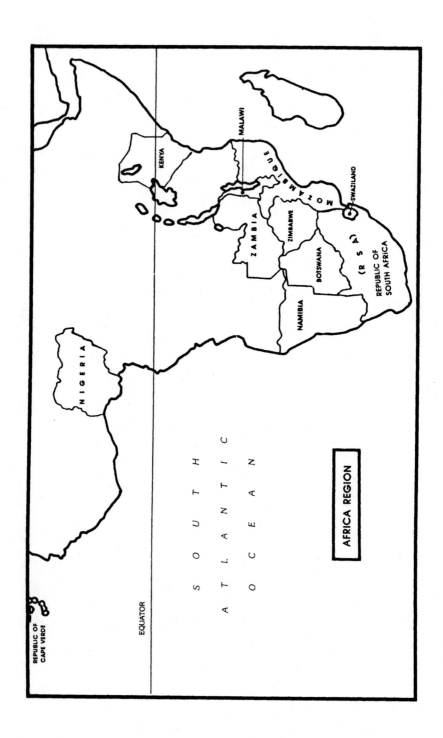

AFRICA REGION

A. SWAZILAND: WHERE IT BEGAN

1. *The Schmelzenbach Legend*

Africa, the "dark continent" made famous in missionary lore by David Livingstone, Mary Slessor, Robert Moffat, and others, was for many years made the center of missionary focus in the Church of the Nazarene by Harmon Schmelzenbach. Though this hardy pioneer from Archer's Fork, Ohio, lived to serve in Africa only 22 years, the stories of his heroic missionary achievements have become legend.

Harmon, an orphan, prompted by what he felt to be the call of God, made his way to Texas Holiness University, in Peniel, Tex., to prepare himself for Christian service. As time passed, the African mission field loomed larger and larger in his vision. After two years, he could quench the fire that burned within him no longer. He told President E. P. Ellyson that he had to go to Africa *now!*

Friends admonished him to complete his education first, but there was no deterring him. Conceding the issue, the school's faculty and student body sent him forth with its blessing and the promise of five years' support at $200 per year. He sailed from New York on May 5, 1907, aboard the *Durham Castle* along with a party of nine other missionaries from God's Bible School. In this group were two young ladies who were to play important roles in the establishment of the Church of the Nazarene in Africa, Etta Innis and Lula Glatzel.

On June 18, 1907, the band of missionaries disembarked at Port Elizabeth on the southeast coast of Africa, where the independent White Holiness Mission was located. That same year two other young men arrived, Herbert A. Shirley and David B. Jones. The latter was destined to become the leader of the International Holiness Mission work in South Africa. Forty-five years later the IHM joined forces with the Church of the Nazarene.

Harmon had read in his Bible how that "one [shall] chase a thousand, and two put ten thousand to flight" (Deut. 32:30, KJV). On the basis of this he concluded that if he were married, his effectiveness as a missionary would be increased 10-fold. Lula Glatzel was the girl of his choice, and they were united in marriage on June 19, 1908, by Rev. Fred Fuge of the White Mission.

Imbued with a true pioneering spirit, they set out for Pondoland in Transkei Territory about 100 miles inland from East London. They had not reckoned with the fact, however, that British law did not allow white persons to live in African homelands unless they were under the auspices of a recognized denomination. That door was therefore closed.

Journeying 300 miles northeastward to the coastal city of Durban, they joined the South African Compounds and Inland Mission and were assigned to the Bethany mission station about 150 miles inland and 15 miles from Estcourt, Natal. Here among the Zulus they gave themselves to intensive study of the language. Harmon proved peculiarly adept and so mastered the language that he spoke it as a true Zulu. At the same time he was receiving valuable on-the-job training and experience in mission operation.

The Church of the Nazarene Enters

While at Estcourt, the Schmelzenbachs received belated word that almost a year before, in April 1908, Schmelzenbach's home church at Peniel, Tex., along with Texas Holiness University, had joined the newly organized Pentecostal Church of the Nazarene. The letter was an invitation for the Schmelzenbachs to join the denomination and open a mission in Africa under its name. No financial support was promised, however.

The challenge was just what Schmelzenbach needed. He was already convinced of the inherent weaknesses of independent missions and welcomed the prospect of continuity that denominational affiliation assured.

Not long afterward, Etta Innis was informed that her home church had also joined the Nazarenes. She had been associated with a mission station at Umtata, about 100 miles northeast of East London.

Before long, she and the Schmelzenbachs got together and began planning the opening of a Nazarene work in Africa. Miss Innis had applied for missionary appointment by the church but had not yet received official acceptance. Furthermore, Schmelzenbach had requested official documents from the church in order to obtain government recognition and authority to purchase property for a mission.

However, the establishment of a central mission board for the new denomination had been slow in developing, so Schmelzenbach was getting confusing signals. The whole matter was finally cleared up when on August 27, 1910, the official documents were received.

By this time, however, the Schmelzenbachs and Miss Innis had already decided that they would open the new mission in Swaziland. In letters to H. F. Reynolds, general superintendent and foreign missions secretary, on August 27 and September 3, Schmelzenbach notified him of these plans, correcting a previous misunderstanding that Natal would be the location of the new work. "There are 90,000 natives and only six white missionaries among them . . . so you can see the need of the field," he wrote of Swaziland.[1]

Strongly influencing the decision was information received from missionaries of the International Apostolic Holiness Union, led by Fred Fuge. In 1909 a scouting party of the IAHU had explored Swaziland, out of which in late June of 1910 they established the Ebenezer mission station eight miles south of the town of Stegi (now Siteki) near the eastern border. Although there was already a mission station at Mankayane, just inside the southern border, led by a Rev. Wehmeyer, and another at Mbabane run by the South Africa General Mission, the northern region was virtually untouched. This was the target area Schmelzenbach had chosen.[2]

As yet Miss Innis had not received her official appointment, but it was agreed that as soon as the Schmelzenbachs had found a location, they would send for her. By the time she received her appointment, the Schmelzenbachs were on their way.

Miss Innis contributed $130 for the purchase of a wagon, while from his personal savings of some $750 Schmelzenbach bought four donkeys and other equipment and supplies, holding some in reserve for possible land purchase. Finally, on October 3, 1910, the Schmelzenbachs, with their 15-month-old son, David, and Billy, a Zulu helper, set out on their historic journey.

The initial route followed was almost identical with that of the IAHU party the year before, the first destination being the Wehmeyer mission station at Mankayane. This first leg took 17 days. On the Wehmeyers' suggestion, Mrs. Schmelzenbach and David remained there while Harmon went on alone to "spy out the land."

On the way he stopped at the South Africa General Mission station in Mbabane. Here he was told of a group of Christians not far from the mining town and government center of Piggs Peak who were calling for a missionary. Arriving at the "Peak," he consulted with the district magistrate, C. Ross-Garner, who told him the area that he had been directed to belonged to the mining company, and no permanent property title could be secured. He did encourage him, however, to bring his family up to Piggs Peak, where he was sure some arrangement could be made.

Back at Mankayane, Schmelzenbach and his family and Billy loaded the wagon and started northward. After a two-week pause at Mbabane where an additional pair of donkeys was purchased, they set out on the most hazardous part of the entire journey. What they thought would take about four days, lasted almost two weeks. When they finally pulled up at the government station in Piggs Peak on December 11, 1910, they were totally exhausted, and only a bit of sugar remained of their food supplies.

Ross-Garner not only gave them food and shelter but told them of an exciting new possibility for a station. Fifteen miles southeast at Endzingeni was a farm owned by a Mr. McCorkindale that was in the recently defined "native area" and therefore up for sale.

The following day Harmon, accompanied by a police guard, walked to the place and consummated the purchase for $425. The owners said they could not vacate the house immediately but would allow the Schmelzenbachs the use of one room until they did. With great faith the little family moved in. They called it the Peniel station.

On the strength of this, also, word was sent to Miss Innis to come to Swaziland. She was to come by rail to Hectorspruit, Transvaal, where Harmon would meet her. On December 21, he left to pick her up, and they did not get back until New Year's Day, 1911. It was a lonely Christmas for Lula and 18-month-old David, but the subsequent companionship of her old friend was rich compensation.

Though the British officials were helpful, they were also limited by legal technicalities. The year 1910 had been a momentous one in South Africa. As part of the consolidation following the Boer War (1899-1902), the Transvaal, Natal, Orange Free State, and Cape Colony had been united to form the Union of South Africa. The homelands of the Tswanas, Sothos, and Swazis were not included in the union but were made protectorates. All white farmers in these areas were to return to the people two-thirds of their land holdings originally granted to them by the Crown. Many felt this reduced their farms to uneconomic proportions, so decided to sell out completely.

One of these was Mr. McCorkindale, who owned Endzingeni, the property Harmon Schmelzenbach had purchased.

But one further condition stood in the way: The Swazi queen mother, known as the Ndlovukazi (She-elephant), must approve the sale of any property to whites. The magistrate advised the Schmelzenbachs not to stay in the McCorkindale house until the requisite permission had been obtained from the queen. So again they set up housekeeping in the 6 x 9-foot donkey wagon, this time with the addition of Etta Innis.

Early on, contact had been made with a group of Christians in nearby Poponyane who had been calling for a missionary (probably the ones referred to by the friends at the Mbabane mission station). Since January 24, Schmelzenbach had been making the 15-mile journey over there to hold services. Under the circumstances it was considered wise to move there, so a native hut was secured, and on March 20 the Schmelzenbachs and Miss Innis moved in. They found the little enclave of three "Christian" families much in need of spiritual help and guidance. But the missionaries were also well received by the people as a whole, and on June 4 the first true convert "chose Jesus." The name of Grace mission station was given to the work. Both a Sunday School and day school were launched by Miss Innis, who was a great believer in winning children.

In the meantime the government, on behalf of the missionaries, sought to obtain the necessary clearance papers from the queen. Weeks passed without any word from the Ndlovukazi, so finally the magistrate suggested that Schmelzenbach himself visit the queen to present his case. He set out on foot the following week on the 65-mile journey.

He was kindly received by the queen, but she was noncommittal, and he had to return empty-handed. But the high commissioner of Swaziland stepped in and personally interceded with the queen on Schmelzenbach's behalf. In mid-May word came through that the requisite permission had been granted, but not before Harmon himself had made a second visit to the queen's kraal. Perhaps word of the arrival of another son, Elmer, had helped to soften her heart.

Missionary Work in Earnest

Harmon had not been idle through these months. On foot and on horseback he traveled from kraal to kraal over the narrow trails, trying to make contact with the people. Even though they were wary of white people and often hid from sight when he approached, Harmon knew that the flimsy grass huts would not stop his voice from penetrating. So, standing alone nearby, he would "preach" the gospel message to the people, "Repent: for the kingdom of heaven is at hand" (Matt. 4:17, KJV).

Eventually he began to make inroads, and by the time they took possession of the new property, he had gathered a small group of listeners and had completed a temporary church building, using materials salvaged from an old goat shed on the farm.

During the winter of 1911 (July 30 to August 3) a very significant conference was held in Mbabane of all mission workers in Swaziland. There were 21 missionaries present representing six different societies. It was a profitable time of fellowship and sharing.[3]

By the last week in August the McCorkindales had finally left, and the Schmelzenbachs moved back to Endzingeni. Miss Innis remained at Grace station two months longer until the arrival of a national preacher named Philip Cele from Natal. Schmelzenbach knew him from earlier days and had invited him to come and pastor the Grace mission. It was a first step toward the establishment of a national church.

When Schmelzenbach wrote to the Nazarene Headquarters in the United States on October 30, 1911, advising them of this action, he received a strong reprimand from Dr. H. F. Reynolds. It was the prerogative of the home church to appoint workers, the letter said. Not intimidated, Harmon politely but firmly replied that it was imperative to use national workers, and he should be granted the freedom to hire them. He was enunciating a basic principle of missionary work later stated well by Rev. H. K. Bedwell: "It is humbling to report, but it is nevertheless true, that more converts are won by the Spirit-baptized nationals than by the missionary."

Unfortunately within six months Philip fell by the wayside, and Miss Innis returned to Poponyane to take care of the little flock that had been gathered. Harmon came upon another African Christian, Solomon Ndzimande from Pretoria, who joined the church and, with his new bride, Martha, became the pastor of the Grace station in 1912.

Miss Innis wrote weekly letters to Dr. Reynolds in which she described the day-by-day activities. She often spoke of the great burden Harmon Schmelzenbach had for the Swazi people. Although their spiritual plight was his primary concern, their physical needs also were great. The many sick people were being exploited by the witch doctors. To help the suffering ones and also find a way to talk to them about Jesus, Harmon began to carry with him simple medical aids. These proved to be so successful they won for the missionary the gratitude of the people but also the growing hatred of the witch doctors. Sensing this open door of medical missions, Harmon began to urge the sending out of nurses and doctors as well as ordained ministers.

Though they had worked so intensely those first two years at Peniel, it was not until 1913 that the Schmelzenbachs won their first converts there. One memorable morning, kneeling in the missionaries' house, Ruth Mongwane and her daughter accepted Jesus Christ. What a day of rejoicing! These two remained loyal workers for the Lord throughout their lives.

It was decided to try holding a camp meeting in Endzingeni, and though 45 Christians attended, most were from Poponyane. As was hoped, many heathen attended as well, opening up a great evangelistic opportunity. The camp meeting was henceforth to become one of the great events of the church calendar in many parts of Africa with thousands attending.

The impact of the gospel upon the Swazi social structure was pronounced. Their native clothing and hairstyles were closely related to the worship of ancestors and to witchcraft. The practice of polygamy and the degrading status of women also ran counter to the gospel message. New converts literally washed the witchcraft off their bodies and out of their hair and discarded their heathen clothing. The outward badge of the Christian therefore came to be the wearing of Western-style clothing, along with physical cleanliness.

But of still greater significance was the treatment of women. Parents sometimes abused the lobola system and arranged the marriage of a daughter to the man who would pay the highest amount for her. It did not matter if he was perhaps old and already had a sizable harem. Whenever girls rebelled at going to live with a man under such circumstances, they sought refuge at the missionary home. Peniel mission thus became a haven for such girls, and the missionaries became involved in many an argument with parents, chiefs, and rejected suitors.

By 1914 several major changes had been made in the administration of the Nazarene missionary program, including the provision for more adequate salaries and the setting up of an operating budget.

It came none too soon, for the Schmelzenbach children were beginning to show signs of malnutrition, Lula was reduced to one dress, and, to top it all, Harmon's horse had died. He had had to use money saved for the children's education to replace the animal so his evangelistic work could continue.

A secondary result of the new financial policy was that the Swazis themselves began to develop a deeper sense of responsibility. They brought offerings to the missionaries, mostly in the form of produce. Gudlamuzi provided milk for the Schmelzenbach family for many years. This was the forerunner of a heightened stewardship emphasis in which the principle of tithing was taught. Offerings of money were taken, but more likely than not the contributions took the form of grain, produce, eggs, chickens, and so forth.

Daniel Dlamini, a crippled man, played a key role in the development of the church. Converted in 1913, he received a little education at Endzingeni and by 1914 was pastoring the church that was later known as Mayiwane. This was the first truly national Swazi church—one that did not begin with a missionary pastor.

Another national worker was reached in the person of Josef Mkwanazi. He had been converted under the ministry of Malla Moe, a remarkable old Scandinavian holiness missionary. While serving on the Swazi police force at Piggs Peak, Josef felt called to preach the gospel. He became Harmon's devoted assistant throughout the coming years.

When the rainy season ended in April 1913, Schmelzenbach began the construction of a more substantial church building at Peniel. He wanted to build it of stone with a corrugated iron roof. This meant hauling 200 wagonloads of stone from a location four miles away and many loads of the sheets of iron from the railway 70 miles away. Eventually the 22 x 32-foot building was completed in time for dedication by the visiting general superintendent, Dr. H. F. Reynolds, in July 1914. Sixty years later this same building was restored as a historical landmark, the original stone walls still intact.

Regular workers' meetings were begun with missionaries and nationals discussing problems and methods and learning more of God's Word. These meetings were the forerunner of quarterly pastors' conferences, which became a feature of the mission calendar. The nucleus of the growing church had been established in the hills of northern Swaziland.

Dr. H. F. Reynolds Visits

On July 7, 1914, Dr. H. F. Reynolds arrived in Africa in the course of a round-the-world missionary journey. He was met at Lourenzo Marques, Mozambique (then Portuguese East Africa), by Harmon Schmelzenbach, and together they went by train to Hectorspruit and thence by wagon to the mission. This last leg of the journey was a rugged three-day trek through lion country.

The last of the corrugated iron for the roof of the church had been installed just in time for the building to be dedicated by the visiting dignitary. Also in the course of the visit, Harmon Schmelzenbach and Etta Innis were officially ordained to the ministry. The visit of the general superintendent brought a great lift to the little band of missionaries and the 60 Christians who, by that time, had been won to the Lord.

With renewed vigor Harmon began to organize churches as fast as he could find national pastors to man them. He launched a two-year training program for probationary members. New missionary recruits soon arrived, and the prospects brightened.

The first of the new workers were Rev. and Mrs. Herbert A. Shirley, who joined them in 1915. They had been working with another mission in Natal. Not long after their arrival, Mrs. Shirley became ill and died. Herbert carried on alone for several years, his special interest being the printing of gospel literature. He later married Etta Innis.

In 1916 funds were made available by the family of Mrs. Susan N. Fitkin to build a hospital. Her 10-year-old son, Raleigh, who had professed a call to the mission field, had died, and the family wished to establish this memorial in his name. Schmelzenbach's dream of a medical work was being realized.

It was decided to build the hospital at Piggs Peak, where a 10-acre tract of land had been given by the government and a missionary cottage had already been erected. Construction began in April 1919 under the direction of Peter Nielson, who was sent to Africa in 1917 to take charge of the building programs, thus freeing the missionaries to continue their regular activities. The hospital was completed in 1920, and the station was named the Fitkin Memorial. Miss Lillian Cole, R.N., who had arrived in August 1916, took over the direction of the hospital.

The first crisis she had to handle was the great flu epidemic. Single-handedly she had to take care of 18 bed-patients besides the constant throng of outpatients. During that time the Schmelzenbach twins, James and Catherine, died.

With the war over, and travel abroad once more possible, Schmelzenbach sent his wife and family home for a rest, but he remained at the task. There was also an influx of new missionaries to expand the work—Rev. and Mrs. Joseph Penn, Ora Lovelace, Eva Rixse, and Minnie Martin. The day school program at Endzingeni was expanded, and both a day school and a much-needed Bible school were launched at the growing Fitkin Memorial station. Thirty students were soon enrolled at the latter.

About this time, Schmelzenbach asked Josef Mkwanazi to become his full-time assistant. Josef had proved himself an able church planter, and together these two men traveled the countryside, proclaiming the gospel message with fearless abandon.

They became particularly burdened for the people of the nearby lowveld. Here malaria and blackwater fever made this a "white man's grave." But Harmon dreamed one night that on the Judgment Day he faced one of the chiefs of the lowveld who blamed him for their damnation because the missionary had failed to take the gospel to them. From then on he was committed to go down into the lowveld with the message of Christ. The decision was costly, for it was the diseases of the area that ultimately took his life.

In July 1920 the Charles S. Jenkinses and Minerva Marshall arrived on the field, to be followed by the F. B. Janzens and Louise Robinson. The Janzens were stationed at Peniel, while the Joseph Penns and Miss Robinson were assigned to the rapidly expanding work in Sabie, Eastern Transvaal (which see).

The First Doctor

When Dr. C. E. West at the age of 50 came to Swaziland in 1921 to serve in the hospital, there was a flurry of excitement, for a true hospital at Piggs Peak was now a possibility. But the British government would not recognize his United States credentials. So, after some years of fruitless effort to be accredited, he was transferred to China in 1925. Prompted by Dr. West, the missionaries were having second thoughts about the location of the hospital. It was in a somewhat isolated area where there was no great concentration of people. This was a particular matter of discussion on the occasion of Dr. H. F. Reynolds' second visit to the field in 1921, but no specific decision was made concerning relocation.

Of immediate significance relating to Dr. Reynolds' visit was the reducing of Grace station to just a preaching point, and the opening of work in Siteki (then called Stegi) in the Lubombo Mountains of eastern Swaziland 70 miles from Endzingeni. It was a strategic town on the main "highway" to Lourenzo Marques on the coast 70 miles farther east.

Rev. and Mrs. F. B. Janzen and Myrtle Pelley, a registered nurse, were assigned the task of opening up this new work. While a clinic and a church were being built, the Janzens lived at the Ebenezer station of the IAHU, eight miles south. They filled in for the regular missionary who was on furlough.

As elsewhere, they soon found Christian girls coming to the mission, seeking escape from unwanted marriages, thus incurring the displeasure of the chiefs. But the helpful ministrations of the clinic in the community offset the opposition.

Isolation was a problem. It was 75 miles by road across the dangerous lowveld to Mbabane, the Swazi capital, where the nearest government doctor was stationed. It was about the same distance to Endzingeni over a treacherous road that included crossing the wild Komati River at Balegane. A mission station was established here, and Schmelzenbach put together a raftlike ferry that was available at the crossing for the use of the missionaries.

The work of the Bible school at Piggs Peak under the leadership of Ora Lovelace became more and more strategic as the work grew. Classes in theology, Bible, and church management were augmented with opportunities for practical training in preaching and personal evangelism in the surrounding churches. One time in the early days of the school a great spiritual deepening time came that will ever be remembered by those who were there. Rev. Shirley had overheard the students talking among themselves of the need for an infilling of the Holy Spirit to counter the powers of the evil spirits around them. So he instructed the students to build a small hut in which he placed a bench, a mat, and a Bible. It was to be a prayer hut, he said, and the students were to take turns there, reading the Bible and praying. The hut was never to be empty. Within a week this chain of prayer brought a transformation that set a new course for the national ministry in Africa. The Holy Spirit came upon the school in revitalizing power.

Schmelzenbach's Health Breaks

Harmon Schmelzenbach was an energetic man, constantly on the go and utterly selfless in his dedication to the missionary task. He had always loved the out-of-doors and was an outstanding marksman, winning riflery contests year after year. But recurring bouts with malaria brought on by his frequent trips into the lowveld began to take their toll. In 1920 he had his first major setback of malaria, complicated by the dreaded blackwater fever. It almost took his life. Again in 1924 he was stricken, but this time with the added complication of typhoid fever.

Though now physically weakened and unable to carry on as before, his zeal was undiminished, and he urged upon his fellow missionaries and national pastors the need for establishing new centers. Great was his rejoicing when the Swazi queen sent word that she was granting him complete freedom to establish churches in her country wherever he wished. He needed only the permission of the local chief.

The Bremersdorp Hospital

In 1925, in response to a request to the government for a place to relocate the hospital in a more populous area, a grant of 35 acres of land was given the church near the town of Manzini (then known by its Dutch name of Bremersdorp). The tract was strategically located on the main road from Mbabane, the capital, to Siteki and Lourenzo Marques. It was also near the royal kraal.

A missionary home was in the process of being built on the property when Dr. and Mrs. David Hynd, with their daughter Isabel and baby Samuel, arrived from Scotland to supervise the setting up of the mission complex with the new hospital as its focus. Under the doctor's forceful and energetic leadership the hospital was completed and ready for dedication on July 16, 1927.

Among the visitors on dedication day was young King Sobuza II. Present also were Ada Bresee and Susan Fitkin. They were officially representing the General Nazarene Women's Missionary Society, but they were also the principal donors of the funds for the project. Besides the hospital itself, a large stone church had been built, along with the medical superintendent's home and a nurses' residence. From then on the Manzini station with its Raleigh Fitkin Memorial Hospital was the dominant center of Nazarene work in Africa.

During Mrs. Fitkin's visit, the Swaziland NWMS was officially organized and became a powerful force as the missionary wives and pastors' wives joined forces with the women of the church. Many of the men became associate members.

The mid-1920s brought many other changes in missionary life, notably in the matter of transportation. In 1925 Rev. Janzen at Siteki became the first of the missionaries to own an automobile. Only his mechanical genius kept the Model-T Ford running between Siteki and Mbabane. That same year the Hynds secured a Dodge touring car, which found much use in the district medical work. The next year Harmon Schmelzenbach himself acquired an Overland Whippet on whose spare tire cover was painted the word *Pendukani* ("Repent"). He became known by that name throughout the country. It was a fitting symbol of his evangelistic passion.

A commercial bus line was begun from Breyten, the nearest rail point in the Transvaal, into Mbabane and later on to Manzini and Siteki. The line carried mail, so postal service was greatly speeded up. The bus itself was just one step above a truck, with its plank seats and no ventilation. Windows had to be left closed to keep out the choking dust, but that made the interior stifling hot. When rains came, the dust became slippery mud, increasing the hazards for the drivers but improving the overall comfort of the passengers.

Another development of this period was the establishment of stores at many points along the way as the people developed a taste for Western goods. With this commercial expansion came a related desire for education. In the absence of a public school system, mission schools flourished. Louise Robinson, who was first assigned to Sabie in the Transvaal, was moved to Endzingeni in 1924 to take charge of the girls' school. In the ensuing years she had hundreds of girls under her care for various periods of time. Not only were the three Rs taught, but farming as well. The mission land produced all the meat, fruit, and produce needed for the dormitories.

But the work of the various mission stations was not without opposition. The lives of missionaries and national workers were often threatened, and Christians were beaten by relatives. The point of greatest tension was over Christian girls refusing to marry heathen men. Some cases ultimately were tried in the courts.

The early 1920s were also marked by an abortive attempt to restructure the method of supervision of the mission fields. In 1924 Dr. George Sharpe of Scotland was appointed by the General Board to be superintendent of India, the Near East, and Africa. (Latin America and the Orient were also assigned superintendents.) However, financial pressures forced the abandonment of the experiment, and in 1926 Dr. Sharpe, who had made Swaziland his headquarters, returned to the British Isles.[4] Nevertheless, it was during the Sharpe regime that the groundwork was laid for the moving of the hospital from Piggs Peak to Manzini. During this time also, annual council meetings of the missionaries were begun.

A crucial weakness in local missionary administration was developing, however. Although the nationals were used plentifully in preaching and in pastoring of churches, the direction of the overall program was in the hands of the missionaries. National laymen were little involved. As Dr. Dan Dlamini, mayor of Manzini, expressed it years later: "It was in the areas of administration and church government that the missionary failed to teach the African." By 1933, however, positive steps were being taken to remedy the situation.

As the latter years of the decade of the 1920s came on and the Great Depression struck, financial support from the homeland began to shrink. But the national pastors loyally stood by and found ways to support themselves. Fortunately, before the financial pinch another group of missionaries had arrived in 1928: Rev. and Mrs. W. C. Esselstyn and Misses Mary Cooper, Fairy Chism, and Anna Lee Cox. They came at a crucial time, for the health of the founder of the mission was failing rapidly.

Death of Harmon Schmelzenbach

The year 1928 was General Assembly year, and the Missionary Board cabled Harmon Schmelzenbach that they wished him to attend the event. It was there he presented the most electrifying missionary message ever delivered before a Nazarene audience. It was titled "A Cry in the Night," based on a graphic description of the destruction of a village in the valley of the Komati River by a raging flood. A witness of the tragedy described the terrible scene sometime later to Schmelzenbach. From the high bank the man had watched the brown waters rise about the village until enveloping night obscured his view. During the night he could hear only the frantic cries of the inhabitants that slowly diminished as, one by one, they were swept away in the flood. By morning the entire village and its occupants had disappeared.

Never was the urgency of missions more eloquently pictured.

God used the message to awaken many young people to the call to missionary service and inspired missionary support throughout the churches as never before.

Schmelzenbach was urged to remain in the United States because of his failing health, but in response to his impassioned plea that he be allowed to die among his people, he was sent back in December of that year. Three months later he was forced to turn over leadership to Rev. C. S. Jenkins.

When it was clear he was soon to die, word went out to as many of the pastors as could be reached, and dozens made their way to the bedside of their stricken leader. He passed into a coma May 22, 1929, and died just before midnight.

At the funeral, the huge throng of mourners sang the songs "Wonderful Story of Love" and "Just Inside the Eastern Gate." In a simple, pine box lined with sheets hurriedly put together by W. C. Esselstyn and H. A. Shirley, his body was carried to its last resting-place near the original stone church he had built some 20 years before.

But what God had wrought in those 20 years! The work had spilled over into neighboring Transvaal to the west and north and to Mozambique on the east. Twenty-four missionaries, located at seven mission stations, plus 143 African workers were preaching, teaching, and nursing for the Lord. There were 110 organized churches with an estimated membership of 3,000. A hospital, several day schools, two Bible schools, and four annual camp meetings in various areas were reaching many thousands of people.

The passing of Harmon Schmelzenbach marked the end of an era. But that he had built the foundations well is attested by the fact that there was no break in the ongoing program, this in spite of the worldwide financial crisis whose initial effects were already being felt.

2. *Growth in Swaziland*

Though the work in Africa now extended beyond the boundaries of Swaziland, this country was still the hub of activity. The loss of the founder was a source of great sadness, but there was the attendant challenge to pick up the torch and carry forward the work that he had initiated.

The national church, despite decreased allotments, began to bear increasing responsibility for the financing of new projects. The principal channel of funds was the Missionary Society, whose membership now approached 1,000. Not only was this organization active in establishing new churches, but they raised funds to purchase an ambulance for the hospital and printing equipment for Rev. Shirley's press. In true missionary spirit, they also built a home for girls over in Mozambique.

The expansion of the Shirley Press resulted in a larger production of tracts and other literature aids. The eight-page Zulu paper, *Umphaphamisi,* increased in circulation to 1,000, while a paper in the Shangaan language, *Mutwalisi,* was up to 650. The first book in Zulu, a translation of C. E. Cornell's *Hints to Fishermen,* was a needed personal evangelism manual published with funds supplied by the national church.

The hospital, aided by special contributions and some government support, continued to expand its facilities to include a children's ward, maternity ward, male and female medical and surgical wards, X-ray equipment, and a modern sanitary system. Dr. Mary Tanner arrived to augment the staff and launch a training program for nurses. The first graduating class of nursing assistants received their certificates in 1931. The Raleigh Fitkin Memorial Hospital had become Swaziland's finest medical center.

When Dr. J. B. Chapman, general superintendent, visited the field in 1931, he found a well-established and smoothly functioning work in Swaziland. But he was particularly impressed with the potential for the work in the mining towns in neighboring Transvaal, the story of which will be related elsewhere.

Meanwhile, at Endzingeni (now known as the Schmelzenbach Memorial station) Louise Robinson's work in the girls' school had been taxing available facilities. On her own, she raised the money, helped make the bricks, and supervised the construction of a dormitory, classroom buildings, and a new tabernacle. This was followed by a dispensary and some outstation churches. She was putting into action her well-known motto: "If you don't like it, change it!"

The Bible school at Piggs Peak was also running at capacity. In 1933 the decision was made to relocate the school at Siteki. With Rev. W. C. Esselstyn in charge, new buildings were erected and a farm secured to supply food for the college. The students operated the farm.

In the mid-1930s Miss Evelyn Fox arrived, and under her guidance the hospital became a registered nurses' training college. This gave permanence to a training program for nurses that had been begun by Dr. David Hynd in 1928. In 1936, of the first nine students who wrote the government examinations, eight were successful. It was a remarkable achievement. The T. Ainsworth Dickson Nurses' Home was dedicated the next year. Another nurse, Elizabeth Cole, arrived and soon became involved in special ministry to the lepers at the government Umbuluzi Leper Colony. Here she gave 24 years of dedicated service and was decorated by the queen of England for her work.

The need for a teachers' training program was evident; and in 1936, under the leadership of Margaret Latta, a Scottish missionary with the necessary British credentials, the Nazarene Teachers' Training School was established at Manzini. A year later, Bertha Parker was on her way from Canada (also with British qualifications) to assist in this new project.

The Manzini station was assuming the classic proportions of a mission compound. It was fenced against intruders and contained several missionary homes, a large hospital, a nurses' home, a nurses' training school, a church, homes of national workers, along with primary, secondary, and teacher training schools with related dormitories.

In 1938 an orphanage was added to the complex to care for babies abandoned at the station, particularly twins who, in those days, would have been killed since they were considered children of witches. (As national customs changed, the orphanage finally became unnecessary and was closed in 1972.)

Church Government

The African church was maturing, aided greatly by the quarterly meetings of the pastors. But lay leadership was not being developed to the extent needed. In response to a suggestion made at one of these quarterly meetings, the Mission Council in 1933 established a commission "to explore the best way to develop self-government in the churches."

The commission went to work and by 1937 was ready to submit its recommendations. They were in the form of a proposed constitution for self-governing churches. This document, published in the official minutes of the Mission Council, included a structure similar to the church board in which laymen were moved into positions of responsibility. But in a society long dominated by the rule of chiefs, the democratic procedures envisioned in the proposals took root slowly. Nevertheless the groundwork for a fully indigenous church was established.

District organization similarly advanced. A committee called Umlomo (the mouth) was established to serve as a liaison between the national church and the missionaries. They were particularly helpful in relating the customs of the people to the rules and practices of the church and working out necessary adaptations. The quarterly meeting, which previously had largely fulfilled this function, assumed a decreasing role in church affairs and eventually was discontinued in Swaziland.

One outcome of the new organizational trend was the establishment of Bible conferences, specifically intended to involve the laymen. The first one was held at the Siteki Bible school at the time of the dedication of its facilities in 1937.

First Ordinations

A milestone in African missions was reached when in August 1939, the first Swaziland ministers were ordained by Dr. J. G. Morrison, general superintendent. They were Solomon Ndzimande, who had been Harmon Schmelzenbach's earliest associate; Josef Mkwanazi, the first African district leader; Samuel Dlamini, who shortly after served as an army chaplain in North Africa; and Enoch Dlamini. During that same visit, Dr. Morrison ordained four more pastors in Mozambique.

These two landmark events were an encouraging climax to a decade of consolidation. There had also been a strong emphasis on the building of institutions, notably the Raleigh Fitkin Memorial Hospital, but the day schools and teacher training had also greatly expanded. In addition, the Bible school had been relocated and upgraded. The results to be achieved by these institutions in terms of evangelism admittedly would be long-range, but the fact remains that during this decade of institutional development, church membership in Swaziland dropped. Due to inadequate and inaccurate records it is not known whether the announced drop from 2,300 to 1,480 is a valid evaluation, however.

World War II (1939-45)

The beginning of hostilities in World War II, in September 1939, placed heavy demands on a depleted missionary staff. Those due for furlough were rushed home while it was still possible. But no replacements could be sent out. As the war progressed, supplies became increasingly difficult to obtain. Building programs ceased. Travel was restricted as gasoline was rationed, and vehicles had to be patched up to keep them in a semblance of running order.

C. S. Jenkins and Joseph Penn, who had served as field superintendents following the death of Harmon Schmelzenbach, were now both in the United States, so the mantle of leadership fell on W. C. Esselstyn. Except when on furlough, he was to serve in this capacity with great distinction for 26 years.

The printing press operated by H. A. Shirley, which had been located at Arthurseat in the Eastern Transvaal, was moved to Manzini in 1942. Larger equipment and facilities became available despite war restrictions, and this phase of the work continued to grow. By 1944 the Zulu paper, *Umphaphamisi*, had a circulation of 5,000, and the Shangaan paper, *Mutwalisi*, 2,800. Hymnals in both languages were being printed. Quarterly Sunday School lessons, catechisms, books, and pamphlets numbering in the thousands came from the presses. Steps were made to publish a Zulu translation of the *Manual*.

Another development of 1943 was the division of the African work into two districts. The Mozambique area, including the satellite mine work in the Transvaal, was separated from the Swaziland field. District organization for each, including national leaders and annual assemblies, were set up with the missionaries providing supervision and guidance. The goal was to develop full indigenous leadership.

By the end of 1943, the total missionary staff on both districts was down to 30, only 4 of whom were men. The women heroically carried the load, however, and in the midst of adversity the work grew. Revivals broke out, and the Bible conferences that now were held at several points rivaled the camp meetings as sources of spiritual fire. Attendance at these was in the thousands. The Bible school at Siteki was running at capacity, giving promise of increased national leadership.

In these years when the overworked missionaries were growing weary and some were ill, Dr. David Hynd, the only resident doctor in the hospital, became a legend. On call 24 hours a day, he would often work virtually around the clock, finding sleep in a convenient chair whenever he had a free moment.

The heavy duties in no way diminished the missionaries' vision for the future. In 1944, as the inevitable conclusion of the war drew near, Dr. Hynd drafted a "Memorandum on Postwar Advance," for presentation at the annual Mission Council Meeting. It was enthusiastically endorsed, and a Committee on Postwar Advance was set up. The following recommendations of this committee were adopted and forwarded to the General Board in Kansas City.

> 1. That the Department of Foreign Missions send out an experienced and successful elder to start work among the English and Afrikaans speaking people of Southern Africa.
>
> 2. That funds be appropriated to start work among the Coloured peoples of Southern Africa—those people of mixed cultural heritage.
>
> 3. That work be started among the African people living in the African towns adjacent to the cities of the land. In these towns lies the greatest concentration of people in Africa.
>
> 4. That a commission be appointed to investigate the country for a new area where work could be started among people who have not yet heard the gospel.[5]

The report recommended the sending out of 33 more missionaries in addition to those requested for the white work. It should be noted that the L. C. Ferees had already resigned from the Nazarene missionary staff to begin an independent work among the white people. This was indicative of an already-felt need in this area.

The program outlined was an ambitious one, but most importantly it plotted a new direction for African missions. Evangelism was its keynote, and it was to involve both missionaries and nationals in a great outreach program.

Postwar Expansion

Before the war was over, restrictions had eased sufficiently for 4 new missionaries to be sent out along with 2 veterans. The new missionaries were Paul Schmelzenbach, a son of Harmon, whose wife, Mary Kate, was also a nurse, and Dr. and Mrs. Lauren Seaman, who came to serve in the hospital and help relieve the heavy load on Dr. Hynd. They were followed in 1945 by the veteran C. S. Jenkinses and 12 more new recruits. The new workers were rapidly pressed into service, while needed language study became a secondary priority. Long-range effectiveness was no doubt hampered thereby, but the emergency was considered acute.

In 1946 another 5 furloughed missionaries and 15 new ones arrived. Although not all of these were assigned to Swaziland, the absorption problem became difficult. There was too little housing, and there were too few veterans to help orient the new ones to their tasks. The Africa field had been granted the missionary force that had been requested, but the planners had not reckoned with the problems such a sudden influx would create.

To complicate matters, a number of new missionaries became ill, while others were frustrated, disillusioned, and discouraged. The "mortality rate" was high as many remained no longer than a single term, if that. At the same time, it must be remembered that a large backlog of missionary candidates had accumulated during the war, along with a pent-up desire on the part of the church to get missionaries onto the field. The prime motivation was to "send forth labourers."

The medical work profited greatly by the release of wartime restrictions. With new doctors and nurses and much sophisticated equipment obtained as war surplus, the hospital entered a new period of expansion. Nursing graduates were becoming available to man clinics that were built at each mission station. This situation was further strengthened in 1948 when the nurses' training college, now under the direction of Miss Dorothy Davis, received full government accreditation. It became the most highly rated training program in the country.

To control and direct this rapidly expanding area of the work, a Health Center Council was created. The enormous contribution of Dr. David Hynd, who had masterminded the medical work from the first, was recognized by King George VI of England. On the occasion of the king's visit to South Africa in 1947, he bestowed on Dr. Hynd the high title, Commander of the Order of the British Empire. Ten years earlier the doctor had been accorded the lesser title, Officer of the Order of the British Empire. His fame as a missionary physician was widespread in the land.

With the arrival in 1947 of 10 additional missionaries, the work in Africa reached a stage of explosive outreach.

Visit of Dr. Hardy C. Powers

Eight years had passed without a visit from a general superintendent when in 1947 Dr. Hardy C. Powers came to spend five weeks touring all areas of the African field. He held three ordination services. At the one in Swaziland seven received elders' orders: James Malambe, first pastor at Manzini; Phineas Dlamini, Simon Dlamini, and Ephraim Shongwe (all of whom later became district superintendents), Timothy Gininda, Simeon Mapanga, and Gideon Nkambule.

A major purpose of Dr. Powers' visit was to explore the possibilities of opening up work among the Afrikaans and English population of South Africa. It was his favorable report to the General Board in January 1948 that set in motion this new project. The European work was assigned to the Department of Home Missions and will be discussed separately.

The work in Swaziland, which had already shown a disappointing decline in prewar years, continued to sag from 1,480 to 1,247 members. Some seemed to see in this an indictment against institutional missions, pointing out that while the hospital and schools were flourishing, evangelism languished. But there were several mitigating factors. Not the least of these was the extensive government reforestation project in the Endzingeni/Piggs Peak area that forced large numbers of people to relocate, greatly depleting the churches there. Also, inadequate record keeping may have presented a false membership picture.

Another factor was the emphasis on evangelism to the neglect of discipling of new converts. The pastors needed to be trained in the art of getting the people established in the faith. Too many members were being lost out the "back door." At the same time, however, missionaries and national pastors were feeling the need for a revival of the spiritual fervor that had characterized the earlier days, and they began to pray earnestly for a new moving of the Holy Spirit upon the work.

As was noted already, the returns in institutional work are more long-range than is the case with direct evangelism. This was to be proved in subsequent years as the country became seeded down with teachers, nurses, and others who had come up through the Nazarene school system. Also, more homes and communities were opened to the gospel through the compassionate ministry of the hospital and related dispensaries and clinics than will ever be known. There was, indeed, an eventual turnaround in the statistics.

The Mid-Century Crusade for Souls

The churchwide emphasis on evangelism during the 1948-52 quadrennium came at a strategic time on the African field. The people responded enthusiastically. For the first two years of the "Crusade for Souls" each one pledged to try to win one person to Christ each quarter. In 1950 the emphasis switched to visitation. Thousands of contacts were made.

Also in 1950 Dr. Hardy C. Powers made a second trip to Africa, this time spending a full two months. The focus of his visit was the official organization of the European District. He also visited Cape Town, exploring the possibilities of starting a work among the Coloured people (those of mixed race). A great gathering of Nazarenes from all over Southern Africa that met in Tavane, Mozambique, was a highlight of the visit. The meeting did much to unify the people.

A new organizational structure was worked out for the nonwhite work. There were now three districts or regions: Swaziland, Mozambique, and the Transvaal. Each region had its own sessions during the annual council meeeting, but there were also general sessions. Each had its own Executive Committee to handle regional business between council meetings. One field superintendent, Rev. W. C. Esselstyn, served all areas, and the combined Executive Committee formed a Field Executive Committee. This new structure was maintained well into the 1960s.

Swaziland Church Expands

Though the Church of the Nazarene was reaching out ever farther in South Africa, the central focus was still in Swaziland and more specifically at Manzini. The hospital continued to expand its facilities. Its nursing school was graduating skilled workers to serve in the hospital, its satellite dispensaries, and government institutions. The teacher training college was likewise sending out qualified teachers whose Christian witness was to strengthen the church in the more remote areas of the country.

The missionaries whose responsibilities were with the institutional work became involved on the weekends with opening new churches in the surrounding countryside. The church on the mission station, under African leadership, increased in membership to over 500. In 1946 a more commodious building, the Sharpe Memorial Church, was erected to accommodate the large crowds. Pastor Jotham

Magagula was giving excellent leadership. Fifteen churches have been organized from outreach Sunday Schools conducted by this one church.

Hospital Development

Missionary doctors were added to the staff during the 1940s and 1950s in the persons of Dr. Kenneth Stark, Dr. Samuel Hynd (son of the hospital's founder), Dr. Evelyn Ramsey, and Dr. Paul Sutherland, who arrived in 1960. But the increasing load was still too much to handle, so the concept of having doctors come to the field for short periods to offer relief to the beleaguered medical staff was proposed. Dr. Paul McCrory and Dr. Howard Hamlin were the first to vounteer, each spending six weeks at the Raleigh Fitkin Memorial Hospital in 1961. The Hamlins spent another six weeks there in 1962 and, feeling that it was God's will that they give themselves to full-time service, applied for regular missionary status. This was granted in January 1963, and later that year Dr. Hamlin left his well-established Chicago practice and moved to Manzini.

The first two years, his surgical expertise was shared one week out of each month with the Ethel Lucas Memorial Hospital in Acornhoek, Transvaal. The 250-mile journey between the two hospitals over poor, unmarked roads was arduous enough, let alone the extremely demanding operating schedule at ELM. It eventually proved too much for the doctor and had to be stopped. In 1965, when Dr. Samuel Hynd went on furlough, Dr. Hamlin became superintendent of the Manzini hospital.

After a year's furlough, the Hamlins returned to Africa in 1969, this time to be stationed at the Acornhoek hospital. Dr. John Sutherland (older brother of Dr. Paul), who had been stationed there since 1955, had had to return to the United States because of his wife's health. About the same time, Dr. Evelyn Ramsey was transferred to the hospital in Papua New Guinea. The demands upon the staffs at both hospitals were therefore unabated.

Then, in the early 1970s there were some very significant developments on the medical scene. Dr. Samuel Hynd, medical superintendent of the Manzini hospital, recognized that a major renovation and rebuilding project was urgently needed. The facility was not only inadequate but rapidly decaying. It was too extensive a project for the church to shoulder, so Dr. Hynd contacted the Protestant Central Agency for Development Aid, an organization in West Germany, to

see if they would be interested in helping. They had already contributed heavily to the building of the teacher training college on the
Manzini station. (The state church in West Germany, which is supported by taxes, is required by law to allocate a certain percentage of
its income to projects in developing countries.)

The response was that they would assume two-thirds of the cost
(approximately $1 million U.S.). Dr. Hynd then contacted a similar
agency in Holland, the Interchurch Coordinating Committee for Development Properties, which agreed to assume the other one-third.
By October 1974 the necessary agreements were signed, and the
reconstruction began.

The project was hardly under way when tragedy struck the
Hynd family. On New Year's Day, 1975, Dr. Hynd's wife, Rosemary,
was fatally injured in a freak accident in the driveway of their home.
It was a devastating experience not only for the doctor but for the
entire missionary family.

Despite his deep grief, Dr. Hynd pursued the heavy tasks that
had been laid on him both as hospital superintendent, practicing
surgeon, and supervisor of the building program. This included the
establishment of preventive health clinics in outlying areas—a stipu-
lation in the agreements with the West German and Holland bene-
factors. When construction was completed in December 1976, almost
the entire hospital had been replaced with well-designed, substantial
facilities that ranked the institution among the finest of its kind in the
Third World.

It now became the task of the church to provide the funds and
personnel to operate the enlarged facility and its satellite clinics. It
proved to be a greater burden than had been anticipated. Certainly
the management of such an institution was too much for an already-
extended medical staff, and despite assistance from the government
of Swaziland, the financial situation also became more and more critical. Not the least of the problems was securing adequate staff.

On May 1, 1978, Dr. Hynd resigned to go into private practice.
This marked the end of more than 50 years of dedicated hospital
leadership under the Hynds, first by Dr. David Hynd, the pioneer, and
then by his son, Samuel.

In August 1978 Howard Miller, business manager of Northwest
Nazarene College, was sent to take charge of the financial affairs of
the hospital. This move, along with other internal adjustments, avert-
ed a potential disaster. But not all the problems were solved. There

were indications that the government was wanting to take over administration and operation of the hospital and its satellite clinics. A financial crisis in October 1982 brought church leaders and government officials to the conference table.

The church made clear its intention to continue to provide competent medical care for the people. It was already operating the only nurses' training college in the country. The recruitment of adequate medical personnel was proceeding in line with expanding demands. But the continual need to update the hospital services in line with new medical technology demanded an investment difficult for the church to assume. The government was prepared to provide assistance.

This assistance was not to be interpreted as a wedge to control. It was agreed to name the Raleigh Fitkin Memorial Hospital as the official hospital for the Manzini District. One of the RFMH medical officers was to be named the district medical officer. The hospital was to be further upgraded and designated as the major referral center in the country. A new mental hospital was scheduled to be built by the government on mission land, further extending the scope of medical care provided. All these moves had the endorsement of the General Board.

To formalize the agreements, Regional Director .Richard Zanner entered into a five-year interim pact with the minister of health (to be replaced then by a permanent agreement) in which responsibilities and obligations of both parties were clearly delineated. In essence, the operating budget would come from the Swaziland Health Authority as part of the national budget, but the full responsibility of directing the hospital was to be in the hands of the Church of the Nazarene.

The School Program

The day schools also intersected with government programs, but here the problems were less complex and the opportunities broader. Most of the main churches conducted primary day schools, but district focus was at the secondary and teachers' college level, where outstanding work was being done. There were three Nazarene high schools in Swaziland: Siteki, Manzini, and Endzingeni. The latter was for many years plagued with facility problems—in particular, deplorable housing facilities aggravated by an inadequate water supply and no electricity. By 1985, however, all this had changed, and it was now recognized as a quality school along with the other two.

The teachers' college in Manzini was running at about 100 students. So highly rated was the school that it was receiving 2,500 applications for admission each year, of which only 50 could be selected. Graduates were similarly in great demand. The long-range effect of having the elementary schools of the land filled with Nazarene teachers is incalculable.

The secondary schools likewise had far more applicants than they could accommodate. These three institutions were totally under the auspices and control of the church. The academic achievement level in each was well above average by government standards. Already these graduates were assuming leadership roles in community and national government. This could be decisive for the future of the nation.

A very significant part of the high school program was the religious phase. In 1978 Rev. Juliet Ndzimandze was appointed school evangelist. She scheduled regular visits of a week's duration in each school, speaking to and counseling with both students and teachers. She averaged about 1,000 converts a year. A graded follow-up program based on Charles Shaver's *Basic Bible Studies* was instituted. In 1984, when Rev. Ndzimandze became a district evangelist, her place was taken by Grace Masilela, a converted witch doctor and former prophetess of the cultic Zionist movement. Such direct spiritual ministry as these evangelists gave was unusually significant in the lives of those hundreds of students.

A New Nation

Although by covenant Nazarene missionaries are not allowed to involve themselves in any way with the politics of the countries in which they are working, the Swaziland missionaries could not help but be apprehensive as the day of independence for the nation approached. Under King Sobuza II, the country had known long years of political calm. The security and stability that the British presence afforded was particularly valuable. How well this calm could be maintained under purely national rule was uncertain.

After careful preparation and with due fanfare, Swaziland became an independent nation on September 6, 1968. The following Sunday was declared a national day of prayer—a significant fact indeed. Following the granting of independence, the country was to be governed by a Westminster (British) constitution in which power was shared by King Sobuza II, his ministers, and an elected House of

Assembly. The first elections were held in 1972. King Sobuza's party ran a full slate of candidates and won all but three seats in the parliamentary assembly.

But the presence of even so limited an "opposition" was quite foreign to a people unaccustomed to democratic procedures. There was no apparent complaint when, in 1973, King Sobuza summoned the nation to a conference in the ancient capital of Lobamba and in their presence tore up the constitution. Once more the country was back to a monarchy. One of the ministers in the government was E. V. Dlamini, son of a Nazarene pastor. A later addition was Dr. Samuel Hynd, who was minister of health until 1983. The king himself was, over the years, very friendly toward the church, and several of his wives attended services. The Swaziland government has continued to be the most stable of all the new nations of Africa, even after the death of King Sobuza in 1983.

Two Districts Created

In 1969 Rev. E. B. Shongwe retired as district superintendent. Rev. Leonard Sibandze succeeded him and served until 1982. Under his leadership the work made great strides. He was strong on Christian Service Training, and a well-trained laity has been the result, though the lack of national pastors was a problem. Nonetheless, 17 new churches were planted under his leadership, and membership increased 63 percent. Finances jumped a phenomenal 730 percent from a few thousand dollars to $105,000 per year! These gains showed that the district merited regular (Phase 4) status, which was granted in 1980.

Upon Rev. Sibandze's retirement, Rev. Solomon Magagula was elected district superintendent, and aggressive growth continued. By 1985 there were 80 organized churches on the district with 5,486 members. It was the largest district in Africa.

Because of comity agreements with other missions in the early days, the Church of the Nazarene did not attempt to evangelize in southern Swaziland. But it was obvious that much of the area was not being reached by any mission.

In 1975 Rev. Samuel Dlamini was asked to go to Nhlangano, near the southern border, to start a new work. This became the mother church of the Swaziland South District, of which Rev. Dlamini became the district superintendent. By 1985 there were 13 churches and three preaching points on the district with a total membership of 506.

Ambitious plans to reach a goal of 45 organized churches by 1990 and regular district status by 1995 were announced. Extension classes from the Swaziland Nazarene Bible College in Siteki for the training of present and prospective pastors was part of the strategy for growth.

The Swazi church grew strong and spiritually mature. Along with the spirit of evangelism and outreach was the application of effective administrative techniques by the pastors. Leadership seminars and workshops across the country in 1983-84 were of great value. There was still opposition from traditional elements of the culture, but there was deep dedication to God and the church among both leaders and rank-and-file members.

B. BEGINNINGS IN THE EASTERN TRANSVAAL

The opportunity was now given to the missionaries to prove that the stated goals of the Committee on Postwar Advance were no idle words. They had been given the missionary force they considered necessary, and the church back home was rising to the challenge to give "A Million for Missions." To actualize those dreams meant reaching out into new cultures and into new types of ministry.

But it was not entirely virgin territory. Already foundations had been laid in various places outside of the Swaziland core. Now the challenge was to build on these as well as to find and exploit new opportunities.

1. *Sabie*

Harmon Schmelzenbach's dream to get the gospel out to every place where there was need, made him somewhat of an explorer. He and Josef Mkwanazi roamed many miles out to find new areas of gospel need. Word reached them that a great missionary opportunity existed in the gold-mining town of Sabie in the Drakensberg Mountains of Eastern Transvaal, about 75 miles north of Peniel station (over 100 miles by road).

The opportunity to work in the mines lured many of the Blacks in surrounding areas to such mining centers as Sabie. Some men came with their families, but most of them came alone, contracting to work in the mines for a period of six months to two years and then to return to their families. Thus there grew up around the mines large shantytowns built willy-nilly by the workers themselves as temporary shelters while serving their contracted time. It was estimated at one time 100,000 people lived in and around Sabie.

Heretofore, Schmelzenbach's work had been largely in a village and rural setting. Here was the challenge to present the gospel where there was a high concentration of people. This radical new venture began in early 1920 when Rev. and Mrs. H. A. Shirley moved to Sabie to establish a mission station. Within a year they were joined by the J. F. Penns and Miss Louise Robinson.

To meet the needs of the people working in various shifts, both day and night schools were conducted along with regular evangelistic meetings.

When Nurse Lillian Cole and Miss Maude Creators were sent to help the Shirleys and their coworkers, a much-needed clinic was added to the program. Louise Robinson described the earlier "dispensary" as consisting of "a medicine cabinet containing a cure for everything: sulphur for itch; aspirin, quinine, and Epsom salts for malaria; iodine, boracic powder, and permanganate for disinfectants, and a pair of forceps for toothache."

It was while he was at Sabie that H. A. Shirley was able to make a major step forward in his long-felt desire to develop a literature ministry. Although his equipment was limited, he began printing tracts and publishing the Zulu preachers' magazine, *Umphaphamisi* ("The Awakener"). Miss Minerva Marshall, who had come out to teach the children of the missionaries, prepared a Zulu hymnal *Izihlabelelo Zokudumisa* ("Hymns of Praise"), which was printed on the Shirley Press. It has continued to be a powerful evangelistic tool. A Zulu translation of C. E. Cornell's *Hints to Fishermen* was the forerunner of several books and pamphlets that came from the little printshop.

Not only was Sabie becoming a busy, flourishing station, it was extending its influence far and wide in a sort of chain reaction. Most of the miners were drawn from the tribes of the bushveld to the east. Naturally, the new converts asked the missionaries to come to their home areas to preach. Thus there developed a string of outstations reaching out as far as 60 miles. A more promising missionary center would be hard to find.

But two developing factors over which the missionaries had no control were to profoundly affect the work at Sabie. One was the shift of gold-mining activity to the more highly productive deep mines along the Witwatersrand in the Johannesburg area. The alluvial gold deposits at Sabie were nearing exhaustion.

The second factor was an extensive reforestation project, similar to the one in northern Swaziland. Tremendous quantities of mine support timbers were needed for the rapidly expanding deep mines along the reef, but since there were no indigenous forests anywhere near, the establishment of tree farms was necessary. The grass-covered mountains of the Sabie area were found to be ideal for the growing of eucalyptus and pine. To make way for these new forests, the people were moved out of the area in large numbers. The combination of factors produced a rapidly dwindling population that, as early as the mid-1920s, was adversely affecting missionary work. One by one missionaries were assigned elsewhere until finally the Sabie station was closed. It was the end of a short-lived era.

In the light of the dwindling possibilities in the Sabie area, in 1922 the Joseph Penns opened a station 16 miles to the east on the fringe of the mining area but still in the mountains. It was appropriately named Bethel, for there the Penns won the hearts of the people and carried on a highly effective ministry.

2. *Arthurseat*

Though Sabie itself was closed, Bethel and the other eight outstations continued to flourish. The main group of these was farther east from Bethel, down in the bushveld. One was at Arthurseat, seven miles from the railway station at Acornhoek. At first the mission property was leased, which limited permanent development. However, in 1947 a large, 600-acre farm, of which the leased property was a part, became available. The proceeds from the sale of the Sabie property were used to purchase the farm. The church was thus able to develop a major station here.

Meanwhile Rev. Shirley had moved his printing equipment to Arthurseat in 1935. In 1942 the press was again moved, this time to Manzini, where it remained until Rev. Shirley's death, March 17, 1945.

When the Shirleys left Arthurseat, Rev. and Mrs. Carl Mischke took over the work there and remained for 15 years. They were joined by the Elmer Schmelzenbachs, under whose leadership much of the development of the station and the present Eastern District took place.

It was at Arthurseat in 1947 that Dr. Hardy C. Powers ordained the first Eastern Transvaal elder, Enos Mgwenya. He later became district superintendent.

From 1943 onward the main evangelistic growth of the church shifted to the Eastern Transvaal and Mozambique. This area was a major center of evangelism for nearly four decades. During the late 1940s, the Eastern Transvaal Zone had grown to such size that it was able to challenge all of Swaziland successfully in Sunday School competitions. The camp meetings soon became the largest in Africa, and church growth was excellent, with up to 60 outstations and preaching points in the mid-1960s. Even the all-Africa missionary councils were shifted during the 1950s to Arthurseat. It was here also that the merger of the IHM and the Church of the Nazarene took place on November 29, 1952, just as it was on this mission station that the gavel was struck to organize the European District in 1950.

Many of the national leaders who made possible the expansion of the work into such areas as the Witwatersrand locations, the Northern Transvaal, and Blouberg in the 1960s also came from this area.

In addition, Arthurseat was the center of 16 church-operated schools with an enrollment of over 10,000 students. Though in the late 1960s the South African government assumed responsibility for education throughout the country, Nazarene-educated laymen continued to make their mark in church and community affairs.

3. *Blouberg*

Item 4 in the postwar plan was that a brand-new area be found in which to begin Nazarene work. In 1947 such a place was singled out in far northern Transvaal, 300 miles north of Acornhoek, where few white men had ever been and where the name of Jesus had never been heard. There a mission station was built at the foot of the Blaauberg Mountains (now spelled Blouberg). This was a strongly Pedi community with a few pockets of Shangaans, totaling some 40,000. Although there was some opposition at first, the chief was friendly, and the dispensary that was established soon became widely known. Uniquely, it was to Blouberg that the first African missionary, Richard Mamiane from Arthurseat, was sent. In addition to his evangelistic work, it was he who put up the church building as well.

Rev. and Mrs. George Hayse were chosen to begin the work here. Miss Kathryn Dixon, R.N., also joined them and became a well-known and much-loved person as she rode about in her little donkey cart by day and night, ministering to the sick and suffering.

4. *Idalia*

In the late 1940s, also, a farmer by the name of Beukes at Idalia just outside the southwest border of Swaziland offered the Church of the Nazarene a piece of property for a mission station. Again the question was asked whether the church should invest in an area so lightly populated when populous areas were calling for missionaries. Nevertheless, there was no missionary work in the area, so the offer was accepted, and the Paul Schmelzenbachs were sent to establish a mission. His break in health, forcing his return to the United States, was a setback, but Rev. and Mrs. Joseph Penn, Jr. (another second-generation missionary) successfully took over the work that, though in the Transvaal, became a part of the Swaziland District.

5. *Naboomspruit*

Naboomspruit, about halfway between Blouberg and Johannesburg, was the center of a large European farming area in which there were thousands of Black workers. Here in 1948 Mr. and Mrs. Theron, following the suggestion of Rev. and Mrs. L. C. Feree, offered the church a farm on which to build a mission. The cry for missionary help in the Johannesburg area was mounting, but still it was considered wise to accept the offer and send a missionary couple. The Wesley Meeks were chosen for the task the following year.

C. THE WITWATERSRAND MINES AND MOZAMBIQUE

1. *The Mines Around Johannesburg*

The Witwatersrand (commonly called the "Rand" or "Reef") is a range of low hills along a mile-high plateau running in a shallow arc generally east and west for about 100 miles with Johannesburg about its center. It was here in 1885 that gold was discovered, setting off a boom that, far beyond its financial impact, was to have a profound sociological effect upon South African life from then on.

As happened at Sabie and other earlier mining areas, African laborers flocked to the mines, signing contracts to work for periods of from six months to two years, then to return to their homelands. Clustered around each mine were the makeshift shelters these workers built for themselves. More deplorable living conditions could hardly be imagined.

The mine owners sought to alleviate these problems by building barrackslike buildings to house the workers. But although this served to reduce the squalor somewhat, it did not remove the basic social problems inherent in such a crowded situation. These housing compounds became breeding grounds for all sorts of moral evil and violence.

However, though these workers' areas were hotbeds of sin, they also offered unprecedented opportunities for missionary activity. Nowhere was there such a concentration of people who could be so readily reached with the gospel message. In an effort to meet the spiritual and social needs of the men, various religious bodies built chapels around the fringes of these compounds. It was considered too dangerous for missionaries to venture into the compounds themselves, though some did. To many of the men these mission centers became havens of refuge—if they could withstand the taunts and threats of their workmates who tried to keep them away.

As many as 40 tribes were represented in the labor force, but almost one-third of the workers were Shangaans from Mozambique (then Portuguese East Africa) 500 miles to the east. It was among the latter that Rev. and Mrs. I. O. Lehman began an independent work in 1920. So effective was their ministry that when their converts returned to their homeland after their periods of service (limited by Mozambique law to 16 months), they began sharing the gospel with their friends and neighbors. Some even began regular preaching services and built meeting places. A focal point for this work was Manjacaze in the Gaza area, 150 miles northeast of the capital city of Lourenzo Marques (now Maputo).

The Lehmans visited there occasionally and assisted in establishing churches, but it was basically a project of the Shangaans themselves. They early learned the principles of self-support, and a truly indigenous church developed. Also, due to the fact that it was men who had taken the initiative, it was male leadership that thereafter characterized the Mozambique work. Elsewhere, women were the dominant force.

In 1922 the Lehmans, lacking adequate home backing and seeking to give their work a stronger base and a more certain continuity, asked the Church of the Nazarene to take it over. They and the Schmelzenbachs had both worked with the South Africa Compounds Mission and were well acquainted. This opened up two entirely new areas of ministry for the church: one almost 300 miles west of Swaziland in the Johannesburg area of the Transvaal, and the other an equal distance to the northeast in Mozambique.

2. *Mozambique*

When the work of the I. O. Lehmans was taken over by the Church of the Nazarene, it was agreed that the Lehmans themselves would continue their activities in the compounds at Johannesburg while their coworker, Miss Bessie Tallackson, along with Rev. and Mrs. C. S. Jenkins would go to Mozambique to take charge of the work there. Also there were the Emil Sywulkas and Sophie Pfankuchen.

At first the Jenkinses were reluctant to move, for they were just getting their roots down in Swaziland. However, they ultimately bowed to the repeated requests of the Mission Council and moved to Manjacaze. It was not long until they felt completely assured they were in the place God wanted them. Their ministry among the Shangaans of Gazaland in the following years was outstanding.

The acquisition of the Lehman work greatly increased the size of the missionary program in Africa. The Johannesburg/Gazaland work listed 572 full members and 256 probationers, while all the other African work had but 178 full members and 306 probationers. The missionary force now totaled 22.[6]

With the nucleus of returning mine workers and a responsive populace, churches and preaching points were rapidly opened up. By 1925 Rev. Jenkins had gathered around him a considerable group of preachers. However, most of them had limited training. To give them needed help, he requested the publication of a preachers' magazine in Shangaan. It was thus that *Mutwalisi* was added to Rev. Shirley's printing program. It later became a general magazine in the style of the English *Herald of Holiness*.

One great handicap to progress was the lack of permanent buildings. The church could not obtain title to any land, and without this security it was considered unwise to invest in substantial structures. There was also the budget pinch brought on by the mounting financial crisis in the homeland in the late 1920s. The reduced funds also meant smaller allowances for the national pastors, but without complaint they trusted God to supply their needs. The spiritual deepening resulting from such exercise of faith precipitated a far-reaching revival that began spontaneously at a regular quarterly meeting of the preachers in 1927 and spread to all the churches. This unusual visitation of the Holy Spirit went on for three years as people flooded the churches to pray and to praise God. Confession and restitution were the order of the day.

A by-product of this revival was that many felt the call of God to the ministry. Several were sent to the Bible school at Piggs Peak for training, but the language problem in itself proved to be a difficult hurdle. There was an obvious need for a Bible school in Mozambique to train pastors for the rapidly expanding work. A first step was to transfer Miss Eva Rixse to Manjacaze to launch such à program.

Then in 1930 a government decree was issued that no church could operate unless it had permanent buildings. Furthermore, no mission could be established within five miles of an existing church. The presence of a large Roman Catholic church in Manjacaze meant that the Nazarene mission was in forbidden territory.

The wisdom of having erected only temporary structures was confirmed, for the mission had to abandon its station. But how could a new location be found and permanent buildings erected before the prescribed deadline? Desperately the missionaries sought for a place to relocate. But the search seemed fruitless, and as the final date approached, plans were tentatively made for the departure of the missionaries.

Just when the cause seemed lost, Rev. Jenkins was approached by the Methodists to see if the Nazarenes would be willing to take over their well-developed station at Tavane, 20 miles north and farther inland on the same narrow-gauge rail line that ran from the forests of the interior down through Manjacaze to the port city of Villa de João Belo. In a consolidation move, they had decided to dispose of the Tavane property. The question now was whether the Department of Foreign Missions would be willing (or even be able) to purchase the property, what with the financial depression on and retrenchment the order of the day.

The station met all the government qualifications, but by now the time factor was critical. Telegrams were sent to Kansas City, and the people were called to special prayer. Communications flew back and forth, arrangements were hastily made, and on the last day before the new law came into effect, the property transfer was completed.

Along with the main station, a number of outstations were also involved in the transaction, most of which became part of the Nazarene work. As a result, outstations and preaching points doubled from 20 to 40 that year, and membership jumped from 717 to 934. Growth of the church through the next decade was outstanding.

Yet another roadblock was to be put in the path of the mission by the government. An order went out that no one would be granted permanent residence unless they had passed an examination in Portuguese. In addition, all teachers and leadership personnel would have to pass government examinations, and schools would have to be taught in Portuguese. This necessitated special language study for all current and future missionaries. The only day school to survive was the one at the main station in Tavane.

But there was much encouraging development. It was in Gaza that the Men's Missionary Movement, a logical outcome of the strong male leadership, came into being and subsequently spread throughout the other African areas. They called themselves the *Isitimela* (train) while the NWMS (the women's movement) took the name *Ndlopfu* (elephant). Soon Nazarene churches everywhere were filled with songs about the train and the elephant. The men would sing, "We are the train that carries the load," while the women would respond with equal fervor, "We are the elephant that pushes the train." Soon they had a new song, "If We All Work Together." The friendly rivalry was a powerful force in sponsoring mission projects.

The Methodist property the Church of the Nazarene acquired at Tavane included a clinic and a nearby government leprosarium that housed 100 patients. Miss Estelle MacDonald was sent to operate this phase of the work, and later she was joined by Miss Myrtle Pelley. It became one of the busiest clinics in Africa. For a time, there was even a Portuguese doctor on the staff, and the development of a full-fledged hospital was seriously considered, but this never came about. The government moved the leprosarium to an island down near the coast 70 miles away, but the missionaries continued to hold services there occasionally.

A milestone on the Mozambique field was reached in 1939 when four of the pastors were ordained by General Superintendent J. G. Morrison: Daniel Muketi Muyanga, who had been Rev. Jenkins' first helper; Paul Siweya; John Mazivila; and Zephaniah Mhula. By then, membership in Mozambique had reached 2,206, largest in the Africa field. This represented an annual growth rate of 21 percent.

Impact of World War II

When World War II broke out in 1939, missionaries due for furlough, or overdue, were rushed home while the sea lanes were still open. Among these were the Jenkinses. Replacing them in Gaza was Rev. Glenn Grose, who had taken his master's degree in Portuguese to qualify for teaching in Mozambique. Significant expansion of the educational work was anticipated.

He had been there only a short time when he went with a group to hold Christmas services at the island leper colony. On the return trip to the mainland, the boat capsized. Rev. Grose was the only one who could swim, so he had to help others to safety, but he himself drowned. It was a tragic blow to his family but also to the work in Mozambique. At the same time, however, it seemed to have the effect of inspiring the national leaders to assume greater responsibility, and a new intensity of effort was apparent. The people were further saddened on October 22, 1945, when Daniel Muketi Muyanga died. He had been a stalwart leader of the church, particularly during the war years when the Jenkinses were in the homeland.

The Bible conferences that had been so successful at Siteki were

introduced in Gaza. They soon rivaled the camp meetings in attendance.

The great influx of new missionaries sent to Africa following
World War II did not greatly help Mozambique, for the government
severely restricted the number of missionaries it would admit, and
furthermore it insisted that they all be stationed at Tavane. Despite
these hindrances the work continued to expand, reaching 3,318 members by 1950 with 80 outstations plus other preaching points. There
were outstanding revivals throughout the district, but medical and
educational work was greatly restricted. Even the Bible school suffered and in 1949 had to be closed.

In 1954, however, the Bible school was reopened under the dynamic leadership of Miss Lorraine Schultz. She was to direct this
institution until 1975. An expanded curriculum, including a fourth
year of specialized training, resulted in a highly qualified group of
ministers being available. Since instruction was given in Portuguese,
it was possible to use textbooks prepared for the Cape Verde Bible
College. Miss Schultz's first assistant was Benjamin Langa, who was
followed by Noë Mainga. The latter's untimely death in 1975 was a
serious blow to the Mozambique church.

The reopening of the Bible school in 1954 was in part necessitated by the considerable expansion of the work when the International Holiness Mission joined forces with the Church of the Nazarene in 1952 (see the following section). Their work was centered to
the west at Mavengane and was under full national leadership. Special instruction was therefore felt necessary as part of the assimilation
process.

The addition of the IHM work also made a division into two
districts advisable. This was done the year following the merger. It
was not long until a third area, the Limpopo District to the south, was
set apart. Under outstanding national leadership, all three districts
moved rapidly toward self-government. It was none too soon, for the
storm clouds of political upheaval were beginning to envelop the
nation.

To help offset the severe restrictions on day schools, Miss Mary
Cooper and "Auntie" Marito Mundlovu organized among the juniors
and teenagers monthly day-and-a-half teaching sessions called Mintlawa (meaning "groups"). Basing the program on the Laubach
method of "Each one teach one," hundreds of them learned to read
their Bibles. They were also taught the domestic arts and hygiene. By

1972 there were 10 centers with a total of 1,700 enrolled in the Mintlawa.

As the 1950s wore on, there came a disturbing decline in membership. It would have been easy to blame this on mounting government pressure and the general political unrest, but neither missionaries nor national leaders were willing to accept this explanation. Instead, they pointed out that fewer revivals were taking place than in the heyday of the work. They therefore gave themselves to fervent prayer for a spiritual reawakening. Their deep heart-searching resulted in a great outpouring of the Spirit that produced a new surge of growth. The result was an increase in membership during the next decade to 10,000.

The Tavane District became the largest in Africa at that time with nearly 4,000 members and 77 churches. A milestone was reached when its district superintendent, Rev. Benjamin Langa, was named an official delegate to the 1972 General Assembly. The Mavengane and Limpopo districts grew to 40 churches each.

In 1972 the Lourenzo Marques District was organized under the leadership of Rev. Simeão (Simeon) Mandlate and soon became the fastest-growing district in Africa. Here the TEE (Theological Education by Extension) classes proved extremely beneficial in preparing workers for the rapidly expanding program. Rev. Mandlate gathered around him a well-trained group of pastors and built attractive churches. His district, though small in area, had the distinct advantage of a high concentration of people in this metropolitan area. It was in Lourenzo Marques that the largest Nazarene church in Africa was located.

But in the mid-1970s the winds of political change grew to hurricane force as the country anticipated its independence from Portuguese rule (consummated on June 25, 1975). When independence came, the Marxists had prevailed and immediately set to work to rigidly curtail missionary activity, particularly by the missionary leaders.

Armand Doll, after 17 years as mission director, stated in his report to the Mission Council in Pretoria in July 1975 that he and his wife, Pauline, planned to leave on furlough in September. The missionaries returned to Mozambique on July 10, and two weeks later the primary school, the dispensary, and some of the mission vehicles were taken over by the government. Two government informers were sent to live at the mission.

On August 28, Armand Doll was arrested without charge and put in prison. The following day, Hugh Friberg was likewise imprisoned. Lorraine Schultz and Pat Buffett, along with Evelyn Friberg and her two children, managed to drive to South Africa five days later. All the other missionaries had left before the final crisis, leaving almost everything they owned behind. Hugh Friberg was released on April 27, 1976, but Armand Doll was not set free until September 19, after being held one year and three weeks.

The five national superintendents, Revs. Benjamin Langa, John Muchave, Lot Mulate, Simeon Mandlate, and Marcelino Rupia, assumed the burdens of leadership in a new light. They were completely on their own except for what guidance they could receive from Mission Director Frank Howie, who had to remain in the Republic of South Africa. The Tavane station was gone, but most of the other churches continued to operate, and even new places were opened. In 1985 there were 214 churches and preaching points with a total membership of 7,974.

3. *Developments in the Mine Work*

While the Mozambique work was flowering, the mine ministry back along the Rand was not forgotten. True, it was frustrating work because of the lack of permanence, for the men were constantly moving in and out. But regular preaching schedules were established. Because the mine work was chiefly among the Shangaans of Mozambique, there was a lively connection between the two areas. It seemed logical to consider them as one district, even though the methods of missionary operation were so greatly different and many hundreds of miles separated the two.

The Crown Mines, one of the largest operations in the Johannesburg area, became a major center of activity, and in 1931 the Ainsley Memorial Church was built there. It was a large, brick structure seating 350 comfortably but many more in African style (on the floor rather than on benches). On the occasion of his visit to Africa in 1931, General Superintendent J. B. Chapman preached here to a capacity crowd. He was deeply moved by what he saw and upon his return to the United States wrote of the great challenge of this work. For a number of years, however, the compounds remained a somewhat neglected field of activity, upstaged by the more traditional activities elsewhere.

In the late 1930s, Rev. Joseph Penn, Sr., then superintendent of the African field, began to make more frequent visits to the various compound churches and also followed up on invitations to newly developing areas. An outcome of this increased activity was the establishment in 1940 of a mission station at Boksburg, 15 miles east of Johannesburg. It was basically a large home from which the resident missionary could keep a reasonably active contact with the churches and preaching points scattered along the 50-mile stretch of the Reef in which the church was working.

4. *The African Suburbs*

About this time an industrial revolution of sorts was taking place in South Africa. The Johannesburg area was once again the center of activity as manufacturing plants sprang up all over and new cities emerged. Black laborers, lured by the new jobs, streamed toward the cities. Now, however, many brought their families with them, compounding the problems of finding a place to live.

At first there grew up around these industrial centers shantytowns little better than the conglomeration of hovels that clustered around the mines in the earlier times. Sanitation systems were virtually nil, water supplies were contaminated, and diseases took their deadly toll. Attempts were made to develop more adequate housing areas called "locations," which provided some relief but did little to solve the deeper social problems.

Crime and violence became a way of life often fired by intertribal rivalries. Lawless bands of youths, called "tsotsis," roamed the narrow streets uncontrolled, and terrorists exacted "protection money" from the frightened inhabitants. Even the witch doctors, who provided a nostalgic tie to former tribal religions, took advantage of the situation. They found ready customers for their charms and medicines "guaranteed" to give protection and/or bring prosperity.

In the desperate struggle for existence, women sold their virtue, and even 10-year-old girls were involved in prostitution. It was estimated that two-thirds of all the babies born in the locations were illegitimate. At the same time, because of disease and malnutrition, 65 percent of the children died before they reached the age of 2.

Political subversion also found fertile ground here. Communism, the historic "scavenger of revolutions," worked through the organization called the African National Congress to foment unrest and rebellion.

Following World War II, the government moved in to try to stem the tide of lawlessness and insurrection. They ultimately banned the ANC, but more importantly, they launched a massive slum-clearance program. The miserable shantytowns were replaced with modern, planned cities with tree-lined, paved streets. The brick houses were plain in design but were equipped with electricity and modern sanitation systems. Here the Africans could live in dignity and reasonable security.

In the light of this significant development, it is not surprising that one of the four key recommendations of Dr. Hynd's Committee on Postwar Advance was "that work be started among the people living in the African towns adjacent to the cities of the land." But in spite of the great influx of new missionaries and funds, the church was still slow to move into this area of ministry.

The first significant expansion came in 1948 when a promising opening was found at Witbank, a coal-mining center 100 miles east of Johannesburg. Rev. and Mrs. C. F. Church were sent there to establish a station. The church was officially organized in 1951. Meanwhile the Morris Chalfants, working out of Boksburg, had organized a church at Jabavu, and a fine building was completed there in 1950.

In late 1952, when the International Holiness Mission joined forces with the Church of the Nazarene, the work in the Johannesburg area received a substantial boost, for this had been one of their major areas of operation. They added both experienced personnel and new centers from which to work.

But the church was missing out on a golden opportunity to secure building sites in the new locations. As these new African towns were planned, church sites were designated at strategic places. So far, none of these had been secured for the Church of the Nazarene. These plots were available under certain conditions:

1. That the church be officially registered

2. That there be an adequate following to justify the granting of a site

3. That the church refrain from political involvement

4. That within a year a building of approved design and construction be erected

Somewhat belatedly, the decision was made to launch the location work in earnest. Upon their return from furlough in 1954, Rev.

and Mrs. George Hayse were transferred from Blouberg to Johannesburg to lead the project. No greater contrast in missionary strategy and activity could be found. The Hayses had enjoyed the work in Blouberg and were reluctant to leave the people with whom they had labored for so many years. However, feeling it was God's will, they accepted the new assignment. Subsequent developments proved Rev. Hayse to be indeed God's man for the hour.

His initial course of action was to secure some of those church sites that had been set aside by the town planners. His first visit was to the office of the manager of native affairs for the proposed township of Katlhehong. Upon hearing that Rev. Hayse represented the Church of the Nazarene, the man's face brightened, for he had been a regular listener to "Showers of Blessing," broadcast from Lourenzo Marques. Obviously he was impressed with what he had heard.

There was a map on the wall, showing the first phase of the Katlhehong project, which would accommodate 50,000 of the ultimate 250,000 planned for. Twenty-five red pins studded the map, marking the available church sites. Few had, so far, been selected, so Rev. Hayse was able to secure a choice lot near the center of the city.

The missionary lost no time in hiring a crew, having architectural plans approved, and launching construction. Long hours and hard work resulted in the completion in two months of the beautiful Barton Chapel. With money raised at the dedication service, a comfortable four-room parsonage was built next door for the national pastor. Then it was on to the huge township of Soweto, where an excellent site at Dube was secured.

At Orlando Rev. Hayse found a centrally located tract of land he felt would be ideal for a district center. But when he inquired of the authorities, he was told rather bluntly that all church sites had been taken. A few days later, however, the official called Rev. Hayse and told him he wanted to show him a piece of land that he thought the missionary would be interested in. Amazingly it was the very site he had been originally attracted to! He was told the land was designated for "municipal use," but since it was to become a "district center," they could bend the rules enough to make it qualify as "municipal use." Within a few months a spired church seating 1,000, homes for the pastor and the district superintendent, a storage building, and a dining hall were erected on the site.

And so it went as new sites became available and new churches were erected. The official Rev. Hayse had originally contacted called one day to suggest that since he was in on the planning of all the new developments, he would be glad to assign sites to the Church of the Nazarene as soon as they became available. In a short time, 17 of these plots were held by the church.

"These were not small, skimpy, second-rate sites near the railway tracks or on back streets," said Rev. Hayse, "but centrally located property next to parks, traffic squares, or near government buildings and schools, where everyone would see them."

But the requirement that churches were to be constructed on the property within a year posed a problem. Furthermore, the buildings would have to conform to strict codes. No mud-and-thatch shelters would do.

This massive building program called for an all-out effort, and Rev. Hayse proved equal to the task. Feverishly he raised funds, dickered for materials, and superintended the building programs. He was often seen in overalls himself. His ability to get the most out of every dollar and at the same time meet or exceed the strict building code requirements was quickly recognized.

Most of the money needed came from the United States, including Alabaster funds. Interested churches and individuals also contributed generously, among these being Mr. George Jetter, who paid for eight of the buildings. Mr. Willie Young, a Swazi storekeeper, also financed one—the first of several he was to pay for in the following years.

Sites in other cities began to open up in a similar manner, including Bloemfontein, 300 miles to the southwest in Orange Free State; Vlakfontein, 45 miles north; and the burgeoning industrial center of Ga-Rankuwa, 75 miles north. Three hundred miles south on the road to Cape Town lay the diamond fields surrounding Kimberley, where in the suburb of Galeshewa a site was granted. As fast as tracts could be secured, buildings were erected until by 1965, 30 churches, most with parsonages, were already built, and others were under construction. Rev. Hayse's vision reached out to anticipate 100 churches in these great suburban centers.

All the churches were manned with national pastors. At first their support was subsidized, but a system of decreasing outside support was worked out in anticipation of normal growth so that the churches would be fully self-supporting in 10 years.

A large 40 x 90 green tent was often used for services during the construction period to capitalize on the interest of the people in the building activity and to gather a nucleus for the new church. This tent was also used for later evangelistic meetings, which met with great success under the leadership of Rev. Jack Riley. But these tent revivals were often disrupted by rowdies, most of whom were strong nationalists. They were bent on ousting the white people and intimidating any who cooperated with them. They scoffed at the "white God" the missionaries proclaimed. The tsotsis also harassed the Christians and their meetings. But the day came when many of them sought God's forgiveness at the altars and became loyal and ardent followers of Christ.

A major step forward for the location work was taken in February 1965, when the first annual district assembly was held at the district center in Orlando.

D. THE INTERNATIONAL HOLINESS MISSION

One of the most significant events in the history of the African mission field took place near the close of 1952 when the International Holiness Mission of Great Britain, with its substantial work in Africa, united with the Church of the Nazarene. The events which precipitated the union began with the death of Rev. David B. Jones in Durban on January 14, 1950. For 42 years he had labored in Africa and was the founder and leader of the IHM work there.

Direction of the missionary program fell to Rev. Maurice Winterburn, secretary of the home board, who was not unaware of the precarious position of the organization. Extensive expansion moves had overextended the support capability of the home constituency. Survival demanded drastic retrenchment or the discovery of a new source of support.

Over the years, beginning with the early close association of David Jones and Harmon Schmelzenbach, there had been frequent fraternization between the workers of the IHM and the Church of the Nazarene. It was only natural, under the circumstances, that thoughts should turn to a possible amalgamation of forces. After initial overtures, it was felt that such a move could be to mutual advantage. There followed a period of intensive study and working out of details that culminated in the act of union in Leeds, England, on October 29, 1952. Exactly one month later, at the Arthurseat station in Eastern Transvaal, the uniting convention of the missionary phase was held.

1. The History of the International Holiness Mission

The parent organization of the International Holiness Mission came into being in England in 1907. David Thomas, a drapery merchant in Battersea, a suburb of London, was instrumental in bringing together a group of independent holiness churches into a kind of fellowship, loosely organized, but with a common, passionate interest in world evangelization.

One of their number, David B. Jones, caught the vision and ere the year was out left for South Africa. He did not go under the auspices of the IHM, however, but was associated with an undenominational group. He landed at the same time and place as Harmon Schmelzenbach, and there the two eager pioneers established a lifelong relationship. Though their paths led in different directions, they kept in touch with each other throughout the years. In fact, the Schmelzenbachs' first daughter was born in the Joneses' home near Johannesburg.

Because he had no support from the homeland at first, Rev. Jones temporarily had to give up his dream of opening up mission work in a pioneer area and went to work in the Johannesburg mines. In 1911 he was married to Miss E. M. Harold, and together they set up housekeeping near the Ferguson Compound in Johannesburg.

In their home the African work of the International Holiness Mission was launched. It was not until 1913, however, that the work was officially adopted by the IHM in England to the extent that they gave regular financial support.

The work had hardly gained a foothold before World War I began in September 1914. The finances that had just begun to come in were cut off, and D. B. Jones had to return to work in the mines. Every spare moment, however, he spent ministering to the miners in the nearby compounds.

Following the war, Mrs. Jones journeyed to England for furlough, and while there recruited workers for the field. Rev. H. C. Best and Misses Latham and Marsh responded. Soon after their arrival H. C. Best and Miss Latham were married.

The original work in the mining compounds was expanded. Also since most of the mine workers were Shangaans from Mozambique, it was natural to consider a follow-up ministry among these men when they returned to their homeland. Rev. and Mrs. Best were chosen to go to Mozambique for this purpose. In 1922 they established their first base at Chaimite on the Limpopo River in the Gaza area. This was a little south of Manjacaze, where the Jenkinses had recently begun work for the Church of the Nazarene.

Back in the Johannesburg area the work continued to expand. A mission was started at Benoni to the east of the city, and in 1921 a farm was purchased at Kempton Park to the north. This farm, which they named Rehoboth, became the headquarters of the IHM work, and a Bible school was built on the property in 1923.

In 1924 one of the IHM missionaries joined Mr. Tudhope of the independent Bob Street Mission in Regents Park, Johannesburg, ministering to the white people of the city. Twenty-five years later this same church joined the Church of the Nazarene and became part of the South Africa European District.

Problems in Mozambique

It became apparent rather soon that Chaimite was an ill-selected site. Malaria and blackwater fever were rampant, and the ever-present hordes of mosquitoes made life miserable. The river, too, was subject to rampaging floods during the summer rains. So in 1925 the mission was moved to Magude. The clinic flourished but government restrictions limited other activity. Nor was the health problem of the missionaries fully solved.

In the meantime, Simone Ndhlovu (the Elephant Man), a graduate of the Rehoboth Bible School, had returned to his native land and began preaching at nearby Emaplankweni. He met with such opposition, however, that he decided to move across the border into Eastern Transvaal. Here, at Livydale, he purchased a small farm and built a church where he could preach. Glowingly he reported to the missionaries back in Mozambique about the beautiful country and the response of the people to the gospel. He urged them to join him there.

The missionaries were intrigued by the reports they heard, and in late 1929 Rev. Henry Pope was sent to investigate. He discovered that it was, indeed, an attractive area. Not far away was the Cottondale siding on the Selati Railroad line. What is more, a large adjacent tract of land had recently been subdivided into farm plots that were for sale.

Rev. Pope was impressed with the possibilities but was not authorized to make any commitments at that time. However, he was back again in April 1930 to perform the marriage ceremony for Simone and his bride, Phazimane (Rosia), but more importantly, to purchase a piece of land for the mission. He selected a 500-acre tract five miles from Simone's kraal toward Cottondale. On this property were to be built three separate stations about a mile apart in the form of a triangle. One, the Salem station, would be for the Pedis; another, the Hebron station, would be for the Shangaans; and the third, at the northern apex of the triangle, would be a medical clinic and school center.

This last would be called the Ethel Lucas Memorial station in honor of a young woman in England who had died. Ethel was the daughter of Frank Lucas, pastor of the Southampton church. She was always frail, suffering from a severe heart ailment, but worked tirelessly to bring in money to build the first hospital.

The Cottondale Mission

Later that year, the Stricklands, the Whites, and Misses Doris Brown and Tabitha Evans made a historic 60-mile trek from Magude to the new location, leaving the work in Mozambique in the care of the nationals. Work began on the mission complex.

Because of the ravages of termites, steel-framed and -sheeted buildings were erected. The dispensary or clinic was of particular significance. Although the law allowed only six beds in the dispensary, two government doctors promised to conduct weekly clinics at the dispensary. They took turns coming from the nearest hospital 80 miles away at Pilgrim's Rest. The foundation was being laid for a full-fledged hospital, but it would be 20 years before a missionary doctor was stationed there. That doctor was T. Harold Jones, younger son of the mission's founder and superintendent, Rev. D. B. Jones.

Seven hundred miles to the north lay the isolated Mozambique province of Tete. Here in 1931 the Bests were granted permission to open a mission near Furancungo. With the temporary assistance of the Stricklands, a home, a church, and a clinic were built of native materials, and the mission was given the high-sounding but prophetic name of Plus Ultra ("More Beyond"). When the Bests furloughed in 1934, Rev. and Mrs. Henry Pope took over the work. For 18 years they served in this remote and primitive region.

Meanwhile, back at Cottondale, some problems were developing. It was discovered that in the rainy season the valley between the dispensary located at the apex of the triangle and the other two stations became a raging river. For weeks, the two lady missionaries at the clinic and school would be isolated. Would it be wiser to build an all-weather road and bridge across or to relocate that part of the mission complex on the same side as the others? The greater question was: If this were to develop into a hospital, as it seemed destined to do, would it not be better located at a more accessible point such as on the railroad?

Transfer to Acornhoek

With the added recommendation of the district commissioner and other medical men, a 10-acre tract of land was secured for the clinic at Acornhoek, the next station up the line from Cottondale. The laborious task of dismantling the existing buildings and transporting the material by oxcart to the new site eight miles away was begun in 1935. By the close of 1936 a new dispensary, school, church, and adjunct buildings were completed. A leader in this complex operation was Reginald Jones, son of the mission's founder, who had been appointed in 1932. The wisdom of making this move was quickly apparent.

In 1939 the Rehoboth Bible School was closed, and the mission headquarters was moved to Cottondale. Then in 1940 the government gave the mission a concession of land including some farm buildings in a new native reserve at Islington, seven miles down into the bushveld from Cottondale. The only condition was that a clinic be built there. A great number of people were being moved into the area from the overpopulated lands near the mountains, and this made it a fertile ground for missionary effort.

After their marriage in January 1940, Reginald and Nurse Lillian Jones were placed at Islington. The clinic they developed became an important auxiliary to the more elaborate facility at Acornhoek, to which they were transferred in 1942.

About the same time, Harold Jones, who had been head of Rehoboth Bible School until its closing in 1939, began his medical school training at the Witwatersrand University in Johannesburg, one of the finest such institutions in the world.

By the time the war broke out in 1939, the Acornhoek clinic had grown from a 6-bed-and-many-mats-on-the-floor dispensary into a 66-bed hospital. Lillian Jones and her helpers were in constant demand, and the patient load forced almost continual expansion of buildings despite limited funds. Additional wards were added until a 300-bed capacity was reached. A nurses' training school was also begun. Government agencies were generous in their grants to the hospital, and local donors helped meet many needs, making possible the phenomenal growth of the institution.

Postwar Expansion

Following World War II there was a surge of growth in all areas of the IHM work. In 1945 Rev. and Mrs. I. E. Dayhoff of the Hepzibah

Faith Mission joined the IHM and opened work at Lorraine in the Eastern Transvaal, about 70 miles north of Acornhoek. Again, a condition for permission to establish the mission was that a dispensary be established. This phase of the work was carried on by Hazel Pass. In 1946 a farm was donated for the establishment of a mission at Carolina, 150 miles southeast of Johannesburg, and the C. H. "Happy" Stricklands were assigned to open that work.

In 1947 the Rehoboth Bible School was reopened at Modderfontein near Johannesburg after an eight-year lapse, under the leadership of H. K. Bedwell. That same year, the Letaba Mission near Lorraine was purchased from the Pilgrim Holiness church, and a clinic and dispensary was set up there. Miss Doris Brown was the nurse. Also a high school program was launched at Cottondale by Miss Miriam Evans. The Courtney-Smiths arrived in 1947 and were stationed at Islington.

Rev. C. V. Blamey joined the mission and was assigned to the work at The Downs in the Drakensberg Mountains north of Lorraine. The property had been given to the church by English farmers. He was followed in 1949 by the Rex Emslies. The final flurry of excitement in the decade was the arrival of Dr. T. Harold Jones, now graduated from medical college, to take charge of the Acornhoek hospital. The supporting staff of missionary nurses included Misses Minnie Hope (later Singleton), Joan Bradshaw, Abigail Hewson, and Hazel Pass.

Joining Forces

Talk of merger with the Church of the Nazarene both in Great Britain and on the mission field was no doubt hastened by the sudden death of the IHM leader, David Jones. But the unity of purpose and doctrine shared by the two groups, along with the close association that had existed between them over the years, made merger as logical and easy as the confluence of two streams.

On November 29, 1952, at the Arthurseat mission station the union was consummated. Dr. Hardy C. Powers, general superintendent, and Dr. Remiss Rehfeldt, general secretary of the Department of Foreign Missions, were present for the historic event.

The merger added 31 missionaries, 100 national workers, 10 mission stations, a hospital, and a Bible college to the Nazarene work in Africa. Since the IHM did not keep membership statistics, it is not known exactly how many nationals came into the church. However, the year after the merger, membership growth moved up from 6,493 to 7,459. This would indicate that the merger added about 1,000 members.

2. *Postmerger Developments*

The most immediate effect of the merger was found in the Bible college, where the Rehoboth school (by then at Cottondale) was merged with the Nazarene one at Siteki, Swaziland, and H. K. Bedwell became the principal. For the 16 years he was at the helm, he placed a strong emphasis on preaching.

The merger also brought a great impetus to the camp meeting movement. There were now 10 annual camp meetings in the various fields, with attendance running into the thousands. The camps usually started on Thursday and continued over the weekend. Some had well-constructed tabernacles, while others, such as in Gaza (Mozambique), used simple brush arbors. It was a colorful sight indeed to see the people coming in over the trails, carrying bundles of bedding, cook pots, food, and clothing on their heads.

The usual daily program began with an early morning prayer meeting at six o'clock. After breakfast there was the morning service, which continued until noon. After lunch a similar service continued until evening. There was a mixture of singing, preaching, exhortation, and teaching. The night service was a great evangelistic meeting often attended by many heathen.

Sunday was a climactic day with a baptismal service and Communion at the close of the morning service. Baptisms were usually conducted in a nearby stream, though sometimes a big tank on the platform served the purpose. Another feature of the Sunday services was the march offering in which each one laid his gift upon the altar. In the evangelistic services the altars were lined with seekers, as were many of the front rows of seats. Everyone prayed at the top of his voice. The spiritual results were profound.

The Ethel Lucas Memorial Hospital at Acornhoek was another important adjunct that continued to play a significant role in the work in Eastern Transvaal. As years passed, however, there was increasing government pressure to nationalize it. Finally the law was made that all foreign personnel were to be replaced by nationals as soon as the latter became available. By then the hospital was receiving full government support, and although missionaries were permitted to carry on their usual religious activities, it appeared the end was near.

Anticipating the changeover, the name of the hospital was changed in 1975 to Tintswalo Hospital, and most of the missionary staff were reassigned elsewhere. The government found great difficulty, however, in attracting capable doctors and nurses to this out-of-the-way place and soon were urgently appealing for the missionaries to stay. Though the hospital was no longer an official institution of the Church of the Nazarene, gospel influences thus remained strong.

Most importantly, the union with the IHM brought into the Nazarene work a band of experienced and dedicated missionaries who, like the Bedwells, found channels of effective service in the broader potential afforded by the amalgamation. These subsequent developments will be discussed under the various regions of the African work.

E. EXPANSION IN THE REPUBLIC OF SOUTH AFRICA

1. *The Republic of South Africa North*

Seeking to meet the needs of the many Black tribal groups, estimated to be over 70, the government of the Republic of South Africa has been creating a number of self-governing Black states within the republic, such as Lebowa, the Pedi homeland; Bophuthatswana, land of the Tswanas; and Venda, farthest north of the homelands. The Church of the Nazarene has structured the administration of its work largely along the lines of these tribal groupings.

The oldest Nazarene work in the Republic of South Africa began in the Eastern Transvaal as an extension of the pioneer station at Sabie. Here also Rev. I. E. Dayhoff, formerly with the IHM, labored faithfully for 41 years. Located in this area is Blouberg, the first new field opened as part of the Postwar Advance in 1947 by Rev. and Mrs. George Hayse. Familiar places like Acornhoek and Arthurseat are in this section, which, in the first district structuring, became the Eastern Transvaal District and later the Republic of South Africa North. With the strong move toward nationalization, this total area was eventually divided into eight different districts.

In 1976 the **Eastern District** was set apart as a national-mission district, and Rev. Hannibal Sebati was appointed district superintendent. In 1985 there were 45 churches here with 2,897 members. The area is financially impoverished, which has prompted the development of self-help programs. Also there are only 25 trained pastors, so the churches have had to rely on lay leadership. In 1983 Rev. M. Ribisi became district superintendent. In the early 1980s this area saw a great influx of refugees from neighboring Mozambique.

Farther out is the **Northeast District,** where in 1974 Rev. Abram Maenetśha was elected district superintendent. He was followed by Rev. M. Ribisi. When he then took over the Eastern District, Rev.

Makhubela was elected in his place. By 1985 there were 17 organized churches with a total membership of 777.

The historic **Blouberg** became the center of another district when the former Northwest District was divided into three districts, Northwest (later Seshego), Blouberg, and Northern (later Venda). In 1985 there were 10 organized churches and 4 preaching points on the Blouberg District with 510 full and probationary members. Rev. Daniel Mokebe was the young district superintendent who, with his wife, Pauline, was also actively involved in the Pedi translation program of the Africa Literature Board. The problem on his district was also the need for pastors. Although a rural area, this is the heart of the Pedi homeland, and a well-developed district center included a medical facility operated by missionary nurses Juanita Pate and Janie Semlar. However, the medical work was taken over by the government in 1980.

The name of the Northwest District was changed to **Seshego** in 1978 with Rev. R. M. Ribisi continuing as superintendent. The name was changed to relate it to the name of the temporary capital of Lebowa. The main city of the area is Pietersburg, an industrial center, while nearby is the University of the North. Lebowa, with over 1 million population, is internally self-governing, though the Republic of South Africa still gives assistance. In 1985 there were 13 churches with 350 members on the district.

Two of the more distant Seshego churches were assigned to the new pioneer district of **KwaNdebele** in an area to which many people were migrating. That district now had four churches and a membership of 122. In 1985 the Seshego and Blouberg districts were rejoined to form the **Northwestern District.**

The name of the Northern District was changed to the more identifiable designation of **Venda District,** which is taken from the name Vhavenda, the smallest ethnic Black group in South Africa and farthest north homeland. The mountainous Venda area was proclaimed an independent republic on September 13, 1979, though it had been self-governing since 1973. The work of the Church of the Nazarene here was launched in 1973 by Dale and Pat Stotler. By 1985 there were five churches with 226 members. A distinguished member of the church is Mr. B. T. Mashamba, the chief health officer of the government and a world authority in the knowledge and treatment of tropical diseases, especially malaria.

On the western side of this northern part of the Republic of

South Africa in the general area of Pretoria, the capital, lies the home-land of Bophuthatswana, made up of eight isolated sections scattered generally along the border of Botswana. The South African government has been seeking to link up these scattered segments by buying up the land that lies between them. (The word "phutha" in the name means "to bundle together.")

The pioneer missionary of this area was Rev. J. C. B. Coetzer, who began an independent work in the Vryburg area that in 1961 was united with the Church of the Nazarene. This was the area in which the famous missionary, Robert Moffat, had worked 150 years before, so the Christian witness among the Tswanas was of long standing.

The **Bophuthatswana District** was made a national-mission district in 1977 with Rev. Wilton (Dalton) Maenetja appointed as superintendent. In 1979 it was considered wise to divide the district into **Eastern** and **South** districts, the latter a pioneer district under missionary Ken Rogers. There were six churches in the Eastern District with a total membership in 1985 of 168. Growth has been slow, largely because of a lack of pastors, particularly Tswana-speaking. A bright hope lay in a new radio ministry. The program "Mokhosi wa MuNasarene" ("The Voice of the Nazarene") has prompted response even from inside the neighboring republic of Botswana.

The people of the South District basically live in locations around the large cities such as Kimberley, Vryburg, and Mafikeng. The capital of Mmabatho is also here. Again the problem is to find and train pastors. Because of the employment situation, TEE is the best method to develop the workers needed. The 1985 membership was 198 in six organized churches.

2. *The Republic of South Africa South*

By 1980 there were three Black districts in the southern area of the republic: KwaZulu, Southeastern, and Southwestern. A large segment of the Black people on these districts are Zulu, and their biggest concentration is in Natal, where they constitute 80 percent of the population. They live in about seven somewhat scattered enclaves that take up about 35 percent of Natal's territory. The tribal chiefs wield great power, but there is a KwaZulu Legislative Assembly that began to meet formally in 1972.

The **KwaZulu District** was actually begun in 1962 through the pioneer efforts of Rev. and Mrs. Reginald Jones. They found in the locations around the big cities many displaced Nazarenes who had gone there to work. A Swazi pastor, Rev. Gininda, was brought down to preach to the Zulus, while the Joneses ministered to the Shangaans. The superintendent was Rev. Samuel Ndhlovu. In 1985 there were 23 churches on the district with a total membership of 813.

In 1975, in response to a need for a Zulu Bible college, Rev. and Mrs. Philip Bedwell were appointed to open the KwaZulu Nazarene Bible College. It is located on a beautiful site overlooking the Indian Ocean and has become a valuable training center for both existing and future pastors, plus numbers of laymen.

The **Southeastern District** is actually an extension of the work in Swaziland. Its beginning churches were the Idalia and Carolina missions, originally opened by the International Holiness Mission. There has been a considerable migration of people from Swaziland into this area of the Republic, and the Nazarenes among them have formed the nucleus of some congregations. Up along the Swaziland border the work is quite strong. The district superintendent is Rev. Frank Mncina, and the total membership in 1985 was 1,085. Most of the churches operate day schools. The government pays the teachers and provides subsidies for buildings. Some of the teachers serve as local pastors as well. Miss Irma Koffel has administered this significant phase of the work.

The **Southwestern District** takes in the heaviest-populated part of South Africa including the Johannesburg area and the teeming location city of Soweto. Here District Superintendent Minaar Zwane has led 37 churches with a total membership of 764 (1985). He has been crippled considerably by the fact that many of his churches do not have pastors. The potential for the district is enormous if adequate leadership can be found.

F. TRANS SOUTH AFRICA

The most prominent ethnic group in South Africa apart from the European and the Bantu is what is known there as the Coloured race (those of mixed blood). They number 1.5 million and thus constitute a significant segment of the total population. Yet they are in many respects a forgotten people.

The Coloured people originated with the coming of the white settlers to the Cape area over 300 years ago. The intermingling of the two racial groups over the years produced a mixed race that Betty Emslie describes as a "friendly, happy, and singing people." Yet they stand in a sort of no-man's-land, not fully accepted by either Black or white. They are, however, basically European in customs and lifestyle, most of them speaking Afrikaans but many of them English. Among them are numbers of business and professional people, well-educated and prosperous. Yet they have been an isolated group, set apart socially and, for the most part, economically.

Recognizing the unique problems this mixed-race group posed, the government built a number of cities in strategic areas. Among the larger of these modern complexes are Mitchell's Plain, near Cape Town, with 250,000 people; Atlantis, also near Cape Town, with 500,000; Ennerdale, just south of Johannesburg, with 150,000; and Phoenix, north of Durban, which houses 160,000. As these cities were being constructed, property was secured and Nazarene churches built. A great potential for evangelism existed here, and the development of the Trans South Africa field closely followed the establishment of these communities.

1. Johannesburg Beginnings

When the Morris Chalfants were assigned to both the Black and Coloured work in the Johannesburg suburbs, they experienced unusual success among the latter. The result was the organization in 1948 of the first church among the Coloured people at Protea.

The majority of the Coloured population, however, lived in the vicinity of Cape Town. Therefore when Dr. Hardy C. Powers visited the field in 1950, he spent some time in that area investigating the possibilities of opening work there. In the meantime, it was felt necessary to organize the three existing churches in the Johannesburg area into a separate district. This was accomplished in 1951. Rev. George Taylor became superintendent of the Northern District in 1974 and remained in office until his death. Rev. Peter Wagner succeeded him. Membership in 1985 stood at 807 in 14 organized churches.

An unusual aspect of the Coloured work was the large number among them who felt a call to preach. To provide them the necessary training, the former IHM Bible school facilities at Rehoboth in suburban Johannesburg were reactivated for this purpose. In March 1954 the school began operation under the leadership of Rev. J. F. Penn, Jr.

In 1960 the school was transferred from Johannesburg to Ottery, a suburb of Cape Town. It still carried the Rehoboth name but was upgraded to college status. Rev. Philip Steigleder became principal, to be followed a few years later by Rev. Raymond Thorpe and then Rev. Ronald Calhoun. Three main buildings were erected, including a dormitory for singles and a home for married students along with an administration building with classrooms and dining hall. A three-year Bible course, meeting the requirements for ordination, and a two-year Christian Workers' course for lay leaders were offered in the beginning years.

In 1978 a beautiful new campus was developed and occupied in Port Elizabeth under the leadership of Rev. Don Scarlett. This was a significant step forward.

2. *Expansion to the Cape*

It was the products of the Bible school that made possible the launching of the work in the Cape Town area. Here the Church of the Nazarene was able to secure sites in the new suburban towns of Factreton, Matroosfontein, Steenberg, Sunnyside, and Bonteheuwel. In 1955 construction began in the various buildings through the use of Alabaster funds.

In 1973 the Western Cape National-Mission District was formed, and Rev. Layton B. Smith was named superintendent. The district had over 800 members and was 85 percent self-supporting. By 1980 membership was up to 1,767, and mission district status had been achieved.

The final step was to become a regular (Phase 4) district. At the 25th anniversary district assembly in 1982, it was a momentous moment when the assembly delegates voted to accept the challenge and request regular district status to take effect at the 1983 assembly. When this was consummated, the district became part of the Republic of South Africa jurisdiction rather than Trans South Africa. By 1985 there were 23 organized churches with 2,664 members. Rev. L. B. Smith, who had been the first national district superintendent elected in 1973, was continued in office.

3. The East Indians and the Natal District

Before the turn of the century the first immigration into South Africa from India took place. The industrious workers were brought over to develop the sugarcane fields on the southeast coast. Their descendants and subsequent immigrants, now totaling half a million, form the largest ethnic group in the city of Durban and outnumber the white population of the province of Natal. Among their number are prosperous business and professional people, but there are also many at the opposite end of the economic spectrum. As a whole they are a tolerant, intelligent, and ambitious people with an insatiable desire for education.

The Indians largely adopted Western ways, including the English language, but ancient customs still persist. A delightful carryover is the wearing of beautiful saris by the women. Three-quarters of the Indians are Hindus, and most of their homes have shrines. But their public religious processions have greatly decreased in recent years, and attendance at the many temples has declined.

Work among the Durban Indian people was begun in 1963 under the leadership of the Joseph Penns, Jr., in the suburb of Merebank. A church was organized there the following year, and the pastor installed was from the Lenasia Church in suburban Johannesburg. The latter was the first Nazarene Indian congregation in Africa, though they were not officially organized and had no building. They worshiped in a school building until a site was granted and a church finally built. The church was then organized with 14 members.

A second church was begun in Chatsworth, a new town that eventually would house 200,000 Indians. A well-located property in a shopping center was secured and another attractive Alabaster church built. Wayside Sunday Schools and cottage meetings were launched to attract people to the church, and the work continued to grow.

One secret of the 10 percent-per-year growth in the Indian church was the strong lay participation in outreach. Another was the Sunday School emphasis. It was not unusual for Sunday School attendance to run 5 to 10 times the church membership. Music, both instrumental and vocal, also was characteristic of the church. District singing competitions were instrumental in drawing young people into the church.

The Natal District was officially organized by Rev. Rex Emslie in 1972 and became a mission district in 1976, with Rev. Ahmed Subjee the elected superintendent. There has been remarkable growth, but a major drawback has been that less than half of the organized churches had their own buildings. By 1985 there was a total membership of 1,869.

4. *The Eastern Cape District*

In 1969 Rev. and Mrs. Don Scarlett and Rev. and Mrs. George Meyers pioneered a work among the Coloured population in Port Elizabeth. Services were held in a schoolroom that was soon overcrowded. In 1971 property was purchased and a church built in the suburb of Schauderville. Under the leadership of the pastor, Rev. J. Hamilton, the church was self-supporting within three years. It also spawned three other churches in the area.

Progress was such that a new district was formed called the Eastern Cape District. The first assembly was held in 1974. In 1978 it became a national-mission district, and Rev. Peter Wagner was appointed superintendent. By 1980 membership was up to 318, and by 1985 it had reached 528 with seven organized churches. The moving of the Nazarene Bible College from Cape Town to Port Elizabeth was a great boon to the work in this area. (It will be recalled that it was at Port Elizabeth that Harmon Schmelzenbach first set foot on African soil.)

G. CENTRAL AFRICA

1. *Northwest Mozambique*

The first penetration of the Church of the Nazarene into central Africa was in the far northwest Mozambique province of Tete. Here in 1938-39 the L. C. Ferees had done some exploratory work, but for various reasons the attempt to open a work never materialized. The International Holiness Mission, however, had some years before opened a work at Furancungo that, with the merger with the Church of the Nazarene in 1952, became a part of the Nazarene field.

The Henry Popes had labored in Furancungo station in lonely isolation for 18 years. The strongest phase of the program was the medical clinic, which was desperately needed in this remote area, but the results in terms of conversions were disappointing. With the reassessment of the total missionary program that the merger occasioned, there was serious question as to whether this distant, struggling station should be continued. The imminent retirement of the Popes made an early decision imperative.

A commission appointed to investigate the situation visited the field in 1954 and again in 1955. Their conclusion was that the potential for development of the work was limited, particularly because of increasing government interference. Nevertheless, one more effort was made to salvage the work by sending Rev. and Mrs. Norman Salmons to Furancungo. They served there with some success from 1954 to 1969, being joined by Fairy Cochlin in 1964.

When the Salmonses went on furlough in 1969, Oscar and Marjorie Stockwell took charge of the work amid mounting apprehension concerning the political situation. Indeed, only one year later the missionaries were forced to depart, leaving the work in the care of the nationals.

2. *Malawi*

With the possibility of finding a new mission field in central Africa, in the course of their investigation of the Tete situation, the commission visited nearby Malawi. They were greatly impressed with both the need and the opportunity. Other than Johannesburg, it was the most populous area in Africa south of the equator. Hundreds of thousands lived along the shores of the great lake, third largest in Africa, which formed the country's central core. The fact that the prevailing religion was Muslim would perhaps make missionary work more difficult here, but the people seemed open and friendly. The footprints of Livingstone, the great missionary explorer, were also to be found here.

The lake teemed with fish, and the nearby forested hills harbored abundant wildlife. Where cultivated, the land yielded rich harvests with tea a principal export product. But in contrast, the people themselves were abysmally poor. Outside of the cities living conditions were primitive.

As soon as the decision was made to open a work here, property was secured at Chipoka, a lake port that was also a railhead. In 1956 Rev. and Mrs. James Graham and Rev. and Mrs. Maurice Hall moved temporarily into a two-room mud hut there and began to carve out a new work.

The first rainy season soon showed the error of their site selection. Violent storms forced the closing of the port, and consequently no trains came for long periods. Roads became impassable, even to jeeps. For six months the missionaries were virtually immobilized. The one helpful result was that they had abundant opportunity to work on their language studies in which they became very proficient.

When they were once more able to get about, they began to search for a more advantageous location. They decided on Fort Johnstone at the southern tip of the lake. Here they met with good success, and that year, 1957, Malawi was made an official district.

The first expansion move was to Limbe, 100 miles south, in the industrial area of the country. Here a Bible school was opened, and by 1965 enrollment reached 38 and by 1975 had climbed to over 50. At first the Bible school was to serve the entire central Africa region, but in 1973 it was decided to begin a separate school in Zimbabwe (then Rhodesia). The principal at Malawi, Rev. Jack Barnell, was assigned the task of opening the new school. Rev. Tom Waltermire took his place at Limbe. The fact that all instruction was in the Chichewa language of Malawi was a factor in the decision to have a separate institution, but the political situation was also becoming critical.

The response to the gospel in Malawi was phenomenal. By 1970 there were 1,061 members, and this number doubled in the next five years. Superintendent Fred Manda placed strong emphasis on pastoral visitation, and as a result his pastors average 200 visits per month. A similar emphasis on tithing (both money and produce) soon brought several churches to the level of self-support.

In 1976 Malawi South was set apart as a national-mission district, and Rev. Albert Mphamba was appointed superintendent. In March 1981 the Central District reached that status, and Rev. Kalitera was appointed superintendent. At the same time the pioneer North District was launched.

Though divided into the three districts, there was close cooperation at all levels of church operation. A uniform policy for all pastors was formulated. This included educational subsidies for their children, and family medical and pension plans. Annual national retreats for laymen and for ladies, as well as seminars for pastors, were held. A strong cooperative program of evangelism was instituted with a national evangelist holding services in every church during each year.

In an effort to alleviate the chronic poverty problem and develop self-support, the Africa Regional Office set up grain mill projects on the three districts beginning in 1983. These mills provided employment, made processed food available for those living in urban areas, and provided an income base for local church and district support.

Church growth in Malawi was outstanding. In 1980 the South District had 2,466 members, but by 1985 this figure was up to 3,264 with 33 organized churches and 40 other preaching points. The Central District in 1985 reported 1,540 members in 21 organized churches and 6 preaching points. The pioneer North District with 6 churches had a membership of 166. Ambitious goals the districts had set for themselves were all surpassed. The combined membership of 4,970 was more than double what it was 10 years before.

3. *Zambia*

The work of the Church of the Nazarene in Zambia actually had its beginning in the heart of one of its people who had gone down to Johannesburg to work and was saved in one of the churches there.

When he returned to his home near Lusaka, the capital city, he began to preach the gospel. About the same time, in the mid-1950s, Rev. J. J. Scheepers, pastor of the European congregation at Potchefstroom, Republic of South Africa, moved to Lusaka and launched a church among the white people of the city. This early organization, however, did not survive.

The commission members who explored the area in connection with the Tete investigation visited Lusaka and heard the plea for a missionary to reach out to the Black population. In response, in 1958 the Edwin K. Wissbroeker family were sent to Lusaka, where a solid foundation was established. A growing nationalism made progress slow until adequate national pastors were trained. The first class of three was ordained by Dr. George Coulter in 1973.

A unique opportunity was given to the church to provide Bible instruction in the public schools. The missionaries and national preachers were soon conducting 24 such classes each week. A colportage work was also set up in which Bibles and religious books were sold in the village and city markets.

Along the northwest border of Zambia, next to Zaire, lies one of the richest copper-producing areas in the world. As in the Johannesburg area, large African townships were established around the many mines, offering a great opportunity for ministry. In answer to the challenge in 1964, Rev. and Mrs. Jay Hunton were stationed at Kitwe, the center of the mining area. Subsequently church buildings were erected at Chikumbi and Bancroft.

In 1976 Nicolas Chirwa was ordained by Dr. George Coulter, general superintendent, and appointed the first national superintendent of Zambia. In 1979 the Zambia Bible College was opened on a campus that a Work and Witness team from the Washington Pacific District helped develop.

In 1980 Zambia was divided into two districts, North and South, and goals were set for development of all phases of the work: membership, finance, Sunday School, youth, and NWMS. At the time of the division, total membership was 535. By 1985 the combined membership had more than doubled to 1,167 (713 in the North and 454 in the South). There was a total of 13 organized churches and 10 other preaching points. A significant move was made in 1982 when Rev. and Mrs. Ignatius Chavunduka were assigned to open an English-speaking church in Lusaka. It was officially organized in 1983.

As in other areas of Africa, the matter of self-support was a difficult challenge. On the South District an agricultural project was begun in 1981, raising sugar beans and seed maize to finance district projects. Zambia North followed suit. Alabaster funds also played an important role in the building of churches and parsonages. In addition, $10,000 went toward the construction of a second building at the Bible school in 1983. By 1985 well over half of the 13 organized churches were fully self-supporting.

4. *Zimbabwe*

This newest of African nations (achieving independence on April 18, 1980) was formerly known as Southern Rhodesia or, more recently, simply Rhodesia. Because it was the center of conflict between Black and white rule, missionary work was not easy. But here again, the advent of national leadership marked the major upturn in church growth.

The work in this area was launched in 1963 when a church was established in the Salisbury area. The next step was into the African suburb of Harare, where a building was erected. The national pastor installed there was Rev. Enoch Litswele from the Transvaal, who was very much a missionary.

The next step was into Bulawayo, and within a decade there were nine churches in the two centers along with other preaching points. In 1973 Rev. Ignatius Chavunduka became the first national superintendent. The Sunday School became a strong emphasis and, as in Zambia, an opportunity opened to teach religious education courses in the local primary and high schools.

A well-trained ministry is characteristic of this work. Of the 14 pastors, 13 are Bible-college trained, and 1 is a layman. Of the 19 congregations, 2 are English-speaking, 1 in Salisbury (now Harare), and 1 in Bulawayo. Revs. Larry Wright and Jim Sage were early pastors, respectively, the latter also serving as mission director.

It became necessary, because of the unsettled political situation, to establish a separate Bible school in Zimbabwe. The first principal was Rev. Jack Barnell, to be followed by Don Bell, a lay missionary.

With the coming of independence in 1980, the Zimbabwe Nazarenes, under the leadership of their new district superintendent, Rev. Paul Mukome, set about to build a truly interracial district united in Christ. Training programs were designed for all levels of leadership.

Mission Director Jim Sage put together an in-depth discipleship training program based on Don Wellman's *Dynamics of Discipling,* which
was used with success among the pastors.

By 1985 there were 19 organized churches with a membership of
932.

H. EUROPEAN SOUTH AFRICA

When Dr. Hardy C. Powers visited Africa in 1947, it was the first time in eight years that a general superintendent had been there. The intervening period, principally marked by the trauma of World War II, had brought vast changes to the land and its people. The missionary program of the Church of the Nazarene was itself going through a revolution of sorts as it began to burst the confines of its original Swaziland bounds.

1. *English and Afrikaans*

This explosive vision was capsulized in the four-point program outlined in 1944 by the Committee on Postwar Advance and reiterated in 1945 and 1946. Item No. 1 on the list was that work be started among the English- and Afrikaans-speaking people of southern Africa. This idea was not new, for the need for a holiness message among the European population had long been recognized. True, South Africa was the home of the great holiness exponent Dr. Andrew Murray, and a number of independent holiness churches were in operation, especially those related to the Africa Evangelistic Band. But there was no denominational thrust.

Perhaps the first to catch this vision was Mrs. Laura H. Feree, who with her husband, Rev. L. C. Feree, had come to the field in 1925. They were first stationed in Mozambique but were later transferred to the mine work at Boksburg. Here in the Johannesburg area they caught the vision of the need for Nazarene work among the white population. Mrs. Feree's tool was the *Herald of Holiness,* which she distributed in great quantity. She spoke to white audiences at every opportunity and even gave herself to the study of Afrikaans so she could speak to Afrikaner as well as to English congregations. The J. F. Penns, who followed the Ferees at Boksburg, caught the vision too; and though the war restrictions temporarily thwarted expansion into this area, the pent-up desire to enter this entirely new field was to bring early results. No wonder it assumed No. 1 position in the postwar "to-do" list.

A central purpose of Dr. Powers' 1947 visit was to explore the possibilities of the white work. He even visited a Portuguese congregation in Lourenzo Marques, led by Dr. E. A. Riberro, which had expressed a desire to affiliate with the Church of the Nazarene. Dr. Powers went home convinced that it was time to move and reported so to the General Board at its January 1948 meeting. A basic decision was made that such work be under the Department of Home Missions rather than Foreign Missions.

Rev. C. H. Strickland, pastor of Dallas First Church and former superintendent of the Florida District, was selected to launch the work. But when Dr. Powers approached the Stricklands about the matter, they were frankly negative at first. However, the Lord began to lay the burden of Africa upon them to the extent that a few weeks later Rev. Strickland called to say that if the position was still open, he and his wife, Fannie, were ready to go.

The Stricklands were immediately placed under appointment, but there were months of tedious waiting for residence permits. Just before they were to leave, Rev. Strickland was involved in an automobile wreck that he miraculously came out of unscathed; and while on their way to Africa, the family came close to a fatal crash at the fog-shrouded airport in Accra, West Africa. It seemed an ominous beginning. But on August 28, 1948, the Stricklands landed in Johannesburg ready to study the situation and plan a strategy for opening up the work.

They had already studied the historical background of the people they sought to minister to. The Afrikaners, descendants of the original Dutch and Huguenot settlers, constituted the larger segment (60 percent) of the total 2.4 million white population. The animosities that grew out of the Boer War (the Second War of Independence), 1899-1902, had largely dissipated, but the character of the two groups was still distinct. The Afrikaners were conservative and their religious roots ran deep. Almost all were members of the Dutch Reformed church. The English were, by contrast, liberal, secular, and religiously indifferent. Whether the opposition of the strongly Calvinistic Afrikaners would be harder to break than the apathy of the English was yet to be seen.

The critical question to answer at the outset was whether it was possible to minister to both simultaneously or whether separate districts should be formed. The decision to follow the former course was to have long-range significance. The bilingual problem was not easy to handle, but the result was a church of unique character that bespoke the message preached.

The first step was to purchase a house in Discovery, a suburb of Roodepoort near Johannesburg, to serve as a district parsonage. From here there was ready access to the white population in the area and also to the capital city of Pretoria, 35 miles to the north.

Rev. Strickland contacted the congregation in Lourenzo Marques and scheduled a revival meeting with them for November 14-21, 1948. Helping greatly to publicize the meeting was the regular broadcasting of "Showers of Blessing" over a powerful local station that had begun the year before. At the close of the meeting the church was officially organized with 13 charter members. Rev. Kenneth Babcock, one of the Mozambique missionaries, was named as pastor. Thus the first European church in southern Africa was neither Afrikaans nor English, but Portuguese.

An unusual development was that the European church had pastors available before it had churches. The first of these was Rev. J. J. Scheepers, a former missionary to the Congo and an outstanding minister of the Zion church, a small holiness movement. He threw in his lot with the Church of the Nazarene in June 1949. Shortly after, he was joined by Rev. Hendrik J. Senekal, who was reached through listening to "Showers of Blessing" and came to offer his services to the church.

Mrs. Feree's distribution of the *Herald of Holiness* was productive, bringing in two other pastors, Rev. J. MacLachlan and Rev. Stafford Finnemore. Next came the able and talented Rev. Christoffel D. Botha, to be followed within a year's time by half a dozen more. As fast as ministers became available, revival campaigns were arranged and new churches organized. In such a way a campaign was begun in Pretoria in August 1949, which culminated in the organization of a church and the installation of Rev. Senekal as pastor. By December the congregation had bought a vacant church building in which to worship.

Now that the purchase of church property came into the picture, unexpected legal complications arose. Churches not registered with the government prior to 1945 could not hold property. Apparently the laws that allowed missions to hold such titles did not carry over to the European segment, for the church had bought numerous properties in the Transvaal. The impasse was resolved when, on checking the records, it was found that in 1915, Rev. Harmon Schmelzenbach had officially registered the church in South Africa. At the time, Swaziland, as a native preserve, was considered under the jurisdiction of the government of South Africa, so the official registration granted to him covered the entire union. The long-range effect of that action he had no way of knowing.

On November 4, 1949, the third church was organized at Parys in the Orange Free State on the main road to Cape Town. Rev. Scheepers became its pastor. By July 1950 three more churches had been organized, one at Potchefstroom, the oldest town in the Transvaal, and the other two in the twin cities of Vereeniging and Vanderbijl Park, centers of the growing iron and steel industry. In the latter city the first new church building was erected on a superb site donated by the city. The cost was underwritten by Kansas City First Church in honor of Dr. R. T. Williams, and dedication ceremonies were conducted by Dr. Hardy C. Powers on October 28, 1950.

The latter event marked the climax of a historic week in which the first district assembly of the European District was held in the Parys church on October 24. Rev. C. H. Strickland was appointed district superintendent; Mrs. Strickland became missionary society president; Rev. J. Lazarus, district secretary; Rev. J. MacLachlan, district treasurer; and Chris Botha, NYPS president. An Advisory Board and Church School Board were also elected. Within a decade there were 25 churches with a membership of 608. These churches were spread all across southern Africa, including Durban, Natal; Klaserie, in the Eastern Transvaal; Lusaka, Zambia; and Cape Town. In addition, satellite missions were started by several of the churches. Although the majority of the churches were within 50 miles of Johannesburg, the most distant churches were 1,800 miles apart. Some congregations were English-speaking, some were Afrikaans, and a few had dual congregations using the same facilities.

2. *South Africa Nazarene Bible College*

The May 1952 issue of the district's bilingual news bulletin, *The South African Nazarene,* announced that the General Nazarene Young People's Society had taken on the project of helping to start a Bible college for the district. This was featured at the General Convention at Kansas City in June, and $20,000 was raised for the purpose. This was invested in property in Potchefstroom that would accommodate about 25 students. The facilities of the nearby Potchefstroom church would be available for use as well.

A governing council for the proposed school was selected in November 1952, which in turn elected Rev. Cyril J. Pass as principal. The college officially opened January 9, 1954, with an enrollment of seven. Fourteen courses were offered to meet the full ordination requirements. Nearby Pastors J. MacLachlan and J. J. Scheepers along with Rev. Charles Strickland and Rev. Pass shared the initial teaching load. The following year, Rev. Floyd Perkins, who had been pastor of the Lourenzo Marques church, was transferred to the Johannesburg Central Church and joined the Bible college faculty. In 1955 he became principal of the school.

3. *Publishing Program*

Classes at the Bible college were conducted on a bilingual basis, but since initially none of the textbooks were available in the Afrikaans language, this necessitated an enormous translation project. In the first six months of operation 750,000 pages of Afrikaans study sheets were duplicated. This monumental task could not have been accomplished without the acquisition of some printing equipment, and the Stricklands' garage became a miniature printing plant. The Nazarene Publishing House in Kansas City donated an offset press, which was put to use in preparing Sunday School literature in Afrikaans, as well as other items. This printing operation also became a book depository and distribution center for English materials.

In 1963 the Shirley Press, which had been located in Manzini, Swaziland, was united with the European operation. Thus the Africa Nazarene Publishing House came into being in Florida, a suburb of Roodepoort, where the college itself had moved. The pooling of equipment and personnel seemed a wise move, but working with 11 different languages was difficult and frustrating. It was not until 1972, under the leadership of Alfred Mills, that the Publishing House finally reached the break-even point financially.

In the meantime, the presses had turned out great volumes of material that were invaluable in the ongoing of the work on the various fields. The Nazarene hymnal was printed in six languages including an Afrikaans-English edition. Church papers in the pattern of the *Herald of Holiness* were published in Zulu, Pedi, and Shangaan. Rev.

H. K. Bedwell, a strong supporter of the publishing program, edited a Zulu *Preacher's Magazine.*

In 1966, under the leadership of Dr. A. F. Harper, a four-year Sunday School curriculum was prepared to be used on all fields. This was enlarged to a six-year cycle in 1976. Over the years special teachers' quarterlies and children's materials were added.

In January 1982 the Evangelical Literature Association of Southern Africa (ELASA) was organized. Participating groups were the Church of the Nazarene, the Free Baptist church, the Free Methodist church, and the Wesleyan church, all of them committed to holiness doctrine. The initial cooperative effort was in the production of four levels of Sunday School literature, but expansion into the areas of youth work and evangelism was planned.

The rapid expansion of the missionary work into new language groups only compounded the work of Africa Nazarene Publications. The 16 staff members in the main office plus 4 in the branch office in Swaziland could not keep up with the existing load of writing, translating, and checking, let alone initiate badly needed new projects.

In March 1983 Dr. Bennett Dudney, director of Publications Services in Kansas City, met with the African Publications Board and the Curriculum Committee to seek a solution for the problem. The outcome was the setting up of literature development committees in each of the 15 language groups where the Church of the Nazarene was then operating. The initial task was to set priorities and goals. The development of adequate literature for both indoctrination and training was considered of prime importance.

4. *College Expansion*

In the meantime the Bible college itself, under the leadership of Rev. Floyd Perkins, had acquired a more adequate property in Florida and had expanded its curriculum and faculty. An affiliation was worked out with Canadian Nazarene College for the granting of degrees.

In the early 1970s Rev. David Whitelaw became principal of the Bible college, and in 1973 a potential campus site was procured between Johannesburg and Pretoria. The facilities in Florida were proving inadequate for the growing college. Unfortunately they were unable to go ahead with building on the new property, and alternate plans were drawn to provide new facilities on the old site. The closing of the printing plant there in 1976 provided a basic classroom and administration building.

In 1976 Rev. Whitelaw was elected the first South African superintendent of the European District, and selected to succeed him at the college was Rev. Ted Esselstyn, a second-generation missionary then serving as principal of the Lula Schmelzenbach Memorial Nazarene Bible College at Arthurseat, Eastern Transvaal.

5. *Later Developments*

In 1980 Rev. Whitelaw resigned the superintendency to pursue his doctoral studies at the University of South Africa in Pretoria. Dr. Richard Zanner, who had just been appointed regional director for the Africa field and thus would be moving to Africa from West Germany, was asked to serve temporarily as superintendent of the European District. At the 1980 General Assembly the district was recognized as a regular district. By 1985 its membership had reached 1,888 with 28 organized churches. Rev. Jerry Jennings was elected district superintendent to follow Dr. Richard Zanner. He is the son-in-law of Rev. Chris Botha, the first district NYPS president and one of the early pastors on the district.

I. THE REPUBLIC OF CAPE VERDE

When Portuguese adventurers began to sail the seas on exploring and trading expeditions in the 1400s, they chanced upon a group of volcanic islands 300 miles out in the Atlantic off the western hump of Africa. Though they were mostly barren, they were named the Cape Verde (Green) Islands after the African coast adjacent to them and were claimed for Portugal. There were 15 islands in all, but only 9 were habitable.

The islands became a stopping-off place on the trade routes of the Atlantic. Slave ships on the way to the United States were frequent visitors, and for one reason or another many black slaves remained on the islands. The government also used the islands to isolate criminals from Portugal. Traders and sailors added to the mix until a unique diverse population was developed. Their language was officially Portuguese and religion Roman Catholic.

There was not much about the islands to attract settlers, for food was scarce and droughts frequent. But some did make their homes there, and a population of over 300,000 was eventually reached. But it was hard to hold the young people for whom the sea was an alluring highway to more intriguing lands in which to live.

1. John Diaz, the Pioneer

In earlier years particularly, many of the inhabitants were seamen. One of these, a Mr. Diaz, was making a trip to the United States in 1889 and took his adventurous 16-year-old son, John, with him. The young man chose to stay, settling first with the Cape Verdian community in New Bedford, Mass. While there he was converted in a Protestant mission. After two years he moved on to Providence, R.I., where he came in touch with the People's Church, of the Association of Pentecostal Churches of America, where he was led into the experience of entire sanctification.

Feeling the call of God upon him to preach the gospel, he began ministering to his own people in America. He was instrumental in leading a number of people to Christ, including his own father. But friends in the church began to urge him to return to the place of his birth to preach the gospel. They promised to support him to the extent of $16.00 per month. So John J. Diaz set out in 1901 aboard an old sailing vessel bound for his home island of Brava, one of the smaller of the Cape Verdes, located in the southwest extremity of the island chain.

After his 12 years absence, both family and friends welcomed him warmly. But when the purpose of his coming was made known, even his family turned against him. Twice he was mobbed and beaten, narrowly escaping death. Four times he was jailed. His followers were likewise ill-treated, but from these fires of tribulation great giants of the faith emerged, and the church grew. In 1915, with the help of funds from the United States, a church building seating 300 was built.

In the meantime, in 1907 the Association of Pentecostal Churches of America had united with Dr. Bresee's Church of the Nazarene to form the Pentecostal Church of the Nazarene, and so John Diaz automatically became a Nazarene. The changed relationship did not alter the situation greatly, for he labored on in isolation. Twice Dr. H. F. Reynolds, general superintendent and Foreign Missions secretary, tried to reach the island of Brava but was unable to do so.

In 1920 a day school was opened in Brava that soon had an attendance of 100. The teacher, E. P. Tavares, was employed by the Nazarene General Board of Foreign Missions. This did much to win the goodwill of the people. In 1932 José Freire, a Portuguese Protestant evangelist, held a meeting up on the island of São Vicente that was so successful that another Church of the Nazarene was organized there. Even without a pastor and with only occasional visits from Rev. Diaz, the church flourished under the care of an outstanding layman, Augusto M. Miranda.

Finally in 1934 it was arranged to have the Nazarene missionaries, Rev. and Mrs. Charles S. Jenkins, stop off in the course of their journey home from Africa on furlough to hold eight weeks of evangelistic meetings on the islands. The Jenkinses were missionaries to Mozambique (then Portuguese East Africa) so knew the language. Their effective ministry resulted in the conversion of scores of people. For Rev. Diaz it was an overwhelming experience. For 34 years he had labored without a single visitor from his own church.

2. *The Everette Howards Arrive*

The Jenkinses went on to the United States and in the course of their deputation ministry spoke often of their experience in Cape Verde. As a result, they were largely influential in persuading a young Kansas pastor and his wife, Rev. and Mrs. Everette Howard, to volunteer for missionary service in the Cape Verde Islands. Their arrival at Mindelo on the island of São Vicente, March 9, 1936, after five months of language study in Portugal, marked the beginning of a new epoch in Cape Verdian missions. They received a tumultuous welcome when they finally reached Brava and were soon installed as pastors of the church. Some months later, after the Howards had the work well in hand, the ailing John Diaz returned to America. This great warrior of the faith passed away in 1964, never again having returned to his native islands.

The earlier persecution, though not as severe, was still present, showing up particularly as new islands were "invaded" by the church. Everette Howard proved to be an undaunted and fearless worker whose missionary exploits have been recorded in numerous volumes. Ever driven to expand the work, he moved from island to island, establishing churches in Santo Antão, Fogo, Santiago, Maio, São Nicolau, and Sal, in addition to the ones on Brava and São Vicente. On some of these islands several churches were soon flourishing.

One of the first ventures was to the island of Fogo, next to Brava. Here Rev. Howard met Jesuino Monteiro, who had been converted in the United States and had returned to his homeland 17 years before. For all those years he had prayed that God would send a missionary their way. He was known among his people as the "little religious man." He became a pillar in the new church.

One of the most difficult obstacles to overcome was that of transportation between the islands. Small sailing vessels, often barely seaworthy, were the only means of communication. The island chain was in the shape of a horseshoe with the open end, 150 miles across, facing west. Many harrowing days and nights were spent in those island-to-island crossings. An added hazard was the lack of docking facilities in most places. Only God's miraculous care kept the missionaries alive.

Rev. and Mrs. George Keeler came to Cape Verde in 1937 but had to return to the United States the following year for health reasons. The next missionary to come to the islands was a Britisher, Rev. Clifford Gay. He arrived in 1939 after he had been thwarted from going to his planned destination of Angola, another Portuguese colony in southern Africa. For many years he served as a bachelor, until in 1955 he was married to an Irish nurse, Charlotte Mann.

In early 1938 Dr. and Mrs. J. B. Chapman visited the Cape Verde Islands in the course of an extended missionary journey. It was the first time a general superintendent had come to this field. It was not long afterward, February 1940, that Mrs. Chapman passed away. Dr. Chapman wrote a biography of her life, the proceeds for the book going to the building of a church in the capital city of Praia on the island of Santiago. By a strange providence, Rev. Howard was able to purchase a large, beautiful block of land there for an unbelievably low price. On the property was erected an imposing building seating 1,000, plus overflow space for 500 more. It was called the Maud Chapman Memorial Church.

The dedication day in August 1947 was one of the high points in the history of the Church of the Nazarene in Cape Verde. Oddly enough, it was on the day following Dr. Chapman's own death. By this time the prestige of the Church of the Nazarene had been established in the islands, and government officials and prominent businessmen were being numbered among its members and adherents.

3. *Expansion After World War II*

In 1946 Rev. and Mrs. Earl Mosteller had arrived on the field, beginning an illustrious missionary career that later was to take them to Brazil, Portugal, and then the Azores in pioneering roles. They were followed in 1948 by Rev. and Mrs. Ernest Eades, who served effectively in various capacities for 12 years. Then in 1949 Lydia Wilke, a missionary nurse who had served in Swaziland from 1940 to 1946, began 14 years of fruitful work on the islands. Her nursing skills were much in demand, and for a time she operated a mobile clinic on the island of Fogo. She reported as many as 4,000 treatments a year. However, health problems made it impossible for her to continue, and the medical program came to a virtual stop.

In 1950 Dr. Samuel Young, general superintendent, visited five of the islands, traveling in the flimsy, interisland sailing vessels of the time. In 1954 Dr. Hugh C. Benner was the first to fly in, but after that there was no visit by a general superintendent for nine years. Then Dr. Powers, visiting in Lisbon in the course of a European tour, was able to secure passage on a diplomatic flight to Cape Verde. In his subsequent report to the General Board, it was Lisbon that had captured his attention. "I strongly recommend," he said, "that the Department of Foreign Missions consider opening a church in Lisbon." It was not until 10 years later that this was accomplished, however. Subsequent visits to the islands were made by Dr. Samuel Young (1967), Dr. Eugene Stowe (1970), Dr. Edward Lawlor (1974), Dr. V. H. Lewis (1977), and Dr. Orville Jenkins (1981).

In 1951 Mrs. Garnet Howard suffered a severe heart malfunction that necessitated the Howards returning to the United States. Though their service was cut short, they had seen the work spread throughout the island chain in spectacular fashion. In those 16 years there had been some remarkable answers to prayer, bodies had been healed, and outstanding conversions had taken place, even among the priests of the Catholic church. Perhaps the most storied miracle of all was the opening of a spring of water high in the volcano crater on the island of Fogo (Fire). God rewarded the importunate faith of those mountain-dwelling Christians with a water supply that has continued to flow ever since.

When the Howards left, Rev. Mosteller became mission director and served in that capacity until commissioned to open the work in Brazil in 1958. His first major move was to establish a seminary for the training of pastors. In a remarkable way outstanding national leaders had been raised up to fill the pulpits of the many new churches, but up to then no formal training had been provided for them. In 1953 Rev. and Mrs. J. Elton Wood arrived on the field to take over the leadership of the new seminary. For many years Rev. Wood guided the training of preachers, at the same time pastoring churches and evangelizing as needed. On occasion he also served as mission director. In 1976 the Woods were transferred to Brazil to take over the direction of the seminary there.

In the meantime the Roy Hencks had come in 1959 to assist in the seminary, while the Duane Sraders arrived in 1971 to help fill the void left by the departures of the Ernest Eadeses a couple of years before and Paul and Nettie Stroud, who served from 1967 to 1971.

On July 5, 1975, the Cape Verde Islands became an independent republic, no longer a Portuguese colony. Though the country was spared armed revolution, it was a disruptive time. But the church moved on without interruption. However, with the possibility that all missionaries might have to leave, Cape Verde was moved quickly from a pioneer district to a national-mission district, and Rev. Francisco Xavier Ferreira was appointed as the first national district superintendent. As it turned out, under the new government the church was given more recognition and freedom than ever before. It was given equal rights with the Catholic church and exemption from the payment of import taxes. The switch to national leadership in the church doubtless had something to do with this attitude. Rev. Ferreira was succeeded by Rev. Gilberto Evora in 1978.

The printing of Portuguese literature has been a special contribution of the Cape Verdian Nazarenes to the worldwide missionary program of the church. Mozambique and Brazil, in particular, looked to Cape Verde for their literature needs. The first steps in this work were taken in 1937 with the formation of an editorial committee to see what could be done to meet the need for holiness literature in Portuguese, of which there was virtually none.

In the early 1950s Humberto Pires Ferreira, government administrator on the island of Brava, resigned from his distinguished post to move to the Nazarene headquarters on São Vicente to begin a publication program. Starting with a simple mimeograph, more and better equipment was added through the years. *Editora Nazarena,* as the program is called, is probably the world's largest producer of Portuguese holiness literature. In 1973, one of its capable staff members, Rev. Jorge de Barros, was asked to move to the Nazarene Headquarters in Kansas City to head the Portuguese program of the International Publications Board.

Another phase of Portuguese missionary outreach in which the Cape Verde Islands took the lead was the international radio program, "A Hora Nazarena" ("The Nazarene Hour"). Rev. Barros was the speaker on this program, which is now broadcast over 40 stations in several countries.

Despite the ravages of a devastating famine brought on by a prolonged drought in the late 1970s, the national leaders carried on heroically. A great exodus of the people, principally to Portugal, Brazil, and the United States, took away many pastors and church members, yet the net membership continued to grow, particularly in the Sunday School. It should also be noted that in both Brazil and Portugal, these former Cape Verdians formed the nucleus of several congregations in these other countries to which they had migrated.

In 1980 the Sraders were forced to leave because of critical illness in the family, leaving the Roy Hencks as the sole remaining missionary couple. The Sraders were transferred to Portugal, and Paul and Nettie Stroud returned to Cape Verde after a 12-year absence in late 1983. He became mission director. He also directed the Bible school while the Hencks were on furlough.

A unique construction and repair project called Operation Neemias (Nehemiah) was instituted on the islands. An annual offering was received from each church, and a committee selected the place where it would be used, either for the repair of an existing structure or for a new building. The first project was a parsonage in Porto Novo. The district giving was augmented by Alabaster funds, and in addition a special gift from Salem, Oreg., First Church was received for the building of a church in Ribeira Brava.

By 1985 there were 18 organized churches on the islands, 7 of them fully self-supporting, and 31 other preaching points. Total membership stood at 2,205.

J. THE NEWEST FIELDS

1. *Namibia*

Southwest Africa, or Namibia, is a sparsely populated land on the South Atlantic coast of Africa. Since World War I it had been mandated to the Republic of South Africa; but finally after frequent altercations with South Africa and intervention by the United Nations, guerrilla war, and white/Black confrontations, a semblance of independence was secured in 1978.

In the midst of this milieu, the Church of the Nazarene sought to establish its presence in the country. In the early 1970s Harmon Schmelzenbach III and Dr. Harold Jones made a 6,000-mile trek throughout Namibia to explore the possibilities of establishing a mission in this somewhat forbidding land. They were intrigued by what they saw and heard, and presented a strong recommendation that work be started as soon as possible.

Prayer meetings were begun in a home in the capital city of Windhoek in August 1973, which led to a two-week evangelistic campaign November 4-18. At the close of the meeting a church was organized with 19 charter members. In April 1974 Rev. P. J. van den Berg came to pastor the flock.

The work faltered, however, and reverted to regional office jurisdiction. However, a house was purchased in Windhoek to serve as a base of operations. Previous contacts were renewed, and services were begun first in homes and then in a rented hall. The congregation was primarily Afrikaans speaking. In 1978 the Ralph McClintocks were transferred to Namibia.

In May 1979 a well-located but rundown church building was purchased at an auction, and renovation activities brought notoriety to the Church of the Nazarene. Rev. Oscar Anderson, who had previously worked in Southwest Africa and had many contacts, came to pastor the church.

Property was purchased in the busy port city of Walvis Bay, and

sights were set on launching a work in the booming city of Swakop-
mond, site of the largest uranium mine in the world. In a country so
rich in natural resources, a self-supporting church would be expected
quickly; but the obstacles of political unrest and the multinational
character of the populace called for special strategy. In 1980 a pioneer
district was formed, and by 1985 there were three organized churches
with a combined membership of 50. The Mike Shalleys took over the
leadership in Namibia in 1985.

2. *Nigeria*

Nestled into the corner of the Gulf of Guinea on Africa's west coast is
the Republic of Nigeria. Its 360,000 square miles of territory with 80
million people give it a population density of 222 per square mile. It
was once a British colony but won its independence in 1960 and
became a republic in 1963. But it has been plagued with political
unrest and intertribal warfare that has also had religious overtones.
The north is dominated by Muslims and the south by Christians.

In the 1960s a Nigerian student, Samson Udokpan, journeyed to
the United States to work on a master's degree at North Texas State
University in Denton, Tex. There he and his wife were reached by the
Church of the Nazarene, and he even received a district minister's
license.

When he returned to Nigeria, he encouraged his brother, John
Udoh, an independent minister, to try to get the Church of the Nazarene to come to the Cross River State of Nigeria. Samson himself
became a leader in government as minister of education and of lands.

Correspondence was carried on with the Church of the Nazarene
for a number of years, during which time other independent groups
expressed similar interest in joining. Finally, at the 1976 General Assembly the challenge to enter Nigeria was enthusiastically accepted.

Missionaries George Hayse, Jack Riley, and Don Messer visited
Nigeria at different times, seeking official registration for the church
and visas for missionaries. They were unsuccessful and realized that
any church development would have to come from within the country. So Mr. Udokpan was invited to join a REAP team (a Nazarene
outreach program titled Resources for Evangelism And Projects) that
would plan to visit Nigeria two or three times a year to conduct classes
on the doctrines, polity, and practices of the Church of the Nazarene.
The first visit was made in March 1980.

Fourteen churches had been started by Rev. John Udoh, all within 10 miles of the mother church at Ndiya. He and four of his pastors were received as full members of the Church of the Nazarene, and the 1,000 or so church members became probationary members until such time as they became acquainted with the doctrines of the church. Some other independent groups also wanted to join.

Rev. Udoh visited the 1980 General Assembly and en route was ordained by Dr. George Coulter at the New England District Assembly. He was then appointed district superintendent of Nigeria. The proposed training sessions by the REAP team enjoyed a measure of success, though less than hoped, but nonetheless 30 churches with a total of 1,373 members gave promise of a booming district if the doctrinal and organizational problems could be worked out.

But the resolution of the issues involved was slow in coming. Besides, the government was wary of recognizing any organization with ties to the Republic of South Africa—and that is where the first Nazarene emissaries had come from. Attempts to obtain visas for Rev. and Mrs. Wilfredo Manaois of the Philippines in order to lead an all-important Bible school program were thwarted. The international nature of the Church of the Nazarene was apparently not considered by the authorities. There was also rather strong sentiment among Rev. Udoh's men against any outside supervision or control.

Despite the seeming confusion that existed, however, the work in Nigeria under Rev. Udoh's leadership continued to show growth. Membership in the 30 churches had reached 2,275 by 1985. But as time passed the creation of a true Church of the Nazarene from this base was seemingly more and more distant.

3. *Botswana*

Situated in the very heart of southern Africa is the country of Botswana, a 220,000-square-mile area of rolling plains dominated on the southwest by the inhospitable Kalahari desert. This arid plain covers 80 percent of the country and is the home of the diminutive, nomadic Bushmen. Most of the 1 million population are concentrated in the southeast along the Limpopo River, where the capital of Gaborone is located. Once known as the British protectorate of Bechuanaland, the country became an independent republic in September 1966.

Here are found evidences of David Livingstone's pioneer missionary efforts. Though officially only 15 percent of the people are now classified as Christians, there was a time when the main tribal leaders were counted among Livingstone's converts, and by the turn of the century the country was heavily influenced by Christianity. The situation has greatly deteriorated.

In anticipation of possible expansion into Botswana, the Church of the Nazarene was registered there in 1971, at the direction of the general superintendent and the executive committee of the RSA North field. But it was not until 1984 that steps were actually taken to establish a work there. This country was one of five chosen to be entered in celebration of the 75th anniversary year of the Church of the Nazarene in 1983.

Early in 1984 Ron and Sara Willard with their two daughters moved to Gaborone and located a plot of ground on the west side, not far from the ruins of Livingstone's famed mission station. Here with the help of two Work and Witness teams from Detroit First Church, the first building was erected—a missionary home with a wing to be used eventually for Bible college classes.

Within a year, two other properties in the Gaborone area were purchased. Out of the first established congregation came the first national pastor, Rev. Ivan Maswabi. In 1985 this pioneer area reported 12 members.

4. *Kenya*

Another of the five new 75th anniversary fields to be opened was the Republic of Kenya. This East African nation of 225,000 square miles, sitting astride the equator, is desertlike in the north, but a mountainous plateau along the western side provides more moderate temperatures and adequate rainfall for agriculture. This area is dominated by Mount Kenya (17,058 ft.), and here is located the capital city of Nairobi. Along the southeast is the 300-mile shoreline of the Indian Ocean and the port of Mombasa. Kenya has been an independent nation since 1963 and enjoys a stable government. British influences are still strong, and English is an official language along with Swahili, a mixture of Bantu and Arabic.

Kenya has long been friendly to Christian missions, and 37 percent of the people are Protestants; 22 percent are Roman Catholics. Though close to Muslim-dominated northern Africa, only 3 percent follow that faith. There have been as many as 30 missionary organizations at work in the country, but nevertheless urgent calls were being received for the Church of the Nazarene to come. The doors were wide open.

Careful study was made of the potential for missionary work, and in 1984 Rev. and Mrs. Harmon Schmelzenbach III were appointed to open the field. In October 1985 they were able to purchase a small hotel in Nairobi on a 1.2-acre plot of land. This provided a headquarters center as well as missionary residence. Rev. and Mrs. Roger Gastineau were transferred from Zambia to pastor the first congregation that was gathered here.

Rev. and Mrs. Dan Anderson were appointed to open a work in the western side near Lake Victoria, while a German couple, Rev. and Mrs. Fritz Bode, were assigned to work among the Masai people.

Leo Mpoke, the first Kenyan Nazarene, was directly involved in the distribution of some $229,000 worth of food, medical, and other relief supplies contributed by the Church of the Nazarene during the great famine of 1985. Parts of Ethiopia and Sudan as well as Kenya were included in the program. Mr. Mpoke continued in charge of compassionate ministries there but was also made director of development for eastern Africa.

At the close of 1985 Kenya was still a pioneer area, with but one organized church with a membership of 67. However, prospects were bright with several promising preaching points developing.

5. *Ciskei / Transkei*

On the southeastern coast of South Africa, two Black African republics were developed in the vicinity of East London: (1) the Ciskei, an area of about 7,700 square miles stretching inland from the Indian Ocean south and west of East London; and (2) the Transkei, situated to the north of East London between the Indian Ocean and the inland kingdom of Lesotho. Both are inhabited by Xhosa people, of which there are 5 million in all of South Africa.

In 1978 an investigating committee of Nazarene missionaries and national leaders visited the area with a view to opening work in one or both of the republics. The result was that in March 1979, Joe and Ellen Penn, upon returning from furlough, were assigned to begin a mission in Ciskei. An early move was to set up a tent revival in the largest city, Mdatsane, about 12 miles west of East London. Out of this a small nucleus was gathered, worshiping first in a community hall when available, and finally locating in a small garage. Called to pastor the little congregation were Benjamin and Selinah Ngqakayi, recent graduates of the KwaZulu Nazarene Bible College in Natal.

One of the early stalwarts was Mrs. Ruth Ngubelanga, who had been sanctified in 1964 in a revival sponsored by the Dorothea Mission near East London. The evangelist at that time was Rev. Minaar Zwane. Now a Nazarene, he was also the evangelist at the Penns' meeting. For 15 years Ruth had prayed for a holiness church to be established among her people. She was overjoyed to learn that her former spiritual mentor had returned, this time to assure her that the Church of the Nazarene had come to stay.

The Penns returned to Natal shortly after Ben and Selinah arrived, and it was not until January 1981 that the Jack Rileys arrived to give direction to the work. They soon had established a number of cottage prayer groups. Property was purchased and in September 1981 construction began on a combination parsonage/chapel. In December there was a "triumphal march" from the old garage location to the new building.

On December 4, 1981, Ciskei became an independent republic. The president, Dr. L. L. Sebe, was a Christian and from the outset gave full support to Christian missionary activity. One of the members of his cabinet had spent considerable time in Swaziland and knew of the great work of the Church of the Nazarene in that country. It was through him that Dr. Sebe became acquainted with Jack Riley.

The outcome was the moving of Nazarene missionaries into key places of influence, particularly in the areas of education, agriculture, and industry. This unique deployment of missionaries was called the Ciskei Experiment.

Beginning in January 1983, Stan and Jo Doerr, John and Sandy Estey, and Ralph and Beth McClintock arrived to fill places of leadership and service in the government. Ralph McClintock rose to become director general of the Department of Transport and Aviation and technical advisor to the president. Dr. and Mrs. Glenn Fell and Dr. Dorothy Diggs taught at the Fort Cox College of Agriculture and Forestry.

All this provided a wide-open door for the Church of the Nazarene throughout the country. Though such service was of technical nature, the prime goal of evangelism was not lost sight of. All those involved in these specialized ministries took part also in the missionary program.

The Mdatsane church outgrew its chapel, and prefab buildings had to be added to absorb the crowds. In January 1984 construction began on a large complex to include a youth center, sanctuary, and administration offices. In the meantime, church work was begun in the city of Zwelitsha, which became an organized church in 1984. In the neighboring republic of Transkei a regular radio broadcast was launched as an entrée to the people both there and in the Ciskei. John and Sandy Cunningham came to Ciskei to lead in the area of church growth.

In July 1982 Jack Riley began a long, two-year struggle with cancer. He carried on heroically between four major operations but finally succumbed July 15, 1984. His funeral was held in the new youth center, which had been dedicated at Easter time. Tom (no relation) and Faye Riley took over the unfinished task, and the sanctuary was ready for dedication on November 24, 1984.

By 1985 there were two organized churches with a combined membership of 47, but there were exciting prospects for the future.

K. MEETING THE CHALLENGE OF THE 1980S

Rapid changes were taking place on the African continent both politically and within the church. Drawing the many facets of the work together was not easy. In the Nazarene African field there were 18 different language groups in a dozen republics, some of which were quite new and struggling with great internal problems. Racial confrontations created unrest as Black Africa struggled to its feet economically and politically. All this had its effect on the church community as well.

To meet the challenge and opportunities of the new Africa that was emerging, the Church of the Nazarene sought to develop an effective organizational structure. Before 1970 the central administrative head of all the work in Africa had been the field superintendent. Working with him was a regional advisory committee made up of representatives from each of the fields. It was under the 26-year leadership of W. C. Esselstyn (1941-67) that this arrangement came into full flower. During this time of explosive growth of the Africa field his challenge of "Cape Town to Cairo" was often heard. Dr. Esselstyn was followed in office by D. Herman Spencer, and expansion continued.

By 1970, however, it was felt advisable to reorganize the complex field structure into six autonomous jurisdictions, each with its own superintendent and executive committee directly responsible to International Headquarters in Kansas City. The only function that brought the fields together was in the area of literature and the central Publications Board. Underlying this structural change was the basic goal of indigenization that, because of the many language and cultural barriers between the various fields, had seemed difficult to achieve.

The atomizing of the organizational structure created more problems than it solved, and the value of the integrated arrangement that had existed under the overall field superintendent was increasingly realized. In fact, under the Intercontinental Zone structure (1976-80), Darrell Teare had spent time in Africa to help synthesize the multifaceted work, though he was not resident there. In July 1980 Richard Zanner, then superintendent of the Central European District, was named coordinator of the Africa field, to serve under the director of the World Mission Division. The following year, when the major world mission restructuring plan adopted by the 1980 General Assembly was implemented, he assumed the title of regional director for Africa.

A West German who had once lived in South Africa and in fact had married a South African, Dr. Zanner brought to the task his own unique brand of dynamic leadership. He soon earned for himself the Sotho name *Setsokotsane* ("Whirlwind"). It was not long until he had formulated a master plan for organization and development of the Africa field.

His plan included internal strengthening of the district programs, which led to Swaziland North and South Africa European districts achieving regular (Phase 4) status in 1980, to be followed in 1983 by the Western Cape District.

Also included was expansion into new fields. Two of the five worldwide fields selected to be entered in commemoration of the 75th anniversary of the Church of the Nazarene were in Africa—Botswana and Kenya. Also entered during the 1980-85 quinquennium was the Black Republic of Ciskei.

Construction Projects

A significant facet of the integration effort was the coordination of building programs under the leadership of Richard and Betty Crow, who took over the task in 1982. The standardization of both architecture and construction procedures was a key element in the program he devised. A 50/50 system of financing building projects was worked out in which the local congregation was responsible for 50 percent of the cost in cash and/or labor, while the other half was to be paid through direct donations, Alabaster funds, and/or Work and Witness teams. This plan created a sense of ownership and identification with the buildings of the congregations involved. The plan proved highly successful.

Education Assistance

For many years, at great personal sacrifice, pastors had tried desperately to see that their children were educated. In 1980 the Middle

European District caught the vision and established a fund to help with the education of these African children. The fund was administered on the field by Rose Handloser. But the amount given was insufficient to reach beyond South Africa, so in 1985 this need became a broader compassionate ministries item. Now pastors' children throughout Africa could receive the necessary assistance.

Ministerial Pensions

The need for a ministerial pension plan also had long been felt, but it was difficult to devise a regionwide plan that would apply to all ethnic groups and yet be within the framework of what the districts could afford. A flexible program was devised for the rand monetary area, and parallel ones for other countries.

Radio and Audiovisual Services

Along with the integrated literature program, the potential in radio was also recognized. Bill and Sherrill Wagner pioneered this work. At first they used the recording facilities of Trans World Radio but in 1981 constructed their own studio near the regional offices in Florida, Transvaal.

By 1985 nine 15-minute Nazarene programs were being aired each week over Trans World Radio in Swaziland, CKI in Ciskei, and Radio Pulpit in the Republic of South Africa. Languages used were Pedi, Tswana, Shangaan, English, Portuguese, and Afrikaans. Hundreds of letters were being received, and in 1985 the Jim Buchanans joined the staff to coordinate an extensive follow-up program. The radio program was also providing a significant number of contacts in areas the church had not yet entered.

Another development was Africa Vision Communications to provide audiovisual tools for the churches and schools including slide sets, photographs, videotapes, and motion picture films. Slide sets and tapes of new work and special events throughout the region were also made available. Africa Vision also helped soon-to-furlough missionaries prepare slide sets for their deputation work. Gerald and Gayle Hayse launched this phase in 1983.

Regional Conferences

Africa's own celebration of the 75th anniversary of the Church of the Nazarene took place December 13-15, 1983, on the campus of the

University of Swaziland. More than 1,000 Nazarenes from all over the Africa Region converged there for a time of celebration and learning. Denominational leaders Dr. Orville Jenkins, Dr. L. Guy Nees, Dr. Phyllis Brown, and Rev. Phil Riley were present. To see the love and sharing among the many racial groups united in a great cause was a memorable experience.

To compensate for the fact that representatives of the youth organization were unable to attend the Nazarene World Youth Congress in Mexico in 1983, an Africa Regional NYI Convention was held in 1984. Dr. Reuben Welch and a musical group from the United States made this an unforgettable event for the young people who came from all over Africa.

Training and Education

The selection and training of local leadership was high on Dr. Zanner's priority list. For this purpose various training conferences were held across the region. Ministerial leadership was also given added attention. Since 1983 annual District Superintendents' Conferences had proved to be unusually profitable. Although the main emphasis had been upon spiritual leadership, many practical subjects were now dealt with as well, including personal relationships, management, finances, responsibility, and accountability.

Much thought was also being given to the educational institutions. As of 1985 there were 10 established Bible colleges in the region:

Location	Language	Principal
Cape Verde (Mindelo)	Portuguese	Roy Henck
Zambia (Lusaka)	English	Glenn Kell
Malawi (Limbe)	Vernacular/English	Hilbert Miller (interim)
Zimbabwe (Harare)	English	Jim Sage (interim)
Mozambique (extension)	Vernacular/Portuguese	Simeon Mandlate
RSA (Florida)	English/Afrikaans	Wally Marais
RSA (Arthurseat)	Vernacular/English	Enoch Litswele*
RSA (KwaZulu-Natal)	Vernacular/English	Philip Bedwell
RSA (Port Elizabeth)	English/Afrikaans	R. C. Calhoun
Swaziland (Siteki)	Vernacular/English	P. K. Walker

*Acting principal, Juanita Pate.

The basic diploma course of these schools met the needs for ordination for ministers. However, there was increasing need for more advanced work at the degree level. For this reason, the Africa Nazarene Theological College of Southern Africa was established in 1984. In effect, this was a merger of the three major campuses in Florida, Port Elizabeth, and Siteki. The faculties of these three colleges all became part of the one college, as did their libraries. Each campus had its own principal, student body, and operating budget. But the three campuses were controlled by one administrative committee under the direction of one president, Dr. Theodore Esselstyn. He also served as coordinator of theological education for the region with broad powers. The advanced theological degrees were offered through affiliation with Canadian Nazarene College.

Organizing for the Future

To more easily supervise and develop the various areas of the complex Africa Region as well as to assign countries for possible future development, Dr. Zanner proposed a restructuring of the region into five fields, cutting across racial and political boundaries as follows:

Field	Director	Current Countries	Potential
Africa South	Norman Zurcher	Namibia, Botswana, Venda, Bophuthatswana, Ciskei, Republic of South Africa	Transkei, etc.
Africa Southeast	Peter K. Walker	Swaziland, Mozambique	Islands east of Africa
Africa Central	Jim Sage	Zambia, Zimbabwe, Malawi	Zaire, Angola
Africa East	Harmon Schmelzenbach	Kenya	Uganda, Tanzania, Sudan, Ethiopia, etc.
Africa West	John Seaman	Nigeria, Cape Verde	Ivory Coast, Togo, Senegal, Liberia, Sierra Leone, etc.

The five field directors were to be appointed annually by the director of the World Mission Division with the approval of the general superintendent in jurisdiction. These five, along with Dr. Ted Esselstyn as president of ANTC, would constitute the regional advisory council to work with Regional Director Richard Zanner.

This bold move, which received the endorsement of the general church leaders, was in line with the tenor of the times. Africa, the once-sleeping giant, was stirring, and the church needed to face the challenge with a dynamic, innovative program. The mounting problems of hunger, war, drought, unemployment, and lack of shelter and clothing needed to be addressed through compassionate ministries. The tensions resulting from Third- and First-World peoples rubbing elbows on a daily basis had to be eased through the proclamation of the gospel of love. Above all, the underlying need for a personal spiritual relationship with Jesus Christ remained the overarching purpose of the Nazarene evangel. To the proclamation of this life-changing gospel, the 41,357 members in the African church were committed.

II

ASIAN REGION

- India
- China
- Taiwan
- Hong Kong
- Japan
- Korea
- The Philippines
- Burma

Researchers:

Mary L. Scott—China, Taiwan, Hong Kong, the Philippines
Donald Owens—Japan, Korea

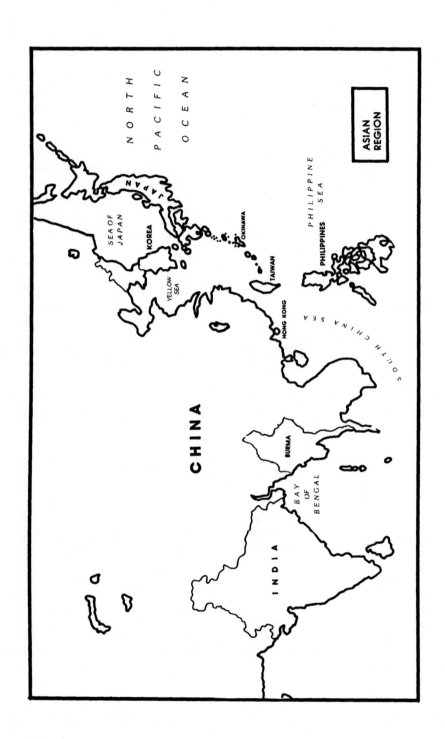

A. INDIA

The exotic land of India for centuries captured the imagination of both adventurers and traders who had heard of the wealth and beauty of this remote land. In fact, it was their search for the jewels and spices of India that led them to the chance discovery of the Americas. Nestled behind the towering wall of the Himalayas in the north and wedging southward almost to the equator, India is a world apart.

It is a land of striking contrasts: high mountains and coastal swamplands; enormous wealth and abject poverty; lush jungle and arid plains; storied wisdom and pervasive illiteracy; rich cultural heritage and a grinding struggle for existence. India is a land of religions, but religions that offer no inner peace or hope.

India extends 2,000 miles north to south and 1,700 miles from east to west, and with a population (1981) of 683 million it has a density of over 550 per square mile, highest in the world among the larger countries. Though there are some huge cities like Bombay and Calcutta, almost 80 percent of the people live in some 700,000 villages scattered about in some areas only two or three miles apart, from which the people go out to work their meager farms.

Early Christian Influence

Hinduism is the religion of 84 percent of the people against which the 2.6 percent of Christians are a tiny minority. Yet India has had Christian influence since the first century. The apostle Thomas is said to have come to southern India, and today's Mar Thoma church is the surviving remnant of that evangelizing effort. The Christian torch was picked up by Syrian missionaries in the fifth or sixth century, and to this day the Mar Thoma people are known as Syrian Christians, and their Scriptures are in the Syrian language of Jesus' day. The group lapsed almost into oblivion after the beginning centuries until about 100 years ago when a revival began among them. Now they number well over 100,000, including those related to the Roman Catholic branch.

William Carey, the British cobbler who has been called the father of the modern missionary movement, landed in India in 1793. There he struggled against great odds to finally establish his historic mission in Serampore. Hindered from doing evangelistic work, he led in the translation of the Scriptures into 40 different languages including the ancient Sanskrit. Many other missions followed and with the help of comity agreements concentrated their efforts in the specific areas assigned to them.

The India mystique caught the imagination of Christians in Europe and America, and when the subject of "foreign missions" arose, this was the country that invariably came to mind. The holiness movement, historically missionary in vision, was caught up in this interest and participated by sending various groups of workers there in the latter half of the 19th century.

1. *Forerunners of the Church of the Nazarene*

It was because of this pervasive interest in India that it became the oldest missionary field of the Church of the Nazarene. It is also the only one in which all three major organizations that united at Pilot Point in 1908 had missionary work under way prior to that historic union. The Association of Pentecostal Churches of America (the eastern branch) had a mission in Buldana, central India; the Holiness Church of Christ (the southern branch), near Bombay; and the Church of the Nazarene (Bresee's group), at Calcutta. Of interest, too, is that the Pentecostal Mission of Nashville, which united with the Church of the Nazarene in 1915, also had a band of missionaries in India when this later union took place. In fact, they had been there since 1903.

The Association of Pentecostal Churches of America

On December 11, 1897, a group of five missionaries under the auspices of the APCA embarked for India, arriving in Bombay January 14, 1898. The original five were Rev. and Mrs. M. D. Wood, who had already served a term in India under another mission, Lillian Sprague, Carrie Taylor, and Fred Wiley. This group was augmented soon after by the coming of Mina Shroyer. They chose to locate first at Igatpuri, a railroad town 85 miles northeast of Bombay. Here they gathered about 16 orphan boys, victims of the recent famine and plague, and opened a school.

In September 1899 the mission was moved to what they felt to be a more advantageous location 300 miles inland at Buldana, Berar. The town of 6,000 was 28 miles from the railroad, but it was a county seat, which provided contact with the hundreds of surrounding villages. The elevation was 2,100 feet above sea level, which also provided a more healthful environment for the missionaries than did Igatpuri.

A six-acre compound was purchased, a girls' orphanage added, and a school begun with an enrollment of 60. Mrs. Wood conducted an extensive medical dispensary and clinic program. Shortly after this move Miss Taylor and Mr. Wiley were married and left to serve in another mission. Miss Shroyer also left.

In 1903 the Wood family and Miss Sprague returned to the United States to solicit funds and recruit more missionaries, leaving the Buldana station in charge of Mr. and Mrs. Fred Moore, who were borrowed from a neighboring mission. Their trip was highly successful, and they returned the following year with several thousand dollars and nine new missionaries: Julia Gibson, Priscilla Hitchens, Gertrude Perry, Mrs. Ella Perry, Mrs. Nellie Barnes, Mr. and Mrs. James M. Davidson, L. S. Tracy, and Elmer Burgess. Several of these were older people who paid their own passage and advanced the money necessary should they have to return. The main group arrived on August 5, 1904, though Rev. Wood and Mr. Burgess had returned two months earlier when the Fred Moores had to go back to their own mission. Miss Sprague did not return until a year later.

With the funds acquired, a 23-acre farm was purchased one mile south of Buldana, and the boys' school was moved there. It was known as the Dhamandari station. In 1904 Mrs. Perry and her daughter Gertrude opened a mission in Chikhli, a key town 14 miles south of Buldana. An abortive attempt was also made to start a work in the railroad town of Malkapur.

The year 1905 was a momentous one for the work. One significant event was the marriage of Gertrude Perry to L. S. Tracy. This necessitated the transfer of Priscilla Hitchens and Julia Gibson to the Chikhli mission. In 1905 also, the Davidsons and Elmer Burgess had to return to the United States for health reasons. This reduced the missionary force to nine. But 1905 also saw a great spiritual awakening on the field, an offshoot of the Welsh revival, which swept through the boys' and girls' schools.

But in the midst of spiritual revival, seeds of discontent were growing in the heart of M. D. Wood. Fiercely independent, he demanded full control of all missionary finances and program, with no interference from the home board. When told flatly that such operation was unacceptable, he began to lay plans to leave. He moved the girls' school from Chikhli, where it had been transferred only two months before, up to the farm near Buldana, and with them Mrs. Nellie Barnes and Lillian Sprague, who were sympathetic to his cause. At the same time he moved the Tracys from the farm into Buldana.

Early one February morning in 1906, L. S. Tracy found a tin box on the porch of the missionary home. In it were papers concerning the Buldana and Chikhli properties, a few coins, and a brief farewell note written by M. D. Wood. Although the Tracys and Mother Perry had sensed that something was afoot, they were ill prepared for what they saw when they hurried out to the farm. There were no missionaries, no teachers, no children, no animals, no equipment. All movable property had been loaded onto bullock carts and moved out. Only faithful Lucas remained to tell what had happened.

The total entourage, consisting of perhaps 100 people and 20 buffalo, could not have been very far along on their journey by then, but the Tracys saw no purpose in pursuing them. As it turned out, the orphan girls were turned over to a Methodist mission at Basim, 85 miles to the southeast, while the remainder went on another 25 miles south and set up a new mission. The work did not last, and soon the group was scattered.

As soon as they could, the bereft missionaries made their way down to Chikhli to tell Miss Hitchens and Miss Gibson what had happened. Together they determined that they would pick up with what was left and start over again. It was not easy, for Rev. Wood had poisoned the minds of the people against the mission, and a long and difficult road lay ahead. On 23-year-old Leighton Tracy lay the responsibility of leadership. With all the institutional work gone, evangelism was the only channel open, and to this they turned their full effort.

In February 1906 Rev. and Mrs. W. J. Rogers arrived on the field. Mrs. Rogers had previously served in India under another board and had inherited a piece of property in Igatpuri, the very town the pioneer missionary party had worked in briefly eight years before. Here the Rogerses began a mission. Their health failed within a year and, deeding the property to the APCA mission, they returned to the United States. Priscilla Hitchens was transferred there from Chikhli, leaving Julia Gibson to carry on that work alone. It was under her ministry that the first Indian convert, Babadi Mhaske, was won in 1908.

The Holiness Church of Christ

The southern branch of the soon-to-be-organized Church of the Nazarene was also caught up in the appeal to take the gospel to India. In 1907 a missionary party consisting of Rev. and Mrs. L. A. Campbell, Olive Nelson, and Rev. A. D. Fritzlan was brought together and set sail November 21. Arriving in Bombay on January 1, 1908, they proceeded to Gujarat, north of the city, where missionary friends were located. They settled in to study the language and do what they could in the mission where they were guests.

In April, word came through to L. A. Campbell that a union was in the offing between the Holiness Church of Christ and the Pentecostal Church of the Nazarene, which had been formed the year before in Chicago. He was instructed to get in touch with the Nazarene missionaries and become associated with their operation. He went to nearby Igatpuri and knocked on Priscilla Hitchens' door. Apprising her of his mission, she directed him to Buldana and L. S. Tracy, the mission superintendent.

Mr. Tracy could not believe what was happening when the slender young missionary appeared on his doorstep and announced that there were four of them ready to join forces in the work. Only shortly before, Tracy's desperate appeal to the homeland for help had been answered with the words, "There is no money. We have no one to send. Hold on!" Doubtless this message had gotten to the Holiness Church of Christ leaders, whose missionaries in India were already looking for a place to begin work. Thus the two were brought together before the actual church union took place on October 13, 1908, at Pilot Point, Tex.

The Church of the Nazarene

The involvement of Dr. P. F. Bresee's group in the India enterprise was the result of overtures from the country itself in which a ready-made opportunity was placed in their laps. The key personality involved was Mrs. Sukhoda Benarji, a high caste Hindu woman of Calcutta who, because she herself had been deserted by her husband when she was but 15, conceived the idea of opening a home and school for similar girls in distress. Trained in a mission hospital as a nurse, she had attended the famous school of Pandita Ramabai. Here was developed her great concern for the young women of her country.

Accompanied by an English lady, Mrs. Avetoom, she went to the United States in 1904 to solicit funds for her project. She met a group in Portland, Oreg., who offered to support her work for one year, and so she returned to launch the Hope School in Calcutta in January 1906. There were 16 girls to start with.

Toward the end of the year of promised support, Mrs. Benarji returned to the United States, this time accompanied by a national preacher who had been helping her, Rev. P. B. Biswas. Through Mrs. E. G. Eaton, whom she had met on her previous trip, she was introduced to Dr. P. F. Bresee, head of the Church of the Nazarene. For two years his church had been talking about sending missionaries to India, and this seemed like a wide-open opportunity to achieve this goal.

On April 30, 1906, the Board of Home and Foreign Missions signed an agreement to assume the support of Mrs. Benarji's mission to the extent of "something over $2,000." Mrs. Eaton herself, along with her husband, E. G. "Papa" Eaton, offered to go to India as missionaries, and later that year they and V. J. Jacques arrived in Calcutta.

A well-developed property just under six acres in extent, three miles west of central Calcutta, was purchased for $26,400. It included three substantial brick buildings and other usable structures in a landscaped setting that they called Hallelujah Village. Here an orphanage, rescue home, and school were launched with a total "family" of about 125 persons including both girls and boys. The work expanded to include schools outside the compound, and special religion classes were held in the public schools as well.

Thus, when the Pentecostal Church of the Nazarene came into being in October 1908, there were three areas in India in which missionary work was in progress: (1) in Igatpuri, 85 miles northeast of Bombay; (2) in Buldana and Chikhli, central India, 300 miles east of Bombay; and (3) in Calcutta in eastern India. It was logical that the question should arise as to the viability of operating in three scattered areas in the same country. Communication in those days was difficult and costly, available funds were limited, and the missionary contingent small. But there was no move to consolidate at this time.

2. The Development of the Three India Fields, 1908-30

The Western Field

Of the three areas, Igatpuri was obviously the weakest. It was considered part of the Buldana (Central) field, however, and thus not expected to survive on its own. Igatpuri was therefore included in the first India Mission Council meeting, which convened in Buldana, June 25, 1909.

Miss Hitchens continued her Sunday School and small day school program alone until she furloughed home in 1911. The Campbells, who had opened the work in Mehkar in 1912, began to experience severe health problems and also lost one of their boys. They spent a brief time at Igatpuri just before returning to the United States permanently in 1915. With that, the work in Western India was about to be phased out when another nearby field moved into the picture. This was the work in the Thana District a few miles closer to Bombay, which had been developed by the Pentecostal Mission of Nashville. When its parent organization united with the Church of the Nazarene on February 13, 1915, the Thana District automatically became a part of the Nazarene work in India.

The Pentecostal Mission, led by Rev. J. O. McClurkan, had also been caught up in the great surge of interest in India at the turn of the century, and in 1903 had sent out four missionaries, Rev. and Mrs. R. G. Codding, Eva Carpenter, and Lizzie Leonard. These were followed by Olive Graham and Jessie Basford. They located their work at Khardi and Vasind, two railway towns 15 miles apart, about 50 miles from Bombay. Miss Carpenter, who pioneered the Vasind mission, served there for 14 years. At Khardi, which was considered the main station, a boys' school was established.

For a time, a mission was conducted at Igatpuri with Miss Leonard in charge, but when her health failed and she had to return home in 1913, this work was closed. Another mission was opened in 1905 at Duhlia, 100 miles farther inland, by Mattie Long and Florence Williams (the latter a sister of Dr. R. T. Williams). Here on a 10-acre tract, a girls' orphanage and school was established. When Bessie Seay arrived in 1909, she was also assigned to this station to set up a medical dispensary. Mrs. Bertha Davis, who had accompanied her to India, became a mainstay at Vasind, while Rev. and Mrs. Hugh Gregory, later arrivals, were stationed at Khardi.

It was an exciting day when word came through that the Pentecostal Mission had become a part of the Pentecostal Church of the Nazarene. It was Rev. R. G. Codding who carried the news to Buldana.

A united assembly was called that was also attended by three representatives from the Eastern field. Such a move had been recommended by Dr. H. F. Reynolds during his visit to the field the year before. The meetings were held in Buldana in June 1915. R. G. Codding, who strongly urged a fusion of the work rather than a mere union, was elected superintendent of the Western and Central fields. The more distant Eastern field, which was also of a different language, was not disturbed. However, a comprehensive India mission policy was drawn up that was so well prepared it became the basis for a missionary policy statement adopted for the entire overseas program of the denomination.

A major move in line with the fusion of the other districts, advocated by Rev. Codding, was the transfer of the boys' school in Buldana to the Khardi boys' school. The experiment was abandoned four years later, and the program was moved back to Buldana, where in 1921 a fine building was erected out at the farm to house it.

Another move to draw the fields together was the interchange of missionary personnel. Among these was the transfer of Mrs. Ella Perry to Khardi, where she developed a flourishing medical work. Tragedy struck on January 24, 1919, when she collapsed at her post and died the next day, a victim of cholera. She was buried at Igatpuri, 12 miles away.

Two months later, the first of the largest contingent of missionaries ever to go to India in one year arrived to aid the overburdened veterans, who by now numbered only six. Of the new missionaries, Viola Willison, Eltie Muse, and Lula May Tidwell, along with Bessie Seay who was returning from furlough, were assigned to the Western field.

Miss Willison was sent to Murbad to take the place of Miss Basford, who had opened the work there in 1916 and was due for furlough. She was later joined at Murbad by Miss Muse. Only two years after her arrival, on February 19, 1921, Viola Willison's missionary career was cut short when she was fatally stricken with malignant malaria. Miss Muse carried on the Murbad work for a while until it was finally turned over to the nationals. Little did she realize then that 10 years later, March 17, 1931, she too would lay down her life in India, a victim of smallpox.

By 1926, after retrenchment had forced the return to the United States of a number of missionaries while others had gone home on extended furlough, the total India missionary force was reduced to four, none of whom were stationed in the Western field. Rev. A. D. Fritzlan, who was at Jamner, the nearest point on the Central field, gave what supervision he could to the work. A critical loss had been the return of the Coddings to the United States in early 1926 when their health failed. It was a combined blow from which the Western field never recovered.

The Eastern Field

With Hallelujah Village a well-established base in Calcutta, the missionaries began to think in terms of outreach. When Misses Myrtle Mangum and Lela Hargrove arrived on the field in 1912, they quickly began to explore the possibilities of evangelism outside the well-churched environs of the city. They came in touch with a small Christian group among the Garo tribesmen in the Mymansingh District, 350-400 miles northeast of Calcutta. These people begged them to come and minister to their group who numbered about 40,000. Accepting the challenge, they went up to this hill country, purchased an acre of land, and with the help of the friendly Garos erected five buildings. Soon they had regular services going and three primary schools. But the Garos were a nomadic people, and establishing roots was difficult.

In 1913 Hulda and Leoda Grebe, both nurses, left for India, arriving in Calcutta in early 1914. Shortly afterward, Dr. H. F. Reynolds, general superintendent and Foreign Missions secretary, with whom they had traveled as far as Japan, landed in India. While he was still there, the Eatons, because of health problems, left for the United States. Dr. Reynolds considered the situation critical enough to call for Rev. and Mrs. L. S. Tracy and Mrs. Perry to come from Buldana to care for the work until a replacement could be sent out. That replacement was Rev. George J. Franklin, who arrived in the summer of 1915 and shortly thereafter, on September 21, married Hulda Grebe.

It became increasingly obvious that for all its fine facilities, Hallelujah Village was not well located. Poor drainage made for malaria infestation, typhoid, and other diseases. Besides, there were many missionary groups already at work in the city. Looking for another more healthful and spiritually productive location in which to work, the missionaries found a 985-square-mile area in the general vicinity of the Garo work that by comity agreements was open to the church. In this section lived 800,000 people. There were 1,528 villages and several large cities. On March 16, 1916, work was begun in the railroad center of Kishorganj, by Myrtle Mangum and Leoda Grebe.

Property was purchased, and the boys of Hope School were transferred there. In August 1918 Hallelujah Village was sold, and the girls transferred to Kishorganj. In January 1919 the Calcutta work was officially closed. In the meantime, Maude Varnedoe had come to replace Myrtle Mangum, who was forced to return home for health reasons in 1917. In 1918 Myrtlebelle Walters was added to the group, to be followed in 1919 by Rev. and Mrs. A. H. Kauffman and Miss Agnes Gardner.

In October 1920 another contingent arrived, including Rev. and Mrs. F. E. Blackman, Ruth Williams, and Lou Jane Hatch. In April 1921 the coming of Nellie Ellison brought to 13 the number of missionaries on the Eastern field. She was the last to be appointed, however. One by one missionaries returned to the homeland or were transferred elsewhere, until by 1925 only 4 remained: Rev. and Mrs. George Franklin, Maude Varnedoe, and Nellie Ellison.

At the time of the move to Kishorganj in 1919, the countryside was going through a crisis of famine and an influenza epidemic, capped by a destructive windstorm on September 25. The government placed Rev. Franklin in charge of its relief program. This won for the mission valuable recognition and goodwill, which was climaxed by Rev. Franklin's being named an "honorable magistrate."

This being a strongly Muslim area meant that the seclusion of women was a dominant practice. They were kept in zenanas (houses of seclusion), which afforded an excellent opportunity for the lady missionaries to visit with them and present the gospel message. Zenana visitation became an important phase of missionary activity.

Another unique ministry was houseboat touring. During the monsoon season roads were impassable, but the streams were full. The logical way to reach the villages to hold services was therefore by boat.

A by-product of the goodwill of the community toward the church was that permission was granted to give one hour a week of religious instruction in eight government schools. This was in addition to the Middle English Girls' School conducted on the mission station, which had an enrollment of 80. The government provided generous support for the mission's school program.

When General Superintendents R. T. Williams and J. W. Goodwin visited the field in late 1929, they found a brick-walled six-acre mission compound containing 8 substantial brick buildings (most of them replacements for buildings destroyed in the 1919 storm) and 12 native-style bamboo buildings. Besides the girls' school, classes were being held for preachers and prospective workers, a medical dispensary was in operation, outstations had been established at Mitamain and Bhatrab, and 5 village weekday "Sunday Schools" were being conducted with an enrollment of 301. Accurate records indicated that in 1929, a total of 396 villages and 776 individual homes had been reached, and 28,000 had heard the gospel preached. All this with a staff of 3 missionaries (Miss Ellison having returned to the United States) and 13 national workers. There were, however, only 38 members and 17 probationers.

At issue was whether or not this work should be closed as part of the general missionary retrenchment brought on by the Great Depression. In the light of what appeared to be a well-managed and active station, it was decided to continue for another year. If there was a significant breakthrough in conversions during that time or a change for the better on the economic front, then the mission might conceivably be continued. It proved to be a vain hope.

Central India

When the India Mission Council Meeting was called in Buldana in June 1911, an important item for discussion was the possible addition of adjacent territory from the Christian and Missionary Alliance and the Church of Scotland, which would almost double the area assigned to the Church of the Nazarene. It would include a section to the west in the Jamner area and another to the southeast in the Mehkar District. It was agreed to take on the added responsibility.

Another important part of the proceedings was the ordination of L. S. Tracy by Rev. Campbell. The recommendation to elder's orders had been passed at the historic General Assembly in Pilot Point, Tex., in October 1908, but only now consummated.

As the council meeting progressed, L. S. Tracy became increasingly ill and conducted the final business of the council from his bed. He had contracted typhoid fever and within hours of the final benediction he was in a delirium. A doctor and nurses were called, but all despaired of his life. Typhoid was almost invariably fatal, particularly with a case as severe as this.

Yet God performed a miracle in response to the importunate prayers of the missionaries and the people in the homeland who had been informed of the critical situation. L. S. Tracy was snatched from the jaws of death, and the slow process of recovery began. So astounded were the people of the community that their hearts became opened to the gospel as never before.

In 1912 work was begun in both of the newly added territories, with Olive Nelson and associate missionary Pearl Simmons at Jamner and the L. A. Campbells at Mehkar. Miss Simmons' work had only begun, however, when she was stricken with smallpox and died.

Miss Daisy Skinner was sent out to replace Miss Simmons, and the following summer (1913) she married A. D. Fritzlan. Miss Nelson was moved to the Buldana station, and the Fritzlans took over the Jamner work. Since Jamner was the only mission station on the railroad (a spur line) and was thus connected with Bombay and the work in Western India, less than 200 miles away, there were high hopes that it would become a center uniting the two fields. There was even talk of building a hospital there. But the only reliable road into Jamner from Buldana, 30 miles away, was a roundabout 75-mile route. Such isolation was a severe obstacle. A shortage of missionaries, including the temporary transfer of L. S. Tracy to the Eastern field, 1914-15, made it necessary for Rev. Fritzlan to superintend the work at both Buldana and Jamner for a time, and ultimately forced a temporary closing of the latter work.

When Dr. H. F. Reynolds paid his historic visit to India in 1914, he found a well-established station at Buldana with a large compound in the town and a 23-acre farm outside with a total of seven buildings. A day school and a dispensary were in operation. The latter, operated by Mrs. Perry, was treating 200-300 patients per month. Besides Buldana, the outstations in Chikhli, Mehkar, and Jamner, plus a number of preaching points, gave signs of growth.

The uniting of the Pentecostal Mission with the Church of the Nazarene on February 13, 1915, added six missionaries to the staff, but despite the added forces, by 1918 furloughs and attrition had reduced the total number of missionaries to seven. All were worn out and needing furloughs themselves. Then on January 25, 1919, came Mrs. Ella Perry's sudden passing at Khardi. The morale of the remaining group was put to the test.

But a surge of missionary interest in the homeland following World War I resulted in the sending out of the large contingent of missionaries previously referred to. The Central field staff was augmented by Rev. and Mrs. K. Hawley Jackson, Rev. and Mrs. F. A. Anderson, Rev. and Mrs. Prescott Beals, Amber Tresham, Ruth Rudolph, and May Bursch. The Bealses were originally scheduled to go to Kishorganj, but they were redirected to Buldana after landing in Calcutta.

In 1919 the Buldana church was officially organized with 24 members, the first in India. It should be noted that there is a historical record of the organization of a church in Buldana on January 29, 1911, with 2 charter members and 6 probationers, but the 1919 date is accepted as official. A beautiful church was erected in 1921 and named the Kansas City Chapel.

The worldwide flu epidemic struck the nation in 1919, and to this was added another devastating famine. The high postwar prices for grain further complicated the problem. Rev. A. D. Fritzlan was placed in charge of the relief program in which the mission provided 4,222 hours of work, with the laborers being paid with grain, clothing, and bedding. The missionaries' efforts to alleviate the suffering during this time won much goodwill for the church.

Just before the Fritzlans furloughed in 1920, after 13 years of continuous service, they began working among the robber caste in the vicinity of Buldana and experienced a significant spiritual breakthrough as over 30 were converted. They were brought into the mission compound where the police continued to keep watch on them for a year or two until they became convinced the conversions were genuine.

In 1921 the first attempt at organizing a girls' school was made at Buldana. Up to this time the neighboring Christian and Missionary Alliance Mission had been taking care of the girls. But the effort to start the Nazarene school was short-lived, and in 1924 the great missionary retrenchment forced an abandonment of the project. Not until 1932 was the school reestablished when a building was erected at Chikhli.

In 1922 and 1923 some 10-day Bible conferences were held at

Buldana for the national workers. These were significant gatherings, for the limited training of Indian preachers had been a weakness of the missionary program. These conferences were the forerunners of a full-scale Bible training school, which took its first faltering steps in 1927.

But the middle 1920s were fraught with discouragement and uncertainty for the work in India. In 1924 came the abortive attempt by the general missions board to appoint three superintendents over various world areas. India was assigned to Rev. George Sharpe of Scotland. The program failed, not because of the personnel involved but due to the financial drain on an already overextended budget resulting from the euphoria of the postwar advance. Rev. Sharpe did make two journeys to India, encouraging the workers and offering helpful guidance.

In November 1925 word came through that eight missionaries were to be returned to the United States as part of the retrenchment program. Then the next year the Coddings had to leave the field for health reasons, which reduced the missionary force to a mere four: the Bealses and the A. D. Fritzlans. In fact, for a short time when the Bealses had to leave for furlough because of Rev. Beals's failing health, the Fritzlans were alone. In 1928 the situation improved with the return of the Andersons and the Bealses. The Tracys, who had been away from the field since 1919, returned in late 1929 just in time for the momentous conferences with General Superintendents Williams and Goodwin in January 1930 concerning the reorganization of the India work.

3. *Consolidation in Central India*

Lines drawn from New Delhi in the north to the southern tip of India, and from Bombay to Calcutta intersect in the Central India field of the Church of the Nazarene. Three hundred miles to the west, not far from Bombay, was the Western field in the Thana District, while 850 miles northeast was the Eastern field centered in Kishorganj.

At issue was whether the financially straitened mission board could support three such widely separated fields in one country, particularly since none, for whatever reasons, were truly flourishing. India was a difficult field at best. The climate was harsh and debilitating, and disease was rampant, which made for a frequent turn-over of missionaries. Of the 47 missionaries who had served on the field to this point (1930), the average term of service had been less than 7 years. Transporting missionaries halfway around the world was costly. Also conversions from Hinduism and Islam were exceedingly difficult to achieve. Church members totaled only 180. Statistics did not tell the whole story, of course, but it was difficult to ignore the fact that the heavy investment in India had not paid off in terms of converts and an established, growing work.

The council elected L. S. Tracy as mission superintendent over his protest that he had been away too many years to have a proper grasp of the work yet. He was also aware of the troubled times ahead both economically and administratively, but he did not shrink from the task once it was laid on him.

The first decision was to close the Western (Thana) District, moving the McKays from Khardi and Miss Mellies and Miss Muse from Murbad to Buldana. National leaders were left in charge of the schools for the time being.

The Eastern field presented a different kind of problem. As already pointed out, it was more isolated from Buldana than was the Western field. It was also in a different language area (Bengali as against the Marathi of the other two districts). Although only the Franklins and Miss Varnedoe remained, the work was progressing reasonably well. In fact, Rev. Tracy declared that there was more to show for the 15 years in Eastern India than in the 25 years in Western India. But it was an area fraught with many problems—floods, famine, and political unrest that frustrated missionary endeavor.

The proposed one-year trial period to see if the work was viable was hardly a fair test since there was no strengthening of the missionary force and no additional financial investment made in the work. The Tracys spent Christmas 1930 at Kishorganj, but there was a shadow over the festivities as plans were being laid for closing the field. In the conference in Buldana the previous January, the die had been cast. On March 1, 1931, the three missionaries sailed for home. The work was left in charge of a national pastor, Samad Babu, with several visits a year being made by the mission superintendent in Buldana until in 1937 the property was sold. One part of the station was reserved for another mission in order to perpetuate a Christian presence in that area.

4. *From Consolidation to World War II*

Adjusting to the new situation was not as difficult as coping with the strictures the depression years imposed. In fact the compact field and the acquisition of a group of experienced missionaries from the Western area signaled renewed activity.

Evangelism

To this point the basic method of missionary evangelization was known as touring. During the cool season, December, January, and February, a missionary (or group of missionaries) with possibly a national pastor and other helpers would tour neighboring villages, taking with them tents to live in and other camping equipment. Bamboo poles and canvas were used to build a shelter in which to hold services. During the day, services were conducted on the streets and in the bazaars, literature was distributed, Scripture portions were sold, and personal contacts made. At night, services were held in the central location. After a few days, the touring group would move on, and the national pastor in the area would follow up on the interested persons, hopefully leading them on to baptism.

In 1931 a new dimension was added to the touring program with the institution of "inquirers' meetings." As a climax of the three months of touring, the people who had been reached were invited to meet in a central location where a much larger canvas tabernacle was erected. The people came prepared to stay four or five days for intensive religious instruction. In the afternoons, men's, women's, and children's meetings were held separately. One hundred fifty adults plus many children attended the first such meeting, and thereafter this became a regular event.

These inquirers' meetings gave birth to the annual jungle camp meetings that began in December 1932. Property seven miles north of Buldana was secured, and a large canvas-covered tabernacle with woven bamboo walls was erected. The people came with their cooking equipment and necessary food (even sometimes including water buffalo cows for milk) and set up shelters surrounding the tabernacle. Services began with an early morning prayer meeting and continued throughout the day with a great evangelistic service each night. A significant feature was the small-group encounter sessions held each afternoon at various places in the surrounding jungle. Many spiritual victories came from these group meetings. Neighborhood people attended the evening services, and many of them were won to Christ.

That first camp meeting was considered by many to mark a turning point in the India church. It should be noted that it had been preceded in November by a meeting of the national workers led by Rev. Tracy. He and others had sensed some troublesome personality conflicts and animosities that had developed within the group, but in a profound melting experience the workers were drawn together in love and contrition. The effect of that event carried over into the camp meeting that followed. It is little wonder that the results of the latter were so far-reaching.

It was in 1932 that Chikhli took on stature as a mission center. In July the church there was officially organized, the second church on the India District. Also the girls' school building was erected there, the largest building project undertaken to date. Miss Margaret Stewart came that year to work in the school.

In September 1933 the first annual district meeting was held in the Buldana church. It was conducted like a miniature district assembly, including reports by pastors and other workers. Year by year, Sunday Schools and missionary and youth societies were organized, and their reports were added to the agenda. Within three years there were eight organized churches. Each church was challenged to launch another church, and new preaching points were opened up. These developed into "probationers' classes" (embryo churches) and then into regular churches. Another by-product of the annual meeting was the launching of the district paper in Marathi, an eight-page publication called the *Nazarene Evangel*.

In 1934 Rev. and Mrs. L. S. Tracy retired from the leadership of the district. Twenty-eight years before, the task had been thrust upon him when Rev. Wood abandoned the mission, and he had steered the work through many of its crises. His place was taken by Rev. Prescott Beals, who was now a veteran of 14 years experience.

The Washim District Added

Just before L. S. Tracy left India, he received a letter from Rev. LeRoy Lightfoot, district superintendent of the Methodist Episcopal mission field that bordered the Nazarene work on the southeast, in which he proposed to transfer this area to the Church of the Nazarene. The Methodists had decided to concentrate their efforts in urban areas. This territory, about 80 miles long, and 50 miles wide, was similar in size to the existing Nazarene field with also a comparable population of 800,000. Even its Christian population of 400 was about the same. It would, therefore, double the existing territory.

The main city in the area was Washim (then called Basim), in which there was a mission compound with several good buildings including two missionary bungalows, two school buildings (currently boys' and girls' schools), a brick church and parsonage in the town, and several outstation buildings. (It was here that M. D. Wood had left his group of orphan girls when he defected nearly 30 years before.)

On November 28, 1934, a letter was drafted by the India Mission Council to the Department of Foreign Missions in Kansas City, strongly recommending that the new territory be added. It would be in line, they said, with the decision made four years before to consolidate the Nazarene work in Central India. It would also provide two missionary residences that were needed, and the two large school buildings on the Washim compound would fill two important needs: One could be used for the Bible training school now temporarily housed in Buldana, and the other for the proposed hospital. Buildings for both of these institutions would have had to be built anyway.

To finance the purchase of the buildings, it was proposed that the properties on the Thana District and at Kishorganj be liquidated and the proceeds be invested here. Also, money that had already been sent in for the "Benson Memorial Bible School" totaling some $3,200 was available. Apparently there had been considerable agitation from the homeland to reopen the Eastern field, and it was hoped that this new challenge might ease that pressure. The Methodist church valued their property at 80,000 rupees (about $30,000); and when the Church of the Nazarene offered only $10,000, it was refused. The compromise figure agreed upon was $15,000, payable one-fourth down with three additional annual payments.

In January 1935 the General Board authorized the acceptance of this new field and ordered the purchase of the property. It was a significant milestone in the history of the India work when in July the official transfer of the territory took place. It now remained to make the most of the new facilities and opportunities thus afforded.

Some of the Methodist national workers and many of the church people transferred their membership to the Church of the Nazarene. To help weld the two sections together, a two-weeks preachers' meeting was held in Washim and later on, in November, a camp meeting was held there. It was a good means to acquaint the new people with Nazarene beliefs and ways of doing things.

With the new territory came the need for increased missionary staff. Rev. and Mrs. Ralph Cook arrived in November 1935, and in 1936 Rev. and Mrs. J. W. Anderson and Dr. Orpha Speicher.

The Bible Training School

The building in Washim formerly used as a girls' school was readily adapted for the Bible training school. This institution had first been launched in Buldana in 1927 but fell victim to the lack of workers during the retrenchment. Then when the McKays were transferred to Buldana with the closing of the Western field in 1931, they opened the school again, only to have it closed a year later when they furloughed. Upon their return the school was begun once more in December 1934, with Mrs. McKay in charge. It was the first institution to move to the new Washim station in July 1935.

A three-year course was set up with a six-month term each year (July to December). From mid-December to mid-March the students were involved in touring, giving them valuable practical experience. On weekends and market days they also engaged in street evangelism. Two Indian men served with Mrs. McKay on the teaching staff, S. Y. Salve and Prasadrao Manerikar. The first year of operation at Washim the enrollment was 19.

Then tragedy struck on November 29, 1935. As the McKays were driving from Buldana to Washim, an accident caused by a tire blowout took the life of Mrs. McKay and their young son, John T. ("Buddie"). But the work of the Bible school continued under Rev. McKay's leadership. In 1940 Rev. Leslie Fritzlan became the director as during the war years the two missionary couples remaining in India, the Bealses and the Fritzlans, struggled to keep as much of the work going as possible. The Bealses headquartered in Buldana, and the Fritzlans in Washim.

Though the Bible school enrollment was never large (seldom over 20), the institution had a significant effect upon the work, particularly in its early days as the district began to move rapidly toward national leadership. There came also an upsurge in conversions and church organizations.

Another phase of the educational program was the Junior Bible School in Buldana. This was a lay training program that developed out of the inquirers' meetings. The latter had been held for many years at the close of the touring season and eventually were concentrated in Buldana.

The Medical Program

From the earliest days of Nazarene missions in India, medical dispensaries and clinics were in operation as personnel to handle them was available. The pioneers were Mrs. M. D. Wood and Mrs. Ella Perry. Though Mrs. Perry had no formal training, she won an outstanding reputation as a practical medical practitioner. It was while she was administering medicine to a patient in Khardi that she herself collapsed and died within 28 hours. Over the years, several of the missionaries who came to India were registered nurses and used their skills to aid the suffering.

Though there was no organized medical program, from the earliest days there was talk of establishing a hospital on the field. In fact, as earlier stated, when the town of Jamner was added to the Nazarene territory in 1909, there was talk of building one there, but this never materialized. However, when the Washim area became a part of the Nazarene field, and a building that would lend itself to adaptation as a hospital was thus acquired, the development of a medical facility became a top priority.

One of the first missionaries to be appointed after the Washim addition was Dr. Orpha Speicher, who arrived in 1936. This multi-talented lady wrote an epic chapter in the story of medical missions in India. Almost single-handedly she brought into being the Reynolds Memorial Hospital. The U-shaped, mud-walled school building that she inherited was in a state of disrepair and filth; but with such help as could be commandeered, she joined the scrub- and paint-bucket brigade to bring the building into some semblance of orderliness and cleanliness befitting a hospital. The building was ready to receive women and children patients in June 1938. Dr. Speicher had only one missionary nurse to assist her and a few untrained Indian helpers.

The next problem was to get people to come to the hospital for treatment. Fear, mistrust, and superstition were hard to overcome. But once the barrier was broken, progress was rapid and expansion of the hospital was soon necessary. Here again Dr. Speicher stepped in as architect, construction boss, materials procurer, carpenter, and bricklayer, all the while continuing her medical ministrations. The present modern 105-bed hospital is a monument to her skill and planning as well as her arduous personal labor.

Toward a National Church

Rev. Prescott Beals was an ardent believer in an indigenous church, and he carefully trained pastors and national workers in the leadership arts. Without a Bible training school this was often a matter of personal coaching. He also began urging the general church leaders to organize the work into a national district with Indian leadership throughout.

At the 1936 annual district meeting, besides electing nationals to various district offices and the leadership of the missionary society and youth auxiliaries, a straw vote was taken for district superintendent. The results were not to be announced, so presumably it was a test to see what kind of leadership the India church would elect if given a ballot. Apparently the results were reassuring.

On October 9, 1937, Dr. and Mrs. J. B. Chapman, general superintendent and wife, arrived for a six-weeks stay in India, during which an intensive study of the field was made. Dr. Chapman became convinced that the district was ready for organization; and on November 24, when the fifth district assembly was convened, he pronounced: "I hereby declare this to be the first annual district assembly of the Church of the Nazarene in India." There were eight churches with 603 members. Henceforth the missionaries would assume an advisory role except those involved in the institutions.

In the assembly the first six Indian elders were ordained by Dr. Chapman: Samuel J. Bhujbal, S. Y. Salve, W. H. Kharat, David Bhujbal, G. S. Borde, and B. D. Amolik. When the time came to elect their own district superintendent, the vote went to Samuel Bhujbal, eloquent preacher, skillful organizer, and ardent evangelist.

Samuel Bhujbal was a product of the Vasind church on the old Thana District, where he was converted under the ministry of Dr. H. F. Reynolds in 1921. He was sanctified at the Buldana church four years later. He ministered in the Murbad church where a school for high caste children grew in one year from 25 to 120. In 1926 he became a teacher in the boys' school in Buldana. Following the sweeping revival at the jungle camp meeting in 1932, he organized 15 students into a number of bands who reached 40 villages during the touring season that followed. Thus began his ascendancy as a spiritual leader among his people.

The wisdom of organizing a national district at this time was abundantly confirmed when, two years later, the nation was swept into World War II and subsequently all the missionaries save two couples (Bealses and Fritzlans) were forced to return home. The work was structured to carry on on its own if necessary. The fact is, the India church actually grew during those difficult years.

The war was to affect the work in many ways. Invasion by the Japanese was threatened, and though it never materialized, the country was under wartime footing with the accompanying scarcities and restrictions. In faraway Manila, two missionaries on their way to India were interned by the Japanese in Santo Tomas prison in January 1942. Dr. Evelyn Witthoff and Nurse Geraldine Chappell languished there until the war was over.

5. *The Post-World War II Era*

The India field took on a different character after World War II. Largely unscathed by the international conflict, the country was nonetheless affected by the global unrest. Many of its young men served in the armed forces abroad and brought back new ideas and different mores that impacted the deeply ingrained life-styles of the populace. The drive for political independence was the most significant result of this new attitude, and on August 15, 1947, this was consummated when colonial ties with Great Britain were severed. The new constitution was ratified January 26, 1950.

It is only natural that this new national spirit would affect the missionary program. Again the wisdom of creating the national-mission district before the war was confirmed. The organizational structure was in place and during the war had had opportunity to function—indeed the national leaders were forced to exert leadership because of the limited missionary force.

But there were other factors that contributed to make 1947 a watershed year in the history of India missions. One was the infusion of a host of new missionaries. In a period of one year, more than 20 missionaries arrived on the field, some of them returnees but most of them newcomers. To be sure, added help was needed, but this sudden influx had its drawbacks, for the housing and effective deployment of such a large group was difficult. The result was disillusionment and frustration for a number of them. But for all the confusion, there was also the injection of new ideas and enthusiasm that revitalized the work.

Three areas of expansion were to evolve in the coming years: (1) development of the educational work, both in the Bible training school and in the day schools; (2) the extension of the hospital and other medical work; (3) the opening of work in the cities. This is not to say that the established evangelistic ministries such as touring, camp meetings, and church planting were curtailed. In fact, the Bible school program was more specifically tied to evangelism. But it should also be noted that, following independence, the government applied increasingly greater restrictions on the admission of missionaries. It became almost impossible to obtain visas for any other than professional people—doctors, nurses, and teachers.

Education

a. Nazarene Christian Coeducational School. The girls' school located in Chikhli and the boys' school in Buldana 14 miles to the north were long-standing institutions, but it appeared to the missionaries that there was considerable duplication of effort, particularly in the classroom phase. During the war, Mrs. Beals had done some experimentation with mixing boys and girls in the lower grades and saw no reason why this could not be extended. As a result, when the Ralph Cooks returned to India in 1946, Orpha Cook was put in charge of organizing a coeducational school in conjunction with the girls' school in Chikhli.

The plan was to build a dormitory for the boys across the road where they would eat and sleep. In classes and chapel, however, boys and girls would be together, though in the tradition of the segregation of the sexes in India, they would sit on opposite sides of the room. Such an innovative venture caught the attention of the government authorities, and they were so impressed with the success of the idea that little by little all government schools went coeducational. John Meshramkar, formerly head of the boys' school, was named headmaster (principal) and continued in that capacity for many years. Missionaries who directed NCCS after Mrs. Cook included the Leslie Fritzlans, the John McKays, the Cleve Jameses, the William Peases, and Miss Jean Darling.

In 1970 Rev. S. P. Dongerdive, who had previously served as chaplain in the Reynolds Memorial Hospital and on the faculty of the Bible training school, became the first national director of the coeducational school. Enrollment in this very successful institution averaged between 240 and 310. The decline in more recent years to the lower figure has been because the high school students, though boarding at NCCS, now attend the public high school. Though there was considerable government pressure to add the upper grades to the NCCS program again, enrollment continued to decline until in 1982 the school was closed.

b. Bible Training School. The Bible school, which had been kept alive during the war by Leslie Fritzlan, became the responsibility of John Anderson when he returned to India in 1946. Despite his efforts and those of Earl Lee who followed him in 1949, the school went through an up-and-down period. A key problem was to find students with adequate educational background to master the courses offered. It was considered ill-advised to lower the standards for the ministry, but making too high a demand cut enrollment. In addition, there were those who desired to attend the school who did not plan to be preachers, so educational standards were of minor concern to them. Compounding the uncertainties was the pressure to move the school back to the Dhamandari campus at Buldana. In fact once or twice classes were held there for a term. A Junior Bible School, actually an extension of the inquirers' classes, had been held there for many years.

It was not until 1962, when Mrs. Hilda Lee Cox took over the school at the beginning of the Coxes' second term, that the school finally got on its feet. She accepted the fact that the needs of both laymen and ministerial students needed to be met and so tried to serve both. A strong English program was instituted to prepare the ministers for seminary so they would be prepared to take advanced training. At the same time the importance of training strong laymen was not lost. Each year one or two of the ministerial student graduates would go on to seminary, usually to the South India Bible Institute, which had a holiness orientation.

Two who came to Nazarene Theological Seminary in Kansas City were to play important roles in the future of the India church. Padu Meshramkar graduated from NTS in 1970 and returned with the Coxes to India. Rev. D. M. Kharat was then in charge of the school, having taken over when the Coxes left on an extended furlough in 1967. After a term of service teaching in the school, Padu Meshramkar became director in 1973. The enrollment continued to run just under 20, but with a high morale and strong evangelistic emphasis, the impact of the school became significant.

By 1978 missionaries were no longer teaching at the Bible school. Well-educated and highly qualified Indian teachers had assumed total responsibility for the school, both administratively and in the classroom.

The other who attended NTS with Padu Meshramkar was Suresh Borde, who upon his return became head of evangelism on the India field. He died in October 1976 while pastoring a new work in the city of Nagpur, 150 miles northeast of Washim.

Reynolds Memorial Hospital

Though the work of the Reynolds Memorial Hospital was greatly restricted during World War II, it did remain in operation, using national personnel. When Dr. Speicher returned in 1944, several moves were begun that greatly broadened the ministry of the institution. The first was the establishment of a nurses' training school, which was Miss Jean Darling's major assignment when she arrived on the field from Canada in 1945. The graduates have not only staffed the Nazarene hospital, but many have carried their Christian witness as they have gone to serve in various government hospitals. The high quality of the graduates became broadly recognized. One of the early graduates was Nalini Yangad, who is now superintendent of nurses in the hospital.

The next major move was to open a men's wing in the hospital and add surgery facilities. Kansas City First Church took up an offering of $15,000 to build a home for the first resident male doctor, Dr. Ira Cox, Jr., who was a member of that church. He and his wife, Hilda Lee, and their three children arrived in India in 1952 to begin these two phases of the hospital program.

As indicated earlier, two important additions to the medical staff, Dr. Evelyn Witthoff and Nurse Geraldine Chappell, had originally set out for India in 1941 but were interned in Manila by the Japanese for the duration of the war. Miss Chappell finally arrived in India, along with the Earl Lees, in the fall of 1946; Dr. Witthoff in April 1947. Dr. Witthoff's chief function was to supervise the dispensary and clinic work. Major dispensaries were at Chikhli, Mehkar, and Pusad, while regular clinics were scheduled in numerous surrounding villages. For a time, Dr. Witthoff operated a well-equipped, mobile clinic. Assisting in the dispensary work were principally Geraldine Chappell, Agnes Willox, and Hilda Moen. Esther Howard and Norma Weiss, besides serving the hospital, were involved in the nurses' training program, as was Carolyn Myatt, who is now administrator of the hospital.

Dr. and Mrs. Donald Miller came to India in 1960 and served two terms before leaving the field in 1971. Then in 1973 a new "first" took place with the coming of Drs. Albert and Rosa Ainscough from Argentina. Not only were they unique in that both were medical doctors, but they were the first missionaries to be sent out by the Argentina Church of the Nazarene. They helped fill the void created by the loss of Drs. Miller and Cox, who had left not long before. They served until 1978, during which time he also was mission director for a year. When they returned to Argentina, they resumed the pastorate of a church they had started years before in Buenos Aires.

In the meantime, Indian doctors were being added to the staff, among them Dr. Kamalakar Meshramkar, a second-generation Nazarene, who became medical superintendent of the hospital when Dr. Orpha Speicher retired in 1976.

Reynolds Memorial achieved an outstanding record of service over the years. Widely acclaimed by the India authorities, its ministry touched the lives of some 25-30,000 patients every year. Every one received the spiritual ministrations of the hospital chaplain as well as of the Christian doctors and nurses, and the long-range effects of such a ministry were incalculable.

The Call of the City

Historically, apart from a brief ministry in Calcutta at the beginning of the century, the work of the Church of the Nazarene had been concentrated in the rural towns and villages, of which there are some 700,000 in the country. In the 80,000-square-mile area of Central India allotted to the Church of the Nazarene, there are about 1,800 villages and a total population of 1¼ million. This is an imposing missionary challenge, but for the most part it is a scattered constituency.

Not so with the huge masses concentrated in the great cities like Calcutta (by 1981, 9.2 million), Bombay (8.2 million), Delhi (5.7 million), Madras (4.3 million), and several others over 2 million. Comity agreements that restricted the work of each missionary group to a designated area were not in force in any city over 100,000. Here was a mission field unique and challenging.

The spiritual need in the cities had been a concern of the India missionaries for many years, but it was not until after the war that the necessary personnel were available to do anything about it. Thus in 1946 the Ralph Cooks were asked to investigate the possibilities of opening work in Calcutta or Bombay. But in this postwar situation the cities were in foment, and housing was virtually impossible to obtain, so the idea was temporarily shelved. Then in the early 1960s Hari Saraf began a small work in Bombay largely on his own. Rev. Samuel Bhujbal, for many years India's district superintendent, moved to Bombay and took over this work and developed a unique family ministry.

This was also the time of the great exodus of young people to the cities. The interior Nazarene field was not untouched by this movement that saw numbers of Nazarenes moving away, principally to the cities of Bombay, Aurangabad (150 miles east of Bombay), Nagpur (150 miles northeast of Washim), and New Delhi, the capital, far to the north. Although many were lost to the church, a group in the Santa Cruz area of Bombay began sporadic meetings in the 1960s. They did not have the initiative or leadership at that time to organize a regular church program, however. But this meant that with Samuel Bhujbal's work there were at least two potential churches in this metropolis. It was the opening wedge of city work in India that was to see significant expansion in the years to come.

In 1962 Luther Monmothe was sent to Aurangabad, a city of then 200,000, to see about opening up a work. A good group of Nazarenes was already there. In 1974 property was purchased and a church erected. S. T. Gaikwad, who had just concluded a 15-year term as district superintendent, was installed as pastor. The William Peases were later sent to open work six miles away in the "new city" section.

In 1974 Bronell A. and Paula Greer were appointed to officially organize the Western Maharashtra District to include the Bombay area and Poona. (The former Central India field became the Eastern Maharashtra District.) A property at Khandala, about 35 miles southeast of Bombay toward the city of Poona, was offered to the church rent free for five years. On it were several buildings that could be used for various functions, and thus it could serve as a district center. The Harold Harrises were assigned to Bombay in 1976, and new house churches were begun there as well as in Poona. A two-acre property was purchased in Poona and a church built.

After a revival meeting at Nagpur, conducted by Rev. Suresh Borde and Dr. Albert Ainscough, a church was organized on July 18, 1976, in this burgeoning industrial city of 1 million. The nucleus of 30 charter members was also largely made up of Nazarenes from the old Central District, and the congregation was soon self-supporting. Suresh Borde continued as interim pastor for this congregation until his sudden and untimely death three months later. Miraculously, a prime piece of property was secured and a new building erected. Sumant Mhaske became pastor.

Meanwhile, the capital city of New Delhi, 1,000 miles north of Buldana, was coming into the picture. In June 1977 John and Doris Anderson, upon returning from furlough, were assigned to open a work there. The metropolitan area, made up of two cities—the old and the new—presented a great challenge. Several Nazarenes had moved there and formed a starting nucleus. Within a year six Bible study groups in three different languages, one of them English, were under way in the city. A predominantly Hindi-speaking church was added, paving the way for the organization of a pioneer district in the fall of 1979. The total membership of the two churches was 41. Not long after, a third church was added, and within a year the district's membership was up to 141 and steadily increased to 189 in 1985. In that year Dr. V. K. Singh became the first national superintendent of the Delhi District.

In late 1979 M. V. Ingle was named superintendent of the Western Maharashtra District, and the Bronell A. Greers moved to South India to organize the Tamil Nadu District. Here a group of independent holiness congregations had expressed a desire to unite with the Church of the Nazarene. There were three churches with a total of 106 members.

Radio and Correspondence Courses

Another avenue of outreach begun in 1959 was the radio program "Tilak and Christ." (Tilak was a revered poet/philosopher of India whose writings were used as a drawing card to the listeners.) This 15-minute weekly broadcast over powerful Radio Ceylon was the brainchild of Bronell A. Greer. Handling the technical phase of recording the program at Washim was Wallace Helm, and the national director was Manohar V. Ingle. A correspondence course was offered on the program, which drew excellent response. As many as 3,000 letters a year have been received, and answering these has been a ministry in itself. The contacts made have been particularly useful in those cities where the Church of the Nazarene is operating and where personal follow-up is possible. The radio program has done much to familiarize the general public with the name of the church and its teaching.

6. *South India Field*

With the promising developments in South India, it was deemed wise to set this area apart as a separate field. Rev. Arlen Jakobitz was appointed mission director of the North India field, which included the districts of Eastern Maharashtra, Western Maharashtra, and Delhi. Rev. Bronell A. Greer was appointed mission director of the South India field.

The first district assembly of the South field was held on January 18, 1981, with General Superintendent Greathouse presiding. Two districts were established along provincial lines—Tamil Nadu and Karnataka/Andhra Pradesh. By mid-1985 the work had grown to 19 churches and 831 members.

This fertile mission field had had a long history of Christian influence. Eighty percent of India's Christians live in this area. It was here that the apostle Thomas is reputed to have come with the gospel message and to have died in Madras. A holiness tradition had also been established principally through the World Gospel Mission, which was very supportive in the launching of the Nazarene work.

The area of most active cooperation was in the South India Biblical Seminary, which the World Gospel Mission had founded in 1937. In return for Nazarene financial support, the seminary worked out an agreement in 1981 whereby one-third of the governing board and one-third of the available student openings would be reserved for Nazarenes. The principal in 1985 was Rev. Frank Dewey, a Nazarene, but in India under the WGM board. The executive secretary was Rev. Bronell A. Greer, and the registrar was another Nazarene, Rev. Subhash Dongerdive. Most of the faculty and staff, however, were non-Nazarene, in keeping with the interdenominational character of the institution. One hundred eleven students were enrolled in 1985.

Besides its academic program, the seminary also had a Department of Health and Rural Development that conducted a variety of activities from baby clinics and health education to animal husbandry. Food-for-work schemes, tailoring institutes, seed and fertilizer supply, well drilling, and housing were typical of the self-help programs instituted. Another facet of the curriculum was the popular Vacation Bible School program in which materials and assistance were provided for some 200,000 students of many denominations each year.

Compassionate ministries were a significant part of Nazarene missionary work in South India, and village health care, food projects, vocational training, and so forth were provided. But the central goal of evangelism was not lost sight of. "We need Christ's help to balance, as He did, physical concern with His clear statement that only those born of the Spirit enter the kingdom of God," wrote Bronell A. Greer in the district paper, *Pavithravanti* (October 1985, 5). The steady growth in both number of churches and membership was witness to the fact that this prime goal was being pursued successfully.

The severe government restrictions on the admission of missionaries to India largely dictates a fully indigenous church. Even professional missionaries such as doctors, nurses, and teachers are by government decree to be replaced by nationals as they become available. Training for church leadership is a top priority. The exodus of young people to the cities has hampered this to some degree. At the same time, pastors will need to be specially trained for city work. The strategies are vastly different from those used in the traditional rural setting. With a population growth in India of 12 million a year, the process of urbanization would increase in coming years, presenting a still greater challenge to the church.

Despite the problems, the work in India has moved ahead. By 1985, membership in the North field had reached 3,195 in 53 organized churches. These figures combined with those of the South field gave all-India totals of 4,026 and 72 respectively.

B. CHINA

1. *Mainland China*

a. *Northern Field*

China, for millennia a remote and inscrutable land, swathed in mystery, rarely opened its windows, let alone its doors, to outsiders or foreign influences. Yet in A.D. 536, Jaballaha, a Nestorian priest, brought the Christian message overland from Syria and received the blessing of the emperor. Because the Nestorians were also learned in the sciences, they remained a strong influence in the land for eight centuries. Then they strangely disappeared.

From then on Christian influence, basically Roman Catholic, came and went with passing dynasties and revolutions, until finally, in 1754, an edict was passed prohibiting Christianity and banishing all missionaries from the land. At the same time Buddhism, the most dominant religion, and Taoism received the support of the ruling powers. Ancient Confucianism, while not a true religion because it has no deity, also remained an influential ethical force.

But by the turn of the 19th century the situation had altered somewhat, and Robert Morrison of the London Missionary Society arrived in China to become the first Protestant missionary. Jesuit missionaries, defying the 1754 edict, had already established themselves and stubbornly opposed Morrison's coming. To avoid problems, he settled in Macao, Portuguese outpost on China's southeast coast where foreigners were free to reside. Here he set to work with Dr. Milne to translate the Bible into Chinese. The task was completed in 11 years and, along with it, a Chinese grammar and a six-volume dictionary. But Morrison's evangelistic efforts were less auspicious. It took 7 years for him to win his first convert, and even after over 25 years he had won only about a dozen.

Then came the Opium Wars of the late 1830s and early 1840s and the treaties that opened up China not only to international trade but to missionary work as well. The promising condition did not last, however, for steadily rising opposition to foreign intrusion finally erupted in the Boxer Rebellion. Though the rebellion itself was quelled, the antiforeign sentiment that provoked it was only heightened.

The ancient system of ruling dynasties finally came to an end when after the revolution that erupted on October 10, 1911, a republic was established in 1912 with Sun Yat-sen as provisional president. He immediately resigned and Yüan Shih-k'ai was elected in his place. But it was far from a united country, for local warlords actually ruled. It was not until Generalissimo Chiang Kai-shek became president in 1928 that the country was truly brought together as a constitutional republic. Of particular significance was the fact that he was a Christian and was strongly supportive of missionary efforts.

Chiang's first challenge came from the Japanese, who had long sought to seize Chinese territory. In 1931 they moved into the northeast provinces and set up a puppet state in Manchuria. With the outbreak of World War II, they expanded their intrusion to include much of the country, but had to return all occupied territory in the surrender treaty of 1945.

The next challenge came from the Soviet-supported Communists who, even before World War II, had been infiltrating from the north. From 1946 to 1949 civil war continued between Nationalists and Communists that ended in the retreat of Chiang's forces to Formosa (now Taiwan) and the setting up of a Communist government in Peking (formerly Peiping). Mao Tse-tung became dictator and Chou En-lai premier. With that, the so-called Bamboo Curtain fell, and China's "People's Republic" became isolated from the rest of the world for a quarter of a century.

Nazarene Missions in Old China

It was in the midst of this political and military foment that the Church of the Nazarene sought to establish an effective missionary presence in China. Its work was launched in those beginning years of the republic when the doors were first opened wide for Christian missionaries.

At a meeting of the general missionary board on October 9-12, 1913, it was officially voted to establish a Nazarene work in China. Available to launch this effort were Rev. and Mrs. Peter Kiehn, who had already spent a five-year term in China under an independent mission in Tsaochowfu. They not only had an intimate knowledge of the field but had valuable connections with existing missionary endeavors. Using this information, Dr. H. F. Reynolds had been in correspondence with other missions in the country regarding the obtaining of a territory in which to work.

By mutual agreement among the various missions, the entire country had been divided up among the various groups so there would be no overlapping of missionary efforts. These comity agreements, as they were called, did not include the major cities, which were considered open to all groups. For the Church of the Nazarene to begin work, one of these established missions would have to release a section of its territory to the newcomer. It was thus that the National Holiness Association offered part of its assigned area to the Church of the Nazarene. The section granted was just north of where Rev. Kiehn had previously worked, so he was familiar with both the language and the people.

On the afternoon of December 16, 1913, the *Tenyo Maru* sailed out through San Francisco's Golden Gate, headed for the Orient. On board were Dr. H. F. Reynolds and 10 missionaries, some bound for Japan, some for China, and some for India. The China missionaries were Rev. and Mrs. Peter Kiehn with their son, Arnold, and Miss Glennie Sims, the latter from Pasadena College.

Dr. Reynolds stopped off with the Japan-bound missionaries to make necessary arrangements for the work there, while the Kiehns and Miss Sims went on to Shanghai, and the India missionaries to Calcutta. After landing, the Kiehns and Miss Sims traveled northward about 700 miles to Tsinanfu where they stayed with missionary friends, the Geislers, until the arrival of Dr. Reynolds on January 31, 1914.

It was decided that Miss Sims would remain at Tsinanfu for language study while also tutoring the two Geisler children. The Kiehns and Dr. Reynolds set out westward on an arduous four-day trip by mule cart to the National Holiness Association headquarters in Nankuantao, 120 miles inland.

The missionary party was warmly greeted by Rev. Woodford Taylor, superintendent of the NHA work, and immediately discussions began concerning the future of holiness missionary work in China. One possibility explored was the union of the two groups under the banner of the Church of the Nazarene, but this did not materialize. The decision was finally made to turn over to the Nazarenes 4 1/2 of the

10 counties in western Shantung province that the NHA had originally been assigned. In addition, they offered to send one of their able pastors, Rev. C. H. Li, to assist them in launching a work.

With Rev. Cecil Troxel of the NHA as a competent guide, the area was thoroughly studied. It was about 100 miles long and 30 miles wide and included within its boundaries 10 cities, several market towns, 2,000 villages, and a total population of about 1 million. The countryside was flat, with the Yellow River cutting across the southeast corner.

Having decided to make the walled city of Ch'ao Ch'eng their headquarters, the Kiehns moved there on April 5, 1914, and rented a small compound that had been previously occupied by the Chinese NHA pastor. Within the compound was a building large enough for a chapel, while the remaining buildings were used for living quarters.

As the missionaries worked to repair and adapt the buildings for their use, they never lacked for an audience, as the people crowded into the small compound to watch the activities of the foreigners. They were intrigued by Mrs. Kiehn's big feet that enabled her to walk like a man, unlike those of their own women whose feet had been bound between the ages of six to eight and thus were deformed. (The custom had been outlawed in 1853 but was not enforced.) They were curious, too, to know what the missionaries ate to make their skins so white. As the missionaries talked with them and treated their minor ailments, fear and prejudice gradually melted away.

In the fall of 1914 Miss Sims joined the Kiehns. Her task was to open a girls' school and a boys' school. (The segregation of the sexes was a deep-seated tradition in China.) To open a girls' school at all was unique, for in a land where only 2 percent of the women could read or write, this was a new concept. Two Chinese teachers were hired for the school program.

The ready response of the people to the gospel was evidenced by the fact that in May 1915, the first 10 Christians were ready for baptism. The following Sunday the first Church of the Nazarene in China was organized with 16 full members and 40 probationers.

Miss Ida Vieg, a member of the Church of the Nazarene in Portland, Oreg., had gone to China on her own and was teaching in an NHA boarding school in Shanghai. In the course of his exploratory trip, Dr. Reynolds met her there and urged her to apply for regular missionary service with the Church of the Nazarene. Though she was quickly appointed, it was not until May 1916 that she officially joined the missionary staff. She worked with Miss Sims in the day schools as well as in village evangelism among the women. By then, enrollment in the schools was running about 30 boys and 20 girls.

The original compound was soon overcrowded, but an appeal to the mission board for money to buy a more adequate property went unheeded for lack of funds. Undaunted, the missionaries themselves pooled their personal resources, and this amount combined with other gifts solicited from friends in the homeland was used to purchase property on the west end of town. With a special gift of $1,000 from Rev. S. C. Brilhart, a California pastor, a fine chapel was built in memory of his son Clifford who had recently drowned while on a hunting trip. Even then, in a short time multiple services were needed to accommodate the crowds who came.

In 1917 a large corner lot became available. The original buildings there had burned down during a revolt, and several squatters had built shanty homes on the land. Besides paying the owner for the land, it was necessary to pay off these homeowners to get them to move elsewhere. They were allowed to take all the building materials they could salvage as well. The first building erected on this commodious property was a missionary home, built in late 1918 with funds contributed by Mrs. Lizzie Fraley of Los Angeles First Church in honor of her late husband.

By this time Rev. and Mrs. O. P. Deale had joined the missionary force in late November 1917. Also before the year's end, Miss Pearl Denbow, a veteran of five years with the South China Holiness Mission, had arrived in Ch'ao Ch'eng. With these added forces, plus other Chinese workers, the village work began to expand. This included a mission in Puchow, an important county seat 30 miles southwest down near the Yellow River. It was a market center serving over 1,000 villages.

Expansion to Tamingfu

Thirty-five miles northwest of Ch'ao Ch'eng, in the southern panhandle of Hopei (Chihli) province, was the large, walled city of Tamingfu. Its population of 40,000 within the walls and 30,000 in the suburbs made it a dominant center. In fact, 2,000 years before, it had been the capital of the Chinese Empire. Rev. Kiehn felt that this would be a strategic location in which to establish a Nazarene mission.

Already operating in Tamingfu was the South Chihli Gospel Mission under the direction of Rev. H. W. Houlding. Over the years, he had brought to China over 100 missionaries. Among them was Rev. Jacob Kohl, a Pennsylvanian who had moved to Los Angeles and there had been brought back to the Lord and sanctified under the ministry of Dr. P. F. Bresee. He joined the church and with Dr. Bresee's blessing and probably the church's financial support, he went to China and served with the South Chihli Gospel Mission. He labored diligently for 15 years, taking only one three-month furlough during that time. In this sense, he was the first Nazarene to be a missionary in China, though not serving under its board. Why he did not join up with the nearby Nazarene work in Ch'ao Ch'eng when it was begun is not known, but probably his presence in Tamingfu had something to do with the expansion of Nazarene work in that direction.

Rev. Kiehn naturally conferred with Rev. Houlding concerning his desire to launch a mission in Tamingfu and found him very responsive. In fact, he offered the Kiehns living quarters in their own large compound inside the city's west gate. The Kiehns moved there in March 1919.

In June of that year, Dr. H. F. Reynolds again visited the China field, and a major item of discussion was the newly opened mission station. Rev. Houlding offered to the Church of the Nazarene five counties north of Tamingfu that had been assigned to his mission, adding another million people to the church's responsibility. This added territory was granted on condition that the church would establish a Bible training school there as well as a hospital. With that in mind, plus the fact that Tamingfu was now near the center of the enlarged field, the decision was made to establish the mission headquarters there.

Several other factors confirmed the logic of this move. Besides being the most important city in the Nazarene territory, it was only 45 miles from the main line of the Peking-Hankow railway. Also, a strong military post was maintained in the city, which would offer some protection from bandit gangs who roamed the countryside, and also from political uprisings.

Rev. and Mrs. L. C. Osborn, of Rev. Houlding's South Chihli Gospel Mission, had already made application for transfer to the Nazarene mission board and had been officially accepted. Dr. Reynolds received them into church membership, and at the meeting of the Mission Council in Ch'ao Ch'eng, Rev. Osborn was ordained and assigned to take charge of the work there.

The church lost no time in honoring its commitment to establish a medical and educational work in Tamingfu, for the following year it sent out a number of missionaries to fill these roles. A medical doctor, Dr. R. G. Fitz, and his wife arrived, along with Rev. and Mrs. F. C. Sutherland, Rev. and Mrs. A. J. Smith, and Rev. and Mrs. H. A. Wiese. Also joining the staff was a veteran China missionary, formerly with the Mennonite mission, Miss Catherine Schmidt. She was assigned to help the Kiehns in Tamingfu while the newcomers went to language school in Peking.

Hardly had the rejoicing for this great leap forward subsided when a great famine struck that part of China. There was no rain for 13 months, and an estimated 20 million people were starving. At one point it was reported that 10,000 were dying each day of hunger or cold.

On November 27, 1920, Rev. Kiehn sent a cablegram to Kansas City: "Famine terrible. Nazarenes help." A sum of $1,000 was sent immediately, and a China Famine Relief Fund was set up to which the church people responded with contributions totaling $25,000. The significance of this amount is indicated by the fact that 3¢ a day would keep one person from starving.

Rev. Wiese and Rev. Smith were called from their language study to assist in the relief program, which was carried out in three major ways: (1) a work program; (2) a school program; and (3) grain tickets.

Just before the famine struck, a 20-acre plot of ground in the north suburb of Tamingfu had been purchased for the headquarters of the church. One of the first necessities, especially in China, was to build a wall around the property. As part of the relief program, about 500 men were employed to do the work in exchange for millet soup prepared three times a day in five large vats. The workers were housed in temporary mat sheds on the property. Here the gospel was presented to them daily. The nine-foot wall was made of mud brick reinforced with fired brick around the bottom and capped with tile to keep the rains (which eventually would come) from melting the mud bricks.

Another work project was upgrading the crooked 45-mile mule track between Tamingfu and the railroad at Hantan, into an auto road. This project, sponsored by the International Red Cross, was directed by Rev. Kiehn. Wages were paid in grain.

While the men were involved in the work projects, Mrs. Kiehn held daily classes for over 600 women, many of them young mothers with children. Canned skim milk was given to the children, which greatly improved their health.

In Ch'ao Ch'eng the International Relief Commission gave the Nazarene missionaries thousands of dollars to distribute at their discretion. Since this was a straw-braiding center, the mission bought up the output of about 1,000 women. While the women were working, they were taught to read the new phonetic script. By the end of the project, over 100 had learned to read.

Schools were established for boys who were paid five pennies a day to attend. At Ch'ao Ch'eng 400 were enrolled, and another 200 at Puchow. In Tamingfu, about 30 girls who had been sold by their parents to secure money for food, were "redeemed" by the missionaries and placed in regular classes. These girls, along with others, became the nucleus of the Nazarene Girls' School.

Besides the work and school programs, grain tickets were provided for those unable to work. The grain was furnished by the International Relief Commission. It took careful management to avoid graft and hoarding of the available supply. Rev. Wiese, who was helping Rev. Osborn at Ch'ao Ch'eng in his investigation of homes to determine actual need, wrote of his visits in over 700 homes: "We found the empty earthen vessels in which food was once kept. We found the people eating dried sweet potato leaves that had been cured to feed the stock, or eating leaves from trees."

Though the relief work taxed the strength of the missionaries and limited evangelistic activities, their unselfish, compassionate ministry broke down walls of prejudice and suspicion and paved the way for a more ready acceptance of the gospel.

In the spring of 1921 the famine was broken with the harvest of a wheat crop. The crisis past, the missionary staff was deployed to begin again their normal activities. The Fitzes and Smiths were assigned to Tamingfu, the Wieses to Puchow, the Sutherlands to Ch'eng An, and the Deales to Kuangp'ingfu. This made five stations where missionaries were in residence, the last two being new. In October 1921 Miss J. Hester Hayne, a registered nurse, and Miss Blanche Himes, a teacher for the missionaries' children, arrived on the field.

Yet another crisis arose in the summer of 1922: The Yellow River, appropriately called "China's Sorrow," breached its dikes, and large areas in the southern end of the Nazarene field were flooded. Rev. Wiese, stationed in nearby Puchow, was asked by the International Relief Commission to assist in the distribution of wages to the 10,000 men who were working to rebuild the dikes. Ten pounds of grain a day was the established payment. He personally distributed over 30,000 bags of grain. As the emergency deepened, Rev. Osborn was called from Ch'ao Ch'eng to supervise, with others, another work force of 5,000.

In the midst of the problems, God blessed the work of the missionaries. A new church building in Ch'ao Ch'eng was filled with more than 1,000 worshipers in its opening service on Christmas Day, 1921. The following week the new station at Ch'eng An, 35 miles northwest of Tamingfu, had between 400 and 500 in attendance in a revival meeting that had a profound effect on the whole town.

Education

As earlier noted, education played an important role in the missionary program from the very first. From the original 2 schools begun in Ch'ao Ch'eng in 1914, with an enrollment in the boys' school of 19 and in the girls' of 14, the number of schools had grown by 1925 to 39. This included 1 boys' high school with 40 enrolled. Total grade school enrollment was 767 boys and 201 girls. All the schools met government standards, and almost all teachers were Chinese. Bible classes and regular chapel services were what made these Nazarene schools unique. Enrollment rapidly declined after 1925, as political unrest enveloped the country. In 1928 the government ordered all mission grade schools closed.

But adult education also played an important role. Each station had separate classes for men and women, which were highly successful. Men's classes were usually held in the off-farming season, and special instruction was given to those who seemed to have the potential to become evangelists, pastors, or farmer-preachers. There was a growing recognition of the need for a central training institution to prepare pastors for the growing number of congregations.

In the first fully organized Mission Council meeting, held in late 1922, it was recommended that a Bible training school be launched, offering a two-year course for young men entering the ministry and special classes for the present national pastors. A uniform course of study for the women's classes in the various churches was also recommended, for Bible women played an important role in the Chinese church.

Thus on April 4, 1923, a Bible training school was launched at Tamingfu under the direction of Rev. F. C. Sutherland. The initial enrollment was 25. Later a women's Bible training school was begun, and by 1925 the respective enrollments were 22 and 25. Though the men's enrollment reached a peak of 35 the following year, the lack of teaching personnel coupled with unsettled conditions in the country brought a decline, and eventually the Bible schools had to be closed in 1928.

The training of preachers and Bible women continued on a tutoring basis until in 1935 the Bible school was reopened with 36 students. Reflecting the rapid growth of the church, in five years' time enrollment was up to 125 with a waiting list of 200. Sixty student evangelistic bands fanned out over the countryside on weekends.

Medical Work

Initial medical work in China consisted of the simple ministrations of Mrs. Kiehn as she sought to relieve the physical suffering of those who came to her for aid. As many as 40 were treated in one day for various ailments. It was a helpful avenue to reach into the Chinese homes. The people soon realized that the missionaries were not there to exploit them (as they had been warned the foreigners would do) but rather to serve them.

Because in those days medical facilities were few, the missionaries felt that a hospital would be of untold benefit in relieving the widespread physical suffering. At the same time it would help to open the people's hearts to the gospel message. There was also the promise made to Rev. Houlding when the five-county area north of Tamingfu was turned over to the Church of the Nazarene that a hospital would be built there. The coming of Dr. R. G. Fitz in 1920 was a confirmation of that commitment. It remained now to organize a full-fledged medical program.

Dr. Fitz spent his first year in Peking, not only in language study, but taking special courses in the Peking Union Medical College in order to qualify for full government certification. On September 10, 1921, he opened a dispensary at Tamingfu.

His first report to the Mission Council in November read in part: "In the two months which have passed, there have been 415 patients registered for treatment, 1,081 treatments given, 16 operations performed, three of which were under general anesthetic."

In 1922 a small, two-story dispensary/clinic with an operating room and a few wards was built. Miss Hester Hayne, a registered nurse, had arrived in 1921 to take charge of the nursing phase. In a short time the dispensary was treating an average of 40 people a day.

But the building of a hospital was the ultimate goal; and when Dr. Reynolds was present at the 1922 Mission Council Meeting, a building committee was set up with instructions to visit the Presbyterian mission hospital and obtain all the information they could on what would be needed.

In the meantime a group of Nazarenes in southern California had organized in 1921 the Nazarene Medical Missionary Union to promote the cause of medical missions. The need for a hospital in China became its prime interest. As president of the group, Rev. C. J. Kinne, along with William P. Trumbower, went to China to survey the situation. They visited other mission hospitals in the country and spent a week watching the operation of the dispensary/clinic at Tamingfu. They charted the number of people who came and the nature of their ailments. They noted that in the first 18 months of operation people from 579 separate villages had come for help.

When the two men returned to the United States after five months of thorough study, they were convinced that a much larger hospital was needed than their particular group could finance. They therefore proposed that it be made a churchwide project and that the institution be named in honor of Dr. P. F. Bresee. The General Board authorized the plan, and August 24-31, 1924, was set aside as a week of self-denial in which the proceeds would go toward the building of the Bresee Memorial Hospital.

Rev. Kinne was appointed superintendent of construction and returned to China that fall in time for the groundbreaking ceremonies. The first goal was to erect a central, four-story unit with men's and women's wings to be added as finances permitted.

Rev. Kinne wasted no time in assembling the necessary materials —rock cut to order from the mountains; lumber from Tientsin, 300 miles away; brick and tile from the surrounding area. An 8,000-watt electric plant came from England, and plumbing fixtures and a windmill came from the United States. The logistics of shipping all this material to the site was a complicated task in itself.

In a year's time enough of the building was completed so that on October 17, 1925, the dispensary/clinic was able to move in, and by January 1 both men's and women's wards were occupied. The first stories of both wings were enclosed so that inside finishing could proceed during the winter.

A major concern was to find an adequate water supply to serve the 100-bed hospital. A good underground water source was down there, but a layer of quicksand between it and the surface thwarted efforts to reach it. While in prayer concerning the matter, Rev. Kinne received the inspiration for a unique plan. He set the men to digging by hand a large hole 15 to 20 feet in diameter. At a depth of 20 or 25 feet and well above the quicksand level, water began to spurt into the excavation, soon creating a great pool fully adequate to serve not only the hospital but the entire mission compound in which 200 people lived. The water was pure and abundant, even in times of drought.

Dr. C. E. West was transferred from Swaziland to China when he was unable to obtain British certification in Africa, and was present for the opening of the hospital. His coming made it possible for the Fitzes to return to the United States for furlough. He served not only as doctor and medical superintendent but as pastor of the English church in Tamingfu. In February 1926 Rev. Kinne returned to the United States. Though his departure was hastened by word of his wife's failing health, she passed away just before his leaving for home.

An important phase of the hospital development was the establishment of a training school for men and women nurses, which was launched on October 22, 1926. Miss Mary Pannell, R.N., who had completed a year of language study, came to aid the limited nursing force in this new project.

In addition to the hospital work, the beleaguered medical staff also conducted field clinics in surrounding towns and villages. A Chinese preacher was always taken along to present the gospel to the crowds that gathered.

Evangelism

The heart of any missionary program is evangelism, and in this respect the China field had remarkable success, particularly during the golden years following World War I. In 1920 there was but one organized church, the one at Ch'ao Ch'eng, which had 78 members. In 1921 the Tamingfu and Ch'eng An churches were organized with 55 and 24 members respectively. By 1922 there were six churches with 213 full members, 270 probationers, and 625 enrolled in the Sunday Schools. The number of full members tripled in the next three years, and probationers more than quadrupled.

Particularly significant was the great growth in outstations.

Around Tamingfu alone there were 15 such preaching points. In all there were 35 outstations. Dr. Reynolds visited the field in 1914, 1919, and 1922-23. His enthusiasm was expressed after his 1919 visit as follows: "The outlook for an aggressive and permanent work in this great district could not be brighter. The possibilities . . . are limitless."

The decision in 1923 to open the Bible school in Tamingfu was significant, for the need for national pastors and evangelistic bands for the growing church was acute. Along with this was the organization of women's missionary societies and youth organizations.

The hospital, completed in October 1925, as did its predecessor, the dispensary/clinic, provided an open door for evangelism as each patient was confronted with the claims of the gospel. The people saw Christian love in action through the ministrations of doctors and nurses, and much of the antiforeign prejudice melted away. The selfless service of the missionaries during the crises of famine and flood in the early 1920s also opened many doors. In fact, there were more calls for services to be held in various places than could be filled.

There were reports of great spiritual breakthroughs, such as 110 being baptized in one service at Tamingfu and 590 seekers in the course of a revival meeting in Puchow. At Fanhsien, an outstation 10 miles from Ch'ao Ch'eng where special services for the women were held, between 50 and 60 sought for spiritual help. In Kan Lo, an outstation of Ch'eng An, a five-day meeting under a rented straw tent resulted in 100 conversions.

Fairs and marketplaces provided golden opportunities for evangelism, and it was a familiar sight to see the Christians distributing tracts and personally witnessing to the throngs. Tents were used in village evangelism. The meetings usually lasted four days with four services a day. Often open-air meetings were held where the slope of the land provided a natural amphitheater. One such meeting held by Rev. Wiese won 77 converts.

Laymen's evangelistic bands were organized for village evangelism. At one time 448 laymen were involved in this kind of ministry. It is little wonder that the church grew so rapidly during those golden years of 1920-25.

The Opposition

A constant threat to missionary effort was the presence of robber bands who roved the countryside. They were not opposing missionary efforts as such, but their presence struck fear in the hearts of the people so that they would not venture forth from their homes. The bandits pillaged, robbed, kidnapped for ransom, and sometimes murdered. When robber bands were known to be in the vicinity, walled cities closed their gates except for a short time during the day. The lives of missionaries, as foreigners, were particularly in danger. For two months, the Deales could not leave Kuangp'ingfu.

This situation of anarchy was heightened when the founder of the Chinese republic, Sun Yat-sen, died in 1925. With that came a great power struggle. Warlords who represented remnants of the old Manchu dynasty, which had been deposed in 1911, seized the opportunity to assert themselves. In early 1926 Dr. West reported that four large armies were fighting each other for supremacy in the area of the Nazarene field. Government forces were inadequate to quell the insurrectionists.

When Nationalist armies confronted the army of warlord Feng T'ien at Tamingfu, the mission hospital became a busy place caring for the wounded. The missionary personnel of both hospital and school were pressed into service to meet the emergency.

In their usual fashion, the Marxists, accurately dubbed the "scavengers of revolutions," moved into the situation. Calling the attention of the people to the special concessions given to foreigners after the Boxer Rebellion (always a lingering sore spot), they stirred up animosity against all outsiders except, of course, the Russians. Chinese Christians, naturally loyal to the missionaries, suffered severe persecution.

Undaunted, the missionaries and their faithful church members moved on with their activities. On May 30, 1926, a beautiful new church was dedicated at Ch'eng An. The building was made possible by a $1,000 gift from William Trumbower, the California layman who had worked with Rev. C. J. Kinne in the planning of the hospital at Tamingfu. And when the Mission Council met in September 1926, they reported that despite the persecution "there is a greater demand for preachers and teachers to be sent to the villages for opening new work than we are able to supply. . . . The awakened interest and desire create an urgent demand for more missionaries."

In the early summer of 1926 an epidemic of smallpox had broken out; and among the victims was Dr. West, the only doctor at the Tamingfu hospital. For days he hung between life and death. While lying helpless on his hospital bed, the Lord laid on him a burden for spiritual revival among both the missionaries and the Chinese. He promised God that if he were healed, he would give himself to deep intercession for revival.

Almost instantly healed, Dr. West returned to his heavy duties at the hospital. But he also spent many hours a day in prayer and, for one two-week period, fasted as well, eating only a little fruit once a day. Other missionaries joined him in intercession and heart-searching. The result was a glorious visitation of the Spirit that swept away interpersonal problems and inspired the entire Nazarene community to renewed evangelistic endeavor.

The revival spread from Tamingfu to Ch'ao Ch'eng and other stations. A spirit of confession, contrition, and intense seeking for a deeper relationship with God prevailed. The Chinese testified that they now had *je hsin* ("hot hearts"). The revival continued for several months.

On March 18, 1927, Rev. Osborn wrote of the happenings at Ch'ao Ch'eng as follows: "Praise God for a mighty revival in our midst! It began over three months ago. For over three weeks there was no definite preaching, though four long meetings were held practically every day. One Sunday morning over 100 seekers were at the altar. . . . The Chinese church is shouldering responsibility and pushing forward as never before."

In less than a month from that date a political crisis erupted. The United States Consulate ordered all the missionaries to go to the coastal cities for safety. Leaving the work in charge of the national leaders including Dr. Chu at the hospital, the 13 Nazarene missionaries set out for Tientsin. They arrived on April 9, after miraculously reaching the railroad at Hantan just in time to catch the only train that had passed through in two weeks. It was also to be the last one for many more weeks.

Because of the uncertain future, it was decided to bring back to the United States six of the missionaries whose furloughs would soon be due. This included the A. J. Smiths, and Misses Blanche Himes, Ida Vieg, Glennie Sims, and Hester Hayne. The Osborns and Deales, along with Dr. C. E. West and Misses Mary Pannell and Margaret Needles, remained in Tientsin, working as they were able in Christian activities. One of their ministries was among U.S. Marines stationed there.

Meanwhile, the Nationalist government, still somewhat anti-foreign in sentiment, ordered the registration of all private (including mission) schools. They passed a law that prohibited making study of the Bible and chapel attendance mandatory. It also required the display of a large picture of Gen. Sun Yat-sen in the assembly hall, with a three-minute period of silence to be observed in his honor each week. Rather than concede to these orders, the mission schools were closed in 1928.

Rev. Osborn was allowed to make periodic trips to Tamingfu to check on the work, to advise and encourage the people, and to take money to them. Although he discovered that as many as 1,000 soldiers had occupied the mission compound at one time, the buildings were comparatively undamaged.

On his third trip in, Rev. Osborn and a Chinese pastor with him were arrested by the Nationalists as spies and held captive for 19 days in a Roman Catholic church in Kaichow. Their imprisonment was a blessing in disguise, for while they were in custody at Kaichow, a contingent of the northern rebel army stormed the mission compound at Puchow, demanding a large sum of money from "the foreigner." They had doubtless heard that Rev. Osborn was scheduled to visit the station. The only damage inflicted was the bursting of a bomb on the roof of the dining hall.

By the summer of 1928 Generalissimo Chiang Kai-shek had successfully established his government in Peking. Rev. Kiehn, who had been sent back to China to appraise the situation, recommended to the General Board that since the political climate now seemed stable, the missionary activities shouuld be resumed. Accordingly, the missionaries were returned in the late summer of 1928, over a year after they had been evacuated. Miss Needles did not return, however, for in the interim she had married a Methodist missionary, Rev. Horace Williams. Also Dr. West had returned to the United States to attend the 1928 General Assembly. However, the Kiehns and C. J. Kinne had returned to China, and with the Osborns, the Deales, and Miss Pannell they took up their various posts in the interior. They were warmly received. All except the Osborns, who returned to Ch'ao Ch'eng, were stationed at Tamingfu.

The Rebuilding Years

Rev. Kinne set to work immediately to complete construction of the hospital. On October 30, 1929, Dr. and Mrs. Fitz returned, and they were a great help in bringing about the completion of the building project, all the while working in the medical program as well. The construction work was completed in the spring of 1930. The Wieses had also returned in the fall of 1929, though not yet under official appointment, and his expertise in electrical work was put to good use in that important phase of the building program. Also added to the missionary force as bookkeeper and accountant was Miss Catherine Flagler, who had been serving in China under the National Holiness Association.

At the annual meeting of the China District on June 21, 1929, all the Chinese workers and delegates from the 31 main stations and outstations were present. The national leaders were showing fine capability in the management of church affairs.

In late 1929 General Superintendents R. T. Williams and J. W. Goodwin visited the China field and brought great inspiration and encouragement to the workers. In the course of their visit they dedicated the Bresee Memorial Hospital (though it was not fully completed) and the E. F. Walker Memorial Church in Kuangp'ingfu. They also participated in the graduation exercises on November 11 of the first class of nurses from the hospital nursing school.

In 1930 Miss Myrl Thompson, R.N., arrived in China and went to Peking for a year of language study so that she would be ready to take the place of Miss Pannell, who was due for furlough the following year.

Evangelism was given renewed emphasis, and soon many baptisms were being reported. The use of tents was particularly effective, and eight were in use throughout the district. In the fall of 1930 a large tent came as a special gift from the United States and proved to be a great help. More calls for meetings were coming in than could be filled. The churches were flourishing as before.

The momentum was to be slowed once again, however, this time by the depression, which drastically reduced the funds available for the work. Missionary activity was reduced to somewhat of a holding pattern. Though many of the Chinese workers had to seek secular employment, the pastors, for the most part, continued their work, though on a reduced scale.

During the summer of 1931 the missionary force, except for the Fitzes, was forced to evacuate once again to Tientsin. It was felt that in Dr. Fitz's position he would be the least likely to be molested. Furthermore, as it turned out, his presence on the mission property helped to protect it from potential looting and damage.

As was feared, a bandit gang of 1,000, led by their chief, Black Heart, seized the walled city of Tamingfu. Orders were issued to bring

Dr. Fitz in from the Nazarene compound outside the north wall of the city as a hostage. Twice Dr. Fitz refused to leave. Fortunately, by night-fall government troops had moved into the mission compound. This provided some protection for the missionaries but also made it a bat-tleground. An eight-inch shell crashed into a bedroom of the Fitz home, but miraculously Mrs. Fitz, Elizabeth, and Baby Guilford were not killed.

The Fitz family took refuge in the basement along with six or seven Chinese families until the shelling ceased about 10 days later. Through the treachery of disloyal Chinese, Black Heart and his band were able to escape. Once more the missionaries returned to their posts.

In January 1933, Rev. Kiehn asked to be relieved of the super-intendency of the field, and Rev. Harry Wiese was elected in his place. In the meantime Miss Hester Hayne had graduated from medical school and now was ready to return as an M.D. to the hospital. After two years' internship at the Peking Union Medical College, she took up her duties in 1936. Also in 1934 Dr. and Mrs. Henry Wesche, who were operating a clinic for the NHA 25 miles from Tamingfu (she as a nurse), offered their services to the hospital on a part-time basis. Their schedule was three weeks per month in the hospital and one at their own clinic. In 1939 they began full-time work at the hospital.

Another staff addition in the fall of 1934 was Miss Bertie Karns, who was assigned to teach the missionaries' children, thus releasing their mothers for more active participation in the missionary pro-gram. She had already served a term (1919-23) in Japan.

In 1935 Dr. J. B. Chapman, general superintendent, and Mrs. Chapman visited the field. While there Dr. Chapman challenged the national leaders to become self-supporting and thus achieve district status. The depression years, when funds from abroad had been greatly reduced, had shown the people how well they could function on their own. A related need was to reopen the Bible school, which was done in September of that year with an enrollment of 40.

Missionary efforts received the unqualified support of Gener-alissimo and Madame Chiang Kai-shek, who in a series of meetings with missionaries in each provincial capital paid generous tribute to what they had done for their country. The generalissimo asked for missionary support of the New Life Campaign, a program to lift the moral life of China. The goal was to stamp out the evils of opium, gambling, and prostitution.

By 1935 there were 22 organized churches plus 32 outstations. Full membership had reached 1,321 with 547 probationers. There were 13 missionaries and 72 national workers. Once again momentum was building, and although wary eyes were cast to the north where Japan had occupied Manchuria (1931) and threatened further conquest, there was no thought of holding back.

In 1936 Dr. Hester Hayne's return made it possible for the Fitzes to leave for a much overdue furlough. Also the Osborns and Miss Thompson furloughed, and Miss Karns returned to Japan. But taking their places were the returning Sutherlands, the Pattees, and Miss Rhoda Schurman. Rev. and Mrs. Geoffrey Royall, who had spent a year as missionaries in western China, were also in the party that sailed for China on September 12. Shortly after their arrival, Mrs. Susan Fitkin and Miss Emma Word, president and secretary of the Nazarene Women's Missionary Society, visited the field.

At the annual council meeting in 1936 a program for attaining self-support was set up by which churches that had been in operation seven years could start weaning away from outside support. With membership rising substantially and Bible school enrollment up to 55, the missionaries were full of optimism and requested three new missionary couples and three single ladies. This call became more urgent when in the spring of 1937, Miss Ida Vieg passed away, a victim of cancer. She was buried in the mission compound in Tamingfu, the first and only China missionary to die on the field.

The Japanese Invasion

In July 1937 the shots fired at Marco Polo Bridge near Peking signaled the invasion of China proper by the Japanese. At the time, several of the Nazarene missionaries were on vacation at Peitaiho near the coast. These were Dr. and Mrs. Wesche, the Pattees, the Kiehns, the Royalls, and Miss Schurman. Because of the new danger, they proceeded to Tientsin. At Tamingfu were Dr. Hester Hayne, the Wieses, the Sutherlands, and Misses Flagler and Pannell.

On August 22 the American consul general in Hankow warned the missionaries of possible military action in their area and suggested they withdraw to places of safety if possible. Four successive telegrams were sent to them, each more urgent than the preceding one. To fail to follow the consul's advice meant to forfeit American protection and aid.

In the meantime, full-scale preparations were made on the Tamingfu station in case of attack—dugouts built, fire-fighting equipment prepared, and air raid drills conducted. Five large United States flags flew from high posts, and flags painted on reed mats were placed on the roofs of various buildings.

The first bombs hit the nearby Tamingfu airport on Sunday morning, October 10, 1937. When a more severe attack came on Tuesday, evacuation of the missionaries seemed judicious. The Wieses, however, chose to remain to do what they could to protect the property. The Kiehns up at Ch'eng An also remained at their post.

At 6 A.M. Wednesday morning, the 13th, the Sutherlands with their five children, Dr. Hayne, and Misses Pannell and Flagler set out on foot for the coastal city of Tsingtao, 300 miles away. After a harrowing 13 days they reached their destination, covering the last part of the journey by train. Miss Flagler was ill and overdue for furlough, so she sailed for the United States on November 13. When the fall of Tsingtao also seemed imminent, the rest of the group moved up the coast to Tientsin where the other missionaries were waiting.

The Japanese forces advanced relentlessly down the Peking-Hankow railroad; and Hantan, 45 miles north of Tamingfu, fell on October 16. The army advanced to Ch'eng An where Rev. and Mrs. Peter Kiehn were stationed. The invaders met stiff resistance there and lost 200 men, so retreated momentarily. The next day, with an augmented force, they stormed the city and in revenge killed 2,000 men—almost every civilian man inside the city walls. Among them was Mr. Lu, dean of the Nazarene Bible school, which was now closed. The Peter Kiehns and all the Christians who had taken refuge in the Nazarene compound outside the city walls escaped unharmed.

Meanwhile the Wieses in Tamingfu prepared their basement bomb shelter for the expected attack, the same room the Fitzes used at the time of the bandit attack. It was only 6 × 14 feet with a 6-foot ceiling, yet as many as 20 people were crowded into it for safety at one time.

The major attack came on November 10. From 9 in the morning until 4:30 in the afternoon there was the constant roar of planes overhead and the bursting of bombs. The main points of attack were the airport, a quarter of a mile to the north, the army barracks to the west, the normal school to the east, and the walled city to the south. No bombs fell on the mission compound itself.

Should the missionaries try to escape before the army arrived? As they prayed, the scripture came to Rev. Wiese, "Stand still, and see the salvation of the Lord" (Exod. 14:13, KJV). The direction was clear that he should stay, but at three o'clock in the morning of November 11, under cover of darkness, Mrs. Wiese and the children set out on foot for Ch'ao Ch'eng, which, at the moment, was out of the line of battle. The journey took two days, but with the help of friends they made it safely.

The night of the 11th the Japanese ground forces reached Tamingfu. They knocked down a section of the mission wall, and a contingent marched through the compound. There was no sign of life, so, firing some random shots into the Wiese house, they marched on. The little group huddled in the basement heaved a sigh of relief.

A few days later Rev. Wiese ventured forth to survey the situation. The city was obviously in Japanese hands, and the missionary knew that sooner or later he would have to make his presence known. Carefully he made his way to the military headquarters inside the city and introduced himself to the Japanese officials. He found them quite congenial and received their permission to carry on his missionary activities. One of the first things he did was to go and get his family at Ch'ao Ch'eng. It was none too soon, for on December 9 bombs began to fall there, and the large church in the mission compound was destroyed along with one of the missionary homes.

Because of the unsettled conditions, village evangelism was curtailed, but Rev. Wiese conducted all-day Bible classes on the Tamingfu mission compound. Later these were cut down to half-day sessions with a special emphasis on holiness. The missionaries in Tientsin kept busy with language study, conducting Bible classes, and holding services. The national pastors, for the most part, stayed at their posts through all the turmoil. Some reported a spiritual deepening as the people were forced to a greater trust in God.

In March, Rev. Sutherland and Rev. Royall ventured back to Tamingfu to see what the conditions were. With Rev. Wiese they paid a short visit to Ch'ao Ch'eng. While there they arranged for roof repairs on the salvageable buildings to protect them from the elements until permanent repairs could be made. They were also able to transfer money to the area pastors who had received no financial support for three months.

Conditions stabilized sufficiently that Misses Schurman and Pannell, Dr. Hayne, and Rev. Pattee were able to return to Tamingfu for Easter services. One by one all the others went back to their posts except the Wesches, who sailed for the United States on furlough. In the early fall of 1938, Rev. and Mrs. Osborn returned from furlough, and with them was Miss Evelyn Eddy, a new missionary nurse, who enrolled in language school in Peking. A revival spirit prevailed among the churches as once more the missionary program began to roll. The reopened hospital was ministering to 250 patients a month and administering thousands of cholera injections. The nurses' training program was also reopened.

The Kiehns, who had been laboring at Ch'eng An in the northwest part of the field for almost 10 years, returned to the United States when two of their children graduated from high school that summer.

On September 22, 1938, the 13 remaining missionaries met for their first council meeting in two years. The theme was Thanksgiving —praise for God's protection during the hostilities, for the minimal damage sustained to mission property, for the way the lives of the Christians had been spared (at most only 12 had been killed), for the return of the Osborns, and for Miss Eddy's coming.

For the two-year period, 8,000 gospel services had been held, with 867 converts and 193 baptisms in the 51 churches and preaching points. People involved in evangelistic bands numbered 448, and 108 had enrolled in the Bible school when it was reopened in the fall of 1938 under the leadership of Rev. Sutherland. The number could have been much higher had there been room.

Though it was not safe for the women to go out on evangelistic trips, 20 of the men students, organized into five teams, went out into the countryside during the one-month Chinese New Year break. They held services in 133 villages with a total of 22,156 attending the open-air meetings. There were 86 new converts besides many others who experienced spiritual revival.

In early May there was a unique visit to the field by Rev. Hiroshi Kitagawa and his brother Shiro from Japan. When the people of the Japanese church heard of the destruction of the Ch'ao Ch'eng church by Japanese bombs, they took up an offering of 350 yen to help in the rebuilding of it. These brethren were personally delivering the offering as an expression of Christian love. While there the visitors, accompanied by three of the missionaries, called on the captain of the Japanese garrison in the city and were graciously received. The captain spoke highly of Rev. Wiese's work.

In the fall of 1939 Dr. and Mrs. Wesche returned from furlough, and with them were Mr. and Mrs. Arthur Moses. Mr. Moses was to be business manager of the hospital, while his wife, a registered nurse, would assist the overworked hospital staff. In an extensive report of the work in China, Rev. Osborn indicated that missionary activity was apparently back in full swing. "Our hearts are welling up within us as to what God is doing in our midst," he wrote. Then, in the spring of 1940, the Wieses went home on furlough, having been in China over 10 years in their second term.

Because of visa complications, Michael and Elizabeth (Fitz) Varro, who were under appointment to China, were unable to go as scheduled, but Miss Mary Scott did make the journey. Arriving on September 12, she entered language school at Peking.

A month later, as the missionaries were gathered for their annual council meeting, the American consul, who was closely monitoring political conditions, sent a message advising that all who were not absolutely essential to the work should return to the United States. By this time the missionaries were somewhat inured to such warnings and were reluctant to go. However, they realized the importance of setting up a complete contingency plan with the Chinese leaders in case evacuation of missionaries became necessary.

By March 1941 conditions were such that it was deemed wise to return a large number of missionaries: Rev. and Mrs. Sutherland, Rev. and Mrs. Royall, Mrs. Pattee, Mrs. Moses, Mrs. Wesche, Dr. Hayne, and Misses Schurman, Pannell, and Eddy. Despite the departure of most of the hospital staff, eight Chinese nurses, six men and two women, completed their studies and graduated from the nurses' training school on May 12.

In July a very talented Chinese lady doctor, Dr. Liu, joined the hospital staff. With the medical program curtailed by the departure of the missionary nursing staff, Dr. Wesche decided to return to the United States. Dr. Liu carried on heroically until the hospital was forced to close its doors in the latter part of December.

It was with mixed emotions that the five remaining missionaries, Rev. and Mrs. Osborn, Rev. Pattee, Mr. Moses, and Miss Mary Scott, met for the annual council meeting in September 1941. On one hand, the reports were encouraging: 54 organized churches and 91 out-stations were in operation with 2,120 full members and 3,412 proba-tioners; 42,000 Gospel portions and 50,000 tracts had been distrib-uted; 130 students were enrolled in the Bible school, and 5,300 patients had been in the hospital. But on the other hand, a cloud of apprehension hung over them as they planned for the future.

On the morning of December 8 (December 7 in the United

States) a Japanese officer arrived on the mission compound to announce that Japan and the United States were at war, and as enemy aliens, the missionaries were put under arrest. They were given two hours to pack two suitcases and a bedding roll apiece and then were escorted into the city. The men were taken to the military police headquarters and the two ladies to the Mennonite missionary compound, where they found 11 others being held. Rev. Pattee and Mr. Moses were released after 2 days to join the other missionaries, but Rev. Osborn was held for 36 days undergoing repeated interrogation but not being physically harmed.

By the time Rev. Osborn was finally released and taken to the Mennonite compound, only three Mennonite missionaries were left plus the five Nazarenes. They settled into a routine of Bible reading, prayer, and study, preparing their own twice-a-day meals. Finally, on June 5, 1942, Rev. and Mrs. Osborn, Rev. Pattee, and one of the Mennonite missionaries were taken to the coast and put on board the repatriation ship, *Gripsholm*. Then in September the remaining four, Rev. and Mrs. Brown (Mennonites), Miss Scott, and Mr. Moses, were transferred to the Oriental Missionary Society compound in Peking, where they were united with several other missionaries whom they had previously known.

This pleasant association, even under a prisonlike situation, was broken when all the missionaries were transferred to a civilian internee camp in Weihsien, Shantung, about 100 miles inland from the port of Tsingtao. In September 1943 Mr. Moses was selected to return on the second *Gripsholm* repatriation trip, while Miss Scott remained a prioner of war until liberated by American parachutists on August 17, 1945.

Post-World War II Developments

With the signing of the surrender documents and the withdrawal of Japanese troops from China, hopes were high that the missionaries would once more be able to return and pursue their work. Dr. C. Warren Jones, Foreign Missions secretary, stated that not only was the church planning to rehabilitate the former field but also "to open another 1,000 miles from the old field." As it turned out, the second option was the only one open.

Unknown to all, as the Chinese troops were being pushed south by the invading Japanese, opportunistic Communist guerrillas, called the Eighth Route Army, had been moving in to consolidate their positions in the north and east sections of China, especially in the rural areas. When the Japanese troops were withdrawn in 1945, these Communists, with Soviet support, were almost immediately in control of most of the northeast part of the country, including the Nazarene field.

Rev. Wiese and Rev. Pattee left for China on May 8, 1946, on a fact-finding mission to determine what course of action should be taken. While still in Tientsin they were visited by one of the pastors, Chia Ju Tso, who told them what had been happening. Throughout the war, the churches had continued to operate, as members of the evangelistic bands filled in for pastors who had been taken away. Many new preaching places had been started as well, principally house churches. But now, under the Communists, the churches were undergoing severe persecution. Pastors were being imprisoned, and two were known to have been killed.

At Peking Rev. Wiese and Rev. Pattee were advised not to attempt to go to Tamingfu. Other missionaries who had tried the same kind of exploratory trip had been arrested and imprisoned, and only strong protest from the American consul got them released.

It was decided that Rev. Pattee would make a secret trip in, confer with the church leaders, and hopefully get back out before any action could be taken against him. It was the opinion of the Chinese pastors that the presence of foreigners, particularly Americans, would only aggravate their situation. If they were going to be permitted to carry on at all, they would have to go it alone.

From that time, communication with the Nazarene work in the North steadily diminished. What fragmentary reports did filter through were ominous and discouraging. "Some are suffering, and others will be called upon to give their lives for their testimony," wrote Rev. Wiese in 1948. "Any moment . . . you can be sure that one or more of our preachers will not only be in prison but be in a torture chamber or hung up by a rope tied to the hands, which are joined behind the back—a most painful way to be hung up."

It was reported that when Pastor Chia returned to Tamingfu after conferring with Rev. Wiese and Rev. Pattee in Tientsin earlier, he was jailed and finally executed. The accusation was that he had conferred with a foreigner—an American. All the leading pastors had been brought to trial and punished time and again for refusing to give up their ministry. At least two and possible several more were reported to have been executed.

b. Southern Field

With the northern field indefinitely closed, it was now the task to explore possibilities for a new location in South China, the option already proposed. There were two prime considerations: (1) to choose a place not likely to come under Communist rule, and (2) to find an area where the mandarin or northern dialect was used, so the missionaries would not have a language problem. (Of the many dialects in China, the major ones are Mandarin, principally in the North, and Cantonese in the South.) On Rev. Wiese and Rev. Pattee was laid the task of choosing the location.

In initial correspondence with the National Christian Council in Shanghai, four possible areas were proposed, of which two were selected by the Nazarene missionaries for final study, one in Szechuan Province and the other in Kiangsi. Several weeks were spent in examining every aspect of the situation—terrain, people, climate, accessibility, religious backgrounds, availability of property, and so on. Neither area was without its problems, but when all factors were carefully weighed, Kiangsi was selected.

When the purpose of the missionaries' investigation became known, people in the area from all walks of life expressed their delight and urged the missionaries to come. Chinese officials were extremely cooperative. Instead of the missionaries being called "foreign devils," as was done in the North, they were almost venerated here. The people knew that they had come not to exploit them but rather to help them, and so were quick to express their feelings accordingly.

The city of Kian was targeted for the starting point. There were unexpected problems in securing adequate buildings, and the rented quarters the two missionary families had to move into left much to be desired. Also, the first services in August 1947 had to be held in a rented salt shop 12 × 22 feet in size.

Nevertheless 98 were in attendance at the opening service, and even more the second Sunday. Being 750 miles south of the original field also placed them in a warmer climate, and August temperatures were high. The little salt shop was like an oven, but the people were reluctant to leave when the services were over. They lingered to ask questions, discuss the Scriptures, and learn songs. Rev. Wiese wished he had a tent that would seat 500, for he was sure it would be filled every night.

Shortly afterward, the Pattees moved to Kanhsien, a city about

100 miles south, to open up another station. This had once been a Methodist center, and a number of former members of that mission were among the 100 or so who began attending the Nazarene services.

There was great rejoicing when two Chinese pastors from the original North field succeeded in escaping the Communist net and made their way safely to Kian. They were a great help in launching the new work. They also brought firsthand reports of what life was like under Communist rule. Up to that time, at least, the church was carrying on.

Two weeks before Christmas, Rev. and Mrs. Michael Varro and Misses Ruth Brickman and Mary Scott arrived on the field after an arduous journey inland from Shanghai—two days by train and three by truck. Mrs. Varro, daughter of Dr. and Mrs. Fitz, knew the language, as did Miss Scott, but Miss Brickman had to go to language school at Wu Han. Rev. Varro picked up the language with the special help of his wife as he remained actively involved in the work.

The Christmas program in Kian was a red-letter event. A hall rented for the occasion was packed with an audience of 2,000. During the program, Pastor Yu presented a powerful message on "Peace, and the Prince of Peace."

By March 1, 1948, the Kian congregation moved into its new tabernacle with 355 attending the opening service. Notably, leading citizens of the city were being reached, with businessmen, bankers, and teachers numbered among the converts. Six whole families were won in the opening months of the work.

On April 2 Dr. and Mrs. R. G. Fitz and their son Guilford sailed for China. Dr. Fitz conducted revival meetings in both Kian and Kanhsien with a good response.

A prime need was the establishment of a Bible training school, and though a campus was not yet available, classes were begun at the mission compound in Kian on October 12, 1948. There were 26 students enrolled.

That year the NWMS raised almost $75,000 to be used for a Bible school in the field, to be named the Fitkin Bible Training School. About $6,500 was used for the purchase of land and the building of the wall. However, because of the Communist takeover, no buildings were erected. The amount remaining in the fund was parceled out to various education projects in other fields, including $24,000 to the

Bible school in Japan and lesser amounts to the Philippines, British Honduras (Belize), Lebanon, and Swaziland.

In November 1948 Dr. Orval J. Nease, general superintendent, visited the field, and there was eager response to his messages. At the Sunday morning service 400 were in attendance, and 20 seekers bowed at the altar at the close. In the afternoon, John Ch'i was ordained by Dr. Nease, and the elder's orders of Rev. Yu and Rev. Ma were recognized. These, with Rev. Hsu, who had been ordained by Dr. Williams in North China in 1929, formed the core of the national leadership for the new field.

But while Dr. Nease was still in Kian, the first warning came from the American consul that the Communist armies were once more on the move against Chiang Kai-shek and his Nationalist forces. Their obvious intent was to seize control of all of China. Evacuation of all possible personnel, especially women and children, was advised. There was opportunity to discuss with Dr. Nease what should be done and to work out plans of action in the various possible contingencies. The earlier experience in the North gave some idea of what might be expected.

The initial move was to follow the consul's advice and proceed with a partial evacuation. Thus, on December 8, 1948, Mrs. Varro and her three children, Mrs. Pattee and her daughter Grace, Mrs. Wiese and her two children, and Guilford Fitz left for the coast and there boarded a ship for the United States.

The seven remaining missionaries—Dr. and Mrs. Fitz, Misses Scott and Brickman, and Revs. Wiese, Pattee, and Varro—planned to stay as long as conditions allowed. The agreement was that when the Communists crossed the Yangtze River, 150 miles to the north, it was time to get out.

Evangelistic work continued in the cities and villages but with a heightened sense of urgency. On April 17, 1949, 27 were baptized at Kian, among them a prominent businessman, Mr. Chou. The Bible school was enjoying a good year, and an outstation had been opened at Yu Tu, a Buddhist stronghold.

A second warning came from the American consul, but the missionaries were hoping to hold out until the end of the school year. However, a cablegram came from Dr. Nease on May 4, in which he advised the missionaries to put into effect immediately the evacuation procedures agreed upon. Quickly the necessary steps were taken to leave. Instructions were given to the national leaders, last-minute packing was done, and the 1946 Ford that had been purchased for just such an emergency was readied for departure.

On the morning of May 11 the Chinese Christians and the missionaries gathered around the automobile for a farewell prayer together. Committing each other to God's care, the missionaries, with heavy hearts, set off on the 150-mile journey westward to the nearest railroad leading down to Canton. The railroad to the north, though closer, was already cut off. A month and a half later the Communists occupied Kian.

When the missionaries left, there were 70 full members and 200 probationers in two fully organized churches and three preaching points. (One of the latter, Yu Tu, was organized after the missionaries left.) It is estimated that between 400 and 500 converts had been won.

Scant information was received concerning this field after the departure of the missionaries. In 1950 word came through that the Bible school was still in operation with Rev. Hsu as the head. The enrollment was 53. All five stations were still in operation with the same pastors. One report indicated that eight converts had been baptized.

The abortive 21-month effort to make a fresh start in South China was costly, but it could not be written off as a wasted investment. Indeed there was unmistakable evidence that the work continued under national prearranged leadership. As in the North, however, there was mounting pressure from the Communist authorities, who were bent on snuffing out all religious activity.

c. *The Bamboo Curtain Falls*

By late 1949 the Communist takeover of the China mainland was complete. Chiang Kai-shek and the remnant of his army, along with thousands of refugees, had escaped to the island of Taiwan. There they confidently awaited the opportunity to return to the mainland and oust the Communists. As the years passed, however, such a hope gradually faded and a new Republic of China took form and prospered on the island.

Meanwhile, on October 1, 1949, Mao Tse-tung became president and supreme dictator of China with Chou En-lai as premier. The storied Bamboo Curtain was drawn, behind which China was to remain in almost complete isolation from the rest of the world for a quarter of a century. Heavy censorship shrouded the stories of what was actually taking place, though hints of repressive and harsh control measures were widespread.

By 1965 things were not going well, and Mao launched the highly touted Cultural Revolution in an effort to bring the country back into line with hard-line communism. Three years of near civil war forced him to back off, and instead the military took over with generals as heads of state in three out of every four provinces. By 1969 there began a softening of relationships with other countries and, at the same time, a growing cleavage with the Soviet Union.

Though a significant breakthrough came with the visit of President Nixon to China in 1972, it was the 1976 deaths of Mao and Chou and the ensuing internal power struggle that changed China's course.

Visitors to China became a common sight but only in highly controlled areas. Much of China was still cut off from the outside world. Yet more and more the veil was being lifted.

The Church Survives

The big question was: Had the church survived in these years of upheaval and isolation? For many years gospel radio programs had been beamed into China from powerful shortwave stations, but there was virtually no way of knowing whether they were being heard. Had atheistic communism been successful in snuffing out the Christian message? Specifically, was the Church of the Nazarene still functioning in North and South China? Bob Sutherland, son of the former missionaries Rev. and Mrs. F. C. Sutherland, wanted to find out the answers.

Through a contact made with a travel agent by Bob's brother-in-law, it was learned that a trip into the interior might be possible, so negotiations were begun to make the journey. A party was organized including two of Bob's brothers, John and Frank; two sisters, Margaret and Ellen; and one of the Wiese girls, Pauline (now Mrs. Morse), all of whom had lived in China as children. Invited to join them were Dr. Guy Nees, World Mission director; Dr. Don Owens, regional director; Rev. Jack Holstead, superintendent in Hong Kong; and Rev. John Pattee, the last missionary to have had contact with Chinese Nazarenes.

In November 1982 the group entered the country through Hong Kong and proceeded to Peking (now called Beijing). From there they set out by train with a government guide for Han Dan, the nearest railhead for tourists from their ultimate goal of Da Ming (Tamingfu), 50 miles farther on. But at Han Dan the officials refused to let the group continue on the basis that Da Ming had not been cleared for tourists, and the group did not have the required special permits to go there. After considerable fruitless haggling during which the authorities became increasingly adamant, the party was finally hustled onto a midnight train headed back to Canton. It was particularly frustrating to the five Sutherlands, who at that point were only 10 miles from Ch'eng An, the city where their parents had been stationed in the early 1920s.

But the party was in Han Dan long enough to discover a former Nazarene church there. It was now a "Three Selfs" church, but still visible on the wall behind the pulpit was the painted motto in Chinese characters: "Holiness unto Jehovah." The pastor, Mrs. Wu, was not there, but it was reliably reported that there were at least 30 places in that county alone where services were being held, most of them in homes.

In 1983 Irma Fitz Deale, daughter of Dr. and Mrs. R. G. Fitz, who had grown up in Da Ming and was still fluent in Mandarin Chinese, began teaching English at the Chang Chun Geological College in what was once Manchuria. Through the persistent efforts of the friendly president of the college, the way was cleared for her to visit the city of her birth "for a few hours."

Accompanied by the foreign affairs officer from the college, she made the historic journey in the spring of 1984. She was able to take a few pictures of the old mission compound where she had lived as a girl and also parts of the city itself. The ancient wall had been torn down, but the original gates remained. Most importantly, she made the warm acquaintance of Miss Huang, magistrate of the city and county.

In the spring of 1985 Irma wrote to Miss Huang and asked if she could make another visit. She was cordially invited to do so. This time she ventured to ask if she could return in the fall and bring her sister Maxine (now Mrs. Henry Fritz) from the United States.

Thus in September 1985 the two women, with the genial cooperation of the foreign affairs officers assigned to them, were given a red-carpet welcome to Da Ming. They were able to explore in much greater depth than Irma alone had been able to do. The original Nazarene compound, which was now a county headquarters, was greatly changed, but several of the original buildings were recognizable. The hospital, now "a little decrepit looking," was apparently being used as an apartment house.

The women wanted desperately to contact any of the Christians who might still be around, but did not know how to go about it. It could arouse suspicion with the authorities. But while they were taking pictures of a former Mennonite church (now a warehouse hidden behind a newer building), an old man stepped out from the ever-present crowd of curious onlookers and said, "Ping An, Ah-li-lu-ya!" ("Peace, Hallelujah!") He was a former member of that church and still a Christian. He remembered having been treated by Dr. Fitz in the Nazarene hospital. Soon others stepped forward, including Mr. Chang, the son of a seamstress who once did work for the Fitzes.

Quickly the web of acquaintances grew as the word spread as to who these American visitors really were. Among them was Li Mo-si, son of the former gatekeeper on the Nazarene compound. He named off all the former missionaries and inquired about each. That evening he brought with him Wang Yu-shen, son of the Fitzes' cook, and the four shared happy reminiscences. "There are many, many Christians here," the visitors were told.

Although it has been difficult to obtain accurate statistics, the Chinese Church Research Center in Hong Kong estimated in 1985 that there were 30 million Christians in China as against only 1 million when the Communists took over in 1949. Some unofficial estimates ran as high as 60 million Christians. No wonder a government newspaper confirmed a "Protestant revival fever" throughout China. Two new churches a day were being opened in China, and literally thousands were reported to be turning to Christ daily.

What this portended for the future of the Church of the Nazarene in China could only be conjectured. There was every evidence, however, that the door of opportunity to reach the most populous nation in the world with the gospel was once more at hand. Even though probably no missionaries could be sent, the foundation for a strong national Christian church, under whatever name, was already in place.

2. *Taiwan*

One hundred miles off the southeast coast of mainland China lies the subtropical island of Taiwan, named originally in 1590 by Portuguese sailors Ihla Formosa ("Island Beautiful"). The name stuck even though the island fell under the influence of Dutch and Spanish traders in the 1600s, then passed under Chinese influence until finally won by the Japanese in 1895. The latter's defeat in World War II brought the island back under Chinese control, and only then did the name Taiwan ("Terraced Bay") displace the original Formosa.

Dutch Reformed missionaries were the first to bring the gospel to the island. From 1627 to 1664 they labored with good success, reportedly winning 6,000 converts. But the ruthless warrior Koxinga (of Japanese and Chinese extraction) exterminated the missionaries and their converts, and for 200 years a state of anarchy existed; the Chinese influence was finally confirmed in 1885, when the island became officially a province of China. There followed an extensive migration from the mainland.

Though after the Sino-Japanese War in 1895 the Japanese won control of the island, the Chinese population outnumbered the Japanese five to one. Shortly before and during World War II the flow of Chinese from the mainland was stopped by the Japanese, but it picked up again after the surrender. (At the same time, the Japanese residents were deported to their home islands.)

In 1949 Taiwan became the refuge of Chiang Kai-shek's retreating Nationalist forces along with thousands of civilians seeking to escape the Communist takeover of the mainland. The population has since ballooned to 19.5 million, three times what it was at the beginning of World War II, of which 98 percent are Han Chinese, 18 percent of whom are from the mainland. Nearly 400,000 aborigines remain, mostly in the high mountains along the eastern side of the island. The chief religions are naturally those of mainland China: Buddhism, Confucianism, and Taoism.

Missionary Activity

Though missionaries began work again in Taiwan as early as 1865, their activity was limited until after World War II when the doors were opened wide to missionary activity. Many former missionaries to China were reassigned to Taiwan, and a number of new missions were opened up. By 1955 it was reported that there were 49 missions with 371 missionaries at work on the island. However, the Church of the Nazarene seemed slow to move into the open door.

In 1948 Rev. and Mrs. Peter Kiehn, veteran China missionaries, though officially retired, went on their own to Taiwan to, as they put it, "spend a few more years in gospel work among the Chinese people." They opened an independent gospel mission and Bible school and started several churches.

In the fall of 1954 Rev. and Mrs. L. C. Osborn, similarly motivated, desired to give a few more years with their beloved Chinese and sailed for Taiwan. Though they also were not official missionaries of the Church of the Nazarene, Rev. Osborn was asked by the church leaders to look over the situation and give his judgment as to the advisability of opening up a Nazarene work there. As the Osborns moved from place to place in their evangelistic work, they became convinced that a golden opportunity awaited the church here. His recommendation was that two missionary couples be sent immediately. "The field is white unto harvest, and the grain bending low," he said.

The logical move would be to send former China missionaries, but by this time most of them were involved in other responsibilities. Therefore, the choice fell on an experienced missionary couple from elsewhere, Rev. and Mrs. R. Ray Miller. They were currently serving in Trinidad after a term of service in Africa under another missionary board. They arrived in Taipei on December 12, 1956. A month later, Rev. and Mrs. John Holstead arrived as first-term missionaries.

As always, there was the question of how and where to start. Rev. Kiehn, now past 70 and wanting to retire, offered to turn over his independent work to the Church of the Nazarene. However, there were some complicating factors that made it seem advisable to start from scratch. Thus the beginning was made in the Millers' home.

No doubt the presence of the Kiehns and Osborns helped spread the word concerning the coming of the Church of the Nazarene. This was probably why two holiness congregations begun in 1954 and 1955 in the northern towns of Yang Mei and Ta Hsi asked to become affiliated with the church. Thus by the end of 1957 there were already four churches operating, though all were not yet fully organized.

Besides regular church services held Sunday and Wednesday nights, English Bible classes were held regularly. An unusual opportunity opened up when the Church of the Nazarene was allowed to conduct services twice a week for the Women's Anti-aggression League (a women's group gathered to sew for the Nationalist army). Another door opener was the distribution of clothing. In response to a plea from the missionaries to the homeland, boxes upon boxes of used clothing were sent to Taiwan. With refugees pouring in from the mainland with virtually nothing but the clothes on their backs, this kind of material assistance was the means of reaching the hearts and homes of many hundreds of people.

Ch'iao Ai, a refugee village built largely with funds from overseas Chinese, became a major distribution center for the clothing and thus a logical place to start a church. A lot was purchased, and the Bertolet Memorial Chapel was built. In nearby Chung Li a high-school-level vocational school was launched to educate young people from the mountain tribes. Classes in trade skills were taught along with Bible, music, English, and Mandarin. It was hoped that a number of these young people who were being converted through the influence of the school would take the gospel back to their homes. It was thus that the church made valuable contacts that would bear fruit in the years to come.

1958, the Golden Anniversary Year

The Church of the Nazarene commemorated its 50th anniversary in 1958, and the year-old church in Taiwan wanted to get in on the celebration. The first major event of the year was the visit of Dr. Hugh C. Benner in March. He visited not only Nazarene congregations but government relief centers, where he was often invited to preach. "It was most heartening," he said, "to sense the open-mindedness toward the gospel of Christ."

Another significant happening that year was the opening of the Taiwan Nazarene Theological College on October 3 with an enrollment of 14 students. Pending the acquisition of a permanent campus, a large house in Taipei was rented for the school's use. Immediately following the opening of classes came the Week of Witnessing in which 4,000 people were reached with personal testimonies. Each also received a gospel tract. Those witnessing wore a special printed badge with the Chinese characters, "Calling You."

Special services were held in October at Yang Mei and Ta Hsi in which there were many converts. October 12, the Anniversary Sunday, was celebrated in all the churches with great rejoicing. It was a significant opportunity to tell the story of the Church of the Nazarene to these new adherents. Two weeks previously, plastic bags with the words "Fiftieth Anniversary Offering" printed on them had been distributed. Members and friends were urged to bring in 50 coins or 50 paper bills as a thank offering to God on this day of celebration. An astounding total of 4,000 Taiwanese dollars was received!

At a rally on Monday night in the "garden" of the rented school property, the filmstrip *50 Golden Years* was shown. A tape-recorded translation of the script was used. A special program followed in which special greetings and good wishes were read from the Free China Relief Association and the Chinese Women's Anti-aggression League with whom the Church of the Nazarene had been working.

On November 1 the Osborns, who had been engaged in interdenominational evangelism, were officially appointed as Nazarene missionaries. Since they were beyond retirement age, this appointment was renewed annually until they finally returned to the United States in 1963. Their first assignment was to launch a church in Taipei, which to this point had been meeting in the Miller home.

On January 1, 1959, evangelistic services began there in a rented store building. So successful was the meeting that a substantial church was organized that the Osborns continued to pastor for the remainder of their time in Taiwan. In 10 years' time this church had spawned nine others in this great metropolis of 2 million people.

In April 1959 Rev. and Mrs. George Rench, who had been pastoring the Chinese Church of the Nazarene in Fresno, Calif., arrived in Taiwan. After a year in language study, Rev. Rench was placed in charge of the Bible school. A pressing task was to locate a suitable permanent site for the institution. In 1960 an eight-acre, hilltop site overlooking the beautiful Tan Shui River valley, 10 miles north of Taipei, was acquired. The tract involved parts of 18 farms, and it took six hours of patient negotiations to finalize the purchase. It was not until 1963, however, that the first building was completed and dedicated.

In 1960 Miss Bernadine Dringenberg, a nurse who had already spent a number of years in Taiwan, joined the Nazarene missionary force, bringing that group to nine. By now there were 14 churches and preaching points with 445 full and probationary members. Bible school enrollment stood at 25. In March 1961, the first graduating class of 6 received their diplomas. The following year Rev. and Mrs. Phillip Kellerman were added to the missionary staff.

Dr. V. H. Lewis, general superintendent, visited Taiwan in March 1962, at which time he organized the first Taiwan Nazarene Mission Council. That fall the council elected as field superintendent, Rev. Harry Wiese. At the time, he was on furlough from the Philippines, but due for transfer to Taiwan at his request. The Wieses had already given distinguished service in both the North and South fields in mainland China and knew well the customs and language of the people. They arrived in Taiwan in February 1963.

In promoting the 1962 Thanksgiving Offering, the general leaders had stated that it took $6.00 a minute to operate the missionary program of the church and suggested that individual churches could assume a certain block of time. The Taiwan church rose to the challenge and said they would seek to cover 13 minutes, or a total of $78.00. Each church was given a goal—the largest being $31.00 and the smallest 50¢. Only one church failed to reach its goal, but some went over so that the total came to $78.10! Most significant was the fact that the Taiwan church for the first time had caught a vision of world evangelism in which they could participate rather than only receive.

In March 1963 General Superintendent Samuel Young and Foreign Missions Secretary George Coulter visited the field. A highlight of their visit was the dedication of the first building on the Bible school campus. It was a milestone in the progress of the Taiwan field.

Later that year, Rev. and Mrs. Jack Messer joined the missionary staff, replacing the Osborns, who were at last retiring after a distinguished career that began as Nazarene missionaries in Old China in 1919. Taiwan had not seen the last of them, however, for in 1965 they were asked to come back to conduct evangelistic campaigns, which they did for seven months.

For the third year in a row, the Taiwan field was visited by a general superintendent in March 1964. It was Dr. V. H. Lewis' second trip to the island. He was greatly heartened by the spirit of both missionaries and nationals. Night services were held in the headquarters church at Shihlin, a suburb of Taipei, with many oustanding spiritual victories. He noted that Bible school enrollment was 22, with 10 of those due to graduate at the close of the school term. In August, Miss Patricia Burgess joined the faculty of the school.

Vacation Bible Schools were proving to be valuable outreach programs, with 22 being conducted the previous year with a total enrollment of 2,112. Two kindergarten schools with enrollments of 95 and 80 were also providing entrées into numerous homes.

The Christians among the 200,000 or more tribespeople of Taiwan suffered greatly under Japanese rule, particularly in the period preceding and during World War II. Yet despite the prohibition against missionary activity among the tribes and the persistent persecution, the Christians kept up their witness and their numbers actually increased in the midst of adversity. At war's end, missionaries who were once more able to enter these mountain areas found 7,000

Christians and 22,000 more waiting for baptism. These responsive people constituted a great challenge to missionary endeavor.

The Church of the Nazarene established its foothold among these people in its early vocational school for young tribesmen living in the Taipei area. Most of these students were from the southern Paiwan tribe, the largest of the seven main aboriginal groups. It was through this connection that the Nazarene missionaries were invited to their villages to present the gospel.

In 1964 Rev. Holstead, in one of his earliest contacts with these people, arranged to hold a service in the isolated village of Ahkala. To reach the place, one had to cross a river on a flimsy swinging bridge. Since it was harvesttime, the service could not begin until 9:30 P.M. But the crowd that gathered seemed to enjoy the service, and apparently no one was in a hurry to leave. At the conclusion of the message, near midnight, there were many hands raised for prayer. "In the loneliness of that dark night, high in the mountains of Taiwan, among people who a few generations ago were fierce headhunters, I felt the closeness of God as I had never felt it before," wrote Rev. Holstead of this experience.

At the time, the mountain dialects had not been reduced to writing, but even when, a few years later, the Gospels and Acts were translated into the language, few were educated enough to read it. But the work moved ahead, and before long there were six Nazarene churches in the southern mountains. Philip was the first tribesman to become a preacher, and he worked among his people with zeal and vision. It was a sad day when he passed away early in his ministry, for he was an inspiring leader who had already established two churches.

One of Dr. Lewis' recommendations on the occasion of his 1964 visit was that a work be opened in the large southern port city of Kaohsiung. This would also put a missionary in the area of the tribal churches to give encouragement and supervision. The Kellermans were chosen for this task.

Innovative Ministries

In 1966 the first Nazarene Youth Institute was held on the Bible school campus, with 39 registered for the four-day event. Prayer meetings, classes, morning and evening preaching services, and afternoon recreation filled the days with intense activity. The spiritual results were particularly rewarding, with almost everyone finding victory at the altar during the institute. The dynamic effect upon the local churches as the young people returned was felt throughout the district.

The following year 90 high school and college youth attended the institute, and this annual event continued to be a key item on the district calendar. Significantly, it was directed by the nationals rather than the missionaries. Mr. Hsieh and his committee of three Chinese pastors guided the program.

In 1968 came another first on the Taiwan field—a Nazarene Women Workers' Retreat. Betty Lin, the director, and her committee set a goal of 100 percent attendance of pastors' wives and women workers. It was suggested that all children save babes-in-arms should be left at home. Despite the consternation of husbands unaccustomed to doing domestic chores and caring for children, the plan worked, and 21 enrolled for the retreat, along with six babies.

The special speaker for the occasion was Gladys Aylward, the "Small Woman" of China, whose legendary missionary exploits on the mainland had made her name a household word. The two-and-a-half-day program passed all too quickly, but the blessing of God that fell upon the closing service was long to be remembered.

Tragedy Strikes

Betty Lin, a graduate of the Taiwan Nazarene Theological College, had also attended Bethany Nazarene College in the United States for two years (1964-66). She was looked to as an emerging leader in the Taiwan church. Her direction of the women's retreat was illustrative of her efficiency and dynamism. Her chief role was as a teacher of theology and church history in the college and as a translator of books. She worked closely with Miss Burgess both at the college and in district evangelistic endeavors. Christian Service Training, Vacation Bible Schools, and youth work were their special concern.

The two women had been on a special evangelistic mission among the mountain churches of the South when on Monday, February 24, 1969, the commercial plane in which they were flying back to Taipei crashed. Both were killed. It was a tragic blow to the work in Taiwan.

The District Grows

When the Wieses retired in 1966, Rev. John Holstead was elected field superintendent. That same year, Rev. and Mrs. John Clayton were added to the missionary staff, and the following year Rev. and Mrs. Stephen Rieder were transferred to Taiwan from Korea.

Dr. Orville Jenkins, general superintendent, visited the field in 1969 and ordained five Chinese preachers. Two of these were transferring their credentials from a sister holiness denomination.

With the arrival of Rev. and Mrs. Jirair Tashjian in September 1970 and Mr. and Mrs. Willis Zumwalt in July 1971, the missionary staff was up to 12. However, when the George Renches were on furlough in May 1970, they had been approached about the matter of opening up work in Indonesia. Thus when they returned to Taiwan in July 1971, it was only to serve there until necessary permits and visas could be obtained for them to go to Singapore and eventually Indonesia proper. The Renches' ultimate departure for their new field in May 1973 left a significant gap in the missionary ranks.

But the end was not yet. In January 1974 the General Board voted to open up work in Hong Kong, selecting the Taiwan superintendent, Rev. John Holstead, for the task. Another leading couple was thus taken from the Taiwan ranks after serving nearly 18 years there.

About 1967 the Taiwan church leaders adopted a plan called STEPS, which would bring every church to the level of self-support in 10 years. It was a simple plan used effectively on other mission fields whereby at least within each successive year, the local church would assume 10 percent more of the subsidy it had been receiving from the general church. If the church wished to speed up the process, so much the better. The people were quick to respond to the challenge, and by July 1970 two churches had already become self-supporting. By 1975, two years ahead of schedule, all 27 of the fully organized churches had reached the goal. This meant that they were paying the pastor's salary, local church expenses, and a district home missions budget besides.

The churches also responded to the challenge of world missions. Their early effort in 1962 to "operate the church worldwide for 13 minutes" by raising $78.10 was but the beginning. By 1970 the district was setting goals of $400 and $450 (U.S.) for their Thanksgiving and Easter offerings.

About the same time, the Alabaster offering idea was being proposed. It was not difficult for them to recognize that many churches on their district as well as the Bible school buildings had been financed largely through Alabaster funds. Now it was their turn to share with others. Their only objection was that the Alabaster boxes provided from Headquarters were too small! Instead they used an orange, plastic bottle. Many stories emerged of sacrificial gifts contributed to this phase of the world outreach program of the church.

When the Holsteads were transferred to the Hong Kong work in 1974, Rev. Phillip Kellerman, the oldest missionary on the field in point of service, was elected mission director. By this time the missionary force was down to four couples: the Kellermans, the Tashjians, the Zumwalts, and the Rieders. In August 1976 Rev. and Mrs. James Williams joined them. As more and more nationals were trained and were assuming positions of leadership, the need for missionaries decreased. By then there were 21 Chinese pastors, 14 of whom were ordained.

When Dr. Eugene Stowe, general superintendent, and Dr. Jerald D. Johnson, executive secretary of the Department of World Missions, visited Taiwan in September 1975, the district took two major steps toward becoming a regular district. First, Rev. Pan Ming-Ting, one of the earliest pastors on the Taiwan field, was appointed by Dr. Stowe to be the first Chinese district superintendent. Second, because the district was already 50 percent self-supporting, it was moved all the way from pioneer district status to a full mission district, bypassing the national-mission stage. At this level they were entitled to send four delegates to the 1976 General Assembly.

In 1984 a sweeping revival broke out among the Paiwanees, a tribe numbering 50,000 where there were seven Nazarene churches. The death from leukemia of the nine-year-old son of Pastor and Mrs. John Liou was used of God to spark this great awakening that spread much beyond the bounds of the Church of the Nazarene. The result was a wave of growth that had a ripple effect over all of Taiwan. District Superintendent Kou Min-Hua was a strong supporter of this revival movement. Under the leadership of Mission Director Willis Zumwalt, by 1985 there were 28 organized churches on Taiwan with a total membership of 1,548.

The theological college at Kuan Tu continued to serve the district well with an enrollment of 19 students, 10 of them full time. Since Jim Williams had resigned from the college, the coming in August 1985 of a British couple, Robert and Rhea McMurdock, was a great boon to the school. They had formerly served in Taiwan under the Finnish Missionary Society.

3. *Hong Kong*

The British crown colony of Hong Kong at the mouth of the Pearl River on China's south coast has long been considered one of the most strategic ports in the world—certainly in the Orient. Its free-trade status has made it one of the greatest transshipment ports. The name is derived from two Chinese words, *Hong* ("fragrant") and *Kong* ("harbor"). It indeed has a very beautiful and commodious harbor.

The colony consists of mountainous Hong Kong Island (35½ sq. mi.) with Victoria, the capital city, on its north shore; the city of Kowloon (3 sq. mi.) on the mainland; and the New Territories, a 355-square-mile area of the mainland and numerous adjacent islands that were leased from China in 1898 for 99 years. Crowded into this tiny area are perhaps 7 million people. (The official population of 6 million is swelled by uncounted numbers of refugees.)

The first wave of refugees swept in after the second Chinese-Japanese war in 1937, but a large number left or were killed during the Japanese occupation during World War II. The influx since then has been largely due to the Communist takeover of mainland China.

Ninety-eight percent of the people of Hong Kong are Chinese, and the religions of China—Buddhism, Confucianism, and Taoism—prevail. But because of the British influence, there are more Christian churches here than in any other Oriental city. Six percent of the population are Protestants, and 6 percent Roman Catholic. It was the enormous influx of people (mostly from China proper) after World War II that made Hong Kong one of the most challenging areas for missionary work in the world.

Along with Taiwan, Hong Kong offered an entrée to the Chinese people that had been denied the church when the Communists took over the country in 1949. Suggestions had been made from time to time that the Church of the Nazarene should enter this wide-open door; and in 1970 Dr. Orville Jenkins, general superintendent, in the course of a visit to other fields in the Orient, made an investigative stopover there. He was much impressed with what he saw, and he recommended that consideration be given to opening a work in the colony.

In 1973 Dr. and Mrs. Eugene Stowe also paid a visit to the island. So positive was their feeling that a work should be launched that a recommendation came before the General Board at its January 1974 meeting to proceed immediately. Rev. John Holstead, field superintendent of Taiwan and at that time on furlough in the United States, was named to head the project. Only limited preparatory work had been done beyond basic surveys, so the Holsteads had to make their way through a maze of basic decisions as they established the pattern of operation. The situation was unlike any other in the world, and precedents to follow were few.

The Holsteads, Jack and Natalie, and their three children, Kathy, John, and Kian, landed at Kowloon's Kai Tak Airport on July 17, 1974, to begin their new adventure. The initial task was to find a place to live and to arrange for the schooling of their children. They also wanted to get a quick overview of the task before them. They found costs astronomically high but were successful in finding an apartment in Kowloon. After a two-week trip to Taiwan to pack personal belongings left there when they went on furlough, they were ready to begin their appointed task in early August.

Permanent resident visas were not granted until six months later. The process of registering the church was lengthy and involved also, but in due course both documents came through about the same time.

Where to begin and how to start were the next two questions to be answered. The teeming masses and the evidences of wickedness and immorality on every hand ("a veritable Sodom," Rev. Holstead termed it) presented a bewildering challenge. With prices so high, any wrong move would be costly, so a careful analysis of the situation was necessary.

The language problem was a considerable hurdle, for though the Holsteads were fluent in Mandarin (the official language in Taiwan and also almost all mainland China), nearly everyone in Hong Kong spoke Cantonese. Mandarin has only four tones; Cantonese has seven, which made the transition difficult. They spent eight months in full-time study at the Hong Kong Language Institute. The director of the institute was the one who had been their language teacher in Taiwan 17 years before.

The search for property was begun soon after the Holsteads arrived and continued concurrently with the intensive language study. All land in Hong Kong is in the name of the British crown, so what the property seeker buys is a 99-year lease, hopefully renewable. These leases are sold at public auction to the highest bidder. Since land is so scarce, the bids are high.

In February 1975 Dr. Eugene Stowe, general superintendent, and Dr. Jerald Johnson, executive secretary of the Department of World

Missions, stopped off for a day in Hong Kong to confer with Rev. Holstead on the property situation. The decision was made to first explore all the possibilities for purchase (or lease/purchase agreement) of property rather than rent. With that in mind the missionary began an intensified search and study of the entire area.

A chapel for sale in the New Territories and a kindergarten and church complex on Hong Kong Island owned by another mission group were checked out. Two hundred real estate developers were apprised of the church's search for property. Dozens of interviews were held with the missionaries and national leaders of other groups. One hundred fifty proposed sites were examined carefully

The Government Housing Authority provided a list of 32 different "housing estates" (low-cost, concrete housing units in which 43 percent of the population lived). Here the church could rent space at a subsidized rate. Each of the estates housed from 25,000 to 80,000 people. Rev. Holstead conferred with those who were already doing missionary work in some of these places and found the situation less than promising.

In September 1975 Dr. Stowe returned to Hong Kong, at which time Rev. Holstead laid out the results of his arduous search during the preceding months. In the light of his findings, it was decided to rent property for the time being in order to get the work started, provided this could be done within the limit of $1,000 per month. The search for a permanent location would be continued, however.

Within a month a lease was signed for space on the 10th floor of the newly completed Hang Lung Center, a 28-story commercial complex in the Causeway Bay area. There was just under 1,000 square feet of space, but it was near a main block of elevators, and rest rooms were nearby. The rent, including utilities, and the taxes came to $850 a month.

Regular Bible studies and Sunday services were begun in November. The meetings were all advertised in newspapers and on radio, and letters were sent out to a mailing list that had been compiled through the previous year. Personal contacts were also made in the building in which the "church" was located, and an intensive calling program was instituted in the area. Within a half-mile radius of their location there were no other churches, yet in that same area it was estimated that over a million people lived—the most densely populated section of the city and also the fastest growing.

Soon several families and single young people were attending the services, and some significant contacts were being made.

In 1976 the property search came to an end when the entire 20th floor of the new Causeway Commercial Building was purchased, which provided room for a 150-seat auditorium and Sunday School classrooms. The church was officially organized with 13 full and probationary members and a thriving youth organization. Among the members was a graduate of an evangelical Bible school, Sam Chung, who was already proving to be a great blessing to the work. He was a native Cantonese but also fluent in Mandarin and English and so was able to help the Holsteads in communication with the people.

The work received a great boost in its beginning months with a three-day visit from the Northwesterners choir from Northwest Nazarene College. Their performance in the city hall brought wide exposure for the church through extensive radio and TV coverage of the event. The group also sang at the annual meeting of the Hong Kong Evangelical Fellowship, which introduced the Church of the Nazarene to the other Christian organizations of the community and lent credibility to the new Nazarene work there.

In September 1979 reinforcements arrived in the persons of Rev. and Mrs. William Selvidge. In 1980 the Holsteads furloughed and, along with Samuel and Winna Chung, now pastors of the Causeway Bay Church, attended the General Assembly in Dallas. The one congregation now had 39 members, and the Sunday School averaged 55. A thriving ministry to youth was particularly significant, since half the population of Hong Kong is under 18 years of age.

In March 1982 the first mini-district assembly was held with General Superintendent Greathouse and Regional Director Owens present. A highlight was the ordination of Samuel Chung.

Shortly after the assembly, persistent efforts on the part of the missionaries were finally rewarded when a small commercial area at Tai Koo Shing was leased to the church. This new section of the city with 80,000 people offered a great opportunity. With a strong nucleus of members from the Causeway Bay Church a second congregation came into being with the Selvidges as pastors.

When the Selvidges furloughed in 1983, Louise Law became pastor of the Tai Koo Shing Church. This Hong Kong native had been converted in the Parkhead Church in Scotland while in nurse's training and had subsequently graduated from the Australian Nazarene

Bible College. It was a shock to the church when, six months after taking the pastorate, she succumbed to cancer at the age of 31.

In the meantime the Causeway Bay Church had become fully self-supporting and was a 10 percent-plus church in world mision giving. Eighty percent of its members were tithers.

In October 1984 a small, second-story apartment was rented at Shau Kei Wan on Hong Kong Island, and a third church was organized there under the leadership of Daniel and Fanny Lam. In January 1985 Patrick and Leona Fung united with the Church of the Nazarene and became pastors of the Tai Koo Shing Church.

With the three congregations totaling 129 members, and all national pastors, a solid foundation had been laid. But with the looming prospect that on July 1, 1997, the British would be turning the colony back to the People's Republic of China, a real challenge faced the young district. Training of future leaders in holiness doctrine became a priority. With the help of the church in Taiwan, Chinese literature was made available, and a Chinese version of the "Showers of Blessing" radio program was being aired all over China. Hong Kong could well be the springboard for a future thrust into the mainland.

C. JAPAN

Japan, or Nippon ("Rising Sun"), is an island nation extending some 1,250 miles north to south off the east coast of Asia. There are four main islands (among hundreds)—Honshu in the center with Hokkaido on the north and Kyushu and Shikoku to the south. Six out of seven of its 147,000 square miles are mountainous with 500 volcanoes, few of them still active. The remaining arable land is intensely farmed to help feed its nearly 120 million people, 75 percent of whom live in the cities.

Shintoism ("the way of the gods") was the original, indigenous religion of Japan in which the spirits of nature (animals, trees, rivers, etc.) and of ancestors were worshiped. It was a state religion taught in the schools until abolished after World War II, along with emperor worship. Buddhism, however, had long been the dominant religion, having come across from nearby China about A.D. 500. One hundred thousand of its temples dot the land. Confucianism and Taoism also have a considerable following.

Christianity came in the form of Roman Catholicism in the 16th century; but when in 1637 all foreigners were expelled from the country, Christianity was also banned. Many thousands of its followers were ruthlessly tortured and killed. The doors to the outside world remained tightly closed for 230 years until in the 1870s they were once more pushed ajar. Protestant churches and missions quickly seized the opportunity and sent in some outstanding missionaries. Despite mounting opposition from the Buddhists, who saw their religious monopoly broken, the gospel began to take root.

1. Early Beginnings of the Church of the Nazarene

The starting point for the work of the Church of the Nazarene in Japan was the historic early capital city of Kyoto. The first missionaries were Miss Lillian Poole and Miss Lulu Williams who were already in Japan, sent out in 1905 under the auspices of the Holiness Church of Christ to work in Tokyo under the Oriental Missionary Society (later the Japan Holiness church).

In 1907 these two ladies had been transferred to Kyoto, 250 miles to the west, where they began work among the children and taught English-language classes. When the Holiness Church of Christ in the southern United States became a part of the Church of the Nazarene at Pilot Point, Tex., in 1908, these two missionaries in Japan were asked to open a work for the young denomination in that country.

They continued essentially what they had been doing and slowly brought a Christian influence into the community. But not until reinforcements arrived in 1910 was there promise of establishing a permanent work. Among the new arrivals was Miss Minnie Upperman, who had served with the original two in earlier years in Tokyo. There was also J. A. Chenault (who, soon after arrival, married Miss Upperman) and Rev. and Mrs. J. W. Thompson. The coming of these reinforcements made it possible for Miss Poole and Miss Williams to return to the United States for a much-needed furlough. Mrs. Chenault's knowledge of the language and the customs of the people made her a valuable leader of the now-blossoming work.

But the encouraging prospect soon dimmed when within a short time, both couples encountered health problems. First the Thompsons had to return home, and in 1912 the Chenaults. No resident missionaries were left, no property had been acquired, and no firm nucleus of believers had as yet been brought together to give continuity to the mission.

Providentially, just at this critical time Mrs. I. B. Staples and Miss Cora Snider of Los Angeles were making a tour of Japan and became aware of the situation. So concerned was Miss Snider that she offered to remain in Japan for two years to keep the work going. Mrs. Staples promised to return also as soon as family arrangements could be worked out.

Shortly afterward, Rev. and Mrs. J. I. Nagamatsu, who had been in the United States studying at Pasadena College, returned to Japan and began working with Miss Snider. But progress in Kyoto was slow, and when an apparently more promising area opened up at Fukuchiyama, 40 miles northwest, they decided to move there.

In 1914 the initial stop on Dr. H. F. Reynolds' first around-the-world missionary tour was Japan. Arriving with him were the two former missionaries Lulu Williams and Lillian Poole, returning from their extended furlough, and new recruits Rev. and Mrs. L. H. Humphrey. It was Dr. Reynolds' judgment that Kyoto was the more strategic point at which to establish a base, so he located the returning missionaries and the Humphreys there, naming Rev. Humphrey superintendent of the field.

Soon after, Miss Snider's failing health forced her to return to the United States, leaving to the Nagamatsus the sole responsibility for the work in Fukuchiyama. They acquired an old hospital building that was converted for church and Sunday School use plus a weekday kindergarten. By 1920 they had gathered a membership of 84, and before long they had 10 Sunday Schools going with a total enrollment of 700.

Meanwhile, when Mrs. Staples returned to the United States in 1912, her whetted interest in Japan prompted her to reach out to Japanese nationals in the Los Angeles area. She began ministering to those who worked in the citrus groves in the vicinity of Upland, where she and her husband lived. Among her converts was Hiroshi Kitagawa, whom she encouraged to enroll in Pasadena College and who was ordained by Dr. P. F. Bresee in 1914. He and Mr. and Mrs. Staples set out for Japan late that year (arriving on January 5, 1915) and began evangelistic work in Rev. Kitagawa's birthplace of Kumamoto on the southern island of Kyushu.

At first unmarried, Hiroshi Kitagawa soon took care of that matter with the help of Bishop Nakada of the Japan Holiness church, who introduced him to Miss Toyoko (Ruth) Nagai and performed the marriage ceremony. Mrs. Ruth Kitagawa proved to be a superb worker at the side of her husband in the coming years.

The work in Kumamoto grew rapidly, and on April 4, 1915, Mission Superintendent L. H. Humphrey organized there the first official Church of the Nazarene in Japan with 18 charter members. Rev. Kitagawa was appointed pastor, while Mrs. Staples carried on evangelistic work throughout the island of Kyushu. Mr. Staples gave loyal support by handling the business affairs of the Kumamoto church and serving as district treasurer. Soon property was purchased for a parsonage, a missionary home, and a school.

An unusual characteristic of the Japan work from the start was the number of converts who professed a call to preach. This prompted the launching of a Bible training school in the fall of 1915 with Rev. Kitagawa in charge. A few miles north of Kumamoto in the large coal-mining city of Omuta, a work was begun in March 1916. It was carried on by Bible school personnel until the arrival of Miss Bertie Karns, who took up residence in the city in April 1920.

Meanwhile, back on Honshu Island, the Fukuchiyama church had been officially organized. The revived work in Kyoto took on permanence when it, too, was organized and property was rented on Gojo Street. This became a center of intense evangelistic endeavor.

But ill health, which before had decimated the missionary force, again dealt a blow when Rev. Humphrey and Miss Poole became too ill to carry on and had to return to the United States in 1915. Miss Williams was left to carry on alone in Kyoto.

The mission board moved quickly to fill the gap, however, and in February 1916 Rev. and Mrs. William A. Eckel and Nobumi Isayama arrived on the field. For almost two years the Eckels had been leading the Japanese work in the Los Angeles area, having taken over from the Stapleses when the latter went to Japan. Nobumi Isayama, one of Mrs. Staples' converts, had been a valuable assistant and interpreter for the Eckels and had recently graduated from Pasadena College. Though not ordained, he was named pastor of the Gojo Street mission.

In 1917 Miss Ethel McPherson arrived, and she and Miss Williams started a second mission in Kyoto on Theatre Street. Also arriving were Rev. and Mrs. P. C. Thatcher, who opened a mission in Okayama in 1918. They were ably assisted by a Japanese preacher who had been studying in the United States and had recently returned. They had a good measure of success in spite of some adverse circumstances including health problems experienced by Mrs. Thatcher. The building they erected remained in continuous use until destroyed during World War II. When the Thatchers were forced to leave in December 1919, Miss Gertrude Privat ably took over. Within a year she opened a branch Sunday School, and the attendance soon reached a total of 100, counting both places.

With the Kyoto work well in hand, the Eckels and Isayamas moved to Kure in September 1918. This was a new naval base 200 miles west of Kyoto. Westerners were not allowed to take up permanent residence here, so the activities of the Eckels were somewhat restricted. However, Rev. Isayama secured property, and a new mission was launched. By the time Dr. H. F. Reynolds visited there the following year, 12 converts were ready for baptism. A crisis in the Kyoto work made it necessary for the Eckels and Isayamas to return there, but Shiro Kitagawa, a brother of Hiroshi and a recent graduate of the Bible training school, was available to assume the leadership of the Kure church.

From time to time other missionaries arrived on the field but for various reasons served for only short periods. Retrenchment after a period of overextension was one explanation of why some missionary careers were cut short. Among the names that appear on the records are Miss Ethel McPherson and Miss Helen Santee (who labored with Miss Williams in Kyoto about a year), Rev. and Mrs. Henry Howard Wagner, Rev. and Mrs. C. H. Wiman (who later served in Peru), Rev. and Mrs. C. Warren Jones (later general secretary of Foreign Missions), Rev. and Mrs. Paul Goodwin, and Rev. Frank Smith. Not all were officially appointed missionaries but worked there on their own. In spite of this great turnover of missionaries, the church continued to grow. This is a tribute to the outstanding national leaders whom, from the earliest days, God gave to the work.

2. *An Organized Mission District*

On the occasion of his 1919 visit to Japan, General Superintendent H. F. Reynolds organized the Japan District with five churches: Kyoto, Kure, Kumamoto, Fukuchiyama, and Omuta. With their satellite Sunday Schools and preaching points, the total number of members and adherents was estimated to be about 1,600.

The first official assembly was held in Kyoto in November 1922, with Dr. Reynolds presiding. Rev. J. I. Nagamatsu was elected district superintendent. When, a few months later, Rev. Nagamatsu decided to return to the United States, Rev. Hiroshi Kitagawa, head of the Bible school, was appointed to replace him. Thus began his long and distinguished career as a leader in the Japan church.

The second district assembly was held in November 1924, under the leadership of Rev. Joseph Bates. (He had been elected superintendent of the Oriental work by the Board of Foreign Missions in an ill-fated organizational attempt to strengthen the supervision of overseas fields.) During the interim, only one additional church was reported—the Honmachi Church in Kyoto.

In 1921 the Bible training school had been transferred from Kumamoto to the more central location of Kyoto and was attached to the newly organized Honmachi Church. The strategic impact of the Bible training school at this time cannot be overstated. Rev. Hiroshi

Kitagawa remained its inspired leader until his appointment to the district superintendency in 1923.

In 1928 the third assembly was held, conducted by Rev. Hiroshi Kitagawa. By now there were eight churches, and at the fourth assembly held the following year, still another was reported. This 1929 assembly was marked by the visit of two general superintendents, Drs. J. W. Goodwin and R. T. Williams. At the assembly Rev. Shiro Kitagawa was ordained.

The inspiration provided by the presence of these church leaders made the 1929 assembly a watershed year for the church, for from then on there was marked expansion. By 1931 there were 16 churches, and in 1932, 22 were reported. By the time of the fifth district assembly, conducted by General Superintendent J. B. Chapman in 1935, there were 33 churches with 1,675 full members. Thirteen of the churches were fully self-supporting, and two were Korean congregations located in Kyoto and Osaka.

Two of the newer churches were in Tokyo. For years plans had been discussed to open work in the sprawling capital, but not until a group of navy wives began meetings in their homes did a breakthrough come. By 1933 a sufficient number of people had been brought together to organize two churches with Rev. Eichi Kuboki as pastor of both.

Although national leadership had been dominant during those first 30 years on the Japan field, at the 1935 assembly a major step forward took place when the 131 delegates voted to assume the responsibility of full self-government and self-support. Rev. Shiro Kitagawa was elected district superintendent and his brother Hiroshi their delegate to the 1936 General Assembly. Nine ministers were ordained by Dr. J. B. Chapman, the presiding general superintendent.

When the action of the assembly seeking full district status came before the General Board for final approval in January 1936, that body recommended that two districts be created. The western one, the Kansai District, which was the older and more established area, would be a regular district, as voted, while the eastern (Kanto) district would remain a mission district. The dividing line would be generally north and south in the vicinity of Nagoya, about 75 miles east of Kyoto. Kyoto and Tokyo would be the respective headquarters cities.

The plan was not well received in Japan, but in spite of the unpopularity of the division, a great wave of evangelism swept through the Japanese church. On the wings of a strong emphasis on prayer, evangelism became the keynote in every area. Tent meetings were especially popular and productive. There were 17 tents in constant use during the summer months. Each church also held a weekly street meeting, at which invitations were given to attend the nearby Nazarene church. Large meetings in rented auditoriums were also held, particularly in the colder months, but these proved to be less productive than tent and street meetings. Street parades replete with brass bands or other instrumental groups were often used for advertising. The excitement and color thus generated brought out great crowds of people to the meetings.

Further supporting these evangelistic efforts was the liberal distribution of tracts and other religious literature. In a country with an almost 100 percent literacy rate, this was a powerful tool that the church was quick to exploit. A modest printing operation was begun to provide the needed literature.

Tokyo became an area of concentration on the Kanto District, and within two years 10 churches were organized in this metropolis of 5 million. As churches mushroomed, the training of national pastors in this area became imperative. Instead of sending their prospective preachers to Kyoto and possibly losing them to the Kansai District, their own Bible training school was set up in connection with the Shimokitazawa Church in suburban Tokyo. This move reflected an unfortunate rivalry between the two districts.

The Son of Righteousness was indeed beginning to rise in this Land of the Rising Sun, and, despite the crosscurrents, a bright future lay ahead for the Church of the Nazarene. But it was the sinister forces outside the church that were soon to thwart the efforts toward spiritual revival.

By the late 1930s the power of the military leaders in the government was becoming apparent. In 1931 the first step had been made toward the realization of their imperialistic dreams when the Japanese moved into the Chinese province of Manchuria. From there, in 1937, they advanced into China itself. At the same time, there began an internal purge of any movements within the country not wholeheartedly endorsing the government's aggressive policies. The Christian church and all related institutions were on this list. Western missionaries were particularly suspect. Undercover agents attended services to check out activities and teachings and often demanded advanced scripts of sermons. Shintoism, the national religion of Japan, received favored status with the government.

Quietly the United States Embassy passed the word to their citizens in Japan to return home, but the missionaries were reluctant to leave. One day a Tokyo friend of Rev. Eckel whispered to him, "Get out of Japan while you can, or you may never make it." The man seemed to have some inside information and asked Rev. Eckel not to tell anyone what he had said. The missionary took the warning seriously, and gathering a few personal belongings, he and his family prepared to leave as soon as they could. Fortunately they found passage on a departing ship. As they bade a tearful farewell to the little band of Japanese leaders who came to see them off, Rev. Isayama spoke for them all when he said, "Missionary, we want you to know that we will shed our blood if need be for Christ who shed His for us."

The only Nazarene missionary left was Miss Bertie Karns, who had returned to Japan in 1936 after serving about a year and a half in China. Living in a less vulnerable area than Tokyo, she chose to remain longer. She finally left on one of the last ships to depart for the United States before the bombing of Pearl Harbor.

As government pressure on the Christian church was steadily increasing, it was a question whether the Japanese delegates to the 1940 General Assembly to be held in Oklahoma City should or would be allowed to leave the country. Rev. Hiroshi Kitagawa and Rev. Nobumi Isayama, the elected delegates, were key Nazarene leaders in Japan, and if they failed to get back, the result would be crippling. The government did allow them to go, however, and this gave them a valuable opportunity to discuss future strategy with church leaders in the United States.

One decision, which ultimately proved academic, was to unite the two districts. This would not only help to heal the rift between the districts but would tighten the organization and thus increase the chances of survival. Rev. Isayama was chosen to be the overall leader. But by the time the men got back to Japan, they discovered that the government had done some tightening up on its own. The order went out that no church could use its own name but would be assigned a number by which it would be identified. Furthermore, only 11 numbers would be issued and these only to those churches with substantial enough constituencies to merit such recognition.

The scramble for these numbers was already on. Number 1 had been assigned to the Presbyterian church; No. 2 to the Methodist church; No. 3 to the Congregational church; No. 4 to the Baptists; No. 5 to the Lutherans; No. 6 to the Oriental Missionary Society; and No.

7 to the Japan Evangelistic Band. There were four holiness groups, including the Church of the Nazarene, that were considered individually too small to be recognized by the government.

The need for swift action to cope with the situation prompted Bishop Tsuchiyama of the Free Methodist church to meet the returning Nazarene ministers at the dock when they landed. A meeting of the leaders of the four groups had already been arranged, and after an all-night session it was decided that they would unite under the name of Seika Kyodan (the Sanctified or Holiness church) and make application for a number. Besides the Church of the Nazarene and the Free Methodist church, there were the Scandinavian Alliance Mission and the World Missionary Society (Tokyo Division).

Bishop Tsuchiyama was elected as moderator of the group, and Rev. Hiroshi Kitagawa was asked to head a joint Bible training school. The Seika Kyodan was assigned No. 8.

When all numbers were finally assigned, the leaders of each were required to elect a general moderator. He was to be the liaison with the government through whom all orders were to be passed on to the individual groups. Rev. Mitsuru Tomita of the Presbyterian church was elected as the *tori* or general superintendent.

One year later, the government went a step further and ordered that the numerical groupings be dissolved and all 11 organizations carry the single designation, *Nippon Kirisuto Kyodan* (the Christian Church of Japan). The next step was to close all their schools except two—one for men and one for women. Government control of the church was now virtually complete.

While the war with China had begun in 1937, it was largely an operation of the military, which affected the homeland very little. But after the monumental decision was made to move against the United States by bombing Pearl Harbor, it was a matter of total mobilization. Every aspect of Japanese life was affected.

When, after three years, the counteroffensive of the American forces finally brought Japan within the range of its bombers, the devastation and privation mounted. By the time the war was over in mid-August 1945, much of their country lay in ruins.

What went on within the church during those years is hard to imagine. In Tokyo all but 2 of the 10 Nazarene churches were destroyed, and 10 elsewhere were also lost. All the pastors were forced into secular work or were drafted into the military. All 12 pastors in the western section were drafted. Rev. Saegusa was shot in the chest and was reported killed in action, but he survived and is still (1985) pastoring a church. Rev. Michio Nagasaka was sent to China, where he became ill and died. Rev. Takamatsu was sent to Manchuria; and seven years after the war was over, his wife received word that he had died in a Soviet prison camp in Siberia. Rev. Shiro Kano, whose story is graphically told in Alice Spangenberg's *Oriental Pilgrim,* was killed in the South Pacific.

One of the many fascinating stories of wartime heroism relates to Rev. Nobumi Isayama and his new church building in Tokyo. One night after a bombing raid, that entire section of the capital was in flames that threatened at any moment to engulf the church. Inside the building, the beleaguered pastor prayed that God would somehow spare his church. If not, he vowed, the same flames that consumed his church would consume his body also. Then a miracle happened. A sudden shift in the wind turned the flames away from the church, and it was spared destruction though it was in the center of ruin.

An inventory following the war revealed that only 10 of the original 28 church buildings in Japan remained. Nine of the original 35 pastors were lost. Of the 2,500 members, only 1,800 could be accounted for. The process of reconstruction for both nation and church would be difficult but challenging. The fact that the occupation forces were directed by a Christian statesman, Gen. Douglas MacArthur, augured well for the rehabilitation of both.

3. *The Post-World War II Years*

One of General MacArthur's first edicts was a Bill of Rights that included the following provisions: (1) All prior legislation that impaired freedom of thought, religious assembly, and speech was null and void; (2) All extralegal secret societies and spying organizations were forbidden; (3) No public funds could be diverted to support the Shinto religion. Such legislation opened wide the door for unprecedented missionary activity.

Another step toward reestablishment of the church came through Nazarene servicemen who were in the occupation forces. Many made a determined effort to find traces of the former Nazarene work and also contributed funds for their rehabilitation. Dr. Howard Hamlin, attached to General MacArthur's staff as assistant chief of the Surgical Section and chief of the Orthopedics Division of the 49th

General Hospital in Tokyo, was able from his vantage point to make an invaluable contribution to the reestablishment of the church.

Lieutenant Doyle Shepherd of the air force was so impressed with the need as well as the opportunity for Christian work in Japan that he and his wife offered themselves to the church for regular missionary assignment. They were officially appointed by the General Board in January 1948. Without even returning to the United States, he resigned his commission on the spot and began full-time missionary activity. When the work in Okinawa was begun in 1957, the Shepherds took the lead there also.

Major Robert H. Shaw was attached to the military government in the northern island of Hokkaido. The Shaws conducted English Bible classes in their home with such success that several churches were organized out of their converts.

When the Korean conflict broke out, Robert Shaw, now a lieutenant colonel, was transferred to Pusan where he gave invaluable assistance in the establishment of the Church of the Nazarene in that country.

Chaplain Joseph Pitts, searching for the probable remnants of Nazarene work in Tokyo, came upon the still-intact church of Nobumi Isayama. Working in the yard were the pastor and his wife, who were overjoyed to see him. They had been praying for just such an eventuality.

Among other personnel in the occupation forces who helped reestablish the links with the Japanese church were Orval Nease, Jr., Chaplain Lowell George, Glenn Overholt, Raymond Bolerjack, Ardee Coolidge, and Viola Roberts.

But the real reconstruction began when Rev. W. A. Eckel returned to Japan in January 1947. During the war he had been superintendent of the Rocky Mountain District and resigned that post to return to his former field of labor.

When his ship, the *Marine Falcon,* docked at Yokohama, he was greeted warmly by Lieut. Doyle Shepherd and Eckel's longtime colaborer, Rev. Nobumi Isayama. The latter was thin and haggard and dressed in worn and ill-fitting clothes that bespoke the hardships he had been through. But the beaming smile and hearty "Amen" as he greeted the missionary reflected his indomitable spirit. To him it was the dawning of a new day.

Word spread rapidly that Rev. Eckel had returned, and among those who came to greet him at the Dai Ichi Hotel were eight of the former pastors. Then word came that Hiroshi Kitagawa was coming to Tokyo from Kyoto. The man Rev. Eckel met at the station was so changed that he hardly recognized him, but the fervent "Praise the Lord!" that came from his lips as the two shook hands thrilled the heart of the missionary.

Wisely, Isayama and Kitagawa had laid claim to all missionary property in their own names in order to hold it. Now the business of legally reestablishing the church structure and transferring deeds to the name of the denomination had to be worked out. It was a tedious process. The three leaders then made plans to tour the entire country to assess the situation and lay plans to revitalize the work that had been so disrupted.

Establishing a Headquarters

One goal of General MacArthur's occupation policy was to break up the large landholdings of the formerly wealthy and redistribute the land. Not only did this make property readily available, but values dropped precipitously. The church made the most of the situation, and about 45 parcels in various parts of the country were acquired. In the following years, a church was built on each one, many also with parsonages and kindergarten schools. Dr. Hamlin was influential in having deeded to the church a beautiful tract in Oyamadai, a section of Tokyo, for a headquarters location. On this a two-story main building and several residences were erected to accommodate the district headquarters and the Bible college.

In January 1948 Rev. Eckel returned to the United States to report to the General Board concerning his findings. The wide-open opportunity and the urgency of the situation were the keynotes of his glowing report. Immediately plans were made to send Dr. Hardy C. Powers, general superintendent, and Dr. John Stockton, general treasurer, to Japan to appraise the possibilities.

With the Hamlin home as their base of operation, the two men were able to have interviews with several top officials, including Gen. Douglas MacArthur. They were strongly encouraged to invest heavily in the Japanese work, and Rev. Eckel's report of the great potential for expansion was readily confirmed in the minds of the visiting church leaders.

The training of ministers was a No. 1 priority. By 1949 there were 45 churches in operation; and to serve these, many of the available pastors had to be circuit riders on foot, by bus, or on bicycle ministering to several congregations. Growth would be stifled unless more pastors became available.

In commemoration of Mrs. S. N. Fitkin's long service as president of the Women's Foreign Missionary Society (1915-48), a churchwide offering of $70,000 had been raised to build a Bible training school in China to be named in her honor. However, due to the Communist takeover there in 1949, this plan had to be tabled. It seemed appropriate to divert $25,000 of this fund for a similar school in Japan, and Harrison Davis of Pasadena College was appointed to assist in organizing the school and to supervise the building.

The Oyamadai property in Setagaya Ku was chosen to accommodate both headquarters and Bible college, as mentioned above. Here, on March 10, 1951, the groundbreaking ceremony was held, and on April 13, 1952, the Susan N. Fitkin Memorial Building was dedicated. Five days later 16 students registered and began the four-year course of study. The following year 12 more enrolled, bringing the total to 28. Rev. W. A. Eckel was named president, and Rev. Makoto Oye dean. Instructors included Rev. Hiroshi Kitagawa, Rev. and Mrs. Harrison Davis, and Revs. Makoto Oye, Aishin (Ross) Kida, Susumu Okubo, Yozo Seo, and Nobumi Isayama.

Later a church building was erected on property across the street from the seminary and dedicated to the memory of Mrs. W. A. (Florence) Eckel, who passed away in June 1952.

The rapid expansion of the Japanese work called for a strengthened missionary force. Several new recruits were thus commissioned. Besides the Doyle Shepherds and Harrison Davises already mentioned, the Hubert Hellings and Merril Bennetts arrived in 1952, the Bartlett McKays in 1954, the Maurice Rhodens in 1956, the Wendell Woodses in 1959, the Charles Meltons in 1960, and Miss Jean Williams in 1961. In 1952 Miss Catherine Perry, who had gone to Japan under the United States government to serve with the Atomic Bomb Casualty Commission, was appointed a missionary by the General Board and a year later she married Rev. Eckel.

Education Program

With Japan's rapid recovery from the ravages of war came an intense interest in education. It seemed an open door for the church, so when a high school and junior college complex in Chiba City, across Tokyo Bay, became available (partly through earlier ties formed by Chaplain Geren Roberts and Dr. Howard Hamlin), Dr. Eckel contacted Headquarters in Kansas City on the matter. After a visit in 1959 by Dr. Hugh C. Benner, general superintendent, who voiced his approval, the General Board agreed to taking over the property. In April 1960 Rev. Eckel was named chairman of the Board of Regents of the school. Rev. Harrison Davis was transferred from the Bible college to become president of the junior college, while Rev. Hiromichi Oba was continued in his position as principal of the junior and senior high schools. The combined enrollment of the latter reached 687 in 1964.

Although in many ways this was a successful venture, it was never truly a Nazarene mission school, and to continue to fund its operation was considered an unwarranted expenditure of missionary funds. To resolve the matter, a new educational corporation was organized to operate the junior college under the name Japan Nazarene College, while the high school continued as a separate entity under the direction of its founding body.

At the time of the division, the junior college acquired a seven-acre plot of land and constructed the main building. Enrollment was restricted to 120 because of the limited size of the facilities and faculty, but it enjoyed the distinction of being an accredited institution of higher learning. Rev. Harrison Davis, following an extended furlough for advanced studies, returned to Japan and served as president of the newly incorporated institution from 1965 to 1984. Under his leadership the school gained acceptance and a reputation for solid scholastic work. Over the years new buildings and faculty members had been added. The enrollment increased to its present (1985) student body of 185. Following Dr. Davis's resignation, Rev. Fred Forster served one year until his furlough. The school board then appointed Rev. Yozo Seo acting president in 1985.

The Department of English Literature of the junior college trained young people for business and teaching fields, while its Department of Religion included all course work required by the *Manual* of the Church of the Nazarene for ordination. The seminary, a separate institution operating on the headquarters property in Tokyo, provided an additional three years of graduate work. Enrollment at the seminary has ranged between 3 and 10 since the mid-1960s.

In the postwar years, religious radio became popular, and the Church of the Nazarene played its part. Rev. Bartlett McKay, who was very knowledgeable in this area, set up a recording studio at the mission headquarters in Tokyo. Eight programs a week were produced and taped for broadcasting from both the Tokyo/Yokohama and

Osaka/Kyoto areas, which had the highest concentrations of people. Soon responses to "The Nazarene Hour" were averaging about 100 per month. For 18 years Rev. Yozo Seo, dean of the Department of Religion at the junior college, was the principal speaker. He is also an able translator of books and a capable author in his own right. He became chairman of the Evangelical Publishing Association, an organization of holiness denominations in Japan committed to the task of publishing holiness literature. The EPA has already published over 60 volumes, 15 of which were written by Nazarene authors and released through the Nazarene Publishing House.

In the early 1980s the cost of air time had risen so much that the church was forced to cancel its broadcasting contracts. As an alternative plan, weekly programs were aired from Guam on a strong shortwave band. But the results were very disappointing, and the broadcasts were terminated. In 1985 the Radio Committee began negotiations with a company on the west side of the main island (Honshu) where the programs could be aired over stations that reach a large radius.

With the closing of the 17th district assembly, held March 20-22, 1964, Dr. and Mrs. W. A. Eckel concluded their ministry in Japan. Dr. Eckel had arrived in Kobe, Japan, 48 years before on February 25, 1916. Apart from the war years, he had given 42 years of service on this field. His name was synonymous with the Church of the Nazarene, and he was well known both within and without the church.

He had been vitally related to the Japanese church almost from its infancy and had seen it grow to 54 organized churches and 92 preaching points with 48 ordained elders and 28 licensed ministers and other workers. Total membership had reached 3,608.

By the time Dr. Eckel left, Dr. Aishin (Ross) Kida had become district superintendent, to be followed in 1967 by Rev. Takichi Funagoshi. In 1970 Rev. Tsurutaro Sakurai was elected to the office, and in 1973 Rev. Sadao Harada. An unofficial three-year pattern seemed to have been established. A new twist came in 1976 when Rev. Sakurai was elected to a second term. Rev. Shin Kitagawa, son of the pioneer, Hiroshi Kitagawa, then succeeded him in 1979. It was at this assembly that General Superintendent Strickland read the official proclamation recognizing Japan as a regular district. In 1983 Rev. Shinobu Dohi became district superintendent.

Through the years the Japan church followed the policy of assisting with all travel and lodging for delegates to the district assembly. In order to meet the challenge of being a regular district and yet remain financially solvent, the assembly passed a resolution to hold the district assembly every other year. In the interim year a miniassembly was held, with about 55 pastors and several laymen gathering to conduct the required session.

A major move was made in October 1964, when two-thirds of the Setagaya Ku property was sold for $750,000 and the headquarters offices temporarily moved to the Florence Eckel Memorial Church building across the street. The seminary was moved to the junior college campus in Chiba, but it was soon realized that it would be better to be separated from the junior college. By action of the General Board in January 1970, the Japan Theological Seminary was relocated in Tokyo in the new headquarters building that had been completed in February 1967. Dr. Ross Kida served as president until 1976, when Rev. Yozo Seo was elected to leadership. Rev. Masanao Tanimoto succeeded him in 1979, to be followed in 1983 by Rev. Masao Fujii. The teaching load was carried principally by local pastors. Small enrollment, never over 15 (1967) and as low as 6 (1976), was a continuing problem.

In the early 1960s an English-speaking church was organized in Tokyo to minister principally to United States servicemen and their families. It was called the Far East Church of the Nazarene. A serviceman, Gerald Bohall, served as pastor for the first few years, followed in 1963 by Rev. Ralph Wynkoop, whose wife, Dr. Mildred Wynkoop, was president of the seminary and also teaching at the junior college. From 1967 on, missionaries served as pastors for varying periods, among them Rev. Merril Bennett, Rev. Hubert Helling, Rev. Fred Forster, Dr. Chester Mulder, and Rev. David Cox. U.S. servicemen, such as Richard Schwartz, often assisted as associate pastors.

As the number of servicemen in the country rapidly declined in the 1970s, Japanese people began moving into the housing areas being vacated. As a result, the Far East Church became quite cosmopolitan. During this transition period, pastors have been Rev. Doyle Shepherd, Rev. Donald Byrnes, Rev. Wendell Woods, and Rev. Larry Wagner.

4. *Okinawa*

The Ryukyu Islands, about 100 in number, stretch some 600 miles southwestward from Kyushu toward Taiwan. Near the southern end of the chain is the largest of the islands, Okinawa, 65 miles long and from 2 to 12 miles wide. The Ryukyus for centuries had been under Japanese control, but in 1879 the area was made a prefecture (province or state) of Japan, its people becoming Japanese citizens.

During the occupation following World War II, the islands were under United States mandate. Millions of dollars were poured into the area to rebuild its economy following the devastation of the war. Its great airfields, which were the launching areas for the final bombing forays on Japan, were later strategic to the United States in the Korean and Vietnam wars. Okinawa was therefore aptly designated the "Keystone of the Pacific."

On May 15, 1972, the United States government's administrative control over the Ryukyu Islands came to a close, and they were once more a prefecture of Japan.

At the beginning of World War II there were only about 12 Protestant churches in the Ryukyu Islands with about 1,000 members. These were largely wiped out in the conflict. But immediately after the war many Christian missions were begun, supported strongly by interested servicemen of the occupation forces and particularly by the chaplains. These various missions (Methodist, Baptist, Presbyterian, Japanese Holiness church [Oriental Missionary Society], and Salvation Army) joined forces under the name United Church of Christ of Okinawa.

The Church of the Nazarene began work independently in 1957, but the first steps in that direction had been taken back in 1953. Dr. Eckel was urged by an Okinawan man he met in Japan, to open work among his people. In response Dr. Eckel journeyed to the island and conferred with various persons including Chaplain Charles Crouch and Miss Viola Roberts. The tentative strategy planned was to send two couples, one Japanese and one missionary, to open the work. The logical target area would be the capital city of Naha with its population of 350,000.

Finally, in December 1956, the Japan Mission Council decided it was time to take action. But none of the missionaries volunteered to go, and when a straw vote was taken, the result was indecisive. The matter was tabled until the next day. That morning (January 1, 1957)

Mattie Shepherd divulged to her husband at the breakfast table that the day before she had voted for them to go to Okinawa. Why would she do such a thing without consulting him? he wanted to know. But his remonstrance was hollow, for he admitted that Okinawa had been on his own mind and heart for some time. He had made it a matter of prayer, and to him this was the confirmation he needed.

When the council reconvened that morning and Dr. Eckel opened the subject of Okinawa for discussion once more, Doyle Shepherd could hardly wait to tell what had transpired earlier in their home. He recalled the time in November 1946, when listening to Dr. Howard Hamlin speak at a GI Gospel Hour in Tokyo, he and Ardee Coolidge (who later went to Argentina) answered the call of God to missionary service. The call to Okinawa, he said, was as clear as the call to Japan itself had been back there.

At about the time God was speaking to the Shepherds about Okinawa, he was laying a similar burden on the pastor of the Meguro Church in Tokyo, Rev. Shigeru Higuchi. When a few days later Dr. Eckel approached him and his wife about going to Okinawa, they readily said yes. It was not the first time Okinawa had been brought to his mind. As a boy he had been strongly influenced by a Christian teacher from Okinawa by the name of Tonaki. Then during the war he was sent to Mongolia, where he became ill and was hospitalized. While thus out of action, his battalion was transferred to Okinawa, where most of his friends were killed. He was moved to a hospital in Peking, China, where he heard via radio the Japanese emperor's words of unconditional surrender.

Returning to his home, he began attending the Congregational church, where he met his former teacher, Tonaki. At Christmastime he gave his heart to the Lord. He enrolled in the religion department of the junior college in Chiba, where he came in touch with Dr. Eckel and other Nazarene national leaders. He was so impressed that he joined the church and upon graduation was appointed pastor of a new church in Ushiku, in Chiba Prefecture.

In April 1957 an advance party consisting of the Eckels, Ross Kida, Shigeru Higuchi, Hubert Helling, and Doyle Shepherd went to Okinawa to establish a beachhead. A house was purchased in Naha on a tract of land large enough for a future church building. However, when the two couples arrived three months later to begin work, the owner of the land had changed his mind about the property and doubled the price. An adjacent tract was acquired, however, and until a building could be erected, services were held in a rented house.

The next target area for a church was Mashiki, 10 or 12 miles north of Naha. The Naha church accepted the challenge of opening work here, and on January 15, 1959, Operation Mashiki was held. Twenty or more new Christians trudged up and down the streets in the drizzling rain, distributing handbills and tracts. Services were held in rented quarters until a tiny Alabaster church was built in 1961 under the leadership of Rev. Merril Bennett, who had been transferred there from Japan in 1960.

In the meantime, while Rev. Shepherd had been looking for land on which to build the Mashiki church, a Mr. Miwa, who lived at Gusukuma, halfway between Naha and Mashiki, offered to sell the church a beautiful tract overlooking the China Sea. Although the Mashiki area was the prime target at the moment, the property was purchased and services begun in the Miwa home. The Los Angeles District provided funds for a church building in Gusukuma.

Christian missionary efforts on Okinawa were vigorously opposed by the powerful, militant Soka Gakkai religious sect, which has Buddhist roots. On the other hand the American Christian servicemen gave encouragement and support. They also held monthly fellowship meetings among themselves.

In September 1961 regular Sunday afternoon English services were begun in the little Alabaster church in Mashiki. The leaders of this work were Air Force T/Sgt. Thomas L. Blaxton, an ordained elder, and Marine Chaplain Harlan Shippy. Rev. Blaxton had worked with Rev. Shepherd earlier when both were stationed in Hokkaido, Japan's northern island. Providentially, after a tour of duty in the United States, Rev. Blaxton had been reassigned to Okinawa. Being attached to the chaplaincy office, he had access to the religious preference cards of 14,000 airmen, and through this, numerous contacts were established. Soon the church, which could hold at best only 25 or 30 people, was crowded out; so the servicemen told Rev. Shepherd that if he could get the money to build another wing on the church, they would pay back the cost.

By the time the church was officially organized in September 1962 as the Keystone Church of the Nazarene with 24 members, most of the $7,000 building cost had already been paid back. Full payment was completed the following year. Rev. Thomas Blaxton became the pastor of the church and served until the air force transferred him to Kyushu 17 months later.

Rev. Shepherd assumed the pastoral duties and was responsible for securing an ideal piece of property in the Chatan area north of Mashiki. When the Shepherds returned to the U.S.A. in 1966, Rev. Wendell Woods became the missionary in charge and pastor of the Keystone Church. In 1967 Rev. William Kelvington was appointed pastor. During his ministry the new Keystone building was completed at Chatan in 1968. In 1970 Dr. George Taylorson began an effective five years of service there. He invited the local Japanese congregation, which had been meeting in rented quarters, to share the Keystone facilities.

In 1975 Missionary Fred Forster became pastor, and some important changes were effected. Among these were the completion of the second story of the fellowship hall for a parsonage and the addition of a third congregation, a Chinese church, to share the Keystone facilities. When the Forsters furloughed in 1980, Rev. Dean Flemming became pastor, to be followed by Rev. David Kennedy and then Rev. Levi Johnson.

Although the English congregation had declined from its peak of about 250 in the mid-1970s due to the partial withdrawal of the United States occupation forces, attendance by 1985 was still averaging over 140.

In the early 1970s a piece of property was purchased for a parsonage in Chatan Village. Years later this became the site for the Chatan Japanese church. An attractive building was constructed and designated the Shepherd Memorial Church. Both the Japanese and Chinese congregations that had been meeting in the Keystone Church now had permanent homes.

By 1985 there were six churches in the Okinawa Prefecture. These with the 67 other churches in Japan proper reported a combined membership of 4,840.

D. KOREA

Korea, situated in the heart of the Far East, remained for centuries a strangely remote land, ethnically pure, and tied to its ancient traditions. It has been aptly called the "Hermit Nation." Even the Church of the Nazarene passed it by as it established work in the country's more dominant neighbors, China and Japan.

But the beautiful Land of the Morning Calm was not wholly out of mind. In 1936 Sung-oak Chang,* a young Korean student who had gone to Japan to further his education, crossed paths with Rev. W. A. Eckel and Rev. Nobumi Isayama. These men were able to help him become established in the Christian faith and encouraged him to return to his homeland and start a Nazarene church there.

He successfully launched a work in Pyongyang, the capital city of what is now North Korea, and then went down to Seoul, present capital of South Korea, to establish another church. In the latter place he secured an assistant by the name of Huk-soo Sung. The work was officially under the supervision of the Japan mission, but the relationship was apparently quite tenuous. There is record that both Rev. W. A. Eckel and Rev. Nobumi Isayama held meetings in Korea, and both were enthusiastic about the potential for missionary work there. In fact, Rev. Eckel was so enamored with the country, he offered to go himself. At the same time, however, he objected to the fact that the support of the Korean work had to come out of his already strapped budget for Japan.

At the close of World War II, as part of the mandating of former Japanese territory, Korea was divided at the 38th parallel, with the northern part being assigned to the Soviet Union and the southern part to the United States. Under the occupation policies of the Soviets, Communist doctrine was vigorously promoted in their area, and the persecution of Christian communities became standard procedure. It

---

*Strictly speaking, the Koreans write their surnames first (for example, Chang Sung Oak), but for various reasons it has been decided to use the Western style in this book and hyphenate the given names.

was the opposite in the South, where the MacArthur policy of freedom of religion and the encouragement of Christian missions was the rule.

The result was a mass emigration of Christians from the North into South Korea. Rev. Sung-oak Chang and most of his congregation were involved in the exodus and joined forces in Seoul with Rev. Sung and his people. Several Nazarene servicemen in the occupation army were regular attenders at the church, bringing encouragement to the people and cementing the ties to the denomination. The records reveal very few other lines of communication, however.

1. *Rev. Robert Chung*

The Church of the Nazarene was to find another channel through which to reach Korea in the person of Dr. Robert Chung, one of the country's best-known evangelists. His personal story and the providential circumstances that led him into the Church of the Nazarene are witness to the "wondrous ways" in which God builds His kingdom.

In 1907, during a time of great spiritual revival in Korea, a lanky, red-whiskered, Presbyterian missionary by the name of Hunter came to a small village near Pyongyang to preach to the people. He was a novelty in the village because the Koreans are ordinarily small of stature with black hair and flat noses. Hunter's height, red beard, and long nose brought him much attention, particularly among the small boys of the village who had never before seen a Caucasian. But response to the gospel that the man preached was limited until a prominent citizen by the name of Kang was converted. Thus began a great turning to the Lord that swept through the entire village. Among those converted was the 13-year-old grandson of Kang, Nam-soo Chung. He in turn led several of his friends to the Lord. He was a special favorite of the missionaries, who gave to him the Western name of Robert.

In his late teens and early 20s, Robert Chung became involved with C. H. Ahn, a leader in the nationalist movement seeking to thwart the intrusion of the Japanese into their country. Robert, a promising leader, was sent to Seoul for special training in revolutionary tactics. When Mr. Ahn was imprisoned for a time for his activities, young Robert took care of him, providing him with food and other comforts.

Finally, Mr. Ahn decided to flee the country, taking Robert with him. They stowed away on a Chinese junk loaded with salt, which took them across the Yellow Sea to China. From there they made their way to Vladivostok, near the eastern terminus of the Trans-Siberian Railroad. They then made the long journey by train to Europe and crossed the Channel to England. From there they took a ship to the United States, arriving in October 1911.

Their final destination was California, where Robert found employment. Things did not go well, however, and finally in company with a newfound friend, Joseph Chae, he boarded a train for Cincinnati. On the train they made the acquaintance of a tall, white-haired man who successfully persuaded Robert to go to Asbury College in Wilmore, Ky. That man was the president of the college, Dr. H. C. Morrison.

At Asbury, Robert went through a time of spiritual struggle that culminated in a mighty baptism with the Holy Spirit. He committed himself to the ministry of the gospel and upon graduation in 1926 returned to his homeland. He organized the Korean Holiness Evangelistic Band and for a number of years was an independent evangelist having his own tent and a supporting cast of musicians. He frequently returned to the United States to muster financial support, principally from Methodist holiness camp meetings. His ministry throughout the land was blessed of God, and he became known as "The Billy Sunday of Korea."

With the outbreak of World War II in 1939, the Japanese rulers began to look with suspicion on any movements that had connections with the United States. Missionaries in general, and Robert Chung in particular, were suspect and were subjected to strict surveillance. After Pearl Harbor the opposition intensified. Robert Chung was imprisoned for a time and suffered torture. Forced to cease his evangelistic activities, he retired to a rural area where he farmed until the end of the war.

In 1947 he returned to the United States, renewing old acquaintances and holding services. In the course of his travels he met Dr. C. Warren Jones, then executive secretary of the Department of Foreign Missions, who urged him to join the Church of the Nazarene and set up a missionary program in Korea. He was familiar with the church, for a number of his Asbury classmates were Nazarenes, and he had spoken in their churches. He had also met Dr. W. A. Eckel of Japan and the two Nazarene preachers, Chang and Sung.

Following Dr. Jones's suggestion, he returned in 1948 and contacted several of the independent pastors with whom he had worked in earlier years. He also talked with the two Nazarene ministers who doubtless welcomed association with such a famous evangelist.

In October of that year, a meeting of interested pastors with General Superintendent Orval J. Nease was arranged in Seoul. A tentative church organization was set up, and the credentials of seven elders were recognized, including those of Robert Chung and the two Nazarene pastors, Chang and Sung. A five-man committee was set up with Robert Chung as chairman to direct the church's affairs. Nine congregations with 835 adherents were involved.

These independent-minded pastors and churches were wary of any kind of superintendency or missionary intrusion and were adamant about the five-man committee arrangement. This made it difficult for Robert Chung to implement the administrative structure of the Church of the Nazarene. Indeed, it never was accomplished with that group, for catastrophic events soon altered the picture drastically.

2. *The Korean War*

At dawn on June 25, 1950, the armed forces of North Korea swept across the 38th parallel against the hapless South Koreans, who were totally unprepared for such an invasion. Though the outmanned and outgunned defenders attempted some delaying action, there was a steady retreat toward Seoul, and the fall of that city seemed imminent.

Sensing the impending disaster, Robert Chung loaded his family and possessions into his 1947 automobile and headed south, miraculously making it through to the port city of Pusan. There he sold the car and bought passage on a ship headed for the United States for military supplies. Thus the family escaped the privations of the ensuing war. It also gave Rev. Chung opportunity to speak in a number of Nazarene churches in the United States, inspiring prayerful interest in the Korean work.

When the uneasy truce was signed at Panmunjom in 1953, plans were made for Robert Chung to return to continue the development of the Korean work. In early 1954 he made a brief inspection trip in which he discovered that a number of the churches had been destroyed or damaged, and one of the pastors, Rev. Huk-soo Sung, along with many church members had been killed. Reporting back to

Dr. Remiss Rehfeldt, then executive secretary of the Department of Foreign Missions, he secured the promise of funds for reconstruction and also the assurance that a missionary couple would be sent.

But when the Chungs returned to Korea to once more set up the church structure, they found the welcome was somewhat less than cordial. Possibly there was resentment that they had fled the country and had not experienced any of the suffering the others had had to endure. But also the spirit of independence still prevailed, and on second thought several of the pastors decided that they did not wish to continue working with Rev. Chung or the Church of the Nazarene. Added to this, the one remaining original Nazarene pastor, Rev. Chang, had become full-time chaplain of the Young Chun prison near his former church in Seoul and was no longer available. The frustrated leader was left with eight congregations, only four of which had church buildings, and about 400 adherents.

3. *The First Missionaries*

The first Nazarene missionaries, in the persons of Don and Adeline Owens, arrived in Seoul on May 29, 1954. Graduates of Bethany Nazarene College, they were pastoring at Fairbury, Nebr., when they offered themselves for missionary service and were placed under general appointment. They were assigned specifically to Korea after the Panmunjom truce was signed. They were the fulfillment of the promise made to Robert Chung that a missionary couple would be sent to help him.

It is reported that some of the pastors who met the new missionaries were somewhat dismayed at their youthfulness. "They have sent us Boy Scouts," they moaned. But in true Korean fashion, the Owenses were welcomed warmly. The name the people gave them, *Oh Eun-soo*, was a spin-off of their English name but also meant "Someone who has received much grace." God gave Rev. Owens the seal of His blessing when in the first service after his arrival 30 people came forward to receive Christ as their Savior.

An initial task was to work out property settlements with the defecting churches whose buildings were legally in the name of the Church of the Nazarene. There was also the task of repairing the remaining buildings and providing chapels for the house churches. Alabaster funds were provided for this, and helpful GIs obtained trucks to transport material, supplies, and equipment to the building sites. The help and support of American military personnel in many ways was of immeasurable value during this time.

An early task also was the organization of a Bible school, because indoctrination of the present pastors and the training of new workers was a pressing need. A fire-gutted former missionary home was purchased and rehabilitated for this purpose. The second floor was converted into an apartment for the missionaries. The school was opened in September 1954 with 23 students, 8 of whom were pastors.

The only teachers available were the Owenses, for by this time the Chungs had returned to the United States to retire in Florida. Their departure took place only three months after the Owenses had come, and the young missionaries were left with a staggering task. Many loose ends had yet to be gathered together, and a viable program for development and expansion needed to be set in motion.

The quick moves to repair and build churches, to provide parsonages, and to distribute the huge quantities of food and clothing generously supplied from overseas boosted morale among the churches, and a spirit of optimism and courage began to grow.

Mr. Yoon-kyu Jun proved to be an invaluable assistant in these beginning days. He was the Owenses' interpreter as they taught their classes in the Bible training school, and he later became a professor himself.

In early 1955 Dr. Remiss Rehfeldt visited Korea and conducted a preachers' meeting. Many organizational matters were clarified at this time. Also it was decided to make plans to officially organize the district with delegates from the churches electing their own national leaders. A busy time lay ahead for the missionaries who, besides conducting the complex affairs of the church, were struggling through language school, trying to learn the difficult Korean language. In addition, the church *Manual* that Robert Chung had helped translate had to be printed and the pastors instructed in the necessary preparations for the proposed assembly.

In mid-July 1955 a three-day preachers' workshop was held to instruct the pastors in the basics of church government. Thus, when the assembly convened on August 30, the business flowed smoothly. The evening services of the three-day meeting were also times of spiritual blessing as several sought and found the experience of entire sanctification.

When it came time to choose a district superintendent, there was only one Korean ordained elder on the district who qualified for election, Rev. Kee-suh Park. The assembly elected Rev. Don Owens as superintendent, but on the advice of Headquarters in Kansas City it was considered better to have a national in that position. Therefore, at the General Board meeting in January 1956, Rev. Park was appointed district superintendent. He had already proved himself to be a capable church planter, for he was responsible for four of the congregations that had come into the church back in 1948.

At the assembly, the Ways and Means Committee, composed of all pastors, took significant action concerning self-support. Each local congregation was to assume a portion of the pastor's salary. That salary was set at $26.00 a month plus $3.00 for each member of the family. An additional $5.00 was allowed for city pastors because their expenses were obviously greater. To take care of any special needs such as medical expenses, an emergency fund was set up to be administered by the District Advisory Board. The offerings in each church on the first Sundays of March, June, September, and December were sent in for this fund.

The orderly organization of a national district produced a healthy sense of responsibility. Pastors and people alike rallied to the new challenge. An awareness of their own mission to promote scriptural holiness in the framework of the Church of the Nazarene was established.

There began a surge of growth that was to gain momentum in the years that followed. A key method of church planting was the "Moving Nazarene Family" idea. A family would move into a new community and begin holding Bible studies in their home. If interest grew, a house church would be organized and a property search begun, leading to the building of a church. Sometimes a tent would serve as a temporary meeting place. Bible school students or neighboring pastors would hold the regular services until a full-time pastor could be supported.

When a church was ready to build, Alabaster funds would be requested, but always the local group was expected to contribute half the cost in either funds, material, or labor.

By the time the third district assembly convened on March 12, 1957, there were 45 delegates representing 23 churches with a total membership of 1,332. In June of that year Rev. and Mrs. Eldon Cornett and their two sons arrived on the field and immediately began intensive language study at a mission language school and also under the tutelage of a private teacher, Mr. Seung-jin Kim. Mr. Kim continued as a translator and teacher in the Bible college. Within a year the Cornetts were involved fully in the work of the college and in other phases of the work.

4. *The Korean Bible College*

The original buildings that had been purchased in Seoul for the Bible school were woefully inadequate to take care of the school's growing needs, let alone the mission headquarters offices and missionary residence that were also there. In 1956 Rev. Owens began searching for a possible site for a future campus.

Early in 1957 an available 21-acre tract was found just west of the city on the highway to Kimpo Air Force Base. The $5,000 cost was paid from Alabaster funds. The low price was doubtless because part of the land was owned by the government, and only user's rights would be granted. To build on that part would be a somewhat precarious venture. The mission negotiated with the authorities for months, seeking to obtain a clear title, but without success. Not until the existing government was overthrown by a military coup in 1961 and a more accommodating regime installed was a clear title to the entire tract issued. This unusual answer to prayer inspired the faith of the people.

In the meantime, the first class of five students graduated August 1, 1958. At the same time, four Korean pastors completed the home course of study. The education program was already paying off.

That summer the buildings in Seoul had been sold to help launch the building program on the new site. An extensive project was undertaken with nine separate structures being erected. On the first week in January 1959, the school, under the name Nazarene Bible College, moved into its new quarters, which consisted of a main administration and classroom building, dormitories for men and for women, and a dining hall. In addition there were three Korean teachers' homes and two missionary homes. The prudence of this move, despite the uncertainties of ownership at that time, became obvious when, 10 years later, this property that had been purchased for $5,000 was now valued at $1.25 million and was still rising.

The fourth district assembly convened here in March 1959, with Dr. Hugh C. Benner presiding. It was the first visit by a general superintendent since 1948. During the assembly, dedication ceremonies were held for the new campus, and at the closing service, 10 men were ordained to the ministry. Statistically, there were now 28 fully organized churches and preaching points, 2 of which were totally self-supporting. There were 35 national workers including 11 ordained elders, 4 missionaries, and 1,888 members.

At the fifth assembly in March 1960, Missionary Eldon Cornett presided, since the Owenses were home on furlough. Two new churches were reported. At the sixth assembly in 1961, there was a change in leadership when Rev. Chong-soo Kim was elected district superintendent. He had been a successful businessman prior to his conversion and had served as district treasurer since the inception of the district, so he was a well-qualified leader.

That year also, the Charles Strouds joined the missionary staff. He was an experienced builder whose skills were particularly valuable at this time of expansion, and she was an excellent musician. After taking language training at Yonsai University, they began teaching at the Bible college and holding evangelistic services.

General Superintendent Samuel Young and Dr. George Coulter, then executive secretary of the Department of Foreign Missions, were present for the eighth district assembly in April 1963. By this time there were 39 organized churches, 5 of them self-supporting, with a membership of nearly 3,000. There were 52 national workers. During the visit of the church leaders, a Far East Servicemen's Retreat was held in Seoul with about 40 United States armed forces personnel and their wives in attendance.

Church planting and self-support were twin themes of the district program in those years. In two years' time 8 more churches were added, while those achieving self-support jumped from 5 to 11. Total membership in 1965 was 3,820.

Early in the Korean work a system for reaching the level of full self-support was worked out in which the mission subsidy granted a church was reduced annually by 10 percent. Theoretically, in 10 years a church would become self-supporting, though many achieved this goal in much less time. The incentive was that the district would thus have more money to invest in opening new churches.

As an extension of the Bible college, teams of teachers went out to the churches to hold three- to five-day leadership training courses. Doctrine, Bible, teacher training, and evangelism were the main subjects. This produced a strong laity and knowledgeable delegates for the annual assemblies. A district paper, *Nasaret Sori* ("Nazarene

Voice"), was also useful in keeping local churches informed and involved.

In 1965 the Owenses returned to the United States on their second furlough, at the conclusion of which he became a professor at Bethany Nazarene College. They were replaced by Rev. and Mrs. Paul Stubbs, who had previously been associated with the Oriental Missionary Society in Seoul, teaching in the school that served missionary children and others in the foreign community. They were already oriented to the field and moved swiftly into the work.

In the latter half of the decade there was rapid growth. District Superintendent Kim was a resourceful church planter, and congregations sprang up both in the city and in rural areas. Revivals broke out in many of the established churches. One instrument God used greatly was the Bible college quartet organized by Rev. Stubbs.

In 1967 Rev. and Mrs. Stephen Rieder from Pennsylvania joined the missionary force, and for a brief time there were four couples on the field. But in 1968 the Strouds returned to the United States and assumed a pastorate in Oklahoma.

By 1970 there were 70 congregations with 6,155 members. At the beginning of the decade the corresponding figures had been 30 and 1,698. The work had been growing, but progress had perceptibly slowed in recent years. The emergence of strong but unyielding personalities among the national church leaders created crosscurrents of criticism and disloyalty that adversely affected the work. At the 1970 district assembly, the validity of the ballot that reelected Chong-soo Kim as district superintendent was questioned, and an acrimonious debate arose on matters of parliamentary procedure. The missionaries were frustrated in their efforts to calm the troubled waters because they could ill afford being accused of choosing sides.

As a result of the altercation, the rapid growth of previous years ground to a halt, and the future of the work was in jeopardy. General Superintendent Orville W. Jenkins and Foreign Missions Executive Secretary E. S. Phillips made a trip to Korea in 1971 to seek a solution to the problem. Their decision was to have the Don Owenses return to Korea for a short assignment along with the Paul Stubbses, who had been home on furlough. At the same time the Eldon Cornetts and Stephen Rieders, who had unwittingly been caught in the cross fire and who were due for furlough anyway, were returned to the United States. This strategic move produced the desired result of reconciliation. But more importantly, the Spirit of God came upon the people in a healing wave that not only restored peace and confidence but set the church off on a new sweep of revival and expansion.

In March 1972 Dr. Orville Jenkins returned to conduct the district assembly at Chun-ahn. Smoothly the organizational and policy matters that had caused the rift in the first place were resolved, and in an atmosphere of revival proportions, Dr. Jenkins ordained 19 Korean pastors.

5. *Golden Years of Growth*

At the 1972 assembly the proposal was made that the district be divided. A committee was appointed to study the matter. When, at the conclusion of the General Assembly in Miami that summer, District Superintendent Kim accepted the invitation to become the pastor of a Korean congregation in Chicago, it seemed an appropriate time to follow through on the proposed division. The study committee that had been set up was now called upon to carry the matter through to implementation.

Thus in September 1973 a special assembly was called, presided over by General Superintendent Eugene Stowe, in which the Central and South districts were organized. In the naming of the districts there was perhaps the veiled hope that in time the Korean nation would once again be unified, and North Korea would become accessible to the gospel. In such case, a true North Korea District would come into being.

The Central District selected as its leader Rev. Moon-kyung Cho, who had been with the church since Robert Chung days, had taught theology and Greek in the Korean Nazarene Bible College, and was currently pastoring the largest Nazarene church in the country. He had been ordained by Dr. Benner in 1959.

The South District elected Rev. Jung-hwan Oh as its superintendent. He also had been ordained by Dr. Benner in 1959 and was in the first graduating class of the Bible college in 1958. For nine years he had been the treasurer of the combined districts. His special skill was in church planting.

Earlier in 1973 the great Billy Graham campaigns had been held in Korea, and a climate of response to the Christian gospel had been created throughout the nation. Over 80,000 accepted Christ in the course of the various campaigns around the country, and in the final rally in Seoul, an estimated 1.1 million attended. It was the largest gathering in Christian church history. The students of the Nazarene Bible College actively participated in the Seoul campaign.

The effects of the Graham crusade rippled out through all the evangelical churches, but the Church of the Nazarene, partly because of encouraging developments within its own organization, reaped the most bountiful harvest of all. Within a year the number of churches leaped from 79 to 125, and membership more than doubled from 7,126 to 16,532.

In August 1974, Explo '74, sponsored by Campus Crusade for Christ, was held in Korea, when some 300,000 received special training in personal evangelism, discipling, and personal Christian living. Once more the nation was exposed to the gospel in a dramatic way. On Saturday afternoon the delegates, armed with the familiar *Four Spiritual Laws*, attempted to reach the entire 6 million people of Seoul. It was an unprecedented experiment in saturation evangelism.

Following Explo '74, the Nazarene Korean pastors and hundreds of laymen retired to a mountain retreat and spent five days in intensive Bible study and prayer, led by their district superintendents. The result was an intensified vision of what could be accomplished in the propagation of the gospel in Korea. The two districts in their first year of separate operation gained a combined total of 2,222 members.

Rev. A. Brent Cobb, who had been appointed to Korea in 1970, became the mission director in 1975, replacing Rev. Paul Stubbs, who returned to the United States. There followed a period of unusual progress. The Korea Nazarene Theological College with its 70 students was under the capable leadership of William Patch, who was elected president in 1975. He and his wife, experienced educators, came to Korea in 1973 as lay missionaries to teach in the college. A Korean, Rev. Young-baik Kim, was dean of the college and also the featured speaker on one of the two national radio programs sponsored by the Church of the Nazarene.

Rev. and Mrs. Kenneth Schubert were added to the college staff in 1974. Then in 1977 the coming of Dr. and Mrs. Donald LeRoy Stults gave an additional vital lift. The Timothy Mercers, who arrived in 1979, also taught at the college.

The government Ministry of Education was exerting increasing pressure that the college would have to be accredited or cease functioning. It was also made clear that such accreditation could not be obtained if the college remained at its Seoul location. In June 1978 the decision was made to sell the college campus and accompanying mission property and relocate. In December the sale of a majority of the land was consummated for $4.5 million. With this capital, in March 1979 a 32-acre tract was purchased in Chonan, 50 miles south of Seoul, and a 4-story, 76,000-square-foot college building valued at $2.25 million was completed in 1980. This paved the way for the first stage of accreditation in June 1981, followed in March 1985 by full accreditation as a four-year college-level institution. Enrollment began to rise, reaching 93 by 1985 with 160 anticipated by 1987.

In February 1982 the remainder of the Seoul property was sold for $1.4 million. It was agreed that the total income from the property sale ($5.9 million) would be divided three ways: a small portion would be set aside for replacing missionary homes that had been on the original property, while 70 percent of the remainder would go for college relocation, and 30 percent for home mission programs, buildings, and land.

In line with the practice of other denominations, it was decided to invest the district's share in an income-producing office building. A beautiful nine-story structure containing 84,600 square feet was built in the south coast city of Taejon and dedicated on October 26, 1984. It was valued at $2.6 million. After payment of the residual debt on the project was completed, rental income would go to home mission projects and a college scholarship fund.

During all this feverish real estate activity, there developed much mistrust and suspicion among the pastors and churches about how the money was being spent. It was a turbulent time that left wounds that were slow to heal. Nevertheless positive moves were being made to expand the Korean work.

It was obvious that development thus far had followed the Seoul-Taejon axis with a heavy concentration in the vicinity of Seoul. In an attempt to correct this situation, in March 1981 the Korea East District was split off from the Central District, with the veteran Rev. Ki-suh Park being appointed superintendent. The new district began with 8 organized churches and 294 members. About the same time, the Korea Honam District to the southwest was split off from the South District with Rev. Jung-moon Suh, NYI president of the South District, being appointed superintendent. This new district had a healthy 16 churches with 1,201 members.

The following year, the southeastern part of the country was set off from the South District to form the Korea Yongnam District with

7 churches and 369 members. Rev. Young-sup Ahn, pastor for 15 years on the Central District, was named superintendent.

By 1983 all three of the new districts had reached mission phase. Korea Central had attained regular district status in March 1981, while the South District was expected to reach that level in 1986.

By 1985 total membership in Korea stood at 28,006 with 161 churches. During the quinquennium giving had tripled, going from $770,980 (U.S.) in 1980 to $2,232,096 in 1985. The mission director during all this reorganization and growth was Rev. Kenneth Schubert, who was originally appointed in 1979.

E. THE PHILIPPINES

The Republic of the Philippines consists of an archipelago of some 7,000 islands off the southeast coast of Asia. They stretch over 1,100 miles from Taiwan in the north to Malaysia on the south. Almost all the over 50 million inhabitants are concentrated on the 11 largest islands, of which Luzon and Mindanao are the principal ones. English and Tagalog are the two official languages.

The islands came under United States control in 1898 as part of the settlement of the Spanish-American War. Occupied by the Japanese during World War II, the country became an independent republic in 1946.

Three hundred years of Spanish domination of the Philippines prior to the United States takeover brought with it the Roman Catholic church. During that era, religious freedom was unknown, and there was tragic exploitation of the land and its people by the Roman church. Despite the injustices inflicted upon them by the church, the vast majority of the people remained strangely loyal, and even today 80 percent are nominally Roman Catholic.

Though religious freedom was declared by the United States, the existing property holdings of the Roman Catholic church were recognized, which meant a continuation of much of their power. But at least the door was now open to Protestant missions. Old-line denominations such as the Methodists, Baptists, and Presbyterians quickly seized the opportunity to launch missionary work. In fact, the first distinctly Protestant sermon was preached in Manila while the Spanish-American War was still in progress. At first, comity agreements were worked out to give each organization specific territory and thus avoid competition, but these boundaries have since been abandoned.

It took World War II to bring the Philippines into national and world attention. It was from these islands that General MacArthur escaped in the dark days following Pearl Harbor, vowing that he would return, which indeed he did as he splashed ashore on the island of Leyte on October 20, 1944.

Thousands of United States servicemen were in the Philippines at the close of the war, among them many Nazarenes who were interested in the potential there for missionary work. Chaplains J. E. Moore, Jr., A. Bond Woodruff, and Joseph Pitts, in particular, were to figure strongly in the launching of the work there.

1. *Early Nazarene Beginnings*

Though the Nazarene missionary program in the Philippines was not officially begun until after the war, its roots go back much farther.

Large numbers of Filipinos had migrated to the United States in the earlier years of the century, most of them settling along the West Coast. Among them was a young student by the name of Marciano Encarnacion, who came over in the early 1920s. He came into contact with the people of the First Church of the Nazarene in Seattle, where he was converted and sanctified. Through that church's influence, and doubtless with its financial backing, he went to Northwest Nazarene College to complete his high school in their academy. He returned to Seattle and began his studies for a degree in pharmacy at the state university.

Upon graduating in 1926, he returned to his homeland, hoping and praying that missionaries would soon be sent. Missionaries or no, Marciano started evangelizing on his own, preaching whenever he had opportunity and traveling about as much as his pharmacy job in Baguio City would allow. He was rewarded with a number of converts at several places between Baguio City and Manila.

The nature or extent of the contact maintained between Mr. Encarnacion and his friends in the United States are unknown, but the Philippines were not out of mind as far as the general church was concerned. Dr. J. G. Morrison, then secretary of the Department of Foreign Missions, in an editorial in the November 1928 *Other Sheep*, expressed his concern for the Philippines. "Would God the Church of the Nazarene could enter that opportune field," he wrote.

In 1935 a Filipino evangelist, saved in a Methodist mission in the Philippines and sanctified while attending God's Bible School in Cincinnati, made application to the Nazarene mission board for missionary service in his homeland. But the church had apparently not sufficiently recovered from the depression to consider opening a new field.

In 1939 Rev. W. A. Eckel visited Manila to look into the spiritual needs of thousands of Japanese who had migrated there, but in the process he caught a vision of the need and challenge of this field. "The country is largely Catholic," he wrote, "but is under the Stars and Stripes—a free land in which to preach."

Then came the liberation of the Philippines following World War II and the great influx of American servicemen. Chaplain J. E. Moore, Jr., of the army's 86th Division in Manila was aware of previous Nazarene influence in the islands, and with the official blessing of the church leaders, he began to search for these roots. Through Colonel Lindval of the Salvation Army he was directed to Marciano Encarnacion in Baguio City, the summer capital, 150 miles to the north. But he had no specific address, so when he arrived, Chaplain Moore stepped into a drugstore to see if anyone there might know about the pharmacist he was seeking. Who should be behind the counter but Mr. Encarnacion himself!

When the chaplain told him why he was looking for him, the man broke down and cried. Then with shouts of joy he exclaimed, "For 20 years I have been praying for a Nazarene work in the Philippines!"

Chaplain Moore was transferred out before a mission could be started, but a fellow chaplain, A. Bond Woodruff, picked up where he had left off.

The decision was made to begin work at Cabanatuan City, a provincial capital of 20,000 population about halfway between Baguio City and Manila. Here there was a nucleus of Christians, most of whom had been converted under Marciano's ministry. Also it was his hometown, and his sister Paulina's home was available as a meeting place. The Christians canvassed the area and announced services and also held street meetings. The response was encouraging, and on May 19, 1946, the first Church of the Nazarene in the Philippines was organized with 29 members. Mr. Encarnacion was appointed pastor and treasurer. Chaplain Woodruff was also transferred home, but by now the work was well enough established to continue.

The third chaplain, Rev. Joseph Pitts, had been returned to the States before these developments, but he had taken with him a great burden for the Philippines. He prayed earnestly that God would call someone to that needy field. As the months passed, he began to hear the voice of the Holy Spirit saying, "Why don't you go?"

Convinced the call was of the Lord, he offered to go back as a missionary for the church. He was quickly placed under appointment, and in January 1948 he and his family were on their way. They landed at Manila on February 10 and were met by Marciano Encarnacion, who took them to Cabanatuan City.

For six months the Pitts family lived in Cabanatuan City, working out from there into other towns and villages. Open-air meetings were the chief method of evangelizing. One place where they found good response was Cabu, where a large Japanese prison camp had been located during the war. However, a church was not organized yet, principally because of the political unrest in the area. Ever since the United States had granted independence, establishing the Republic of the Philippines on July 4, 1946, and even before, Communist rebels had sought to overthrow the government. This People's Liberation Army ("Huks" for short) was quite strong in the Cabanatuan City area.

Iloilo

In July 1948, in response to a request from a Rev. Catalina, pastor of a Filipino church in the United States, the Pittses went to Iloilo on the island of Panay, about 350 miles south of Manila, to visit a group of holiness people there. They had been apprised of Rev. Pitts's coming and gave him an enthusiastic reception. After discussing with them the doctrines and practices of the church as outlined in the *Manual*, Rev. Pitts was confident that the people were ready for membership, so a church was organized with 45 members. However, all were listed as "probationary" members for the present.

The missionary then held meetings at Manbusao, a town of 19,000 also on Panay. So great was the response that at the close of the meetings several leading citizens tried to exact a promise from Rev. Pitts that a missionary would be sent there. All he could assure them was that if another missionary were sent to the Philippines, he would see that their town was visited often.

Balacag, Pozorrubio

An invitation came for Rev. Pitts to hold a service in an independent chapel in the out-of-the-way village of Balacag. The congregation was worshiping in a small bamboo building with a thatch roof and dirt floor. At the close of the service, 18 people came forward for spiritual help. Instead of a single service, meetings continued for two weeks, and at the conclusion, Pastor Veras and his people expressed their desire to become Nazarenes. A probationers' class of 30 was begun with regular instruction being given on the beliefs and rules of the church.

In late 1948 while General Superintendent Orval J. Nease was in Korea to receive Robert Chung's group of congregations into the Church of the Nazarene, he made a brief visit to the Philippines and while there officially organized the Balacag church. Two years later, with Alabaster assistance, they built themselves a larger and more permanent frame church to worship in.

In the summer of 1948 General Superintendent Hardy C. Powers and General Treasurer John Stockton visited the Philippines briefly in the course of their investigative trip to Japan. A service in the front yard of the Pittses' home attracted a large crowd.

Aringay

During the war, Chaplain Pitts had one day picked up a Filipino guerrilla soldier who had obtained a few days' leave to go to see his seriously ill daughter. Though it would take him considerably out of his way, the chaplain felt moved to take the soldier all the way to his home in Aringay on the Lingayen Gulf north of Manila. Not only that, he went to get some medicine for the sick child. The family was greatly impressed by this kindness.

Two and a half years later Chaplain Pitts, now a missionary, and Marciano Encarnacion were in the area to visit some converts from a meeting the latter had held there 10 years earlier and to explore the possibilities of establishing a work there. After a time of fellowship with these people, Rev. Pitts decided to look up the family he had befriended during the war. Stopping at a store to seek directions, he was recognized by a lady who was much interested to hear that he had returned to the Philippines as a missionary. When asked if he were planning to start a work in their community, he said he would at least like to pitch a tent somewhere and hold meetings. She immediately offered her own front yard.

It was an unusual coincidence that this woman happened to be the sister-in-law of the soldier Rev. Pitts had helped. Thus he was able to meet the family again and visit with them.

But it was several months before the tent meeting could be arranged. With the nucleus of Mr. Encarnacion's converts and the friends Rev. Pitts had reached through his kind gesture, a successful evangelistic campaign was held, which lasted a month. Oddly, the soldier, a key person in the chain of events, refused to enter the tent. He did occasionally linger on the outside, however, and heard the gospel preached. The seed sown bore fruit when two years later he finally yielded his life to the Lord.

The people wanted regular services continued, so Mr. Encarnacion acceded to their request to become their leader. For six years they met under one of the houses. (In that low-lying area the houses were built high off the ground on stilts.) With the financial help of a United States congregation, plus the sacrificial labors and gifts of the people themselves, a new chapel was finally completed and dedicated on February 19, 1956.

Baguio City

During their brief visit to the Philippines in 1948, Dr. Hardy C. Powers and Dr. John Stockton toured Baguio City, beautifully located a mile above sea level. Its population at that time was 32,000. The visitors were impressed with the location and urged Rev. Pitts to move there from Cabanatuan City and make this a headquarters for the church. The presence of an American school there where the Pitts children could be educated was an added incentive. The Cabanatuan City church, which added 16 new members on the closing Sunday of the Pittses' leadership, was left in the hands of a national pastor.

Services in Baguio City were begun in the front room of the Pittses' rented home, and in two years' time average attendance grew from 18 to 45.

Pinamalayan

Among the early converts in Baguio City were a barber and his wife who were to play a key role in the opening of work in Pinamalayan. In 1949 the Lopez family moved from Cabanatuan City to this city on the island of Mindoro, 90 miles south of Manila. There Mrs. Lopez began a Sunday School in her home with 25 or 30 children. In response to her urging, a series of evangelistic services was held there with the music being provided by Mrs. Pitts and her three children and the preaching by a young man from the Cabanatuan City church. Some services were held in the Lopez home, some in a converted store building, and some in the open air. A sufficient number were converted to begin regular church services. A hall was rented for the purpose, and when the newly converted barber, Jose

Carpio, asked Rev. Pitts if there was some place he could preach, he was sent to lead this group of Christians. Unfortunately this work did not survive.

In two years' time, however, the work of the Church of the Nazarene had touched three islands—Luzon, Panay, and Mindoro—with several preaching points and Sunday Schools. The church was beginning to find rootage in Philippine soil.

2. *Expansion in the 1950s*

A major step forward came when Rev. and Mrs. John Pattee were added to the missionary force on September 6, 1950. They were experienced workers, having served nine years in North and South China. In their 21 years of service in the Philippines they became much loved and revered. A two-story missionary home was rented in Baguio City, with the Pittses moving into the upstairs and the Pattees on the lower floor. The living room doubled as a meeting place for the congregation for about a year. During that time the Sunday School grew to an average attendance of 70, which taxed available space to the limit.

A Christian Workers' Institute was held in this home with an attendance of 23, including both pastors and laymen. It was the first attempt to give formal instruction in Nazarene doctrine, history, and polity. Evangelistic services were held each night with an emphasis on holiness. These institutes were to play an important role during the coming years in training nationals for church leadership.

In January 1951 a Preachers' Institute was held in which the challenge was laid down to enter new cities with the message of full salvation. The following month, Rev. Pattee, assisted by some of the pastors, began a month-long evangelistic campaign in Binalonan, about 20 miles south of Baguio City. The meetings, held mostly in the town plaza, attracted considerable attention, and a sufficient number were converted to continue regular services. Eventually a church was organized, and a full-time pastor was installed. Services were also held in the nearby rural community of Laoac, three miles to the west, where a strong church was organized. Some three or four years later the people there constructed their own church building with the help of a $500 gift from the United States.

By 1952 there were 5 organized churches with 14 other Sunday Schools and preaching points. Sunday Schools were averaging 550 in attendance. Importantly, there were 11 national workers helping to reach their own people for Christ.

Bible Training School

The training of these national workers and the preparation of new pastors to take care of the expanding work became a matter of prime concern. Early in 1952, in the course of a search for a suitable location for a Bible school, an outstanding piece of property overlooking La Trinidad Valley was discovered. This 11-acre, pine-covered tract, three miles north of Baguio City, was purchased from the sister of the mayor of La Trinidad, who also granted permission to pump water from a spring that lay outside the property line, thus assuring an adequate and pure water supply. One other advantage of this site was that La Trinidad was one of the few cities that provided electricity around the clock.

In honor of Mrs. S. N. Fitkin, who retired from the presidency of the Nazarene Foreign Missionary Society in 1948, the organization raised $74,277 to build a Bible training school in South China.[1] But when that field had to be closed by the Communist overthrow, the money was diverted to other such schools in the Orient. Of this amount, $9,274 was granted to the Philippines, which made possible the purchase of the property at La Trinidad, which cost $11,250.

Temporary buildings were erected so that classes could begin as soon as possible. On August 2, 1952, the first class of 35 students enrolled. Five or six different language groups were represented, but since English was the common second language for all, classes were taught in that tongue.

The Pitts family returned to the United States for furlough in time to attend the General Assembly in June 1952, leaving the Pattees alone on the field. However, on August 28, 1952, three new missionaries arrived to help them—Rev. and Mrs. Adrian Rosa and Miss Frances Vine. Rev. Rosa, like Rev. Pitts, had served in the armed forces in the Philippines and from that time had felt a call to return as a missionary. He was an experienced builder who took charge of the construction of the permanent buildings on the campus, thus releasing the Pattees to visit the churches and hold evangelistic meetings. Miss Vine became a teacher in the Bible school, beginning a long period of dedicated service in this capacity.

Sunday evening services were begun in the Bible school chapel. On Sunday mornings and afternoons the students were involved in holding services in surrounding areas, one place being 60 miles away. But in La Trinidad Valley were many Igorot tribesmen who needed to be reached with the gospel, so in January 1953 a full schedule of services was begun for them at the chapel. The results were encouraging, as attendance climbed to 130 in two years' time.

In February 1953 Dr. and Mrs. G. B. Williamson visited the field. During their stay they conducted the annual ministers' conference, which for the first time was held at the Bible school. The students, many of whom were already pastors, benefited greatly from the ministry of the Williamsons.

During the long vacation period from mid-March to early July, teams of men students were sent out to the churches to help the pastors and at the same time to gain practical experience for themselves. Also, Miss Vine taught teams of women students how to conduct Vacation Bible Schools. Not only were the children led into the Christian way through this ministry, but this became an avenue into the homes.

The full course at the Bible school required five years. The fourth year was spent in full-time work in one of the churches or in a church planting project. The other years were spent at the Bible school. This kind of curriculum brought a unique balance of the theoretical and the practical.

Manila

For five years Nazarene workers had skirted the great city of Manila, which at that time had a population of about 1.5 million—one-tenth of the population of the entire country. Its great airport was the crossroads of Far East air traffic. Its magnificent harbor drew shipping from all parts of the world. And the 100,000 students in its many colleges and universities made it an unrivaled educational center. The Church of the Nazarene needed some measure of presence here.

While the Pittses were home on furlough in 1952-53, they met a Filipino war bride by the name of Mrs. Purcelley in Houston. She told them of her plans to return to visit her mother in Manila and of her desire while there to help establish a Church of the Nazarene in that city. They gave her their blessing and helped her with some suggestions for people to contact.

Within two months of her arrival in Manila, with the help of some Nazarene air force personnel, she was able to begin a thriving Sunday School. Then, after much persuasion, her mother granted a

20-year lease to the church on a choice building lot for one peso a year (50¢). It would have been better for the church to have a clear title, but the lady could not quite bring herself to sell the property. Nonetheless it was considered secure enough to erect a chapel on the property. The pastor of the Cabanatuan City church was transferred to the new project. When Rev. and Mrs. Roy Copelin arrived in August 1954 they were located the first year in Manila to help establish the work there.

When General Superintendent George Coulter and his wife visited the Philippines in 1965, he urged that plans be made to purchase a permanent property in Manila. A suitable site was located in the Parañaque section of the city, and in July 1967 a groundbreaking service was held.

Construction was completed in the spring of 1968, and 65 persons attended the dedication services. In early 1969 property was acquired in the new suburban capital of Quezon City, and the Capital City Church was completed there in 1970. It later became known as the Parkway Church.

Lo-o Valley

Two Igorot boys, Antonio Lumiqued and Paul Bayan, while attending high school in Trinidad, were converted in the Bible school chapel and felt the call of God to return to their own people and preach the gospel. Their home was in the remote valley of Lo-o, 60 miles north of Baguio City. It was accessible only by a tortuous mountain road. The inhabitants were almost all Igorot tribesmen.

In 1955 Rev. and Mrs. Pitts and Rev. and Mrs. Copelin, along with Antonio and Paul, who were by then enrolled in the Bible school, made a scouting trip into the area. It took six hours of precarious driving to reach their destination.

It was indeed a beautiful valley, and the people were warm and hospitable. When a service was held on the schoolhouse porch, however, the adults did not come. The evidence of heathen practices and superstition were all around. But a few weeks later, when Rev. and Mrs. Pattee and a converted Catholic priest went up there to hold evangelistic services, the response was much more encouraging.

When vacation time came, Antonio and Paul went up to the Lo-o Valley; and with the help of a grant of $100 from the mission, the generous contribution of lumber from a local mill, and the hard work of many neighbors, an attractive thatch-roofed chapel was erected, complete with benches. The land on which it was built was donated by Paul's father, who was a well-known tribal leader. Though still not a Christian, he was willing to go along with his son's project. The chapel was ready for dedication in June. Another beachhead had been established for the Church of the Nazarene.

Medical Missions

Although mission plans for the Philippines did not include medical work, Mrs. Pattee was a registered nurse, and her skills were often used in ministering to the physical needs of the people, particularly in the more remote areas. She gave as many as 3,000 treatments a year, besides making and distributing many gallons of ointment for the treatment of the prevalent skin diseases. As always, such ministrations were an effective means of opening the hearts of the people to the gospel.

3. The First District Assembly

On May 23, 1955, Dr. Remiss Rehfeldt, executive secretary of the Department of Foreign Missions, arrived to conduct the first Philippine Mission District Assembly at Baguio City. It was a historic event for this field. All the pastors were present, representing 17 churches and 10 preaching points. Also in connection with the assembly, the fifth annual Christian Workers' Institute was held. These institutes were proving to be valuable adjuncts to the mission program, in which both pastors and laymen were given instruction.

Following the assembly, the Pattees and Rosas returned to the United States on furlough, and Rev. Roy Copelin was placed in charge of the Bible school. In October 1956, Rev. and Mrs. Bob McCrosley joined the missionary team, followed a year later by Rev. and Mrs. Harry Wiese, veteran China missionaries. The arrival of the latter was a stabilizing influence following a leadership crisis that had resulted in the Pittses' resignation and their return to the United States in 1957.

The Anniversary Year—1958

In March 1958 the district assembly was held at the Bible school with General Superintendent Hugh C. Benner as the presiding officer. In the Sunday afternoon service, seven pastors were ordained. It was also the 10th anniversary of the official beginning of the Philippine work, and though progress had not been spectacular, there was cause for celebration. There were now 16 churches plus several preaching points with 538 full and probationary members. With 54 enrolled in the Bible school, there was great promise for future expansion.

The 1958 school year opened in July with revival services each night. Although the meetings were scheduled for one week, they continued for a month with much prayer, fasting, confession, and restitution. The same outpouring of the Holy Spirit came upon the annual Preachers' Meeting in November.

The overflow of this revival inevitably reached the local churches. The Cabanatuan City church, the oldest on the district, had a visitation of the Spirit as the people became sensitive to the need for tithing. Rev. Wiese, who had become superintendent of the field when the Pittses returned to the United States, strongly felt that this was the secret of the church becoming both self-supporting and self-propagating. He emphasized this in all the churches he visited, and one after another experienced new spiritual vitality as they rose to the challenge of giving to the work of the Lord. Outreach was also greatly intensified, and within one year of the anniversary assembly the number of churches and preaching points had doubled to 33. Five of them were now partially self-supporting.

Such explosive growth called for added missionary assistance, which came in 1961 with the arrival of Rev. and Mrs. Charles Tryon and family. They were assigned to the Igorot work in the Lo-o Valley.

A youth institute attended by about 150 each year and boys' and girls' camps with 50 enrollees each were profitable ventures. The annual training institutes were continued also. General Superintendent V. H. Lewis, who was present for the 1962 Missionary Council meeting, was impressed with the high morale and esprit de corps of the missionary family.

The Ronald Beech family arrived in January 1963, and in March, Miss Norma Armstrong. The Beeches were initially stationed in Manila, where they underwent intensive study of Tagalog. Miss Armstrong was assigned immediately to the Bible school. In September 1963 Rev. and Mrs. Robert Latham were added to the missionary staff, and in 1965 Rev. and Mrs. Denny Owens.

Expansion to Samar and Mindanao

It was in 1963 that the island of Samar was entered. This largest of the central islands on the Pacific side had long been a concern of the church leaders. In April of that year, Rev. Contado, pastor of the Iloilo church on Panay, moved with his family to Balangiga on the south coast of Samar. He rented one of the familiar stilt houses and began services in the space underneath it. Rev. Bob McCroskey and a group of musicians from the Bible school came to assist in the opening services. There was determined opposition, but the gospel found root, and in a few years' time there were three churches on the island.

When Dr. V. H. Lewis paid a second visit to the islands in 1964, he ordained seven more men, all of whom were graduates of the Bible school, and recognized the credentials of a minister joining the Nazarene ranks from another group.

The large island of Mindanao, at the south end of the archipelago, constituted a strong challenge to the Church of the Nazarene. This heavily populated island is inhabited largely by Moros who are of Malaysian origin and Muslim in religion. Rev. and Mrs. Denny Owens, who had been on an extended furlough for health reasons, returned in 1976 and were assigned the task of beginning a mission on the island. Eventually churches were started in Valencia and Malaybalay in the north and Marbel in the central part.

Another challenge lay in reaching the Negritos, the true aborigines of the islands, numbering about 60,000. They are pygmies averaging under five feet in height and have black skin and kinky hair. Most of them live in scattered tribes that roam the forested mountains and valleys of the larger islands, principally in central Luzon.

Mr. Valmonte, a Christian Filipino who owned land in the mountains above Clark Air Force Base north of Manila where some of the Negritos lived, became burdened for these people. He spoke to his pastor and the missionaries about the matter, and plans were made to try to reach these shy tribesmen. But before the plans could be carried out, Mr. Valmonte died. However, the vision did not perish with him, and a few months later, Rev. Copelin with some members of the church hiked back into the mountains to visit these people. They presented the gospel the best they could and established some lines of communication, but regular services were not begun.

The city of Angeles, also near Clark Air Force Base, presented a different kind of challenge. The city of 100,000 was morally corrupt, as are many such centers near military establishments. But the degree of evil only heightened the challenge. In August 1965 the Ronald Beeches moved there and began prayer meetings in their home and in the homes of others. These were soon crowded out, and the need for a church building became urgent.

In their search for property they were miraculously led to a choice tract situated between two large housing areas, one Filipino and the other American. The Mission Council promised to provide the $6,000 cost of the lots if the people would build the church. They accepted the challenge and on June 25, 1965, a groundbreaking service was held. Servicemen from Clark were deeply involved in the project.

Exactly three months later the first service was held in the building, with 83 people in attendance. The church was officially organized on November 18 with 11 full members plus some probationers. In less than two years' time regular attendance was averaging well above the 100 mark.

4. *Becoming a National District*

The 13th district assembly, held in March 1967, was a significant event in the history of the Philippine work. The Mission Council recommended that year the election of a Filipino as district superintendent. This meant that the district would have to assume his support. The assembly voted to accept this responsibility and elected Rev. Andres Valenzuela to the office. He had a long record of proven service on the district, having been one of the first graduates of the Bible school and a member of the first group of elders ordained by Dr. Benner in 1958.

During the assembly, eight more ministers were ordained by the presiding general superintendent, Dr. George Coulter. Reports of substantial progress in all areas gave evidence that the Philippine work was firmly on its way.

That fall, special visitors to the field were Mrs. Louise R. Chapman, general NWMS president, and Evangelists Rev. and Mrs. Don Silvernail, who held a revival meeting at the Bible school. Dr. and Mrs. Ralph Earle were special workers at the annual Preachers' Meeting held later on La Trinidad campus.

Rev. Andy Hayes was the evangelist for the annual camp meeting in 1968. He was accompanied to the Philippines by his wife and the Bernard Farrs of Modesto, Calif. The big camp meeting tent had been the gift of Rev. Hayes's father.

The development of a truly indigenous church was slow in coming, but the election of a national district superintendent was a major step in that direction. Where the church was lagging was in self-support. Pastor Carolino Fontanilla of the Pico church in La Trinidad was a pioneer in correcting this situation. He was convinced that a self-supporting church would grow faster and be a stronger church. The necessary exercise of faith and trust in God would also bring spiritual returns to the people, he said.

When he first presented his plan to his church, he got mixed reaction. Some even dropped out, frightened by the financial demands this would make on them. Some were critical of the pastor whom they felt was becoming "money conscious." Some accepted the idea in principle but took a "not yet" attitude.

But the pastor had analyzed the situation well, and he pointed out to the congregation its capacity to give. If they would all do their share, he said, they would have more money than was now being received from the Mission Council. The people accepted the challenge, and immediately tithes and offerings began to increase. In the first year of the experiment, income doubled. And just as Pastor Fontanilla had predicted, there was comparable growth in every area of the church. Attendance in Sunday School and church also doubled. More members were received in the first two years of self-support than in the previous seven years. Personal evangelism bands were organized, and twice-a-week Bible studies were begun. The church truly came alive and set an example for the entire district to follow.

In 1970 Rev. and Mrs. Gordon Ingles joined the missionary force, and the following year the David Brownings were transferred from Guyana to the Philippines, the latter to fill the place left vacant when the Pattees retired. Also coming in 1971 was Miss Charlotte Wuster, who was assigned to Faith Academy, a school for missionary children in Manila.

The 25th Anniversary

To celebrate the 25th anniversary of the district in 1973, a special evangelistic thrust was led by District Superintendent Valenzuela and Missionary David Browning. A series of revival meetings was held throughout the district over a period of four months. A special drawing card for the meetings was a musical group called the Woodland

Trio. Their leader was Tommy Chamos, former leader of the popular combo group called The Fugitives. He and his wife had been wonderfully converted in the Baguio City church and had enrolled in the Bible school, seeking God's will for their lives. It was there that God directed him to organize a Christian musical group. The name Woodland Trio arose from the fact that the inspiration for forming the group came to Tommy while he was meditating alone out under the pine trees on the campus. These singers were greatly used by God during the four-month crusade and also in the coming years.

The statistics at the end of 25 years were outstanding. Eighty-two churches and preaching points on five different islands were reported, 25 of the churches being self-supporting. There were 1,442 full members and 487 probationary members. Thirty-one of the pastors were ordained. Enrollment in 43 Sunday Schools was 5,773. Many of the churches were fully organized with both NWMS and NYPS groups whose total membership stood at 1,442 and 1,248 respectively.

In June 1964 the Visayan Nazarene Bible College had been launched by the Copelins at Iloilo. It was initially a two-year Bible school to serve the southern islands. When Stanley and Flora Wilson returned from furlough that summer, he became the first president of the college. Total enrollment in the two Bible schools had now reached 63.

Divide and Multiply

This was an opportune time to consider division of the district. Not only the number of churches but the geographical spread (some 800 miles) made supervision difficult. Because of the problems of interisland travel, only the pastors could make it regularly to district gatherings. Few of their wives and almost no laymen could afford the costs. Therefore, at the close of the 1973 assembly, two separate districts were formed, the Luzon District and the Visayan District.

The first assembly of the southern (Visayan) district was held in April 1974 at Iloilo City with General Superintendent Eugene Stowe presiding. There were 17 churches represented. Rev. Wilfredo Manaois was appointed assistant superintendent, and the following year at the second assembly he was officially elected district superintendent.

With the formation of the new district came a strengthening of the Bible school at Iloilo. Its former two-year program was expanded to four years. Following this move, enrollment jumped to 50.

The scattered nature of the Philippines field adapted it well to the new training concept of Theological Education by Extension (TEE). This work was directed by Miss Frances Vine, and about 50 people were enrolled. In this program, short courses were given at strategic centers for new Christians and Christian workers. Content was similar to courses taught at the Bible schools, but advanced work was also offered to pastors. It was a matter of taking the school to the people so there was no disruption of the students' regular activities. In this way more could be trained than would be possible in a residential school situation. Furthermore, the students were not pulled out of their own churches where they were greatly needed, nor were they culturally uprooted. Too often students leaving rural areas and going to school in the city were reluctant to return to the more primitive life in the country. A cultural gap developed that made them "foreigners" in their home communities.

The formation of the two districts did indeed result in rapid expansion. By 1977 the Luzon District under Rev. Valenzuela was up to 2,047 members, more than the total of the combined districts at the time of the division four years before, and an increase of 368 in that one year. Eight new churches had been organized, and eight others started.

Similarly, the Visayan District under Rev. Manaois reported that same year 13 new churches, making a total of 40 with 1,155 members. Back of this advance should also be noted a plan for evangelism worked out in 1975 by Missionary David Browning. It was a 10-year program involving the continued efforts of individual churches, the evangelism commission, the missionaries, the two Bible schools, and the new churches themselves with each assigned quotas to reach each year. If all went according to plan, by 1985 the number of churches would be 250 as against the 1975 total of 55. Full mobilization would be required to make the plan work. According to the chart, the objective by 1980 was 126 churches. The actual total was well beyond the goal.

Two New Pioneer Districts

In order to further expand the work, in 1977 two new pioneer districts were created, Manila Metropolitan and Cebu. Rev. Peter Burkhart, outstanding church planter, who with his wife had arrived on the field from Guyana only the year before, was assigned the Manila project. For all the advances in other areas there were still only two churches in this great metropolitan area of then 5 million people and rapidly growing even larger.

The island of Cebu presented a great challenge since its capital, Cebu City, was a university center. A third-story office area was rented that would provide space for a district office, a classroom for leadership training, an apartment for the missionaries (Rev. and Mrs. Denny Owens), and a small auditorium seating 150 for church services. At the time, there were four preaching points on Cebu but no organized churches. However, the district also included the islands of Samar, Leyte, and Mindanao. Churches were already organized on Samar at Salcedo, Balangiga, Magtino, and San Antonio, and several other preaching points were being opened. Valencia in northern Mindanao was being reactivated, and a work among the Igorots on that island was projected.

5. *Expansion in the 1980s*

The Luzon District, mother district of the Philippines field, continued to grow under the gifted leadership of Rev. Meliton Bernabe. A former member of the faculty of Luzon Nazarene Bible College, he was elected to the district superintendency in 1980. During the subsequent quinquennium, membership swelled to 2,600, a 13 percent increase in the last year alone. The climax came in 1985 when the district attained Phase 4 (regular) district status.

An area of rapid growth was in the northeast province of Isabella, where five new churches were organized. Then when the Robert McCroskeys returned from furlough in the summer of 1985, they were assigned to open a pioneer district south of Manila that held great promise.

In the southern islands, ambitious plans for expansion were taking shape. Because of developments in the islands of Mindanao, Samar, and Leyte, it was considered wise to move the Visayan Nazarene Bible College to a more central location. The task of finding a site was a priority assignment for the college president, Rev. Alvin Orchard, when he returned from furlough in 1985. Rev. Roy Copelin, who had directed the school in the interim, continued in that role at the Iloilo campus, while the Orchards settled on the island of Cebu. The addition of the Duane Batys to the missionary staff gave added impetus to the work of the southern field.

In the meantime the Luzon Nazarene Bible College continued to grow commensurate with the growth of the district. Rev. Ernesto Rul-loda was elected president in 1984.

Asia-Pacific Nazarene Theological Seminary

Of great significance not only to the Philippines but to the work throughout the western Pacific was the opening of the Asia-Pacific Nazarene Theological Seminary in 1983. Dr. Donald Owens, director of the Asia Region, assumed the added responsibility of president of the institution. The administration building was dedicated by Dr. W. M. Greathouse in January 1983, and regular classes began for the second semester. In September 1984 Dr. LeBron Fairbanks, formerly at European Nazarene Bible College, became president. The cosmopolitan student body represented the countries of Korea, Japan, India, New Zealand, and Swaziland, besides the Philippines.

Plans for the Future

In February 1985 an interdenominational National Church Growth Strategy Congress was held in Baguio City. The theme was "A Church in Every Barangay [Village] by A.D. 2000." Delegates from many denominations and mission organizations left the congress with the conviction that this ambitious goal could be reached.

In March in Manila, and in April in Cebu, Nazarene leaders came together to discuss plans for Nazarene participation in the program. Strategies and goals were presented to the Second All-Philippines Leadership Conference in November. The following targets were adopted: 20,000 Nazarenes, 500 churches, and 20 districts by the year 2000. The plan was called Vision 20-20. With the current statistics revealing a membership of 8,083 in 126 churches and seven districts, these were ambitious goals, but at the recent rates of increase were quite within reach. Mission directors Merrill Williams (Luzon) and Kyle Greene (Visayan/Mindanao) were fully supportive of the program, as were the national district superintendents: Meliton Bernabe (Luzon), Andres Valenzuela (Metro-Manila), Herminio Tabuena (Western Visayan), Jose Causing, Jr. (Central Visayan), Stephen Azura (Eastern Visayan), and Honorio Mateo, Sr. (Mindanao).

F. BURMA

The inscrutable land of Burma, walled in physically by mountains to the north, east, and west, and existing in self-imposed isolation from outside influences for decades, offered an intriguing challenge for missionary endeavor.

Situated on the Bay of Bengal between Bangladesh on the west, and principally China and Thailand on the east, most of Burma's 262,000 square miles are covered with dense forest. Twenty percent of its 36 million inhabitants are urban, and half of those (3½ million) live in the capital city of Rangoon. It is famous for its rice (once known as the rice capital of the world), teakwood, jade, and opium. It has also been called "The Land of Pagodas," bespeaking the fact that 75 percent of the people are Buddhists.

The Burmese are of Tibetan ancestry, and for thousands of years the area was ruled by China. In the 19th century Burma became a part of the British Empire and in 1937 was granted self-governing status within the Commonwealth. Following occupation by the Japanese during World War II, on January 4, 1948, Burma became an independent nation. Gen. Ne Win rose to power in 1962 and forced out both the Indians, who had dominated the government, and the Chinese, who had controlled commerce. This with the socialization of the economy produced an isolation that threw the country far behind economically. Only recently, perhaps because of a developing petroleum industry, has there been evidence of an upturn.

Protestants constitute only 3.2 percent of the population, two-thirds of whom are Baptists.

The Church of the Nazarene in Burma

When the Nazarene church leaders were selecting the five new mission fields to be opened in celebration of the 75th anniversary of the denomination, Burma came into the picture as an unusual opportunity and challenge. In the files in the missionary office were letters from a group of Christians there who were interested in affiliating with the church, though the matter had not been pursued. Such requests were not new in the missions office, and seldom were they productive, but the possibility was there to be explored.

A more tangible direction to follow lay with a young Burmese student, Robin Seia, who was about to graduate from Fuller Theological Seminary in California. He was a member of Pasadena First Church of the Nazarene and held a minister's license from the Los Angeles District. He was ready and eager to return to his native land and establish the Church of the Nazarene there. He was the bridge to Burma that the church chose to take.

Robin Seia was born in Kalenyo, northwest Burma, of Christian parents. To further his education he enrolled in Madras Bible College in India in the late 1970s and four years later, upon graduation, returned to Burma's capital city of Rangoon. There in 1981 he organized a small Evangelical Fellowship. But while Robin was in Madras, Dr. John Stott had visited the school and, recognizing the unusual ability of this young Burmese student, encouraged him to go to the United States and take graduate work at Fuller Theological Seminary. He promised him financial assistance. Robin decided to follow through on this offer and in May 1982 set out on this new adventure.

Soon after he arrived in the United States, he accepted an invitation to attend Pasadena First Church and was quickly enveloped by this caring congregation. He found in Pastor Earl Lee great encouragement and support as he was led into a deeper understanding of holiness doctrine and experience. He became a thoroughgoing Nazarene and earned the confidence and support of the church.

It was thus that Robin Seia, upon graduation from Fuller, returned to his native land in June 1983, armed with authority to establish the Church of the Nazarene there. He lost no time, for on July 15, 1983, he organized the Trinity Church of the Nazarene in Rangoon. Most of the 30 charter members were from his former Evangelical Fellowship. Within another month he had registered the Church of the Nazarene with the Burmese government, a certification that was to be renewed every two years.

In August 1983 Seia held services in Whang-ge near the Thai border and organized a second church with "50 believers." In early September he journeyed to his hometown of Kalenyo, where 70 people of Methodist background were organized into a church. In the nearby village of Tuivar were "150 believers," which gave promise of another organization. In December 1983 Dr. Donald Owens, regional director for Asia, spent a week with Seia, inspecting the southern work and making plans for future development.

But it was in the northwest area that the people who had earlier contacted the Church of the Nazarene were operating, and they considered Robin Seia's coming to their "territory" an intrusion. This group of about 200 members, led by Davis Laliana, had split off from the Assemblies of God over the tongues issue. While seeking some other affiliation, they came across the book *You and Your Church,* by Harold W. Reed, and decided that such a denomination was what they were looking for. Hence their letter to Headquarters. They, of course, received a courteous but noncommittal reply merely expressing interest in their proposal. But this had been interpreted as authorization for them to proceed. Thus, on October 15, 1980, they had organized "The Church of the Nazarene (Holiness Church of Burma)."

In September 1984 a letter was dispatched from this group to Kansas City, repudiating the leadership of Robin Seia and calling attention to the fact of their earlier organization. This prompted a quick trip in October by Dr. Owens to straighten out the situation. The upshot was that the denomination's support of Robin Seia's leadership was confirmed.

Also on this occasion $100,000 was committed for the purchase of a substantial building in Rangoon to house a church, parsonage, district office, bookstore, and recording studio. An additional $5,000 was promised for the launching of a radio ministry and a translation program.

In March 1985 Dr. William Greathouse, general superintendent, accompanied by Dr. Owens, visited Burma and officially organized the work there as a national-mission district with Robin Seia as superintendent. By this time he had gathered around him three other pastors, and together they ministered to four organized congregations and three additional preaching points with a combined membership of 346. All this had been accomplished without the presence of a missionary, a significant first in world mission annals.

III

EUROPE/ MIDDLE EAST REGION

- Italy
- West Germany/Switzerland
- Denmark
- Sweden
- The Netherlands
- Portugal
- France
- Spain
- The Azores
- European Nazarene Bible College
- Holy Land
- Jordan
- Syria
- Lebanon

Researchers:

John E. Riley—Italy, Middle East, Portugal
John C. Oster—Middle Europe

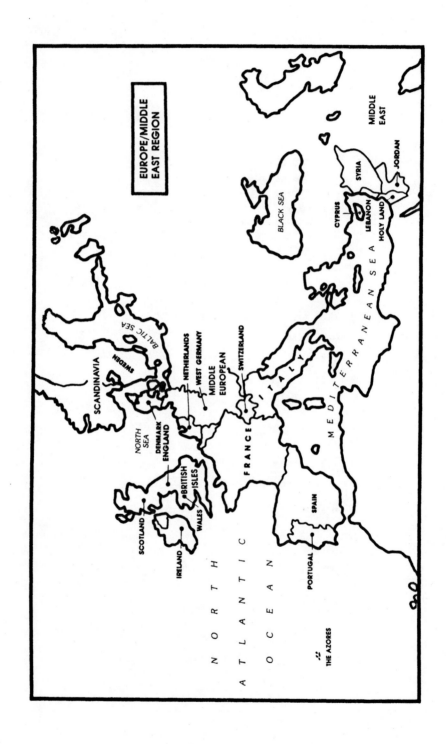

EUROPE/MIDDLE
EAST REGION

A. EUROPE

The huge land mass of Eurasia is geographically divided by an ill-defined line running north from the Caspian Sea through the Ural Mountains to the Arctic Ocean. To the west is Europe, to the east, Asia. Next to Australia, Europe is the second smallest continent, yet it is the most crowded. Asia has more people but has a comparably larger area.

Europe has been called the cradle of civilization, for it has had more influence on world history than any other part of the globe. Its people have migrated to every part of the earth, and wherever they have gone they have left their mark. Though the great colonial empires of Britain, Germany, France, Spain, Holland, and Portugal have largely disappeared, the political and cultural influences of their occupation still remain. Scarred by two world wars and divided by opposing ideologies, Europe is still a center of world focus.

Europe is itself bisected by a not-so-mythical line called the Iron Curtain, which separates the Soviet bloc from the Allied nations of the West. Only outside the Iron Curtain is free religious activity possible. Here is found the power center of the Roman Catholic church in Rome, the cradle of Luther's Reformation in Germany, and the heart of Reformed theology in Holland. Thus Western Europe does not lack for religion, but it is a decaying, formalized religiosity, lacking the vitality of evangelical faith. Most European countries have a state church that is supported by taxation.

From its earliest days the Church of the Nazarene had been at work in the British Isles, but it was not until after World War II that it began its ministry on the Continent. First it was to Italy, then to Germany, Denmark, Sweden, the Netherlands, Portugal, Switzerland, France, Spain, and the Azores. Each has its unique story of how the work was begun and how it has developed over the years.

1. *Italy*

The boot-shaped peninsula of Italy, jutting down out of the heart of Europe into the Mediterranean Sea, was once the center of the great Roman Empire, which in its heyday stretched from the British Isles to India. But Italy also was and is the center of the Roman Catholic church. It would seem that as the former waned, the latter rose to become in its own way a world power whose influence girdles the globe.

Some have seemed to see a fading of Catholicism's power, yet millions around the world still look to Rome, and the dominance of this religion in Italy itself is still unquestioned. Any religious activity there must reckon with that fact.

In the early years of the Christian Church, Rome was a prime target for evangelism. Paul had his sights on that great center as indicated in the letter he wrote to them before his work was cut short. But he would not have been the first Christian there. Acts 2:10 refers to "visitors from Rome" being present in Jerusalem on the Day of Pentecost. And we know that about A.D. 49, Priscilla and Aquila, early evangelists, were compelled to leave Italy where they had evidently been preaching. We also find reference to "the saints . . . who belong to Caesar's household" (Phil. 4:22). Paul, a Roman citizen, did spend his last years there, but as a prisoner just before his martyrdom.

It was in Rome that the early Christians, under severe persecution, fled to the catacombs, those subterranean burial places beneath the city, to find protection and a place to worship unmolested. Even so, thousands lost their lives for their faith until in the time of Constantine, Christianity received official sanction. From that point, a new empire began to emerge in the form of the Roman Catholic church, which leaped political boundaries and became both a temporal and spiritual power.

But not all those claiming to be Christians in Italy have been Roman Catholics. In 1179 Peter Waldo, a merchant of Lyons, founded the Waldensians, a group of dissenters who rebelled against the heresies, formalism, and corruption that had crept into the Roman church. Their emphasis was on Bible reading, preaching, and primitive purity of living. They were the first true Protestants. Though their influence spread around the world, they never became a dominant force. Even in Italy they are today outnumbered three to one by the Pentecostals, who at 100,000 members constitute the largest Protestant body in that land. Most major denominations have some measure of missionary endeavor in the country.

Nazarene Missions

The Church of the Nazarene found its roots in Italy itself in the person of Rev. Alfredo del Rosso, a holiness preacher born in Poggibonsi, not far from Florence, on July 7, 1890. While he was yet a boy, his mother left the Catholic church and joined the Waldensians. Thus Alfredo was trained in Waldensian schools and was converted at age 17. Responding to a call to the ministry, at 22 he entered the Waldensian College and Theological School. While there he was led to a church where he learned of the experience of entire sanctification and was filled with the Holy Spirit.

He had just begun his first pastorate in 1915 when he was called into military service in World War I. Leaving the army as a captain in 1919, he became pastor of a Baptist church in Civitavecchia, not far from Rome. His preaching of holiness doctrine was not welcomed, so in 1926 he joined the Apostolic church and began a work for them at Grossetto. But after only three years he became at odds with the church's teaching on tongues, and so began an independent work in Civitavecchia. Eventually this fiery preacher had congregations in four cities—Florence, Rome, Civitavecchia, and Montalcino. But persecution was heavy, and he was forced for a time to flee the country. While abroad, chiefly in Switzerland, he took advantage of the opportunity to learn other languages and became reasonably proficient in four of them. He also developed his considerable talents as a songwriter and translator.

Once again, in 1941 Rev. del Rosso was called into military service in World War II, emerging in 1945 with the rank of major. His linguistic ability made him a valuable assistant to the Allies following the hostilities.

Under the new political regime, Rev. del Rosso was able to return unhindered to his ministry, supporting himself by managing a Salvation Army canteen. He was especially interested in the American GIs and began conducting prayer meetings for them on Friday nights. When two Nazarene soldiers, Albert Carey and Charles Leppert, testified in these meetings to being sanctified, Rev. del Rosso became excited. Upon questioning the men, he discovered that the doctrines he had been preaching coincided with those of the Church of the Nazarene. The servicemen had a *Manual* and other pertinent books sent to him and urged church leaders to use this base to start a Nazarene work in Italy.

Thus in 1947 Dr. H. V. Miller, general superintendent, in the course of a European trip, visited Rev. del Rosso. So impressed was he with the work he was doing as well as with the man himself, Dr. Miller arranged to have him visit the General Assembly in St. Louis the following June. Two months later his ministerial credentials were recognized, and his four missions became a part of the Church of the Nazarene. Each had a constituency of about 30 members.

The domination that the Roman Catholic church held over the Italian people was a major obstacle to the growth of the church. For example, at first no Protestant church could own property. To circumvent this, a "Nazarene Company" was formed with del Rosso and his pastors as stockholders. They built churches in Florence and Civitavecchia that were eventually transferred to the Church of the Nazarene when the latter was officially recognized. In 1948 a revised constitution guaranteed religious freedom, and though this was reconfirmed by the High Court in 1957, it was not truly enforced until 1960. Also, those who left the Catholic church to join the evangelicals were severely persecuted and ostracized.

In 1952 the work in Italy was placed under the jurisdiction of the Department of Foreign Missions, and Rev. and Mrs. Earl Morgan were appointed to the field to assist Rev. del Rosso. They established their base of operations in Florence. Here property was acquired by the Nazarene Company in 1953, and a two-story building was erected containing both a chapel and living quarters. A fledgling Bible school was also begun.

The Morgans were transferred to Lebanon in 1961. The year before, Rev. and Mrs. Robert Cerrato, he an Italian-American, had come to Italy. Rev. Cerrato was to serve as field director and pastor of the Florence church. The situation was not entirely new, for he had been in Italy as an American GI in World War II. It was during the Cerratos' term of service that the Church of the Nazarene was given official government recognition, which made it possible to hold property in the name of the church. The first property acquisition under the new relationship was a meeting hall in Catania, Sicily, in 1961. Here about 1950 an independent congregation under Angelo Cereda had joined forces with del Rosso. It has since become one of the leading churches on the district.

A Bible correspondence course was begun, and the news bulletin

Araldo di Santita ("Herald of Holiness"), which Rev. del Rosso had been publishing, was renamed *Il Nazareno* and sent to an enlarged mailing list. Assisting in the work for a few months were Rev. and Mrs. Vincent Adragna.

When the Cerratos returned to the United States in 1964 after four years of very effective leadership, they were succeeded by Rev. and Mrs. Paul Wire. While they were in Italy, Mrs. Seba Agostinelli in 1966 donated a parcel of land in Sarzana on the coast northwest of Florence, and a church and parsonage were erected on it.

In the spring of 1967 the first district assembly was held in Florence. The historic event was marked by the ordination of four ministers by General Superintendent G. B. Williamson: Angelo Cereda, Mario Cianchi, Vicenzo Inzo, and Luigi Morano. That same year Rev. and Mrs. Roy Fuller arrived to bolster the missionary force; and when, in 1968, the Paul Wires returned to the United States, Rev. Fuller became the mission director. He continued in that capacity until in 1977 he was transferred to Quebec to lead the French-speaking work there.

In 1966 the European Nazarene Bible College was opened in Switzerland and became the training center for Italian pastors. Among the earlier students was Salvatore Scognamiglio, who in 1977 was appointed as the first national district superintendent. Other outstanding students have graduated from the college over the years, providing excellent leadership for the churches.

In 1969, under the leadership of the Fullers, a fine property was purchased in Rome, and the headquarters was moved there. In 1974 a building was erected in Mancalieri on land donated by Mrs. Olimpia Serra, which was dedicated the following year by Dr. Edward Lawlor, general superintendent, at the time of the annual district assembly held there.

About this same time missionary reinforcements arrived in the persons of Rev. and Mrs. Howard Culbertson (1974) and Rev. and Mrs. Thomas Long (1975). Both of these talented couples moved quickly into the life of the church and within months had assumed the pastorates of the Florence and Catania churches respectively. With the departure of the Fullers in March 1977, Rev. Long became mission director. On August 26, 1977, the Russell Lovetts joined the missionary force.

A full district program has been conducted including preachers' meetings, missionary and Sunday School conventions, young people's and family camps, as well as the annual assemblies. A regular weekly radio broadcast, "L'Ora Nazarena," was launched in 1976, using the powerful Trans World Radio station in Monte Carlo. The translation and publication of books and other holiness literature in the Italian language, along with a hymnal, also has aided the work greatly.

As years passed, government restrictions were relaxed more and more. By the late 1970s Nazarene pastors had equal rights with parish priests, including the performance of marriages and other religious rites and participation in national health and pensions programs. At the same time, the district has made good progress toward self-support and involved itself in church planting. An added step was the purchase of property in Calatafimi in 1979.

Rev. Salvatore Scognamiglio continued as district superintendent, and by 1985 he was able to report 11 churches with a total membership of 320.

2. *West Germany / Switzerland (Middle European District)*

West Germany is an economic miracle. Rising out of the ashes of World War II, it became in less than three decades an industrial giant and an economic world power. It lies in the heart of Europe, where for centuries its influence, both economic and cultural, has reached out to girdle the globe. Here the great musicians—for instance, Brahms, Bach, and Beethoven—placed their imprint on the music of the world, and here Gutenberg revolutionized the printing industry with the invention of movable type.

Here also Martin Luther launched the Protestant Reformation, which broke the hold of decadent Roman Catholicism upon the religious world. And Germany was the home of Peter Böhler, the Moravian, whose profound influence on John Wesley ultimately sparked the great 18th-century revival in England.

But the land of Luther and the Moravians today stands in desperate need of spiritual revival. Its materialistic society, related tenuously to a state church system that is itself weak and ineffectual, has little time for matters of the spirit. Yet the inner hunger is there for spiritual reality, and the challenge before the evangelical church is to step into the vacuum with the vibrant, vital, life-changing message of the gospel.

The Church of the Nazarene Enters

For some years following World War II there had been conversation about the Church of the Nazarene entering Europe. Servicemen and chaplains in the United States occupation forces were particularly concerned that such a work be started, and offered their support. Finally in 1957 the Board of General Superintendents suggested to Dr. Hardy C. Powers that in the course of his journey to conduct the British Isles assemblies, he make an exploratory trip to West Germany.

He was greatly impressed with what he saw. To him, the time seemed ripe to make the move to the Continent. And what more exciting challenge could be presented to the church for its golden anniversary year of 1958? At the General Board meeting in January, the project was officially endorsed. Rev. Jerald Johnson, successful pastor of the First Church of the Nazarene in Eugene, Oreg., and a member of the General Council of the Nazarene Young People's Society, had already been approached by Dr. Powers about going to Germany, and his nomination was enthusiastically approved. His wife, Alice (Schmidt), a Canadian of German parentage, had reasonable proficiency in the language, which was to prove of distinct advantage, particularly in the early days.

The opening of the European work was well publicized at the quadrennial Conference on Evangelism that January, and the General Council of the NYPS committed the organization to the goal of raising $15,000 for the purchase of a parsonage. (About $27,000 was actually received.)

Assured of the backing of the church in this significant venture, the Johnsons and their two young sons took off for Germany in March 1958. Their instructions were to launch the work in Frankfurt. That was all. No prior contacts had been made, no study of the situation they would find, and no strategy worked out for getting started. They were on their own. But they were also fortified by the promise God had given them from Isa. 55:5: "Behold, thou shalt call a nation that thou knowest not, and nations that knew not thee shall run unto thee because of the Lord thy God, and for the Holy One of Israel; for he hath glorified thee" (KJV).

After spending a day at the Servicemen's Retreat in Berchtesgaden, they were driven to Frankfurt and let off at the Frankfurter

Hof Hotel, which was to be their home for about 10 days while they tried to find a house to rent—no easy task in one of the tightest housing situations to be found anywhere. They had to settle for an apartment, for no houses were available.

Among the first tasks was to make some friends and to get the church properly registered with the authorities. After two months, Thursday night Bible studies were begun in the Johnsons' living room, to which their neighbors were invited. Among the early attenders was Johnny, the 16-year-old page boy they had met at the hotel. He was eager to learn English and found the Johnsons willing to help him. The arrangement was mutually beneficial, for Johnny had many contacts and invited numbers of his friends to attend the services. Little by little the circle grew.

Rev. Johnson wrote out his messages in German and had them corrected by his language teacher before reading them to the people. It was a good learning technique. He set as his goal to preach in German in six months. He made it in five! For his wife, Alice, it was a matter of brushing up on her German in which she was soon very proficient.

In the summer of 1958 an article appeared in the state church paper decrying the lack of fervor and dedication in their church. It cited as an example to emulate the Church of the Nazarene in the United States and lauded its evangelical fervency. "What would happen," the article concluded, "if our church could be like that?" Little did the writer know that at that very time, this Church of the Nazarene had moved into their midst. And what more opportune publicity!

An excellent piece of property was purchased, and construction began on a parsonage. The spacious two-car garage section was made into a cozy chapel seating 60. There regular Sunday services were begun, and the church was officially organized in the fall of 1958 with 7 members. Then construction began on the church building itself.

When the leaders of the state church saw the size of the foundation, they became alarmed. Previous threats had not frightened off the new church. Letters sent to all their constituents warning them against attending the Nazarene services had proved to no avail. In fact Rev. Johnson thanked them for the publicity. The time had come for them to take more drastic action, so a letter was sent to Rev. Johnson asking him and his wife to meet with the officials of the state church. It seemed more like a summons, and Rev. Johnson refused to attend until they assured him the meeting was merely for the purpose of getting acquainted. It turned out to be the kind of grilling session the Johnsons had expected, however, and it was made quite clear they were persona non grata in Germany.

When one of the men accused them of being a fly-by-night sect, Rev. Johnson had a perfect answer. He pulled out the article that had appeared in their own church paper two years before, commending the *Church* of the Nazarene—not a *sect* but a *church.* After about an hour and 40 minutes of questioning, one of the churchmen finally said, "Well, Herr Dekan, we have 10,000 members in our church with an attendance of 300. Don't you think we should let the pastor work on the other 9,700?" ("Dekan" is the equivalent of "superintendent," for the Johnsons were facing the official board of the state church.) An elderly gentleman asked to make a comment. "Herr Dekan, I have been listening to this pastor and his wife and have come to the following conclusion: This is a young church that has not as yet lost its first love." The Church of the Nazarene had won the day, and though by no means was all ecclesiastical opposition silenced, it put the Johnsons in a commanding position.

Construction went on, and as soon as it was possible, a chapel was prepared in the basement, while construction was continued upstairs. Finally, at the end of two years, the great day of dedication arrived. The building contained not only a commodious sanctuary seating 300, but Sunday School rooms, an apartment for the pastor, men's dormitory for the Bible school, kitchen and dining room facilities, and a printshop. The original building continued as the district parsonage and a women's dormitory.

Expansion Beyond Frankfurt

While the building program was going on, new openings were being found for the church in other areas of the country. The first of these was at Kaiserslautern, 75 miles southwest of Frankfurt, where there was also a large United States military base. The attractive church that was built housed both a German and an American congregation. Then came Hanau, 10 miles east of Frankfurt, which was started by a layman and became Richard Zanner's first pastorate.

Following these came Stuttgart, Mannheim, Wuppertal, and Kassel. In 1961 a Bible school was opened in Frankfurt to train pastors for the expanding work. So successful was it that when the European

Nazarene Bible College opened in Switzerland in 1966, the German people were rather reluctant to give up their school to become a part of the new and larger institution.

An important breakthrough was the opening of work in West Berlin, the landlocked city of 2.25 million people. Rev. Gerhard Bröhl, formerly of the Salvation Army in Wuppertal, offered to go to open the work. At first, services were held in the pastor's fourth-floor apartment, but soon after they began, a visitor to their service from Texas, Elmer Trimble, was led of the Lord to contribute enough money to purchase property for the construction of a church building. By the time they were ready to move into their attractive chapel, the church was fully organized with 15 members.

Capable German leadership made possible the outstanding growth of the church, particularly in those beginning years. In the decade of 1965-75, the Church of the Nazarene was recognized as the fastest-growing denomination in the country. Richard Zanner, Hugo Danker, Rudy Quiram, and Gerhard Bröhl, among others, were unusually gifted men who helped make this possible.

Richard Zanner grew up in Nuremberg, Germany, during the war years and in 1953 emigrated to South Africa. There he met and married a young lady from the European Nazarene church. He was later converted and enrolled in the Bible college. There he was sanctified and called into the ministry. He went home to Germany to visit his ailing father and while there was persuaded by Rev. Johnson to remain and minister in Germany.

His first pastorate was at Hanau, but soon Rev. Johnson called him as his assistant in Frankfurt so he himself could give more time to district and Bible school responsibilities. It was not long until he was the full-time pastor, and when the Johnsons returned to the United States in March 1969, Richard Zanner was nominated by Dr. G. B. Williamson as district superintendent in his place. The people enthusiastically voted their endorsement. He served with distinction there until in 1980 he was named the regional coordinator for all of Africa.

Hugo Danker, whose mother had been converted in the Nazarene mission in Guatemala, is a product of the German work. He was saved and sanctified in the Frankfurt church and graduated from the Bible school there. He was the very successful pastor at Hanau for almost 17 years and then assumed a full-time position as district leader of church growth and evangelism. He became superintendent of the Middle European District in the place of Rev. Richard Zanner when the latter moved to Africa.

When Rev. Zanner became district superintendent in 1969, his successor in Frankfurt was Rev. Rudy Quiram. He was born in Romania, grew up in Germany, was educated in the United States, married an American girl, and then returned to Germany. In 1975 he was loaned to an Evangelical Free church in Thayngen, Switzerland, and while still serving there launched in July 1978 the first Nazarene church in Switzerland at Neuhausen, later becoming its full-time pastor. The College Church at ENBC in Büsingen was considered a German church and had been organized in the early days of the college.

Work among Nazarene servicemen had been encouraged, and by 1985 there were four organized congregations near American bases, a fifth group that did not have a pastor, and three home Bible study fellowships. At the same time, there were 16 German congregations, giving a total membership on the district of 817. Stewardship and tithing had been themes stressed from the beginning as the churches were encouraged to become fully self-supporting and also contributors to the worldwide mission program. Easter and Thanksgiving offerings became big events. The success of this emphasis is indicated by the fact that total giving jumped from $63,500 (U.S.) in 1970 (the first year they were on their own) to $427,925 by 1980.

Outstanding laymen in the churches along with an emerging group of talented young pastors gave promise of a great future for the Middle European District.

3. *Denmark*

Jutting northward from West Germany is the peninsula that, along with adjacent islands, constitutes the country of Denmark, ancient land of the Vikings, of Hans Christian Andersen, and of the storied Tivoli gardens. It is a fairy-tale land of quaint villages and great museums that depict a glorious past when the Vikings controlled the North Atlantic and may well have been the true discoverers of the North American continent.

The tiny country of only 16,000 square miles and 5 million population is a welfare state that from the national treasury provides everyone's needs from the cradle to the grave. But the luxury of worryless existence economically has produced a pervasive malaise and melancholy. The taxes to support the system are unbelievably high, the level of morality is incredibly low, and the suicide rate is among the highest in the world. Worst of all, its churches are virtually empty. Fewer than 2 percent of the people attend with any regularity. The basic religion is that of the state church, which teaches that salvation is by infant baptism, and no moral or ethical demands are involved beyond that.

"One who listens carefully," writes John M. Nielson, "hears an echo from Laodicea: 'You say, "I am rich; I have acquired wealth and do not need a thing." But you do not realize that you are wretched, pitiful, poor, blind and naked'" (Rev. 3:17).

Into this center of appalling spiritual need, the Church of the Nazarene has established itself to help fan the flickering gospel flame into life once more.

The Church of the Nazarene

The pioneers for the church in the Scandinavian countries were Rev. and Mrs. Orville Kleven. He had been born into a Norwegian family in Minnesota, while she had been born in Denmark. There was a growing interest in their hearts toward their ancestral land, and on their own they went to Norway where, with the aid of relatives, they arranged a series of evangelistic campaigns, even over in Sweden. Meetings were also scheduled in Germany, and while there they discussed with Rev. Jerald Johnson the possibilities of opening up work in Scandinavia.

Rev. Johnson, following the suggestion of General Superintendent Hardy C. Powers that Germany should be considered the base from which other European countries might be reached, had earlier visited Denmark with such expansion in view. Together Revs. Johnson and Kleven went to Copenhagen and there purchased a corner property in Rødovre, a suburb of the capital city. A former dance school on the property lent itself to conversion into a chapel.

The Klevens moved to Denmark and opened services in the new property on November 5, 1960. It was a slow process to attract a congregation, but the Klevens patiently worked at the task until they were able to organize the first church there at the time the property was dedicated by Dr. Hardy C. Powers, general superintendent, in November 1961.

In 1966 Rev. Gunnar Gunderson from Norway became pastor of the Rødovre church and served until 1969. He was followed by Frank Morley from England, who remained until 1973.

In 1965 an old farmhouse was purchased at Mosede, 10 miles down the coast from Copenhagen, in an area destined to become a flourishing suburb. Miss Clara Christensen, an ordained elder and former teacher in Canadian Nazarene College and Northwest Nazarene College, felt called to return to her parental homeland after retirement to help establish the church there. She moved into the remodeled house and began a children's work. In the fall of 1966 when she was called to teach music at the newly opened European Nazarene Bible College in Switzerland, Rev. and Mrs. Kleven moved out to Mosede and continued the work there for two years. After this others picked up the task, including Ulf Kristofferson, who labored there for five months while the Klevens were on furlough. On the Klevens' return they were transferred to Stockholm, Sweden.

A church was finally organized in Mosede in 1973, and Niels Eliasen, who had been assisting in the development of the church, was named pastor. It was largely a youthful church supported by 20-30 young adults with over 100 children and teens in the Sunday School.

The Northwest European District

In the late 1960s with the beginning of the work in Holland, that country, Denmark, and Sweden were separated from Germany (Middle European District) to form the Northwest European District, with Rev. Jerald Johnson elected to serve as district superintendent along with the Middle European work. In 1969 Rev. Orville Kleven took over as acting district superintendent for a year. He was followed by Rev. Ray Lunn Hance, who served from 1970 to 1972. Next came Rev. Murray J. Pallett, who remained until 1976. It was during the latter's term that Denmark was again separated to form with Sweden the Scandinavia District. (The First Church of the Nazarene had been organized in Stockholm, Sweden, on May 22, 1966, but was at that time dormant.) Rev. Pallett served as superintendent of both the Northwest European and Scandinavia districts.

In June 1975 Rev. and Mrs. John M. Nielson arrived in Denmark to pastor the Rødovre congregation. Although the church had been without a regular pastor for two years, plans for relocation were already under way. A fine property was purchased, and an attractive building was erected. Dedication services were held in March 1977. The church had an expandable seating capacity of 225 and was designed to serve as a district center. Besides Sunday School and fellowship facilities, space was provided for the expanding literature program of the district.

Before 1975 there was virtually no holiness literature in Danish and even little evangelical material. A concentrated translation and publication program was instituted, and in a short time Sunday School and Vacation Bible School materials, the *Manual,* music (including a hymnal), plus a number of books and a Danish edition of the *Herald of Holiness* were available. It was a remarkable achievement.

In the meantime, Niels Eliasen had begun a children's work in Solrød as an extension of the Mosede church. In 1978 Rev. and Mrs. Doug Terry were appointed to the Denmark field, and after a year of language study, they moved to Solrød to develop a regular congregation and build a church and parsonage.

The Mosede church moved and built a beautiful building in Greve under the leadership of Rev. Eliasen. He continued to pastor the church after his election as superintendent following the departure of the Palletts in 1976.

In the meantime, by an unusual providence, Peter Thomsen, a native of Copenhagen, came in touch with the Church of the Nazarene and after a year at ENBC, became pastor of the Rødovre church. (The Nielsons had had to return to the United States upon the expiration of their visas.)

There was the unmet challenge to return to Sweden where Nazarene roots still remained, and also to explore some contacts already made in Norway. Finland, though not, strictly speaking, a Scandinavian country, also was offering a challenge. Some services had been held there, and several Finnish students had attended ENBC.

4. *Sweden*

The kingdom of Sweden is a beautiful country of lowlands, lakes, and mountains lying on the eastern side of the Scandinavian peninsula. It is 1,000 miles long and 300 miles wide at its widest point. Most of its 8 million people live in the southern half. Its standard of living is among the highest in the world, and its literacy rate is almost 100 percent.

As in Denmark, religious life is centered in the state church, to which 99 percent of the people belong. There were also the same problems of materialism, secularism, and spiritual indifference. Could the Church of the Nazarene make an impact on such a society?

The Church of the Nazarene

The stronger contacts for the Church of the Nazarene were in Norway rather than Sweden, but an interesting providence intervened to direct attention to Sweden. Dr. Hardy C. Powers and Rev. Jerald Johnson were flying from Germany to Copenhagen, Denmark, at Thanksgiving time in 1961 for the dedication of the new property there, when fog forced their flight to be diverted to Stockholm, Sweden. Thus faced with the necessity of staying over a day waiting for weather conditions to improve, they decided to explore the city. Renting a car with an English-speaking driver who could answer their multitude of questions, they toured the entire metropolitan area.

Dr. Powers was greatly intrigued by the situation, and in his report to the General Board in January 1962 he said, "The doors in Sweden are wide open to the Church of the Nazarene." But no official action was taken until the time of the meeting of the Board of General Superintendents in the fall of 1963. Dr. Powers was asked to visit Stockholm for further exploration in the course of his regular November trip to Europe. The result was a recommendation passed by the General Board in January 1964 that work be started in Sweden.

In the meantime, negotiations were already under way with Rev. H. E. Hegstrom, an evangelist in the church who spoke the Swedish language, concerning his opening the work. Feeling that it was God's will, he finally committed himself to the task and was officially appointed on April 11, 1964. Five months later he and his wife were on their way.

Landing first at Frankfurt, Germany, District Superintendent Jerald Johnson took them by car northward through Denmark and across the Skagerak Strait by ferry into Sweden. They drove into Stockholm on a full-moon night on September 21. Despite the acute housing shortage, they managed to secure an apartment that they were able to move into on October 1.

The Ground Is Broken

The Hegstroms spent the first few weeks visiting various churches, seeking to determine the worship habits of the people and to get a sense of the general religious climate. Colonel Perry of the

Salvation Army was particularly friendly and helpful. All the while, Rev. Hegstrom was brushing up on his rusty Swedish, while Mrs. Hegstrom was starting from scratch in learning the language.

Two factors impressed them as they visited the other churches: One was the lack of cordiality toward visitors, and the other was the limited number of children. This was a cue to them to make friendliness and Sunday School work distinctive characteristics of their new work. The real challenge was to break through the pervasive apathy of the people toward religious matters.

In March 1965 General Superintendent Dr. G. B. Williamson, Rev. Jerald Johnson, and Dr. O. J. Finch were traveling over Europe in search of a site for the proposed European Nazarene Bible College, and thus visited Stockholm. At that time regular services were not yet being conducted. However, following the district assembly held the next week in Frankfurt, the Hegstroms returned to Stockholm, ready to set up a schedule of services.

A downtown KFUM hall (similar to YMCA) was rented, and a 12-day evangelistic campaign was conducted from April 20 to May 2, with the Klevens from Copenhagen as special workers. Eighty-four different individuals attended the services, seven of whom responded to the invitation to seek spiritual help. Regular Sunday afternoon and evening services were continued thereafter with a beginning attendance of over 20. A group from Olivet Nazarene College, whose students had contributed $3,000 for the Swedish work, visited at the end of May. Then in both June and August, Dr. Richard Taylor, of Nazarene Theological Seminary in Kansas City, conducted one-week campaigns with good results.

The dearth of holiness literature in Swedish constituted a handicap. Here Colonel Perry was very helpful in translating portions of the *Manual* and some small books on the subject of entire sanctification. These were distributed freely to interested persons.

In May 1966 Rev. Jerald Johnson conducted a week of special meetings, at the conclusion of which, on May 22, he officially organized the First Church of the Nazarene in Stockholm. That same week the first piece of property was purchased—a parsonage in which midweek prayer services were begun. Sunday night services were continued in the downtown hall. Here also a series of evangelistic services were conducted in August by Dr. and Mrs. C. William Fisher with good results.

When Rev. and Mrs. H. E. Hegstrom left Stockholm in 1968 for the United States, Rev. and Mrs. Orville Kleven were transferred there from Denmark and spent a little over two years in diligent effort. However, the work in Sweden never attained sufficient momentum to carry on, and when the Klevens departed, the work was temporarily closed.

At this point, the Scandinavia District consisted of the work in Denmark where, in 1985, three organized churches were in operation with a combined membership of 48.

5. *The Netherlands*

The picturesque land we familiarly call Holland immediately conjures up visions of windmills, wooden shoes, dikes, and tulip blossoms. It is a quaint land, much of which is below sea level and protected by a 150-mile network of dikes. Along its dikes and canals, pumping windmills have played an important role in the nation's ongoing struggle with the sea, though they have been largely replaced by electrical equipment.

Holland won its independence from Spain in 1581 and embarked on an era of discovery and colonization abroad, and economic and artistic advance at home. A brief interlude of French occupation was ended in 1815, and in 1830 Belgium formed a separate kingdom. Holland's largest colonial holding was Indonesia, which won its independence in 1949, but Dutch seamen left their mark in many areas of the world.

Holland is now heavily industrialized, but the sea still calls many; and Rotterdam, its second-largest city, handles more cargo than any other ocean port in the world.

Possibly because of early Spanish influence, 40 percent of the people are Roman Catholic. The 40 percent Protestant population is largely connected with the Reformed church, of which there are several branches.

Enter the Church of the Nazarene

Uniquely, the beginning of the work of the Church of the Nazarene in the Netherlands came by invitation resulting from a remarkable chain of events. The chief characters involved were Jeanine van Beek, a Dutch Nazarene lady from New Zealand, and Cor Holleman, a sales representative for a Dutch paper company, who with his wife,

Miep, had found a deep experience with Christ keyed to the concept of full surrender to God.

Miss van Beek was visiting in her native Holland while on her way to assume the pastorate of the Wuppertal church in West Germany when she met a mutual friend of the Hollemans, Hetty van Houweninge. Through their conversations, Hetty and the Hollemans discovered that their spiritual experiences corresponded to the doctrinal teachings of the Church of the Nazarene, of which they had never before heard. Continuing their spiritual search, in the late summer of 1966 Cor and Miep Holleman and their children visited European Nazarene Bible College in Switzerland to learn more about the church. They decided that Miep and the children would stay for the fall semester, while he went back to his work in Holland.

Meanwhile Dr. and Mrs. Willem deVries had also met Jeanine van Beek and made a visit to the college in Switzerland. There they discussed for many hours with Rev. John B. Nielson, the rector, the beliefs and practices of the Church of the Nazarene. On the way home, they stopped in Frankfurt, Germany, to talk with Rev. Jerald Johnson. They told him of their group in Holland, the Hollemans among them, who had been studying and praying together. Through their contacts with Jeanine van Beek and the college, they had become convinced that the Church of the Nazarene interpreted for them doctrinally what they had been seeking experientially.

Of their conversation with the deVrieses, Rev. Johnson later wrote: "Such eager, open, and sincere seeking is not often found. . . . [The group they represented] were nearly all professional people, well established in life as far as material things were concerned. They had merely become convinced that the Church of the Nazarene had the message they were seeking and the message they felt all of Holland was needing."

Haarlem Church Organized

The deVrieses invited Rev. Johnson to come to Holland and meet with their group to discuss the Church of the Nazarene. The result was what Rev. Johnson described as "an exciting evening." He was invited to return to organize a church. In January 1967 the official organization took place with seven charter members. Rev. Johnson assigned himself as pastor and commuted the 300 miles from Frankfurt to take care of the little flock until more permanent arrangements could be made.

A young Dutch pastor in South Africa was contacted, but he had just applied for missionary service and was going to Swaziland. But God had His man in Cor Holleman, who felt led to offer himself for service to the church. It would mean sacrifice, for his salary would be cut to about one-third of what it was. He would also have to work on the course of study for ministers, but he was already well educated and was a diligent student. In October 1969 he was ready for ordination at the hands of General Superintendent Samuel Young.

Through the assistance of a capable lawyer, the Haarlem church was incorporated, and the Church of the Nazarene received official recognition as a denomination in Holland. This opened the way for the purchase of a large three-story home, the main floor of which was remodeled into a chapel with the pastor's home upstairs. Rev. John B. Nielson, rector of the Bible college, preached the dedicatory sermon.

With the addition of the Holland congregation it was decided to separate the Netherlands, Denmark, and Sweden from Germany to form the Northwest European District. Their first miniassembly was held at Haarlem in 1968. The three churches involved—Haarlem, Copenhagen, and Stockholm—had a total membership of only 49! Rev. Jerald Johnson served as district superintendent until Rev. Ray Lunn Hance was ready to take over in the spring of 1970.

The Haarlem church continued to grow until the original chapel was completely crowded out. An excellent one-acre tract of land was purchased just off one of the city's major boulevards, and a prefabricated chapel erected. It was dedicated on November 22, 1970, with 175 in attendance. This building served until a beautiful permanent church building was completed in 1973. Funds for the new church were provided by Rev. Dowie Swarth, a retired district superintendent who had emigrated to the United States from Holland in his youth. A substantial inheritance had come to him in his later years that he wanted to invest in the work of the Church of the Nazarene. And what more appropriate place! He was able to be present for the dedication. By then the membership had grown to 51.

Reaching Out to New Areas

Now well established themselves, the Haarlem congregation began to look for a place to start another church. They chose the city of Zaandam (Koog aan de Zaan), a suburb of Amsterdam seven or eight miles northeast of Haarlem. The leader selected for the new work was

Jan Spijkman, a businessman from their own membership who the previous year had been studying at ENBC in Switzerland.

The year 1974 also witnessed the beginning of work in the great port city of Rotterdam, Cor Holleman's hometown. Here an imposing abandoned church building seating 1,100 people became available. Situated in the heart of a developing shopping and recreation center, it was valued at $1 million, but the purchase price was only $160,000. Renovation of the huge structure was a formidable task, but the remodeled sanctuary was ready for use on November 16, 1975.

In the meantime, while Rev. Murray Pallett, district superintendent, carried on the renovation project, Cor Holleman, who had been named pastor of the church, was away with his family, spending a year in the United States for deputation services and seminary studies. While there a strategy for developing the church was worked out with Dr. Raymond Hurn, then executive secretary of the Department of Home Missions. The plan included the sending of Gary and Lavonna Moore to lead a youth program and Merritt and Linda Nielson to direct the music and publicity. Both arrived in September 1975 and with Cor Holleman, who had returned in July, went to work on the renovation. The auditorium was reduced by walling off balcony areas until the remaining part seated 350. The opening day crowd was over 300, but then attendance dropped back to an average of 20-25. The church was officially organized in March 1976 with 12 members.

At first growth seemed slow, but in the spring of 1977 the area Youth for Christ leader began attending, and most of his group followed him. Within a year attendance was averaging between 160 and 175, and membership reached 81 in 1980. It was a youth-oriented church with 65 percent of the congregation under 25 years of age.

When Cor Holleman became pastor of the Rotterdam church in 1974, he was replaced in Haarlem by Rev. Stephen Gunter, who, with his wife, Roxie, gave excellent leadership to the church until they returned to the United States in the summer of 1976. Their place was taken by Rev. Johannes Smink, a native Hollander who had been pastoring the Wuppertal church in West Germany.

In 1976 Cor Holleman was appointed district superintendent when Rev. Murray Pallett returned to the United States. He continued to pastor the Rotterdam church. When the Merritt Nielsons completed their second two-year term there, Jan Spijkman took his place as associate pastor. The vacancy thus created at Zaandam was filled by a recent graduate of ENBC, Jan van Otterloo, who had been the top engineer with the Burroughs computer company.

In the spring of 1981 Sunday evening "get acquainted" services began in Vlaardingen, near Rotterdam. Regular Sunday morning services began in January 1982. Six months later the church was officially organized with 18 members, and by the end of the year there were 30 members. Though in rented quarters, the church was flourishing under the leadership of Ed and Cobie Meenderink, both graduates of ENBC.

By 1985 the Netherlands District (formerly Northwest European) had 456 members in 5 churches. The infant days were now past, and an exciting period of expansion lay ahead.

6. *Portugal*

The Iberian Peninsula, the southwestern projection of Europe that reaches down to the Strait of Gibraltar separating it from Africa, contains the two nations of Portugal and Spain. Portugal, on the west side, is about one-sixth the size of Spain, but its population of just under 10 million makes it much more densely populated than its neighbor, which has 40 million people. The northern part of Portugal is generally mountainous, cool, and rainy, while to the south are rolling plains with a somewhat warmer climate. The capital of Lisbon is on a landlocked harbor at the mouth of the Tejo River.

Living as they did on the westernmost point of Europe with the alluring Atlantic Ocean at their doorstep, it was only natural that the Portuguese should become great seamen and explorers. The names of Bartholomew Dias, Vasco da Gama, and Ferdinand Magellan are in the Hall of Fame of the world's greatest explorers.

With exploration came colonization, and among Portugal's acquisitions were Brazil, Angola, Mozambique, Portuguese Guinea, Portuguese Timor, the Cape Verde Islands, and Goa, along with some lesser areas. Even with the loss of Brazil in 1822, the total remaining colonial empire was still 23 times the size of Portugal itself. By 1975, however, virtually all the colonies had won their independence.

After many centuries as a monarchy, in 1910 Portugal became a republic. But it was not democratic, for ruling the country were autocratic dictators who favored the wealthy landholders and continued to hold the masses in poverty. Furthermore, although the constitution promised religious freedom, the Roman Catholic church was accorded preference and continued to wield great power.

In 1974 a bloodless revolution brought on general elections.

However, no party received an outright majority, so there was considerable jockeying for political advantage. It was out of this foment that the colonies won their independence and, more importantly, that the power of the Roman Catholic church was broken. Nonetheless, Portugal remains 90 percent Catholic.

Nazarene Missions

Though the Church of the Nazarene had been actively working for many years in the Portuguese territories of Brazil (1958), Mozambique (1922), and the Cape Verde Islands (1901), and many missionaries had lived briefly in Portugal during their periods of language study, no mission work as such had been conducted there. The fact was that new Protestant churches were virtually excluded from the country until the 1974 revolution. By that time, the Church of the Nazarene was already laying the groundwork for its mission there.

At the January 1973 meeting of the General Board, official action was taken to enter Portugal, and Rev. and Mrs. Earl Mosteller were named to pioneer the work. They had first served for 12 years in the Cape Verde Islands and then had pioneered the work in Brazil beginning in 1958, so a more qualified couple could not have been found.

When they arrived in Portugal on September 1, 1973, they were greeted by a group of 18 friends of their former years in Cape Verde. They called themselves the "Embaixadores Nazarenos" (Nazarene Ambassadors) and were led by a former Cape Verdian pastor, Rev. Joao Filipe Gonçalves. It was a joyful time of reunion.

The first service was held the following day in the home of Maria de Conceição Ferreira with Rev. Teobaldo Mello, another former Cape Verdian pastor, bringing the message. From their very first day it was obvious to the Mostellers that the church already had a sound footing on which to build.

With consummate wisdom born of much experience, Rev. Mosteller went about the task of making contacts and obtaining necessary government approval for establishing the work of the Church of the Nazarene. At the time, this would also mean recognition of the church in the "overseas provinces" as well, which would include Mozambique, Cape Verde, and Angola. However, by the time the long process was completed in 1976, the latter countries had been granted their independence.

Along with pursuing the necessary government certification was the securing of a place to worship. Until the certification came through, the purchase of property was not possible, nor was an assemblage of more than 25 legal. The homes of the people, the Mostellers' apartment, and a rented hall served until, on December 9, 1973, the board of the Amoreiras Church, a Plymouth Brethren congregation, agreed unanimously to allow the Nazarenes the use of their building when it was not otherwise occupied. It so happened that the pastor of the church had participated in the dedication of the Maud Chapman Memorial Church in Praia, Cape Verde, in 1947. In fact Rev. Mosteller himself had preached in this same church on his way home from Cape Verde on his first furlough, 24 years before. The use of such an established church freed them from the 25-person limit as well.

Sixty-six people gathered for the first Nazarene service in the Amoreiras Church on January 13, 1974. Services continued there until the middle of 1977, and although these were restricted to Sunday afternoon hours and two smaller meetings during the week, attendance of 100 was common, with as many as 200 for special events. In 1975 Rev. José Delgado, a former Cape Verdian, became pastor of the Lisbon church.

Two missionary couples sent to Portugal for language study before going on to Mozambique were a great help in the opening days of the work. They were Rev. and Mrs. Gary Bunch and Rev. and Mrs. Jon Scott. When the door was closed for them to go on to their intended field, they were officially appointed in January 1976 to remain as missionaries in Portugal.

In the university city of Coimbra, 100 miles north of Lisbon, services were begun on January 18, 1975, in the home of Julieta Santos, the mother of Dr. Odette Pinheiro, a Nazarene physician who later went to Kansas City and graduated from Nazarene Theological Seminary. Rev. Acacio Pereira, a converted ex-priest from Mozambique, was the preacher. In September of that year the Jon Scotts were stationed in Coimbra, and services were begun in their home. Attendance at Sunday School on the opening day was 21, with 23 at the preaching service. During Easter Week of 1976, the congregation moved into a remodeled, rented hall, and Gabriel Rosario became the full-time pastor.

Meanwhile, the tedious task of getting the church incorporated continued. With the help of Dr. José Bravo, a member of the Plymouth Brethren congregation whose church the Nazarenes were using, the bylaws of the church were drawn up in proper, legal form, and submitted for government approval on September 3, 1975. Four weeks later, on September 29, in the presence of 10 Portuguese citizens, a notary public made the declaration concerning the existence of the Church of the Nazarene. This was followed by the printing of the bylaws in a government bulletin and the publication of the church's constitution in the daily newspaper, *O Jornal Novo,* all of which were prescribed legal steps.

On January 6, 1976, the following communication was issued by the Ministry of Justice: 'I communicate to you that, on the fifth of January, 1976, by order of His Excellency, the Minister of Justice, recognition of the Church of the Nazarene was authorized, being registered in a book for that purpose existent in the office of the Ministry of Justice." It was now official. The Church of the Nazarene could own property, advertise, distribute literature, conduct a radio ministry, and so forth.

On March 10, 1976, the first district assembly was held with Dr. Jerald Johnson, then executive secretary of the Department of World Missions, in the chair. The Lisbon church, with 80 members, all listed as probationary, was the only organized congregation. A second miniassembly was held in November 1976.

Outstanding people had begun attending the services, and many valuable contacts had been made for the church. An influx of former Nazarenes from Mozambique as well as Cape Verde was adding new strength to the congregations. Through a guest book and other means, a mailing list of 3,000 names was developed, which reflected a great reservoir of friendship and interest. Invitations to the Mostellers to speak in various independent churches helped broaden contacts even further. A unique ministry to the gypsies was very fruitful. A month-long visit by a group of Student Mission Corps young people added impetus to the work, as did the launching of the Portuguese "Showers of Blessing" program, "A Hora Nazarena."

But perhaps the most significant event in the early years of the work was the visit and ministry of the Northwesterners from Northwest Nazarene College in the spring of 1978. The college choir appeared on Portuguese television, in the newspapers, and before two university audiences and other groups. The national television network videotaped them for five hours in the gardens of Jeronimos Monastery, a famous Lisbon historical landmark. Portugal's foremost newspaper gave them three-column-wide coverage on the front page. Whether singing to capacity crowds at Lisbon University, on the steps of the National Assembly, or in the local churches, the choir was enthusiastically received. As many as 4,000 at a time listened at their open-air concerts. During their four-day stay they rendered 30 concerts or miniconcerts. The Church of the Nazarene was publicized as never before.

An emphasis on youth work resulted in the development of a youth camp. Several young people there responded to the call of God to the ministry, and in 1979 there were 10 Portuguese students enrolled at European Nazarene Bible College in Switzerland.

The influx of refugees from Cape Verde, Mozambique, and Angola—more than a million as of 1979—drove property values very high just when the church was seeking to acquire needed land and buildings. But the large numbers of displaced persons created a great opportunity for ministry, of which the missionaries sought to take advantage. Numerous preaching points were opened up in an effort to discover the most productive areas in which to plant churches.

In 1980 Rev. and Mrs. Duane E. Srader were transferred from the Cape Verde Islands and opened work in the northern city of Porto. Two years later, when the Earl Mostellers were asked to open the new field in the Azores, Rev. Srader was appointed district superintendent and mission director of the Portugal field.

In February 1983 a month-long chain of prayer was organized. The results of this continuous prayer vigil were almost immediate. New churches were established, and there was heavy involvement of Work and Witness teams in construction programs. One of these was the Alameda church, built in memory of Garnet Howard of Cape Verde fame. The rise in value of the American dollar also made the purchase of buildings possible. As a result, 8 new churches were organized between 1980 and 1985. In 10 years' time, 10 buildings had been purchased or built, and 16 others rented for either churches or parsonages. Ten national pastors and two missionary church planters were at work with 9 organized churches, 10 other regular preaching points, and a total of 419 members.

7. *France*

On the western edge of Europe across from the British Isles lies the Republic of France, beleaguered victim of two world wars and numerous revolutions, yet somehow durable and resistant enough to emerge from each with strength and prestige. It is now the world's fifth-greatest industrial power. Largely divested of its colonial empire, which once included Indochina, Morocco, Tunisia, and other large African territories, it retains only a small presence in various parts of the world, most of which "colonies" are considered departments (states) of France itself.

France is one of the strongholds of the Roman Catholic faith, which claims 90 percent of the population. Protestants total only 1 percent, yet among them are sincere evangelicals who carry a great burden for their countrymen for whom religion is a matter of form, and secularism holds sway.

The Church of the Nazarene Enters

In 1977 Walter Crow and Dr. Paul Orjala, both former missionaries to Haiti, made an exploratory trip to France to appraise the possibilities of opening a work there. The report was encouraging, so the Walter Crows and the David Fraleys were appointed to undertake the task. Both couples and their families arrived in January 1979. The Crows, having served in Haiti for 13 years, were acquainted already with the French language, whereas the Fraleys' first few months were largely spent in language study.

The first organized services began as a Bible study in the home of the Crows. Shortly thereafter they heard that the Anglican chapel in Versailles was no longer being used for Sunday morning worship because the English-speaking congregation had grown too large. Excited Anglicans agreed to rent their chapel to the Church of the Nazarene. The first regular services were held there in January of 1980, and the church was officially organized in May of that same year.

In the fall of 1984 Serge Ricard, a recent graduate of ENBC, began his pastoral career in the church. In 1985 the Anglican church agreed to sell the property to the Church of the Nazarene. With space for Sunday School and office use being available for lease just next door, the Versailles church had room for growth.

An independent Haitian congregation in a new suburb of Paris sought affiliation with the Church of the Nazarene, but this promising prospect never materialized. However, the contacts made gave good portents for the future.

A third Bible study group had been started by a former Cape Verdian Nazarene, Noel Alves. He had followed God's leadership to come to France to study for the ministry in the hope that he would be able to serve the Church of the Nazarene someday. By the time contact was made with Rev. Crow, his group had already outgrown its space and was looking for other facilities for worship. One of the members of the Haitian group had told Rev. Crow of an old movie theater for sale in Paris. It turned out to be the same building that Mr. Alves had claimed in prayer for the Church of the Nazarene 11 years earlier! The building was purchased in 1981, and the congregation officially organized that same year with Noel Alves as pastor. The building was remodeled into a sanctuary and several classrooms.

When in 1982 Rev. Crow became rector of European Nazarene Bible College, the Russell Lovetts were transferred to France from their previous assignment in Italy to serve as mission director and district superintendent.

During Dr. Orjala's sabbatical leave from the seminary in Kansas City, he and his wife, Mary, spent seven months in France in 1985 helping with the work there. From that experience they felt God's leading to offer themselves for full-time service there. They were officially appointed mission directors by the General Board in February 1986. Their prime task would be to train prospective pastors for the work.

In 1985 the existing two congregations reported a total membership of 50.

8. *Spain*

Though Nazarene work had begun in Portugal in 1973, it was not until 1981 that its neighbor on the Iberian Peninsula, Spain, was entered by the church. This country, whose Christian history dates back to the beginning, was once on the target list of the apostle Paul, had his life been spared (Rom. 15:24). The Early Church fathers Irenaeus and Tertullian spoke of the Christian community there. This land was probably the ancient Tarshish of the Old Testament.

The Spanish, as were the Portuguese, were great explorers and colonizers, their influence being concentrated in the New World area that is still referred to as Latin America. Although Spain's colonial empire has largely disintegrated, the Spanish language and culture continue to dominate the area from Mexico all the way to the southern tip of South America. By treaty, the eastern hump of South America was left to Portugal (see Brazil).

Three-fourths of Spain's nearly 200,000 square miles is an almost treeless plateau, but the coastal regions are adequately watered for agriculture. Most of Spain's 40 cities are within 50 miles of the coast, either Atlantic or Mediterranean, but the capital of Madrid is near the center of the country.

Though Spain is almost totally Roman Catholic, in 1967 religious freedom was proclaimed, which legally made possible a Protestant presence for the first time. For many years the Spanish radio program "La Hora Nazarena" had been broadcast from the Trans World Radio station in Monte Carlo. In September 1974 Rev. Hugo Danker of West Germany was asked to investigate the possibilities for Nazarene work in Spain. His report was enthusiastic. "I have never known a country with a greater opportunity to present the gospel than in Spain today," he wrote. Leading Protestants in the country were urging the Nazarenes to come. But it was not until 1980 that the decision was made to enter this promising field.

A Nazarene Work Is Begun

In January 1981 Tom and Barbara Long and their four children moved to Madrid, a city of 4 million people, to launch the new project. While getting settled and beginning language study, they attended the Open Bible Church, where they were cordially received. There they met a Mr. Loyola, who introduced them to Rev. Ramon Blanco, pastor of an independent church on the other side of the city. It so happened that he had just retired and was looking for someone to take over his work. His church was in a five-story building that he owned and also wished to sell.

Negotiations were begun with Headquarters in Kansas City, and the purchase of the building for $200,000 was approved—an unbelievably low price. The building contained two apartments, Sunday School rooms, a recreation hall, a bookstore, and an attractive sanctuary complete with piano, pulpit furniture, and pews seating 150 people. Also involved was a small nucleus of 15 people that was organized into a Nazarene church in March 1982.

After the Longs returned from a summer furlough in 1983, Bible study groups were begun in several homes, and by 1985 two of them, Alcala de Henares and Fuenlabrada, were meeting in their renovated, storefront buildings. Both were officially organized in December 1985.

Of particular significance to the future of the work was the ministerial training program that was instituted. Seventeen students were involved in the program, each of whom was required as part of his training to begin and nurture a Bible study group. In addition, several Spanish students had attended or were attending the European Nazarene Bible College in Switzerland. Their first national pastor (actually an Italian), Giampaolo Morano, was ordained in 1985. An ENBC graduate, he was director of the ministerial training program and associate pastor of the Madrid church.

Pursuing some valuable contacts, work was opened in the summer of 1984 in the southwestern city of Seville under the leadership of Rev. and Mrs. Harry Stevenson. These natives of Ireland had been serving in Bolivia since 1971 and brought valuable expertise to the task. Then in early 1985 the Victor Edwardses from the British Isles, who had been serving in Argentina and Paraguay since 1963, were transferred to Spain to open work in Barcelona in the far northeast on the Mediterranean Sea.

By the time of the fifth district assembly in December 1985, there was still only one organized church but five other growing congregations and 121 members in this promising new field.

9. *The Azores*

The Azores are a group of nine Portuguese islands out in the Atlantic, 800 miles west of Portugal and 1,000 miles southeast of Newfoundland. The islands are of volcanic origin with a total area of 890 square miles. The population is a little over 300,000, of whom one-quarter live in the capital city of Ponta Delgada on San Miguel Island. There is a large American air base on Terceira Island.

When the Church of the Nazarene selected the Azores as one of the five new fields to be opened in the denomination's 75th anniversary year, the decision was based on firm evidence of its potential for success. For a number of years the Portuguese program "A Hora Nazarena" had been broadcast there. There were also several subscribers to the Portuguese *Herald of Holiness,* and among a band of refugees from Mozambique were some Nazarenes. Correspondence had been carried on for some years through these contacts.

To further check out the possibilities, in October 1982 Earl and Gladys Mosteller had been sent to "spy out the land." They spent three weeks in the islands, visiting all nine of them and following up on earlier contacts. They found that five of the islands had no evangelical work whatever, and none of the few churches on the other islands had more than 40 members. Though Roman Catholicism was the dominant faith on the islands, they seemed wide open to the gospel. The people were friendly and hospitable, and the press was supportive.

The Mostellers, veterans of 12 years service in the Cape Verde Islands, 15 years in Brazil, and 9 in Portugal, gladly accepted the assignment to launch the new work. The task was not new to them, for they had started the work in both Brazil and Portugal. They arrived in July 1984 and set about to have the church legally registered. They were able to purchase a home for $60,000, which was half the value of the land alone. Here they began gathering a congregation. There were 43 present in their first public service held in a rented hall.

Knowing that a number of Work and Witness teams would be coming to the islands, two floors of a four-story building were purchased to be remodeled as dormitories for these visitors.

By the end of 1985 there were two congregations totaling about 50 people, one in the capital and one on Terceira Island. Two pastors had been recruited, and more than 20 were already enrolled in Bible studies. Rev. Ernest Eades, a former colleague of the Mostellers from Cape Verde days, was called out of retirement to head up the training program. Over 500 individual contacts had been made, which indicated warm interest and response.

10. *European Nazarene Bible College*

Wherever the Church of the Nazarene has gone, one of its early priorities has been to establish a school for the training of qualified national pastors. In this respect Europe offered a special challenge, for here was an advanced culture with a rich theological heritage. Just as quality buildings had to be erected if the church were to make an impact in the communities they served, so well-educated men were required to man the pulpits.

There were other important considerations. One was the fact that the Church of the Nazarene was virtually unknown. It had to build its own credibility with knowledgeable and loyal leaders. Then, too, Wesleyan theology was little known. In the Calvinistic stronghold of Europe, Wesleyan pastors needed to be skilled in their doctrinal position to hold their own. Most of all, if the goal of a totally indigenous church were to be achieved, capable leaders would need to be trained for the task.

Out of this need came the fledgling institutions launched in Florence, Italy, and Frankfurt, Germany. But it became obvious as the work expanded to other areas of Europe that it would be impossible to staff and maintain separate schools in each country. At the same time there was a certain cultural commonality that made a central school possible, even though several languages were involved. The logistics would need to be worked out, but the basic decision was made to launch a single, international school to serve all of Europe except the British Isles, which had its own college. It was a daring idea.

Choosing a Site

The obvious choice for a location was that most neutral of all countries, Switzerland. But at the time, Switzerland was not permitting new foreign groups to enter, and certainly not to purchase property. Thereupon a search committee began to seek a location elsewhere, but perhaps some place near the Swiss border. It was thus that Rev. Jerald Johnson and Rev. Richard Zanner, while on another errand to Innsbruck, Austria, discovered the small German enclave of Büsingen, wholly inside the northern tip of Switzerland. How this tiny 3.5-square-mile area became isolated is a quirk of history that the residents have learned to live with. Büsingen is politically German but economically Swiss. What this meant was that if the college were located here, it would be on German territory (which already recognized the Church of the Nazarene) yet have all the advantages of a Swiss location. Visas and work permits for students could readily be obtained from the German authorities located in nearby Singen.

The location committee (Revs. Kleven, Wire, Hegstrom, and Johnson) were called to meet in Büsingen in June 1965 to explore the possibilities further. While they were eating in the restaurant of a small hotel on the main street, they told the manager and his wife of their mission and asked if they knew of any suitable property in town that might be for sale. Quickly they responded that the very building they were in was on the market. That night after they had thoroughly examined the building and other smaller structures on the seven-acre tract, they decided that they would contact the owner the next morning to see if a deal could be worked out.

The price the man asked was so much in line with what they had expected to have to pay that no one thought of making a counteroffer. A telegram was sent to Kansas City recommending the purchase, and permission to proceed was soon granted.

Dr. G. B. Williamson, general superintendent in jurisdiction, selected Rev. John B. Nielson, pastor at Lowell, Mass., and former faculty member of Eastern Nazarene College, as the founding rector (principal) of the school. He and his wife, Marguerite, and their two younger children, Patricia and Bill, arrived in Europe in August 1965. Their first task was to prepare the hotel for school use. Many of the needs, such as dormitory rooms and eating facilities, were already there, so renovation rather than alteration was the principal task.

The next challenge was to gather a student body. A prospectus was hastily prepared outlining courses and class schedules principally built around the *Manual's* course of study for ministers. The decision had early been made that classes would be taught in English, so any students who came would be expected to have a reasonable facility with that language.

The College Begins Operation

The European Nazarene Bible College began operation in January 1966, with 12 full-time students representing six countries—Germany, Italy, Sweden, Finland, Denmark, and England. Among them was Salvatore Scognamiglio, who later became national superintendent in Italy. By the second semester, enrollment was up to 18. Assisting the Nielsons with the teaching at first were Rev. and Mrs. A. J. Finkbeiner. They were followed shortly by Miss Jeanine van Beek and Miss Clara Christensen. Visiting professors from England and the United States augmented the faculty for varying periods.

By the time the Nielsons returned to the United States in 1969, a total of 16 students had graduated. Dr. Richard Taylor served as rector for the year 1969-70, after which Rev. Bill Prince took over. It was during his term that a new, three-story building was erected that provided faculty and married students' apartments, library, student lounge, and shop.

In 1976 Dr. Bennett Dudney became rector, and the following year Dr. LeBron Fairbanks was appointed academic dean. Under their leadership, the curriculum offerings were expanded to include an A.B. program in conjunction with Mid-America Nazarene College. The first three students in this program were graduated in 1978.

In the spring of 1979 construction began on the first phase of another major building to provide chapel, library, classrooms, student lounge, and additional dormitory space. Building codes were strict, and structures had to be built to last 200 years, so costs were high; but with the help of three Work and Witness teams the total was held down to some degree. The building was completed in 1981, and shortly afterward Dr. Dudney resigned to become director of Publication Services within the Division of Communications for the Church of the Nazarene. His place was taken by Rev. Walter Crow, then superintendent of the new work in France and a former missionary to Haiti.

In its first 20 years ENBC graduated over 180 students, and their impact upon the work in Europe, both in clergy and laity, was being increasingly felt. Enrollment had reached 43 by 1985.

B. THE MIDDLE EAST

The Eastern Mediterranean has for millennia been the "crossroads of empire." Here East meets West. Here was the home of the patriarchs, the land of the Israelites, the birthplace of the Savior, and the launching pad of the Christian Church. This also was the no-man's-land where the warring empires of Babylon, Persia, Assyria, Egypt, Greece, and finally Rome contended for supremacy.

Here the followers of Muhammad in the seventh century moved into the religious vacuum created by the dispersion of the Jews and the failure of the Christian Church. In turn, it was here that the Crusaders from Europe sought unsuccessfully from ca. A.D. 1100 to 1300 to oust the Muslims from the land of Palestine.

And here the United Nations created in 1948 a new land of Israel to which multiplied thousands of Jews from over 100 nations of the world have come to establish themselves once more in the Land of Promise. But this has not been without conflict and ill feeling, and the result has been an uneasy and often volatile situation that has defied peaceful settlement.

The city of Jerusalem itself epitomizes the conflict between the dissident factions. Legally, by United Nations action an international city, it came under Israeli control by virtue of the Six Day War in 1967, though this has never been officially recognized. Included in this is the ancient Temple Square atop Mount Moriah, which is now dominated by the magnificent Muslim shrine, the Dome of the Rock, and the nearby Al Aksa Mosque. No religious Jew will enter the Temple area, however, as long as it is "desecrated" by a Muslim shrine. But it was on this very location that Solomon's magnificent Temple once stood, and later Herod's. The high western wall of this Temple area is the storied Wailing Wall to which the Jews flock daily to pray for their beloved Jerusalem.

The Old City itself is divided loosely into four sectors—Christian, Armenian, Arab, and Jew. The Armenians, who once made up a strong Christian community, have dwindled considerably in recent decades.

When Palestine became a British protectorate in 1917 as General Allenby peacefully took the country from the Turks, the Balfour Declaration provided for a national homeland there for the Jews. This gave great impetus to the Zionist movement, whose goal was the return of Jews to the land of their forefathers. However, they came against extreme opposition from the Arabs. It was only after the partitioning in 1948 that the real influx of Jews began.

The 3 million Palestinians, displaced from their former homeland when the nation of Israel was carved out, continued their unrelenting refusal to cooperate with the United Nations mandate. The 450,000 who remained inside the Israeli borders accepted the situation with extreme reluctance, but there were also the 650,000 Arabs isolated in the West Bank and Gaza Strip areas who were also subjected to Israeli authority after the Six Day War.

It was in the midst of this area of foment that the Church of the Nazarene sought to develop a viable missionary presence. It was the Great Commission in reverse—carrying the gospel back to where it started. The Nazarene work has been centered in Israel, Jordan, Syria, and Lebanon. The total population of the four countries is approximately 17.5 million of which, outside of Israel, over 90 percent are Arabs. The 425,000 Armenians, emigrants from the area of Turkey early in the century because of religious persecution there, are concentrated in Lebanon and Syria.

1. *Holy Land*

One sees more religion in Jerusalem than in almost any place in the world, but it is basically legalistic. There are three regular holy days each week, Friday for the Muslims, Saturday for the Jews, and Sunday for the Christians. In addition there are many other holy days observed by each. But one senses little deep piety except perhaps among the Hasidim sect of the Jews and the many Muslim pilgrims who come to pray in the Dome of the Rock. The Muslims still hear the call to prayer from the mosques five times a day, but few Arabs pay attention. And among the immigrant Jews, political considerations loom much stronger than the religious ones. Though there is a religious mystique that is perhaps the binding cement holding the country together against fierce odds, the dominant forces in the country are commercial and educational, coupled with the underlying sense of racial pride and great human drive.

The Christians in Israel number a little over 75,000, most of whom are Arabs and members of one or more of the branches of Catholicism and Eastern Orthodox faiths. Most of the Christian sacred sites in the country are marked by Roman Catholic shrines. There are perhaps 3,000 Protestant Christians, and a mere handful of these are Jewish. The largest Protestant body is the Church of England.

The Church of the Nazarene in Israel

It has been estimated that a million and a half Armenians in Turkey were massacred from 1895 to 1915, while hundreds of thousands fled for their lives to Syria, Lebanon, and Palestine. These refugees became the seedbed for the work of the Church of the Nazarene in these countries. Rev. Samuel C. Krikorian, himself an Armenian, was the first missionary, arriving in Jerusalem on October 7, 1921.

An aunt of Samuel, Miss Rebecca Krikorian, had gone to the United States in 1895 to raise money for a Christian mission in Aintab, Turkey, where Samuel had been born two years before. Shortly after she left Turkey, the first massacre of Armenians took place, and from then on she expanded her appeal to include relief for destitute Armenians.

Since Samuel had been spared the fate of his family, his aunt felt that surely he was destined for some great work for God. For years she sought to arrange for his coming to the United States and finally succeeded in 1909. He began his schooling in Philadelphia. In the course of her travels around the United States, Miss Krikorian came into contact with the Church of the Nazarene in California and decided that Samuel should attend Pasadena College. He graduated from there in June 1917 and joined the Church of the Nazarene in December.

Both Samuel and his Aunt Rebecca felt the call of God to open a mission in Jerusalem and approached the Foreign Mission Board about starting a Nazarene work there. The project was approved in October 1919, and both of the Krikorians were appointed to go. Miss Krikorian never made it, but after nearly two years of deputation work, Samuel sailed for Palestine in August 1921.

There were possibly 5,000 Armenians in Jerusalem at the time, most of them related to the Gregorian church. Rev. Krikorian was bitterly opposed by these church leaders. But a much more critical obstacle arose when the British occupation authorities told him he could not open a mission unless he likewise operated an orphanage.

Shortly after receiving this news, Dr. H. F. Reynolds, general superintendent and general secretary of Foreign Missions, visited Jerusalem. When apprised of the problem, Dr. Reynolds suggested they spend a night of prayer concerning the matter out on the Mount of Olives, which they did. With the dawn came the assurance in their hearts that God was moving on their behalf. Indeed, within a few days the orphanage project was taken over by another group, and the church was granted the necessary permit to launch a mission. Rev. Krikorian set to work immediately, and during the ensuing year moved among the people, gathering a nucleus for a church.

In 1922 the Alvin H. Kauffmans were transferred from India to Jerusalem to superintend the work. With the help of the rector of the Anglican church, a building was rented near the Jaffa Gate on the road to Bethlehem, and regular services were begun in December 1922. On April 6, 1924, the Church of the Nazarene was officially organized with 21 members.

A month before the organization of the church, Rev. Krikorian had married Miss Hranoush Yardumian, a Beirut schoolteacher. She and her sister helped start an elementary school in connection with the new church. Many of the children had been attending a Roman Catholic school, and a recent ruling had been made by the priest that no one could attend the school who did not also attend Sunday services in the Catholic church. There was no way out but for the Nazarenes to start a school of their own.

In the fall of 1924 Rev. Moses Hagopian arrived to augment the missionary force. He was an Armenian who had escaped to the United States from Turkey in 1912 and had graduated from Northwest Nazarene College in 1921. After a few months in Jerusalem he was transferred to the port city of Haifa, 60 miles northwest. Here at the foot of Mount Carmel he launched an Armenian mission in February 1925. It had been open less than a year when for lack of funds it had to be closed.

Rev. Hagopian then did evangelistic work in Lebanon and Syria. While in the latter country, he found his sister who had once been imprisoned in Turkey. He had not seen her for many years. He brought her back to Palestine with him, and together they started a mission in Jaffa (the biblical port city of Joppa, now a suburb of Tel Aviv).

In 1928 ill health made it necessary for the Hagopians to return to the United States, and the Jaffa mission was placed in charge of Rev. G. Manoushagian.

That same year the Kauffmans returned to Palestine after a three-year furlough, during which time Rev. Kauffman completed his work for an M.A. degree in missions at Hartford Theological Seminary. He had also been conducting services in which he raised money for a church building in Jerusalem. The uncertainties of using rented property, plus the fact that the building the congregation was then using was crowded out, was a strong basis of appeal.

Immediately upon his return, Rev. Kauffman began to search for property. None was available in the crowded Old City, and since Jerusalem at that time was not divided, the logical place to look was in the New City on the west side. A choice 100 x 200-foot lot was found on Julian Way, a main thoroughfare and directly across from a new million-dollar YMCA Building. Nearby also the elaborate King David Hotel was about to be built. The purchase of so valuable a property for only $12,000 was a great answer to prayer.

Construction was begun on a stone building on the back of the lot that would provide church facilities on the first floor and a pastor's apartment above. The plan was to construct a more commodious church building on the front of the lot when funds became available. As it turned out, it was never built.

The new facilities gave an air of permanence to the church's program, and the work continued to grow. Membership reached 60, Sunday School attendance was averaging 200, and there were 40 in the youth group. The elementary school had an enrollment of 60, and among its graduates going on to high school were two young men who in the future were to play significant roles in the work of the church in the Middle East. One was Berge Najarian, an Armenian, born in Egypt, who years later, after obtaining college and seminary training in the United States, returned to the Middle East as a missionary. The other was Puzant Krikorian, brother of the pastor, who went on to medical school in Beirut, Lebanon, and upon completion of his studies operated the Christian Medical Center Hospital in Beirut. He was largely instrumental in the opening of Nazarene work in that city in 1948. Still another elementary school graduate was Paul

Manoushagian, who became an assistant librarian at Harvard University.

Most of the church members were Armenians, but a few Arabs were being reached, among them George Shammas, who later became pastor of an Arab congregation in the Old City.

As the influx of Jews continued to mount, friction between them and the Arabs correspondingly increased. By 1936 open clashes erupted. By this time the Kauffmans had been brought back to the United States for their protection and did not return until 1937. The work of the church, under the leadership of Rev. Krikorian, continued without interruption, however.

World War II saw no significant effect on the work except that the Kauffmans were again returned to the United States in 1939.

The pent-up emotions finally erupted in May 1948, when the British evacuated Palestine. Furious battles were fought between Arabs and Jews. The United Nations, in one of its earliest major actions, stepped in, enforcing an armistice and imposing a settlement by arbitrarily partitioning the country into Arab and Jewish segments. Part of the demarcation line ran through the city of Jerusalem between the old and new sections, the former in Arab and the latter in Jewish territories. This was a major source of contention for the Jews that they steadfastly refused to accept. The new state of Israel was thus born in turmoil, and its history ever since has been turbulent.

The Armenians, though not directly involved in the issue, scattered in all directions, settling for the most part in neighboring countries, but others making it to Europe and America. The Jerusalem church was decimated. Not only did they lose the Armenians, but since it was in the Jewish sector, it lost its Arab members as well, as no one dared to cross the line.

When Rev. and Mrs. Alexander Wachtel arrived as missionaries to the Israelis in 1952, they found only one Armenian family in the church, the Dadians. In a short time they, too, had departed. Rev. Wachtel, born an American Jew and raised in orthodoxy, was converted as a young man and graduated from Eastern Nazarene College and Nazarene Theological Seminary. He had the natural qualifications for dealing with his own race. But the problems the Wachtels faced were many. They had a church building that was unusable because of its dangerous location. Attendance at services was meager. What is more, the new government had strict rules against Christian evangelistic activities. Nevertheless the Wachtels carried on valiantly with Saturday night services in Jerusalem while often commuting to Nazareth and Haifa to help there. Finally it was decided to close the Jewish work in Jerusalem and the property was sold in May 1973. The Wachtels completed their term of service in 1974.

In 1955 Misak Sarian, who lived in Nazareth, was led into the experience of entire sanctification and began conducting services in his own home. Later, as attendance rose, an apartment was rented for the purpose. In May 1957 an excellent piece of property was purchased for $6,000. After overcoming numerous legal roadblocks, a church building was erected and dedicated in 1961. There was a chapel and classrooms in the first floor and a pastor's home on the second floor toward the back. Though Nazareth is in Israeli territory, the church was largely an Arab congregation and proved to be among the more successful Nazarene enterprises in Israel.

In 1962 the work in Haifa was reopened when, after 18 months of negotiations, a substantial residence was purchased there for $28,000. In September the Sarians moved there from Nazareth. The latter church was left in the charge of a new missionary couple, the Allen Hollises. The work was apparently going well in both places, but when the Hollises returned to the United States in 1964 and the Sarians accepted a pastorate in Canada in 1967, the rising hope began to dim once more. For a number of years only sporadic services were held anywhere in Israel—"Seven black years," Rev. Wachtel called them.

In August 1971 hope revived once again when Rev. and Mrs. Earl Morgan arrived in Nazareth to pick up the work once again. Rev. Morgan had been a missionary in Italy from 1952 to 1957 and then was transferred to Lebanon, where he served until 1963 (including a year back to Italy). Because of his wife's declining health, he took a pastorate in the United States until she passed away. In 1971 he married Norma Wiese, a missionary nurse from India, and soon they were on their way to Israel.

The work was moving well once again, and a church was organized in December 1972 with 13 members. Services were also held at Issfieh on Mount Carmel and at Jdeidy in the Vale of Acre.

On December 31, 1972, Samuel Sabbah, an Arab who had graduated from European Nazarene Bible College, and his Finnish wife, Maiju, were appointed to pastor the Haifa church. Then in 1975, when the Morgans went to the United States on furlough, Rev. and

Mrs. Arnold Finkbeiner came to serve the Nazareth church for a year as interim pastors.

After serving for one year, the Finkbeiners returned to the United States, and Rev. and Mrs. Merlin Hunter were transferred from Trinidad to Nazareth. Upon their return from furlough, the Morgans took over the Jerusalem center, and he was named district superintendent and mission director.

In February 1981 an educational building was begun in Nazareth, and shortly thereafter the Lindell Brownings arrived to replace the Hunters. The Brownings had been in language study in Jordan for 20 months. With the help of five Work and Witness teams the building was finally completed in 1984. This made possible the launching of a preschool, which provided a valuable entrée to the community. Within four months the enrollment had climbed to over 50.

In the meantime, it had become advisable to close the Haifa and Jdeidy work.

The Arab Sector of Jerusalem

With the partition of Palestine into Arab and Jewish states in 1948, which included the division of Jerusalem itself, the Nazarenes living in the Arab sector of the city were no longer able to attend the church that was on the Jewish side. Rev. and Mrs. Vartkes Keshishian, who had been involved in the church in the New City, therefore asked permission to try to establish a work in the Old City. Rounding up what members could be found, they arranged to hold services in the Christ Church Hostel, thus keeping a nucleus alive.

However, it was not until the middle of 1960 that steps were taken to establish a permanent mission in Arab Jerusalem. A valuable piece of property was purchased just north of the Damascus Gate, not far from the American Consulate and Gordon's Calvary. Plans for a building program were interrupted by the Six Day War in 1967, in which the Old City along with the West Bank, the Gaza Strip, and the Golan Heights were occupied by the Israelis. This removed the no-man's-land that had separated the two sections of Jerusalem, but tensions remained that made the carrying on of an Arab church in the former building ill advised. The members of the original congregation were now scattered anyway.

Finally, in 1970 construction began on a Nazarene International Center. The building was financed largely by the Russell L. Price family of Long Beach, Calif. Besides the church auditorium itself, the building contained facilities for entertaining visitors and living quarters for the Najarians, who were serving as superintendents of the work in Jordan. The building was completed and dedicated by Dr. Samuel Young, general superintendent, in 1971.

Technically, Israel and Jordan were at war, since in the partitioning of Palestine in 1948, the West Bank was made part of what was known as Transjordan. In April 1949 it became the Hashemite Kingdom of the Jordan. Israel was, therefore, occupying Jordanian territory. The Allenby Bridge, the main crossing of the Jordan River east of Jerusalem, was strictly controlled. Yet Rev. Najarian was allowed to cross over regularly and occasionally take others with him, such as General Superintendent Edward Lawlor in 1973 and Dr. and Mrs. John Riley in 1974.

Rev. Najarian continued to serve the Jerusalem congregation until 1976, when the Earl Morgans, who had been serving in Nazareth, were transferred there. In April 1982 the name of the district was changed to Holy Land to help erase the political overtones of the former designation of Israel.

Branch Sunday Schools had been operated in Taybe and in the Old City that in 1985 became regular preaching points. Youth meetings were also begun with volunteers Wayne and Nancy Goldsmith and Butros Grieb. The latter had been converted in the Nazareth church and, feeling a call to preach, had enrolled in the Arab Bible College in Bethlehem. Also George Kuttab returned from the United States and added strength to the Old City congregation.

In 1985 Rev. and Mrs. Christopher Grube arrived in Israel to begin language study and add to the missionary staff there.

2. *Jordan*

Prior to World War I, all Palestine on both sides of the Jordan River was under Turkish rule. After the war, the League of Nations gave Great Britain a mandate over the area. They, in turn, separated the two parts, setting up Arab rule in what was called Transjordan and gradually relinquishing control to them. In May 1946 Transjordan became completely independent.

Meanwhile the Zionist movement, aided by the Balfour Declaration, had resulted in an enormous influx of Jews into the area west of the Jordan. There was a great clamor to make this area a Jewish national home, but the British would not yield to the pressure and turned the matter over to the United Nations. The U.N. arbitrarily divided the territory between Jews and Arabs, drawing the lines generally according to population concentration. The Arabs never accepted the partitioning, and continued fighting went on between the factions.

A mass migration of perhaps 500,000 Arabs across the river into Jordan following the partitioning had a profound effect on the country. How could a nation already impoverished absorb a sudden one-third increase in population?

Providentially, in 1947 Rev. and Mrs. William Russell of the British Isles had been sent out by the Church of the Nazarene to assist Rev. Krikorian in opening up work among the Arabs of Transjordan. They were in Jerusalem in language study during the height of the turmoil. When the crisis arose in 1948, the Krikorians, who had been on furlough, hurried back to assist.

Among the Palestinian refugees were a number of members of the Jerusalem church who had settled mostly in Amman and Zerka in Jordan, and in Beirut, Lebanon.

The Krikorians decided to move to the capital city of Amman. When they arrived from the United States, the word was already out among his old Jerusalem friends that services were to be started there. A church was soon organized, and Rev. Jamil Chamichian, one of the Jerusalem Nazarenes who had been Sunday School superintendent there, was installed as pastor. In 1952 a building was erected.

Services were soon begun in the Jebel-Amman section of the city, and before long there was another organization. Their building was completed in 1955.

Meanwhile, in April 1949 the Russells had moved to Zerka, 15 miles north of Amman. Here Rev. Krikorian's sister-in-law, Miss Puzantohie Yardumian, had been holding Bible study meetings for women and Sunday School for the children. Here also lived George Kuttab, an Arab Christian who was an able assistant in getting the work under way. Other Jerusalem Nazarenes helped form the nucleus of a thriving church, among them the Tashjians, whose son Jirair was years later to become a missionary for the Church of the Nazarene in Taiwan. A church and a day school building were erected in 1954. Enrollment in the school quickly grew to 200.

In 1956-57 an international crisis arose in which Jordan broke relations with Great Britain. Since the Russells were Britishers, it was considered advisable to have them leave. For about five years the work was in the charge of national pastors with limited supervision for a while from the missionaries in Syria. There was no slackening of activity in Zerka, however, and in 1962 a large, attractive church was erected to complement the earlier two buildings. The congregation, pastored by Rev. Kamal Kusus, as well as the school, were having a growing influence in the city and surrounding area.

In 1961 Rev. and Mrs. Berge Najarian arrived on the field. He became superintendent of the work and with the exception of furlough years served in that capacity until May 1976. During the latter years, after the erection of the church in East Jerusalem in 1971, he supervised the work from there.

The fourth church was organized in the town of Karak in 1963. The work in this hilltop city had been opened in September 1962 by Rev. Jacob Ammari. In this congregation was a brilliant young virologist, Dr. Mukhles Amareen.

In 1964 the Ivan Lathrops were appointed to the Jordan District, but in 1967 they were transferred to Lebanon where in 1971 he became field director of the Syria/Lebanon District. In 1976 Jordan was added to his jurisdiction, and ultimately (1980) the three were united as the Middle East National-Mission District.

3. *Syria*

The Arab country of Syria, like most of the Middle East, came under Turkish domination in the middle of the 16th century. Though there were stirrings of Arab nationalism as early as the 19th century, freedom from Turkish rule did not come until World War I.

The Arabs fought on the Allied side and assumed that independence would be granted after victory was achieved. However, in 1916 a secret pact was signed between Britain and France, designating their respective future spheres of influence in the Middle East. To France was mandated the Syrian area, while Britain was to control Palestine.

The French territory was divided into two states, Syria and Lebanon. On September 16, 1941, Syria was proclaimed a republic by France and achieved full independence on January 1, 1944. Eighty-eight percent of the population of over 8 million are Muslims.

Nazarene Missions

The work of the Church of the Nazarene in Syria began somewhat concurrently with that in Palestine, though it was slower in developing. The first services were held in Bludan on July 7, 1921, under the pioneer leadership of Rev. Mulhim Thahabiyah. Bludan, a village 25 miles north of Damascus, was his hometown where he had been born 28 years before. In 1911, at the age of 18, he had emigrated to the United States with his father to avoid being drafted into the Turkish army.

He came in touch with the Church of the Nazarene, was converted, called to preach, and went to Olivet Nazarene College, where he graduated in 1920. He was ordained that year by Dr. R. T. Williams and appointed as a missionary to Syria. When he arrived on Christmas Day, he was warmly received by his family, most of whom he was able to lead to the Lord. Neighbors and friends, largely members of the Greek Orthodox church, were also won. When church services were officially begun, the priests rose up in violent opposition. In spite of this the work grew rapidly.

A visit by Dr. H. F. Reynolds, general superintendent, in 1921 was a great encouragement to the lone preacher. At that time a building lot was purchased, but no structure was built for some time.

In 1922 an elementary school was established with an initial enrollment of 75. It soon was up to 200. Preaching points in Zahlah and Zebdani were also opened. It was not until 1925 that the Bludan church was officially organized with 20 members.

Through the years, Rev. Thahabiyah heroically labored alone, receiving occasional visits from Rev. A. H. Kauffman, who was stationed in Jerusalem and for three years (1937-39) was superintendent of the Middle East Mission District. Rev. Moses Hagopian from the Palestine area also evangelized in Syria. It was not until 1944, when France lost her mandate over Syria and an Arab government was in power, that the Church of the Nazarene received official government recognition.

The following year, Rev. and Mrs. Don DePasquale arrived to assist in the work, and several forward moves were made. The Thahabiyahs moved to Damascus and began services in their home in the Bab Touma (Gate of Thomas) section of the city. In 1946 permission was granted by the government to open an elementary school in the city, which in three years reached an enrollment of 150.

Another boost for the work came on February 7, 1946, when an Armenian congregation led by Rev. Nerses Sarian joined the Church of the Nazarene as a body.

In October 1955 Rev. Thahabiyah retired, and leadership of the

Syria-Lebanon field was turned over to Rev. DePasquale, who served until 1969. By then there were 10 organized churches in Syria with 10 additional preaching points. Membership stood at about 300, of which 225 were full members. Thirteen Sunday Schools were averaging about 500, and two elementary day schools were in operation.

But several factors brought on a somewhat static situation in all of the Middle East. One was the exodus of the Armenians, who had constituted the most fertile area for Nazarene work because of their deep Christian roots. At the same time, the prevailing Islamic faith of the Arabs was hard to penetrate. The overarching problem was the seemingly endless warfare between the various political and religious factions. In the case of Syria, by a government decree all missionary activity was forbidden, which resulted in the withdrawal of all missionaries. Fortunately the loyal nationals carried on heroically despite the restrictions.

4. *Lebanon*

The Lebanese people, descendants of the ancient Phoenicians, were for centuries the victims of international incursion as one world power after another ruled the area. Not until the League of Nations mandated the area to France after World War I did this tiny country, pressed against the Mediterranean Sea, become a nation. In 1945 it became an independent republic. The majority of its approximately 3 million people were Christians (mostly Maronite Catholics), and therefore it was considered a Christian nation. Rich in natural beauty, Lebanon was for many years the educational and financial center of the Arab world and enjoyed a level of peace unknown elsewhere in the Middle East. Its capital, Beirut, was the heart of communication and finance of the eastern Mediterranean area.

Civil Conflict

When the republic was established in 1945, the Muslims and Christians worked out an agreement whereby the president of the country would be a Maronite Christian and the prime minister a Suni Muslim. The remainder of the government was to be divided but maintain a Christian majority.

In 1975 the mounting tensions throughout the Middle East spilled over into once-peaceful Lebanon and erupted in bloody fighting between Muslims and Christians. A complicating factor was the presence of some 270,000 Palestinian refugees living in city slums and in squalid settlements along the Israeli border to the south. Incited by the Palestine Liberation Organization, terrorist attacks were made across the border that embarrassed the Lebanese government, who wanted no part of the Palestinian issue. Nevertheless, retaliatory strikes by the Israelis made Lebanon a battleground of this conflict.

But as the Muslim population of Lebanon proportionately increased, the demand for more equitable representation in the government increased, fueling the fires of discontent to the point of civil war. This only aggravated the PLO issue. In the end, Beirut not only lost its prestigious position as an international center, but the once-beautiful city lay virtually in ruins.

Nazarene Missions

Rev. Moses Hagopian, whose principal ministry had been in Palestine in the 1920s, also held evangelistic meetings in neighboring countries. Thus he was the first Nazarene voice in Lebanon, though he established no specific mission center.

When Lebanon and Syria were outlining the constitutions of the respective republics they would become in 1945, the evangelical communities organized with government approval the Supreme Council of the Evangelical Community in Syria and Lebanon. The Church of the Nazarene had one representative from each of the two countries on this council, although there was as yet no established work in Lebanon.

Following the 1948 Palestinian War of Partition, many of the Nazarenes in Jerusalem, both Arab and Armenian, fled to Beirut. There this loyal group of about 35 got together in the homes for fellowship and worship. Rev. Krikorian came up from Jerusalem to help in the purchase of a building site in the suburb of Sioufi. Plans were drawn for an impressive five-story building on a hillside to house both a church and school. Staff apartments were also included. During the two-year construction period the chapel of the Christian Medical Center was used for worship. This distinguished institution had been developed by a Nazarene physician, Dr. Puzant Krikorian, and a partner. He continued to be a valued member of the congregation.

Both Arabic and Armenian services were conducted in the new building, which was known as the Ashrafieh Church. Elementary and secondary day schools were launched with enrollment soon reaching 300.

In 1954 Rev. and Mrs. Donald E. Reed arrived as the first missionaries to Lebanon, and a Bible school was begun in the Ashrafieh building. In the 15 years the Bible school was in operation, it supplied most of the pastors for the Middle East area. However, as years passed, the central purpose of the school dimmed. Syrian students, non-Nazarene in most cases, used the school only as a stepping-stone to the United States. As a result, the Bible school was closed in 1969, though the elementary and high schools were continued.

In 1956 preaching services were begun in the Sin-el-fil section of Beirut, and a building accommodating a church and school was erected. Here again services were conducted in both Arabic and Armenian languages. In the place of the Reeds, the Oliver Karkers arrived in 1966 and remained until 1971. In 1967 the Ivan Lathrops were transferred there from Jordan, and in 1969 the Gordon Johnstons and the Larry Buesses arrived. The work took on momentum.

But in October 1975 civil conflict erupted, and all the missionaries were forced to get out of the country, leaving the national leaders to carry on as best they could. The Sin-el-fil Church, which had been used as a command post by the military, was completely destroyed by bombs; and the large Ashrafieh building was damaged, although it continued in limited use.

The Johnstons, expecting the birth of a child, could not leave with the others but took an apartment in the south end of the city near the airport so they would have an escape route if necessary. They remained until after the baby arrived on Thanksgiving Day. The missionaries evacuated to Europe, where they found places of temporary service in the church there.

The following year the Lathrops and Buesses returned to Jordan. From here Rev. Lathrop made frequent trips into Lebanon to give direction to the work. With great courage and optimism the people of the Sin-el-fil Church rallied to reconstruct their building. But the political unrest worsened once more, and in 1980 it became necessary for all foreign personnel to leave. During these troubled years great heroism had been displayed by both nationals and missionaries. Despite flying bullets they stayed at their posts, until only by a miracle were they able to escape. For nine days the Alajajis hid under a staircase with their tiny baby and barely survived. The final chapter of that story is yet to be written.

Out of the 1975 crisis came a recognition of the need for a national church organization, and soon after the missionaries returned, the necessary steps were taken to accomplish this. In 1978 Rev. Habib Alajaji was appointed superintendent of the Syria/Lebanon District. When in the following year Rev. Alajaji accepted the pastorate of the Armenian church in Glendale, Calif., Rev. Jacob Ammari was elected in his place. In 1980 the Syria/Lebanon District and the Jordan District were combined to form the Middle East District under the superintendency of Rev. Ammari.

At that time four churches, all in the north side of Beirut, remained in operation. Besides Ashrafieh and Sin-el-fil, there were churches in the Judeideh and Dekweineh sectors. Each church had both Arab and Armenian congregations; but since most members and pastors were Syrian with some Jordanians as well, this made it difficult to attract Lebanese, who have a proud national heritage and are slow to associate with others.

But such problems became academic with the violent upheavals that took place in the 1980s. Civil war, factional conflict, and rampant terrorism reduced the once-beautiful city of Beirut, the capital, to a no-man's-land. In 1985 Rev. Thomas W. Schofield, regional director, was able to go into Beirut and visit with Rev. Ammari. Surprisingly, he found two churches and a day school still in operation but under extreme duress. The future looked dark indeed.

The 1985 statistics for the Middle East District revealed that eight churches were in operation with 259 members.

IV

MEXICO, CENTRAL AMERICA, and CARIBBEAN REGION

- Mexico
- Guatemala
- Belize
- Nicaragua
- Costa Rica
- El Salvador
- Panama
- Honduras
- The Caribbean
- The Bahama Islands
- Guyana
- Suriname
- Caribbean Nazarene Theological College
- North American Indian District

Researchers:

Honorato T. Reza—Mexico, Central America
Ruth O. Saxon—The Caribbean
W. Howard Conrad—Guyana
F. Charles Scrivner—North American Indian

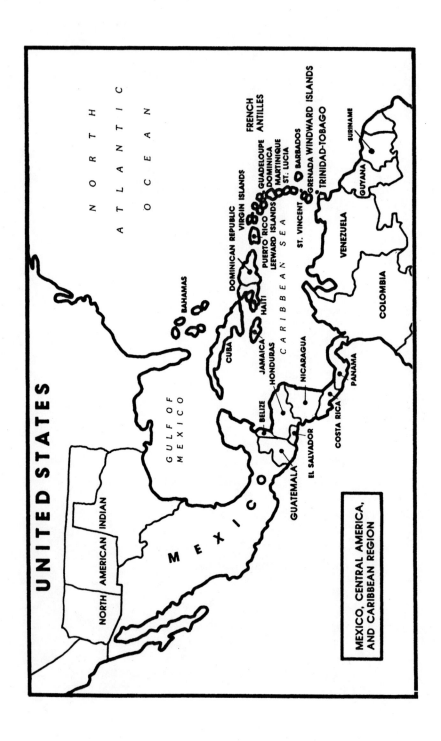

UNITED STATES

NORTH AMERICAN INDIAN

M E X I C O

GULF OF MEXICO

N O R T H   A T L A N T I C   O C E A N

BAHAMAS

CUBA

DOMINICAN REPUBLIC

HAITI

JAMAICA

VIRGIN ISLANDS

PUERTO RICO

LEEWARD ISLANDS

GUADELOUPE

DOMINICA

MARTINIQUE

ST. LUCIA

FRENCH ANTILLES

BARBADOS

ST. VINCENT

GRENADA

WINDWARD ISLANDS

TRINIDAD-TOBAGO

C A R I B B E A N   S E A

BELIZE

GUATEMALA

EL SALVADOR

HONDURAS

NICARAGUA

COSTA RICA

PANAMA

COLOMBIA

VENEZUELA

GUYANA

SURINAME

MEXICO, CENTRAL AMERICA,
AND CARIBBEAN REGION

A. MEXICO

Bordering the United States on the south is the third-largest country on the North American continent, The United Mexican States, or simply, Mexico. This sprawling 760,000-square-mile land, which measures 2,000 miles between its east and west extremities, consists of lofty mountains, fertile valleys, coastal jungles, and arid central plains. Its nearly 80 million inhabitants are largely a mixture of Spanish and Indian blood, estimated to be as high as 80 percent. Although perhaps only about 50,000 pure Indians remain, Indian culture and influence are strong, for here was the home of the storied Mayan and Aztec civilizations, which flourished before the Spanish conquest.

Mexico has been an arena of conflict for centuries. In its struggle for national identity it has been an ideological battleground in which extreme elements have struggled for supremacy. Still short of its goal of stability, it has nonetheless made giant strides in recent decades. The late discovery of vast petroleum deposits presages a new day for Mexico. Profound economic and sociological changes will be felt in this land that up to now has struggled with grinding poverty among the great majority of its people.

The Religious Climate

Mexico is nominally 96 percent Roman Catholic and has strict laws against foreign religious incursion. But before these restrictions were passed and all outside missionaries were out of the country, the seeds of the gospel had been planted, and the present growing Protestant community attests to the effectiveness of that sowing.

In the second half of the 19th century James Thompson, as he did in several South American countries, successfully established some of his famous schools in which the Bible was the main textbook. With the added influence of Francisco Penzotti, the Bible was widely distributed in Mexico and often with the blessing of the priests.

It is reported that in 1861 a small company of Protestant believers, all Mexicans, began holding services in the northern city of

Monterrey, and six years later another group began meeting in Zacatecas near the heart of the country. The first Protestant church was organized in Mexico City in 1869 by the American Foreign Christian Union.

The Presbyterians opened work in Mexico in 1872, followed a year later by the Methodist Episcopal church. The Baptists came in 1881, and before the turn of the century the Congregationalists, the Disciples of Christ, the Episcopalians, and the Quakers had all established missions.

1. *Roots of the Church of the Nazarene*

In 1903, five years before the Church of the Nazarene officially came into being at Pilot Point, Tex., Rev. Samuel M. Stafford, a native New Yorker but apparently under the sponsorship of the Texas Holiness Association, established a pioneer mission in Tonala, in the southern state of Chiapas. There with the help of Rev. Edwin H. Hunt, a carpenter by trade, he built a large church building, including space for a school and later a parsonage. Funds for the total project were provided by J. T. Shingler of Donalsonville, Ga. Uniquely, the city archives of Tonala and nearby Arriaga record that both towns were laid out by our missionaries and are recognized even today, according to the mayor of Tonala, as "the best-planned cities in this whole section of the country."

Rev. Hunt remained to pastor the new church for a year and then went into colportage work. He became proficient in the language of the people and translated the Gospel of John into the Zapoteca dialect.

Doubtless as an appreciation gift for help in planning the town of Arriaga (then called Jalisco), an attractive piece of property was given to the church; and in 1906 Rev. and Mrs. Charles Quesenberry arrived from Texas to launch the work there. Rev. and Mrs. J. W. Sewell arrived shortly afterward to assist with both churches, later to move on to establish a new work in Teloloapan in the state of Guerrero.

Also in 1906 Dr. A. G. Lowe, a Chicago physician, established a practice in Arriaga and gave immense support to the mission program throughout Chiapas as a self-supporting missionary. Also associated with him was a Dr. Dilley.

Meanwhile, in 1905 Rev. Carlos H. Miller had gone to Mexico City to open a church there. He already had experience working with

Mexicans on the Texas border and had some contacts in the capital. There he began a mission in a rented hall on Mesones Street a few blocks from the main city square. For a short period of time he had the help of Rev. and Mrs. J. Howard Estes, who in 1909 moved to Tonala.

The following year, 1910, the Millers were called to assist in an unusual colonizing project near Tonala. With the blessing of District Superintendent Stafford, a group of about 30 Texas Nazarenes, led by Rev. J. D. Scott and Dennis Rogers, bought a large tract of land at Arriaga and began a farming and stock-raising program for the purpose of helping to support the mission's work. An ambitious printing project was also instituted, with D. C. Ball arriving in 1911 to serve as its director. A school had been established in 1909 under the direction of Rev. and Mrs. J. Eaton Wallace of New York, and Mrs. Henryetta Richards of Chicago arrived soon after to assist them. A Nazarene colony of sizable proportions was developing.

Rev. Stafford had attended the historic 1908 General Assembly at Pilot Point, Tex., and had stirred up considerable interest in the Mexican work. Missionaries who returned with him at that time were Rev. and Mrs. J. D. Franklin, Miss Julie Payne, and Miss Carrie Lewis (who later married Rev. E. H. Hunt). After leading in the erection of a beautiful church at Arriaga, the Franklins and Miss Payne were assigned to open work in San Jeronimo (now Ciudad Ixtepec), 150 miles west of Tonala. There another fine church and parsonage were erected.

It would appear that explosive growth was in store for the work, but at the peak of expectations came the rumblings of a national revolution, which effectively shut down all missionary activity. The missionaries, under duress, decided it was best to leave. In May 1912 the last of the colonists, 27 in all, including a few remaining missionaries, were loaded on a train and under escort of 500 soldiers, were taken to the port of Salina Cruz for passage to the United States.

The Carlos Millers chose to remain in Tonala in hopes that the situation might change, but they soon decided to leave also. They later went to Argentina to help Rev. Frank Ferguson establish a mission and in 1927, after eight years of effective service, returned to the United States. Here they spent the rest of their days working among Spanish-speaking churches with Rev. Miller pastoring the First Mexican Church of the Nazarene in Los Angeles. Dr. H. T. Reza says of him, "He understood the Latin culture better than any other Nazarene man then living."

A New Mexican Church Emerges

Out of the ensuing chaos came two major factors that were to alter profoundly the direction of the missionary program in this country. One was the emergence of Dr. V. G. Santin as a national church leader, and the other was a government edict issued in 1917 that, among other things, stated that all clergymen engaged in active service in Mexico must be native-born citizens.

a. Dr. Vicente G. Santin was born in Toluca, just west of Mexico City, in 1870. His father, a Methodist minister and one of the earliest Mexican converts to Protestantism, died when Vicente was only 12. The young lad who first had attended a Presbyterian school was transferred to a Methodist orphanage. Upon completion of high school, with the help of interested friends who provided a scholarship, he entered Colegio Central in San Luis Potosi in 1890. In 1893 he was appointed a pastor in the state of Veracruz but continued his studies to become a medical doctor. Despite his heavy study program, he became a highly successful pastor. He was both an excellent preacher and administrator and was in great demand as a speaker.

Upon his graduation from medical school in 1905, he launched into a medical career that won him as much recognition as his preaching. But popularity proved his undoing, and he found it necessary to resign from his church, one of Mexico City's finest.

One Sunday morning in early May, he was walking aimlessly along the streets of the city, still trying to adjust to this new experience of having no pulpit to fill. After some time he came to Mesones Street and heard the joyous sound of familiar hymns coming from a nearby building. Strangely drawn to the place, he entered to find a small group of people worshiping. He listened with excitement to the sermon. During the altar call at the close, Pastor Carlos Miller, possibly recognizing the visitor, looked directly at Dr. Santin and said, "And you, sir, seated there on that bench, God has brought you here because He needs you for a great work." Dr. Santin stepped forward and at the humble altar confessed his backslidings and wept his way back to God. Later he followed the call of God to holiness, and inscribed in the flyleaf of his Bible are the words: "I was sanctified October 7, 1907. Blessed be the Lord!"

The young doctor became more and more involved in the work, and Rev. Miller trained him for leadership in the church. By the time the missionary left in 1910 to become a part of the ambitious project down in Arriaga, Dr. Santin was ready to take over the work in Mexico City. There followed a long and distinguished career as a minister and leader in the Mexican church. He died in 1948.

b. In 1917, as an outcome of the revolution that had begun in 1910, the National Constitution of Mexico was revised. Concerning religious activity the following principles were laid down: (1) all clergymen engaged in active service must be native-born Mexicans; (2) all primary education must be secular, thus doing away with parochial schools for children of that age; (3) clergymen were not permitted to criticize the government or the constitution, nor were they allowed to vote or hold public office; (4) no political meetings were to be held in churches; (5) religious periodicals must not comment on political matters; (6) all clergymen must register with the government, which was to determine the number of clergymen who would be allowed to function in a particular area; (7) no religious services were to be conducted in private homes.

Some of these regulations constituted no problem, but others had a devastating effect on the work of the church. Except for Dr. Santin, there had not been time to train adequate national leadership to take over the existing churches. Where there were buildings, the congregations carried on the best they could; but without the possibility of developing house churches, outreach was severely handicapped.

The one bright light was Dr. Santin. Through eight dark years he kept the Mexico City church open in spite of what J. D. Scott described as "indescribable persecution." Dr. A. J. Wood, an American medical associate, gave him great support.

In June 1919 Rev. J. D. Scott was sent to Mexico to make a general tour of the country and particularly to visit the former mission stations to see what the possibilities were for rebuilding the work. He was surprised and pleased to discover that though a number of the buildings had been commandeered by the government for soldiers' barracks, field hospitals, and other uses, they were in good enough condition for use. He was particularly impressed with Dr. Santin's work in Mexico City.

The outcome of Rev. Scott's visit was that Dr. Santin was invited to attend the General Assembly in Kansas City in October of that year. During the proceedings, he was named superintendent of the Mexico work, while Rev. Scott was made supervisor of all the Latin American region. With the promise of financial backing by the general church, Dr. Santin went back to pursue with great vigor the task of reopening the work in his homeland. Thus began the second stage of the Nazarene missionary effort in Mexico.

Expansion of the Work, 1919-35

Dr. Santin's first problem was to find pastors to send to these former mission stations. Rev. Jose Mota, one of his faithful helpers in the Mexico City church, was sent to Chiapas to reopen the work in Arriaga (Jalisco) and Tonala. Benjamin Maceda was sent to Oaxaca. He sent Rev. Bernabe Delgado, an older minister, and his brother Josue to the state of Guerrero. Dr. Domingo Ortiz, Rev. Antonio L. Bautista, and Rev. Mariano Lechuga, who was a member of the Mexican Congress, were given assignments in the vicinity of Mexico City. All of these, except Mr. Maceda, were university graduates and seminary trained but largely unschooled in evangelism and Nazarene ways, so growth was disappointingly slow. Also, because of their educational status the ministers catered to the middle class, which was largely indifferent to the gospel appeal. In the South there was a flurry of excitement as former members rallied to the reopened churches, but this too began to fade, for the pastors sent there did not fit in with the worship style of the people.

It quickly became obvious that a training school to develop truly Nazarene ministers was needed. So a Nazarene seminary was launched in Mexico City in 1922. The students simultaneously took classes at the university. Dr. Santin was bent on developing a highly cultured and educated ministry. Assisting him in this work was his son-in-law, Dr. C. E. Morales, in whose home several classes were held as well as in the church.

The first six graduates completed their work in 1926. Two of the class were Dr. Santin's own children, Alfredo and Judith. Two others were soon married and one remained to teach at the seminary, but all found places of active service.

Another supportive phase of the program was the medical work. Two clinics were operated by Dr. Santin in Mexico City from 1927 to 1939. These highly respected institutions won favorable recognition for the church throughout the city.

It was during this time also that a modest publication program was initiated. A paper, *La Antigua Fe* ("The Old Faith"), a youth periodical, *Juventud Nazarene,* and a 325-page, words-only songbook, *Lluvia de Gracia* ("Songs of Praise"), based on *Glorious Gospel Hymns,* were all published.

In 1927 a commodious building to house the First Church of the Nazarene in Mexico City was erected 14 blocks south of the city center.

It had been decided that the Mexican church would concentrate its efforts in the three southern states of Chiapas, Oaxaca, and Guerrero, as well as in Hidalgo, including the capital city itself. But in 1933 an event took place that forced a broadening of those horizons. A Baptist minister, Victor Godinez, was asked to resign from his large congregation in Guadalajara, 400 miles west of Mexico City, because he was preaching scriptural holiness. He and 300 of his loyal supporters began holding services on the patios of various homes, moving each week to a different location because of government restrictions. They adopted the name Evangelical Church of the Nazarene, though there was apparently no knowledge of the larger denomination whose name they had adopted. It also turned out that their doctrines were very nearly identical.

A Nazarene lady, a member of First Church in Mexico City, was visiting relatives in Guadalajara and was invited by them to attend one of Rev. Godinez' services. She was surprised to find what the group's name was and to hear a message much like she was accustomed to hearing in her home church.

The upshot was that communications developed between Guadalajara and Mexico City that climaxed in the acceptance of about 400 of Rev. Godinez' followers into the Church of the Nazarene. At the 1933 District Assembly their pastor's ordination was officially recognized. Five young pastors associated with Rev. Godinez along with their congregations were included in the transfer. The church thus began to blossom in an entirely new area.

As might be expected, there were some indoctrination problems to overcome, and in the accomplishment of this, a key figure was Rev. David J. Sol. He had been remarkably converted in the southern city of Villa Flores in 1928 and enrolled at the seminary in Mexico City in 1931. His many gifts and talents impressed the church leaders; and after he had served a short time in the pastorate, he was appointed by Dr. Santin to be his assistant superintendent in charge of the Guadalajara sector. Here his particular task was to help the many newcomers understand more fully the doctrines and practices of the Church of the Nazarene. It was the beginning of a long period of service as a leader in the Mexican church.

A Time of Adjustment, 1935-53

This period in the life of the Church of the Nazarene in Mexico was one of great activity, yet also of offsetting problems as the districts sought to establish a firm course for the future.

The year 1935 saw the beginning of explosive development in the southern state of Chiapas. The apparent human instrument God used was Apolinar Catalan. As a student at the seminary, he had chosen to take his required year of intern work at Villa Flores, birthplace of Rev. David Sol. He so won the hearts of the people that at the close of the year when he was scheduled to return to his studies in Mexico City, the people pled successfully to have him stay another year.

Apolinar Catalan, with the help of a dedicated group of laymen, successfully launched a number of preaching points that moved on toward full church status. From that time forward this was probably the fastest-growing section in Mexico in terms of church development. Many young people were called to the ministry and went off to prepare themselves for the work.

But the expansion was so rapid that there were not enough trained preachers to man the new churches. To the west, the work in the state of Guerrero was showing virtually no growth, so in 1939 the decision was made at the district assembly to close the work in this area, at least temporarily, and move the ministers to the Chiapas and Oaxaca fields to take advantage of the great opportunities unfolding there. It was not until the 1970s that the Guerrero field was reopened, but soon there were four thriving congregations in this area.

However, while God's blessing was so manifest in the South, in the Central District some conflicts, unrest, and defection were beginning to develop. The center of controversy was the seminary in Mexico City and involved also a resistant attitude toward Rev. Alfredo Santin, who had succeeded his father in the leadership of the district. The institution had done well in providing ministers for the growing Mexican work, but it had been necessary in order to attract sufficient students to lower the entrance requirements and institute a dual curriculum, one of preparatory nature and the other of graduate level. This tended to reduce the educational level of the seminary to that of a Bible institute. At the same time, it more fully served the needs of all of Mexico, particularly in the South, where the educational demands were quite different from those in the city.

Two moves were made to help quiet the situation. One was to

unite the Central and South districts under the leadership of Rev. David Sol, and the other was to close down the seminary. Dr. C. E. Morales, director of the school, became pastor of the Puebla church southeast of Mexico City. There he conducted some Bible and training classes, though on an unofficial basis.

2. *A Training Center for Ministers*

The ultimate solution for the ministerial training needs of Mexico was found in the establishment of an entirely new school in San Antonio, Tex. Several factors entered into this decision:

1. San Antonio was one of the strongest centers of Nazarene work among the Mexicans in the United States, and the Mexican community in the city was also substantial.

2. A training center was needed by the Department of Foreign Missions in which to prepare missionaries going out to Spanish-speaking areas.

3. Under the circumstances a neutral site for the Mexican seminary seemed advisable.

4. A school was needed in which to train pastors for the rapidly expanding Mexican work north of the border.

Such a center had, in fact, been in operation in Los Angeles since 1942 under the auspices of Pasadena College. Dr. C. B. Widmeyer was director of the school, and Rev. Honorato T. Reza, who was later to become a dominant figure on the Mexican Nazarene scene, was dean. Those were World War II days, and the school was housed in a building that the government had taken over from its Japanese owners, who had been interned in the interior of the United States. When in 1946 the Japanese were allowed to come back, the building was returned to them. Thus the school was looking for a new location.

Then in the summer of 1946, the talented young dean was called to Kansas City to organize the newly established Spanish Department of the Nazarene Publishing House. The school's future was in jeopardy.

With all these needs in mind, it seemed that the planting of an entirely new institution in the most Mexican of all United States cities would be an auspicious move. Further confirmation seemed to come when a former Pilgrim Holiness training center there became available for purchase.

In the fall of 1947 the Spanish Nazarene Bible and Missionary Training Institute was officially opened under the leadership of Rev. Hilario S. Pena. Twenty-six students enrolled that first year, all but three of them from Mexico. The missionary training aspect of the projected program never materialized.

The school moved ahead slowly in the beginning years, but when Dr. William C. Vaughters, veteran missionary from Guatemala, became director in 1955, major changes took place. The curriculum was upgraded and more adequate buildings erected. The name of the school was changed to Seminario Nazareno Hispanoamericano (Spanish-American Nazarene Seminary). The name also reflected the fact that students were coming from other Latin American countries as well.

The need for a larger campus was becoming imperative, and so early in the 1970s a more spacious property was purchased in suburban San Antonio, and a building program was begun. The initial buildings with an estimated value of $300,000 were dedicated on March 3, 1973. In 1974 Dr. Vaughters was called to Kansas City to serve in the office of the Department of World Missions, and his successor at the seminary was Rev. Marshall Griffith.

The influence of the Spanish seminary on the Latin American work was great indeed. Its scores of graduates are found in every Spanish-speaking country, some of whom are district leaders. A number serve in the International Publications offices at Headquarters in Kansas City.

Seminario Nazareno Mexicano

As years passed, however, there had been a growing desire to provide for advanced ministerial training in Mexico itself. Expansion into the cities also demanded a more highly educated clergy. A step in this direction was made when in 1978 the Mexican extension program of Nazarene Theological Seminary (Kansas City) was launched. This program consisted of two 30-day sessions of intensive study per year at which classes were taught by at least one visiting professor from the parent seminary, by Dr. Sergio Franco, who was director of the program, and by other guest lecturers.

In November 1979 the development of a full graduate seminary in Mexico was proposed, and in February 1980 the General Board authorized the establishment of such an institution. The plan involved the selling of the San Antonio property and investing the proceeds in a new campus somewhere "in or near Mexico City." The sale, which was consummated in 1980, netted $1 million. A year later Seminario Nazareno Hispanoamericano ceased operation after 34 years of effective service.

A Board of Regents for the proposed seminary was selected which in September 1980 elected Dr. H. T. Reza, then director of the International Publications Board, as president. A site selection committee inspected several possible locations and settled on a beautifully located 10-acre tract in the south part of Mexico City. The property was purchased in February 1981, and the board went to work on drafting a constitution and bylaws to govern the operation of the seminary. Also there were many legal details to work out and design concepts to study.

On March 26, 1982, a groundbreaking ceremony was held and construction began on the brick-and-wrought-iron fence around the entire property. Preliminary plans were developed calling for "six modest buildings." Instructions were that the campus was to be built without incurring any debt.

Legal complications arose, particularly with reference to the property title, and the project was stalled for a year and a half. Then in December 1984 came a dramatic breakthrough. The title problem was resolved, construction permits were granted, and contracts signed with architects and builders, all within a span of three weeks. Construction on the buildings began in earnest on January 7, 1985. To accelerate the process, two companies were put to work at the same time on separate parts of the project.

Some United States churches and individuals became interested in the work, and their financial contributions made possible the expansion of the building program to include a chapel auditorium to seat 400, a library, residences, and maintenance structures for a total of 10 buildings. Official dedication took place on January 25, 1986, and classes began the following week. Enrollment soon passed the 50 mark.

In the interim, beginning July 1982, an innovative program of area satellite extension classes in various centers was instituted to replace the former extension system out of Kansas City. Over an eight-month period each year, highly qualified professors shuttled between six selected centers, giving one-month concentrated lectures in each place. Students commuted to classes from the surrounding areas or arranged for board and room on their own except in the larger Mexico City center where nearby residences were rented for dormitories as needed. Full academic credit was given for work done in these satellite sessions.

By late fall 1985, 11 students had completed all the courses necessary to receive the bachelor of theology degree, and in mid-November the first graduation exercises were held out in the nearly completed campus auditorium.

It was recognized, however, that the seminary could not meet all the ministerial training needs for Mexico, for many did not have the necessary educational qualifications for entrance. For this reason, two Bible institutes were opened, one in the northwest at Ensenada and the other in the south at Tuxtla Gutierrez. A minimum of junior high standing was required for admission. Further down on Mexico's "educational pyramid" was the Bible school level for those with only a minimal grade school background. The Huasteca Indian Bible School in central Mexico is an example of this. The base level of religious education is in the Sunday School, Vacation Bible School, and other such local programs.

3. *The Latin Publications Program*

One of the most significant developments for the Mexican church during this 1935-53 period took place not in Mexico itself but in Kansas City. Here in July 1946 the Spanish Department of the Nazarene Publishing House was launched.

As before stated, several publications had already been produced in Mexico. Plans for expansion of this phase of the work were already under way, including the preparation of a hymnal, when at the 1944 General Assembly in Minneapolis, authorization was given for the organization of a Spanish Department at the Nazarene Publishing House. It would be under the direction of the Department of Foreign Missions (now World Mission Division) and use the equipment and facilities of the Publishing House. It would serve not only Mexico but also all Spanish-speaking areas. Already there were 11,000 members on these fields, and rapid growth was being experienced.

Rev. H. T. Reza, who had been associated with Pasadena College and its Spanish auxiliary, was called to head up this new venture and arrived in Kansas City July 10, 1946. The first publication, the monthly *El Heraldo de Santidad* ("Herald of Holiness") appeared in October of that year. Three months later, two Sunday School quarterlies came out: *El Sendero de la Verdad* ("Bible School Journal") and *La Antorcha Dominical* ("The Young Torch," geared to children). Several other periodicals were soon added, including a preachers' magazine and a Spanish version of the youth magazine, *Conquest*. Much of the material in early publications was translated from English periodicals, but as rapidly as possible original articles by Spanish writers were introduced.

Under the aggressive leadership of Rev. Reza, an intensive book program was also begun, including such substantial volumes as *Introduction to Christian Theology*, by Wiley and Culbertson, and many Christian Service Training books. A crowning achievement in the early days was the publication of a hymnal, *Gracia y Devocion* ("Praise and Devotion"). Rev. Reza himself translated many of the hymns. The book and music program has vastly expanded over the years.

The quality and variety of Nazarene Spanish materials was recognized among Protestants generally, and soon over half the sales were to non-Nazarene markets. In 1971 the name was changed from the Spanish Department to the Latin Publications Division, when the Portuguese language was added. It now operates under the more inclusive International Publications Board, whose assignment is worldwide.

During the 1980-85 quinquennium, four major projects were launched in Spanish: (1) the translation of the 10-volume *Beacon Bible Commentary*; (2) a stewardship packet sent annually to all Spanish churches; (3) a lay Christian training program called IPC (Instituto de Preparacion Christiano); (4) the ministerial course of study leading to ordination. The latter was designed and written entirely by Spanish-speaking nationals including the work manuals and textbooks where needed.

4. *The Emergence of the District Structure*

Up to the late 1930s Nazarene work in Mexico was concentrated in metropolitan Mexico City, the southern border states, and the cluster of churches recently added in the Guadalajara area to the west. With the exception of some scattered work along the United States border, the broad expanse of northern Mexico was untouched by the church.

In 1939 Rev. Enrique Rosales, who was an assistant to Rev. E. Y.

Davis and later to Rev. Ira L. True in the Texas-Mexican work, felt the call of God to witness to his own people in Monterrey, the steel city about 150 miles south of the border. He began services there on October 18 and met with eager response. He brought in outside evangelists and organized a Bible class program to prepare workers to open new churches. So rapid was the growth that by 1952 there were 36 organized churches in the area with 49 other preaching places. Membership stood at 1,779. Rev. Roberto Moreno became superintendent in 1962. The district has since been divided twice.

The Period of Reorganization, 1953-85

The Mexican Church of the Nazarene has had to adjust its structure to comply with the unique government regulations under which it has had to operate. Chief among these restrictions is that it has been extremely difficult for missionaries to work there since 1912. This has not been without positive value, for it forced the Mexican church to "go it alone," and a strong, indigenous organization developed from the earliest days. Generous financial support and careful supervision have come from the general church, but an authentic Mexican church has emerged. Excellent national leadership has resulted in vigorous growth that by 1985 had seen four of the eight districts (the South, Central, Northeast, and South Pacific) achieve regular district status. By 1985 total membership had grown to 21,722.

Another unique feature is that the church owns no property in Mexico. All real estate is in the name of the government. This situation is not as uncertain as it sounds, however, for there is a tacit agreement between the church and the government that when a church is properly registered and complies with all regulations imposed by the state, the buildings and property it builds, and in a sense owns, are exclusively hers to use until such time as they are no longer needed.

Furthermore, the church cannot be incorporated as a legal entity in Mexico. However, it does have a government-recognized Board of Administration, which at first was made up of the district superintendent and the Advisory Boards of each of the districts. With the proliferation of districts, however, the size of the board became unwieldy. It now consists of the eight district superintendents and one layman elected from each district. Dr. H. T. Reza has served as adviser.

This board keeps the official registry of all pastors, sees that all properties are duly registered, and also administers the insurance and pension plan for its pastors, which is funded half by the Mexican churches and half by the World Mission Division. The board meets officially once a year. The general superintendent in jurisdiction conducts the annual assemblies on each district.

Democratic procedures have been encouraged as a matter of church policy through the years. It was thus a significant event when in 1974 the districts, for the first time, elected their own superintendents. Heretofore they had been appointed by the general superintendents.

A Unified Church in Mexico

To draw together the variety of cultures and worship styles of the Mexican Nazarenes was not a simple task. The extremes were represented by the formalistic and cultural group of the Dr. Santin tradition, and the free-worshiping people of Pentecostal background brought in by Rev. Enrique Rosales. There was also some confusion in matters of holiness doctrine and organizational procedure.

When the general superintendents began their cycles of four-year periods of jurisdiction, they began to work toward a greater unification of the various areas. Dr. G. B. Williamson (1948-52) felt a strong emphasis on holiness was needed. Dr. Hugh C. Benner (1952-56) and Dr. Samuel Young added the organizational factors and encouraged integration with the general church. It was Dr. Benner who inaugurated the insurance program for pastors, and Dr. Young who gave special attention to the legal matters and laid the groundwork for the establishment of the Mexico Board of Administration.

In the adjustment period of the 1960s, Dr. V. H. Lewis (1960-64) emphasized strongly the organizational structure as prescribed in the *Manual* and sought to bring the Mexican churches into line. He organized areawide and district conventions in which he brought in general church leaders such as Dr. George Coulter (then Foreign Missions secretary) and Dr. Mary Scott of the NWMS.

The visits of the Nazarene Evangelistic Ambassadors in 1964 and 1966 were also valuable in drawing together the Mexican church and the general organization. Between these two visits, a National Pastors' Conference was held November 13-17, 1967, in Cuernavaca. The results of this were far-reaching, for not only was there great spiritual uplift, but new guidelines were set for furthering the work of the national church.

From 1973 to 1985, Dr. Jerald D. Johnson gave significant guidance and leadership to the developing Mexican church, first as executive director of World Mission (1973-80) and then as general superintendent in jurisdiction (1980-85). During this time the number of districts doubled to eight, four of them attaining regular status. A new generation of church leaders emerged, prominent among whom were Revs. Jose Palacios, Jonas Aquino, Samuel Ovando, Antonio Alvarado, Carlos Martinez, Manuel Gurrion, and Armando Cortez. These strong men not only provided aggressive leadership in their own constituencies but became responsible members of the international church.

Another link was forged with the organization of the missionary language school in Mexico City for outgoing missionaries to Latin countries. This program continued until 1974, after which new missionaries were assigned to attend the prestigious interdenominational language school in San Jose, Costa Rica.

The literature program through the Spanish Department of the Nazarene Publishing House, already referred to, was also an important contributor to the development of an integrated, truly Nazarene program in Mexico.

"La Hora Nazarena"

The story of the Church of the Nazarene in Mexico would not be complete without reference to the impact of the Spanish radio broadcast, "La Hora Nazarena." This program, which is produced in Kansas City and blankets the entire Spanish-speaking world on 700-plus radio stations, was originally a spin-off of the English program, "Showers of Blessing." It began in 1953, but it was not until March 1, 1961, through the efforts of Rev. Moises Esperilla, that the broadcast went out over a Mexican station. Even then it had to be sponsored by a commercial organization—in this case a bakery in Hermosillo.

Soon opportunities came to broadcast on more powerful stations, including a 600,000-watt station in Mexico City with its six 50,000-watt satellite stations scattered across the country. The station owners offered a three-month trial of the program. In 1965 these became regular outlets. At one time, of the more than 700 stations carrying "La Hora Nazarena," over 70 were in Mexico; but in subsequent years there was a considerable reduction in that number. However, the program still blankets the nation.

The radio program, in which Dr. H. T. Reza was for 23 years

principal speaker, has been a means of bringing the name of the church as well as its message before the people. When new places are entered by the church, often the radio program has paved the way, for people have been listening to "La Hora Nazarena."

Mexico's Eight Districts

As previously stated, there were a number of shifts of district boundaries as various parts of the Mexican work expanded and a new potential for growth was envisioned. The newest were the East District, which included the Yucatan peninsula, historic home of the Maya Indians and now a popular tourist area, and the South Pacific District, which included the state of Oaxaca and eastern Chiapas. The list of districts with their number of organized churches and membership in 1985 was as follows:

District	Churches	Membership
Central	59	4,593
East	18	1,303
North	16	488
Northeast	37	3,580
Northwest	28	2,006
South	59	3,647
South Pacific	53	3,944
West	30	2,161

This represents a grand total of 21,722 members and reflects a growth of 7,646 since 1975—a remarkable increase of 54 percent.

National Events

Some large national gatherings involving some or all of the districts significantly lifted morale among Mexican Nazarenes. In 1971 the first National Youth Conference was held in the government resort at Oaxtepec on the West District. Young people from Northwest, North, Central, and South districts participated. Speakers for the event were Rev. Paul Miller of the International Youth Department in Kansas City and Dr. H. T. Reza of the Latin Division at Headquarters. Lasting results have accrued from this gathering.

In 1974 the first National Laymen's Conference was held on the West District. It was at this conference that Samuel Ovando answered the call to missionary work. He was the first Mexican-born missionary and was a leader in opening up the Colombia field. He became assistant director for Mexico in the Mexico/Central America region in 1985.

In 1978 the first National Conference on Holiness was conducted. Speakers were General Superintendent Greathouse; Dr. W. T. Purkiser, former editor of the *Herald of Holiness*; and Dr. H. T. Reza, by then executive director of the International Publications Board. The conference had a great unifying effect in the Mexican church.

The possibility of opening up work exclusively among the Aztec Indians in the area of San Luis Potosi (West District) and among the Tarahumarah Indians on the North District became a topic of interest and concern. First contacts with the Aztecs had been made by Rev. Carlos Stopani as early as 1953. Also, as previously noted, a Bible school had already been launched among the Huasteca Indians in central Mexico. The presence of concentrations of Indian tribes in other areas as well raised the possibility of forming a separate Mexican Indian District.

The pastors and laymen of the Church of the Nazarene in Mexico have come alive to the church's potential as a leading evangelical force in their country. Exciting years of progress lay ahead in this dynamic republic.

5. *The Mexican Border Work*

Through these years of reorganization there was a considerable shift in boundaries as the church sought to find an efficient alignment of churches both for adequate administration and for outreach. For a time, some of the districts straddled the United States border, for there had been a growing development of Mexican churches chiefly in California and Texas. The story of this latter development needs to be told.

The pioneer of the work among the Mexicans within the United States was Mrs. May McReynolds. She had joined the South Pasadena Church of the Nazarene around the turn of the century. As the wife of a railroad agent, she came into contact with many Mexican track laborers and became burdened for their spiritual welfare. As she had opportunity, she spoke to them about her Lord; and finally in 1904, following her husband's death, she began to devote full time to this type of evangelism.

Starting with house-to-house visitation, she soon had regular services under way. A permanent location was secured in the heart of the Mexican section of Los Angeles, and a mission was organized that in May 1906 became an officially organized church. The Los Angeles First Church gave financial support to the project.

Also, in 1917 work began among the Mexicans in El Paso, Tex., under the leadership of Mrs. Santos Elizondo, and spread to the neighboring city of Juarez across the border. Rev. S. D. Athans came to assist with the El Paso work, while Mrs. Elizondo concentrated her efforts in Juarez. Rev. Athans also conducted a Bible school to train workers.

As the work grew, the one supporting church (Los Angeles First) found the load too great, and so in 1917 the Southern California District took over the sponsorship. Missions were opened in the Pomona Valley; in San Diego; in Deming, N.Mex.; and in other places until in 1925 all were united to form the Southwest Pacific District under the leadership of Rev. and Mrs. E. Y. Davis, formerly missionaries in Cuba.

In 1925 Enrique G. Hampton, a member of the San Diego Mexican congregation, became interested in opening a work in Ensenada, 65 miles south of the border in Baja (Lower) California. A mission was opened, and in spite of early opposition, a flourishing work emerged, which had among its members city officials, businessmen, and professionals. By 1985 it had become one of the largest churches in Mexico under the leadership of Rev. Carlos Martinez.

In 1928, under the leadership of the Hatfield Memorial Church in San Antonio, a Mexican mission was opened on Ruiz Street in that city. In 1933 Rev. Enrique Rosales united with the Church of the Nazarene and became pastor of this group. It was officially organized in 1935 and became a part of the Southwest Pacific (later Southwest Mexican) District.

In 1937 Rev. Carlos Stopani, who had settled in Tijuana, just south of the California border, began services there that culminated in the organization of a church. One by one new churches were organized on both sides of the border, including Tecate and Mexicali on the California side, and San Luis and Hermosillo in Mexico. In Baja California the work extended southward to Maneadero, San Vicente, Chapultepec, Rosario, and La Paz. All were under the supervision of the Southwest Mexican district superintendent, Rev. Ira True, who had served since 1945. When he retired in 1963, the district was renamed the Western Latin American District. In 1972 a division of the 61 churches was made. Those on the Mexican side formed the

Mexico Northwest District, with Rev. Roberto Moreno being appointed superintendent. The churches north of the border retained the name of the Western Latin American District and continued under the superintendency of Rev. Juan E. Madrid, who had served since 1963. It became a regular district in 1985 under the leadership of Rev. Raymond Z. Lopez.

Meanwhile, in 1946 the San Antonio-Monterrey District, formed in 1942 under the leadership of Rev. Ira True, was likewise divided at the U.S.A./Mexican border. The Mexican churches became the Mexico North District under Rev. Enrique Rosales, who had the previous year become superintendent of the original district when Rev. Ira True was transferred to the newly formed Southwest Mexican District.

The United States phase, centered in San Antonio but including churches in several other states, formed the Texas-Mexican District. Rev. Fred Reedy was named superintendent and served until 1949. Then after a two-year term by Rev. E. G. Wyman, Rev. Everette Howard, veteran missionary from Cape Verde, was appointed in 1951. In 1962 the district was renamed the Central Latin American District.

After a highly successful 20-year term of service, Rev. Howard was succeeded by another veteran missionary, Rev. Harold Hampton, who had been serving as superintendent of the Eastern Latin American District since its organization in 1958. He was followed by Rev. H. O. Espinoza. In late 1982 Rev. Joe Dimas was appointed superintendent.

The Eastern Latin American District

There was a time when the Latin population in the United States was dominantly Mexican. In recent decades, however, a great influx of immigrants, chiefly from Cuba and Puerto Rico, has altered the balance so that now only half of the 15 million Spanish-speaking people in the United States are Mexican. The main concentration of non-Mexican Latins is on the Eastern seaboard.

Recognizing the potential for a Nazarene ministry among these people, Rev. Robert Goslaw, superintendent of the New York District, took the lead in launching the work. He brought in Dr. H. T. Reza from Kansas City to survey the situation and recommend a course of action. Chosen to direct this new venture was Rev. Harold Hampton, most recently a missionary in Puerto Rico, who had earlier served in Belize and Guatemala. The starting point was a small nucleus of Puerto Rican Nazarenes who had been meeting for a number of years in a hall on Stanton Street in Manhattan. The million and a half Puerto Ricans in New York City constituted a prime field.

By the time the Hamptons left in 1971 to take the superintendency of the Central Latin American District, there were 14 organized churches, 5 of which were self-supporting, with a total membership of 584. Appointed to take Rev. Hampton's place on the Eastern district was Rev. David Iglesias, of Puerto Rican parentage but born in New York City. At the time of this change of leadership the name of the district was changed from the Spanish East District to the Eastern Latin American District. In 1974 Rev. Jose Cardona became district superintendent.

Through the restructuring of districts to achieve internationalization of the Church of the Nazarene around the world, the three Latin districts in the United States became part of the work in that country rather than being related to the Mexican field. The 1985 statistics for the three fields were as follows:

District	Churches	Membership
Western Latin America	31	1,622
Central Latin America	31	1,582
Eastern Latin America	10	548

A fourth Spanish district, the Southwest Latin American District, made up of the states of Arizona, Colorado, New Mexico, and west Texas, was organized in 1985. Rev. Moises Esperilla, successful church leader from Mexico, was named district superintendent with headquarters in Albuquerque, N.Mex.

B. CENTRAL AMERICA

Central America consists of seven republics that form the narrowing bridge of land between Mexico and South America. The entire area is 218,000 square miles in extent, and the estimated population is about 20 million. The Spanish traditions are dominant except in tiny Belize, which was originally a British colony (British Honduras). From 80 to 90 percent of the people in Central America are mestizos (a mixture of Indian and Spanish), but both Belize and the highland area of Costa Rica are dominantly European. Along the eastern coast (Caribbean Sea) there is a concentration of Blacks. Various Indian tribes, chiefly Mayan, continue their colorful way of life in isolated areas, principally in Guatemala.

The entire area has been an ideological battleground with generally unstable governments, frequent military coups, and disturbing Communist influence. Economically the nations are struggling. Natural resources are limited, and agriculture is the main source of livelihood. The chief export crops are bananas and coffee, with sugar a third significant product.

Five of the republics have frontage on both the Pacific and the Caribbean, while Belize has only a Caribbean coast and El Salvador only a Pacific exposure. Transportation is generally poor, but uniquely one of the greatest traffic arteries of the world is located here—the 50-mile-long Panama Canal, which cuts through the narrow isthmus connecting North and South America. The Pan-American Highway, which runs the length of the region, has been a great boon since its completion in the 1960s.

The Central American countries are tied together by such common bonds as religion, language, and climate. Nominally, 95 percent are classified as Roman Catholic, although only 5 percent of these are regular church attenders. Guatemala is an exception with more than 20 percent of the population being evangelicals. Spanish is the official language in all republics except Belize, and a subtropical climate prevails. The low-lying jungles, principally on the coast, are hot and humid, while in the higher elevations of the interior the climate is more temperate. The entire region is somewhat mountainous.

Religious Influences

As in other areas of Spanish exploration and conquest, the conquistadores of the early 16th century brought with them, by order of the crown, a number of priests. These men not only exerted religious influence but wielded strong political power as well. Though their purpose was to Christianize by persuasion, considerable force and coercion was exercised. Contrary or resistant movements were ruthlessly crushed. The native Indians who were trapped in the web of this formal and austere religion learned little or nothing of the true Christ who came to save them from their sins and give them a life of inner peace.

The story of the missionary effort of the Church of the Nazarene in the countries of Central America will be presented in the order in which each was entered: Guatemala (1904), Belize (1930), Nicaragua (1943), Costa Rica (1954), El Salvador (1957), Panama (1960, although work began in the Canal Zone in 1953), and Honduras (1970).

1. *Guatemala*

The largely mountainous country of Guatemala was once the heart of the ancient Mayan Empire, which flourished 1,000 years before the coming of the Spanish conquerors led by Cortez. It thus became a colony of Spain from 1524 to 1821. After the defeat of the Spanish it became a member of the United Provinces of Central America, but this attempt at unifying the countries soon failed, and in 1839 Guatemala became an independent republic. Although plagued by political violence in recent decades, the country has moved forward. Fortunately the unrest has not hindered the work of the church to any great degree. The main concentration of the population is in the southern half of the country, but the northern section, called the Peten, once a remote jungle plain, is opening up to settlement, particularly since the discovery of oil there and the advent of air transportation.

Seventy percent of the people are Indian, descendants of the mighty Mayans. Mestizos and Ladinos make up 30 percent of the population.

Protestant Influence

The first Protestant penetration came through an English adventurer, Frederick Crowe, who, after his conversion under a Rev. Henderson, missionary in Belize (then British Honduras), joined 80 others in a colonizing venture in neighboring Guatemala. He was to be the teacher in the new community of Abbottsville on Lake Izabal, but evangelization was his purpose. In January 1841 he began three years of ministry both in the colony and in surrounding communities. His preaching was violently opposed by the Roman Catholic hierarchy, and the Scriptures he distributed for the British and Foreign Bible Society were designated as forbidden books.

Fearlessly, Crowe took his Bibles into the interior to Salama. Forced to leave there, he went south to Guatemala City, where he established a school and kept his Bible distribution low key. Nevertheless the Catholic leaders were successful in having him banished from the country in April 1846. Concerning this aborted missionary effort, Dr. James Hudson writes: "After 5 years of many conflicts and frustrations, one man's attempt to establish the evangelical church in Guatemala had failed. It was to be 36 years before another attempt would be made."

The next missionary effort came through an invitation from Gen. Justo Rufino Barrios, who later became president of Guatemala. In the course of a visit to the United States, he asked the Presbyterian church to send representatives to his country. Rev. John Clark Hill made his way to Guatemala in 1882, his expenses being paid by the government and a personal bodyguard being provided for him. The school he established in Guatemala City was attended by the children of high government officials.

The Presbyterians were followed by the Central American Mission, a Dallas organization led by C. I. Scofield of Bible study fame.

Forerunners of the Church of the Nazarene

The Pentecostal Mission of Nashville, in line with its particular interest in Latin America, sent Rev. and Mrs. J. T. Butler with their daughter, Ruth, and Mrs. Emma Goodwin to Guatemala in 1901. They settled in El Rancho, then the terminus of the railroad being built from Puerto Barrios on the Caribbean coast in to Guatemala City. Soon they moved on to Zacapa. They were followed in 1902 by

Rev. Conway G. Anderson and Miss Daisy Ifert, who were soon married.

Mrs. Butler fell victim to yellow fever during an epidemic of tropical diseases and was 1 of 500 who died in that area. To spare the life of his infant daughter, Rev. Butler returned to the United States. There he remarried and returned to open a work among the Blacks in the Caribbean port of Livingston. Meanwhile Mrs. Goodwin became ill with the prevailing disease and had to return home where she soon passed away. Likewise, the Conway Andersons a few years later took ill and had to return. They never recovered and soon died.

In November 1904 Rev. Anderson's 21-year-old nephew, Richard, and his 19-year-old bride, Anna Maude, arrived in Guatemala. After a brief stay in Livingston they moved to Zacapa. Here they too came down with yellow fever and almost died. In November 1905 after they had recovered sufficiently, they moved to Coban at the invitation of the Butlers who had moved there from Livingston in February of that year. In this beautiful capital of the province of Alta Verapaz, at an altitude of 5,000 feet, the climate was much more healthful, and the opportunities for missionary work much more extensive.

Rev. Butler was anxious to start a literature ministry, but using commercial printers who were unsympathetic to his cause was not very satisfactory. He returned to the United States in 1906, where with the aid of John T. Benson he purchased some basic printing equipment to take back with him. Also returning with him in 1907 was Miss Augie Holland, an experienced printer from Mr. Benson's staff, and Miss Effie Glover. *El Cristiano* ("The Christian") soon began publication and continued as a valuable adjunct to the work for 42 years.

Miss Holland remained for three years before returning to the United States. She later returned for a two-year term (1918-20) and also served in Belize when that work was begun. Miss Glover married Amos Bradley, a missionary of the Friends church, and joined that group.

In November 1908 the Richard Andersons returned to the United States for furlough and while there purchased a power-operated press. When they went back to Coban in the latter part of 1910, one of Rev. Anderson's first tasks was to erect a building to house the rapidly expanding literature ministry. At the peak of its production, the press was turning out 1.5 million pages of holiness literature a year. Its materials were being used in Mexico, all of Central America, and even in Argentina and Peru. With the beginning of the Spanish Department of the Nazarene Publishing House in 1946, most of its publication program was absorbed by the new central agency. In appreciation for his years of service, the printing plant was turned over to Isidoro Lopez, who, with Gonzalo Juarez, had learned the printing trade from Augie Holland and had carried on the work after she left.

In 1910 a school was established by Miss Eula Fay Watson, later assisted by Miss Willie Barnett and Miss Carey Cassey. But when they all departed, Mrs. Anderson had to take over. Lack of organizational structure and the involvement of more than one missionary agency in providing personnel and support made for rather erratic progress in those earlier years, though valuable groundwork was laid, and significant projects were launched.

Joining the Church of the Nazarene

When the Pentecostal Mission elected to become a part of the Church of the Nazarene in April 1915, the missionaries individually had the option of joining or associating with another group. The Butlers chose to return to the United States and became members of the Methodist Episcopal church, while others either returned home or worked out other affiliations. This left the Andersons alone to officially launch the Nazarene mission.

It was decided to continue to make Coban their base of operation with the goal of reaching the entire northern part of Guatemala, including the Peten. Comity agreements had already reserved the southern section of the country for the Presbyterians and the Central American Mission.

As soon as possible, Dr. H. F. Reynolds, general superintendent, was dispatched to Guatemala to analyze the situation. The obvious need for more missionaries resulted in the sending out in 1917 of three new recruits: Miss Eugenia Phillips, who took over the school program, and Rev. and Mrs. J. D. Franklin, experienced missionaries from Mexico. The following year Miss Augie Holland returned for an additional two-year term. In 1919 Miss Sarah Cox arrived, and 1920 brought Rev. and Mrs. J. D. Scott, also veterans from the Mexican work. Rev. Scott was named mission director. He was a skillful administrator and in those early days laid the groundwork for a strong, indigenous church.

Miss Neva Lane, who was to give more than 30 years of service to Guatemala, began her work in 1921. That same year, Rev. and Mrs. R. C. Ingram arrived to begin a long and distinguished missionary career. Rev. and Mrs. Ira L. True, also closely associated with the Mexican border work in subsequent years, served in Guatemala from 1921 to 1924 before being transferred to Peru for one year.

With the coming of the Franklins in 1917 came the first expansion move for the mission. At Salama, 45 miles south of Coban in the department (state) of Baja Verapaz, a work was opened that soon spawned an outstation in Rabinal. The nearby former mission at San Jeronimo was also reopened. Unfortunately the Franklins became seriously ill with malaria and in 1922 had to return to the United States, where Rev. Franklin died the following year.

During the 1920s still other missionaries were added: Rev. and Mrs. E. Y. Davis, Rev. William Coats (who married Eugenia Phillips), Miss Bessie Branstine (who married an outstanding national leader, Rev. Federico Guillermo), and Miss Leona Gardner. But illnesses, coupled with cutbacks resulting from decreased missionary giving in the homeland, decimated the talented missionary force. In the midst of it all, Guatemala's able leader, Rev. J. D. Scott, was chosen by the missionary department in 1925 to be supervisor of all the Latin American work of the church. Even though Guatemala was part of his jurisdiction, the loss of his direct leadership was sorely felt.

With the reduction of staff from 13 in 1922 to 4 in 1928, the future looked bleak indeed. Nor was the situation to be improved with the onset of the depression years. Only 3 missionaries were appointed to Guatemala in the 1930s: Rev. and Mrs. Russell Birchard and Miss Marilla Wales. Mrs. Birchard was a daughter of the R. S. Andersons and a trained nurse.

But despite the limitation of missionary forces the work moved forward with the help of outstanding national leadership. When Dr. J. B. Chapman visited the field in 1931, five Guatemalan pastors were ready for ordination. By the end of the 1930s there were 19 organized churches with over 700 members and a strong movement toward self-support.

The Education Program

Although the publications activity of the mission was the dominant feature of the work in the early decades, education was also a concern from the beginning days. The school established in Coban in 1910 by Miss Eula Fay Watson, sister of Mrs. R. S. Anderson, was attended by the children of many of the leading citizens of the town and was helpful in opening doors for the gospel message. But with uncertain support and changing personnel, it did not reach a firm footing until the coming of Miss Eugenia Phillips in October 1917.

The original school became a girls' school, and in February 1921 a school for boys was opened under the direction of Miss Sarah Cox. Mrs. E. Y. Davis served but one year in 1925 before ill health forced her return to the United States. Mrs. Anderson stepped in, as she had done before, to direct the boys' school; while Miss Neva Lane, who had arrived in 1921, took over the girls' school. In 1928 the two were combined to form a coeducational institution under the direction of Mrs. Eugenia Phillips Coats. A secondary school was added in 1932.

In the coming years these schools established an outstanding record of success. Former students today occupy significant positions of leadership in the church and community. One of them married a German businessman, and many years later she was a leader in the opening of the Nazarene work in Germany. Her son, Rev. Hugo Danker, became superintendent of the Middle European District.

To develop national pastors to take the place of the dwindling missionary staff in the 1920s, a Nazarene Bible school was begun in Coban in 1923. Miss Cox was transferred from the boys' school to lead this new project. Rev. J. D. Scott (the mission director), Rev. Ira True, Miss Eugenia Phillips, and Miss Bessie Branstine (Guillermo) all gave leadership to this work in its earlier years. When Rev. Russell Birchard arrived in 1934, this became his prime project, and the school came into its own as a training center for Guatemalan pastors. Rev. Harold E. Hess was added to the staff and became head of the school in the mid-1940s.

In 1952, a fine 10-acre property was purchased on the outskirts of Coban, and the attractive campus developed there was named the G. B. Williamson Nazarene Bible Institute.

Work Among the Indians

An estimated 90 percent of the population in the Nazarene field speak one or more of the three Mayan languages: Kekchi, Pokomchi, and Rabinal-Achi. Yet the church's work had been among the Spanish- and English-speaking population. It was through the avenue of Scripture translation that ministry to this neglected Indian population was launched.

William Sedat, a native of Germany, began work with the Wycliffe Bible Translators in 1936 among the Kekchi Indians. Theirs was an unwritten language, so his first task was to develop an alphabet and then a dictionary. He also wrote a grammar that became a standard government textbook. The next step was to be in the translation of the Scriptures. He returned to the United States, where he taught at Pasadena College for a time and in 1940 married Miss Elizabeth (Betty) Rusling, a Nazarene missionary he had met in Guatemala. This led to his joining the Church of the Nazarene in 1943.

Together the Sedats returned to the field in 1945 to begin in earnest the translation of the New Testament into the Kekchi language. That task completed and published by the American Bible Society, they turned to the Pokomchi language, but the work on this was interrupted by Dr. Sedat's death in 1971. The task was picked up by his wife, Betty, who carried it through to completion. It was a monumental achievement for both.

Although most of the Sedats' time was consumed in translation work, evangelism was not neglected. The Kekchi church at San Juan Chamelco, which is the largest such building in Guatemala, is a monument to their efforts. The Indian phase of the work has grown dramatically. In 1957 the ratio of Indian to Spanish-speaking membership in Guatemala was about 1 to 3. By 1967 it was about 1 to 1, and by 1977 it was 3 to 1—completely reversed from 20 years before.

The work among the Rabinal-Achi Indians was initiated by Rev. Robert Ingram in the early 1940s. He had arranged a series of special meetings among them with Rev. Felipe Pop and became so burdened for the people, he moved his family to San Miguel. He learned the language and established churches in both San Miguel and San Gabriel.

The work began to grow, but so did opposition. A group of Rabinal Indians actually requested the Guatemala president to have the Nazarene Chapel in San Miguel closed (a request he refused). But by 1956 the situation had so changed that 200 Indians signed a petition requesting the Church of the Nazarene to send James and Lucille Hudson to live among them. In 1960 the Hudsons founded the Rabinal-Achi Bible School in San Miguel.

Major Educational Changes

In January 1967 the General Board voted to establish a central Spanish ministerial training college in San Jose, Costa Rica, to serve all of Central America. Such a move would obviate the need for the Williamson Bible Institute in Coban.

Anticipating this major change, in 1968 the Kekchi Indian school, Centro Educacional Kekchi, was transferred from San Juan Chamelco to the Coban campus. This school had been established by the Sedats in 1953 and was currently under the direction of Rev. Guillermo Danneman Paau. When the Seminario Nazareno de las Americas was opened in Costa Rica in 1970, the Williamson Bible Institute was transferred to the Costa Rica campus.

By 1975 it was realized that there was still a need in Guatemala for a training school in Spanish at the secondary level. Thus the Nazarene Theological Institute was founded that year in Guatemala City with Dr. Jonathan Salgado as director. The Rabinal-Achi Bible School at San Miguel was also transferred to this more adequate campus.

Medical Work

In 1926 an infirmary was opened in Coban under the leadership of Miss Bessie Branstine, a registered nurse who had gone to Guatemala on her own because the mission board did not have the funds to send her. It was called the Casa de Salud Nazarene ("Nazarene House of Health") and earned an enviable reputation in the medical community. When Miss Branstine married Rev. Federico Guillermo, leadership of the clinic was picked up by Mrs. Margaret Birchard when she arrived in 1934.

Miss Evelyn VerHoek came to Guatemala in 1951. She was a registered nurse, and the medical clinic at Tucuru was her center of activity for many years. Thousands of patients were treated here and in the surrounding area. So insistent were the appeals for medical help that at one time the church considered the opening of a hospital, but the needed financial support for such a venture was not forthcoming.

Entering Peten

The isolated and almost impenetrable northern jungle region of Guatemala became the object of concern early in the church's missionary activities. In 1917 two Nazarene Guatemalan preachers visited Peten, testifying to the people and distributing tracts. Then in 1920 Rev. J. D. Scott, while serving as an interpreter for a group of oil prospectors, had an opportunity to go into the Peten. He was greatly moved by the spiritual need. In 1926 two more Guatemalan preachers, Matias Velez and Jose Figueroa, made an extended trip through the territory, holding meetings in Flores and other places and winning several converts.

On a second journey a year or so later, they effected a partial organization in Flores, which was completed in 1931 by the mission superintendent, Rev. Robert Ingram. In 1933, on a second trip up to the Peten, this time accompanied by his wife, he arranged to have Miss Leona Gardner assume the pastorate of the Flores church. She remained for two years.

During a third trip by Rev. Ingram, accompanied by two Guatemalan preachers, meetings were conducted in several towns, a camp meeting was held, and a church organized at San Andres. Since visits from the missionaries were few, it was fortunate that among the people themselves were some excellent leaders. It was not until 1947 when the Earl Hunters were sent there that a permanent missionary presence was established. They remained until 1951. The work in this region showed excellent growth.

Meanwhile, the work in the Livingston (Caribbean) area, which had had to be abandoned in the pioneer days because of the ravages of malaria and yellow fever, was revived under the leadership of Rev. and Mrs. William Vaughters, who came to the field in 1945. A missionary home was built on pillars in Livingston, which gave space for holding services underneath, and the family moved in in 1947. Later a fine church was built in the center of town.

The work grew, and by 1952 when the Vaughterses moved to Coban to direct the district's evangelism and day school programs, a national pastor was able to take over. Several churches were opened up in the Lake Izabal region.

William Vaughters was named superintendent of the field when Rev. Ingram returned to the United States in 1953. He served only one year, but in that short span major steps were taken toward nationalization of the work, such as involving Guatemalan leaders in the stationing of pastors and the budgeting of mission funds. A national, Rev. Federico Guillermo, was appointed assistant superintendent.

Toward Self-support and Self-government

As already indicated, the development of a fully indigenous church in Guatemala had been a prime goal. A sense of responsibility was encouraged and became a characteristic of the churches. By 1960 the Mission Council felt that the district was ready for the appointment of a national superintendent. The result was the naming of Rev. Federico Guillermo to the post in November 1960 by Dr. George Coulter, then general secretary of the Department of World Missions. His announcement on behalf of the Board of General Superintendents was made at the district assembly in San Jeronimo amid great rejoicing.

Ten years later, the membership on the district had grown from 1,800 to 4,200, and there was talk of setting apart the Northeast District as a regular district—fully self-supporting and self-governing. It was a historic moment when on January 16, 1974, the General Board voted to make the Northeast Guatemala District the first world mission area to become a regular district.

By 1980 membership was up to 9,975. There were now three districts in Guatemala, and the Northeast was by far the largest with 8,560. The Southeast reported 874 members, and the Southwest 541. For the second decade in a row, total membership had increased over 130 percent.

In his book *Guatemala 60 Years,* written in 1976, James Hudson gave the following projections for growth in the decade of the 1980s: three districts, 100 organized churches, 10,000 members, and 15,000 average Sunday School attendance. As can be seen, these goals had already been reached by the beginning of the decade and by 1985 had been far surpassed. By that time there were five districts (with two more about to be organized), 142 churches with a total membership of 18,227, and an average Sunday School attendance of 22,855.

Such growth has not been without sacrifice and hard work. Though the opposition is not as severe as in earlier years when Christians' lives were threatened and some indeed were killed for their faith, heroism is still a hallmark of the Guatemala Christians. Evangelism is a keynote of their program. Twelve annual camp meetings and evangelism conferences underscore this emphasis.

2. *Belize*

Like a spreading fire, the missionary program of the Church of the Nazarene began to move out from Guatemala into surrounding countries. The first to be entered was the tiny British colony of British Honduras, lying between Guatemala and the Caribbean coast. This country, self-governing since 1964, has been called Belize since 1973. It is only 174 miles long (north to south) and 68 miles across at its widest point with a total area of 8,866 square miles. Its population is about 150,000. Although the pure English population is small, English is still the official language of the country.

In 1930 two Mayan Indians who had been converted in the Flores church in the Peten region of Guatemala felt the call of God to carry their witness into this neighboring country. Making their arduous way through the intervening 60 miles of jungle, Teodoro Tesucum and Encarnacion Banos reached the border town of Benque Viejo. Here they testified to the people and found encouraging response. Their subsequent report to Field Superintendent Robert Ingram resulted in Rev. and Mrs. Ingram visiting the area in 1933 in the course of their trip to the Peten. What they saw confirmed what had been reported to them, and at Rev. Ingram's suggestion, in 1934 the Guatemala Mission Council appointed Leona Gardner, veteran of nearly 25 years in Cuba and 7 years in Guatemala, as the first missionary to that country. She was joined in 1936 by Augie Holland, the multitalented missionary who had launched the highly successful printing program in Guatemala several years before.

These two elderly ladies carried on a beautiful, caring ministry in the Benque Viejo area until in 1938 Miss Gardner, now 75, returned to the United States. Miss Holland remained until 1943 when the Harold Hamptons, who had arrived in Guatemala in 1941, were appointed to take over the work. In 1943 Joyce Blair, a registered nurse, began a long career of outstanding service in the medical clinic in Benque Viejo. When she retired in 1976, her place was taken by Nurse Connie MacKenzie, the first missionary sent out by the Coloured and Indian District of South Africa. Some years after the Benque Viejo clinic was opened, another was started at Crooked Tree with Mrs. Lucille Broyles in charge. Between them, as many as 18,000 persons were treated in one year.

Since British Honduras had no public schools, the Nazarene children were forced to attend Roman Catholic schools, where they were constantly harassed and abused. The need for a Nazarene day school was pressing, and to organize one the Ronald Bishops were sent out, arriving in June 1944. Before long 9 schools were in operation and ultimately 16. Mary Lou Riggle, who arrived in 1965, gave outstanding leadership to the school program.

By 1946 there were seven mission stations with about 300 members, and the missionary staff had been augmented by the coming of Rev. and Mrs. David Browning and Miss Ruth Dech. By action of the General Board, in 1946 British Honduras was made a separate district apart from Guatemala with Rev. Harold Hampton as mission director. Reinforcing the missionary force in those years were the W. C. Fowlers, the Leonard Yorks, Miss Lois Santo, and the Robert Ashleys.

On June 8, 1950, the Fitkin Memorial Nazarene Bible College was launched in Benque Viejo with Rev. David Browning as director. In a few years' time enrollment was holding at about 20, and an agricultural program was added. The college was to fill an important place in the life of the district until the advent of the seminary in San Jose, Costa Rica (Spanish), and, in a measure, the Caribbean Nazarene Training College in Trinidad (English). These schools made the operation of the small Bible college no longer viable.

In 1959 veteran India missionary Rev. Prescott Beals was sent to British Honduras to serve as mission superintendent while Rev. Ronald Bishop was on furlough. Rev. Beals then remained for three more years as principal of the Bible college. Mrs. Bishop's tragic illness that befell her during their furlough made it impossible for the family to return, so Rev. Beals carried on for the full four years. It was during his leadership that a sweeping districtwide revival broke out. But his term was also marked by the devastating hurricane of 1961 that virtually destroyed the capital and severely damaged much of the coastal area.

Even before the country became self-governing in 1964, there had been increasing emphasis on public education and health programs that resulted in an eventual phasing out of the Nazarene day schools and a greatly reduced activity in the clinics. But the program of evangelism and church planting went on. A significant expansion took place among the Mayans in the southern Toledo District under the leadership of the Tom Pounds, beginning in 1973.

In 1970 Belize became a national-mission district, with Rev. Alvin Young being appointed the first national superintendent. He was reelected for a four-year term in 1973. In 1977 Rev. Onesimo Pot was elected to the office.

By 1985 Belize had become a regular district, and membership had grown to 1,305 in 22 organized churches. Rev. Pot was elected the district superintendent representative for the Caribbean Region on the General Board for the 1985-89 quadrennium.

3. *Nicaragua*

Nicaragua is the largest of the Central American republics, with 57,000 square miles of territory. It has a 200-mile coastline on the Pacific side, and 300 miles on the Caribbean. It is a land of many volcanoes and is generally mountainous. One-third of the 2.9 million people are concentrated on a 12-mile-wide strip of land between the two large inland lakes, Managua and Nicaragua, and the Pacific Ocean. Ninety-five percent are Roman Catholic. Mestizos make up 70 percent of the population, but there is also a strong Caucasian community of about 400,000, mostly of Spanish descent.

Like several of the neighboring republics, Nicaragua was conquered by the Spanish in 1552 and did not gain its independence from them until 1821. It became a republic in 1838. A revolution in 1979 brought into power the Sandinistas, who had strong Communistic leanings. Thus Nicaragua became the most strongly Marxist nation in Central America. The political situation remained unstable, however, as contra rebels continued to battle Sandinista forces. Outside support for both sides aggravated the conflict.

David Ramirez and the Church of the Nazarene

The story of the beginning of the Church of the Nazarene in Nicaragua is centered around one person, David Ramirez. He was born on December 12, 1880, in the village of Popoyuapa on the outskirts of the Nicaraguan city of San Jorge on the shores of Lake Nicaragua. At the age of 19 he was converted under the influence of a missionary named Leonore Blackmore, who arranged for him to go to the United States for advanced education.

In this new situation he drifted away from his religious moorings. But concentrating on his studies, he went on to become an accomplished pianist and earned a doctoral degree. He also achieved financial success, but all the wealth he amassed was lost in the stock market crash of 1929. To some degree he returned to his former religious interests by becoming involved in mission work in Chicago. This led to his return to the Lord in repentance and faith.

He was invited to the First Church of the Nazarene, where in 1937 under the ministry of Dr. H. V. Miller, the pastor, he was sanctified. He began to sense the call of God to return to his own country with the message of salvation. So in August 1937, with the promise of financial support from the church, he went back to his hometown of Popoyuapa.

But repeated attacks of malaria, which settled in his already weak eyes, finally caused total blindness within two years. This limitation, plus the violent opposition of the priests, greatly restricted his witnessing efforts, but he prayed earnestly that God would send a Nazarene missionary to Nicaragua.

Alerted to the situation, Rev. Robert C. Ingram of Guatemala made an exploratory trip to Nicaragua, during which he visited David Ramirez. This resulted in a request that a missionary couple be sent there. Rev. and Mrs. Harold Stanfield, pastoring in Hemet, Calif., were selected for the task. They left Los Angeles on September 13, 1943, and after a time of orientation in Guatemala, went on down to Nicaragua. David Ramirez was overjoyed when the new missionaries landed on his doorstep on December 10.

Nazarene Work Begins

The first services in San Jorge were held on December 26, 1943, on the patio of the home of the Francisco Peralta family, with whom Rev. Ingram had become acquainted on his earlier visit. On August 20 of the following year, the first church in Nicaragua was organized with 24 charter members.

The securing of a permanent location for a church was difficult because of threats made to anyone who dared sell the Protestants any property. But despite this, a fine piece of land one mile from the lakeshore was secured, and on September 30, 1945, the first Nazarene chapel was dedicated. From this point on the work in Nicaragua grew rapidly. Missionary reinforcements were quickly sent out. Miss Cora Walker, a registered nurse, arrived in 1945 and opened up a medical work. At first she rode about on her horse from place to place, carrying her medicines and equipment with her, until a fine, four-room dispensary was completed in 1947. Miss Lesper Heflin arrived in 1948 to assist in this work and launched a second dispensary in San Isidro in 1959.

David Ramirez, despite his handicap, did what he could, his main contribution being to help the new missionaries in the study of the language and assisting in the training of the first group of seven potential pastors. His death in 1949 cut short this ministry.

To Esther L. Crain, a former Chicago schoolteacher, fell the task of launching the day school program. The first such school was opened in San Jorge in 1946 with 31 students. By 1975 more than 20 primary schools had been opened. Miss Crain's chief assistant in this work was Miss Mary Wallace, who came in 1956.

Enlarging on the initial work of David Ramirez, a Nazarene Bible Institute was launched in 1948 under the direction of Rev. C. G. ("Bill") Rudeen. On a 50-acre campus on the shores of Lake Nicaragua four substantial buildings were erected. This lovely site became a district gathering place where many memorable spiritual events took place. Subsequent directors of the institute were Revs. Louis Ragains, Robert Wellmon, C. Dean Galloway, Robert Pittam, Marshall Griffith, and Harold Stanfield. The first Nicaraguan director, Rev. Victor Gonzales, was appointed in 1973, but leadership reverted to the missionaries again in 1975 when Rev. Robert Hudson took over.

By the time the Central American Nazarene Seminary, now called the Nazarene Seminary of the Americas (Seminario Nazareno de las Americas), was opened in Costa Rica in 1970 and the Nicaragua school became only a satellite institution, 68 men and women had been graduated. Most of the pastors on the district were products of the school. In 1977 the school was merged with the one in Guatemala.

Supporting Ministries

The dispensary work continued to play an important role in winning people to Christ and making friends for the church. But as public medical facilities developed, particularly in the population centers, the demands for such services diminished.

In 1969 the San Jose dispensary was moved to Ciudad Pantasma in the northern part of the country where the Russell Birchards were stationed, Mrs. Birchard being a registered nurse. A new clinic building was dedicated there on April 8, 1970. When Rev. Birchard died in May 1973 and was buried in Pantasma, Mrs. Birchard returned to the United States. Their place was taken by the Kyle Greenes. Mrs. Greene, also an R.N., served in the clinic until their transfer to the Philippines in 1980.

Another supporting factor was the radio program, "La Hora Nazarena," which has been broadcast continuously since 1953 over the Christian radio station YNOL. Many began attending Nazarene churches because of hearing the broadcast.

Another fruitful ministry was literature distribution. A bookstore was originally opened in Rivas, two miles from San Jorge, to take care of the textbook needs of the day schools, though some religious literature was also available. But when Miss Mary Wallace was assigned the task of developing a more adequate literature ministry, she opened a bookstore in Managua named El Faro Nazareno (The Nazarene Lighthouse) and stocked it with books supplied by the Spanish Department of the Nazarene Publishing House. The store became a strong outreach arm of the Nicaraguan work.

Organizational Changes

From 1943 to 1947 Nicaragua was a part of the Guatemala District, though physically separated from it. In 1947 it became a separate district. That same year, work was begun in Los Chiles, Costa Rica, and later in other towns along the border. Thus in 1963 the Nicaragua-Costa Rica District was formed. This arrangement continued until Costa Rica also became a separate district in 1972 under the superintendency of Rev. Marshall Griffith. Rev. Harold Stanfield was field superintendent of Nicaragua from 1944 to 1958 and was succeeded by Revs. C. Dean Galloway, Bill Rudeen, Marshall Griffith, and Louis Ragains, in that order. Revs. Robert Hudson and Kyle Greene served brief terms in the late 1970s.

In 1972 Nicaragua became a national-mission district with Rev. Ernesto Bello as superintendent. In 1977 the field was divided into the Pacific and Atlantic districts. The Atlantic District, which as yet had no organized churches, was placed under the leadership of Missionary William Fowler. The Fowlers were transferred to the Philippines in 1980, and the district was returned to the jurisdiction of the Pacific District with Rev. Faustino Zepeda as district superintendent. No missionaries remained in the country.

The 1985 statistics revealed a total membership on the Nicaraguan field of 2,669, a 17 percent increase during the previous quinquennium in spite of the growing political unrest throughout the country. There were 52 organized churches and 36 other preaching points.

4. Costa Rica

Discovered by Christopher Columbus in 1502 and colonized by his brother Bartholomew, Costa Rica is the third-smallest Central America country (20,000 sq. mi.) and the only one whose people are mostly of European (Spanish) descent. Most of its 2.1 million people live in the intermountain plateaus of the interior, avoiding the hot and humid coastal plains on both coasts. Ninety percent of the people are Roman Catholic.

Costa Rica's literacy rate of 89 percent is the highest in Central America, its government is the most stable, and its standard of living the highest.

In the latter part of the 19th century, missionaries of the Central American Mission launched the first Protestant work in Costa Rica at the capital of San Jose. They were followed in the early 1900s by the Latin American Mission, whose extensive activity in San Jose eventually included a hospital, a seminary, a printing plant, a radio station, and elementary and secondary schools.

The Church of the Nazarene

The Church of the Nazarene entered Costa Rica by way of its neighbor country to the north, Nicaragua. Since the major concentration of the work there was near the border, the possibility of opening a mission in Costa Rica had been considered from the very beginning. The first move was made in 1947 by Miguel Torres, the pastor of the new work in San Carlos, Nicaragua. He went 10 miles up the Frio River to the isolated town of Los Chiles and began holding services. Under Apolonia Rivera, the next San Carlos pastor, a lot was purchased. Rev. Alberto Zapata built the first chapel for this first congregation to be organized in Costa Rica.

In February of 1954 Alejandro Herrera, on vacation from the Nazarene Bible Training School, was visiting the pastor in San Carlos. On impulse he decided to look up some old friends he had known in nearby San Isidro, Costa Rica. Taking a suitcase full of Bibles with him to sell, he and a companion made their way to the town. But when his former friends found out "Don Alex" was now an evangelical, they turned their backs on him. But he chanced to meet a lady he had once helped in San Jorge, Nicaragua, who gladly opened her home to the young men. They also visited several other towns, holding services and selling Bibles. Thus began the expansion of the work in the jungle area of northern Costa Rica.

In 1961 Rev. Ignacio Hernandez, pastor of the Miller Memorial Church in Managua, Nicaragua, was offered a scholarship to the interdenominational Latin-American Bible Seminary in San Jose, Costa Rica, and a position as program director of the Christian radio station.

(He had held a similar position at station YNOL in Nicaragua.) This, he felt, would give him an opportunity while there to explore the possibilities of opening a Nazarene work in this capital city. A number of Nazarenes were already living there, some of whom, like the Mendozas, he had pastored in Managua. His district superintendent, Rev. Bill Rudeen, not only gave him permission to attend the seminary but authorized him to organize a church if he could.

The Hernandez family arrived in San Jose on February 20, 1963. The very next Sunday they conducted a Sunday School in the Mendoza home with 20 present. The following week regular preaching services began, and the first convert was won on March 17. A temporary location was secured in which to hold services, but it was not very satisfactory, so in August a new location was found. Students from the Latin-American Seminary were a great help, and the work grew. In February 1964 the church was officially organized with 10 full members and 12 probationers.

After a year Ignacio Hernandez returned to Managua, and Rev. Diego M. Ortiz was appointed pastor. The work continued to flourish.

Seminario Nazareno de las Americas

In 1967 the general church took a significant step that would profoundly affect the work in Costa Rica. The organization of a central seminary to serve all the Spanish-speaking fields was authorized, and San Jose was selected as the site of the institution. Rev. Howard Conrad, missionary in Peru, was selected to head the school. It began operation as Seminario Nazareno de las Americas in 1970.

In 1979 Rev. Jerry D. Porter was transferred from the Dominican Republic to serve as rector of the seminary. During his term in office the on-campus enrollment rose from 43 to 86. At the same time, an aggressive extension program was developed throughout Latin America with as many as 3,000 students preparing for the ministry in scores of training centers. The program, called CENETA (Spanish acronym for Affiliated Nazarene Theological Education Centers), combines intensive courses taught in selected centers by professors from the seminary with weekly classes taught by local leaders.

In 1985 Rev. Porter was named regional director for Mexico/Central America and moved to Guatemala City to establish the central office there. Rev. Enrique Guang, a Ph.D. from Ecuador, became the new rector of the seminary. It was hoped that by 1989 a degree program would be offered.

The need for rapid expansion of the work to provide practice preaching locations for the students prompted the separation of the Costa Rica field from its parent, Nicaragua, in 1972. The first superintendent of the Costa Rica District was Rev. Marshall Griffith from Nicaragua. When in 1974 he was called to the presidency of the Spanish-American Nazarene Seminary in San Antonio, he was succeeded by Rev. Allen Wilson. The next step came in 1980 with the election of Rev. Hector Acuña as the first national superintendent.

By 1980 there were 14 churches in Costa Rica with 795 members, but five years later the district was up to 23 churches and 1,314 members, a 62 percent increase. This led in 1985 to the division of the field into North and Central districts. The latter was eligible to become a regular district under Rev. Acuña, while Rev. Jorge Garcia was elected superintendent of the North area.

The country that Francisco Penzotti had written off in 1906 as "having no interest in the Bible" was fast becoming an evangelical stronghold with the Church of the Nazarene a leading Protestant denomination.

5. *El Salvador*

This smallest of the Central American republics (8,260 sq. mi.), yet the most densely populated (4.3 million, or 520 people per sq. mi.) is wedged against the Pacific by its bigger neighbors, Guatemala and Honduras. It is only 150 miles long and 60 miles wide but has much natural beauty. At the same time it is the most highly industrialized country in Central America. Its people are 89 percent mestizos, and Spanish is the official language. As elsewhere in this region, Roman Catholicism prevails.

In the early 1950s the Guatemala Nazarenes began to look toward El Salvador as a place to reach out to with the gospel. The first positive move in this direction was made in 1957 when a Salvadoran Nazarene, Israel Bolanos, early that year, went to Guatemala City and talked with the pastor, Rev. Federico Guillermo, on the matter. He was a graduate of the seminary in San Antonio and had been a pastor but currently was working at the San Salvador airport. He had been hoping the Nazarenes would come to his country, but now he was promising that if a church were established there, he would offer his services as pastor free of charge, relying on his employment to support him.

Thus in April 1957 Mission Superintendent Robert C. Ingram took a party of eight to the town of San Martin and there conducted the first Nazarene evangelistic effort in El Salvador. The meetings lasted less than a week, but they were well attended, and 16 persons were won to the Lord. Israel Bolanos was left to nurture the group as best he could, but his work schedule was such that he could not serve adequately. Besides, driving the 10 miles back and forth posed a problem. As a result the work languished. Each year the Guatemalans talked of going back to El Salvador, but personnel and funds never seemed to be available.

Then in 1963 Guatemala became a national-mission district, and Rev. Federico Guillermo was appointed as its first Guatemala superintendent. What better way to prove that the national church had evangelistic vision than to tackle a challenge such as El Salvador presented? This time the plan was to enter the capital of San Salvador itself.

Two women who had been in the original party six years before, Ernestina Lopez and Amparo Ruano, were sent to open the work. After an intensive visitation program, regular services were begun on May 17, 1964. In August, when Rev. Guillermo and Missionary Lawrence Bryant came to visit, Sunday School attendance was already over 80. Rev. and Mrs. Bryant were soon installed as the first resident missionaries.

By January 1965 the work was going so well that another mission was opened in a residential area of the city. Here the neighborhood was rather sophisticated in contrast to the initial location, which was in a high-crime area. Slowly but surely the gospel message took root. When a disastrous earthquake devastated the city in May, the Bryants won the hearts of many as they gave themselves to the task of helping the people rebuild their lives and homes.

In October 1965 the Stanley Storeys joined the missionary force and opened up a work in Santa Ana, El Salvador's second-largest city. The first services were held there on December 5, 1965, with 40 in attendance. By mid-1966 they were up to 100, and 31 conversions were reported. In November 1966 Guatemalan pastors were assigned to each of the three churches.

It was a memorable occasion when on February 25, 1967, Rev. Guillermo organized the original congregation into the First Church of the Nazarene and on the following day officially organized the second group in the Colonia Centro-America area of the capital. In

August of that year an attractive Alabaster church was dedicated in Santa Ana, and the congregation was formally organized.

In February 1970 El Salvador was organized as a separate district with Rev. Allen Wilson as superintendent.[1] When in the following year he was called to serve on the faculty of the seminary in Costa Rica, his place was taken by Rev. Lawrence Bryant, who remained until his retirement in 1976. He was followed by Rev. Robert Hudson, who served until 1980 when El Salvador became a national-mission district, and Rev. Ramon Campos was appointed district superintendent. There were now 11 organized churches with 575 members and a Sunday School enrollment of 1,189. But this was only a starting point, for by 1985 there were 23 churches and a total membership of 1,768. This was a phenomenal increase of 207 percent in five years!

6. *Panama*

Panama must be considered in two parts: the Republic of Panama itself, which is the last link in the chain of countries connecting North and South America; and the Canal Zone, a 10-mile-wide strip of land 50 miles long, through which runs the Panama Canal.

The Republic of Panama is dominantly Spanish with 70 percent mestizos. But there is a strong Black concentration as well (13 percent). This is also the home of the San Blas Indians and other tribal groups, who make up 6 percent of the population. Ten percent are Caucasian, concentrated in the area of the Canal. Roman Catholicism claims 93 percent of the people.

When it was discovered in the time of the explorers that this narrow isthmus formed a connecting passage to the Pacific, it became a prize that the British captured from Spain but never really controlled. Panama joined Colombia in 1821. Nearly a century later, on November 18, 1903, it declared its independence from Colombia, which had refused to let them negotiate a pact with the United States to allow the latter to build a canal across the isthmus. The project had already been started by the French, who sold their rights to the United States for $40 million.

Panama granted the United States permanent and exclusive use and control of the Canal Zone in a treaty that was finally ratified on February 26, 1904. It provided for an initial payment to Panama of $10 million, plus $250,000 per year beginning in 1913 (eventually increased to nearly $2 million a year). Construction began in earnest in 1907, and on August 15, 1914, the first ship passed through the full length of the waterway. However, it was not until well after World War I, on July 12, 1920, that the Canal was officially opened. The total cost has been variously estimated at about $1.5 billion, but only $380 million for actual initial construction costs.

In 1964 rioting began over control of the Panama Canal, as Panamanians sought to nullify the initial agreements and to seize control of the waterway. Numerous treaty modifications were proposed, but it was not until 1977 that final agreement was reached in which the United States would gradually release control until by 1999 their withdrawal would be complete.

The Church in the Canal Zone

It was into this milieu that the Church of the Nazarene moved on August 22, 1953. That day, through the overtures of E. W. Wilson, chief U.S. Navy radio officer stationed at Gatun, and Col. Arden L. Bennett, a government official who already had Bible studies under way, the Department of Home Missions opened work in Ancon, Canal Zone. Rev. W. A. Jordan had been chosen to launch the work.

A church was organized in Ancon the following week with 15 members. A small school gymnasium in Margarita became the first place of worship until a building was purchased in Ancon in December 1954.

For reasons of health the Jordans were forced to leave within a year, and their place was taken by the Elmer O. Nelsons, who arrived on May 29, 1955.

In March 1956 a second meeting place was opened near Colon on the Atlantic end of the Canal. In 1959 this congregation was organized as the Mount Hope Church. But the work in the Zone was hard to stabilize because of the constant coming and going of service personnel. Nevertheless, the two churches provided a valuable ministry to these people.

Beginning in the Republic

About a year after the Nelsons arrived in Panama in 1955, a family in the church offered them the use of their summer home in the mountains, 80 miles away, for a vacation time. Here, far from the bustle of the Canal, they found a different world that intrigued them.

Walking trips back into the mountains convinced them that here was a wide-open mission field.

When they shared their enthusiasm with Colonel Bennett, who was also interested in the people of the Republic, he suggested that they contact the Department of Foreign Missions to see if they would consider opening a work there. In the meantime, he recommended that they officially register the church with the Panamanian government so they would be ready should the department respond favorably. On February 23, 1957, the registration was completed, and two years later (May 1959) residence papers were granted the Nelsons with the proviso that they would have to move into the country within 15 months—by August 1960.

Reporting to the General Board in January 1960, concerning the work in the Canal Zone, Rev. Nelson took the opportunity to tell of his burden for the Republic. The response was positive, and the Nelsons were sent to language school in Mexico City to prepare for the move. At the General NWMS Convention that June, a $15,000 offering was given for the opening of the Panamanian work.

But the Nelsons' language study was interrupted by typhoid fever attacks that befell both Rev. and Mrs. Nelson and one of the children. By the time they were well again, time was running short on their entrance permits. However, they were promised an extension of time so went on to finish language school. But there was a mix-up in their papers, and the new ones they applied for were not yet ready on their planned departure date. Thus, when they entered the country on June 29, 1961, it was on temporary tourist visas.

The next problem was to find someone who would rent suitable property for a Protestant church to use. Finally such was found in El Carmen, a suburb of Panama City, and the first services were held on October 1, 1961. A nucleus of 16 Spanish-speaking people from the Ancon church gave them a start. The average attendance for October was 28, but this jumped to 71 in November and to 144 in December. Meanwhile, another hitch in processing the Nelsons' immigration papers developed. But just in time, through the aid of the man who had been instrumental in securing the El Carmen property and who was now head of the government immigration office, the papers came through at Thanksgiving time.

On January 28, 1962, the church was officially organized with just 11 members, but there were 83 present in the service, and 13 were at the altar seeking salvation. In September a lot was purchased in Panama City, and the construction of a church building began in April 1963. Despite delays caused by political upheaval, the church was dedicated on February 16, 1964, with over 600 in attendance. Not only did the Panama City church grow rapidly, but churches in other towns were launched including some far to the west near the Costa Rica border. By 1974 there were 11 congregations with a total membership of 348.

When the Nelsons were transferred to the Argentina South District in 1976, leadership passed to the Robert Pittams, who had been transferred from Nicaragua in May 1967. They were followed by the Mark Rudeens, and in 1979 by the Tom Spaldings. This quadrennium of rapid turnover of missionary personnel was also a time of political turmoil and anti-American sentiment throughout Panama. The result was virtually no gain in either churches or membership. The 1980 statistics revealed still only 11 churches and 355 members.

Meanwhile, the activity in the Canal Zone continued. In 1966 this part of the work was placed under the Department of World Missions as part of the Panama District. Up to this time Rev. and Mrs. Ralph Hysong, Rev. and Mrs. James H. Jones, Rev. and Mrs. Fred Agee, Rev. and Mrs. Milton Harrington, and Rev. and Mrs. Richard Leffel had served the churches in the Zone for various periods. After the change in jurisdiction, the names of Rev. and Mrs. Marvin Buell (pastors in Mount Hope) and Rev. and Mrs. Charles Fountain (pastors in Ancon) entered the picture. Later Ancon pastors were Revs. Don Harrison, Mert Winkle, and Paul Barber.

A most significant change came in 1981 when Rev. Jose Gordon became the first national superintendent. There followed a definite upswing until by 1985 there were 17 churches and 609 members on the district.

7. *Honduras*

The last of the Central American republics to be entered by the Church of the Nazarene is also the second largest in size with an area of 43,000 square miles. Of its 2.8 million people, 90 percent are mestizos with a sizable Black concentration on the northern Caribbean coast. Spanish is the official language, and as elsewhere, Roman Catholicism the prevailing religion. Honduras has a 500-mile coastline on the Caribbean and a short 40-mile Pacific shore on the Gulf of Fonseca.

The Coming of the Church of the Nazarene

In February 1969 a group of missionaries from Guatemala and El Salvador conducted a six-day safari into Honduras to explore the possibilities of opening up a mission there. In the party were the James Hudsons, the Samuel Heaps, the Larry Bryants, the William Sedats, and the Stanley Storeys. After visiting the capital, Tegucigalpa, and the second-largest city, San Pedro Sula, the group returned much enthused about the possibilities for evangelism there.

After permission was granted to open a new work, early in 1970 a rental property was secured in San Pedro Sula. Finally, in November of that year Rev. Danilo Solis and his family from Guatemala moved in to open services. Within a month he had gathered a congregation of 11. The church was organized in 1972.

But the work moved slowly, and so in March 1972 the Stanley Storeys made another investigative journey from El Salvador into Honduras. They were soon to furlough and wanted some more firsthand information to give to the Department of World Missions when they appeared before them the next January. Their report was so glowing that they were appointed to go to Honduras at the conclusion of their furlough in June 1973.

When they arrived in San Pedro Sula, the church had been under a supply pastor for four months, Rev. Solis having left to attend the seminary in Costa Rica. The Storeys set to work to restore and enlarge the congregation and to build a missionary home. But on September 19, 1974, a disastrous hurricane inflicted severe flood damage to the home and destroyed all the missionaries' belongings along with that of many of the members, as 8,000 people lost their lives.

Shortly after this tragedy two young men who early in the history of the work had gone to the Costa Rica seminary returned to offer themselves for service in their own country. In December 1974 they were sent to open a new work in Tegucigalpa.

Little by little the Honduran church grew despite severe opposition. In 1976 Mr. and Mrs. Philip Hopkins were transferred from El Salvador to assist the Storeys. Of particular help to the work was the corps of fine national pastors. By 1980 there were 209 members with over twice that number enrolled in Sunday School.

In 1981 the Paul Jetters were transferred to Honduras from the Dominican Republic. The following year he became mission director and district superintendent when Stanley Storey was transferred to the regional office in Guatemala City. By 1985 there were 15 organized churches and 517 members, a quinquennial increase of nearly 150 percent.

C. THE CARIBBEAN

In the missionary annals of the Church of the Nazarene, the islands of the Caribbean Sea cover the entire historical spectrum from the early pioneer to the most recent evangelizing efforts. The first base of activity was established in Cuba in 1902 with the arrival of a group of missionaries under the auspices of the Pentecostal Mission of Nashville, the organization headed by J. O. McClurkan, which joined the Church of the Nazarene in 1915. This group of missionaries had stopped off in Cuba on their way to Colombia, but a war situation in that country prohibited their going on to their planned destination. Finding Cuba to be an equally needy field, they elected to stay and try to establish a work there. One of their number, Miss Leona Gardner, against discouraging odds, remained to serve in Cuba for almost 25 years before being transferred to Guatemala and then to British Honduras for the closing years of her missionary service. The others had left within a short time.

At the other end of the historical spread are such recent ventures as in the French Antilles, where a pioneer district was organized in 1982, and in Suriname, which was entered as a pioneer area in 1985.

The Caribbean area also presents a wide range of ethnic and cultural settings. There are the islands of Spanish heritage along the northern rim (Cuba, Dominican Republic, and Puerto Rico); those of English rootage along the eastern and southern edge (such as the Virgin Islands, Leeward and Windward islands, Barbados, Trinidad, and Tobago); and those of French origin (Haiti to the north, and the islands of Guadeloupe and Martinique on the eastern side). Trinidad, though basically English, has also a heavy concentration of East Indians.

Though close to the Americas, the ties of the Caribbean people are closer to Europe, Africa, and even India than they are to the West. The Spanish republics are probably more a part of Latin-American culture than European-Spanish, however. A number of the English-speaking islands are relatively new independent nations within the British Commonwealth of Nations. The French islands are departments (states) of France itself.

The inhabitants of the English, French, and Creole islands reflect the influence of the earlier slave trade, for the Black population is dominant, particularly in Haiti, which is the oldest Black republic in the modern world. With the emancipation of slaves came the need for another source of laborers, which resulted in the system of contract indenture. This brought many thousands of East Indians to the islands and adjacent areas as contract workers.

The Caribbean field (in 1986 made a separate region) was divided into 21 districts plus the pioneer area of Suriname, and to tell the story of the development of the various areas in any systematized form is extremely difficult. Neither a geographical nor chronological sequence can be completely worked out, so the attempt has been made here to combine the two with some semblance of logic. Starting with the oldest work in Cuba (though it has not been continuous there), the Spanish area will be followed, and from thence along to the Virgin and Leeward islands. Picking up Haiti and Jamaica, the story will then drop down to the southern (English) group where the work is historically older, and then proceed back northward through the Windward Islands to the French Antilles. The Bahamas, somewhat outside the "chain," will then be presented, along with a brief story of the Caribbean Nazarene Theological College in Trinidad, which serves the entire English-speaking area.

Since there is considerable fluidity among the island residents, almost everywhere that new work has been established, people have been found who, on some other island, had come into contact with the Church of the Nazarene. This produced somewhat of a chain reaction that is characteristic of the work in this "Magic Circle of the Caribbean."

Though, predictably, the Spanish and French areas are dominantly Roman Catholic, there have been no legal restrictions to hinder evangelical work. Ecclesiastical opposition has sometimes posed a problem, however. The voodoo religion of Haiti has presented a challenge to the Christian message as has, to some degree, the Hinduism of the East Indians.

1. *Cuba*

The size of the missionary party from Nashville that landed at the port of Trinidad on the southern coast of Cuba in 1902 is not known, but perhaps there were as many as 10. Their measure of dedication to the missionary task was put to an early test when they were thwarted from going on to Colombia. No matter how challenging the Cuban situation was, this frustrating turn of events was bound to have a demoralizing effect. The death of their leader shortly afterward only heightened their apprehensions. The result was that within a year, only three of the original party remained—Miss Leona Gardner and Rev. and Mrs. J. L. Boaz. When the latter couple departed after three years, Miss Gardner was left to work alone.

From 1905 to 1914 Miss Gardner carried on her lonely mission in the city of Trinidad. Results were meager, but one bright light during those dark days was the conversion of a very capable Cuban couple, Teofilo and Juliana Castellanos, who were to be a great help in the work for many years. In 1914 the Boazes returned to superintend the work; and while they were there, their supporting church, the Pentecostal Mission, joined forces with the Church of the Nazarene. This gave new strength to the missionary program.

Dr. H. F. Reynolds, general superintendent and Foreign Missionary secretary, made plans to visit the field, but before he arrived in 1917, the Boazes had again left. The need for reinforcements to help Miss Gardner was quite apparent, and so before the year was out, Rev. and Mrs. J. L. Hinds and Miss Grace Mendell were dispatched to the field. The relief they provided was short-lived, however, for in two years' time the Hindses had to leave for health reasons, and Miss Mendell married a Cuban. Though she remained a sympathetic supporter, she was no longer actively involved.

Near the close of 1919 Rev. and Mrs. E. Y. Davis, who had been working among the Mexicans in the southern United States, were sent to Cuba. A year later, however, the decision was made to close the Cuban field, and the Davises were brought back to work among the Mexicans in the El Paso, Tex., area. Despite the decision from Headquarters, Miss Gardner was firmly convinced that she was where God wanted her, and decided to stay. Supporting herself by her teaching, she carried on her missionary endeavors on the side.

In 1922 the General Board voted to send her financial support, though they stopped short of reactivating the field. So Miss Gardner returned to the scene of her former labors at San Pedro, only to find that her 18 converts had almost all disappeared. It was discouraging to try to rebuild the work, but she kept on courageously until, in 1927, she was reassigned to Guatemala. With her departure, the mission was closed and remained so for 18 years, though Miss Gardner did return for a brief visit in 1938.

In 1945, the year after Leona Gardner died, the General Board voted to reopen the work in Cuba and placed Rev. and Mrs. Lyle Prescott in charge. The Prescotts had opened up the work in the Virgin Islands only a year before and were reluctant to leave there so soon, but they assumed the new task with vigor. After three months of language school in the city of Trinidad, where they found traces of the earlier work, they decided to concentrate their beginning efforts in the capital city of Havana, across on the north coast. There they rented a home in the Santos Suarez section and on May 26, 1946, began public services in their living room. Six months later a second Sunday School was opened, and by the end of the year, six young men had offered themselves as candidates for the ministry.

In March 1947 the first of three property purchases was made, and in a Rally Day on the first anniversary of the opening of services, four Sunday Schools were in operation with a total attendance of 397. In April 1947 reinforcements arrived in the persons of Rev. and Mrs. John Hall.

A country barber from the mountainous area of western Cuba, Hildo Morejon, contracted tuberculosis and was placed in a sanitarium in Havana. There he was reached by some Nazarenes who led him to Christ. Returning to his hometown of Arroyo Hondo in 1949, he led his family and some neighbors to Christ. He invited Rev. Prescott to come and hold services, and the response was so heartwarming that other visits followed. Hildo became pastor of the thriving group. Land was donated by his father, and with the help of a $400 gift from the Southwest Oklahoma District, a chapel seating 100 was built. This church became the center out from which other preaching points were opened.

In May 1950 a 10-acre recreational farm just south of Havana, owned by a wealthy family, became available for sale. It was ideally located on the main paved road leading to the south coast. The tract, which contained a large Spanish-style home, a thatch-roofed garage, and three large poultry houses in an attractive, landscaped setting, was purchased for $13,500. The buildings were later remodeled for Bible school use and others added until an attractive district center resulted.

The very first year, an annual camp meeting program was begun with Rev. C. Warren Jones, Foreign Missions secretary, as evangelist. A 40 x 60-foot tabernacle was built and dedicated by Dr. D. I. Vanderpool on October 31, 1951. It was also in 1951 that the Bible training school was opened with an enrollment of five.

As the work gained momentum, new couples were added to the missionary force: Rev. and Mrs. Ardee Coolidge in 1952, Rev. and Mrs. Spurgeon Hendrix in 1956, and Rev. and Mrs. Howard Conrad in 1957. By then (1957) there were 15 fully organized churches and 20 other preaching points with a total membership of 226. Eighteen students were enrolled in the Bible school. Also that year Dr. G. B. Williamson ordained the first two Cuban ministers.

Still another event of 1957 was the death of Pastor Hildo Morejon's young wife. It was a devastating experience for both Hildo and the district, but so much so for him that he was plunged into spiritual darkness. He did not find his way back until the camp meeting the following year. In a dramatic way, as he sang a solo in one of the services, there was a great visitation of the Holy Spirit upon the people. Hildo had come through with glorious, spiritual victory!

But yet another crisis event of 1957 was the transfer of the Prescotts to Puerto Rico. Rev. Hendrix, who had been in charge of the Bible school, was appointed field superintendent in his place. Rev. Conrad was named director of the school.

All this fell just six months before Castro's successful rise to power. The Coolidges had already left for regular furlough, but the rest of the missionary force was now apprehensive about their future in Cuba. Though they were kept under close surveillance, they were at least not ordered to leave the country. However, it was obvious that the doors were steadily closing, and one by one the missionaries were quietly returned to the United States: the Halls in 1959, the Conrads and the Hendrixes in 1960.

At the request of Dr. G. B. Williamson, general superintendent in jurisdiction, Spurgeon Hendrix, John Hall, and the newly appointed missionary, Ted Hughes, went back to Cuba in the fall of 1960 to see what could be done about the future of the work. During their two-month stay they set up some contingency organization for the district, for it was obvious that a continued missionary presence would be impossible. Early in 1961 Spurgeon Hendrix was able to make another brief trip into Cuba, but subsequent requests for entry visas were refused.

To compound the problem, many of the pastors and people had fled to the United States and elsewhere to escape the consequences of the revolution. "All that was left," wrote Dr. H. T. Reza, "was a number of confused Nazarenes." But there was one stalwart who remained. It was Hildo Morejon, who was named to head the "Executive Committee to handle the Church of the Nazarene affairs." He was, in effect, the district superintendent.

For the next 18 years the curtain was down. Information concerning what was going on in Cuba was hard to come by. However, Dr. George Frame, from the British Isles, was able to make two trips to the island on behalf of the General Board. Contrary to expectations, he presented inspiring reports of how the work was progressing. In spite of extreme privation and government restrictions the church was alive and even growing.

Dr. Reza himself, being a Mexican citizen, was also able to visit on occasion besides using other communication lines. As he monitored the situation, he became increasingly encouraged about the prospects. He wrote to Dr. E. S. Phillips, executive secretary of the Department of World Missions: "One of these days things will change in Cuba, and the gospel will flow freely again like the waters of a strong river."

Even the Bible school continued to operate, but since it was situated near military bases, it was in a precarious location. Finally the Castro government decided to make the Nazarene compound into a military hospital. In exchange for the property, they gave the church a much larger tract west of Havana. It had but one large house on it, but it served the purpose in at least a limited way, and classes were continued.

Through international channels a certain amount of money was funneled into Cuba, but the people themselves bore the major load of support. Nine of the 21 organized churches were fully self-supporting. Quarterly and annual conventions, camp meetings, and revival services continued to be held—not in the same style as before, for government regulations were strict on matters of public assembly, but the essential elements were there.

In 1979 restrictions were sufficiently eased to allow General Superintendent George Coulter to go to Cuba to conduct the district assembly. The high point of his visit was the ordination on June 1 of a class of 14 ministers, 3 of them women, and the recognition of orders of 1 from another denomination. It was the first such ordination in 22 years. Among the candidates was Hildo Morejon. When it came his turn to be ordained, the pent-up emotions of the people broke loose in a flood of praise to God that was indescribable. "I have never seen a service such as this," said one pastor. "It was as though all heaven was concentrated within this building." Dr. Coulter affirmed that this was the highlight of his many years of ministry.

In 1980 came the great exodus from Cuba to the United States under the sanction of the government. Among the hundreds of thousands of refugees were many Nazarenes, even some pastors. The result was a drop in membership that year, leaving approximately 500 full and 100 probationary members. But it was not a mortal blow. One of the most encouraging signs of all was the large number of young people who were associating themselves with the church. In 1985 there were 17 churches reported with a total of 479 members.

What the future held in store for the Cuban Nazarenes was still uncertain, but the courage and dedication of the people gave promise of a continued, dynamic church in this oppressed island.

2. *Puerto Rico*

In 1942, at a meeting of the American Bible Society in New York, Dr. C. Warren Jones, secretary of the Department of Foreign Missions, met a young and very talented Puerto Rican by the name of Juan Lebron-Velazquez. He was the leader of a group of churches in and around the capital city of San Juan. Out of their conversation came a suggestion of the possible uniting of Rev. Lebron's churches with the Church of the Nazarene.

As a result, Dr. Howard V. Miller, general superintendent, visited Puerto Rico the following year and worked out a statement of membership and organization with Rev. Lebron and his people. In January 1944 the General Board approved the agreement, and the group of churches was officially received into the Church of the Nazarene. Rev. Lebron was named superintendent of the work. The general church contributed funds for the erection of two beautiful church buildings in San Juan.

Rev. Lebron's extensive radio ministry was expanded to include not only his Sunday morning program, "The March of Faith," which reportedly reached 3 million people, but a Saturday afternoon program called "Nazarene Spanish News." The English version of "Showers of Blessing" was also aired over four stations.

In 1944 the Lyle Prescotts were sent to St. Croix in the Virgin Islands to take over a previously established work there. But part of their assignment was to supervise the new work in Puerto Rico, 100 miles to the west, and in Rev. Prescott's words, "to make genuine Nazarenes of our Borinquen brethren" (Borinquen being the original Indian name for Puerto Rico). During the one year's duration of the assignment, he visited Puerto Rico eight times, contacting every church and preaching point, accompanied by Rev. Lebron, who acted as his interpreter. But such supervision was not appreciated. To Rev. Lebron this was a violation of the original agreement that no American missionary would be set over him.

The transfer of the Prescotts to Cuba at the end of that year, though not necessarily provoked by the Puerto Rico situation, did relieve the tension temporarily, and for about seven years Rev. Lebron carried on his own program with generous general church support. But also it became increasingly apparent that it was not a genuinely Nazarene operation, and a training school for ministers was considered essential to right the situation. Thus in 1952 Rev. and Mrs. Harold Hampton were transferred there from Belize (then British Honduras) to begin such a program.

The spirit of independency had in no way mellowed in the intervening years, and so violent was the opposition to the new program that Rev. Lebron and some of his group withdrew from the Church of the Nazarene. The matter of ownership of property brought the matter to the courts, and in order to preserve the good name of the denomination, a generous out-of-court settlement had to be made. In order to help mollify the situation and also to keep close to the problem, Dr. C. Warren Jones, Foreign Missions secretary, actually moved to Puerto Rico for six months.

But all was not lost. A loyal group gathered around the Hamptons as they set up a full-orbed district program. New churches were organized, preaching points were opened, and buildings were erected. Out of the shambles grew a thriving church program.

In 1954 Rev. and Mrs. William Porter were sent as missionaries, particularly to strengthen the ministerial training program. That year the Nazarene Bible Institute (Instituto Bíblico Nazareno) was officially launched. When the Hamptons left on furlough in 1957, later to be placed in charge of the Spanish work in the eastern United States, the Prescotts were transferred to Puerto Rico from Cuba.

The ministerial training program was further strengthened in 1958 with the coming of the Harry Zurchers, who had spent 12 years in Peru, and the Edward Wymans. Classes were held in San Juan First

Church with an enrollment of about 60. Only about one-third were involved in the regular ministerial course, however.

A work among the English-speaking people was opened by the Prescotts in the Los Angeles area of San Juan on Easter Sunday, March 29, 1959. There were 13 present. The church continued to grow to what is now known as the Calvary Church of the Nazarene. It was pastored by a continuous line of missionaries including Rev. Cleve James (former missionary to India), Rev. Richard Humston, Rev. Herb Ratcliff, and Rev. Steve Ratlief. After the missionaries left, when Puerto Rico became a mission district in 1976, Mrs. Elna Rogers Worts was called as pastor, to be followed by Rev. Vic Dunton.

In 1960 the General Board voted to open work once again in the Virgin Islands, and the Lyle Prescotts were assigned to the field, much to their delight, for they had happy memories of their earlier one-year stint on St. Croix in 1944-45. They moved in 1961, and Rev. Bill Porter was named Mission Council chairman and district superintendent of the combined fields. He was to remain in that office until a national superintendent was elected in 1976. His efficient, low-key style of leadership helped build a strong national leadership. He also joined the national symphony orchestra as lead French horn player, which gave him an unusual entrée into the business and cultural community, building goodwill for the church wherever the orchestra toured in Puerto Rico and surrounding islands.

In 1966 Rev. and Mrs. Herb Ratcliff were transferred to Puerto Rico from the island of Trinidad, where they had been in charge of the Caribbean Nazarene Training College. The Instituto Biblico Nazareno was at a crossroads, and part of the Ratcliffs' task was to make a thorough study of the institution's program. General educational standards on the island had risen to such a degree that the basic Bible school curriculum was no longer adequate to prepare ministers for the churches. To match the level of their congregations, several pastors were taking university courses, and graduates of the Bible school were going to the United States to take degree courses.

The school was well housed in a substantial two-story building including dormitory facilities in the residential Rio Piedras area of suburban San Juan. But it was becoming difficult to attract full-time students for the limited courses that could be offered. The school had served the district well, but it was apparent that its heyday of usefulness had passed. So in 1971 the Instituto Biblico Nazareno was closed, and the Spanish-American Nazarene Seminary, then in San

Antonio, became the official training school for the Spanish islands of the Caribbean. The property was taken over by the English-speaking Calvary Church, which had been holding its services there for a number of years.

Also in July 1975 the first step was taken toward regular district status for Puerto Rico with the appointment by General Superintendent Edward Lawlor of Rev. Benjamin Roman as assistant district superintendent. The following year he was elected district superintendent by the delegates to the assembly. At the 1977 assembly he was given an extended four-year call by a near-unanimous vote.

The statistics bear testimony to the effectiveness of Rev. Roman's leadership. In 1970 there were 759 full and probationary members. By 1980 this had doubled to 1,554. In 1970 there were 18 churches with only 4 of them self-supporting. In 1980 there were 25 churches, all of them self-supporting. Besides, the district was generously supporting the general church missionary program. By 1976 the district had reached full mission status and all missionaries had left. The last stage of full self-support was reached in 1980, and at the General Assembly in Kansas City in June, Puerto Rico was officially recognized as a regular district. The document was presented to the district assembly on July 18, 1980, amid great rejoicing.

Healthy growth continued, and by 1985 there were 30 churches on the district with 2,059 members. Rev. Roman continued as district superintendent.

3. *Dominican Republic*

Seventy-five miles west of Puerto Rico lies the island of Hispaniola, which is shared by two distinctly different republics, Haiti in the west and the Dominican Republic in the east. The latter was the third of the Spanish Caribbean countries to be reached by the Church of the Nazarene.

Though the actual move into the Dominican Republic did not take place until 1975, there had been considerable preliminary contact. For more than 20 years the Spanish radio broadcast, "La Hora Nazarena," had been aired on some 20 stations in the area, so the name of the church was already familiar. Also the Latin Division of the Nazarene Publishing House had been selling its products to a number of evangelical organizations in the country for many years.

Contacts were further enhanced by the fact that many from the

Dominican Republic had migrated to Puerto Rico and there had come under the influence of the Church of the Nazarene. Relatives and friends back home became early contacts for the church. Rev. William Porter, mission director in Puerto Rico, as a member of the Puerto Rico Symphony, traveled to the Dominican Republic with the orchestra on occasion and had taken the opportunity to appraise the situation there with a view to opening up work for the Church of the Nazarene.

Some Dominican friends of the Porters living in Puerto Rico, the Escarfullerys, gave Rev. Porter the names of two friends whom they felt would be able to help him should the church try to launch a work in their homeland. They were Rev. Andres Rodriguez of the Free Methodist church and José Reyes Castro. On one of his trips to the Dominican Republic, Rev. Porter contacted these men and through them met the two district superintendents of the Free Methodist church. He was warmly welcomed and encouraged to launch a Nazarene work there. "There is more work to be done here than any one church can accomplish," they assured him.

Mr. Castro visited the Porters in Puerto Rico, and they were able to lead him into an experience of entire sanctification. Back home he built a chapel on his own property and offered it to the Church of the Nazarene, but they were not yet prepared to open work in the republic so had to decline the offer. But Rev. Porter's interest was rising, and every official church visitor to Puerto Rico was amply told about the great opportunity on the neighboring island.

The first sign of general church action was a motion passed by the Department of World Missions at its annual meeting in January 1972 that consideration be given to the opening of work in the Dominican Republic. In December 1973, shortly after Dr. Jerald Johnson had succeeded Dr. E. S. Phillips as World Missions secretary, an all-Caribbean conference of pastors and missionaries was held in Haiti under the leadership of Dr. H. T. Reza to plan a strategy for expansion in the entire area. Dr. Phillips had set up the meeting but did not live to attend it. Following the conference, a small airplane was chartered to fly Dr. Johnson, Rev. Bill Porter, and Rev. Louie Bustle to the Dominican Republic for an on-the-spot examination of the situation there.

Dr. Johnson was quickly convinced of two main facts: (1) now was the time to enter this republic of 4 million people, and (2) the man to lead the assault was Rev. Louie Bustle. The next month, January

1974, the General Board adopted the following motion: That work be started in the Dominican Republic with Bill Porter as temporary council chairman of the new pioneer district until the Louie Bustles take further study in the Spanish language.

That year the Bustles took a short, five-month furlough from their work in the Virgin Islands and in January 1975 moved to Costa Rica to study Spanish. In the meantime Rev. Porter was busy laying the groundwork for the new enterprise. A chain of events was taking place that augured well for the future of the work.

The Escarfullerys introduced the Porters to a Dominican doctor living in Puerto Rico who had a house for rent in Santo Domingo. The person in charge of the property, he was told, was Mrs. Liliana Bobea, assistant manager of public relations in a large bank in Santo Domingo. When Rev. Porter called on her to make arrangements for the house, he told her about the plans of the church to open work in her country. Her eyes immediately brightened, and she began to tell of her own conversion a few months before and of her prayers that a way would be opened for her to serve the Lord in some particular way. Was this not the open door?

The following day Rev. Porter was in the office of a Free Methodist lawyer, Rev. Julio Rodriguez, drawing up the papers for the incorporation of the Church of the Nazarene in the Dominican Republic. Since there was as yet no congregation, the sponsorship of some citizen or group had to be obtained. Of course, there was José Reyes Castro, but also the name of Mrs. Bobea (or "Doña Liliana" as she came to be called) came to mind. He called her and found her eager to be a part of the project. From then on this vivacious lady became an ardent supporter of the work. When she was named to handle correspondence related to the broadcast of "La Hora Nazarena" in her country, she was delighted with the opportunity for service.

Finally the Bustles arrived on August 3, 1975, to be met at the airport by the Porters and a group of 12 Puerto Ricans. Among them was Mary Alvarado, district NWMS president, who was there to conduct a daytime Vacation Bible School. An opening series of services had been arranged to be held in the rented parsonage, but after two days it was necessary to move to the front yard. When the rains came, the crowd retreated to the carport. The highest attendance was 126. Among the attenders was Rev. Librado Figuero, a pastor for 33 years who had resigned from his church just six months before and was seeking an affiliation with a holiness church. He became a leader of the new congregation. Also converted in that initial meeting were three young men who professed calls to preach.

The carport served as a chapel for the first seven months until Rev. Bill Griffin and a group from his congregation at Indianapolis First Church came to erect the first church building. It became known as the Las Palmas Church and was organized with 10 full members, to which 14 were added that first year, all but 1 by profession of faith.

But Louie Bustle was a man of great vision. In fact he had told one of the officials at the office of the Social Services of Dominican Churches that he planned to establish 40 churches. The Las Palmas Church was but the starting point. Within a year 12 churches and 2 missions were reported with a total membership of 228. By 1977 the total was up to 21 churches, 2 missions, and 528 members. The next year the figures were 30 churches and 1,079 members, and by 1979, 36 churches and 1,407 members. Nor was the miracle over. The 1980 statistics showed 51 churches with close to 2,000 members. The original 10-year goal of 50 churches had been surpassed in half that time.

Such growth was the product of aggressive planning, consummate faith, and hard work. Every possible avenue for expansion was exploited, and forces of every kind mobilized for action. First there were the missionaries who were sent to assist: Jerry and Toni Porter (October 1975); Paul and Mary Jetter (February 1978); Jerry and Brenda Wilson (transferred from Panama and formerly of Peru, in July 1979).

In 1976 all 52 members of that summer's Student Mission Corps were assigned to the Dominican Republic. It was a daring venture that took meticulous planning. Well-selected adult sponsors for each of the seven teams and experienced Spanish-speaking evangelists were the key persons in a blitz that resulted in the formation of 10 or 11 new churches.

Over the years many Work and Witness teams came from the United States to build chapels all over the country and help make possible the miracle that is the Church of the Nazarene in the Dominican Republic.

Such phenomenal expansion naturally raised the problem of finding and training pastors for the many new pulpits. The key to the substantial growth has indeed been the outstanding Dominican men and women who have been called into the ministry. Along with this has been the related development of the pastoral training program

called SENDA—Seminario Nazareno Dominicano Afiliado (Affiliated Dominican Nazarene Seminary). The program was launched
near the beginning of the work under the direction of Rev. Jerry Porter.

In affiliation with the Seminario Nazareno de las Americas in
Costa Rica, basic courses were worked out under the guidance of Rev.
Howard Conrad, rector of the parent school. The emphasis was, of
necessity, on the practical aspects of the ministry. After two years at
SENDA students could transfer to Costa Rica to complete their work
toward a degree. Only one course was taught at a time, which provided concentrated study for two or three months. This system made
it possible for new students to enter at two- or three-month intervals.
In addition, four-week summer courses were offered, taught by professors from the Costa Rica seminary.

Lacking a central campus, the innovative plan of conducting the
SENDA classes in five different locations was adopted. Local church
facilities were used. This made it possible for pastors to attend classes
during the week and still be close enough to their churches to fill their
pulpits on weekends. Of necessity it was a matter of "building the
wagon while you rode in it." Only local- or district-licensed preachers
were allowed to attend the classes. Almost every pastor took the
courses, and most brought with them young people from their
churches who were planning to enter the ministry. Near-perfect class
attendance and diligent study reflected the caliber of pastors who
were manning the churches. "Truly the greatest miracle of the Nazarene work in the Dominican Republic," wrote Louie Bustle, "has been
the harvesters whom He has called."

In response to an obvious need, work was begun early among the
concentration of Haitians living and working in the Dominican Republic. The Bustles had been in the country less than a week when a
Haitian came to their door, asking to do yard work for the church. He
began attending services and soon brought friends with him. Before
long the pastor of the independent church where he originally attended asked if he and his congregation could unite with the Church
of the Nazarene. Wherever the Bustles went, they discovered the Haitians all seemed aware of the phenomenal growth the church was
experiencing in their neighboring homeland and were unusually responsive.

Among the SMCers who came in the summer of 1976 was
Dwight Rich, son of former missionaries to Haiti. His ability to speak

Haitian Creole was an invaluable adjunct in communicating the gospel to the people. Later, Nazarene translator and teacher Roberto Manoly came for two weeks of services, and soon there were two fully organized Haitian churches. In true Haitian style, these churches spawned others, and soon there were new groups calling themselves the "Church of the Nazarene" and only waiting for official acceptance. "It seems," wrote Rev. Bustle, "that we are just onlookers. God is sending the workers and the churches as we stand by excitedly watching."

With the number of churches reaching the 60 mark and a large measure of self-support being achieved, in 1981 the district reached Phase 3 (mission) status. Rev. Marcos Hatchett, who had been serving as assistant to Rev. Bustle, mission director, was elected the first national superintendent in March 1981.

In 1983 Rev. Bustle was transferred to Lima, Peru, to launch a church planting effort there. Rev. Marshall Griffith, veteran of missionary labors in Nicaragua and Costa Rica, and also for a time president of the Spanish Seminary in San Antonio, became mission director. The work continued to grow, and by 1985 there were four districts, each with a national superintendent. A total of 112 churches was reported with a combined membership of 4,687.

No district in the world of the Church of the Nazarene had ever grown so large in so short a time. Consolidation of such phenomenal gains constituted as great a challenge as the initial evangelistic thrust had been. But there seemed no end in sight as the statistical graph continued its steep upward climb.

4. *Leeward / Virgin Islands*

On the northeast rim of the Caribbean Sea lie the Virgin Islands and the Leeward Islands, the latter so named because they are sheltered from the trade winds. The northern Virgin Islands are British colonies, while the southern group (principally St. Thomas, St. John, and St. Croix) are under the United States flag. It is on St. Croix that the Church of the Nazarene has its work.

Among the Leeward Islands, mostly British colonies, are Antigua and Dominica, where the Nazarene work is located. It should be noted that Dominica (not to be confused with the Dominican Republic and even pronounced differently) is actually in the center of the French Antilles and technically one of the Windward Islands. However, when the district structure was set up in 1975, Dominica was included with the Leeward Islands and indeed was an offshoot of the work in Antigua. In 1985, however, it became part of the Windward Islands District.

In earlier days, the work in the Virgin Islands was associated with the Puerto Rican field because of its close proximity. Also there was no other work in that area at the time. However, the language difference was a hindrance to good administration, so finally in response to repeated requests, in April 1978 the Virgin Islands were officially attached to the Leeward Islands District.

St. Croix

In 1932 a small, independent church was launched in Christiansted, St. Croix, by Rev. Charles S. Mayhew of Barbados. It was never a flourishing work, and when he departed for Puerto Rico in 1943, he left a congregation of only 10 members. He offered this work to the Church of the Nazarene, and in response the following year the Department of Foreign Missions sent Rev. and Mrs. Lyle Prescott to St. Croix to take over the struggling church. At the same time, Rev. Prescott was to give supervision to the newly acquired group of churches in Puerto Rico led by Rev. Lebron-Velazquez.

The basic assignment was handled with reasonable success when within a year the membership was doubled to 20 and some excellent contacts were made for the church. However, the second responsibility produced negative results. As noted earlier, Rev. Prescott made eight supervisory trips to visit the Puerto Rico churches, but Rev. Lebron did not seem to appreciate having a missionary from a neighboring island peering over his shoulder. It was a violation of their original agreement, he claimed. Dr. C. Warren Jones, Foreign Missions secretary, went to the islands to try to resolve the problem. But even the weather was gloomy and with the combination of circumstances, he came to the conclusion that it would be best to back off entirely and move the Prescotts to Cuba. The St. Croix work was turned over to the Pilgrim Holiness mission.

It was a disappointment to the Prescotts, for they had fallen in love with the people of St. Croix, and that love was reciprocated. One lay leader, William DeGrasse, would not give in to the situation at all and prayed daily that the Nazarenes would return.

Twelve years later, in 1957, his faith was rewarded. The Prescotts were transferred to Puerto Rico to fill a vacancy there; and being so close to their former field, Rev. Prescott could not resist making an unofficial journey to St. Croix to visit some of his old friends. He was warmly welcomed, particularly by William DeGrasse, for to him his coming was a direct answer to prayer.

In 1961 the General Board voted to once again open the work in the Virgin Islands. In anticipation of this, the "Showers of Blessing" radio program had been broadcast on the island for a year. The decision was made to establish a base in the capital city of Charlotte Amalie, on St. Thomas Island; but when suitable property could not be found, the Prescotts went down to their familiar territory in Christiansted, St. Croix. Here they found a home to rent and moved their belongings from Puerto Rico in late August 1961.

The first services were held on September 3, 1961, in the home of a Puerto Rican lady at nearby Estate Catherine's Rest. Her invitation to use her home was welcomed because the Prescotts had not yet received permission to hold meetings in their own rented house. When, two weeks later, this permission was granted, a Spanish service was begun there in the morning with an English service at night. About the same time, Rev. Prescott's ministerial credentials were recognized by the government.

Soon a more adequate chapel/parsonage house was located, and around the first of November an evangelistic campaign was conducted there. The average attendance was under 20, and there were only 10 seekers in all, but it was a start. Obviously it was not going to be easy to gain a following.

Rev. Prescott realized that it would be necessary to establish a reservoir of goodwill in the community toward the church. This he did, not only through church services, but also through sacred music concerts (since he was an accomplished pianist), services in retirement homes and prisons, and radio and television performances. He assumed an active role in the Ministerial Association, Community Chorus, Red Cross, and other community enterprises. Even the children were involved and became student leaders in their schools. Such contacts won many friends for the church.

Across the island was the town of Frederiksted where lived a Nazarene couple from Antigua, Rodwell and Elva Buckley. A house was rented, services were begun there on March 25, 1962, and the Buckleys were installed as interim pastors.

Meanwhile an unrelenting search was going on for a permanent property. Finally, on October 23, 1962, a one-acre tract was purchased in the Estate Golden Rock area of Christiansted. Seven months later an adjacent piece of land was added for a total cost of $14,650. Shortly afterward real estate prices began to skyrocket, and in seven years' time a comparable property in the neighborhood sold for $60,000.

A beautiful and substantial church building was erected on the property and dedicated by District Superintendent William Porter on March 21, 1965. General Superintendent V. H. Lewis preached the dedicatory sermon. A comfortable parsonage for the Prescotts was built next door from Alabaster funds.

Following their furlough year in 1966, during which the Carl Mischkes, veteran African missionaries, supplied the church, the first baptisms were conducted with five candidates. Services were held in various other potential locations, and not all were successful, but by 1970 there were four regular preaching points.

On February 12, 1970, tragedy struck when Rev. Prescott was drowned in a fishing accident. Characteristically, he was with a dentist whom he was seeking to win for the Lord. The loss of this gifted missionary leader just when the work was beginning to take hold was a severe blow.

The effort in the Virgin Islands, so well started, could not be abandoned, and a hurried appointment of Louie and Ellen Bustle was made to fill the void. Before their marriage she had gone to St. Croix with a Student Mission Corps team so was familiar with the situation. This dynamic couple were on the job by June 1970.

These were the beginning of boom years for the Virgin Islands, with a large influx of people from other islands seeking to take advantage of high wages and plentiful jobs. Many of them were Nazarenes who quickly allied themselves with the churches in St. Croix. Others, displaced and often lonely, were a fruitful harvest field for evangelism that the Bustles were quick to exploit.

Assuming the Christiansted pastorate temporarily by himself, Rev. Bustle began an immediate search for a permanent pastor at Frederiksted. Through an odd circumstance—the placing of a newspaper ad that was required by law—he came in contact with Rev. Dhanraj Mahabir, a Trinidadian with 10 years of pastoral experience and a graduate of the college of the Church of the Open Bible. He had felt led to move to St. Croix with his family of 10 children and was temporarily driving a taxi. The Lord was already dealing with him about getting back into the ministry when he spotted the newspaper ad.

Rev. Bustle was taken aback when Rev. Mahabir appeared at his door. He had not anticipated *any* answer to his ad, let alone a mature person such as stood before him. They discussed doctrinal and practical matters thoroughly, and Rev. Bustle was impressed. The following day he flew to Puerto Rico to discuss the matter with District Superintendent Bill Porter. They agreed to engage Rev. Mahabir provided he would read certain books of the ministerial course of study, including the *Manual,* and pass two indicated examinations. He was installed as pastor and served there for six months, during which time, in March 1971, the church was organized as a fully self-supporting work.

In the community of Estate Profit in the center of the island a combined Spanish and English work was launched with separate congregations using the same building. Each group was organized in 1972. In 1973 a retired Nazarene layman from Michigan, Lloyd Martz, directed a construction program in which all three congregations acquired new buildings.

When Rev. Mahabir's son, Paul, graduated from a Bible institute in the United States, he assumed the pastorate of the Frederiksted church, while his father moved to the Christiansted church. This released Rev. Bustle for more extensive outreach efforts.

In 1978 in a consolidation move, the Frederiksted congregation united with the English Central Church, using the latter's facilities, while the Spanish church took over the Frederiksted building. The Central Church was officially the Lyle Prescott Memorial Church because the money for it was raised as a memorial to him.

When the Bustles furloughed in 1974 and were reassigned to open the work in the Dominican Republic, this marked the end of resident missionaries in the Virgin Islands. The work became a part of the Leeward/Virgin Islands District in April 1978.

Leeward Islands

The island of Antigua had its first contact with the Church of the Nazarene through Mrs. Lorna James, a native of the island, who in 1956 had gone to St. Croix to find employment. Some years later she moved next door to a Nazarene family who were instrumental in getting her and her son Jeff to attend services. They were converted under Rev. Lyle Prescott's ministry and became staunch supporters.

In 1968 Mrs. James felt strongly moved to return to her native island. Seeking a church home, she visited various churches and in the process met Rev. John St. Louis from the island of Dominica. As usual, she told him about her own church. His denomination was planning to move him to one of the southern islands, so in the interim he visited his home island and also St. Croix, where he made it a point to contact the Church of the Nazarene. He was even invited to preach. He became convinced that he should join the church, and so Rev. Bustle received him into membership. When he returned to Antigua and told Lorna James that he was now a Nazarene, she was both surprised and delighted.

As it turned out, the new preaching assignment in the south never materialized, so Rev. St. Louis secured secular employment to support his family. In the living room of his home he began holding services under the name of the Church of the Nazarene. Lorna James and other friends of earlier church connections formed the nucleus of his group. His home was located on George Street in the Gray's Farm area of the town of St. John's.

A friend of John St. Louis, Rev. Henry Lee, was pastoring a holiness church in the northern part of the city called the Beacon Light Church. They held their services in a school building. Pastor St. Louis urged his friend to join with the Nazarenes.

Rev. Bustle went to Antigua to see both congregations and in October 1973 arranged to have Mission Director Bill Porter and District Superintendent Benjamin Roman of Puerto Rico pay an official visit. On October 15 the congregations were organized as the Beacon Light and Gray's Farm Churches of the Nazarene. The former was an established group, fully self-supporting, but Pastor St. Louis at Gray's Farm had to continue his secular employment.

A pioneer district was formed, called the Antigua District, and Rev. and Mrs. Lawrence Faul, veterans of 22 years in the Caribbean, moved to the island to assume the district superintendency on July 29, 1974.

Just a month before, Pastor St. Louis had been transferred by his company to his home island of Dominica. It seemed to be a deathblow to the young congregation. However, a recent graduate from the Caribbean Nazarene Theological College in Trinidad, Hugh Conner, was available, and he and his wife moved there in August. At the same time Rev. Faul encouraged Pastor St. Louis to start a work in

Roseau, the capital city of Dominica. It seemed to be a part of the divine plan to expand the work to another island.

That summer a Student Mission Corps group conducted a successful Vacation Bible School in the Beacon Light Church, and the first district assembly was held on August 31. Fifty members and an average Sunday School attendance of 98 was reported.

Following Rev. Faul's urging, Pastor St. Louis acquired an old car repair shop in Roseau, Dominica, and with paint and hard work transformed it into a presentable chapel. Opening services were held on October 13, 1974, with Rev. Faul as the special speaker. At first opposition was strong, but Pastor St. Louis hung on, and eventually the congregation began to grow.

Meanwhile there were encouraging developments back in Antigua. Visits from Dr. and Mrs. L. S. Oliver (he the president of the Nazarene Bible College and she the general NWMS president) and Evangelists Rev. and Mrs. W. C. Raker in early 1975 were a great boost to the work. The latter held a three-week meeting in St. Johnston, a suburb of St. John's, which eventuated in a new church organization there on November 30, 1975. A second three-week meeting was held in the village of All Saints near the center of the island, and though attendance was smaller, a church was organized there on June 29. This group did not have a regular pastor until November, but in spite of that, attendance had grown by then to an average of 60.

In June 1975 a 34-member Work and Witness team from Southern Florida built in 15 working days a large steel-and-cement-block church for the Beacon Light congregation. It was financed from Alabaster funds. In the coming years this was to be the rallying center for district events. Rev. and Mrs. Warren Rogers held a series of meetings there preceding the dedication of the building. This was the site of the second district assembly held on August 6, 1975, conducted by Dr. Jerald Johnson, executive director of the Department of World Mission. Though not all were fully organized, five churches were reported with 105 members and a Sunday School enrollment of 319.

Present at the assembly were Missionaries Gene Smith and Robert Ashley, both of St. Lucia, who, with Rev. Faul, had been asked to suggest a new district structure for this part of the Caribbean Islands. They conferred with Dr. Johnson on the matter, and after his return to the United States, the official announcement was made that there would be three districts: Leeward Islands, French Antilles, and Windward Islands.

In January 1976 the first Preachers' Convention was held with Rev. Orville Rees, a former Pilgrim Holiness missionary to the Caribbean, as speaker. In April and May Rev. and Mrs. Harold Hampton held revival services on both islands. One of these, at St. Joseph Village, nine miles from Roseau on Dominica, eventuated in a second church for that island.

In June Rev. Faul teamed with a recent CNTC graduate, Brian Balfour, in a month-long tent meeting in Liberta, second-largest town on Antigua. Regular services continued following the campaign, and the church was officially organized on October 3.

On February 6, 1977, an eighth point was added at Johnson's Point, and in March a Work and Witness team from the Michigan District, led by Lloyd Martz and Albert Conklin, built an Alabaster church at All Saints. The church was dedicated by Dr. Jerald Johnson on June 10, 1977, when he came to conduct the fourth district assembly.

On the island of Dominica there was a Carib Indian reservation from which came a request that the Church of the Nazarene conduct services among them. Pastor St. Louis held occasional services there, but when CNTC student Mackberth Williams was home for the summer of 1977, he pastored the group full time. Beginning again the following summer, he spent his full year of internship (1978-79) on the reservation.

Two young men of the Student Mission Corps gave valuable service in Vacation Bible Schools and tent meetings in the summer of 1977. Out of their work came a new church at Glanvilles on Antigua.

The Leeward/Virgin Islands District

The first visit to the Leeward Islands District by a general superintendent came on March 15, 1978, with Dr. and Mrs. George Coulter present for the fifth district assembly. It was there that the announcement was made of the pending transfer of the Virgin Islands to the Leeward Islands District. As previously stated, this was consummated in April 1978.

When the Fauls furloughed in 1978, they were replaced by the veteran missionaries from Africa, the Paul Hetricks, Sr. The adverse effects of the climate forced them to leave soon, and their place was taken by Rev. and Mrs. Berge Najarian, formerly of Israel and Jordan.

The problem of finding pastors for the expanding number of churches and replacements for the ones who left was a continuing problem. This was somewhat relieved when four CNTC students spent their year of internship (1978-79) on the district, one of these being Mackberth Williams who, as previously noted, went to the Carib Indian reservation. A church was organized there December 31, 1978. About the same time, a small, independent congregation in the village of Bioche, Dominica, joined with the Church of the Nazarene.

With the addition of the three St. Croix churches in 1978, the district quickly moved to national-mission status, and Rev. Dhanraj Mahabir, pastor of the Christiansted church for seven years, was appointed the first national district superintendent in June 1979. When the Fauls returned from furlough at the end of that month, Rev. Faul became mission director. In addition to his work as district superintendent, Rev. Mahabir continued to pastor the Christiansted church until the seventh district assembly in March 1980.

A cloud over that session was the discouraging situation in Dominica. On August 29, 1979, Hurricane David had struck a devastating blow to the island, staggering its already weak economy. The church buildings suffered damage, and a long road to recovery lay ahead.

Dr. George Coulter, who presided over the 1980 assembly, was on his last overseas assignment prior to retirement. The statistical record showed a total membership of 354 in the 13 active preaching points and a Sunday School enrollment of 1,062. Only 5 regular pastors were on the district, however, with lay workers, supply pastors, and students filling in the gaps.

District Superintendent Mahabir went to work on this problem, and by 1985 there were 12 pastors with 17 organized churches and a total membership of 556 for a quinquennium increase of 57 percent.

5. *Haiti*

Haiti, though in the heart of the Greater Antilles, is uniquely different from its Spanish-speaking neighbors. It is officially French, but almost all its people speak Creole. Ninety-five percent are Black, reflecting their African heritage that dates back to slave days. Its population density of 445 people per square mile makes it the most densely populated of Western nations. And the sound of voodoo drums tells of its animistic religious roots even though Roman Catholicism is its dominant religion.

The country is situated only 600 miles from United States shores, yet the Church of the Nazarene was not involved in a gospel ministry to the island until 1948. Even then the contact was initiated from Haiti, not from the church.

The first overtures from Haiti came from Carlos Egen, a law student and schoolteacher who was leader of an independent group of churches he had launched in 1945 after feeling a call to preach. His organization, including two main churches and seven satellite preaching points, had a reported membership of about 600, only 200 of whom would be considered full, baptized members. Seeking some substantial affiliation and the financial resources such a connection might afford, he wrote to Dr. C. Warren Jones, executive secretary of the Department of Foreign Missions, concerning the uniting of his group with the Church of the Nazarene.

Dr. Hardy C. Powers, general superintendent, visited Mr. Egen that year and was favorably impressed, though cautious. At the January 1948 meeting of the General Board, Egen's group was officially recognized, and financial assistance was authorized to be sent to him. Subsequent visits that same year and the next by General Superintendents H. V. Miller and D. I. Vanderpool helped to consolidate the relationship of this incipient work with the missionary program of the Church of the Nazarene.

At the January 1950 meeting of the Department of Foreign Missions, Rev. and Mrs. Paul Orjala were selected as the first Nazarene missionaries to Haiti. After Paul's graduation from seminary in May, they began their active preparation for departure and arrived in Haiti on October 3, 1950. Thus began one of the most thrilling stories of church growth in Nazarene history.

The first task that faced the Orjalas was to tie in with the Egen work, which already had the blessing of the general church leaders. Through this affiliation the door had been opened into Haiti, and government recognition for the denomination had been achieved, but Carlos Egen's vision and ability were too limited. There also seemed to be evidence that he had sought to become part of the Church of the Nazarene for financial reasons, and there were "other problems."

"Our only hope," wrote Rev. Orjala, "is going to be in developing a new generation of young people. We have little hope that the old people can ever change enough to develop a truly Nazarene spirit in our churches."

The Orjalas' opening days were spent in finding a home and

getting the feel of the country. Being forced to use public transportation, since they had no vehicle of their own, may have presented some difficulty, but it certainly brought them in touch with the people. They began their study of Creole and French and visited with government officials to make sure that all legal matters were in order so that the church could operate without hindrance. A key issue was to have the church registered as a denomination, not in the name of a person such as Mr. Egen or even Rev. Orjala.

It had been recommended to the Orjalas that they enter the country on a temporary visa and, once there, apply for permanent papers. But by April 4, 1951, they had exhausted all the legal extensions of the original visa and had not yet received their final permits. They were advised to go to American soil and apply for permanent visas from there. So they spent the next six weeks in Puerto Rico, anxiously waiting for the necessary papers. Haitian friends kept contacting the immigration office frequently on their behalf, and finally, on May 24, they were officially admitted to the country.

The No. 1 priority was to train national preachers for the task ahead, not only Mr. Egen's workers but new ones as well. It was Rev. Orjala's hope that by fall he would have sufficient mastery of Creole and French to open a Bible school. Being a linguist of unusual ability, he was able to launch the Bible school on October 3, 1951, with seven students enrolled. Classes were held three times a week from 4 to 6 P.M. with Bible, doctrine, and music as the subjects taught. (Both the Orjalas were excellent musicians, and this was an avenue to the people that they used with outstanding success.) One of the first enrollees was a young Coast Guardsman, Joseph Simon, who was to become an outstanding pastor and one of the first Haitian elders.

In October 1951 Dr. D. I. Vanderpool paid a five-day visit to Haiti, and in February 1952 Mrs. Louise R. Chapman came. Her mature advice to the young missionary couple was of great value and much appreciated by them.

On January 3-4, 1952, the first Preachers' Meeting was held in the North at Canal Bois. Present also were several ministers from the South, which helped build a team spirit and helpful camaraderie. But there was the lingering problem of what to do about Carlos Egen and his men who constituted the initial corps of workers. Mr. Egen was the heart of the problem, his men being much more cooperative with the new order of things.

As it turned out, Mr. Egen decided on his own that rather than face the issues raised by Rev. Orjala, he would just pull out. The missionary was prepared to start all over again should Mr. Egen's group follow him, but none of them did. All of the pastors and their people in both the North and the South stayed with the church and the Orjalas. Fortunately the crisis did not arise until after satisfactory arrangements had been completed with the government for the Church of the Nazarene to operate in Haiti, so no legal hurdles had to be overcome.

With this weight off his shoulders, Rev. Orjala entered into the task with renewed vigor. And almost immediately phenomenal results were being seen. For example, in a mountain preaching point just 25 miles north of Port-au-Prince 200 conversions were reported in a very short time.

On November 27, 1952, Charles and Alberta Alstott and son, Danny, arrived to begin their first term of missionary service in Haiti. Two days later Dr. Samuel Young, general superintendent, came for an official visit and particularly to interview Max and Mary Alice Conder. This Nazarene couple had been working since 1950 with an independent holiness mission in the North that was about to close. At the General Board meeting the following January, they were appointed associate missionaries and began their work with the Nazarene mission in March.

Property on the outskirts of Port-au-Prince was rented, and a full-time Bible school program was begun there in July 1953. After two semesters it was decided to abandon the program in that location and wait until a permanent campus could be secured and adequate buildings erected. In the foothills 10 miles northeast of Port-au-Prince, an excellent property was purchased; and while the Orjalas were home on furlough in 1955-56, Rev. Alstott began the building program. He had earlier built the first church in Port-au-Prince. Now the initial project was a missionary home that was completed in February 1956. The Nazarene roots were beginning to take hold in Haitian soil.

A Period of Deepening

The Orjalas returned to Haiti in September 1956, and in November another missionary couple, the Brian Vanciels, were added to the team. A year later Rev. and Mrs. Harry Rich came. The main Bible school building was built by Rev. Alstott before he and his wife left on furlough in July 1957. After the Riches arrived, a dormitory and another missionary home were erected. These buildings were still under construction when Dr. Hugh C. Benner, general superintendent, arrived to dedicate the new campus on December 1, 1957. Present for the occasion were several government officials and over 600 members and friends of the church.

Classes began on February 25, 1958, with six students enrolled. Construction continued as the new campus developed into a valuable district center. Here the first Haitian District Assembly was held in September of that year. Though the financial status of the country was poor, the concept of self-support was introduced in the church from the first, and an emphasis on tithing resulted in a 65 percent increase in giving the very first year of organization.

The fall enrollment at the Bible school jumped to 20. An opening revival, led by Pastor Massillon Pierre of the Pont l'Estere church, proved to be a high spiritual experience. Its influence rippled out over the entire field. The first ministers' licenses were granted in December to Jules Boliere, Felix Dauphin, Monneus Fleury, Luc Jean, Massillon Pierre, and Joseph Simon.

The first Nazarene camps were held in February 1959, timed to coincide with the annual Mardi Gras week. A main purpose was to provide a counterattraction for the young people who would otherwise be tempted to participate in the worldly activities of the Mardi Gras celebration. Several camps were held simultaneously over the district with great success.

With the literacy rate in Haiti only 10-20 percent and a government with inadequate resources to support a program of public education, day schools were a prominent part of the various mission programs in the country, and the Church of the Nazarene was destined to follow suit. As Paul Orjala put it: "The Haitian church can never be firmly established and strong until a majority of its members are literate." In July 1959, under the leadership of Rev. Harry Rich, a school building was erected in Port-au-Prince next to the church, the first of many such structures throughout the country.

The literacy problem was compounded by the fact that the country is bilingual. The official language is French, spoken by only an elite few, but the language of the common people is Haitian Creole. Literacy experts from abroad helped in the development of Creole literature, the standardizing of spelling, and so forth. It was not until mid-1960 that the American Bible Society completed its first edition of the New Testament and Psalms in Creole. It was a major breakthrough in the mission program. Rev. Orjala himself was a linguistic advisor to the six Haitian ministers who did the translation.

September 1959 saw the arrival of Missionaries Gene and Catherine Smith and the dedication of the Cabaret church, built by Harry Rich. The contribution of Rev. Rich in the building program was inestimable. It was he who conceived the idea of building churches without walls. This way a larger basic building could be afforded, and the congregations had the challenge to complete the sidewalls at a later date.

The first graduation ceremonies for the Bible school were held on May 6, 1960, when five men received their diplomas—among them Joseph Simon. Rev. Lyle Prescott from Puerto Rico was the speaker for the occasion. Immediately following, the group of graduates was taken on an evangelistic tour in the North, where they received helpful practical experience. That fall, the enrollment at the school was up to 34.

The third district assembly in December 1960, conducted by Dr. Hugh C. Benner, was marked by the ordination of the first Haitian elders: Monneus Fleury, Massillon Pierre, and Joseph Simon. A keynote of the assembly was the emphasis on scriptural holiness and evangelism. An examination of the statistics for the decade of 1950-60 revealed that the Church of the Nazarene in Haiti was on the move.

	1950	1960
Organized churches	1	20
Outstations	12	90
Baptized members	177	1,388
Probationers	557	4,765
Total adherents	734	6,153

Better still, the rate of increase was also going up. The growth rate in 1960 alone was 68 percent. Rev. Orjala cited the reasons for this rapid growth as: (1) the spontaneous personal witnessing of the Haitian Christians; (2) their emphasis upon deep spirituality and separation from the world; and (3) their love of the church.

Of special interest to Rev. Orjala was the adaptation of the musical elements of Haitian culture to the work of the church. This gave the gospel an indigenous flavor as, for instance, when evangelical words were sung to tunes in the Haitian folk music style.

A Period of Advance

The decade of the 1960s was a time of unbelievable growth for the Haitian church. The number of churches and preaching points jumped from 119 to 405 in that period, and total membership (full and probationary) rose from 6,153 to 20,405. It was not unusual for people converted in one location to visit relatives in other communities, witness to them and their neighbors, and then start regular services. Every Christian was a witness wherever he went. Many of these spontaneous preaching points developed into organized churches.

Mrs. Conder, a nurse, had been operating a dispensary in the North from the time they joined the mission in 1953, and in 1959 a dispensary was built on the Port-au-Prince property. The latter was in charge of Mrs. Alstott, who was also a nurse. But though this phase of the work was important, it was not at this time a major aspect of the missionary program. However, the printing of gospel literature was very significant, with Missionary Dave Ford heading the program. By 1970 the annual output of the busy press was nearly half a million pieces. The day school program also caught on, and from the 2 or 3 schools in operation in 1960 there blossomed 44 during the decade with an enrollment of 3,686. The Bible school growth, though less spectacular, was steady, reaching a total enrollment of 43 by 1970.

It was during this decade that Walter and Linda Crow, Elvin and Evelyn DeVore, Bob and Jeanine Brown, Dave and Lois Ford, and Nancy Borden joined the missionary force. Concerning his assistants, Rev. Orjala wrote:

> The Haitian field has been blessed with talented, Spirit-filled missionaries who have not spared themselves to forward the church in every way. They have travelled thousands of miles on horseback, by boat, by jeep, even on foot, to extend the gospel and encourage the Haitian churches. Their normal task in recent years has been to train preachers in the Bible school during the week and then travel on the weekend among the churches. It is perhaps the highest compliment that can be paid to say that they have matched the Haitian Christians in their commitment to the task.

Rev. Orjala complimented as well the national leaders such as Joseph Simon and Massillon Pierre, who were delegates to the 1968 General Assembly. They were preaching to larger crowds than any other Nazarene preachers in the world. But he also paid high tribute to the laymen who, he said, were "New Testament Christians—

people who think that their principal vocation is to win people to Christ." He estimated that 95 percent of the new converts were won through personal evangelism.

In 1964, in the midst of this phenomenal growth, Rev. Orjala received a call to head the missions department of the Nazarene Theological Seminary in Kansas City. It seemed strange to leave in the midst of such a great expansion of the work, but the Orjalas felt it to be God's will for them to move on. At the same time, the momentum that had been reached would make it easier for a successor to pick up the task. That new mission superintendent was Rev. Harry Rich, by now a veteran on the field.

As a prelude to the new decade, in 1969 the decision was made to divide the field into two districts, North and South, with the Artibonite River as the dividing line. Rev. Massillon Pierre was named leader of the northern district and Rev. Florentin Alvarez of the south. This division was a temporary accommodation to the needs of the field until full district organization was effected five years later.

Agricultural and Industrial Development

One of the chief obstacles to the development of the indigenous church in Haiti was the limited economic resources of the country. The average national per capita income was between $50.00 and $75.00 per year (U.S.), and since the Church of the Nazarene was made up almost exclusively from the peasant class, the average for them was even lower. Annual per capita giving in the mid-1960s was about 35¢. Under such circumstances, the achievement of self-support seemed a far-off goal.

This situation gave rise to a new concept in missionary activity. The premise was that if the people could find employment, they would not only better themselves but have money to support the church. Agriculture and light industry thus became target projects of the mission program.

In 1973 Charles Morrow and his family moved to Haiti. He held a master's degree in agriculture from Iowa State University and was a community development specialist. He immediately set to work to teach the people better farming methods. He introduced quality seed to develop diversified crops. Then he brought in high-grade livestock, and soon the people were improving their diets with meat. He brought in purebred poultry, and chicken farms sprouted up around the country. Not only were the nutritional needs of the people being met more adequately, but the sale of surplus products through cooperatives raised their standard of living generally. The ultimate outcome was money for the church through the tithes of the people.

In addition to the agriculture development, Project Autonome was launched under the leadership of Missionary Steve Weber, who arrived in Haiti in 1975. It began with finance, such as the establishment of a Nazarene credit union, and expanded to include various forms of light industry, such as a woodworking factory, a fiberglass industry, a couple of taxis, a printing press, and a clothing manufacturing project.

Vocational Missionary Freddie Williams came in 1980 to develop the building skills of the people. While they learned by building churches, the workmen soon were applying their skills by building or upgrading their own homes or finding jobs as skilled tradesmen in the building industry.

In all, some 20 self-help projects and cooperatives were set in motion. The end result was that by 1980, per capita giving had jumped from the original 35¢ to $2.11. The people were beginning to believe that self-support was a realizable goal within the next decade. In fact, three churches had already reached that level.

With the vocational developments there was also an added emphasis upon compassionate ministries. During devastating famines in the late 1970s, the Church of the Nazarene was given responsibility for the distribution of thousands of dollars worth of aid from abroad and tons of foodstuffs. A portion of these relief items came through the Hunger Fund of the Nazarene Department of World Mission.

The medical needs of the people also were given greater attention. The limited program, begun in 1953, was reorganized in 1964. Nurses were added to the missionary force, and Haitian doctors, dental assistants, lab technicians, and nursing students were employed. In 1978 a missionary nutritionist, Carolyn Parsons, was sent to help in this desperately needed phase of the health program. Besides the dispensary, mobile clinics were set up, and clinics for prenatal care and for children and their mothers were begun.

At the same time, there was a marked increase in the number of day schools operated to well over 100 with a total enrollment of 14,000. In addition 40 adult literacy schools were launched.

But though these innovative ventures captured much attention and interest and indeed were changing the character of the Haitian church, the traditional evangelistic activities were not abandoned.

The church continued to grow, though not as spectacularly as it had in the previous decade.

The Education of Ministers

One dark cloud came across the horizon in 1972 when a critical situation arose that forced the closing of the Bible school. This was a difficult decision to make, but it seemed the only immediate solution to the problem. Nevertheless, there was a mounting clamor from the pastors, most of whom were graduates of the school, to have the school reopened as soon as possible. In the fall of 1975 the doors opened once again. The key individual in this move was Miss Jeanine van Beek, who was transferred from the European Nazarene Bible College in Switzerland where she had been the academic dean. The initial enrollment was 9, but by 1980 this had increased to 22, and by 1985 to 50.

A part of Miss van Beek's time was given to the development of extension courses, particularly for the training of lay leaders, many of whom were pastoring substantial churches. Theological Education by Extension (TEE) was a comparatively new concept in Nazarene missions at the time, but it filled an important need in the Haitian church. The program became known there as Pastoral Extension Training (PET).

Haiti is a land of children, and they have not been forgotten by the church either. Their education, health, and nutritional needs have been met, as well as their spiritual well-being. In1972 Miss Brenda Gould, a child evangelism specialist, went to Haiti and served effectively until 1977, when she was transferred to the French Antilles. Steve and Linda Weber translated and adapted the Caravan program for use in the Haitian culture, then trained the people on how to conduct the program in the schools and churches. In August 1980 Fred Sykes, the general Caravan director for the church, went to Haiti to conduct a week of training classes for Caravan leaders. The program was an instant success, and within a few months 2,000 children were ready to receive their scarves.

Changes were being made in district administration as well. After the temporary formation of the two districts in 1969, the next step up the organizational ladder was for these to become full national-mission districts with the appointment of national district superintendents. In December 1974 Dr. Eugene Stowe, general superintendent, appointed Rev. Delano Pierre as superintendent of the North District and Rev. Florentin Alvarez of the South District. Rev. Terry Read became mission director and served as a most effective balance wheel during the transition. In 1977 Rev. Duroc Placide was elected superintendent in the North, and in 1978 Rev. Herman Andre was elected in the South.

With the creation of two districts, there arose problems concerning the relationship of the church to the government on civil matters such as holding land. The authorities required some single voice to represent the church. As a result a *Conseil National* was created, which was made up of the advisory boards of the two districts. This council was to elect an executive committee consisting of a president, vice president, secretary-treasurer, and a member-at-large. The president was to be the official representative of the denomination before the Haitian government.

All property was registered in the name of the *Conseil National.* In addition, the council supervised all interdistrict activities, such as the Bible college, radio broadcasts, literature distribution, the PET program, relief and development programs, and medical work. (This basic concept was later picked up by other multiple-district mission fields who also needed an official united voice before the government in their respective countries.)

Ambitious goals had been set by the Haitian leaders for the decade of 1975-85. A fundamental change in strategy was to shift the major emphasis from relief and development programs to church growth and ministerial training. Among specific goals was the increasing of districts from two to six, the encouragement of self-support, and an increase in full members to 19,000 (at that time under 7,500). Compassionate ministries and self-help and development programs were to be continued as "important components of a cohesive strategy." The Bible college was to be upgraded to "U" level, and a strong emphasis was to be placed on "the development, production, and distribution of French and Haitian Creole literature."

A unique aspect of the projection was the planning of big events around church growth themes. One of these was a giant, countrywide baptism day. Regional Director James Hudson called attention to the fact that on the Day of Pentecost 3,000 had been baptized, and suggested that on September 30, 1984, mass baptisms be held throughout Haiti with that same goal in mind. On the North Central District a mass rally was held, and 18 pastors baptized 1,044 people in one hour. Reports from elsewhere brought the total to 2,749. This experience triggered a tremendous revival and church growth explosion. By 1985 membership on the six districts totaled 47,746. Just over 19,000 of these were full members, which meant that their ambitious decadal goal had been surpassed. Two of the districts had attained Phase 3 (mission) status. The Haitian church was the largest in the Nazarene world outside of the United States.

6. *Jamaica*

Nestled under the eastern end of the island of Cuba, and less than 100 miles from it, lies the island of Jamaica. It is about 140 miles long and 50 miles wide with a population just over 2 million, 85 percent of whom are of African descent. The island country is about 86 percent literate and, once a British colony, became an independent nation on August 6, 1962. Significantly, Jamaica is 75 percent Protestant, the highest such percentage of any of the West Indian islands with the exception of Barbados.

Nazarene Beginnings

The first tentative probe into Jamaica by the Church of the Nazarene came in the late 1930s when Dr. J. W. Goodwin, general superintendent, in response to a number of suggestions over the previous years, paid a visit to the island. Seeking to discover the potential for a Nazarene work, he contacted the leaders of the Church of God (Anderson, Ind.) mission and found their work to be quite strong. In fact, he preached to an audience of 300 in one of their churches. With such a positive holiness witness on the island, he thought it inappropriate or at least unnecessary to enter this field. The General Board accepted his recommendation, and the matter lay dormant for many years.

Mrs. A. O. (Mamie) Hendricks, who had served with her husband four years in the southern Caribbean, became interested in Jamaica and in the fall of 1955 spent three months there. In the course of her stay she became well acquainted with Mrs. Winston Lyons and Mrs. Lillie Mae Burke. Mrs. Lyons was the leader of the 1,500-member Womens' Club, an organization of businesswomen, while Mrs. Burke was prominent in government circles.

Through Mrs. Lyons, Mrs. Hendricks met the head of Radio Jamaica, whose outlets blanketed the island. The upshot was that "Showers of Blessing" began to be aired over this network on September 2, 1956. Air time was largely paid for in succeeding years by the Hendricks family. There were more responses from the broadcast in Jamaica than from any other airing in the world except for one United States station. Though there was no Nazarene work on the island, the name of the church was becoming a familiar one in innumerable households. In the meantime, Mrs. Hendricks, by personal visits and continued correspondence, was doing her own brand of promoting the church.

It is not surprising that some independent groups became interested in joining the Church of the Nazarene. Each such overture was investigated to determine the motivations of the groups concerned and both the opportunities and liabilities for the denomination should they become affiliated. There were viable reasons why the Foreign Missions Board did not respond to any of these proposals, but this did not mean lack of interest or concern. In fact, almost every year at the General Board meetings, the matter of entering Jamaica was considered.

Finally, in December 1965 Dr. and Mrs. E. S. Phillips visited Jamaica. Their main purpose was to meet with Rev. Oswald Simms, pastor of an independent holiness group of about 60 members. Rev. Simms had attended some classes at Nazarene Theological Seminary in Kansas City, and there was a preestablished rapport.

Dr. Phillips was impressed with the sincerity and dedication of both pastor and people and told them they would be most welcome to join the Church of the Nazarene, but it would have to be on an individual basis, not as a group. The people recognized the wisdom of such a procedure, and over half of them signed an official request for membership.

In January 1966 Rev. and Mrs. Ralph Cook, formerly of India and now serving in Trinidad, were assigned by the General Board to open the work in Jamaica. In a unique sense the English-speaking Caribbean church was being involved in the new venture, both through the selection of the Cooks as leaders, and the continued promotion of this cause by their friend Mrs. Hendricks. In fact, she had been successful at the 1966 assembly of the Barbados District to have them allocate 1 percent of the balance in the district treasury to Jamaica.

The Cooks arrived in Jamaica on March 21, 1966, almost 10 years after the first "Showers of Blessing" program had been aired. On March 27, Rev. Cook preached for Rev. Simms in both morning and evening services with 30 to 40 people present.

But there was a problem over the entrance permits issued to the Cooks by the Jamaican office in Trinidad, and they had to go on to Kansas City and make new applications. After two months they finally received permission to enter the country on a temporary basis that was renewable every two weeks. As soon as they returned to Jamaica, Mrs. Hendricks came and introduced the Cooks to the Lyonses, Mrs. Burke, and other key persons. They found the government particularly responsive to the educational phases of the church's proposed program.

The first major move was to schedule a visit by the Nazarene Evangelistic Ambassadors, a group of college and seminary men from the United States who, with their accompanying evangelists, were holding crusades throughout the summer. They were to come to Jamaica August 26-28, and the 5,000-seat National Convention Hall in Kingston was rented for the event. Since the meetings could not be advertised under the name of the Church of the Nazarene because the government registration papers had not yet come through, the "Showers of Blessing" broadcast was listed as the sponsor.

Evening services were to be supplemented by several daytime appearances in schools, radio stations, and civic clubs. Dr. Paul Orjala, Evangelist Paul Martin, and pianist David Uerkvitz were the scheduled workers.

Meanwhile, Mrs. Lillie Mae Burke had taken it upon herself to see that the Church of the Nazarene was officially recognized. She finally called the acting prime minister at midnight one night and told him of her concern. "Well, Lillie Mae," he replied, "if this is so important to you, we'll see what we can do." The next afternoon the papers were signed.

Thus it was that just six days before the big extravaganza, the Church of the Nazarene was recognized as an official denomination in Jamaica. The name of the church could now be freely used during the meetings.

On the opening night the governor general, Queen Elizabeth's representative in Jamaica, was a guest on the platform and gave words of official welcome, even suggesting that the 450 present urge their neighbors and friends to attend the meetings. Attendance reached 1,000 on the closing night, and there were more than 80 seekers.

The First Church Organized

On October 9, 1966, Dr. E. S. Phillips organized the Crossroads Church of the Nazarene (later renamed Richmond Park) with 44 full members and 8 probationers. Most were from Rev. Simms's congregation, but some were products of the crusade. Rev. Simms was appointed pastor.

Stewardship was strongly emphasized from the first. The people readily adopted Rev. Cook's suggestion that they follow the Nazarene pattern of giving 10 percent of their church income to world evangelism and 5 percent for the Jamaica District. They also assumed the pastor's salary and local expenses. In turn, Rev. Cook promised that the general church would take care of building and property costs.

Christian Service Training courses were taught to develop churchmanship and to produce qualified teachers and lay leaders. "Search the Scriptures" correspondence courses were offered over the air, and hundreds of people enrolled. A full church program, including Sunday School, missionary society, youth organization, and Vacation Bible School, was instituted.

On January 1, 1967, the charter membership list was closed, and in a moving ceremony led by Dr. V. H. Lewis, general superintendent, Pastor Simms was ordained into the ministry of the Church of the Nazarene.

In June 1967 Dr. Uerkvitz returned to give a series of classical concerts in a high school in Montego Bay on the north side of the island. "The greatest cultural event to come to Montego Bay," said the local newspaper. It won many friends for the denomination, but the church was not yet ready to open work in that city.

On November 12, 1967, Mrs. Orpha Cook was hospitalized with a lung problem from which she did not rally, and one week later she passed away. After funeral services in Kansas City, Rev. Cook returned to Jamaica and carried on for another two and a half years. Visits by Rev. Prescott Beals, an old missionary colleague of India days; Rev. Bill Blue, of Fort Lauderdale First Church in Florida; and Rev. Clarence Jacobs, a Jamaican who was pastor of the Miller Memorial Church in Brooklyn, were all a great boost to the work and to the lonely missionary.

Following a tent meeting by a Student Mission Corps team, a second church was organized in Kingston—the Boulevard Church—on October 6, 1968.

Late in 1969 Rev. Simms decided to once more go independent, and some of the members followed him out. Most did not, however, and a strong nucleus was left to carry on. Property had been purchased for the church in Richmond Park in January 1969, on which there was a house that was converted to church use. Then a large adjacent lot was purchased, and with the aid of Alabaster funds construction was begun in 1970 on a beautiful and spacious church building, which was completed and dedicated in 1971. Students of Bethany Nazarene College provided pews and other furnishings for this church, which became a center for district activities.

Rev. Cook had received a letter from a Miss Ethelene Thomas, who was a teacher and community leader at Castle Mountain, south of Montego Bay on the western end of the island. She expressed sincere interest in having the church come to her community, and she even offered land on which to erect a building. Rev. Cook told her a missionary family was soon to come to Montego Bay, and he would tell them to get in touch with her.

That couple who came were the Jerry Demetres, who had been transferred from Barbados to Jamaica. They arrived on April 8, 1970, and services were begun in a small building on the property Miss Thomas had given. In July 1971, with the help of an $8,000 gift from the Los Angeles District, construction began on a large and attractive L-shaped building, one wing of which accommodated a day school directed by Miss Thomas. About the same time, the Demetres began services in the Red Cross Hall in downtown Montego Bay.

On August 18, 1970, the John Smees arrived in Jamaica and soon were installed as pastors of the Richmond Park church. Rev. Smee was thus involved in the big building program there and gave fine leadership to the project.

When the Demetres furloughed in 1971, Rev. and Mrs. Earl Wheeler were transferred to Montego Bay from Trinidad. From here they pastored the Castle Mountain church and continued the services in Montego Bay, finishing out their term there in 1974. By that time a national pastor, Rev. George Thomas, was ready to take over the Montego Bay work, while Rev. and Mrs. William Pease, missionaries from India, were assigned to the Castle Mountain church. They remained for the year 1974-75 while Rev. Pease was convalescing from a cornea transplant operation. They then returned to India.

On July 21, 1972, Rev. Ralph Cook retired from missionary service, and his place as district superintendent was taken by Rev. Jerry

Demetre, who had just returned from furlough. One of his early responsibilities was to direct the construction of a commodious church building in Montego Bay.

The First District Assembly

The year 1975 was a memorable one in the history of the Jamaica work. It was the date of the first district assembly held at Richmond Park in October. Although similar gatherings had been held previously, they were not officially recorded as district assemblies. At the assembly, three men received ordination at the hands of General Superintendent V. H. Lewis: Noel Williams (formerly of the Wesleyan church), Wilford Nelson, and Victor Wright. Ten churches were reported with a total membership of 500.

Not long after the assembly, negotiations were begun concerning the incorporation of the 295-member Gospel Center Association into the Church of the Nazarene. A number of years before, this work had been started in western Jamaica by a dynamic Black woman, Miss Amis. Now at retirement age, she wanted to ensure continuity for her mission, which consisted of a main center called Mount Shiloh where there was a Christian academy (high school) and a large tabernacle for camp meetings and other gatherings. In addition there were about 10 surrounding churches. After careful study by the church, it was agreed to accept the group. Each member was received individually, however.

Rev. Smee realized the importance of training these new pastors in Nazarene ways and supplementing what previous studies they had had. To accomplish this, he moved to Mandeville, where he would be closer to them and yet readily accessible to Kingston for district supervision. Using the extension courses out of CNTC, which were based on the *Manual* course of study for ministers, he held classes and conducted correspondence courses. By 1978 five of the pastors had completed the work and were ordained.

The acquisition of these churches gave new impetus to the Jamaica work. Soon several young people were being called into the ministry and were enrolling at CNTC. There was still need for a training center on the island, however, and property for that purpose was purchased at Mandeville in 1980.

In 1977, at the third annual district assembly, the Jamaica field was elevated to national-mission district status, and General Superintendent Orville W. Jenkins presented the name of Rev. Noel O. Williams, pastor of the Richmond Park church, as nominee for district superintendent. He was elected and in subsequent years was continuously reelected to office.

That same year the Smees had to return to the United States for health reasons, and the following year the Demetres also left. Rev. Williams missed their guidance and help, particularly in the area of ministerial training. Rev. Armand Doll, former missionary to Mozambique, was named mission director and served for two years (1979-80). However, because of political circumstances it was considered wise for him to maintain his home in Florida and commute from there. This limited leadership may, in part, account for the leveling off of the membership total in recent years and an actual decline in 1980 to 1,205. The peak membership of 1,337 was reached in 1979 with 22 churches reporting.

As the group of young pastors began to return from their studies at CNTC in Trinidad, a new surge of optimism and growth began to take hold. In 1984 Rev. Wilford Nelson was named district superintendent, and by 1985 membership was up to 1,510 with 23 organized churches in operation.

7. *Barbados*

The oldest Nazarene field in the English-speaking West Indies is geographically the smallest. Barbados, often called "Little England" because of its lengthy period under British rule and its affinity for things British, extends only 21 x 14 miles. It is the most southeasterly of the chain of islands that make up the Lesser Antilles.

The work on the island began in the heart of Rev. J. I. Hill, superintendent of the Southern California District, who was struggling with what he felt to be a call of God to Africa. While in the throes of decision, he met Rev. J. D. Scott, one of three area foreign mission superintendents that the Department of Foreign Missions had elected in the early 1920s to supervise its work abroad. Rev. Scott's area was the Americas and the West Indies.

He told Rev. Hill of those unevangelized islands full of people of African origin and whose language was English. Rev. Hill was intrigued. Could this be the answer to the tug he felt within? Only a few days later he went to Kansas City to seek appointment as a missionary to these islands.

But it was 1926, and the church was already in a period of retrenchment. Furthermore he was filling an important post where he was, and at 44 he was past the age when missionaries were usually sent out. But so convinced was he that this was God's will for his life, he threatened to go on his own if the church would not commission him. So he was sent on his way with the broad title of district superintendent of the West Indies.

He went to Barbados first because Rev. Scott had visited a group there that called themselves the Church of the Nazarene and had expressed the desire to become officially part of the denomination. In fact, a few months before the Hills went there, Dr. H. F. Reynolds, general superintendent, also visited the group that was led by Rev. S. A. Miller. Another member of the Barbados group was Miss Carlotta Graham, whom Rev. Hill met at the first service he held in Barbados, August 31, 1926.

Carlotta Graham had migrated to the United States 13 years before, had met up with the Church of the Nazarene in Brooklyn, and feeling a call to the ministry, had graduated from Eastern Nazarene College. She returned to Barbados at the time of her mother's death in perhaps 1925 and elected to stay, seeking a place of ministry there. Friends in Brooklyn told Rev. Hill about her, so it was no chance meeting on that first Sunday.

He asked her to become a part of the missionary team, and after some prayer she felt this to be God's open door for her. Leaving her to conduct revival meetings in Barbados, Rev. Hill went on to Trinidad. There he saw evidence of such need that he called for Carlotta Graham to come and help him. And thus it was that in Trinidad she would invest the greater part of her remaining days.

Dr. H. F. Reynolds came in 1927 to hold the first district assemblies on the islands. Though actually only one district (West Indies), sessions were held in Barbados on July 30, and Trinidad on August 16. Eight churches were reported on Barbados with a total membership of 289. Apparently Trinidad, without the running start that Barbados had, did not report any organized work as yet.

The Hills received only a bare subsistence check from Headquarters, but by such activities on the side as raising hogs, dealing in real estate, and refinishing furniture, he was able to put money into the work and won the undying devotion of his pastors.

After two years, spent mostly in Trinidad, the Hills moved back to Barbados, where the greatest number of churches were and where the climate was more healthful for them. In 1930 Rev. and Mrs.

George Surbrook, already on the field working for another mission, transferred to the Church of the Nazarene and served for about four years in both Trinidad and Barbados.

The second district assembly was conducted in 1931 by General Superintendent J. B. Chapman, with sessions in Trinidad on March 13 and Barbados on March 27. Carlotta Graham was ordained at the first session, and S. A. Miller at the second. From then on assemblies were held almost every year, but beginning in 1939 sessions were held in Barbados only. In 1942 Trinidad was set apart as a separate district.

In the mid-1930s Rev. Hill had been confronted with some serious charges of alleged misconduct that threatened to undermine the work or at least destroy his usefulness. However, at the 1936 Barbados assembly session, he received a unanimous vote of confidence on a ballot vote by the 85 delegates, and a subsequent thorough investigation by the general church absolved him of all blame.

In 1937 Rev. and Mrs. Robert Danielson were officially accepted into the missionary force. They had come to the island on their own, bypassing regular channels, and had had to do some backtracking to receive regular appointment. Miss Mamie Bailey, who had come with them, had to be returned to the United States because the board could not afford to send a companion single lady missionary, which they felt she should have.

In 1939 Rev. Hill's health failed. His stomach ulcers, no doubt aggravated by the legal ordeal he had been put through, had become critical, and two months after the assembly, on May 20, he and Mrs. Hill, who was ill herself, were forced to return to the United States permanently. They had served continuously on the field for 13 years with only two short business trips home. During that time the number of churches had grown to 16 with about 800 members.

Shortly after the Hills' departure, Rev. Danielson was named district superintendent. His particular concern was that the church and parsonage buildings be improved. The image of the church was suffering because of the many "mere shacks" that were used for churches. He instituted a construction, repair, and refurbishing program that included the erection of a large stone church in Bridgetown that would seat 800-1,000.

Rev. and Mrs. James Jones and their family arrived as missionaries in December 1945. The following year Mrs. Danielson died, and Rev. Danielson and his two boys returned to the United States. For the next four years Rev. Jones served as superintendent. During the Joneses' extended furlough from 1949 to 1952, the work was in the charge of Dr. and Mrs. A. O. Hendricks. He had been a well-known church leader and college president in the United States, and she was the former Mamie Bailey who had spent a short period in Barbados in 1937.

In 1952, along with the returning Jones family, came Rev. and Mrs. Lawrence Faul and their two children. They were beginning the longest record of missionary service in the history of the Barbados field—17 years. His particular concern in the beginning was the training of ministers, for few of the pastors had had any special instruction. The general education level of ministers needed to be raised as well, for the literacy rate in Barbados is high, and a matching educated ministry was needed if the church were to attract new people.

The year before, however, a more advanced education program had begun when the Nazarene Training College was opened in Trinidad. So in 1953 the first two students from Barbados enrolled there— Miss Eileen Squires and Clyde Gittens (whose name was later changed to Greenidge). They took the special, accelerated, two-year course that was temporarily introduced to speed up pastoral training. They were back in Barbados in July 1955. The island continued to send carefully selected and capable students to the college, so that over the ensuing years a higher percentage of Barbados graduates went on to successful Christian ministry than those of any other country.

At the 1953 Barbados assembly, presided over by Dr. C. Warren Jones, general secretary of the Department of Foreign Missions, a total of 31 churches and 1,217 members were reported.

To this point a weak phase of the program had been in the area of finance. Thus when on September 22, 1955, Hurricane Janet struck, completely demolishing 9 churches and damaging 18 others, the effect was devastating. But shortly afterward, Mrs. Louise R. Chapman, general president of the Nazarene Foreign Missionary Society, came to the district. Visiting at one of the quarterly meetings held regularly on the district, she took a pledge offering to help these churches recover from their losses. She was not impressed, however, with the amount that came in, and so when it came time for her to preach, she used her famous sermon, "If You Don't Like It, Change It!"

At the close of the message she frankly told the people she did not like the offering they had given earlier in the service, so she proposed to change it. God used her dynamic spirit to prompt the people to pledge a total of $1,427.52, a good offering for that time and in that economy. Best of all, a new concept of giving was generated.

On a district tour a short time later in which the speaker was Rev. John S. Lal of Trinidad, tithing was the emphasis. The result was astounding. Most churches more than doubled their giving that year, and 14 of them began giving 10 percent of their offerings for world evangelism.

Hurricane Janet proved to be a blessing in disguise in another way, too, for most of the buildings lost were poor structures anyway. More substantial and commodious buildings replaced them. Several were relocated to more advantageous sites.

While Dr. and Mrs. Hendricks were on the field, they began to cultivate the idea of building a district center, and they and their families challenged the General Board by contributing $8,500 to purchase the necessary property. Other contributions brought the total to over $20,000. Rev. Faul directed the design and construction of a large, open-sided tabernacle on the property, the first of several buildings ultimately erected. Mrs. Louise Chapman was present for the groundbreaking ceremony on October 6, 1955—the same visit in which she had presented her message: "If You Don't Like It, Change It!"

A year later the beautiful tabernacle seating 2,000 was completed, with Rev. Paul Orjala from Haiti as the speaker for the opening convention. A few weeks later, on November 11, 1956, Dr. G. B. Williamson, general superintendent, formally dedicated the structure. Of the total cost of $42,000, some $18,000 remained to be paid. The general church promised to match dollar-for-dollar any money raised by the district to pay off the debt. The Easter offering the following spring was to be applied to this need, and the district's entire $9,000 was raised. "It was a financial miracle," said District Superintendent Jones.

Quarterly district rallies had been started back in J. I. Hill days, but now with a district center these meetings took on new significance. They became a hallmark of the work, and capacity crowds attended the great gatherings.

When the Joneses left the district in 1958 to take up a new assignment in the Panama Canal Zone, Rev. Faul became superintendent. By this time, Rev. and Mrs. Robert Brown had joined the missionary family, serving from 1956 to 1967. They were formerly missionaries to Pakistan under the Calvary Holiness church of Great Britain.

As more and more students returned from the college in Trinidad, the district program was enlarged. In 1961 the first district youth camp was held. The leader was the district NYPS president, Winston Best, a graduate of CNTC, and the speaker was Rev. Russell Brunt of the college faculty. In 1976, with the help of a Work and Witness team from the United States, a separate district youth center was built.

In 1965 tent evangelism was begun, and the following year the NYPS bought a portable organ to go with the district tent. That year, 1966, Barbados received its independence from Great Britain, which heightened the sense of nationalism and perhaps helped to hasten the transfer of district leadership from missionaries to nationals.

During the 1960s several missionary couples served short terms of service in Barbados: Rev. and Mrs. Clayton Garner (1961-65), Rev. and Mrs. Larry Webb (1963-66), Rev. and Mrs. Paul Beals, Rev. and Mrs. Charles Fountain, Rev. and Mrs. Elvin DeVore, and Rev. and Mrs. Jerry Demetre. All of these did missionary work in other fields, and Rev. Demetre was mission superintendent in Barbados while the Samuel Taylors were on furlough, 1969-70. During their next term, 1970-74, the Taylors were the only missionaries on the field—and the last to reside there.

The climax of indigenous development came in August 1971, when Dr. Edward Lawlor, general superintendent, appointed Rev. Clyde Greenidge district superintendent. In the words of Field Superintendent Rev. Samuel Taylor, it was "the crossroad in the history of our work here in the island of Barbados." In 1974 the Taylors were transferred to the Bahamas, and since that time the Barbados District, with national-mission status, has been virtually on its own with occasional visits from the Mission Council chairmen, which have included Rev. Gene Smith (stationed in St. Lucia), Rev. Samuel Taylor (Bahamas), and Robert Ashley (St. Lucia).

By 1976 Barbados achieved mission district status by virtue of achieving 50 percent self-support and was fully represented at the General Assembly that year. One of the lay representatives was Grey Forde from the Speightstown church, who was elected a member of the General Board for the quadrennium representing the Intercontinental Zone II (Mexico, Central and South America, and the Caribbean).

With the achievement of mission district status came the responsibility to elect their own district superintendent. Rev. Greenidge, who had been the appointed superintendent up to this point, received a strong vote to continue with a two-year extended call, which was subsequently renewed in 1978. This was the 50th anniversary year of the district, and various celebrations were planned throughout the year, including a major rally in August commemorating the arrival of the J. I. Hills.

Though the Barbados work showed phenomenal growth in the first years, it subsequently leveled off considerably. The 1985 figures showed 32 churches, the same number as in 1956. Membership stood at 1,828, still short of the oft-repeated goal of 2,000. However, the work had attained Phase 4 (regular) district status and had been experiencing an upturn in growth.

The little island might be considered overchurched, generally, and perhaps 32 Nazarene churches in so small an area is an adequate number. But there are many thousands still who need the Lord, and the challenge to engage in aggressive evangelism still lay before the Barbadian church.

8. *Trinidad and Tobago*

At the end of the island chain of the Lesser Antilles, just six miles from the South American coast, is the island of Trinidad, second only to Jamaica in size among the English-speaking islands of the Caribbean. It is roughly 65 miles north-to-south and 48 miles east-to-west and has a population of about 1.3 million. The people are 43 percent Black and 36 percent East Indian (mostly Hindu but 6 percent Muslim), and the remainder largely mixed.

Twenty miles to the northeast is the tiny, 113-square-mile island of Tobago, which is a ward of Trinidad and thus considered a part of it.

The Church of the Nazarene Enters Trinidad

As noted in the Barbados story, the Trinidad work was a spin-off of the mission in Barbados, 200 miles away. The invitation for Rev. J. I. Hill to visit Trinidad in 1926 came from a Mr. Chester, who had founded an independent church in Port of Spain and had expressed a desire to unite with the Church of the Nazarene. Rev. Hill had been in Barbados only a short while but accepted the invitation and became so intrigued by the possibilities in Trinidad that he called Carlotta Graham to come and assist.

A preaching point was established at Tunapuna, which Miss Graham began to pastor in January 1927. She was to remain there for the next 38 years, building a very strong congregation. An early convert, Elmena Bailey, became her close associate in the work.

But in March 1927 Mr. Chester, disgruntled with the fact that the financial support he expected was not coming from the Church of the Nazarene, chose to pull out of the association. Rev. Hill hurriedly located property in the Woodbrook section of Port of Spain and before the month was up was advertising the beginning of Nazarene services there. A large crowd came that first Sunday, among them the majority of Mr. Chester's flock, and immediately a substantial congregation was brought together. In the first four months, 66 people joined the Church of the Nazarene.

In 1928 the Hills returned to Barbados and supervised the Trinidad work from there. In 1932 a promising young man from Barbados was placed in the Port of Spain church. His magnetic personality resulted in a rapidly developing congregation who were blindly loyal to him. But when it was discovered that he had been pocketing the rental money that Rev. Hill had been sending him, a confrontation ensued that even involved Dr. J. B. Chapman, general superintendent, who had come to hold the Trinidad session of the district assembly. The upshot was that the pastor left and started an independent church, taking most of his congregation with him. The total Nazarene membership in Trinidad was cut in half.

The Port of Spain church, however, continued its program. The people worshiped for a number of years in rented quarters until in 1938, with the help of a $1,000 gift from Mrs. S. N. Fitkin, property was purchased in the St. James area. Construction of a church began in 1939, but in the midst of the project, Rev. Hill's health forced him to return to the United States. Carlotta Graham brought the building program through to a successful conclusion with the dedication taking place on January 28, 1940. It was the first church-owned building in Trinidad. Adjacent property was later purchased, and a larger church subsequently built.

Carlotta Graham pastored both Tunapuna and St. James churches for over five years, and even though those were war years and transportation was difficult, the churches combined to open a mission at Four Roads. It was during this time also that Carlotta Graham purchased a piece of property in Tunapuna, and with the help of a $500 gift from Dr. and Mrs. Haldor Lillenas, a church was built on it. On April 27, 1941, the building was dedicated to the memory of Mrs. Lillenas' father, General Superintendent W. C. Wilson.

The Barbados and Trinidad fields were officially separated in 1942, but no district assembly was held in Trinidad until November 1956! In the interim many changes took place on the field. The first missionaries appointed exclusively to Trinidad were Rev. and Mrs. Lelan Rogers. They arrived in October 1944 to assume the pastorate of the St. James church and the superintendency of the field.

It was during the Rogers era that the first work was opened among the East Indians. Rev. Rogers had come in contact with a young electrician, John Sonny Lal, son of an East Indian contract worker. During World War II, John was working at Waller Air Force Base, and Rev. Rogers was the regular speaker at the Wednesday chapel services there. John, who had already been converted from Hinduism, attended the services, and Rev. Rogers was able to lead him into the experience of entire sanctification. Sensing the call of God to the ministry, he pioneered the first Nazarene work in the South at Couva. Later he opened work at Arima and Five Rivers. It was while he was serving the Arima church for the second time that he passed away at the age of 46. But he had given about 25 fruitful years of service to God and the church.

The Rogerses had been in Trinidad only a year when a call came from a group of three independent holiness congregations in British Guiana on the nearby north coast of South America. They desired to unite with the Church of the Nazarene, and following their being received, the supervision of this new area was added to Rev. Rogers' responsibilities.

In 1946 the Trueman Sheltons arrived in Trinidad to share some of the load. This made it possible for the Rogerses to move to British Guiana in 1947, from which base they supervised the work in Trinidad. The St. James church was flourishing under the Sheltons' ministry when suddenly Mrs. Shelton's health broke, and they were forced to return to the United States. Shortly thereafter, the Rogerses were scheduled for furlough.

The situation would have been critical except that Dr. and Mrs. A. O. Hendricks were available to fill in for a year. But they were interested in more than a mere holding action. Dr. Hendricks, former president of Pasadena College, instituted a training program for the pastors, while Mrs. Hendricks held revivals and directed the building of a church at Arima. Together they supervised the work on the two fields, British Guiana and Trinidad.

The Miller Era of Growth

Just before the departure of the Hendrickses for Barbados in July 1949, the Ray Millers and their two children arrived to take charge of the work. They were veterans of 19 years' missionary endeavor in Africa under the Pilgrim Holiness church, and he had more recently been teaching for several years at Bethany Nazarene College. He brought to the field a stability and expertise that were desperately needed at that time. Public relations and church planting were his forte, and some 25 Sunday Schools and preaching points were opened up throughout the island during his term of leadership.

Rev. Miller also involved himself with several ecumenical activities and encouraged the building of modern and substantial churches. The name of the Church of the Nazarene thus became known and respected throughout the island.

The crowning achievement of their six years on the island was the establishment of the Bible college, which eventually became the training center for all the English-speaking Caribbean countries. The supply of preachers coming from this school made possible the rapid expansion of the field.

During the six-year Miller superintendency, five new missionaries arrived on the field: Wesley and Modelle Harmon, Howard and Dorothy Sayes, and Ruth Saxon. All served on both the district and in the school until the college was made a separate entity. The Harmons and Miss Saxon then gave their full time to teaching. The Sayeses were involved especially in the South where they established churches at Point Fortin and Vance River, and launched Sunday Schools in numerous outlying communities.

When the Millers left on furlough in 1955, subsequently to be transferred to Taiwan, Rev. Prescott Beals, of India fame, took over as superintendent of the field and as principal of the Bible college. When shortly thereafter the Lelan Rogerses left British Guiana (now Guyana), that field, too, was added to Rev. Beals's responsibilities for some months.

Rev. Beals was a warmhearted brother whom the people loved greatly. He was a staunch believer in holiness revivals, and these were encouraged. But he was also strong on organization. Up to that time, following the Barbados pattern, quarterly district meetings were being held at which all baptisms took place and all members were received into the church. Thus the people joined the district organization, not the local church. Rev. Beals set about to correct this situation.

One of his first moves was to set up a joint committee composed of a few Trinidadian pastors (elected by themselves) and the Mission Council Executive Committee. This group functioned much as a District Advisory Board. Then Rev. Beals saw to it that the local churches were properly organized with a complete church program including Sunday School, missionary society, and youth organization.

The climax came with the first district assembly being held November 23-24, 1956, by Dr. G. B. Williamson, general superintendent. Three pastors were ordained: Basil Moses, John Sonny Lal, and Bertrand Doyle. Assemblies were held annually from then on.

By the time of the first assembly, Mrs. Beals's cancer, which had been in remission, flared up again, and it was necessary for her to return to the United States for surgery. Hoping that they might be able to return eventually, Rev. Beals carried on the supervision of the work from the United States with Rev. Sayes as his field assistant. Finally he submitted his resignation on February 15, 1958, and Rev. Sayes was named superintendent in his place, to serve only until his furlough in August of that year. Rev. Wesley Harmon, just back from furlough, then became superintendent and served for five years.

The Sangre Grande church in the far north, the Piarco church (almost 100 percent East Indian), and the San Fernando church (second-largest city) were all organized during this time. In addition, the Canaan church, the first to be organized on the sister island of Tobago, was launched.

An Independent Nation and an Independent Church

On August 31, 1962, the islands of Trinidad and Tobago won their independence from Great Britain. The rising spirit of nationalism made an emphasis on self-support within the church an appropriate and popular theme. This Rev. Harmon emphasized, and the people responded. Giving greatly increased.

Rev. and Mrs. Russell Brunt joined the missionary team early in 1957 and worked chiefly in the school. Rev. and Mrs. Herb Ratcliff were hurriedly transferred from Guyana in January 1957 to head the school and also to help out in the churches as the need arose. After their furlough in 1965 they were transferred to Puerto Rico; then again in 1972 they returned to head the college, which had just that year been separated from the district work.

In 1958 Rev. and Mrs. Ralph Cook, formerly missionaries to India, arrived. Their most significant contribution, besides the opening of the San Fernando work, was the launching of district youth camps and boys' and girls' camps. These became important annual events attracting about 200 participants in each. The Cooks served until 1966, when they were asked to open the work in Jamaica.

Other missionary couples came in the 1960s to serve in various capacities, including Rev. and Mrs. Bill Fowler (1963), Rev. and Mrs. Bob Caudill (1965), Rev. and Mrs. Wayne Knox (1965), Rev. and Mrs. Lauriston Seaman (1965), Rev. and Mrs. Merlin Hunter (1966), and Mr. and Mrs. George Biggs (1967). The Samuel Taylors, who were transferred from Guyana, served but one year, taking the place of the furloughing Fowlers. The Caudills were the first resident missionaries on Tobago. He also directed the construction of three church buildings on Trinidad, led in the enlargement of the St. James church, and served a seven-month stint as superintendent.

The Knoxes were another couple transferred from Guyana, to which they returned in 1975 for two more years. The Hunters' special project was the district bookstore, while the Seamans and the Victor Duntons (who came in 1976) spent short terms in the college. The Biggses gave 12 years (1967-79) to the education program.

The year 1971 was a watershed in the southern Caribbean. For the first time, national superintendents were appointed in Barbados, Guyana, and Trinidad. In Trinidad the choice fell on Rev. Hugh McKenzie, pastor of the St. James church. By the time of the 1974 assembly he asked that, rather than be appointed, a ballot vote be taken on him. Though he received all but 6 of the 59 votes cast, he was aware that his leadership future was uncertain. Within a year he had left the church and subsequently became pastor of an independent congregation in Petite Valley.

At the 1975 assembly, Dr. Jerald Johnson, then executive secretary of the Department of World Missions, presiding in the place of General Superintendent Orville Jenkins, presented two names for district superintendent, Rev. Carl Bompart and Rev. Farrell Chapman. The count was close, but Rev. Bompart received the largest number of votes. However, at the afternoon session he asked to withdraw, and Rev. Chapman was officially appointed.

In 1976 Trinidad and Tobago attained mission district status, having reached the goal of 50 percent self-support. From then on, Rev. Chapman was elected by regular ballot to serve as district superintendent. Reflecting the quality of his leadership, he was selected in 1980 by the general church as a member of a team to go to Nigeria to help train a group of ministers there who were seeking to join the Church of the Nazarene.

Rev. Wayne Knox was the last Mission Council director, his service terminating when he went on furlough in 1975. Since then, only missionaries assigned specifically to the Caribbean Nazarene Training College have been sent to Trinidad. Ruth Saxon was the last missionary to pastor a church, resigning her Santa Cruz pastorate in 1976. Robert Ashley of St. Lucia was appointed mission director in 1976 and served as liaison between Trinidad and the Department of World Mission until 1981. At that time Rev. Tom Pound, former missionary to Belize, was named mission director of the Caribbean. The Trinidad and Tobago District became a regular district in 1982.

In 1983 Rev. Farrell Chapman was elected president of CNTC, and Rev. Carl Bompart was elected district superintendent of Trinidad and Tobago.

Though the numbers of churches remained quite constant at about 23 from the Miller/Beals era (1958) on, membership on the district steadily increased in that same span, reaching 1,898 in 1985 with 25 churches.

9. *Windward Islands*

As previously mentioned, in July 1975 Dr. Jerald Johnson, executive secretary of the Department of World Missions, arranged a meeting on the island of Antigua with Missionaries Gene Smith, Lawrence Faul, and Robert Ashley to decide how best to form the various islands of the Caribbean into districts. Their recommendation, subsequently adopted and put into effect on September 1, was that there be three districts: (1) the Leeward Islands, (2) the French Antilles, and (3) the Windward Islands. Rev. Faul was named mission director for the first, Rev. Smith for the second, and Mr. Ashley for the third.

By this time, work was already in progress in Barbados and St. Lucia and was due to expand to the other two main islands of the Windward group, St. Vincent and Grenada. Dominica, a British island in the heart of the French Antilles, is geographically one of the Windward Islands but for church organization purposes was made part of the Leeward Islands District.

St. Lucia

The 1939 district minutes of the West Indies District contains a report from Rev. J. I. Hill, the district superintendent living in Barbados, of a contact made by Rev. Joseph Garcia with the island of St. Lucia, 100 miles to the west. It seems that Rev. Garcia had been asked to see if he could start a work there, but apparently he was unsuccessful. Shortly thereafter, Rev. Hill returned to the United States, and the matter was not pursued.

But when Missionary Samuel Taylor, stationed in Barbados (1969-74), came across this note in the minutes, he became intrigued. He discussed the matter with one of the Barbadian pastors, Anthony Bailey, who was a native St. Lucian and still spoke the French Patois language of the island fluently. Also he had kept contact with relatives there. So a scouting trip was arranged in May 1971. The two men found not a single holiness ministry on the island.

What was intended to be merely a scouting trip had gone much farther than expected, so Rev. Taylor immediately wrote to Dr. E. S. Phillips, executive secretary of the Department of World Missions, to tell what had happened. To his surprise, the quick reply from Kansas City was to "proceed with your plans to take the Church of the Nazarene to St. Lucia."

Legal registration of the church was completed on January 20, 1972, and a temporary apartment in the city of Castries was secured for Rev. Taylor to live in when he visited the island. Since Haitian Creole is almost identical with the Patois spoken on St. Lucia, Evans Gramon was brought from Haiti to help start the work. The experiment did not work out, however, and Rev. Gramon returned to his home island.

Little by little, contacts were being made with people who, while living on other islands, had had some contact with the Church of the Nazarene. There was, for example, Mr. Kadan, the taxi driver, who had met C. Helen Mooshian, Nazarene evangelist, when she was holding meetings in his home church (Pilgrim Holiness) in Curaçao. There was also Rita Browne, who had migrated to Guyana 20 years before and was converted in the Wismar church. Rev. Taylor had been her pastor there for a number of years before his transfer to Barbados. He learned that she was visiting her daughter in Castries and so looked her up. It was an emotional reunion! The result was that she moved back to St. Lucia in 1972 and began a backyard Sunday School. She was to become a pillar in the church in coming years.

In 1973 a team of four Student Mission Corps workers, augmented by three helpers from Barbados, along with Rev. Taylor, conducted evangelistic services, a Vacation Bible School, and Sunday School classes on the island. Though there were several conversions, there was no follow-up plan save the Sunday School, which was being faithfully conducted by Rita Browne.

The first major step toward an organized work came in 1973 when the Gene Smiths were appointed as missionaries to St. Lucia. However, they were not able to break away from their responsibilities in Haiti until July 1974. In the meantime, the work was carried on somewhat sporadically by the busy missionary staff from Barbados.

In preparation for the coming of the Smiths, Rev. Taylor found an abandoned soap factory in Castries that with an adjacent building seemed to offer possibilities for a church and parsonage setup. With Rev. Smith's permission it was purchased, and with the help of a Work and Witness team from Michigan and Illinois, led by brother Pastors Harold and Bob Harris, the property was renovated into a presentable chapel. As further preparation for the coming missionaries, a Ford van was purchased, and the "Showers of Blessing" radio broadcast was begun. The minutes of the Barbados District for 1974 listed 6 members in the Castries church, though there was no official organization until February 1976. From the start, attendance at services was averaging 25.

Soon after the Smiths arrived in July 1974, a young graduate of the Caribbean Nazarene Training College in Trinidad, Wilvin Clarke, joined them in the work. He was one of the nationals who had worked with the Student Mission Corps team in 1973 and was the first Th.B. graduate of CNTC after its affiliation with Canadian Nazarene College.

In a few months, a larger building was acquired next to the "soap factory" church, and the latter became a youth activity center. In July 1975 Mr. and Mrs. Robert Ashley, lay missionaries, were transferred from Belize to St. Lucia after 20 years in their former post. When the district structure referred to earlier was effected, the Gene Smiths, following their furlough, were transferred to Martinique, and Robert Ashley became mission director of the pioneer Windward Islands District.

Groups of young people from Detroit First Church and Lansing, Mich., South came that summer to conduct Vacation Bible Schools, a kids' crusade, and a youth camp that were highly successful. Then in August, a five-day evangelistic crusade with Rev. and Mrs. Warren Rogers was held in the city auditorium. Out of this meeting came some excellent members for the church, and the name of the Church of the Nazarene became known throughout the city and island.

In September Wilvin Clarke became pastor of the Castries congregation, and in February 1976 the church was officially organized with 11 charter members.

George Leonce, the first St. Lucia student at CNTC, returned to his hometown of Micoud after his graduation and against great difficulty started a work there. Joseph Young, a CNTC graduate from Guyana, became pastor, and eventually a church was organized on February 17, 1980.

When Wilvin Clarke returned to Barbados in 1976 to take a pastorate there, he was succeeded at Castries by an Antiguan, Clifford Warner. He led the Castries church in the opening of a mission in Gros Islet in the north of the island and resigned his Castries pastorate to take over the leadership of this new group. It was organized into a church in February 1978.

St. Vincent

Rev. Harold Harris, one of the brother pastors who led the Work and Witness team that renovated the soap factory at Castries, St. Lucia, had applied to the Department of World Mission for appointment as a missionary, but he was over the 35-year age limit. Dr. Jerald Johnson suggested, however, that he could be used in special assignments, and so in 1975 he and his wife were sent to Guyana. The following year they were scheduled to go to Jamaica, but since they were not granted the necessary work permits, they were hastily transferred to the Windward Islands for a year. With this unexpected help of an experienced couple available, Robert Ashley quickly went to the neighboring island of St. Vincent, about 25 or 30 miles away, and rented a house. It was ready for the Harrises to move into when they arrived from Guyana in March 1976.

The Harrises began immediately to try to find some starting point for beginning a church, but though they talked to dozens of people, there seemed to be no handle to grasp. Easter Sunday came, and in seeking a place of worship, they chose the Methodist church.

Inadvertently they got into the youth service and also, by coincidence, one of the lay preachers, Harold Johnny, attended the same service. Afterward the three met, and Rev. Harris explained the reason for their being on the island. Being a regular listener to "Showers of Blessing," Mr. Johnny needed no further introduction.

"I have just the building you need," said Mr. Johnny. "Meet me tomorrow morning, and I'll show it to you!"

It was a two-story building, formerly used as a discotheque, in the Cane Hall area of Kingstown. It did indeed seem well suited for the work. A low rental figure of only $90.00 a month (U.S.) was agreed upon. Mr. Johnny redecorated the place, benches were built, a sign put up, and newspaper advertisements were run introducing the Harrises and the Church of the Nazarene.

One who saw the ads was Leon Hinds, a taxi driver from Barbados who had been converted in 1944 under the ministry of Rev. Charles S. Jenkins, missionary to Africa. Rev. Jenkins was filling in in Barbados for that particular year. Shortly afterward Mr. Hinds moved to St. Vincent and had been praying ever since (some 30 years) that the Church of the Nazarene would come to his island. He joined in the final preparations for the opening service and, mounting loudspeakers on his taxi, he drove around advertising the big day, May 30, 1976.

Forty-five people attended the opening service, which was followed by a week-long evangelistic crusade with Pastors Wilvin Clarke and George Leonce as speakers and David Harris, Rev. Harris' son, as song evangelist. David stayed all summer, developing an activity program for the young people. When Pastor Clifford Warner came to assist in the St. Vincent field on July 18, the Harrises were able to give extra time to the Rilland Hill work.

The Cane Hall church was organized on October 24, 1976. Leon Hinds, one of the charter members, took a special interest in Rilland Hill and urged that a larger place be rented. He personally supervised the fixing up of the new building that also had been a discotheque. His faith was rewarded when at the first service on December 26, some 180 people were present. This was amazing in so small a community. A schoolteacher, Joseph Abraham, became a pillar in this new congregation and ere long answered God's call to the ministry. He began his studies at CNTC in August 1978.

On the Harrises' second Easter Sunday on St. Vincent there were 222 in Sunday School, 111 in Cane Hall and 111 at Rilland Hill.

Unfortunately their residence permits had run out, and they were assigned elsewhere. The young congregations were now without a pastor, and though various ministers came to the island for short periods, the uncertainty took its toll. Were it not for Joseph Abraham, who gave devoted lay leadership to Rilland Hill and occasionally spoke at Cane Hall, losses would have been even greater.

But in May 1978 Rev. and Mrs. Zephaniah Appalsammy Mahadeo, from Guyana, came to the Cane Hall pastorate and had great success. Within a year he had baptized 20 converts and took 22 into membership. In two years' time Cane Hall membership went from 18 to 52.

The Rilland Hill church was officially organized on September 24, 1978, with 10 members, and in May 1980 Rev. George Leonce became pastor. Rev. Mahadeo was ably assisted by some interns from CNTC who spent their required years of field service on St. Vincent. These were Victor Price, Geoffrey Alleyne, and her own native son, Joseph Abraham.

In September 1980 a Work and Witness team from the Washington Pacific District came to begin the construction of a church building for Cane Hall. They also gave $20,000 to the project. Challenged by this, the congregation also raised $10,000 toward the cost. The new structure proved to be a great asset to the work.

Grenada

The last of the three main islands of the Windward Islands District, Grenada, now became the object of concern for the Ashleys. They had made several investigative trips there but had minimal success until early in 1977, when they made contact with a Mrs. Nelcina Sandy. Once a member of the Point Fortin church in Trinidad, in 1976 she had returned to her native island of Grenada after 30 years' absence. There she had married a childhood friend who was a member of a holiness church, and they were living at a place called Happy Hill. She was delighted to meet the Ashleys, and both she and her husband agreed to help get a work started.

The first step was to officially register the Church of the Nazarene with the government, which was granted in May 1977. Daryl and Brenda Johnson, Student Mission Corps workers from Nazarene Theological Seminary, were then scheduled for a week of opening services in August. Mrs. Sandy had a specific burden for the villages of Fontenoy and Grand Mal and began an intensive search in that area for a suitable place in which to hold the meetings. She met with no success except for an unfinished house in Grand Mal that she hesitated to rent, though time was running out.

On Sunday, August 7, she learned of a three-bedroom house in Fontenoy that had just been vacated, and by 4 P.M. the following day she had the keys. Services were scheduled to begin Wednesday night, so the Sandys and the Johnsons, who had just arrived, went to work building benches and otherwise preparing the meeting place. At the same time they were getting the word around that services were about to begin. Mr. Sandy's open-air bus, Ebenezer, was used to carry material, people, and posters.

Seventy people showed up for the first service. The next day children's services were started, and excitement was high. The first three converts were saved Friday night. Sunday was a rainy day, but there were 52 in Sunday School and 30 in the closing service. The response of the people was warm and encouraging. The Sandys moved into part of the house to serve as pastors of the infant congregation.

Early in 1979 Rev. Zephaniah Mahadeo from St. Vincent held a successful week of special services, and on May 22 the church was officially organized.

In February 1980 Rev. and Mrs. Berge Najarian, former Holy Land missionaries, came, and with the help of another Student Mission Corps group, a very productive evangelistic campaign was held. In the meantime, two former CNTC students, Dawson and Sattie Neckles, had settled in the village of Munich, and with their help it was planned to open a work in that area of the island.

The surprise invasion of the island in October 1983 by United States and other forces thwarted a Communist takeover, and missionary work continued unabated.

The Windward Islands District

The first assembly of the district was held March 13, 1978, in Castries, St. Lucia, with Dr. George Coulter, general superintendent, presiding. Three churches with 60 members constituted the beginnings of this pioneer district. Pastors George Leonce and Clifford Warner were ordained.

By the time of the 1979 assembly there were four churches with 106 members, a 77 percent increase. At the 1980 assembly the district was declared a national-mission district, and Rev. Zephaniah Mahadeo was appointed superintendent. Six organized churches were reported with 152 members. Per capita giving was up to $118.33, a great achievement considering the economy of the islands. Five students from the district were enrolled at CNTC. By 1985 there were nine organized churches with 284 members.

10. *The French Antilles*

One of the newest Nazarene fields in the Caribbean is the French Antilles, situated midway along the eastern rim of the island chain. The main islands of the group are Guadeloupe (actually two islands separated by a narrow channel) and Martinique. As previously stated, they are overseas departments (states) of France and predominantly Roman Catholic. The earlier resistance to the preaching of the gospel was melting in more recent years, however, and the islands seemed ripe for an evangelistic thrust when the Church of the Nazarene launched its effort in the late 1970s.

In May 1976 the Gene Smiths left St. Lucia on furlough, and anticipating their going to Martinique to open up this pioneer district, they took a summer school refresher course in French. Their earlier term in Haiti had given them some French background, though they had worked almost exclusively in Creole. Rev. and Mrs. John Seaman were appointed new lay missionaries to assist the Smiths, but the plan was for them to learn the language on location. As far as was known, there was no foundation whatever upon which to begin the Nazarene work—no property, no people, and no holiness witness.

The Seamans were scheduled to go to Guadeloupe in late 1976, but the imminent eruption of Mount Soufriere, the volcano that dominates the southwestern end of the island, caused the evacuation of 70,000 people to the city of Pointe-à-Pitre where the Seamans had expected to locate. No housing was available. They were, therefore, directed to go to Martinique, where they found a good language teacher and a comfortable basement apartment in the home of one of the evangelical Christians on the island.

The Seamans arrived November 1, 1976, but the Smiths did not come until September 1977. After the Smiths' arrival a small Bible study fellowship was begun in the Smith home with a group of teens and young adults. Unfortunately, the Seamans' language teacher became too ill to carry on, and the young missionaries went through a frustrating period trying to find the instructor they needed. After 18 months on the island they were sent to a missionary language school in France, where they studied from May 1978 to July 1979.

While the Seamans were away, Brenda Gould was transferred from Haiti to develop a children's work, which was her specialty. Since half the population was under 20 and half of those were under 10, this was a fruitful field of work that opened the doors to many a home. Since there was very little holiness literature in the French language, translation became an important task. The help of Roberto Manoly in Haiti was a great asset in this phase of the work. Another prime need was to find suitable property. The culture of the people was such that a good building would be needed. A long and diligent search finally came to a climax in August 1979, when an ideal building was found on one of the main streets in the city of Fort-de-France. A Work and Witness team from the Seamans' home church in Olathe, Kans., came down in December to adapt the building for church use, and immediately afterward regular services began.

But progress was slow, for the people were skeptical of this new group. However, starting with personal neighborhood contacts, friendships were established, and prejudice was gradually broken down. A well-promoted revival campaign in April 1980, with Rev. Adrien-David Robichaud of Quebec, brought the first major breakthrough. "That campaign," wrote John Seaman, "was, in our opinion, the real birthdate of the church here." Soon the church was averaging 50-60 in attendance, and the local people were beginning to assume responsibilities in the work.

The church was organized as the Bellevue Church in March 1981 with a membership of 19. A full program was instituted, including a strong missionary emphasis that included General Budget and Alabaster giving, and short- and long-range plans were made for the future. Brenda Gould launched a Caravan program, and a teen choir and a youth club were begun.

An immediate need was to find and train Martinican pastors. The first break in this direction came when Georges Carole enrolled at CNTC in 1981 to prepare for the ministry. However, since classes are in English, only those, like Georges, who had reasonable proficiency in English could be trained there. A school program for Martinique itself was therefore considered essential.

This critical need was met with the arrival in the summer of 1982 of Teryl and Kathy Ketchum, who had been in language school in France. Starting with the limited school program already under way,

Rev. Ketchum developed a cycle of studies roughly equivalent to the denominational course of studies for ministers. By 1985 10 students were enrolled in the Bible institute, and another 10 had taken at least one class. Three other students who had the necessary knowledge of English had enrolled in CNTC, including Georges Carole, while still another was headed for European Nazarene Bible College in Switzerland.

In 1982 the Godissard Church was organized. It showed good promise until personality problems within the church along with the necessary removal of the pastor brought the church near to collapse. Only one faithful couple, the Emile Rodins, remained. But then François Belrose, a student at the Bible institute, and his wife were asked to lead the congregation. This dedicated couple proved to be God's instrument of healing for this troubled church. Eight months after he took over, François reported to the district assembly that membership was up to 15. It should be noted that the Bellevue Church had "loaned" members to help make this recovery possible.

In September 1984 a third church was organized at Morne Venté. Rev. Georges Carole, with his new wife (and former English tutor), was installed as pastor. He had just graduated from CNTC—its first French graduate. Again the Bellevue Church gave a number of members and adherents to start this new church.

Another role Rev. Ketchum was to fill was as a building coordinator. With property and construction costs high, the young Martinique churches had to rely strongly on Alabaster funds and Work and Witness teams to help meet their building needs. The Bellevue Church, having outgrown their original rented quarters, were able to buy a building directly across the street. This was a much larger house, and when the remodeling was completed, they had a 200-seat sanctuary, plus Sunday School rooms, a fellowship room, and offices.

The Morne Venté Church was the first to have a new building. In this project Terry Ketchum was assisted by Abbie Culp, a layman from the United States who spent six months there. The beautiful, octagonal building, designed by David Hayse, coordinator of the Work and Witness program of the Church of the Nazarene, was built largely by five Work and Witness teams.

The French Antilles District was officially organized in March 1983 by Dr. Mark Moore (substituting for General Superintendent Johnson). By 1985 there were three churches, all with national pastors, and a total membership of 85. Average attendance at services, however, was usually about 200.

Evangelism continued to be an important ingredient in the development of the work, particularly because the holiness message was entirely new to the people. Unusually effective was the ministry of Victor Price from nearby St. Lucia. The developing French literature program of the International Publications Board also gave promise of being an important adjunct to the work.

11. *The Bahama Islands*

The Bahamas, scattered around 70,000 square miles of the western Atlantic just north of the Caribbean Islands and off the coast of Florida, consist of nearly 700 islands, only 30 of which are inhabited, plus over 2,000 cays or islets. Eighty-five percent of the inhabitants are Black, and English is the official language.

An independent missionary, Rev. G. T. Bustin, who had first begun work in the Bahamas, went to Haiti in the late 1940s and established a Bible school near the northern city of Cap Haitien.

Among his converts in the Bahamas was Rosalyn (Rose) Henfield who, with others, went to Mr. Bustin's Bible school in Haiti. There she met and, in 1950, married Massillon Pierre. The young couple pastored one of Mr. Bustin's churches in Haiti for a time, but when their leader left to start a mission in far-off New Guinea and began closing down some of his Haitian work, the Pierres cast their lot with Rev. Paul Orjala and the Church of the Nazarene. Massillon Pierre's great contribution in Haiti has been chronicled earlier in this chapter.

When in the late 1960s Rose's mother, now living in Nassau, became ill, Rose went to be with her. Convinced that her mother needed her, she began putting pressure on her husband to come to the Bahamas. Large numbers of Haitians were migrating there anyway, she said, and he would have ample opportunity for ministry. She appeared to be adamant about it, so Massillon gave in, and in 1969 he and the children joined her in Nassau.

Rev. Pierre found work as a truck driver for a building supply company, but he knew he could not remain long in secular employment. He wrote to the Nazarene Headquarters about opening a work in the Bahamas, and he was given a green light.

Providentially he met Dr. Walker, a physician, who with his schoolteacher wife was much interested in helping the disadvantaged. They had built, mostly with their own hands, a four-story building that included a large auditorium on the second floor and dormitory rooms on the third and fourth. When Mrs. Walker showed the building to Massillon Pierre, it was dusty and festooned with cobwebs. But what an ideal setup for a church! mused Rev. Pierre.

He got permission to use the building and began services there in August 1971. Even though the work was predominantly Haitian and services were conducted in French and Creole, so many English-speaking Bahamians were attracted to the place that soon bilingual services through interpreters were begun. In a few years' time, the church had a membership of 200 and a Sunday School enrollment of over 600. Attendance at services often reached above 400.

Rev. Gene Smith, mission director in Haiti, was asked to supervise the work, and he made occasional visits, but apparently no official organization was effected. When Rev. Smith was transferred to St. Lucia in 1973, Dr. Paul Orjala, serving as interim mission director in Haiti, took over the Bahamas responsibility, making quarterly visits.

Massillon Pierre was quite aware of the cultural gulf between the Bahamians and the Haitians. He also realized the transient nature of the Haitian population, most of whom were waiting to go on to the United States or else were illegal immigrants subject to deportation at any time. If a permanent work were to be established, it would have to be among the Bahamians. This in no way detracted from the need. to minister to the Haitians as well, however, and Massillon Pierre was God's man for this task.

By 1972 Anderson Sands and Freddie Newton had begun separate Bahamian churches in Nassau under the banner of the Church of the Nazarene. The Sands work was beset with problems, and in three years' time, there remained only 14 members, all women. The Newton project, sponsored by Massillon Pierre's church, was actually a mission in a depressed area of Nassau.

When Rev. Samuel Taylor was transferred from Barbados to become superintendent of the Bahamas in late 1974, the situation was not very promising. To add to the problem, Rev. Sands, who was supposed to be working with the government on incorporation papers for the Church of the Nazarene, was not following through properly. Further complications arose with both Sands and Newton, and the situation between them and District Superintendent Taylor deteriorated to the point where their connection with the district had to be terminated. Now free from the friction of these entanglements, the work took on new vigor.

Exciting developments were already taking place. Even before the Taylors' arrival, Massillon Pierre, ever the evangelist, had gone to the island of Eleuthera, about 65 miles east of Nassau, and succeeded in establishing two more Haitian churches there.

In 1975 there was an unusual development on the island of Grand Bahama, 100 miles north of Nassau and only about 65 miles off the Florida coast. Just outside the city of Freeport, two sisters and their husbands, the Outtens and the Rolles, felt led to build a beautiful church building by the sea. Through mutual friends of Rev. Sands they had learned of the Church of the Nazarene and, after meeting Rev. Taylor and studying the church *Manual,* turned their building over to the Nazarenes. A church was organized (called Eight Mile Rock), and in two years' time there were 100 members and a Sunday School of 300.

In the meantime, Rev. Taylor was searching for property on which to erect a church building for Bahamians in Nassau. Finally he located a tract on East Street in the south part of the city near where some new housing areas were being developed, and construction of a church building began in September 1975. The cornerstone was laid by General Superintendent V. H. Lewis when he came to hold the first district assembly in October. By the time of the assembly, the incorporation of the church in the Bahamas had been finalized.

In January 1976 John Forde of Guyana, who had worked with Rev. Taylor in both Guyana and Barbados, came to assist in the Nassau Central Church project. The building was completed in May and dedicated in July, but still it had no members. Immediately following the dedication, however, a group of 40 from the Southwest Indiana District came to conduct Vacation Bible Schools on the district and particularly to help the new Central Church. An excellent group of people was soon drawn to the church, some from the former Sands and Newton organizations, and a substantial congregation developed. This became a center for district activities.

John Forde developed a new church in nearby Yellow Elder, and in less than six months attendance at services was running about 100. The church had an outstanding youth ministry, and out of that group came five or six ministers.

In December 1977 John Forde moved to the island of Eleuthera and began a Bahamian work to augment the two Haitian churches already there.

A group of Nazarenes owned a considerable piece of land at West End on Grand Bahama, about 15 miles from the Eight Mile Rock Church. They offered whatever space was needed to build a church. John Grant, a charter member of Eight Mile Rock, became the pastor of this new congregation.

Attention was finally turned to locating a permanent home for Massillon Pierre's Haitian church in Nassau. A suitable corner lot was found on East Street, the same street Central Church was on but two miles closer to downtown. With the help of Work and Witness teams from South Carolina, Pennsylvania, South Florida, and Kansas districts, a commodious two-story building was erected and dedicated as the Metropolitan Church.

In 1979 the Taylors furloughed, and Central Church had to rely for leadership on lay leaders and occasional visiting ministers until in May 1980 the Russell Lewises, former missionaries to Swaziland, came to pastor the church and to serve as district superintendent. He was followed by Rev. Hilton Outten in 1983. The 1985 statistics showed 11 churches on three islands with 833 members.

12. *Guyana*

In Nazarene missionary history, the small South American country of Guyana is always associated with the work in the Caribbean rather than with the other countries on the continent. Geographical proximity to the Caribbean work makes the association logical, but historically Guyana and its two neighbors, Dutch Guiana (Suriname) and French Guiana, have always been isolated from the rest of South America anyway.

When Spain and Portugal divided the New World between them by the Treaty of Tordesilla in 1494, the British, Dutch, and French were bypassed as far as South America was concerned. Attempts to gain concessions south of the Amazon were refused, so they settled for a toehold in the insect-ridden swamps of the northern coast. On this "Wild Coast," as it was called, the colonies of British Guiana, Dutch Guiana, and French Guiana eventually emerged.

British Guiana became an independent nation on May 26, 1966, and took the name Guyana. Originally peopled principally by British landholders and their African slaves, the importation of contract workers from India to work the sugarcane fields gradually changed the picture. By 1980 some 55 percent of the 820,000 population were East Indian, 36 percent were Black, and the remainder mostly Amerindian, Chinese, and European. It is the only officially English-speaking South American country. It is also the only one in which Roman Catholicism is not dominant. Its people are 57 percent Christian, 33 percent Hindu, and 9 percent Muslim.

Geographically there are three divisions. The coastal area is a swampy band up to 40 miles wide, much of which is below sea level at high tide. A network of dikes built by the Dutch holds back the sea. Ninety percent of the people live in this agriculturally rich area. Some 75 percent of the land surface is in the equatorial rain forest, mostly undeveloped. But from here comes a large amount of the world's bauxite from which aluminum is made. In between the two areas is a grassy, tree-dotted plain. About 80 percent of the population live directly or indirectly from the production of sugar.

The basic ethnic differences between the Blacks and the East Indians have had much to do with the social and political development of the country. The Blacks, almost all descendants of African slaves, are European in culture and English in language. After emancipation in 1807, they rose steadily to the professions, skilled trades, and government positions. The East Indians (mostly Hindus) came as contract workers, and the majority elected to stay when their contracts expired. Though they now outnumber the Black population, they have not been able to rise as high economically. The resulting tension has made it difficult to integrate the two groups.

The Church of the Nazarene Enters Guyana

The work began in Guyana (then British Guiana) through a request from an established group there to have the Church of the Nazarene take over their mission. Rev. William C. Rice had been affiliated with an independent holiness group called the Christian Mission since 1933 and had worked for them in both New York and Trinidad. In 1941 he had been transferred to what was then British Guiana, 375 miles southeast of Trinidad. For reasons not stated, after two years he began an independent work with congregations in Georgetown, the capital, and Wismar, 65 miles up the Demerara River.

Realizing the need for some permanent affiliation, Rev. Rice invited Rev. Lelan Rogers of the Church of the Nazarene in Trinidad, with whom he had had previous acquaintance, to come to visit his work. The stated intent of the requested visit was to see if the Church of the Nazarene would be willing to take over the work. With the approval of the General Board, Rev. Rogers made the journey in 1945, visiting each congregation and acquainting them with the doctrines and practices of the Church of the Nazarene. Their combined boards voted unanimously to join the Church of the Nazarene, and at the General Board meeting in January 1946, the affiliation was consummated. The credentials of Rev. Rice were recognized, and he continued to serve the church there until his death in 1951.

The first year, Rev. Rogers supervised the work as part of the Trinidad District, but in 1947 a separate district was created, and the Rogerses moved to Georgetown. Here the large Queenstown church was built as a district center, and over 700 people were present for the opening services in 1951. Dr. Hugh C. Benner, general superintendent, dedicated the building officially on June 14, 1953. As many as 2,000 have attended Sunday School there in subsequent years.

In 1952 the Rogerses were forced to return home for health reasons, and their place was taken by Rev. and Mrs. Donald Ault. The work continued to grow, and in 1954 another missionary couple, the Herbert Ratcliffs, were sent to assist. In 1955 the David Brownings were transferred there from British Honduras (Belize) and served until 1971, when they were transferred to the Philippines. Other missionaries who have served in Guyana are Rev. and Mrs. Wayne Knox (1957-67, 1976-78), Rev. and Mrs. Sam Taylor (1960-67), Rev. and Mrs. Peter Burkhart (1962-72), Rev. and Mrs. Jerry Demetre (1962-69), and Rev. and Mrs. Robert Brown (1969-79). The latter were British missionaries formerly in Pakistan under the Calvary Holiness church, and then in Barbados since 1956.

Meanwhile, in March 1953 another independent church at Victoria, 18 miles down the coast from Georgetown, was turned over to the Church of the Nazarene. In July 1953 work was begun at Herstelling, 6 miles up the river from Georgetown. On October 25, 1953, the church at Wismar was organized, and a month later their new building was dedicated. March 17, 1954, saw the organization of a church at Friendship near the Suriname border.

In 1955 the important city of New Amsterdam was entered. Beginning in a rented store building, the church grew rapidly, and a lot was purchased in one of the most strategic locations in the city. Here a commodious building was erected and the first services held in 1964. Visitors for that event were the Nazarene Evangelistic Ambassadors in the course of their six-weeks tour of Central America and the Caribbean. Their impact on the city was of untold value to the work.

Churches were organized among both Blacks and East Indians; and with white missionaries as part of the mix, Christian charity was put to the test in district affairs. It should be stated also that it was in the mid-1960s that Guyana was going through its struggle for independence. The Blacks and East Indians were vying for power, and at the same time there was a pervasive distaste for all things foreign (which represented the old colonialism). It was not a healthy situation for missionaries, some of whose lives were threatened, nor for their followers. The problem was not adequately resolved until in 1971 Rev. Joseph Murugan was appointed as the first national district superintendent. He was successful in merging the varying elements on the district.

Under Rev. Murugan's dynamic leadership the work grew rapidly. Within 5 years membership was up 70 percent, and the number of churches more than doubled. At the same time, an accelerated program of self-support was instituted with a view to becoming a regular district in 10 years. The goal was reached in 1982.

In 1977 the District Advisory Board launched a program called "Temple, Talent, Time, Tithe" to spark local church growth. "We are asking our laymen," wrote Superintendent Murugan, "to let God become the Resident in their lives—to be His temple. When that is done, then God can use the talent found in the temple. As they give time and tithe for its development, revival will come." The result, as expected, was that not only were the local churches aroused, but there was a new vision to plant new churches, even over in neighboring Suriname.

To infuse the entire region with this same spirit, James Hudson, regional director, in 1983 appointed Rev. Murugan as project coordinator for the English Caribbean area. In his place Rev. Robert Dabydeen was elected district superintendent of Guyana. Growth continued, and by 1985 there were 45 organized churches with a total membership of 3,770 for a quinquennial increase of 73 percent.

13. *Suriname*

The middle one of the three Guianas on South America's northeast coast was Dutch Guiana, which became the independent republic of Suriname on November 25, 1975. It had been acquired by the Dutch from Britain in 1667 in exchange for New Amsterdam, now New York. Dutch influence is still pervasive, particularly in the graceful architecture, the typical Dutch cleanliness and stability, and in the fact that Dutch is still the official language.

The population is heterogeneous. The original inhabitants, the Amerindians, retreated into the interior when the settlers arrived. Negro slaves were imported to work the sugarcane fields, many of whom escaped into the jungle and became the forebears of the present Bush Negroes. When slavery was abolished in 1863, great numbers of the Blacks migrated to the cities and towns. Their places as laborers were taken by contract workers from China, India, and Java, thousands of whom stayed on. Many of the shopkeepers today, for example, are Chinese. Most of the 365,000 inhabitants are either East Indians (35 percent), Creoles (racially mixed descendants of freed slaves, 30 percent), Javanese (15 percent), or Bush Negroes (10 percent). The people are naturally hospitable, tolerant, industrious, and eager to learn. They like to describe themselves as "the small country with the big heart." Thirty percent of the people are involved in agriculture.

There are three basic geographical areas: (1) the coastal plain, 10 to 50 miles wide, much of which is below sea level and protected by an extensive system of dikes; (2) the forest belt, 30 to 50 miles wide; (3) the remote mountain jungle, of which little is known and which takes up 75 percent of the total area of 63,000 square miles. Ninety-two percent of the land is forested, which provides exotic woods for export. Rice, sugar, and fruit are export items, but by far the greatest resource is bauxite, from which 4 million tons of aluminum are smelted each year. The enormous quantity of electricity required for this operation comes from great power dams in the mountain fastnesses of the interior.

The Church of the Nazarene Enters

The first Nazarene gathering in Suriname was a cottage prayer meeting in the capital city of Paramaribo attended by 18 people on August 29, 1982. Key leaders of the all-Guyanese group were Naraine

Moorgan, Ernest Mangah, and Harry Boodhram. The latter, a nephew of the former Guyana district superintendent, Rev. Joseph P. Murugan, had attended CNTC for two years and also pastored two years in Guyana. On January 3, 1983, he became pastor of the emerging flock.

On February 3, 1983, a letter was sent to Dr. L. Guy Nees, World Mission director, inviting him to come and officially organize the group. The upshot was that Suriname was one of the five world areas selected to be opened by the Church of the Nazarene in its 75th year.

In October of that year, Tom Pound, mission director for the Caribbean area, visited the group and helped them with the initial step of registering the church with the government. The papers were duly signed and submitted, but for some reason no action was taken for a year. Finally, with the helpful urging of the Full Gospel Mission and the Moravians, the government granted the necessary certification. One of the problems was that all the signees were Guyanese, many of whom were there on temporary work permits.

As soon as the clearance came, Rev. Jack Armstrong, veteran missionary currently stationed in Guyana, was asked to come to Paramaribo to officially organize the church. The ceremonies took place on October 28, 1984, with 18 people signing the charter.

In March 1985 the church was visited by Rev. Joseph Murugan, now project coordinator for the Caribbean, and the Guyana district superintendent, Rev. Robert Dabydeen. Also visiting that month was Dr. L. Guy Nees from Kansas City. In May a second congregation was brought together in Liverno, on the other side of Paramaribo. Under the leadership of Patrick Pellew, the 16-member group held regular services in English but also conducted a Dutch Sunday School.

After a visit from Regional Director James Hudson in September 1985, two pieces of property were acquired, and several Work and Witness teams were lined up to erect buildings on them. Anticipated assistance from the Netherlands District in Europe in the persons of Dr. Cor Holleman and Rev. Ed Meenderink gave promise of a breakthrough to the Dutch-speaking community.

Only one country in all of South America remained to be entered by the Church of the Nazarene—Suriname's neighbor, French Guiana. This country of only 23,000 inhabitants was once an infamous penal colony. It was now the site of France's launching pad for space rock   Here lay a challenge for the French-speaking districts of the chu~ ~h to reach out to these people with the gospel.

14. *Caribbean Nazarene Theological College*

The story of the work in the Caribbean Islands would not be complete without a brief account of the development of the Caribbean Nazarene Theological College, which is its integrating institution. Its roots go back to the days of Rev. J. I. Hill, who began the first ministerial training program in his own home in Barbados, a project he continued when he moved to Trinidad in 1927. The program was simple—two or three hours of classes every Friday afternoon.

In 1938, after a visit to Trinidad and Barbados, General Superintendent J. G. Morrison recommended to the General Board that a Bible training school be started to serve the two islands. World War II hindered implementation, however.

Finally, in 1948, when Rev. and Mrs. A. O. Hendricks were in Trinidad for a year, a three-month ministerial training school was held with 50 enrolled. This was an important beginning, and when the Ray Millers came the following year, the establishment of a permanent school became one of their top priorities. A 26-acre campus was purchased in the Santa Cruz Valley about 10 miles north of Port of Spain. The large two-story house on the property was converted to classroom and dormitory use, and three smaller cottages were also used for housing. A mission home was built on the hillside. Later an additional 10 acres was purchased. The orange, nutmeg, cocoa, mango, banana, avocado, and coffee trees and bushes on the property provided both food and income for the school.

Classes began on January 3, 1951, with 16 students enrolled, among them 2 from British Guiana (later Guyana). Because of the urgent need for ministers, an accelerated, two-year course of study was instituted. On weekends, each student had an assignment in one of the existing churches or in a beginning Sunday School.

The Millers carried the full teaching load at first and were aided by their daughters, Mary and Ruth, after their graduation from Bethany Nazarene College. Theopilus Harlow, Mahala Clarke, and Basil Moses, all early graduates, assumed leadership in other phases of the college program.

New missionaries coming to the field usually taught classes in addition to pastoring churches. When Ruth Saxon came in 1954, her primary responsibility was the college with weekend preaching added on.

When the Millers left for furlough in 1955, Rev. Prescott Beals, formerly missionary to India, took charge of the school along with the district superintendency. He did much to create a revival spirit on the campus. He also instituted what eventually became a Board of Trustees by calling together in 1955 the district superintendents of Barbados and British Guiana (Rev. James Jones and Rev. Donald Ault, respectively) to discuss ways to improve cooperation with the school among neighboring districts.

In the fall of 1956 Dr. G. B. Williamson, general superintendent, made his first trip to Trinidad. In the course of his visit he invited Rev. and Mrs. Lawrence Faul from Barbados and Rev. and Mrs. Herbert Ratcliff from British Guiana for discussions on the school situation. The result was the appointment of a curriculum committee consisting of Rev. Howard Sayes (Trinidad), Rev. Ratcliff, Rev. Faul, and Miss Ruth Saxon (representing the college). Dr. Williamson also asked that the Trinidad Mission Council meeting be broadened to an "area committee meeting" to discuss other matters related to the college. Four basic decisions were thus made:

1. That the college should henceforth be considered an area school.
2. That the basic course of study be a three-year curriculum based on the *Manual* course of study for ministers.
3. That new students be admitted each year rather than at the end of each cycle.
4. That the head of the college be authorized to call an annual meeting of an area administrative committee.

In January 1957 Rev. Herbert Ratcliff was appointed director of the college, where he served the remaining 2½ years of his term. Upon returning from furlough in 1960, he began another 5 years in that office.

In January 1960 the college received its own budget allotment from the general church separate from the Trinidad budget, and the area board appointed by Dr. Williamson that year became truly representative. This meant the election of two representatives from each participating field (one being the district superintendent) with the college being represented only by the principal. Henceforth this board would act autonomously without reference to any Mission Council.

In 1966 or 1967 the General Board began appointing certain missionaries directly to the college. About this time also the head of the college became known as president. Rev. Wesley Harmon, Rev.

Russell Brunt, and Rev. Herbert Ratcliff have served in that office for varying periods of time.

It was not until 1974 that the official name of the school became Caribbean Nazarene Theological College. Over the years, 14 of the faculty members have been West Indians, but most have been missionaries, a situation gradually swinging toward West Indian predominance.

An extensive building program has changed the appearance of the campus, thanks largely to the efforts of 21 Work and Witness teams spearheaded by Jerome Richardson of Indiana. Four staff homes, two dormitories, two duplexes for married students, and a large, attractive administration building now grace the campus. The constituency has been enlarged to include all the Caribbean Islands except Cuba, Hispaniola, and Puerto Rico. In addition, Guyana, the Bahamas, and Belize are included.

The curriculum now includes not only the original three-year ministerial diploma course but through affiliation with Canadian Nazarene College, a four-year bachelor of theology degree course is now offered. The first such degree was granted in 1974, and there has been an average of one per year since. A three-year sacred music diploma and a two-year churchmanship diploma are also available.

In 1983, as previously noted, Rev. Farrell Chapman, formerly superintendent of the Trinidad and Tobago District, became president of the college. By the end of the 1984-85 school year, nearly 300 had graduated. The impact of the college upon the Caribbean area is revealed in the fact that four of the district superintendents are CNTC graduates, as are the majority of the pastors in the English-speaking areas. In the administration of the college itself, and in its financial support, the West Indian people were playing an increasing role. It was this indigenous character of the institution that was its genius and that gave promise of increasing value to this area of the church's ministry.

D. NORTH AMERICAN INDIAN DISTRICT

In 1980 the North American Indians numbered well over one and a half million, 300,000 of them in Canada and 1.36 million in the United States. They are the fastest-growing ethnic group on the continent, having doubled in population since 1960. They thus constitute a unique missionary challenge.

The ancestors of the Indians are presumed to have entered the continent by way of the present Bering Strait, which once was a land bridge connecting what is now Alaska and Siberia. Over the centuries they spread across the land and broke up into some 600 tribal groups, many of them quite closely related in language and customs. Because of the accelerating migration to the urban areas in recent years, particularly to California, no more than half of the United States Indians live on the various government reservations scattered across the country. Half the Indian population live in the four states of California, Oklahoma, Arizona, and New Mexico, in that numerical order.

Religious Influences

The Indian is basically a religious person. Living close to nature as he does, he recognizes a power greater than himself and in some form or other worships the "Great Spirit." His belief in an afterlife is apparent in his meticulous burial rites. Significantly, the virtues of honesty, bravery, hospitality, and fair play are strong. Unfortunately the white man's ill-treatment of the Indian has made him mistrusting and rebellious. In his frustration he has sometimes sought to return such treatment in kind, creating a false image of treachery. Another result of the white man's domination has been a loss of self-worth, which has led to a high incidence of alcoholism and suicide.

The Roman Catholic priests, who came with the early explorers, found it somewhat easy to adapt their faith to that of the Indians, even to the displacement of the medicine man, their traditional religious practitioner. They were thus able to establish their missions at an early date.

The earliest Protestant missionary to the Indians was Roger Williams, who in the mid-1600s established a flourishing work in the area of Providence, R.I. Other well-known early missionaries include David Brainerd (Massachusetts, Pennsylvania, and New Jersey), and in the Northwest, Marcus Whitman and H. H. Spaulding. Now there are 36 denominations or religious organizations operating missions among the Indians. Some of them have been at work for 100 years.

The Church of the Nazarene

The Nazarenes founded their first Indian mission in Rhode Island in 1927 through the efforts of Rev. Chester Smith at Wakefield. The next move came in Oklahoma where there was a concentration of Indians, mainly the Cherokee, Choctaw, Chickasaw, Creek, and Seminole tribes. Apparently Rev. C. B. Jernigan, a pioneer leader of the Church of the Nazarene, had made some early contacts with the Indians there. But it remained for District Superintendent J. W. Short to implement a specific ministry among them.

In the mid-1930s, while conducting a revival meeting in the Ponca City church in the northern part of the state, he was invited by a Ponca Indian chief, White Eagle, to hold services among his people in the nearby reservation. The result was the establishment of a work that has had a continuous ministry since then. An invitation to Rev. Short to preach in a Comanche home in the southern part of the state led to the holding of a grove camp meeting near Cache Creek. Out of this grew a strong work. West of Walters, on an acreage donated by Mrs. Blackbear, the Emerson church was built.

The Lawton, Clinton, Watonga, and El Reno white churches all sponsored missions among the Cheyenne and Arapaho in their areas. Many of these Indians became integrated with the white congregations. As a result, most of these early churches do not now exist. However, recognition should be given to Rev. and Mrs. Amos Komah, Rev. D. C. Reynolds, and Rev. C. B. Hildebrand, who were prominent early leaders in the Indian work in Oklahoma.

The most populous of the Indian tribes in the United States are the Navaho, who number over 200,000, most of whom live in Arizona with many also in New Mexico. The first Nazarene mission among them was established in 1943 at Twin Butte, seven miles west of Gallup, N.Mex., by Claude and Gertrude Jones. They were given 1½ acres of land next to the Florence trading post, where they built a church and cabin. It was a small beginning for the Navaho work, which was to see great expansion in later years. At Twin Butte now stands the Florence and Jess Walling Memorial Church, considered to be the finest of the Indian churches.

There were also early missions opened along the Arizona-California border. The work in Somerton, Ariz., near Yuma, was begun by Mrs. Ruth Halford, a notable pioneer in the Indian work. She was a schoolteacher in San Diego and in 1937 began driving to Somerton, 200 miles away, to hold services among the Cocopah. She also made some contacts south of there in Old Mexico. Mrs. Carl Eastman established a mission in Yuma. Then Karney Miller, a chief of the Mojave tribe, invited Rev. and Mrs. Carl Williams to come to Parker, Ariz., to hold services, thus beginning a work there that is still flourishing.

Soon after the opening of the church in Parker, the Williamses began holding afternoon services across the border in Needles, Calif. The work took hold, and in 1943 Rev. and Mrs. Charles Scrivner were sent there to establish a church. The Bresee Avenue Church of Pasadena contributed $300 for the building of a tent home for the Scrivners in which they lived for two years. Another later satellite of the work in Parker was the Poston mission, 20 miles south, among the Navaho and Hopi.

At Winterhaven in the Imperial Valley of southeast California, across the river from Yuma, Ariz., work was begun in the late 1930s among the Quechuan under the sponsorship of the Southern California District, which contributed $300 for the erection of a 30-by-40-foot chapel. In 1943, under the leadership of Rev. and Mrs. T. P. Friday, this chapel was rebuilt and a small parsonage added.

North American Indian District Organized

Although sincere attempts had been made to establish missions among the Indians, the efforts were somewhat isolated and sporadic. The general church leaders realized that only an organized effort would be effective. Thus in January 1944 the General Board authorized the formation of the North American Indian District under the sponsorship of the Department of Foreign Missions. Although there were scattered Indian churches elsewhere, the new district was to encompass the work in the states of California, Arizona, New Mexico, and Oklahoma.

Selected as superintendent was Rev. Dowie Swarth, who took over the task in the late summer of 1944. For two years he had been superintendent of the Arizona District and thus was well acquainted with the great possibilities of the Indian work. Although at that time more Indians lived in Arizona than in any other state, there were as yet only three Nazarene missions there—at Somerton, Yuma, and Parker, all on the western border. In California there were two—at Winterhaven and Needles, both on the Arizona border. In New Mexico there was only the one at Twin Butte, near Gallup. Oklahoma, however, had six missions—at El Reno, Clinton, Cache, Colony, Emerson, and Ponca City.

One of Rev. Swarth's first moves was to call a meeting of the workers in the western area at Eastside Church in Phoenix. Among other objectives, he expressed his concern that the principle of self-support be established from the outset, and budgets based on the tithe of the workers' salaries were established.

The first district assembly (the Indians called it the "First General Council Meeting") was held at Albuquerque, N.Mex., May 1-3, 1945. Many of the delegates had never before been off their own reservations let alone mixed with those of other tribes. But as Rev. Swarth remarked afterward, "To see members of tribes that had never before spoken to each other come together in such warmth and fellowship was truly amazing." Over 700 attended the services, only 60 percent of whom were Christians, which indicated strongly the wide-open evangelistic opportunity before the Indian church.

The Bible Training School

Among the white visitors at the first district assembly was a group from a small New Mexico settlement near Lindrith, about 100 miles north of Albuquerque. There on a 500-acre ranch they had been operating an independent orphanage and Bible school. During the assembly they had heard talk of the need for a school in which to train future Indian workers; so, soon after the assembly Rev. Swarth received a letter from their leader, Rev. Fred Davis, offering to turn over their entire layout to the Church of the Nazarene for the proposed Bible training school. Financial problems had made it impossible for them to continue their own enterprise.

After a thorough study of all the legal involvement including an investigative visit by Dr. John Stockton, general church treasurer, in the summer of 1947, the General Board at its annual meeting in January 1948 gave approval to the project. The board also made a special appropriation of $5,000 to launch the school. Though there were several buildings on the property, much repair and remodeling was necessary before the school could be opened. In this task, Rev. and Mrs. N. A. Malmberg and Rev. and Mrs. R. U. Metzger were of special assistance. The institution was named the C. Warren Jones Indian Bible and Training School in honor of the recently retired general secretary of the Department of Foreign Missions, who had taken a special interest in the Indian work. He actively participated in the work of the school for the first two years.

On September 14, 1948, the school opened its doors to 24 students, representing seven different tribes. When failing health, complicated by the 7,200-foot-high altitude, forced Rev. Malmberg to move elsewhere, Rev. and Mrs. E. H. Timmer came to give leadership through the summer months of building and preparing for the coming term. Rev. Charles Scrivner, with his wife, came that fall to serve as principal. During the previous year Miss Catherine Pickett had also joined the staff and remained a valued worker for many years.

Tragedy struck on the night of December 13, 1949, when fire destroyed the main building, which included classrooms, library, dining hall, and chapel. Lost were all the books, equipment, and much stored food. Undaunted, the leaders of the school, aided by pastors and others, immediately began construction of a replacement building that in 31 days was sufficiently ready for occupancy. It was an amazing accomplishment in the middle of winter.

Rev. A. H. Eggleston was named principal in the fall of 1950 and served for two years. Effort was made to make the school self-supporting by operating a poultry farm and dairy, but the distance from market made this an unprofitable venture. A 17-acre farm had to be purchased six miles south of Albuquerque to provide hay for the dairy.

But the school was proving to be more of a boarding school for grade school and high school students than an institution for the training of Christian workers. Furthermore, the general inaccessibility of the Lindrith property was a growing problem, and when Rev. G. H. Pearson became director in 1952, the decision was made to move the school to the Albuquerque property. It took many months to dismantle and move the buildings and equipment, but with the help of Alabaster funds, the reconstructed campus was ready for occupancy in the fall of 1954.

When Rev. Dowie Swarth retired as district superintendent in 1956, Rev. Pearson was appointed in his place. The vacancy thus left in the school was once again filled by Rev. Charles Scrivner. He was followed by Rev. Merle Gray.

As the years passed, quality government schools had been built throughout the reservations, thus largely obviating the need for the grade and high school programs of the Nazarene school. This part was thus gradually phased out, the high school division finally being closed in 1970.

The name of the institution was changed to Nazarene Indian Bible College, and Rev. Wayne Stark became its director. As a full-fledged ministerial training school, standard GED entrance tests were introduced, and application was made for accreditation by the Association of American Bible Colleges. A strengthened faculty, an enlarged curriculum, and a greatly improved physical plant made possible through the contributions of many Work and Witness teams set the college on a firm course.

In 1984 Rev. Denny Owens, former missionary to the Philippines, became president. By 1985 enrollment had climbed to 40, of whom 16 were resident students, while 24 were off campus.

Expansion of the District

In the beginning years of the Indian District, Rev. Swarth's time was taken up heavily by the school, but nonetheless there were some significant church developments. A new church was begun at Ramah, N.Mex., 30 miles southeast of Gallup, which later spawned the Sand Mountain and Red Lake missions. A church was also begun at Winslow, Ariz., where a large government school was located.

The area of most dramatic early development was on the vast Black Mesa or Low Mountain section of northern Arizona. Decker and Florence Yazzie, well-educated teachers who had been converted in the Winslow mission, became burdened for their people in the huge Navaho reservation up toward the Utah border. The first mission they established was at Smoke Signal, where a church and dispensary were built.

Among the Yazzies' converts were the Riggs brothers, Pete and Alex, who became strong preachers. Pete opened the Twin Hills mission 30 miles north of Tuba City, while Alex launched the Leupp mission, which became the strongest church financially on the entire district. The Riggs brothers are among several Nazarenes who have served on the prestigious Navaho Tribal Council. One of them, Franklin Paul, has been vice-chairman of this council. Other churches in the area are Lee Chee (at Page, Ariz.), Chilchinbito, Kaibito, Shonto (40 miles west of Kayenta), and Window Rock (the capital of the Navaho nation).

Another important development was the establishment of the Western Zone campground, six miles south of Mount Palomar near Escondido, Calif. Camp meetings continued to play a significant role in the Indian work, about 30 such areawide meetings being held each summer. Indian churches were also started in some of the larger cities, such as Tucson, Phoenix, and Albuquerque, to reach the considerable Indian population in these metropolitan areas. The later great influx of Indians to Los Angeles and other California cities opened new opportunities for the urban Indian work there.

One of the most encouraging developments in the district, particularly during the 1970s, was the widespread establishment of Sunday Schools by Nazarene Indian teachers in the government schools scattered throughout the reservations. These teachers were serving in a real sense as bivocational missionaries to their own people. They provided the groundwork for future churches whose pastors will come from the growing number of qualified graduates of the Bible college. This augured well for the future of the Indian work whose growth record for a number of years had been disappointing.

In 1971 Rev. Julian Gunn, a Mojave, was made an assistant to the district superintendent, Rev. G. H. Pearson. Two years later the roles were reversed as Rev. Gunn was appointed superintendent with Rev. Pearson, mission director, as his advisor. In 1976 supervision of the district was transferred from the Department of World Mission to the Department of Home Missions, and further administrative changes took place. A major move came when in 1975 Rev. Pearson was named director of the Casa Robles Missionary Retirement Center in Temple City, Calif., and for the first time the Indian church elected its own district superintendent. Their choice was Rev. Julian Gunn, who had proved himself a gifted and spiritual leader of his people.

Another administrative change came with the election of the first all-Indian college board of trustees. Then in 1978 a 10-year self-support plan for the churches and the district was adopted enthusiastically.

At the 41st assembly in 1985 it was voted to divide into two districts: the Navaho Nation District and the Southwest Indian District. Rev. Johnny Nells was elected superintendent of the former, while Rev. Julian Gunn, who had been superintendent of the combined districts, was elected to lead the latter. The total number of organized churches on the two districts was 32 with a combined membership of 1,587.

V

SOUTH AMERICA REGION

- Argentina
- Uruguay
- Paraguay
- Peru
- Bolivia
- Chile
- Ecuador
- Colombia
- Venezuela
- Brazil

Researcher:

W. Howard Conrad

EQUATOR

VENEZUELA
COLOMBIA
GUYANA
SURINAME
ECUADOR
P E R U
BRAZIL
BOLIVIA
CHILE
PARAGUAY
A R G E N T I N A
URUGUAY

S O U T H
A T L A N T I C
O C E A N

SOUTH AMERICA
REGION

THE SOUTH AMERICA REGION

In the story of world missions, names like Livingstone, Carey, and Morrison, and places like Africa, India, and China immediately come to mind. Not so readily is South America thought of, yet some of the most stirring episodes in missionary annals took place on this continent. It is quite unlike any other mission field, for the history and geography of the land have presented to the Christian Church a challenge that in some ways is more varied and complex than will be found in almost any other part of the world.

The Geographical and Historical Setting

Geographically the continent of South America measures 4,600 miles from north to south and 3,000 miles from east to west at its widest point. About two-thirds of the land lies within the tropics, though the southern extremity extends into the frigid waters of the Antarctic. The heart of the continent is a vast, waterlogged jungle drained by the mighty Amazon, largest river system in the world.

The topography of the continent has had a profound effect on the shaping of its nations and people. The towering Andes mountain chain, which runs the full length of the western side of the continent with more than 50 peaks rising above 20,000 feet, contrasts with the vast flatlands to the east. One-sixth of the continent lies at an elevation above 10,000 feet, but three-fifths is below 1,000 feet above sea level. Most prominent of the high plains is the broad and bleak altiplano of Bolivia and Peru, 2½ miles above the sea. Of the low plains, the steamy jungles of the Amazon basin and the famous pampas of Argentina are the most prominent.

The aboriginal inhabitants of the land are known as Amerindians, many of whom still live a primitive existence in the remote areas. Among the newcomers, the Iberians, descendants of the original Spanish and Portuguese settlers, are the dominant ethnic group. There is also a strong Black element, particularly in the northern fringe, a remnant of the African slave trade. The Creoles, those of mixed race, have become the dominant power in almost every South American country. Superimposed on these basic ethnic groups are the more recent immigrants, mostly from Europe, who have helped produce a cosmopolitan society, particularly in Brazil, Argentina, Uruguay, and Chile.

Great civilizations were in existence in South America's western side long before the early explorers discovered the New World. Principally they were Chibcha in the Bogota area, the Incas in the high central Andes, and the Chimus on the western coastal plain of what is now Peru. The last of these civilizations were wiped out by the Spanish conquistadores, who pillaged their cities and carried off their fabulous treasures of gold.

Spain and Portugal vied for colonization and exploitive rights in the areas of the world their explorers had opened up, and agreement was ultimately reached in the Treaty of Tordesilla (1494) that a north-south demarcation line be drawn 370 leagues (about 1,500 miles) west of the Cape Verde Islands. Everything east of that line would be Portugal's domain, and everything west would be Spain's. This accounts for the large Portuguese colonies that were developed in Africa and the Orient and Spain's dominant influence in the Americas. But this line placed the large eastern hump of South America on the Portuguese side, which explains the fact that Brazil is Portuguese, while virtually all the rest of the continent is Spanish.

Religious Background

With the Spanish conquerors came the Roman Catholic priests, whose teachings accommodated well to the existing pagan animism, creating a kind of neopaganism with which Protestant missionaries had to contend. But even though the Spanish yoke was thrown off in the early 19th century under Bolivar, San Martin, and others, the pervasive dominance of the Catholic church remained. Indeed Catholicism was rigidly enforced to the exclusion of all other religious influences. Protestant missions gained their first foothold through so-called chaplaincies. Small enclaves of resident foreigners (diplomats and businessmen) built chapels and brought in pastors (chaplains) to minister to them in their own language.

The next wedge was through the mass education movement. Anyone who would open a school was welcomed. This opened the door for James Thompson and his so-called Lancastrian schools that used the Bible as a primary textbook. This in turn created a demand for copies of the Scriptures, and the colporteur, a traveling salesman of Bibles and other religious books, became a frontline gospel messenger. The British and Foreign Bible Society and later the American Bible Society thus spearheaded Protestant missions in South America. Possibly nowhere in the story of missions around the world has the Bible been so clearly the basic instrument of evangelization as it has been on this continent.

Though fanatical opposition and persecution of Protestants was standard procedure, such reaction gradually began to crumble, and missionary societies began to infiltrate the various countries. Among the pioneers was Bishop William Taylor, who was instrumental in placing Methodism in the vanguard of missionary activity in South America. By 1890 there were Methodist schools and chapels in most of the Spanish-speaking New World.

The Church of the Nazarene Enters

Official involvement of the Church of the Nazarene in South America did not take place until 1917, when the General Board voted to open work in Peru. Actually it was a matter of assuming the support of a work already begun by Rev. and Mrs. Roger Winans, who had gone there on their own in 1914.

Then in 1919 the second country, Argentina, became a part of the church's missionary program, but the antecedents of this latter work dated back to 1909. The pioneers here were Rev. and Mrs. Frank Ferguson, who first visited South America in 1906. They had gone out under the sponsorship of the Pentecostal Mission of Nashville but apparently were working independently at the time the Pentecostal Mission joined the Church of the Nazarene in 1915. Otherwise, their work would have been automatically transferred at that time, as was the case with other fields.

Since, therefore, the beginnings in Argentina predate those in Peru, our story of Nazarene missions in South America will begin there. After examining the outreach from there into Uruguay and Paraguay, the story will switch to Peru and its extensions into Bolivia and Chile. This will be followed by the more recent Ecuador, Colombia, and Venezuela ventures, with a final study of the Portuguese-speaking work in Brazil, the colossus of South America.

A. SPANISH SOUTH AMERICA

1. *Argentina*

Argentina, second largest of South America's republics, is the "Atlantic Spanish America"—it and tiny Uruguay being the only Spanish-speaking countries on the Atlantic side of the continent. It is slightly over 1 million square miles in area and stretches from the Tropic of Capricorn in the north to 55° south latitude. Almost one-third of its 27 million people are concentrated in the megalopolis of Buenos Aires, the capital. The ridge of the Andes forms Argentina's western border, separating it from neighboring Chile.

The country can be divided into four main geographical areas. In the *mountains* of the west is found the country's mineral wealth and famed alpine resorts. The subtropical, low alluvial plain in the far north, called the *Gran Chaco*, is for the most part a desolate region covered with scrubby brush, where cotton is a principal product. Moving south, rainfall becomes more abundant as the land spreads out into the broad central *pampas*, the country's heartland, in which Buenos Aires is located. This is the ranch country famed for its colorful gauchos (cowboys) and where most of the 6 million European immigrants who arrived between 1850 and 1930 are located. The southern extremity, called *Patagonia*, which begins about 400 miles south of Buenos Aires, is a cold, dry, and windy region in which sheep raising is a principal activity but where, also, oil has been discovered.

Protestantism Comes to Argentina

In this cosmopolitan country dedicated to enlightened humanism, a breakup of the earlier Roman Catholic monopoly was sure to come. Stepping into that vacuum first was the South American Missionary Society, but its mid-19th-century mission to the inhospitable southern tip of the country met with disaster. Then came the more successful work of the Methodist church, the Christian and Missionary Alliance, and the Salvation Army, all before the turn of the century. Mention should be made of the unaffiliated Lancastrian schools of Rev. James Thompson, which were first begun in Argentina about 1820 and later were introduced in other countries. Since, as previously stated, the Bible was the chief textbook, gospel seed was planted that was to bear fruit in years to come.

Twentieth-century missionary movements have brought the total Protestant adherents up to a scant 2 percent of the population, still a tiny minority against the 94 percent professed Roman Catholics. The slow growth of the church has not, however, been primarily because of the deeply entrenched Roman Catholicism but the pervasive materialism and secularism of the people in which getting ahead is the popular religion.

The Church of the Nazarene in Argentina

A prayer list published in 1906 by the Pentecostal Mission of Nashville listed the names of Frank Ferguson and Miss Lula B. Hutcherson under "South America." They had been part of a group of missionaries sent out to Colombia by the same church in 1902 but who had not been able to complete their mission. Cut off in Cuba while on the way, some of the party of perhaps as many as 10 remained a short while there, endeavoring to get a work started. Leona Gardner was the only one who ultimately remained in Cuba.

In the summer of 1906, Frank Ferguson married Miss Hutcherson, and late that year they set out on a journey to South America, seeking a place in which to establish a mission. They toured Ecuador, Peru, and Bolivia and planned to go on to Argentina, but Mrs. Ferguson came down with typhoid fever, and they were forced to return to the United States for recuperation. A year or so later, however, they completed their itinerary, arriving in Buenos Aires in December 1909. Here they found their "Macedonia" and began missionary work. By now they were independent of the Pentecostal Mission and had to supplement the support of a few friends by selling Bibles and religious books.

In 1914 another couple, Rev. and Mrs. Carlos H. Miller, arrived in Buenos Aires. They had had earlier missionary experience in Mexico (he as early as 1906) under the Holiness Church of Christ and then after the union in 1908, under the Church of the Nazarene. He was superintendent of the Nazarene work in the province of Chiapas when the revolution forced the evacuation of all missionaries in 1912. (See the Mexico story above.)

Not content to let their missionary vision die, the Millers, though Nazarenes, accepted an appointment to Argentina under the Christian and Missionary Alliance, arriving, as indicated, in 1914. This brought them into contact with the Fergusons. Since both couples were members of the Church of the Nazarene, they began to urge the church to begin work there and offered their own services for the task.

In 1919 the mission board voted to begin operations in Argentina. The Fergusons were home on furlough at the time, so the Millers began services in their Calle Mendenos home on September 3, 1919.

Among those present was a neighbor, Carmen C. de Garcia, and her three daughters. Lucia, the youngest, a 15-year-old student in a teacher training school, began to pray earnestly for the conversion of the Millers to Catholicism, but in two months' time she herself was the convert and became a devout Christian. She is usually recognized as the first person to join the Church of the Nazarene in Argentina. She went on in her education to receive a doctorate and in 1935 married Natalio Acosta. They made a powerful evangelistic team and were instrumental in opening churches in several cities.

When the Fergusons returned to Argentina in 1920, they started a second congregation in their home in the Villa Modelo section of Buenos Aires, and in June of that year the first seven Nazarenes were baptized. Other house churches were soon begun. In 1921 Rev. and Mrs. Guy McHenry joined the missionary staff and served until being transferred to Peru in 1925.

In 1922 the two congregations with a total of 16 members were organized into a district. Audaciously they set as their goal the evangelization of Argentina, Chile, Bolivia, Paraguay, and Uruguay.

A Christian workers course was instituted to train nationals for leadership, and the first graduate in November 1927 was Lucia Garcia. The following year Miss Soledad Quintana and Antonio Lopez received diplomas. These two were later married. Miss Garcia and Miss Quintana opened the first church outside of Buenos Aires at General Rodriguez.

In 1931 Dr. J. B. Chapman, general superintendent, visited the field and ordained to the ministry Lucia Garcia, Geraldo Jose Marino, and Antonio and Soledad Lopez. Two years later the district's first building, the Castelar Church, was dedicated.

During the great missionary retrenchment in the mid-1920s, the Millers, rather than be returned to the United States, rejoined the

Christian and Missionary Alliance mission. This left the Fergusons to carry on alone, but with an able group of national leaders, the work grew. At the district assembly June 28-30, 1933, five organized churches were reported with 250 members. In October, when the Fergusons left for furlough, the nationals were left completely on their own, with Rev. Antonio Lopez as acting district superintendent. When the Fergusons returned in February 1935, they found the work strong and growing.

On September 16, 1936, John and Marie Cochran arrived on the field to begin a ministry of 36 years in Argentina. They won the love and respect of the people both in and out of the church and did much to shape the church in Argentina in its growing years. Their daughter, Faith, married Ardee Coolidge, and after serving a term in Cuba (1952-57), they were transferred to Argentina. Here they remained for 17 years until being transferred again in 1975, this time to Chile.

When the Cochrans came to Argentina, membership stood at 207; when they retired in 1972, the total was 1,522, which represents an average annual increase of about 8 percent. This is a healthy growth, but especially so in a land of general religious lethargy and dominant Roman Catholicism.

In 1930 Rev. Thomas Ainscough came to Rosario, Argentina, 200 miles up the Parana River from Buenos Aires. He was a Welshman and served first under the auspices of the Emmanuel Mission. He became an independent missionary and organized three thriving churches in Argentina's second-largest city. Although he joined the Church of the Nazarene in 1936, he and his Argentine-born wife, Romana, did not become official missionaries of the church until 1947. His youngest son, Albert, became a medical doctor, and he and his wife, Rosa, also a doctor, served for a term in the Reynolds Memorial Hospital in India—the first Argentine missionaries.

Rev. and Mrs. L. D. Lockwood arrived in 1938, not long before Mrs. Ferguson's failing health forced that pioneer couple to return to the United States after 29 years of faithful labor.

During World War II, when missionary travel to most world areas was impossible, the Americas were still open. Thus Rev. and Mrs. Spurgeon Hendrix began their first term of service in Argentina in 1941. They spent three terms there but also served in Cuba, Chile, and Uruguay—over 36 years in all, before retiring in 1977. Robert and Lela Jackson, both nurses, were on their way to Africa, hopefully, by way of Argentina in 1943, but could get no farther. So they gave two years of splendid service there until the war's end, when they were able to continue their journey. (In 1980 Mrs. Jackson was elected international president of the NWMS.)

As mentioned above, the first visit by a general superintendent took place in 1931 when Dr. J. B. Chapman ordained the first group of ministers. It was not until October 1939 that Dr. J. G. Morrison came for the second such visit. But it was 13 more years before Dr. G. B. Williamson came in 1952. Dr. J. W. Montgomery, district superintendent of the Northeastern Indiana District, paid an official visit in 1939 at which time, under special authority, he ordained three elders.

Argentina shared in the great upsurge in missionary interest around the world following World War II, as a number of new missionaries were sent out in the years immediately following the peace. In fact, Miss Dorothy Ahleman arrived the year before (1944). Rev. and Mrs. Lester Johnston arrived in 1946, and Rev. and Mrs. Ronald Denton in 1947. Subsequently the O. K. Perkinsons came in 1952, and the Melvin Wilkinsons in 1956.

But the 1960s and 1970s saw many crosscurrents politically and economically and not a little ebb and flow of missionaries within the church structure. Ardee and Faith Coolidge, as previously stated, were transferred here from Cuba in 1958 and then to Chile in 1975. The Paul Says, who came to Argentina in 1962, were transferred to the Dominican Republic in 1978. The Harold Rays, who arrived from Guatemala in 1969, were transferred back there in 1974. Miss Ruth Miller came from Nicaragua in 1966, and the Elmer Nelsons from Panama in 1976. But among arrivals during this period were also the "anchor" missionaries, Norman and Joanna Howerton (1964—), Donald and Betty Davis (1960-80), and Victor and Beryl Edwards (1969-82, after a term there under the Emmanuel Mission, 1963-68). Later additions were Douglas and Elaine Perkins (1981-82) and John and Laurel Sluyter (1980-81), following a term in Ecuador (1975-79). Those who served in earlier years were the Donald Crenshaws (1962-66) and the Ron Grabkes (1969-73).

Excellent national leadership has characterized the Argentine field, and the credit for much of this can be given to the Bible training school. As early as 1921 a school was in operation on the field. It offered essentially a Christian workers course with classes taught mainly at night. In the late 1930s the school was moved to more spacious quarters at 884 Donato Alvarez Street, where under the leadership of the Lockwoods a more substantial four-year curriculum was inaugurated. The first graduating class received their diplomas in 1942. In 1945 leadership of the school passed to Rev. Spurgeon Hendrix, with newly arrived Dorothy Ahleman as a leading faculty member. Norman and Joanna Howerton began teaching there in 1980.

The name of the school was later changed to Nazarene Theological Seminary, and the campus was moved to Pilar in suburban Buenos Aires. Rev. Rogelio Fernandez became director with all other staff members but the Howertons nationals. A full residential program was combined with an extension work (CENETA).

Toward a National Church

In the earlier days of limited missionary personnel, national leaders like Rev. Jose Armagno and Rev. Vicente Bustos gave strong leadership to the Argentine work. When the Instrument of Incorporation was drawn up in October 1935, the government required that only Argentinians could attend to the legal matters involved, thus thrusting responsibility on the nationals. The first step toward national-mission status came in 1971 when Rev. Alejandro Medina was officially appointed assistant to the missionary superintendent. In 1972 he was named district superintendent, and in subsequent years was elected by the district assembly. He represented Argentina at the 1976 General Assembly in Dallas but shortly thereafter died of cancer.

Buenos Aires remained the center of the work, but churches were gradually opened in other areas. A major move was to open work in Bahia Blanca, the port city 300 miles to the south, which eventuated in the organization of the South District as a national-mission district with Rev. Carlos Zoroastro as superintendent. He had been elected Central district superintendent after Rev. Medina passed away. Rev. Jorge Cabrera followed him as superintendent of the South District.

At the same time, the work was developing to the north. Also, as a result of an outreach effort of the Formosa Central congregation, a church was organized at Pilar, across the river in Paraguay (see below). The result was the setting up of the pioneer district of Argentina North/Paraguay with Rosario as its main center. Rev. Victor Edwards was named superintendent of the new field and took up residence in the border city of Formosa, Argentina, just 70 miles from the Paraguay capital of Asuncion. He later moved over into Paraguay and superintended the work from there. When in 1983 Paraguay became a separate district, Rev. Ramon Bauza became superintendent of the North Argentine District, to be followed by Rev. Salvador Pereyra.

The year 1980 was significant for Argentina as the Central District became a regular district and elected Rev. Florentino Bauza as its superintendent. The following year Dorothy Ahleman, for many years a teacher in the Argentina Nazarene Bible College, retired from missionary service; while the Elmer Nelsons and O. K. Perkinsons left on furlough, to be transferred to the Dominican Republic and Puerto Rico respectively. This left only the John Sluyters, he serving as mission director; the Norman Howertons, who at that time were in charge of the seminary in Buenos Aires; and the Doug Perkinses as the only remaining resident missionaries in Argentina.

In 1984 the Sluyters returned to their original field in Ecuador, and Rev. Doug Perkins became mission director for a short time of the combined area of Argentina, Paraguay, and Uruguay, known as the Southern Cone Region. He was now residing in Montevideo, Uruguay. This left only the Howertons, who were teaching in the seminary.

In February 1985 the west central provinces of Mendoza, San Juan, and San Luis were set off from the South District to form the pioneer district of Cuyo, with four organized churches. Rev. and Mrs. Wesley Harris, who in 1984 had been transferred to Paraguay from Bolivia to be leaders of that pioneer district, were appointed to also superintend the Cuyo District from there. He also replaced Rev. Perkins as mission director of the Southern Cone Region when the latter left for furlough in 1985.

With 64 organized churches reporting a combined membership of 3,473 in 1985 and an able group of national leaders and pastors to carry on, the work in Argentina held great promise.

2. *Uruguay*

Wedged between Brazil's southern panhandle and Argentina is the tiny but prosperous country of Uruguay. Only about 70,000 square miles in extent, 83 percent of its 2.8 million inhabitants live in the urban centers, over 1 million in the capital of Montevideo alone. Uruguay is a highly socialized state but has struggled with rampant inflation, which has produced some political instability; but the country continues to enjoy one of the highest standards of living on the continent. The people are 90 percent of Spanish descent; independence from Spain came in 1814. Brazil tried to take over the territory but was repulsed in 1828, and Great Britain became an informal protector as the nation struggled to its feet.

The Roman Catholic faith is dominant in the country (66 percent), and only 2 percent are Protestant. The Uruguayans, like their Argentine neighbors, are free thinkers and largely indifferent, if not antagonistic, to religion. Separation of church and state was pushed to the extreme when the president was forbidden to attend church, and religious holidays were secularized. Christmas, for example, was renamed Family Day; and Holy Week, Tourist Week. Indeed, Uruguay is a tourist mecca with its mild climate and white sand beaches. It contains no mountains, however.

All of the unrest, secularism, and economic uncertainty has had its effect on the religious climate. Thirty percent of the people profess no faith. The Waldensians (principally from Italy), the Mennonites, the Methodists, the Church of God, and the Southern Baptists have all established missions here beginning back in 1841, but the impact has been minimal.

The Church of the Nazarene Enters

The Church of the Nazarene could not ignore this missionary challenge, and on January 16, 1949, services were begun in Montevideo by Rev. and Mrs. Ronald Denton, who had been at work in Argentina for almost two years. Three years later the first church was organized on February 17, 1952, with eight charter members. By that time services were also being held in two other locations.

In 1953 the O. K. Perkinsons came over from Argentina, and in 1956 Jack and Janet Armstrong were transferred there from Bolivia. As the work expanded, Melvin and Carolyn Wilkinson were also transferred from Argentina. Ted and Mima Hughes, veterans from Cuba and Nicaragua, were appointed to Uruguay in 1963. He served effectively as both director of the Bible school (1963-80) and mission director (1971-80) until transferred to Chile in late 1980. The Harry Flinners, the Spurgeon Hendrixes, the Robert Wellmons, the Will Haworths, the John Sluyters, and Miss Julie Buchanan also spent short periods on the field.

The total input of missionaries who have served in Uruguay amounts to about 150 years, yet response was slow. However, in 1985 a spirit of revival began, and excellent growth was experienced in several churches. Total membership as of 1985 was 660 in 12 organized churches. A missionary force of only two remained—Rev. and Mrs. Doug Perkins, with Rev. Perkins serving as mission director of the Southern Cone Region.

In an effort to develop the work outside of metropolitan Montevideo, a North Uruguay pioneer area was set apart in February 1985 with one established church and two preaching points as a starter.

Because of high educational standards throughout the country, the establishment of a creditable theological training center has been extremely difficult. Qualified ministerial students were turning to advanced colleges and seminaries in the United States, including Nazarene Theological Seminary. However, the CENETA extension program out of the seminary in Costa Rica was proving to be of increasing value in training pastors.

The future for the work in Uruguay depended on the church's ability to find a formula for reaching a secular society, a problem not unlike that faced in Scandinavia and elsewhere. Outright opposition may be proven to be a better climate in which to produce saints than flat lethargy.

3. *Paraguay*

This 157,047-square-mile republic in the heart of South America is one of the two (with Bolivia) landlocked countries on the continent, although it has access to the sea by the navigable Paraguay and Parana rivers. The population, relatively sparse, consists chiefly of mestizos. The official language is Spanish, but 90 percent of the people speak the Guarani Indian dialect, with most being fluent in both languages. Ninety-seven percent are nominally Roman Catholic, but voodooism and spiritism abound.

The Church of the Nazarene originally came to Paraguay about 1970 when a businesswoman, Apolonia Villalba, in the village of Alberdi, invited the pastor of the Central Church in Formosa, across the river in Argentina, to hold services in her home. These Thursday night services, supplemented by a Sunday School that Apolonia conducted on her own, continued rather regularly for many years with Pastor Florentino Bauza, and later his brother Ramon, playing leading roles. However, it was not until in 1983 when a meeting hall was rented and a pastor installed that the church was officially organized.

Meanwhile in 1978 work had begun in the town of Pilar, 60 miles south downriver, where Apolonia had family and business contacts.

This mission was carried on as a part of Formosa Central's outreach until it ultimately became an organized church. This prompted the aforementioned inclusion of Paraguay with the Argentina North District with Rev. Victor Edwards as superintendent.

In January 1983 Paraguay was made a separate pioneer district with two churches and 27 members with North Argentina becoming a national-mission district. Rev. Edwards continued as superintendent in Paraguay and the following month moved to the capital city of Asunción. A period of rapid development ensued.

Rev. and Mrs. Kenneth Jones were transferred from Peru to assist, and they took over interim leadership when the Edwardses went on furlough in August of 1983. Before they left, however, the Barrio Obrero Church had been organized in the heart of the capital with 17 members. In October 1983 the Lambaré and Loma Pyta churches were organized just outside Asunción.

In June 1984 the Wesley Harrises, who had been serving in Bolivia, arrived in Asunción to replace the Edwardses, who had been reassigned to Spain. In late 1984 four more churches were organized in the vicinity of the capital.

A key problem Rev. Harris had to tackle was lack of buildings. Also some strong opposition from without and some unfortunate defections within slowed growth somewhat, but by the close of 1985 the fledgling district reported nine organized churches with a membership of 404.

4. *Peru*

The second major focus of early Nazarene work in South America was Peru, the land of Pizarro and the Incas. At one time Spain ruled the western coast of the continent and plundered the wealth of the inhabitants of the Andes. Though the Inca Empire vanished, the roots of its communal system still survive as reflected in the respect for social institutions of all sorts, including the church. Unfortunately, the superficial similarities between their system and that of the Marxists have made it easy for them to accept the Communist ideology.

The story of how Pizarro was able to subdue the mighty Inca Empire with only a handful of men (perhaps 200) is a sad one. Unfortunately the Roman Catholic church was able to move in along with him and established an ecclesiastical domain that augmented the political hold that Spain had upon this part of the New World.

Lima became the center of Spanish power—intellectual, cultural, and financial. It became the seat of government for what was known as the viceroyalty of La Plata, which included Argentina, Uruguay, Paraguay, Bolivia, and Peru. At the same time, it became the point of attack of the forces that began to fight for independence. Liberators like José de San Martin, who marched on Lima on July 28, 1821, and Simon Bolivar, who defeated the Spanish in 1824 and occupied Lima two years later, changed the course of Peru and Spanish South America.

Unification of the surrounding territories into a *Gran Colombia* (Greater Colombia) was not accomplished, however, and as years passed, animosities developed between some of the countries. Border clashes continue to the present day.

Geographically, Peru's 1,400-mile coastline runs from near the equator in the north to 18° south latitude, and its 500,000 square miles make it the third-largest country in South America. The population is nearly 19 million.

The territory is divided into three well-defined zones running north and south—the *Costa* (coast), an arid strip 20 to 60 miles wide along the Pacific Ocean, comprising about 12 percent of the land; the *Sierra* (mountains), comprising the Andes Mountains, some of which reach 22,000 feet, and including the 12,000-foot-high altiplano (high plains), constituting 27 percent of the area; and the *Montana*, the jungle wilderness on the eastern slopes of the Andes reaching down to the Amazonian plain.

Two-thirds of the Peruvians live in the 1,400-mile-long coastal region, and half of these in the capital city of Lima, located here. Most of the remainder live in the 200- to 250-mile-wide band of mountains that form an almost impenetrable wall that until recent years defied the efforts of road builders to penetrate to the interior. Here is where most of the true natives live—the Quechua Indians, descendants of the Incas. They are a recluse type of people who live in these remote valleys, slow to accept the outsider. Sixty percent of Peru lies beyond the Andes, but only 8 percent of its people live there. The northern part of the eastern slope of the Andes is the home of the Aguarunas, cousins of the fierce Aucas of Ecuador, and the center of one of the most dramatic missionary developments of the Church of the Nazarene.

Religious Influences

Lima, the center of Spanish political power, became also the center of Roman Catholic domination, and anything that smacked of Protestantism was violently attacked. It was thus that the gospel was held out for so long. It was the same Protestant wedge that had opened up Argentina that opened up Peru—the chaplaincies set up for foreign business and governmental enclaves. The Methodists and Episcopalians also established prestigious high schools that, though breaking down prejudice, were not effective evangelizing institutions. "Accepting quality education," observes Howard Conrad, "seldom included the acceptance of Christ."

An early evangelizing ministry was John Ritchie's Iglesia Evangelica Peruana (Peruvian Evangelical Church). This was a totally national church organized about 1920 under the auspices of the Evangelical Union of South America. The Seventh-Day Adventists went into Peru before the turn of the century, and though over the years they suffered several splits, they boast a substantial membership.

The Church of the Nazarene

The Church of the Nazarene, with 13,169 members, full and probationary (1985), is the fourth-largest non-Catholic religious body in the country. The original comity agreements confined the church's work at first to the far northern departments (states) including the intermountain area. Now its ministry is much more widespread.

The Nazarene work began as a faith venture in 1914 by Roger and Mary Hunt Winans, products of the small Kansas college that became Bresee Bible College, which in turn amalgamated with Bethany-Peniel (Bethany Nazarene) College in Bethany, Okla. They were engaged for about two years in border work among the Mexicans and there acquired facility in the Spanish language. They felt the call of God to Peru, and with the help of friends who rallied to their support, in due course they landed at the north Peruvian port of Pacasmayo. This was once the gateway to Cajamarca, ancient resort city of the Incas, 75 miles inland. There in Pacasmayo they began their first probing missionary efforts, earning their livelihood by teaching English and serving in the colportage program of the British and Foreign Bible Society. But superstitious fear, religious prejudice, and persecution made missionary work difficult and discouraging.

In 1917 the young couple were officially commissioned by the Church of the Nazarene, and reinforcements in the persons of Esther Carson and Mabel Park were sent out. The first real mission station was established at Monsefu, about 20 miles north of Pacasmayo. Here in 1907 an independent work had been started by Mr. and Mrs. A. E. Stevens. When their health broke in 1918, they turned their work over to the Church of the Nazarene. This became the first property owned by the Church of the Nazarene in Peru. That same year a national congregation at Santa Cruz near Pacasmayo was also taken over by the church.

Just when the work was beginning to blossom, however, Mrs. Winans passed away. With so few missionaries the loss of one so capable was a severe blow.

With no prospect of additional missionary forces at that time, Roger Winans gave special attention to developing national workers. In 1919 he took five of them on an exploratory trip throughout the whole area even back into the mountains as far as Cajamarca, Chota, and Jaen, seeking to find the best openings for missionary work. It was during this journey that Roger Winans first heard of the Aguaruna Indians of the Upper Amazon. From then on his soul felt no rest until he was able to take the gospel to them.

Churches were formally organized at Monsefu and Pacasmayo, and in July 1919 the first district assembly was held. Roger Winans took charge of the Monsefu station, while Misses Park and Carson moved to Pacasmayo.

The year 1920 saw several strategic moves. Not the least of these was the marriage of Roger Winans and Esther Carson. This year also marked the arrival of Miss Augie Holland, veteran Central America missionary, who took Miss Carson's place as Mabel Park's companion at Pacasmayo. Buildings were added to the Monsefu station, and Esther Carson Winans launched a Bible school. Though the Pilgrim Holiness church had a station in nearby Chiclayo, it was considered to be a large enough center to accommodate a Nazarene work as well, so a mission work was launched there.

With an adjustment in comity agreements in 1921, a huge northern region reaching back over the Andes was assigned to the Church of the Nazarene. Included in this was the area of the headwaters of the Maranon River, a chief tributary of the Amazon, where lived the primitive Aguaruna Indians of which Roger Winans had heard on his earlier exploratory journey. With the addition of Rev. and Mrs. E.

Rademacher and Rev. and Mrs. D. H. Walworth to the missionary force, there was now the opportunity for the Winanses to investigate the possibilities for opening a work among these remote tribesmen.

In 1922 they moved to San Miguel and began a work in that mountainous area amid fierce opposition. From there the following year they began trips up over the continental divide and down to Jaen and Bellavista. It was an arduous three weeks' trek over treacherous trails. Three days' journey beyond Bellavista brought them to the first Aguaruna outposts. Here at La Yunga on the banks of the Maranon River, the Winanses set up their first mission.

As civilization moved closer, the Indians, who were semi-nomadic anyway, simply moved farther down the river. So the Winanses followed them on down to Yama Yakat, where the first major station was established. Winning the confidence of the wary Aguarunas was a difficult but essential opening task that involved learning their language. No evangelization could take place until this bridge of friendship was built. Mrs. Winans set to work to put the language to writing as an initial step toward translating the Scriptures. She went home on furlough, 1926-27, and returning with her were her parents, Mr. and Mrs. F. W. Carson, who aided greatly in developing the little missionary colony. Elementary industry was introduced by Mr. Carson.

Tragedy struck in November 1928, when Esther Carson Winans died. A brilliant missionary career was cut off in its prime. The elder Carsons remained to care for Baby Jean Esther and to help keep the station going. Later Roger Winans was married to Mabel Park, Esther Carson's first companion in the work at Pacasmayo.

The story of the development of the Aguaruna work is one of the most fascinating in the missionary annals of the church. The years of frustration and agony before the first convert was won, the patient teaching, and careful instruction in Christian ways took decades of arduous toil. A noble band of workers made their contributions over the years: Mabel Park (the third Mrs. Winans), Rev. and Mrs. Baltazar Rubio (Peruvian nationals), Rev. and Mrs. Elvin Douglass (1947-57, thence to the coast until 1980), Rev. and Mrs. Harry Flinner (1954-65), and Dr. and Mrs. Larry Garman (1965—). The Jerry Wilsons and Robert Grays also gave valuable assistance in the work, particularly in the Bible school training program.

Meanwhile, the coastal region in the 1920s and 1930s was not without its disheartening circumstances. The small missionary staff caused by retrenchment and the Great Depression made development of the work difficult. At one time (1926-27) only four missionaries were left on the field: the Walworths on the coast, Augie Holland at a new station in Piura in the far north, and Roger Winans in the interior. Rev. and Mrs. Ira True, active in the Mexican border work in the United States, gave two years to the Peruvian field (1924-25). They were followed by Rev. and Mrs. Guy McHenry, who were transferred there from Argentina (1921-25). They were there only a short while when they had to be recalled for lack of missionary funds to support them. They returned later to serve until 1934. Miss Elsie Hazlewood also served from 1928 to 1934.

For a time in 1934 the missionary force was again down to four with the Walworths on the coast and the Winanses in Aguarunaland. The Walworths wisely concentrated on ministerial training, and national preachers served the churches. It was during this period that such outstanding ministers as Revs. Montoya, Julca, Rubio, and Torres emerged.

Beginning in late 1934, the missionary tide turned, and in rapid succession new workers arrived: Rev. and Mrs. Ira Taylor (1934-56, then transferred to Bolivia), Rev. and Mrs. C. H. Wiman (1935-43), and Rev. and Mrs. Clifford Bicker (1935-37). A tragic automobile accident near Chiclayo in 1937 took the life of Clifford Bicker and a promising young national pastor, Rev. Obando.

Rev. Wiman devised a unique system of ministerial training whereby students alternated two months in the classroom with six weeks of evangelism. So effective was this that by 1940 the church was operating in centers all the way from Pacasmayo north to Talara near the Ecuador border and 100 miles eastward into the mountains. There were nine fully organized churches and 20 other missions with a total membership of 975.

Expansion in the 1940s

The Peru field was the recipient of several new workers during the World War II years and those immediately following. Among them were the O. K. Burchfields (1940-53), the Harry Zurchers (1945-57, then transferred to Puerto Rico), the Elvin Douglasses (1947-80), and the Phillip Torgrimsons (1947-77). Shorter terms were served by the D. L. Larkins (1944-45) and the Harry Mingledorffs (1945-49). Rev. Edward Wyman, who transferred from another mission in 1943, gave excellent service until 1947, when he was transferred to the Spanish seminary in San Antonio and later became a general evangelist in the Latin American area. His special interest while in Peru was the establishment of a Bible and tract depot from which thousands of pieces of literature were distributed. He also launched the Vacation Bible School program, which subsequently became an important phase of the Peruvian work.

At the beginning of the postwar period of expansion a convention was called at Oyotun in the spring of 1945, not necessarily to lay plans for the development of the work, but to gather spiritual resources for the task. It proved to be a time of inner deepening, open confession, and interpersonal healing. The revival spirit generated went out over the whole district and reached a high peak in the district assembly in August of that year. The camp meeting spirit that characterized the sessions became a hallmark of subsequent assemblies.

Dr. H. V. Miller, general superintendent, presided at the 1946 District Assembly, at which time the decision was made to transfer the district center from Monsefu to Chiclayo, nine miles north. It was a larger center, about 30,000 in population, and the general attitude there was less anti-Protestant. Work began on facilities to accommodate district offices, day school, Bible school, and church. By early 1950 the property was ready for occupancy.

The retirement of Rev. and Mrs. Roger Winans in September 1948 marked the end of an era for the Peruvian work. He had given 34 years and she 30 years in developing the field, their crowning achievement being the opening up of Aguarunaland to the gospel.

The 1950s saw another influx of missionaries, some of whom remained for only short terms. Neva Lane was transferred to Peru from Central America in 1950 and stayed until 1954; Marjorie Mayo came in 1950, and her place was taken in 1954 by Mary Miller. The latter, a daughter of missionaries, had wanted to go to Africa, but she accepted her South America assignment with diligence and grace. Her contribution over the years has been immeasurable.

Rev. and Mrs. Clyde Golliher came in 1952 and gave 30 years of distinguished service to Peru. Most of that time he was field superintendent. It was under his leadership that the Peruvian church was led to self-government and self-support. The Harry Flinners, who worked among the Aguarunas, served from 1954 to 1965, until being transferred to Uruguay and then to Chile. Norine Roth came in 1952 and four years later married Howard Grantz of another mission. Together they served on the Nazarene field for a number of years. Rev. and Mrs. Samuel Heap, who had been working for 16 years with the Calvary Holiness Mission in Colombia, became Nazarenes when the CHM joined the Church of the Nazarene in 1956. They were assigned to Peru and served there until 1961, when they were transferred to Guatemala and later to Panama.

The Robert Grays arrived in 1959 to take over the direction of the Bible school, which was averaging about 25 in enrollment. The Howard Conrads were transferred from Cuba in 1961 when the missionaries had to leave that field; they served with distinction, he as president of the Bible school, until 1967, when they were transferred to Costa Rica. There he became director of the Nazarene Central American Seminary.

The Alfred Swains, who opened the work in Ecuador in 1972, served in Peru from 1966 to 1970. Dr. and Mrs. Larry Garman began their phenomenally successful ministry among the Aguarunas in 1965. Evelyn Crouch, after serving from 1965 to 1968, married Samuel Ovando of Mexico, and later they were key leaders in the opening of work in Colombia.

The Jerry Wilsons came in 1967 and in 1976 were transferred to Panama and then to the Dominican Republic. The Mark Rudeens served from 1971 to 1974. They were transferred to Panama in 1975 and then to the Costa Rica seminary. The Donald Coxes served a year (1976-77) before being transferred to Chile, while the Lawrence Bryants, veterans from El Salvador, served from 1977 to 1979. Other missionaries who arrived during this period were the Kenneth Joneses (1970) and the Robert Brunsons (1971).

Toward a National Church

The work in Peru has been blessed with excellent national leaders who have ably assumed responsibility in church planting and pastoral roles. Also, in the early stages of the work, stewardship responsibilities were impressed upon the churches. On the occasion of Dr. H. V. Miller's visit in 1946 the budget system of church and district support was instituted, and the ultimate goal of self-support was set. It would seem that the essential elements of a national church were already falling into place.

But a group of pastors and laymen became impatient with the missionary leaders' promises of self-government and stirred up discontent within the church. They were no doubt affected by the strong nationalism of the times under the Velasco regime. But they also found an unfortunate model in their neighbors of the Pilgrim Holiness church, also based in Chiclayo, in which the nationals of that group had forced out the missionaries altogether in 1969-70.

A dissident group was formed, made up of some half dozen pastors and a sizable group of laymen who formed a National Church of the Nazarene. But so unchristian were their actions and attitudes that the movement became a victim of its own excesses. No doubt some of the complaints were legitimate, but this did not call for such extreme reaction. As the situation cooled, many of their original followers came back to the church, and in the end only a few congregations and four or five pastors were lost to the church. But there is no doubt that this unfortunate schism actually accelerated the process of nationalization.

The area of greatest advance was in the northern provinces. Here the process of moving toward national leadership was begun in 1967 when Peru was made a national-mission district and Rev. Esperidion Julca, pastor of Chiclayo First Church, was appointed district superintendent. When in 1974 the Peru field was divided into two districts, North and South, the North part became a mission district, with Rev. Julca being elected superintendent. When regular district status was achieved in 1976 (the second world mission district to reach Phase 4), Rev. Julca chose to accept the position of head of the Bible school (now a seminary), and Rev. Alberto Zamora was elected to the superintendency of the district. Rev. Modesto Rivera followed him in 1980.

In the meantime in 1970 the intermountain San Martin District had been set off from the North District and in 1982 was renamed the Northeast District; it became a national-mission district. Rev. Alberto Zamora was appointed superintendent and set up his headquarters in the provincial capital of Moyobamba. Although then an isolated area, there had been an influx of thousands of migrants from the northern mountain regions. Among these were dozens of Nazarenes from such places as Chota, Llama, Tacabamba, and Jaen. These were eager to help in the establishment of Nazarene churches in their new homeland. The district has operated without missionary personnel since its inception. Rev. Mario Acuña took over the superintendency when Rev. Zamora had to resign for health reasons. By 1985 there were 19 organized churches with 1,385 members.

With the takeover by the national leadership in the 1970s, missionaries were released to work in other areas of the country, particularly in the south. Here there was a nucleus of three congregations, two in Lima (First and Comas) and one in Chimbote, 250 miles north. The Alfred Swains had pioneered the work in Comas, a suburban area to the north of Lima made up of migrants from the mountains. These people were unusually open to the gospel. The work in Chimbote had been opened in the late 1960s when the Elvin Douglasses were transferred there from the intermountain city of Jaen.

The Howard Grantzes, the Robert Grays, and the Clyde Gollihers moved into the Lima area, including its nearby port city of Callao, and began planting new churches. In 1980 the South District reached national-mission status with the appointment of Rev. Ernesto Lozano, pastor of Lima First Church, as district superintendent.

The 1980s saw a continuation of change in the missionary staff, highlighted by the retirement of two veteran couples. In 1980 the Elvin Douglasses concluded 34 years of service in Peru, and in 1982 the Clyde Gollihers left on their final furlough before retirement after 30 years on the field. Arriving in Peru in 1981 were the Dwain Zimmermans and the Steven Langfords, the latter to serve only until 1984.

In 1982 the Robert Grays were transferred to Colombia, and to compensate, the Louie Bustles were sent to Peru from the Dominican Republic. As mission director, he was to lead a dynamic church planting program. The following year, however, he was appointed regional director for all of South America and moved to Quito, Ecuador. Taking his place as mission director was Robert Hudson, who with his wife, Sheila, had served previously in both Nicaragua and El Salvador.

In 1983 Joan Noonan, veteran of missionary service in Africa, Nicaragua, and Ecuador, was transferred to Peru. That same year Rev. and Mrs. Steven Baker (she the daughter of Elmer and Dorothy Nelson) arrived. They filled in for a year on the Amazon District while the Garmans were on furlough and then were stationed in Lima to direct the extension program from the Chiclayo seminary. There were 350 students enrolled in this program.

Growth in Aguarunaland

Without question the most dramatic area of development on the Peruvian field, if not the Nazarene world, was in the Upper Amazon region among the Aguaruna Indians. Here the work was growing phenomenally under the leadership of Dr. and Mrs. Larry Garman.

The stage was set for this expansion when Rev. Harry Flinner moved the mission downriver from Yama Yakat (the Hallelujah Village of the Winans) to the confluence of the Maranon and Chipe rivers. This placed them nearer the center of the tribe, which, as previously stated, had retreated eastward as civilization approached. A mission home, a chapel, and a clinic were constructed.

Dr. Garman, a chiropractor, took a special course in jungle medicine and a year of Spanish language study before going to Peru with his family in 1965. By the time they reached Aguarunaland, the Flinners had left, so they were on their own. To their basic medical work they added a vigorous program of riverbank evangelism.

The work so prospered that the need for pastors was quickly apparent. Sending the prospective preachers to Chiclayo for training proved to be unwise for a number of reasons. It was better to bring teachers in from Chiclayo to provide short-term instruction "on location." Classes were held in Spanish. With the coming of the Jerry Wilsons, these two-week sessions blossomed into a full-fledged Aguaruna Bible School. In 1978 Eduardo Nayap became the first Aguarunan to take ministerial studies on a college level when he enrolled at the Nazarene Seminary in Costa Rica. Athough Jerry Wilson suffered a severe back injury that forced them to leave, the Bible school continued to operate under the leadership of Dr. and Mrs. Garman. A coastal Peruvian, Abiatar Sanchez, became the director in 1985.

So large had the Aguaruna work grown that in 1982, when the San Martin District was renamed the Northeast District, the Amazon section was made a separate pioneer district. By 1984 it had reached national-mission status, and at the South America regional conference that year, Dr. V. H. Lewis ordained 18 Aguaruna pastors. Rev. Victor Datsa was appointed district superintendent. He was succeeded in 1985 by Rev. Roberto Atamain.

By that time there were an amazing 74 churches and preaching points on the district (67 of them fully organized) with a membership of 2,125. The once-primitive tribesmen were proving to be outstanding Christians and churchmen. Already they were reaching out to their neighbors downriver in a veritable evangelistic explosion.

Theological Education

The training of pastors was a prime need, not only in the practical phases of church leadership, but also in the area of indoctrination. The first such school was established in Monsefu in the early 1920s and for many years operated primarily as a night school. In 1949 a transfer was made to Chiclayo, and a more substantial program was begun. In May 1962 the school, now classified as a seminary, was moved to its present location in Chiclayo. Rev. Robert Gray superintended the construction of a complex centered around a large main building containing offices, classrooms, library, dining facilities, and a chapel. Two dormitories and two faculty residences completed the layout to which a third residence was added later.

The new and commodious quarters permitted an increase in enrollment and an expansion of the curriculum. It was staffed almost exclusively by missionaries at first, but gradually nationals became qualified for teaching duty. Rev. Esperidion Julca was the first national rector. When he retired, Rev. Ernesto Lozano took over.

In the mid-1960s a Nazarene High School was built across the highway from the Bible school, containing offices, eight classrooms, and an enclosed patio. The school was largely financed by Arthur Henley. Prof. Andar Villegas was director of the school, which enrolled 80 students. With the advent of Velasco's nationalist regime in 1968, nationalization of all private schools was ordered even to the expropriation of buildings. Rather than lose this property as well as contr' ' of the institution, the high school project was aborted, and the property was made into a district center. The patio was roofed over to form a tabernacle for assemblies and camp meetings.

Because of the problem of trying to persuade prospective students to go from the capital of Lima to the northern city of Chiclayo for ministerial training, it was considered necessary to open a separate school in Lima. Classes were begun in the home of Pastor Ernesto Lozano who, with his wife, was a student at the university. Rev. Robert Brunson was the missionary in charge. No residence program was attempted, and only subjects relating to pastoral preparation were taught.

During his first term in Peru (1971-75), before being transferred for one term to Panama, Rev. Mark Rudeen began the development of a program of Theological Education by Extension (TEE). This made it possible to take the classroom to the preachers by holding brief series of classes at various centers. The CENETA extension program out of the Costa Rica seminary then took over, and by 1984 there were 350 students enrolled.

Indicative of the dynamic outreach of the Peruvian church was the opening up in 1985 of a pioneer area in the southern part of the country under the leadership of Rev. Steve Baker. The church at Arequipa was the only previous congregation in this part of the country. Other substantial cities, such as Cuzco, beckoned the church.

Meanwhile to the north, plans were under way to divide the North District into four, putting the dictum "multiplication by division" to work. This new structure was scheduled to take effect in December 1985.

As in most areas of the world, the constituency of the Church of the Nazarene in Peru reached far beyond its 13,169 (1985) members. Probably more than twice that number looked to the church as theirs. This constituted a mission field in itself. So far, the national church has evidenced great maturity, and substantial growth has been the result.

5. *Bolivia*

The Republic of Bolivia, fifth-largest South American nation and one of the two landlocked countries on the continent, has an area of about 425,000 square miles and a population of slightly over 6 million. Forty percent of the country is in the high Andes, while the remainder lies in the sloping eastern plain called the *Oriente.* A dominant topographical feature in the southwest part of the country is the altiplano, a largely flat intermountain plateau 12,000 feet above sea level extending 500 miles from north to south and averaging 80 miles across. In the north end of this area, around Lake Titicaca, was centered the great Inca Empire and other great civilizations that preceded it.

Bolivia's people are mostly of indigenous (Indian) background: Aymara, 25 percent; Quechua, 30 percent; mixed (mestizo), 30 percent. The remaining 15 percent are mainly European. The Indians use their own languages, but Spanish is the official language of the country. Sucre is the legal capital, though La Paz is the legislative center. Both cities are in the altiplano, about 250 miles apart. Santa Cruz is a booming city on the edge of the Oriente area.

Bolivia has been the victim of several incursions by its neighbors. It lost its outlet to the sea to Chile, part of its oil-rich chaco (southern Oriente) to Paraguay, and some of its rubber-producing north Oriente area to Brazil. But its minerals, particularly tin, of which it produces 12 percent of the world's supply, provide much of its wealth.

Bolivia has experienced extreme instability of government

throughout its history. The military has frequently taken over control, ostensibly to quell uprisings and revolutions. The nation has averaged about one change of government for every two years of its existence.

The revolution of April 1952 had far-reaching results, for out of it came the nationalization of the tin-mining industry and extensive land reform that broke the old feudalism of the big landholders. It also gave the vote to all, eliminating the old "literacy" and "knowledge of Spanish" requirements. It was a new day for the Amerindian. Even missionary organizations like the Friends and Adventists had to break up their large ranches that they had developed as part of their programs. A rebellion against all things foreign came out of the revolution, however, which unfortunately often included the missionary and his activities.

Finally, after a number of years of military dictatorships, in 1982 a democratic form of government was set up. In 1985 a smooth transition to a new democratic president and congress was made, and an era of stable rule seemed under way.

One of the earliest and now the largest of the non-Catholic missionary groups in Bolivia is the Seventh-Day Adventist church with about 18,000 members. They began work in the Lake Titicaca area in the 1890s as an extension of their strong mission in southern Peru. Education and medicine have been emphasized in their work. They were followed by the Canadian Baptists, the Plymouth Brethren, and the Methodists. A national church, Union Cristiana Evangelica, grew out of two nondenominational missions and became completely indigenous after the 1952 revolution.

The Church of the Nazarene in Bolivia

When Frank and Lula Ferguson made their exploratory journey to South America in 1906-7, they visited Bolivia and preached to the Aymaras, but they ultimately chose to work in Argentina. In 1922 Rev. and Mrs. Ninevah Briles went to Bolivia to work under another mission. They later returned to the United States, joined the Church of the Nazarene, and assumed a pastorate in Indiana.

When the General Board, as part of the missionary explosion following World War II, voted in January 1945 to open work in Bolivia, they asked the Brileses to return there as missionaries for the Church of the Nazarene. They located in La Paz, where they had a number of earlier contacts, and soon three congregations were functioning.

The selection of La Paz had its advantages, since it is the main population center. But its 12,000-foot altitude poses a great health problem for those not native to this rarefied atmosphere. It affects digestion, heart, and nerves—and disposition. Even though the city lies in a canyonlike depression that protects it to some degree from the chilly winds of the altiplano, it is a cold, inhospitable place climate-wise. It is difficult to understand how a city of over a million people could have developed in such a location, but its history dates from the earliest days of the Spanish conquest.

In 1947 the Brileses were joined by the Ronald Dentons, and in 1950 by the Jack Armstrongs. Both new couples experienced health problems and were transferred to the Argentina/Uruguay area. Other early workers included the Earl Hunters, who were transferred from Guatemala in 1952 to take over for the Brileses, who were returning permanently to the United States. There were also the Dale Sieverses and the Frank Van Develders, who could not take the high altitude either.

The mission centers that were opened up usually included a church and a school and sometimes a dispensary. (Mrs. Hunter, for example, was a nurse.) Church and school often came into conflict, however, even though they were intended to be mutually supportive. The problem was that the teachers who were by law government trained and thereby strongly nationalistic, did not easily submit to missionary and/or church control. But the high degree of illiteracy, particularly among the Aymara Indians of the altiplano, made school programs almost imperative if the people were to be reached by the gospel.

At times the medical work flourished with as many as 4,220 people being treated (1972), but this phase of the work was spasmodic. Clinics in the Tiquina Strait of Lake Titicaca, in La Paz, and in Alcoche were conducted by Berniece Andrus, Linda Spalding, Ruth DeBow, and others.

It was not until 1953 that the all-important school for the training of national pastors was begun. Prior to this, pastors were personally taught by the missionaries or in the schools of other missions. After a number of years of operation in various La Paz locations, a fine farm property was purchased down the valley from the city, where a permanent campus was developed. The somewhat lower altitude made this area more tolerable, and the campus became a district center. Giving leadership to these developments was Rev. Harold Stanfield, who served as mission superintendent from 1959 to 1972 (the last year as mission director). During his tenure the work grew from 12 organized churches to 52, with 117 preaching points.

In the 1960s and 1970s, a new group of missionaries came into the picture—as many as 14 being on the staff at one time. But then came the move toward nationalization of the church, and Bolivian leaders began to assume the responsibilities of leadership. The missionary force steadily diminished to 6 (1985).

The roster of this later group of missionaries included Rev. and Mrs. Ira Taylor (1958-68, transferred from Peru in 1958 after 18 years there), Rev. and Mrs. Harold W. Stanfield (1959-72, transferred from Nicaragua), the Vincent Seelys (1959-64), Rev. and Mrs. George Adkins (1960-67), Miss Margaret Primrose (1960-67), Rev. and Mrs. Tom Spalding (1963-79, then transferred to Panama), Miss Bethany Debow (1963-77), Rev. and Mrs. Paul Andrus (1966-75), Rev. and Mrs. Larry Webb (1969-77, after a term in Barbados 1963-68), Miss Caroline Hendrick (1969-77), Rev. and Mrs. Daniel Brewer (1969-85), Rev. and Mrs. Henry Stevenson (1972-84, then transferred to Spain), Rev. and Mrs. Ardee Coolidge (transferred from Chile in 1977 and serving until 1981), Rev. and Mrs. Wesley Harris (1979-84, then transferred to Paraguay), Rev. and Mrs. R. Alfred Swain (transferred from Ecuador in 1982 and now [1985] mission director), and Rev. and Mrs. Randy Bynum (1985).

Toward a National Church

In 1968, under the leadership of interim superintendent Tom Spalding, an in-depth study was made of the first 15 years in Bolivia. Growth had averaged only 63 members per year. Of the 36 national workers only 2 were ordained, and only 16 were involved in church planting; the others were in education. A change of emphasis seemed called for. More importantly, the study called for a more culturally oriented church, such as conducting services in the language selected by the local people and using indigenous music and instruments.

Missionaries began to assume minority roles on committees rather than leadership positions. They were thus involved in the process of making decisions but not in dictating them or merely approving or disapproving them. This placed Bolivia in the vanguard of the indigenous development of Nazarene mission strategy.

Eight new elders were ordained, and all were challenged to spiritual leadership. Church growth immediately accelerated to double its earlier rate, reaching 16 percent to 20 percent per year.

In 1971 Rev. Francisco Paxi was named associate district superintendent and served along with the mission director until 1976 when Rev. Nolberto Vicuña was elected. Rev. Rodolfo Vilela was superintendent in 1977 and 1978, and Rev. Claudio Ticona served from 1979 to 1981. Rev. Carlos Huaynoca was elected as district superintendent in 1982.

In order to better reach other areas of Bolivia, in 1980 the cities of Santa Cruz and Cochabamba were formed into a new pioneer district with four churches and 57 members. Rev. Henry Stevenson was named the district superintendent.

The growth of the work in Bolivia can be seen by recent statistics. In 1975, there were 3,762 members; in 1980, 4,019; and in 1985, 8,058. In 1982 a series of changes took place that have resulted in accelerated growth. The major move was in the area of ministerial training. The Bolivian Nazarene Seminary in La Paz was upgraded to offer the bachelor of theology degree. At the same time, a program of pastoral training by extension, called CENETA, was started in cooperation with the Seminary of the Americas in San Jose, Costa Rica. In its first year of operation in Bolivia 175 pastors and local preachers enrolled in this new program. Through this extension course a pastor can complete his ministerial training in four years. By 1985, 225 students had enrolled in the program. It was now possible for at least 40 lay preachers to become licensed ministers. These local preachers were encouraged to start new churches.

Then in 1984 there was a planned reduction of missionary personnel. Two missionary families were moved to other countries. The Henry Stevensons were reassigned to Seville, Spain, and the Wesley Harrises to Paraguay. Along with this, plans were made to divide the existing districts and involve more national leadership in the direction of the church program.

In January 1985 the La Paz District was divided into three with the splitting off of two new districts. The La Paz District became a regular district with 50 churches and 22 missions and 5,185 full and probationary members. The new Titicaca District with Rev. Francisco Paxi as superintendent was organized with 23 churches and 2 missions and 1,686 full and probationary members. The new Yungas District with Rev. Agustin Ajata as superintendent had 12 churches and 7 missions and 501 full and probationary members.

The Santa Cruz District had earlier been separated from the Cochabamba area to become a pioneer district and now had 6 churches and 2 missions with 204 full and probationary members. Rev. Randy Bynum was named superintendent of this district. A new district, the Central District, was formed from the Departments of Cochabamba, Oruro, and Potosi, with 8 churches and 2 missions and 482 full and probationary members. Rev. Alfred Swain was named superintendent of this pioneer district.

The La Paz, Titicaca, and Yungas districts are bilingual—Aymara and Spanish. The Central District is bilingual—Quechua and Spanish; and the Santa Cruz District has both Spanish- and Guarani-speaking members. The number of organized churches in 1985 was 99 with an additional 35 missions and a total membership of 8,058. Also in 1985 Rev. Eduardo Aparicio was named director of the Bolivian Nazarene Seminary. This was a significant step for the deployment of national leadership in Bolivia.

All of Bolivia was divided among the five districts, and an aggressive program of church planting got under way to extend the church to areas never before reached. The role of the missionaries had changed. While part of their time was given to the development of pioneer districts, their major task now was to support the national leadership and to assist in the program of theological education.

6. *Chile*

The long, narrow country of Chile, situated on the southern half of South America's west coast, is a unique land. It extends 2,630 miles from north to south and averages only about 100 miles wide. In that short distance across, it rises from sea level to altitudes in excess of 20,000 feet along the ridge of the Andes. It contains some of the most fertile soil on the continent and a good portion of its mineral wealth, but a climate that varies from the hot Atacama Desert in the north to cold, fog-shrouded forest wilderness in the south. Between the two areas is the moderate central valley where 75 percent of Chile's 11 million people live. Here is the capital city of Santiago (4.8 million), its port city of Valparaiso (273,000), and the resort city of Vina del Mar (260,000).

The north area was once part of the old Inca Empire, but the Spanish gained control in 1521. Independence was achieved in 1818. As with most other South American countries there have been alternating periods of constitutional government and military dictatorship. Extensive industrialization, particularly after World War I, eventually gave rise to Marxism, which began to infiltrate government until outlawed by President Gonzalez after World War II. In 1958 the tide began to turn again until in 1970 Allende, an avowed Marxist, came to power, only to be overthrown in 1973 by a bloody military coup led by General Pinochet. The purge of Communists that followed left deep scars that will take a long time to heal. Democratic elections have not yet been held to establish a civilian government, but the provisional military government still receives popular support.

Religious Influences

Most Chileans today would call themselves Catholics (unofficially less than 90 percent), but fewer than 10 percent in this secular society are active members. The failure of Catholicism to capitalize on its religious monopoly did open the door to Protestantism, however, and today Chile has the largest proportion of Protestants of any of the Spanish-speaking nations in South America—estimated to be as high as 20 percent. The effect of the Vatican II declaration that opened the door to Protestant missions was also significantly felt in Chile.

James Thompson came to Chile with his Lancastrian schools in 1821, but he did not stay long enough to get them firmly established. When he moved northward to Peru, the schools collapsed. Next came Rev. David Trumbull, who established an independent mission in Valparaiso in 1847 mostly for the English-speaking seamen who came to the port. Not long afterward (1851) the Presbyterians opened the first denominational mission.

The famed Bishop William Taylor (later bishop of Africa) led in the opening of Methodist work in 1877 by the establishment of schools (a standard Methodist procedure). The Christian and Missionary Alliance followed in 1898. The seeds of Pentecostalism were first planted by a Methodist missionary in 1910, and the charismatics soon dominated the evangelical scene.

The Church of the Nazarene in Chile

The work of the Church of the Nazarene in Chile officially began in January 1962, when the General Board voted to assume responsibility for a holiness mission that had been opened 10 years before in the northern port town of Arica. Rev. and Mrs. Boyd Skinner had been working in southern Bolivia under the sponsorship of the Hamilton County, Ind., Youth for Christ when they volunteered to go to Arica and try to open up a mission. In early June 1952 they set out on an exploratory trip to Chile and spent two months making contacts, distributing literature, and testing response. Encouraged by what they found, they returned to Bolivia and began preparations for a move to Arica. Their great adventure began on May 9, 1953. By July 19 a meeting room had been rented and services begun. Within a year, preaching points were established in several surrounding towns and villages as well as others in Arica itself.

In the fall of 1954 Rev. and Mrs. Carlyle McFarland and Rev. and Mrs. Jack Terry joined the Skinners in the rapidly expanding work. The tight housing situation made it necessary for the Terrys to return to Bolivia, but the Skinners and McFarlands continued to open new areas, even in remote mountain valleys.

It became obvious that the group in Indiana could not sustain such expansion, and a broader base of support was needed. It was thus that overtures were made to the Church of the Nazarene to take over the work. The General Board, after careful investigation, voted at its January 1962 meeting to accept the challenge. The work was placed under the jurisdiction of the Bolivia Council with Rev. Harold Stanfield as superintendent. This ready-made field consisted of six churches and eight other preaching points, with some capable national preachers like Maxinio Aguero and Juan Tancara. Pastoral training was difficult, but from 1956 to 1959 a Bible institute was operated in connection with Arica First Church. A very active lay group called Helpers to the Pastor was a powerful force in building the work.

But the arid north held a limited number of people to whom to minister. The more populous and hospitable central valley around Santiago, with nearly 5 million people, presented a challenging field. After an investigative trip by Revs. Stanfield and Skinner, land purchase negotiations and church registration procedures were begun. The first mission was launched in 1966. A nucleus of interested persons had been brought together principally through hearing the broadcast of "La Hora Nazarena." Indiana Nazarenes, under the leadership of Rev. Paul Updike, district superintendent, took a special interest in the Santiago work and provided the money for the first building. In October 1966 the La Granga Church was organized there by Dr. Hardy C. Powers, general superintendent.

Pioneering the Santiago work were Rev. and Mrs. Spurgeon Hendrix, veterans of three terms in Argentina and one in Cuba. Others who came to assist were Rev. and Mrs. Frank Elliott (1969-72), Rev. and Mrs. Charles D. Roberts (1972-77), and Rev. and Mrs. George Adkins (1970-77, transferred from Bolivia). Meanwhile the Chester Naramors were giving leadership to the Arica field (1966-70).

The next step was to the south, where the first evangelistic thrust was made in the city of Lanco in 1973. The following year, Rev. and Mrs. Boyd Skinner took up residence in the city of Concepcion to pioneer a work there. When illness forced them to leave, their place was taken by Rev. and Mrs. Spurgeon Hendrix and Rev. and Mrs. Don Cox. The latter had arrived in Chile two years before and had been working in the Santiago area.

The Bible school, now called Seminario Biblico Nazareno, has been an increasingly important factor in the growth of the work. Beginning with its opening in 1979, the earlier years were somewhat erratic with frequent changes in leadership. The program became stabilized when Rev. Tom Cook became director, and by 1985, 21 students had graduated. (Two of these, Alfredo Veloso and Guido Rosas, are now superintendents of the Central and South districts respectively, which were organized in January 1985.) The addition of another dormitory in 1985 made it possible to accommodate women students.

Miss Mary Wallace, a veteran of 24 years service in Nicaragua before being transferred to Chile in 1980, was a valuable addition to the school. Others of the missionary family have also participated. In addition to the resident enrollment, the CENETA extension program has been in operation out of four centers. Rev. Boyd Skinner is the present (1985) director of the Bible school program.

In 1980 Rev. and Mrs. Kurt Schmidlin, the first graduates of European Nazarene Bible College to become missionaries, arrived and were stationed in Arica. When in January 1985 the Chile field was divided into three districts, Rev. Schmidlin was appointed superintendent of the North District.

The Claude Sislers arrived in 1981 and were at first principally involved in the Bible school. When they and the Coxes returned from furlough in late 1985, their roles were switched, the Coxes joining the school staff, while the Sislers were assigned to open a new work on the South District.

When the Chile field was first separated from the Bolivia work in 1968, there were 3 organized churches and 10 other preaching points with a total membership of 240. By 1985 there were 3 districts, 20 organized churches, 6 other preaching points, and 897 members.

With 11 missionaries serving a constituency of this size, the missionary/member ratio was rather high, but it underscored the church's commitment to this promising field. The emergence of capable national leaders is a key part of the payoff of that investment. Veteran missionaries from other areas, such as the Stanfields and Hendrixes, also lent stability to the work. This tradition was maintained when in 1980 Rev. Ted Hughes was transferred from Uruguay to become mission director in the place of Rev. Stanfield, who was retiring for the second time.

7. *Ecuador*

The triangular-shaped country of Ecuador sits astride the equator (from which its name is derived) on South America's western coast. The offshore Galapagos Islands are also part of the country. Two ranges of the Andes divide the country into three parts: the Coast, the Sierra, and the Oriente.

The low-lying coastal area, though hot, humid, and fever-infested, is a fertile region where a majority of the country's 8 million people live. Here on the estuary of the Guayas River is Ecuador's largest city, Guayaquil, with over a million inhabitants. The central mountainous region (the Sierra) is the principal home of the Quechua Indians, descendants of the once-mighty Incas. The capital city of Quito (775,000) is in this area. The humid jungle of the Oriente on the eastern side of the Andes is inhabited by indigenous tribes such as the Aucas, until recently largely untouched by civilization. The discovery of oil here is having an increasing impact upon the economy of the whole nation. It was the annexation of a large chunk of the Oriente by Peru in the 1940s that created the tension presently existing between the two neighbor nations.

Ten percent of the population is of African origin and is concentrated principally in the northwest area around Esmeraldas. Europeans (another 10 percent) are concentrated in the cities. The 40 percent that are of Quechua (Inca) stock are mainly in the mountains and Oriente, while the mestizos (mixed blood) that make up the other 40 percent are widely scattered, but most live in the coastal region.

As mentioned with respect to other western South America countries, the Incas ruled this area until the Spanish conquest in 1534. After three centuries of Spanish rule, Ecuador won its independence on May 24, 1822, and became part of Simon Bolivar's Gran Colombia federation until 1830. Since then, instability of government has been a hallmark of the country as in many of the South American republics. Between 1830 and 1948, 62 different juntas held power, an average of about two years per government. Even though since 1948 some leaders have served their full four-year terms, there have been a number of coups. Free elections in 1978-79 gave promise of a more stable civilian government after more than a decade of military rule.

Religious Life in Ecuador

In the midst of the ebb and flow of South American political regimes, the enduring quality of Roman Catholic domination of the people is in sharp contrast. Nowhere is this more apparent than in Ecuador, which was the last to open its doors, even though it was but a small crack, to Protestant missions. The first such work began about the turn of the century among the mestizos, but today, after 80 years of effort, the total Protestant community numbers only about 16,000.

As elsewhere on the continent, the Seventh-Day Adventists have a strong work and account for 20 percent of the Protestant community. The various Pentecostal bodies total 30 percent. The Christian and Missionary Alliance has been quite successful with close to 20 percent.

A unique missionary ministry coming out of Ecuador is World Radio Fellowship's huge radio broadcasting facility "The Voice of the Andes" near Quito, with the familiar call letters HCJB (Heralding Christ Jesus' Blessings). Broadcasts from here blanket the Western Hemisphere and beyond with gospel programming—70 hours a day over its multiple transmitters. A staff of over 100 operate the station and related facilities, including a school and a hospital. Its extensive Bible correspondence school reaches almost a worldwide constituency. HCJB was the forerunner of several such gospel shortwave giants in various parts of the world.

The Church of the Nazarene in Ecuador

Interest in establishing a Nazarene work in Ecuador stemmed from the Peruvian field, though the political friction between the two countries was a hindering factor for many years. In 1964 serious discussions began to take place on the matter. Finally in 1968 Clyde Golliher and Phillip Torgrimson took an exploratory journey into Ecuador. Out of this came a request to the General Board that work be opened here, possibly in Guayaquil. Rev. and Mrs. Alfred Swain, who had been working in Lima since coming to the field in 1966, were commissioned to head the new project. Their special training in linguistics was a unique qualification for service in a multilingual situation such as might be encountered.

A more comprehensive survey trip was made in early 1971 by Clyde Golliher and Al Swain, covering all areas of the country. The Quechua area was particularly attractive to the Swains, who had been working among these people in Lima, but the wisdom of beginning in booming, responsive Guayaquil was reaffirmed.

Visas were granted in December 1971, and the Swains arrived in their new field of service February 29, 1972. A strategy of holding street-corner services and establishing house churches resulted in the launching of four congregations within a year.

Six months after the first service, a pastors' training program was already under way. This school was expanded with the coming of John and Sheila Hall in June 1973. He was an enthuasiastic promoter of Theological Education by Extension (TEE), whereby short-term classes would be held in various areas, which involved little disruption of a pastor's regular activities. However, for the Ecuador situation it was decided to use the residence school approach, and a campus was built in Guayaquil. Miss Joan Noonan, who had had four years teaching experience in the Swaziland Teacher Training College in Africa, joined the Bible college staff in 1979. When Ken and Sue Blish arrived in late 1981, he was named director of the Bible school. In 1983, however, it was voted to close the residence phase and concentrate on the extension (CENETA) program. By 1985, 40 students were studying on a weekly basis.

John and Laurel Sluyter served in Ecuador from 1975 to 1980, when they were moved to Argentina. He had been appointed in late 1979 as mission director of Argentina and for several months had commuted between the two countries. The Sluyters returned to Ecuador full-time in 1984. David and Marcia Hayse were appointed to the field in 1976, where his expertise in church building was of particular value in this growing area. This ability also resulted in his being named, in January 1981, mission project coordinator for Mexico, to supervise its many building programs. In 1984 he was called to the World Mission office at Headquarters in Kansas City to become coordinator of the ballooning Work and Witness program.

In 1982 the Al Swains were transferred to Bolivia, and the following year Joan Noonan was moved to Peru. Then in 1984 the John Halls joined the faculty of the seminary in Costa Rica. The end was not yet, for in 1985 the Ken Blishes were transferred to Bolivia. These many shifts indicated principally a sharp increase in national leaders who were ready to assume responsibility.

In the midst of these personnel changes, in 1984 the Ecuador field was divided into two districts, the Coast (Costa) District and Mountain (Sierra) District. Rev. Nelson Murillo, the first national to become a district superintendent, was placed in charge of the Costa District. Rev. John Sluyter, who had just been returned from Argentina, was named superintendent of the Sierra District and served for one year until the arrival of Rev. and Mrs. Dwight Rich to take over this responsibility. Rev. Sluyter became director of the enlarged CENETA program on the Sierra District.

Both districts were ably assisted in several building programs by Craig and Gail Zickefoose, Jim and Frances Jensen, and John and Carolyn Miller, who came to serve for various periods of time. In 1985 the Millers were placed on indefinite specialized assignment to work on building programs in both districts.

A significant event for the Ecuador field was the establishment of the central office for the South America Region in Quito in 1983. Formerly, South America had been included with Mexico, Central America, and the Caribbean under the directorship of Dr. James Hudson. In June 1983 South America was separated, and Rev. Louie Bustle, who had given outstanding leadership in launching the work in the Dominican Republic and who had been stationed more recently in Lima, Peru, was named director. He chose Quito as his base of operations. His wife, Ellen, became his office manager. He found able assistants in Eduardo and Beverly (Armstrong) González, whom he named to direct the extension seminary program (CENETA) for all of South America. They had worked in the seminary in Guayaquil during its last two years of operation while also pastoring a church in the city.

In 1985 the two districts reported 17 organized churches, an equal number of preaching points, and a total membership of 624, up from 188 only five years before or a 232 percent increase in that span.

8. *Colombia*

The far northwest republic of Colombia became the next country of South America to be entered by the Church of the Nazarene. In the beginning it was a venture fraught with frustration and near tragedy. Events conspired to bring the project near to collapse more than once in its first five years, but then the prospects greatly improved.

Only in recent years has Colombia been reasonably open to gospel work mainly because the Roman Catholic hierarchy has been able to exert enough pressure to make Protestant missionary work extremely difficult. At the same time, there are many factors that make Colombia a promising mission field. Not the least of these is its stable, constitutional government. Though socialistic, with the state owning oil refineries, hydroelectric plants, and other industry, foreign investment is invited and protected. It is a country of great natural wealth, and even though the standard of living is not very high, the 78 percent literacy rate is above average and still higher in the cities. All of which creates a positive base for ministry.

Colombia has an area of about 450,000 square miles, somewhat comparable to Peru and Bolivia, and a population of about 27½ million, much higher than either. Its people are 58 percent mestizo (mixed Spanish and Indian), 20 percent European, 14 percent mulatto (mixed Negro and European), and 8 percent Amerindian and Negro. One-third of the country is in the Andes Mountains, which at the northern end consist of three north/south ranges with highland plains between. The remaining two-thirds to the east and south is in the rolling lowlands of the upper Amazon and Orinoco river systems. Most people live in the healthful central highlands.

It was Colombia's fabulous wealth in gold that attracted the early Spanish explorers and made the area a focal point of their search for wealth. The three centuries of Spanish occupation left their permanent imprint on the nation, even though liberation under Bolivar came in 1819 with the formation of Gran Colombia, which included the whole northwest corner of South America. In 1830 Venezuela and Ecuador declared themselves independent states, and the remaining area was called New Granada until in 1866 the name of Colombia was adopted.

As in other Spanish areas of South America, Colombia has had its share of political upheaval and civil war, the most recent being a 10-year struggle from 1948 to 1957 called *La Violencia* (The Violence). It was well named, for it took 250,000 lives. Since the conflict involved a certain amount of Protestant/Catholic confrontation, the cause of evangelical missions was crippled.

A system of alternating governmental administrative power between the liberal and conservative factions was a temporary expedient until in 1974, two-party elections were reinstated. Though the government is now somewhat stable, terrorism has not been quelled. Seeking scapegoats, the insurrectionists have classified everything related to the United States as suspect, and even missionaries (e.g., the Wycliffe Bible Translators) have been falsely accused of being agents of the CIA. Such constant harassment has made missionary work difficult. Finally in March 1981 the army was able to break the back of the M-19 guerrilla movement, and a more normal situation emerged. It was in the midst of this turmoil that the Church of the Nazarene sought to gain a foothold.

Protestant Missions in Colombia

The first Protestant mission was opened in Colombia in 1856, and in subsequent decades several missionary groups established themselves. But since Protestants were generally identified with the liberal political wing (the Catholics being the conservatives), they were classified with the Communists and other rebel groups. Thus, during *La Violencia* Catholic priests took advantage of the situation to persecute Protestants, and thousands of outrages occurred. But converts who remained true during the persecution were of the highest caliber and won the reluctant admiration of their opponents. As in the Early Christian Church, the work grew strong in the midst of persecution.

The Church of the Nazarene Enters

The decision to begin a Nazarene mission in Colombia came at the General Board meeting in January 1974. Rev. and Mrs. Dean Galloway, veterans of 18 years of earlier service in Nicaragua, mostly as mission superintendent, but at that time pastoring in Hot Springs,

Ark., were named to launch the project. They moved to Colombia in 1975.

The first step was to arrange for government permits to open the work, and visas for the workers. In this they were providentially directed to a Protestant lawyer, Mr. Samuel Castro, who within a few months obtained the required papers.

The strategy adopted for the beginning was to launch home Bible studies in four major cities: Bogota (the capital), Cali, Medellin, and Baranquilla. To assist the Galloways, the board appointed Rev. and Mrs. Samuel Ovando. He was a banker from Chiapas, southern Mexico, and a graduate of the University of Mexico who also later attended Nazarene Theological Seminary. Mrs. Ovando, née Evelyn Crouch, was a former missionary to Peru. They, with their three children, arrived in Colombia in the summer of 1976. They were followed in May 1977 by Rev. and Mrs. Phillip "Pete" Torgrimson, he being the son of the veteran Peru missionaries.

But then tragedy struck. Rev. Galloway was discovered to be suffering from terminal cancer and had to return to the United States, where he died a few months later. Shortly after the departure of the Galloways, Samuel Ovando and his daughter were critically injured in an automobile accident. Months of hospitalization followed, first in a military hospital in Colombia and then back in the United States, before Rev. Ovando was able to return to the work.

Meanwhile, to fill in the gap the Harry Nyreens, newly arrived in Costa Rica to teach at the seminary there, were transferred to Colombia temporarily. Another couple, the James Palmers, were also sent. But despite the efforts of the two inexperienced couples the work was stymied for a while. Aggravating their problems was the political unrest of that particular time. But in 1979 the Louis Ragainses, veterans of 25 years in Nicaragua, were sent to Colombia as mission directors, while the Nyreens were returned to their post in Costa Rica. That same year the Ovandos returned to Colombia.

Churches were officially organized in Bogota and Cali, and by 1980 they had a combined membership of 43. From this small base the work began to grow under the leadership of the John Armstrongs in Cali and the Allen Wilsons and Ernest Staffords in Bogota. Allen Wilson was mission director and district superintendent. In 1984 the Robert Grays, formerly of Peru, joined the missionary staff.

Of particular significance was the increasing number of national workers who were joining the ranks and being trained for ministry.

Among them were Samuel Castro, who had originally been instrumental in getting the Church of the Nazarene certified in Colombia. He had now graduated from the Spanish seminary in San Antonio. Another was Christian Sarmiento, who received his master of divinity degree from Nazarene Theological Seminary in Kansas City in 1984. When Dr. V. H. Lewis visited the field in March 1985 three national pastors were ready for ordination: Hector Machuca, Hernan Osorio, and Adalberto Herrera.

By 1985 there were 11 organized churches and 652 members. There had been a 43 percent increase in membership just in the past year. The entire field was then divided into four sections: the Central District, which was at Phase 1 (pioneer) level under the superintendency of Mission Director Allen Wilson; and three pioneer areas—North Coast (Cartagena), Southwest (Cali), and Northwest (Medellin). If successful, such a unique setup for church growth was seen as a possible model for other world areas.

9. *Venezuela*

The last of the major countries of South America (outside of the Guianas) to be entered by the Church of the Nazarene was Venezuela. The vision for this work was first born in the mind and heart of Rev. William Porter, mission director in Puerto Rico, when in 1966 he visited there as a member of the Puerto Rico Symphony orchestra. The great modern city of Caracas with its 3 million people impressed him, and he wondered why the Church of the Nazarene had bypassed Venezuela so long.

Venezuela, whose name means "Little Venice," was so named by the Italian explorer Amerigo Vespucci when he sailed along its low-lying coast. It was originally part of Gran Colombia, which included also the present countries of Ecuador and Colombia, but became a separate nation in 1830. This was achieved under the leadership of the country's national hero and native son, Simon Bolivar.

Venezuela is a country of 350,000 square miles extending 900 miles east to west, and 800 miles north to south. It is bordered on the west by Colombia, on the east by Guyana, and on the south by Brazil, while on the north lies the beautiful Caribbean Sea. There are four geographical divisions: the Andes mountain region to the west, rising to 17,000 feet; the Llanos or Central Plains region; the vast, dense jungle region of the southeast; and the Caribbean coastal plain along the north. In the remote jungle area of the country is found Angel Falls, the world's highest waterfall, 3,212 feet.

Although there remain remnants of the original Indian tribes, the Caribs (east) and Arawaks (west), their numbers have dwindled to fewer than 60,000. The Spanish-speaking population is about 17 million, 65 percent of whom are of mixed ancestry. The early immigrants were Spaniards and Negroes, while in the last 50 years Spaniards, Portuguese, and Italians have formed the basis of the population mix. Prior to 1936, 90 percent was "rural, illiterate, and barefoot," but a change in government in that year brought a great transformation. Now 80 percent of Venezuelans live in cities, 20 of which have over 100,000 population. The country leads the South American continent in gross national product, quality of life index, and political freedom index. Major industries are steel, oil, and textiles. It is the fifth-largest exporter of petroleum in the world. It has 32 universities and institutions of higher learning.

The Gideon Bible Society has been quoted as saying that Venezuela is "the most democratic and least evangelized country in South America." Only 1½ percent are evangelicals. Although the country is 95 percent Roman Catholic, fewer than 10 percent attend church regularly. The result is a rich field for evangelism.

A strong evangelical influence over the years has been Trans World Radio, whose powerful transmitters are located on Bonaire, an offshore Dutch island. Among the programs aired has been "La Hora Nazarena." Over 700 mailed-in responses had been received from Venezuela, which provided some of the original contacts for the church. Another introductory medium was the Spanish literature program of the Nazarene Publishing House. These materials were widely used in the country before Nazarene work was ever started. The name Nazarene was therefore well known and highly respected.

The Church of the Nazarene Enters

In the 1970s, as Puerto Rico rapidly moved toward regular district status, the Porters realized that their missionary days there were numbered. As they looked to the future, Venezuela moved to the center of their thinking. They began talking to church leaders about the matter but were told that it would be 1980 before such a move could be made. So in 1976 they accepted the assignment as district superintendent in New Zealand, returning to the United States for furlough in late 1980. Not long afterward, at the General Board meeting in February 1981, the decision was made to start a work in Venezuela, the last Spanish-speaking country in the Americas, and possibly the world, that the church had not yet entered.

The Porters were, of course, named to launch the work, and in August 1981 they made a 10-day exploratory trip to assess the situation. While there, they started legal proceedings to register the church and obtain entrance visas for themselves. By some remarkable providences that served to confirm their confidence that God was leading in this project, they made some significant contacts. Among these key people was a Christian lawyer who took their legal matters in hand.

A letter was drafted to send to over 500 listeners to "La Hora Nazarena" whose names were on file, telling them that the Church of the Nazarene was coming to Venezuela. They were asked if they would offer their signatures to help the church get government recognition. Over 50 enthusiastically responded. This was a good omen.

In December a second trip was made to contact as many of these people as possible. Within a few days 20 supporters were enlisted, many of them professional people. Homes were offered for prayer and Bible study groups, and the prospects for establishing the Venezuelan work grew ever brighter. A third trip in May 1982 brought even broader contacts that augured well for the future.

In February 1982 the General NWMS Council adopted as its 50th anniversary project a churchwide offering to be received on August 15, 1982, for the opening of the work in Venezuela. The goal was set at $200,000. The Porters were to move to Venezuela six weeks after that, and reservations were made accordingly.

As the time of departure neared, there was rising concern about the visas, which had not come through. The bright light on the horizon was that the special offering had far surpassed its goal (eventually reaching $586,644). After interminable delays the visas were finally granted, and on November 11, 1982, the Porters were on their way, a month and a half behind their original schedule.

The first service was held on the front porch of the Galvis home in Valencia on December 5, 1982. Some months later the pastor of a nearby church passed away, and the congregation offered their fully equipped building to the Church of the Nazarene.

The next move was to Barinas, a city in the lower Andes Mountains, where an independent congregation voted to join the Church of the Nazarene. At the close of a fruitful revival led by a group of pastors from Puerto Rico, the church was officially organized in June 1983—the first in Venezuela. Then came an opening in Calabozo, a city of 60,000 located about 100 miles south of Caracas, where property was purchased and the first of several Work and Witness teams to come to Venezuela erected a church.

After much searching, an excellent property was found on the outskirts of Caracas where a district parsonage, which also contained space for a district office, was built by Work and Witness teams. Reflecting on the frustrating delays from 1980 through 1982 that had kept the Porters from realizing their dream of opening work in Venezuela, they were now seeing how significant that was. For in that interim the oil glut had affected the economy of the country to such an extent that the value of the American dollar there increased by three times. Property and materials that were formerly prohibitive in cost were now manageable.

In the summer of 1983, 20 Nazarene college students in the international Student Mission Corps, assisted by three Puerto Rican pastors and veteran missionary Harold Hampton, held eight evangelistic campaigns in the country. One of these was in a store building in a shopping mall in Caracas that blossomed into a church. By Diamond Jubilee Sunday, October 16, 1983, six new congregations were ready for official organization.

In December 1983 services were begun in Barquisimeto, the fastest-growing city in the nation in the heart of a vast agricultural region. Four months later it too was an organized church. The next move was into the northwestern city of Maracaibo, the center of the petroleum industry and Venezuela's second-largest city. In a matter of weeks a congregation of 40 people was brought together, made up mostly of university students and professionals.

On February 12, 1984, at the San Martin Shopping Mall Church in Caracas, the Venezuela District was officially organized by General Superintendent V. H. Lewis. There were eight fully organized churches and five other congregations with a total membership of 255.

By the time of the second district assembly in March 1985, there were 27 congregations, 15 of which were organized with a total membership of 521. A 100 percent increase or more had been achieved in all phases in one year's time. The highlight of the assembly was the ordination of the first three elders on the district. The training of pastors had been a priority from the first through a strongly organized extension program (CENETA-VEN) out of the Seminary of the Americas in Costa Rica. By March 1985 there were 63 active students, 37 of whom felt a call to the ministry. The principle of self-propagation was also a key to growth. This was summed up in a threefold program:

- Each member win a member
- Each church start a church
- Each pastor train a pastor

Explosive growth was destined to continue as calls continued to come not only from many areas of Venezuela itself but even from the offshore Dutch island of Curaçao. In little more than two years, churches had been established in the capitals of 6 of the 20 states, plus the national capital of Caracas. By the end of 1985 total membership had reached 740.

B. PORTUGUESE SOUTH AMERICA

Brazil

Brazil is the largest South American nation and fifth largest in the world. It is also the only republic on the continent whose language is Portuguese. With 3¼ million square miles of land, it takes up half the continent's area, and its 134 million people account for half its population. Sixty-two percent are of European extraction, 26 percent of mixed blood (European, African, and Indian), while the remainder are chiefly Amerindians and Orientals. Almost 85 percent are professed Catholics, 11 percent Protestants, with spiritists included among the remaining 4 percent. In actual fact, says William R. Read, "the current strength of the Roman Catholic church in Brazil is not much greater than that of the Protestant church" (*Brazil 1980: The Protestant Handbook*).

Mainly because of the vast, 1.5 million-square-mile, sparsely settled Amazonian jungle, 90 percent of Brazil's population live on only 10 percent of the land. The greatest concentration of people is in the industrial area of the southeast in what is called the Magic Triangle, marked off by the cities of Rio de Janeiro (5 million), Sao Paulo (7 million), and Belo Horizonte (1.4 million). The capital of Brasilia, a planned city carved out of bush country 600 miles north of Rio, has a population of a little over 400,000. If the total metropolitan areas of these great cities were included, the official population figures would be almost doubled. Brasilia's satellite cities would bring its total to 1.2 million.

After the Treaty of Tordesilla of 1494 assigned South America's eastern hump to them, the Portuguese did little to explore, let alone develop this vast territory. It did not have the readily accessible wealth of the Spanish West. Feeble attempts at colonization in the 16th and 17th centuries fared poorly, but as always, the Jesuit priests were there to establish a Catholic presence anyway.

During the Napoleonic wars, King João VI fled Portugal in 1806 and established his royal court in Brazil, which thus became an empire until the royal family was banished to Europe in 1889. The subsequent republic period has been a rocky one, often dominated by military rulers as at the present time. But the country is becoming an industrial giant, and though civil and political liberties are restricted, the country enjoys a certain amount of congruity and security.

The Christian Church in Brazil

No country in South America has received more attention from missionary groups than has Brazil. Many thousands of missionaries have gone to that land, the vast majority of whom came from the United States.

The earliest non-Catholic influence in Brazil was an abortive attempt to establish a French Huguenot colony in 1555. Like many other colonists who followed from almost every part of the world, they brought their religious beliefs with them and established ethnic churches. It was not until the latter half of the 19th century, however, that specific missionary work was attempted. Presbyterians, Lutherans, Baptists, and Methodists were involved, and they account for one-quarter of all Protestants in Brazil today.

The phenomenal growth of the charismatic groups is, however, the most significant religious development. Beginning in 1911 with two Swedish-American missionaries who later became associated with the Assemblies of God but were not supported from abroad, the various Pentecostal groups now account for nearly 70 percent of the 6 million Protestant adherents. One of the fastest growing of these groups is the Congregação Crista (Christian Congregation), which began as a single congregation among Italian immigrants but now numbers over 500,000 in membership.

The Church of the Nazarene Arrives

Nazarenes from the Cape Verde Islands had been migrating to Brazil since the 1930s and had been calling for the church to open a work there. Also Ervin and Marjorie Stegemoeller, Nazarene laymen from Indianapolis who were living in Brazil, had been urging the church to move into this wide-open field.

In late 1957 Dr. G. B. Williamson, general superintendent, and Dr. H. T. Reza made a brief survey trip to Brazil, and out of this came the decision to make it a golden anniversary project for the Church of the Nazarene. On January 10, 1958, Rev. Earl Mosteller, mission superintendent in the Cape Verde Islands, received the following cablegram from Kansas City: "Board requests you to open Brazil this year. Cable your approval. Rehfeldt." It was a shock in one sense, but the year before, while on furlough, the Mostellers had heard talk of the possibility of Brazil being made an anniversary project. The challenge intrigued them, for in their travels to and from Cape Verde they had met a number of prominent Brazilians, and the idea of going there had been given more than a passing thought. Thus the cryptic message of the cablegram found fertile ground in the Mostellers' hearts. Leaving their beloved Cape Verde would not be easy, particularly for their three girls, but feeling it to be the call of God, they began their preparations. On July 21 they set sail for Brazil.

Ten days later, after several stops along the Brazilian coast, their boat docked at Santos, port city of the great metropolis of Sao Paulo, 25 miles inland. Here they were met by the Stegemoellers and a Cape Verdian friend, Jose Zito Oliveira, who had emigrated to Brazil two years before.

The decision had been made to make Campinas, about 60 miles farther inland from Sao Paulo, the base of operations, and a search began for housing and a place to hold services. Rev. and Mrs. Charles Gates, also assigned to Brazil, arrived on September 20. Their initial problem was to learn the language in which the Mostellers were already fluent, though their accent was somewhat different (like that between an Englishman and an American).

Much time was spent by the missionaries scouting the metropolitan areas seeking for openings for the church, following up on contacts whose names had been given to them, and building their own mailing list. By the end of the year they had the names of 250 viable contacts. On January 10, 1959, the first Brazilian convert was won even before church services were begun.

Jose Zito Oliveira, the Cape Verdian, felt God's call to become a minister, and the Mostellers began teaching him the *Manual* course of study. It was the beginning of an important phase of missionary activity.

Unable yet to find a suitable place of worship, weekly services were begun on March 18, 1959, in the Stegemoellers' home, with 13 present (only one "outsider"). Within a month attendance had doubled, and both Sunday and Wednesday services were begun.

On April 23, 1959, Ronald and Sarah Denton and family arrived and were stationed in Belo Horizonte. Their previous experience in

Bolivia, Argentina, and Uruguay would stand them in good stead, but converting from Spanish to Portuguese would be necessary. Though the two languages have similar roots, there are distinctive differences that take time to master.

Still lacking a meeting place, the leaders received permission in July to build a temporary tabernacle; but before construction was begun, a strategically located building, not quite completed but two blocks from the city square, was offered to the church. The opening service there, held on August 11, was an eventful occasion attended by the mayor and several other government officials, with the army band providing music. An opening week of nightly meetings with Rev. C. T. Corbett, visiting evangelist from the United States, climaxed with a closing attendance of 200. Some 85 people had responded to the invitation to accept Christ as their personal Savior. Later a four-story building of modern design was constructed on Francisco Glicerio Street, a main city artery. Provision was made for the addition of six more floors. Here is housed the First Church congregation, along with the offices of the mission director, the Southeast district superintendent, and the Brazilian Nazarene Publications.

Services were begun in a Japanese community in Sao Paulo, and negotiations were begun to obtain property in the new capital of Brasilia. On October 30, 1959, the work in Belo Horizonte was officially opened with Dr. G. B. Williamson present. In connection with his visit, the first Mission Council meeting was held, and the first church was organized in Campinas with 14 charter members.

By the time of the 1960 General Assembly, work had been started by the Ronald Dentons in a suburb of the newly dedicated capital of Brasilia, and six young men there had testified to a call to preach. Later that year Rev. and Mrs. James Kratz joined the missionary family. They were followed in 1962 by Rev. and Mrs. Robert Collins, who became involved in the district youth work and in the beginning of the church in Americana.

Years before, Rev. and Mrs. Joaquin Lima had migrated from Cape Verde to Argentina, where they had established the work in Bahia Blanca. When the Church of the Nazarene came to Brazil, they were invited to join in the work and became the first Portuguese pastors there. In 1975 he became the national superintendent of the key Southeast District.

From the start, the concept of the "three selfs" (self-support, self-government, and self-propagation) was strongly emphasized. The matter of self-support, however, seemed difficult to establish, perhaps because missionary subsidies to both churches and pastors had come to be expected, but also because of the ravages of inflation. The fact remains that by 1970, only 1 of the 36 churches and preaching points had reached the goal of self-support. Nonetheless, total membership had reached 828.

The fact that there were only 21 Brazilian pastors in 1970 may have been a cause for concern if church planting were to continue, but the recent graduation of several promising young ministers was an encouraging prospect for the Brazilian church. A more disturbing problem, however, was the infiltration of tongues teaching, which was disruptive to the point of threatening the progress of the work. The Brazilian church weathered the storm successfully but not without some wounds.

A major turn of events took place in 1974 when the Mostellers were transferred to Portugal to pioneer the work there. Rev. Robert Collins was named mission director in his place. In 1975 Dr. and Mrs. Floyd Perkins were transferred from South Africa to direct the Brazilian Nazarene Bible College in Campinas. Dr. Perkins led in the purchase of a piece of property as the first step in a relocation project. But late in the year, Mrs. Perkins became critically ill, which necessitated their return to the United States.

The following year Rev. and Mrs. J. Elton Wood were transferred from the Cape Verde Islands to fill this post. Rev. Wood had served for 23 years in a similar responsibility in Cape Verde. He and his wife had also been involved in the excellent publication program there, which had been supplying books and other holiness literature to Mozambique and Brazil as well as to the Cape Verde Islands. The plan was for them to continue their translation work in their new location. Under Rev. Wood's leadership, an attractive and functional administration building was designed and built on the new campus in Campinas.

In 1973 Rex and Edith Ludwig were sent to Brazil from Panama, and in 1976 they were assigned to open up a pioneer area in the southern panhandle region. It was organized into the South Pioneer District in 1979.

At the 1979 District Assembly in Campinas, Dr. Eugene Stowe, in a special ceremony, commissioned Rev. and Mrs. Stephen Heap, along with João and Ebe Arthur Souza, who were recent graduates of the Bible college, to open a pioneer area in the northeast, 1,700 miles away. The target city was João Pessoa, capital of the state of Paraiba on the eastern hump of the continent. In January 1980 the Jim Kratzes moved to Natal, 100 miles farther north, to open a second church in this new area. Work and Witness teams from Oklahoma and Kansas built an attractive church in João Pessoa, which was dedicated in January 1981 by Dr. V. H. Lewis at the time of the first mini-district assembly.

In January 1983 the Terry Read family was transferred from Haiti to Brazil Northeast to cover for the Heaps, who were about to go on furlough. The Jim Kratzes had returned from furlough in March of that year and resumed work in Natal. In the summer of 1983 the Carl Romeys returned to Brazil from a medical leave and were also assigned to the Northeast District.

The growth of the church in this area was significant. Sunday School attendance by 1985 was over 700 (a 100 percent increase over the year before), and membership was over 300. There were eight organized churches and two districts, one at Phase 1 (pioneer) level and the other a pioneer area.

Because of the great distance between the two sections of the Brazil field, it was voted in 1984 to divide into two Mission Councils. Rev. Stephen Heap was named mission director of South Brazil, and Rev. Terry Read of North Brazil. Meanwhile in the South area, Rio/Sao Paulo had become a regular district and was scheduled for division into two regular districts in 1986. The Minas/Gerais District had reached Phase 3 (mission) status, and the South area under the leadership of the Eldon Kratzes (he being the son of the James Kratzes) had become a pioneer district.

In addition to the missionaries already mentioned, recognition should be given for the labors of others who served for shorter terms: Rev. and Mrs. Roger Maze, Rev. and Mrs. Larry Clark, Rev. and Mrs. James Bond, and Rev. and Mrs. Donald Stamps. By 1985 total membership in the four organized districts had reached 4,226, almost double what it had been in 1980. There were 50 organized churches and 42 other preaching points.

VI

SOUTH PACIFIC REGION

- Australia
- New Zealand
- Papua New Guinea
- Samoa
- Indonesia
- Micronesia

Researchers:

Carol Anne Eby—Papua New Guinea
George E. Rench—Indonesia

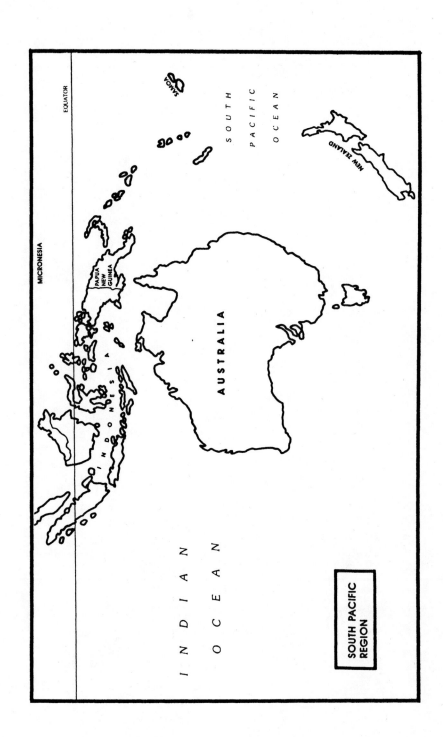

SOUTH PACIFIC
REGION

A. AUSTRALIA

Australia, the last continent to be entered by the Church of the Nazarene, had been largely a forgotten land as far as the holiness message was concerned. Periodically suggestions would come in to Kansas City Headquarters that the church should be established in "the land down under," but no move was made until the mid-1940s.

Here was a land of some 3 million square miles with a population at the time of just over 9 million, most of whom were concentrated on the eastern and southern coasts. Half the people lived in five main cities: Sydney, Melbourne, Adelaide, Brisbane, and Perth. Ninety-five percent of the people were of British descent, and over a third members of the Anglican church (Church of England). The population has since grown to over 15.5 million.

Australia, however, had not been entirely without a holiness witness, for Samuel Logan Brengle of the Salvation Army, and E. E. Shelhamer of the Free Methodist church, among others, had conducted holiness revivals there. Wally Betts, a Methodist minister in Melbourne, was a clear exponent of the doctrine of holiness. In fact, there were scattered groups of holiness believers in various areas. Among them was Alfred C. Chesson in Sydney, who was copastor of an independent congregation with his son Ralph, and a young Methodist home missionary, Harold Madder. They had long been praying for a holiness church in Australia. Another was Douglas Pinch who, with his wife, Maysie, was working among the aborigines in Coraki, New South Wales.

The First Nazarene Roots

It was the life and witness of an American serviceman during World War II that was the catalyst that brought the Church of the Nazarene to Australia. Meredith T. (Ted) Hollingsworth, a British-born licensed minister from Little Rock, Ark., while serving with the U.S. Army Medical Corps in New Guinea, contracted a tropical disease that necessitated his being returned to the United States. Though his orders read that he was to be taken directly home, for some reason he was taken instead to a military hospital in Australia, first in Townsville and then in Brisbane. During his two-months stay at the latter place, he responded rapidly to treatment and was soon out in the city looking for a church group with whom to worship.

He thus came into contact with the Mount Pleasant Gospel Hall, a group that was of Plymouth Brethren background. There, among others, he met 35-year-old Albert A. E. Berg, then an Australian army officer, and Mr. and Mrs. Hubert Kilvert, who were much interested in Ted Hollingsworth's testimony to entire sanctification. This led to inquiry concerning the Church of the Nazarene. What the visitor testified about seemed to them the answer to their personal longing for a closer walk with God. In fact, Albert Berg already had a copy of a book by Thomas Cook titled *New Testament Holiness* and had actually been preaching the experience without himself possessing it at the time. After talking with Ted Hollingsworth, he promised him he would become a seeker for entire sanctification. Spiritual victory ultimately came in January 1945.

Meanwhile, in June 1944 Hollingsworth had been returned to the United States for discharge. Soon after his arrival he wrote to Dr. J. B. Chapman, general superintendent, about the great opportunity open to the Church of the Nazarene in Australia. Dr. Chapman turned the letter over to Dr. S. T. Ludwig, general secretary and at that time head of the Department of Home Missions. He in turn contacted Hollingsworth and asked him to prepare a comprehensive report for presentation to the Board of General Superintendents at their September meeting. They were favorably impressed and sent the report on to the General Board with their recommendation to proceed with plans to take the church to Australia.

Doubtless this chain of events was hastened by an unusual action taken at the June 1944 General NYPS Convention. Without any knowledge of what had been transpiring in Australia, the convention adopted a resolution that read in part: "That the General NYPS Council be authorized to lay plans for the raising of $50,000 during this quadrennium for the evangelization of Australia and New Zealand." It had to be more than coincidence!

The upshot was that Ted Hollingsworth was invited to meet with the General NYPS Council at its January 1945 meeting to lay plans for the project. Then in the General Board meeting that immediately followed, the opening of the work in Australia was officially authorized with Dr. H. V. Miller as the supervising general superintendent.

The first step was to have Albert Berg become a member of the Church of the Nazarene and receive a minister's license. Since there was no church in Australia to join, he became *in absentia* a member of the Warren, Pa., church in April 1945 and was granted a minister's license by the Pittsburgh District. Mr. Berg laughingly related later that when the word got around about his new church affiliation, a friend greeted him one day with, "Good morning, Brother Berg, how is the Church of the Nazarene this morning? Is he well?" As Berg commented, the Church of the Nazarene in Australia was indeed "under my hat."

For a while he faced instense opposition, not the least from his own family, whose Calvinistic roots ran deep. Even his fiancée, Marion Russell, did not go along with him for a while. But eventually attitudes softened, and one by one they and others became seekers after holiness.

Ted Hollingsworth saw to it that Bert Berg was well supplied with holiness literature and information about the Church of the Nazarene. This he distributed among his acquaintances, including his friend Alfred Chesson down in Sydney. Not long after, Chesson was passing through Brisbane on an evangelistic mission and there talked with Bert Berg about the Church of the Nazarene. After a time of prayer and study he, too, decided to join, and within a month (November 16, 1945) he was received into membership and licensed by the Louisiana District. In December 1945 Bert Berg conducted a series of holiness meetings for A. C. Chesson in Sydney, and there he met Arthur A. Clarke, who, the following April, cast his lot with the Nazarenes. The Douglas Pinches (who, as earlier stated, were working among a colony of aborigines) became members, and he received his preacher's license in January 1946.

The Church Begins to Organize

Rev. E. E. Zachary, superintendent of the Kansas District, was named to direct the new work, and he and his family arrived in Australia in October 1946. Within three weeks he held a revival meeting with A. C. Chesson's group in the Campsie area of Sydney and, on November 3, 1946, organized them into the first Australian Church of the Nazarene with 20 charter members. A. A. Clarke was called as pastor.

The second church was organized in Brisbane with 17 members on January 19, 1947, of which Bert Berg's group was the nucleus. The

Pinches' church, Tweed River, was organized in July 1947. Uniquely, it was here that the first Nazarene buildings in Australia were erected—a church and a parsonage. The faculty and students at Bethany Nazarene College provided the necessary funds. One of Rev. Pinch's most faithful helpers was Langus Phillips, a native who was considered pastor of the church. "One of the godliest as well as gifted men I have been privileged to know," wrote Rev. Pinch concerning him. He was both an orator and a musician.

A fourth church was organized in Manly, Queensland. Then in April 1947, A. C. Chesson was led to move to Adelaide, 1,000 miles west of Sydney, to do evangelistic work. Here, through a series of remarkable providences, he was able to bring together a congregation that, toward the end of that year, became the fifth church.

Meanwhile, Bert Berg had been instrumental in leading a young Bible institute graduate, Erle E. Spratt, into the experience of entire sanctification; and when he returned to his home in the great southern port city of Melbourne, he won Stanley Simmons and his wife to the cause of holiness also. When Rev. Weaver W. Hess, from the northwest United States, came to hold a series of holiness revivals in Australia, one of his stops was in Melbourne. Here the sixth church was organized in February 1948 with 12 members. Erle Spratt served as pastor until in September he was called to the Northmead church, and Stan Simmons took his place.

The Northmead church had been organized at Easter time in suburban Sydney, the work having been launched by a lay member of the Sydney (Campsie) church, Edward Clucas. Shortly afterward on April 1-4, the first district assembly was held in Belmore Park, Sydney, with Rev. Zachary presiding. Total membership on the district was reported as 128. An unforgettable outpouring of the Holy Spirit upon the closing services of the assembly was to the young church a seal of God's approval and blessing upon their venture.

Shortly after the assembly, Rev. Zachary and Albert Berg left for the Nazarene General Assembly in St. Louis. While in the United States, Berg spent three months visiting many districts. This served to acquaint him with the church and also gave opportunity for the church to receive a firsthand report of the great workings of God in Australia.

Another significant event of 1948 was the assimilation of a small independent holiness group in Sydney under the leadership of C. A.

Garrett. It was known as the Burwood church, but later it merged with the Campsie congregation to form a new church in the residential suburb of Birrong. Rev. Garrett (ordained in 1953) remained as pastor until called to serve with Dr. Richard Taylor in the newly formed Bible school in 1953.

Since the Zacharys were in Australia on tourist visas that allowed them residence only six months at a time, a more permanent type of leadership was needed. Thus when Dr. H. V. Miller came to conduct the second district assembly in early December 1948 (the second assembly that year), he proposed the election of their own district superintendent. Their vote was overwhelmingly for Rev. Albert Berg, who during the assembly was ordained by Dr. Miller, along with A. C. Chesson, A. A. Clarke, H. L. R. Madder, and W. D. Pinch. Rev. Berg was to serve in the superintendent's role until his death in 1979—over 30 years.

Also at this landmark assembly, the auxiliary organizations were set up. The Nazarene Foreign Missionary Society, under the leadership of Mrs. Grace Dawson (sister of Rev. Berg), and the Nazarene Young People's Society, with Stan Simmons as president, became flourishing activities. The Church Schools Department was less successful. Lacking precedents to follow, a succession of chairmen failed to get an effective program under way.

Five years later in 1953, W. D. Pinch took over the Church Schools assignment. Working closely with Drs. A. F. Harper and E. G. Benson from Headquarters in Kansas City, he was able to put in motion the Cradle Roll, Home Department, Christian Service Training, and Vacation Bible School programs along with promotion of the Sunday School. A rousing annual Church Schools Convention became a part of the district assembly program. The Caravan program was an outstanding success. Here Australian motifs and awards were substituted for the American ones. This gave an indigenous flavor that proved to be very popular.

Also regular district and general budgets were assigned, and soon Australia was a 10 percent district in General Budget giving. A radio secretary was appointed to develop further outlets for the "Showers of Blessing" program, which was already proving to be an effective means of acquainting the populace with the Church of the Nazarene.

The Development of a Bible College

A prime need for the young district was to establish a training center for ministers. As an expression of their concern, in 1951 the district had raised a beginning fund of $1,500 for this purpose. Then in January 1952 the General NYPS Council chose as its 1952-56 quadrennial project the raising of $25,000 for the establishment of a Bible school in Australia—a fitting sequel to their fund-raising effort that had launched the work eight years before. Dr. Richard S. Taylor was selected as the first principal, and he and Mrs. Taylor and son, Paul, arrived in Australia in October 1952.

In February 1953 a six-acre campus with adaptable buildings on it was purchased in Thornleigh, a suburb of Sydney. Dr. G. B. Williamson, general superintendent, who was in Australia to conduct the district assembly, assisted in the consummation of the property deal. After feverish preparation the school opened on March 10, with 10 students enrolled, 7 in residence. The first graduating class received their diplomas in November 1955.

The school played an increasing role in the work of the Australia District and also of New Zealand. An interesting characteristic was that a good proportion of the students were laymen—sometimes almost equal to the number of pastors in training. The result was unusually capable leadership at local and district levels. In 1960 Dr. Taylor returned to the United States to join the faculty of Nazarene Theological Seminary, and Rev. E. E. Young took his place. He, in turn, was succeeded by Rev. Nelson G. Mink in December 1967. A year later Dr. Chester O. Mulder assumed the leadership and served until 1974.

The need for a more adequate campus was an increasing problem, and in anticipation of relocation, the Thornleigh property was sold in 1974. A new campus was purchased in suburban Brisbane, and a large, multipurpose unit built. The new Australasian Nazarene Theological College (now including New Zealand in its constituency) was reopened on March 8, 1976, with Dr. R. T. Bolerjack as principal. He was followed by Dr. Steve Ratlief, and he in turn in mid-1982, by Dr. Robert Woodruff.

In 1984 Dr. Grady Cantrell, recently retired superintendent of the Northern California District, became principal of the college. Serving with him on the faculty were Rev. Ken Koil, Rev. James DuFriend, and former principal, Dr. Chester Mulder. The school was filling an increasingly important place in the growth and development of the church in both Australia and New Zealand.

The Church Grows

By the time of the 1953 assembly there were 12 churches with a total membership of 217. These churches extended all the way from Mackay, 500 miles north of Brisbane, around to Adelaide on the south coast, a distance of over 1,500 miles by road.

Of particular interest was the church at Tweed River, 70 miles south of Brisbane, which had become a center for the work among the aborigines. Most of the 80,000 tribesmen in the country lived in the outback (west of the mountain range along the east coast), but groups were to be found throughout the continent. One area of concentration was along the Tweed River.

Beginning in 1945, Doug and Maysie Pinch had been laboring among these people and found an eager response. Besides their main center at Tweed River, they established five outstations. Several fruitful revivals were held in the area, and there were many baptisms. A dozen young people had shown interest in training for Christian service, but plans to launch a Bible school for these people never materialized. In fact, despite the promising developments, there was apparently a reluctance on the part of the church leaders to invest the limited district funds in the aboriginal work. This phase was therefore left largely to fend for itself. When in 1956 the Pinches took a pastorate elsewhere, Will Bromley, missionary appointee to New Guinea, was temporarily placed in charge of the Tweed River church.

Two more churches were later organized in the Brisbane area, one at Wynnum and the other at Stafford. Both of them were pastored by hardworking Rev. Harold Madder, who was also serving as district secretary and office manager of the Nazarene Book Depository, the latter a very important adjunct to the work. Churches were also organized at Eidsvold, Queensland, 300 miles northwest of Brisbane; at Gawler, near Adelaide; and at the college in Thornleigh, Sydney.

A most significant expansion took place in March 1960 when David and Margy Spall, recent graduates of the Bible college, went to Perth on the western side of the continent to establish a Church of the Nazarene. It was a lonely task, for they were 1,700 miles from their nearest Nazarene neighbor. Furthermore, their sole initial contact in the city was an English lady who had attended the Bible college in Sydney.

The Spalls began services in the living room of their rented house, and for three months their efforts bore no fruit. But then the tide began to turn, and before long an additional work was begun in a nearby town. One of their more fruitful contacts was with United States servicemen stationed in the vicinity.

Out of this initial effort the Mount Yokine church was organized, and in 1981 Rev. and Mrs. John Kerr were called to pastor the work. Because of the extreme isolation of western Australia from the churches on the east side of the continent, a pioneer area was created with Rev. Kerr as leader. By 1985 another church had been organized, which was now pastored by Rev. and Mrs. Geoffrey Burges. The Kerrs had undertaken the launching of another church, and Rev. and Mrs. Byron Blooms had assumed the pastorate of the original Mount Yokine congregation. Total membership stood at 52.

An interesting facet of the Australia field was the development of work among the Greek population, which numbered about 250,000. God providentially provided capable Greek pastors for these churches. The first one was Panagiotis Manetas, who, while serving in the army in his homeland, was led into an experience of holiness under the Oriental Missionary Society. This led to a call to the ministry, and he went to the Nazarene Bible School in Beirut, Lebanon, to prepare.

An elderly Christian woman suggested that he go to Australia to preach, for a large number of Greeks had emigrated there and constituted an open field for evangelism. When he arrived in the late 1960s, he discovered a small group of Greek Christians in Melbourne to whom he became a pastor. Soon a church was organized. Later a second congregation was organized in Sydney with Dimitrios Moschides as pastor.

In 1978 the growth of the Australia District plus the great distances that needed to be covered dictated that the area should be divided. The two districts were named Australia Northern Pacific and Australia Southern. Rev. Berg became superintendent of the northern district and Rev. Jay Hunton, veteran missionary from central Africa, was appointed to the southern district. When Rev. Berg passed away in 1979, Rev. John White was elected in his place. He had been pastor of the Coorparoo church in Brisbane and was district secretary and a member of the advisory board. In 1981 the Huntons returned to the

United States to assume a pastorate, and Rev. Max Stone was elected superintendent of the southern district.

By 1985 there were 26 organized churches in Australia, 12 in the north district, 12 in the south district, and 2 in the west. Membership stood at 318, 393, and 52 respectively for a total of 763. There have been no spectacular breakthroughs in the history of the Australian church, but as the denomination has become better known, earlier prejudices have gradually broken down, and the prospects for growth have become increasingly bright.

B. NEW ZEALAND

The beautiful island nation of New Zealand, 1,200 miles across the Tasman Sea from Australia, is an enchanting land stretching 1,000 miles from north to south. It is said to contain in miniature every type of scenery found in the world—snow-crowned mountains (15 over 10,000 feet), active volcanoes, deep fjords, boiling geysers, green forests, rich farmland, and golden beaches. The 3.2 million population are 85 percent of British descent. There are also 250,000 Maoris of Polynesian background who are the true natives of the country. A highly intelligent and progressive people, they are actively involved in all areas of national life. Seventy percent of the New Zealanders are listed as Protestant, but the sad fact is that only 4 percent of the total population ever attends church.

Enter the Church of the Nazarene

Toward the end of 1950 Dr. and Mrs. G. B. Williamson, in the course of a trip to the South Pacific, stopped in New Zealand to visit an uncle who was an Anglican missionary to the Maoris. Dr. Williamson's subsequent informal report in the *Herald of Holiness* told of "the open door of opportunity" in this dominion.

One who read this report was Rev. Roland E. Griffith of California, who, in the course of an evangelistic tour abroad during the following year, included New Zealand in his itinerary. He lined up 26 revival meetings there with various groups and found eager acceptance of his message. More than 1,000 responded to his invitations to come forward for prayer. But as the months passed, he found a growing resistance to the holiness message, and doors were closing to him.

On an impulse he decided to fly back to the United States to present the need of New Zealand to the church leaders at the General Assembly in June 1952. There he told of his experiences and urged that an organized effort be made to establish the Church of the Nazarene there. The response was immediate, and Rev. Griffith was named to head the project.

The first task was to find a permanent location for the church and a place for themselves to live. Within two weeks of his return to New Zealand, Rev. Griffith located an ideal tract of land on Dominion Road, a main thoroughfare of Auckland. On it was a five-room house and a large, vacant area adjacent, where a church could be built.

Services were begun in rented quarters and in a tent on the property until a temporary basement chapel was completed under the house. Services began there on January 1, 1953, and on May 24, the Dominion Road Church of the Nazarene was organized with 16 charter members. (The number soon rose to 20.)

Construction of a commodious church began that summer with the clearing away of a huge accumulation of rubbish and the laborious blasting of the underlying volcanic rock. No less tedious was the task of erecting the superstructure, which was accomplished largely with volunteer labor. Limited finances also slowed the process. But in two years time the sanctuary was completed, and the building was dedicated on October 1, 1955.

Among the members of the Dominion Road Church was Jervis T. Davis, a former U.S. Marine from Augusta, Ga., who, during a term of leave in New Zealand during World War II, had met and married an Auckland girl, Maisie Stratton. It was not long after they joined the church that Jervis felt called to the ministry, and under his leadership a second church was organized in the beautiful city of Hamilton, 80 miles south. In later years, the Davises were instrumental in organizing both the Breezes Road and Bishopdale churches in Christchurch, a major city on South Island.

In 1958 Rev. and Mrs. H. S. Palmquist were asked to take over the leadership of the work. Their tireless labors began to bear fruit as new churches were organized and the older ones established. One of the major accomplishments of Rev. Palmquist's 12 years of leadership was the purchase of a 20-acre youth campsite, 25 miles north of Auckland and half a mile from the seashore. The bush was cleared away and buildings erected to accommodate 150 campers. All this was accomplished with donated labor, much of it Rev. Palmquist's own. The camp has proved to be a valuable asset to the work.

By the time the district was officially organized in 1967, there were nine churches with 123 members.

In 1970 Rev. and Mrs. Darrell Teare became the leaders of the district. They were followed in 1976 by the William Porters, who had been missionaries in Puerto Rico for 22 years, he as district superintendent for much of that time. When in 1980 the Porters returned to the United States for furlough and eventual assignment to open the work in Venezuela, their place was taken by Rev. and Mrs. Dwight Neuenschwander. They were followed in September 1985 by Dr. and Mrs. Bert Daniels.

One of the more unique churches was the Auckland Otara Church, which was organized in 1973 with 9 members but within five years reached 100. It was made up almost entirely of Niue Islanders, of which there were about 4,500 in Auckland. (They are Polynesian migrants from Niue Island, some 1,200 miles north.)

There was no specific work among the Maoris, for they were largely intermingled with the white population, but in the Wainuiomata Church almost half the congregation were Maoris. Auckland is known as the Polynesian capital of the world, and the church was reaching out to these people.

By 1985 the New Zealand District reported 12 churches and 1 mission with a total membership of 534.

C. PAPUA NEW GUINEA

During the period of worldwide exploration in the 16th century with its exploitation of the treasures of the South Pacific, the large vulture-shaped island of New Guinea seems to have been largely bypassed. Though a few trading centers were established along the coast, little was known of this mysterious land.

With the advent of worldwide missions, there came a flurry of interest in New Guinea along with other South Pacific islands. Beginning in the late 1800s, the London Missionary Society established a foothold in the area of what is now Port Moresby. Roman Catholic, Lutheran, Anglican, and Methodist missionaries soon followed, establishing work in various parts of the coastal areas.

But little did these early settlers realize that up in the mountain fastnesses of the interior dwelt numberless tribes completely isolated from the outside world. They were Stone Age people who knew nothing of metal tools or even the wheel. Then in the 1930s Australian gold prospectors made their way up into the jungle-clad mountains and came back with unbelievable tales of what they had discovered. Missionary interest was aroused, and by 1935 Roman Catholic and Lutheran missionaries were at work in the broad Wahgi Valley of the Central Highlands.

World War II brought most of the island under Japanese control, and missionary activity came to a virtual standstill. But as the counteroffensive developed, Allied servicemen in large numbers came in contact with the New Guineans. Their tales of fascinating encounters with the people captured world interest, particularly of missionary-minded groups. Here was a harvest field like no other in the world—animistic spirit worshipers to whom the gospel of a loving God and a redeeming Savior was completely unknown.

Rev. A. A. E. Berg, superintendent of the newly established Australian District, had heard the stories coming out of his country's island neighbor to the north. The missionary challenge gripped him, and he began talking to the church leaders in Kansas City about the vision he had for this land. While attending the 1952 General Assembly, he had opportunity to talk to the Department of Foreign Missions about the New Guinea challenge. The result was a request that he go to the island and investigate the possibilities. This he did in November of that year, visiting not only the coastal areas but also the remote highlands.

He reported: "There are many thousands of the primitive people in Australia and Dutch New Guinea [the existing names of the east and west halves of the island] who have never heard of Christ and His glorious gospel." Later estimates indicated a population of perhaps 2½ million.

To launch the work would involve a considerable investment that the general leaders felt the church was not able to undertake at the time, so for two years the matter lay somewhat dormant. But 1954 was the 40th anniversary of the Nazarene Foreign Missionary Society, and a New Guinea project to mark the occasion captured the imagination of the organization's leaders. An "old-fashioned march offering" was scheduled for June 20 to launch the work. The response was astounding, as over $102,000 was contributed. Excitement mounted throughout the church as plans for the new venture began to unfold.

In November General Superintendent Hardy C. Powers, accompanied by Rev. Berg, made an exploratory trip to the island that included a flight up into the highlands. Their inspiring report was a feature of the January 1955 meeting of the General Board. At that session Sidney and Wanda Knox were appointed as the first missionary couple. Months of careful preparation followed that culminated on October 14, 1955, when Rev. and Mrs. Knox and their infant son, Geron, landed at Port Moresby on the southern coast.

Selecting a Site

The decision was yet to be made as to where to establish the work. The few coastal towns offered great opportunities for gospel work, but the intriguing challenge was up in the highlands where so few had ever heard the gospel message.

Toward the end of the year, Sidney made an investigative trip up into the Wahgi Valley to try to find a suitable location for the first mission station. In his search he was aided by the Australian government officials who not many years before had established various patrol stations throughout the area.

By January 1, 1956, Sidney had made his decision to locate at

Kudjip in the middle of the broad Wahgi Valley. Four miles north, across the valley, was a small airstrip at the town of Banz, but at that time there was no bridge across the river. But 12 miles to the east was a larger "airport" in the government center of Minj. This field was accessible by road and also could handle the DC-3 cargo planes that would be needed to transport the equipment from the coast, including prefabricated housing components. As an added advantage at Kudjip there was a government rest house maintained for the use of patrolling government officers. The Knoxes received permission to live in this while their own home was being built.

Sidney Knox wrote concerning the chosen location:

> Within a four-mile radius of our land are about 3,000 natives. In the whole Wahgi Valley, there are approximately 40,000 who understand the same language. This will be a very definite advantage to us. In many places here you only go a few miles before getting into a different language. To the back of us, within a couple of days' walk, is a country still partially uncontrolled. We feel this is a great possibility. The country there is extremely rugged. . . . We are the only European mission working in this [Kudjip] area.

The government Lands Department was agreeable to the lease of a five-acre, grass-covered tract. This was to be the scene of amazing development and expansion in the coming years even beyond the dreams of these intrepid missionary pioneers.

On January 9, 1956, the Knox family landed at the Minj airfield. Excitement was tinged with apprehension. "As we looked across those acres and acres of Kunai grass," wrote Wanda, "and at the curious people who didn't understand either what we were saying or what we had come to do, we were inclined to inquire, 'Lord, are You *sure* this is what You had in mind?'"

The high altitude provided a pleasant change of climate from the steamy heat down on the coast. But the newcomers were not without the discomforting presence of an interesting assortment of rats, beetles, roaches, and spiders. Their every move was watched by a curious crowd of spectators who were intrigued by the gadgets the foreigners had brought with them. The simplest tools amazed them, and the prefabricated house was a marvel indeed.

Though the "neighbors" were friendly, the barrier of language proved a difficult hurdle. Pidgin, the go-between language between the English and Wahgi, was the logical avenue of communication, but good Pidgin speakers were hard to find. One afternoon Tal came by to apply for a job and, more impressed by his Pidgin than by his working skills, Sidney hired him on the spot. Tal was a great help, as was his brother Tangip, who later took over as the Knoxes' main interpreter.

While the men worked on the house, Wanda planted the gospel seed with her skillful use of the flannelgraph. She never lacked a group to talk to. When the house was completed, the living room became the gathering place for the people to hear the simple gospel messages. But when the crowds grew to 150 or more, it was obvious that some sort of chapel was needed. Soon a 30 x 60-foot building of native materials was begun and was ready for use on the missionaries' first Easter Sunday in New Guinea.

A second preaching point was opened up soon at the nearby government rest house of Kurumul, four miles east. Here their first convert was an influential elderly lady called Meri Tul-tul. Her death in a drowning accident cut short her testimony among her people but not before she had turned many toward the gospel.

In March 1957 a third preaching point was opened at Kauwi, about four miles from Kudjip on the road to Mount Hagen. This latter was and is the largest city in the highlands, about 30 miles to the west of Kudjip. The church's mission office was ultimately to be moved to Mount Hagen, where Merilyn Bukas, a daughter of Kini, the first convert at Kauwi, served as a secretary for three or four years.

An obvious lack of education among the people prompted the Knoxes to attempt a day school program, which was launched in May 1957. The discipline of following a daily schedule was totally foreign to the New Guinea mind; and this, coupled with the distances the children had to travel, made for erratic attendance. Not until boarding facilities were provided was any semblance of regular attendance achieved.

The Loss of a Leader

Sidney lost the end of one finger in an accident with a power saw in March 1957, but in November of that year a more serious health problem developed. He began to experience abdominal pains that increased in intensity.

On January 3, 1958, the first missionary recuits in the persons of Rev. and Mrs. Max Conder arrived on the field. They were experienced missionaries being transferred from Haiti. Since she was a registered nurse, their coming opened the door to a much-needed medical work.

The day before the Conders' arrival Sidney had experienced an unusually severe abdominal attack, so a few days later he and Max Conder flew down to Madang to pick up some necessary supplies and to visit a doctor. A tumor was suspected and immediate surgery was recommended. It proved to be a malignant growth, with little hope given that his condition could be successfully treated. With beautiful submission to what he felt to be the will of God, Sidney chose to remain on the field "as long as I can in any way contribute to the work of the Kingdom here."

By June it became obvious that he could no longer carry on, so the family (now including Janie, who had been born in New Guinea in 1957) was brought back to the United States. The end came on October 14, 1958, exactly three years from the day the Knoxes had landed in New Guinea. It should be noted that Wanda Knox returned to New Guinea in 1960 and served there until 1975, when she was elected executive director of the NWMS.

In the meantime, in July William Bromley of Australia had joined the Conders, working principally in the area of evangelism. The school was continued with about 40 enrolled, and Mary Alice Conder established an effective dispensary ministry.

In 1959 Rev. and Mrs. Wallace White and their two sons arrived. Wallace and Mona were thrust into leadership responsibilities very soon because the Conders, due to Mary Alice's health, were forced to return to the United States in 1961.

One of the first outpoints opened by Will Bromley was Tun, in a mountainous area nine miles from Kudjip. At first there was considerable resistance to the gospel message, but by 1960, under the anointed leadership of Mona White, a breakthrough came. Soon as many as 250 were attending services, and an enlarged church had to be built to replace the original brush chapel. It was built on 14 acres of land contributed by the people of the area with the provision that a missionary come to live among them and start a school.

In 1963 the promised missionary residence was completed, and in May Rev. and Mrs. Lee Eby and their children, Mark and Lee Ann, arrived to live among the Tongeii people.

In 1965, with money given by Dr. L. C. Philo, the David Philo Memorial Church was completed on the Tun station and dedicated by the visiting general superintendent, Dr. Samuel Young.

Four months before the Ebys arrived, Wanda Knox and Mona White had begun a primary day school at Tun, and the new missionaries continued this program. A national teacher taught the kindergarten, while Carol Anne Eby handled the first and second grades. The school was intended to serve as a "feeder" for the boarding school in Kudjip. This phase of the program became superfluous a few years later with the opening of a government school nearby.

But a more significant challenge was to open before them: that of training national pastors. Wallace White approached Lee Eby shortly after his arrival concerning this and found eager response. It was decided to launch the project on the Tun station.

A Bible School Launched

In March 1964 the Bible school was officially opened with eight students. Most of them did not even know how to read, so the first year was basically a literacy program to give the students an ability to read the trade language, Pidgin. There were few books in the language, but fortunately the four Gospels had been translated into Pidgin. As Lee Eby said: "Wiley's *Christian Theology* and the church *Manual* would have to come later!"

Three years later two of the students, Paul Tagup and Philip Konga, had qualified for graduation. The Bible college continued to grow to an average enrollment of about 20.

Because of the limited space for expansion at Tun, in the early 1970s a 50-acre campus was acquired at Ningei on the Tuman River. It was on this spot in 1967 that the first New Guinea camp meeting was held with over 1,000 people in attendance. It was to become an annual event. On the new property there have been built over the years three missionary residences, three classroom units, a chapel, two national teachers' homes, and 21 residences for single and married students. Besides the Ebys, Clive and Grace Burrows, Ray and Helen Bolerjack, Marjorie Merritts, Wanda Knox, Bruce Blowers, Nancy Seale, the Ron Moores, and Gary Glassco have served on the staff.

In 1975 a most significant step was made when a New Guinean became a member of the faculty. He is John Waka, an earlier graduate of the college who has proved to be a capable and Spirit-filled preacher and teacher among his own people. In December 1980 he moved to Lae to become pastor of the new church there. Other New

Guinea teachers who have served on the faculty include Rev. James Yali, Rev. Taime Marke, Rodney Kuri Gulta, Daniel Tarp Goma, and Anna Laulau.

A major change in the Bible college took place in March 1977 when an English-level program was added. For 13 years the school had been training only in the trade language of New Guinea Pidgin. With the development of town ministries came the need for qualified, English-speaking pastors. By 1980 four students had been graduated from the program. By 1985 total enrollment in the Bible school was averaging about 50. At the same time, an extension program was being developed at Port Moresby to provide the third and fourth years of the Bible school program for the English-speaking students.

In the meantime the regular day school program was being continued at Kudjip. Max Conder supervised the earlier school building program made necessary by growing enrollment. Marjorie Merritts took over this work in 1964 and was assisted by Missionaries Clayton Garner, Merna Blowers, Nancy Seale, Muriel Murray, Mona White, and Mary Lou Tiemann. They brought the program to a high level of academic excellence.

A significant development was the addition of New Guinea teachers. By 1975 the entire staff was made up of nationals, led by Rambai Yano as headmaster. Approximately 75 of the students have gone on to higher education, later to return to places of leadership in the New Guinea church.

Will Bromley began a day school at Singoropa in the Jimi Valley in 1961, with 50 boys enrolled. Among them was Kombek, son of Headman Alu, who in 1976 returned to the school as senior assistant to the headmaster, and eventually became headmaster.

In the early days, the government very much needed missionary assistance in education because of the grave shortage of teachers. This picture vastly changed in later years, and mission primary schools were totally staffed with national teachers. Though all schools are now under the national system, the mission still has a say in the selection of teachers and educational policy in its own schools. Missionaries and pastors provide religious education classes in both mission and government schools.

There has also been developed a strong adult literacy program. This was pioneered in 1968 by Merna Blowers at the Kudjip station. It was expanded to all the main stations, and there have been as many as 20 teachers and 400 students involved at one time. This has proved to be a valuable feeder to the Bible college, the hospital, and other phases of the church's work.

Though the gospel seed was sown carefully, prayerfully, and diligently, securing converts was an arduous and discouraging process. Centuries-long worship of spirits, heathen ways of life, coupled with tribal pressures made it difficult for people to accept this new religion. Some of the early "conversions" proved to be quite superficial, and many fell by the wayside before the gospel really took root in their lives.

The first baptismal service was held in 1964, nine years after the work in New Guinea had begun. Candidates came from four established churches of that time: Kudjip, Tun, Kurumul, and Kauwi.

The Jimi Valley

Typical of the long struggle to win converts is the story of the work in the Jimi Valley, pioneered by Will Bromley. This remote area, three days walk into the mountains, presented an intriguing challenge to Will. He finally talked to Wallace White about his interest. It was agreed to wait until the Tabibuga airstrip, then under construction in the valley, was completed. It would condense the three-day walk into a 15-minute flight. In late 1959 the airstrip was finished, and the two eager missionaries were on the second flight in.

In earlier exploratory trips, Will had picked out Singoropa, four miles west of the airstrip, as a good place to establish a mission station; so, soon after his arrival, he contacted Headman Alu about the need for suitable property. Without their having discussed possible locations, Alu smiled and said, "You can have the ground we're standing on." It so happened that this was the very place Will had secretly hoped to obtain!

In August 1960 Will, with his young cookboy Ap, from the Tun area, flew into Tabibuga. They set up housekeeping in a tent while, with the help of neighbors, they built a house and began to transform the matted jungle into a beautiful garden spot. By the end of October, a church seating 500 had also been completed.

It was a shocking surprise when on the opening day of the new church, no one showed up. Alu had passed the word that their obligation ended with the building of the church, and they had no intention of listening to the white man's talk. What really happened was that the "bush grapevine" reported that the missionary had come to change their customs and culture. Will went directly to Alu and persuaded him to disregard the rumors and to at least give him a hearing. The people did begin to attend the meetings in great numbers.

In 1963 Will Bromley was married to Margaret Robson, a nurse from Australia who had come to Kudjip in 1961 to take over the dispensary there when Mary Alice Conder had to leave. The Australia District financed the construction of a dispensary at Singoropa, and Margaret's ministry there augmented the evangelistic efforts of her new husband.

Two other preaching points were opened in the valley at Kwibin and Waramis, and all three churches were filled with hundreds of apparently eager listeners. But no one made a move to accept Jesus Christ. After seven years without a convert Will became desperate. He deeply examined his own heart to make sure he was not hindering the working of God's Spirit upon the people.

At the close of one Sunday's service, Alu said to Will, "Out at Kudjip there are many Christians. You have been here seven years, and still there are no Christians."

Will replied, "There must be something wrong. Do you think it's me?"

"No," replied Alu, to which Will quickly responded, "Then it must be *you*."

No more was said, but an arrow of conviction went through Alu. It was not long until he gave his heart to the Lord, and like opened floodgates, revival tides began to flow throughout the Jimi Valley.

In January 1969 the first baptismal service in the Jimi Valley was conducted by Wallace White, Will being ill at the time with what was thought to be a case of flu. But when his health did not improve, he was flown out to the hospital at Kudjip. There, three days later, March 19, he died of a heart attack. After funeral services in the Sidney Knox Memorial Church, his body was flown back into the Jimi Valley for burial, according to his stated wish.

Margaret remained to carry on the work until their son, John, was ready for school. The Merle Fetters took care of the work briefly, and then Ap, who had became pastor at Singoropa, bridged the leadership gap until in 1973 Ray and Helen Bolerjack were reassigned from Kudjip to the Jimi. There are now seven churches in the valley, all but one pastored by national pastors who have graduated from the Bible college. Meanwhile Mrs. Bromley transferred to the Kudjip station, where she continued to serve until November 1984.

The Kobon Area

Still farther back into the mountain fastnesses were other isolated valleys that captured the minds and thoughts of the missionaries. Pilots of the Missionary Aviation Fellowship told of seeing numbers of homes on the jungled mountain slopes. It was against the law for strangers to go back in there until government patrols had "secured" the areas, but as soon as they could, Wallace White and Will Bromley organized the first contact patrol into the area. It was a hazardous walk through the leech-infested jungles, over dimly discernible trails, into a land of possibly hostile people. It had been dubbed "the land on the edge of nowhere."

Missionary patrols continued periodically from 1964 until 1969, and valuable relationships were established with the Kobon people who inhabited the Kaironk and Arami valleys. Finally, to Daryl and Elizabeth Schendel was assigned the task of opening up the work in that remote area. A beginning site was selected at Salemp, 19 miles in from the nearest airstrip. There in July 1969, with native materials and with the help of a group of local men, Daryl began building a house. By the end of the year the task was completed, and on January 6, 1970, he took his wife and two children to their new home among the cooperative but only recently peaceful Kobons.

Open-air services were begun on their very first Sunday, and construction of a native-style church building was started. Three miles away another church was soon begun. That same year Yekip, a graduate of the Bible college, moved into the valley to assist the Schendels. Though he was crossing tribal lines, he soon won the hearts of the people. When the Schendels went home on furlough in 1971-72, Yekip carried on the work alone. Upon the return of the missionaries, Pastor Yekip took a leave of absence to return to his own village and "buy" himself a wife. It was a successful quest, and Janie became a very great help to him in his ministry.

Because of the difficulty of transporting food and supplies over the tortuous, 19-mile trail, Rev. Schendel began looking for a suitable place to build an airstrip. To find a reasonably level surface 1,500 feet long in that rugged country was not easy. Furthermore, the thick jungle growth made it impossible to see far enough to determine how much earth moving would be necessary. Finally, a stretch of land along a ridge at Dusin was selected.

With 100 men, 8 wheelbarrows, and a number of hammocklike stretchers carried on the shoulders of two men for carrying dirt, work began in September 1972. Though an unexpected ridge jutting into the path of the runway was discovered as the jungle growth was cleared away, the huge task of building the runway was completed, and on May 17, 1973, the first MAF plane landed.

From the Salemp base, patrols were sent out to other valleys to make new contacts. New Guinea pastors and their families went into these remote areas to minister to the people and tell them of Jesus' love. As in other new areas converts came slowly at first, but in 1974-75 there was a great breakthrough. Eighty-one new Kobon converts were baptized, and two new churches, now fully self-supporting, were organized.

Expansion in the Wahgi Valley

Meanwhile, back at the Kudjip main station and in the Wahgi Valley the work was continually expanding. The town of Banz, main center for the 25,000 Middle Wahgi people on the north side of the valley and the location of the airstrip, was a prime target area. Although services had begun at Wara Kar, three miles away, no help could be expected from that place to expand into Banz, for the people were tribal enemies. But in July 1970 an open-air service was held in the crowded marketplace in Banz at the close of which interested listeners were invited to a service in a nearby hall. Eighty people came!

Within three weeks attendance was up to 300. Then there was a sudden decrease to around 60 caused by opposition from the Catholics, who had been established there for many years and were alarmed at the intrusion. On top of that, the hall the Nazarenes had been using was torn down, and for two years services had to be held out of doors or, for a while, in a carpenter shop.

In 1972 land was granted, and the Norrell-Van Dyne Memorial Church was built. Rev. Norrell was present for the dedication, while New Guinea Missionary Helen Bolerjack represented her family (the Van Dynes), as the church was built in memory of her father.

There was no immediate surge of growth despite the more adequate facilities, but seed was being sown that began to produce a harvest in 1974. Missionary Neville Bartle was the instrument God used for this revival. His unique method of reaching the people was the use of stick-figure charts with which he illustrated the gospel story. Somehow the message came alive to the largely illiterate listeners. Gandi, a native of Banz converted in 1971 and now graduated from the Bible college, became pastor of his home church. He too adopted the stick-figure illustration idea, and revival fires began to spread. The miraculous healing of Bang, a former witch doctor, was a key factor in this dramatic turn of events.

The Mission Hospital

The most significant event in the Kudjip station was the building of the hospital. From the time of Wanda Knox's "backdoor dispensary" there had been the dream of a missionary hospital. Both Dr. Powers and Rev. Berg had envisioned this in their earliest contacts.

The first step in this direction was taken in 1957 when a dispensary building was erected to house Mary Alice Conder's medical work. By the time Margaret Robson (later Bromley) arrived, a "bush ward" had been added. Maternal Child Health Clinics held throughout the area were an added boon to the people.

When Margaret married Will Bromley and moved with him to the Jimi Valley, Mrs. Helen Bolerjack took over. The day she had to single-handedly take care of a crowd of victims of a local tribal fight will never be forgotten. Over the years, her capable ministrations to those who sought her help made the Nazarene dispensary a haven for many suffering people.

In 1964 the Nazarene World Missionary Society was celebrating its 50th anniversary and, seeking a special project to commemorate the event, turned to New Guinea again. Ten years before, on their 40th anniversary, they had launched the work in New Guinea. This time they took a special offering to build a hospital.

Architect Ray Bowman with Wallace White and Dr. Dudley Powers prepared the plans, and a dedicated building contractor from Oregon, Ken Dodd, offered his services to build the hospital complex. He and his family arrived in New Guinea in 1965. Ken Dodd's capable management of the building project, his innovative ideas, coupled with his enthusiasm for the task, made his contribution to the work in New Guinea outstanding. Not only was the hospital complex well designed and constructed, an ingenious hydroelectric power plant was built on the nearby riverbank to serve the entire station. The hydro race, over a mile and a half long, was dug by prisoners under supervision of the prison staff. The government and local people also made substantial contributions of both labor and material.

In the midst of the building project, Dr. and Mrs. Dudley Powers and their family arrived to furnish professional guidance in the setting up of the hospital, to plan the staffing of the hospital, and to begin developing the medical program. How appropriate that the son of the general superintendent who had envisioned the hospital in the first place should become its first resident doctor.

On March 31, 1967, the new hospital was officially dedicated by Dr. Hardy C. Powers. Six thousand people gathered for the occasion. Government officials, businessmen, and representatives of other missions joined in the celebration. A typical New Guinea feast was served, and an athletic field day provided entertainment.

But the 100-bed hospital was to go through rough times before becoming a viable medical institution. The key problem was staffing. Besides Dr. Powers only three nurses—Helen Bolerjack, Virginia Stimer, and Bente Carlsen—were there to carry the load. Not only was there the normal nursing care of the patients along with operating room duty, but there was the training and supervision of nursing aides—"dokta bois" or aid post orderlies. The already established Maternal Child Health Clinics were also to be continued. The load was too great for so limited a staff. The launching of a needed nurses' training school, which failed initially, was picked up years later with great success.

After completing a three-year term (1965-68), the Powers family returned to the United States, and Dr. Glenn Irwin and his wife, Ruth, arrived in November 1968 to direct the hospital. Ruth, a registered nurse, took over the tutoring of the orderlies. Soon a full training program for nurse's aids and registered nurses was launched. It was a memorable day when, on August 7, 1975, the first class of four nurses was graduated from the hospital training school. All had received high grades in their national exams and had already proved to be exceptional nurses. Three of them joined the regular hospital staff.

In early 1969, not long after the Irwins arrived, arrangements were made to have Dr. Evelyn Ramsey stop in New Guinea on her way home from Africa for a short, eight-month term of service in the Kudjip hospital. She had not let it be known that she had been feeling for some time that her work in the Raleigh Fitkin Memorial Hospital in Swaziland was completed. More specifically, she believed God was leading her to the New Guinea hospital as her new field of service. The request from Headquarters coincided perfectly with what she had felt all along to be God's direction. Eagerly she accepted the immediate challenge and at the end of the eight months requested permanent assignment.

Not only were her medical and administrative skills invaluable in the hospital, she was an outstanding linguist. Shortly after she returned to Kudjip in 1970 for her first full term, she began work on a greatly needed dictionary of the Middle Wahgi language into English. Five years later the 459-page volume was published. It represented about 10,000 hours of work sandwiched into the predawn and late night hours. It was a monumental achievement.

When she returned in 1979 for her second term, after an extended furlough, physical problems forced her to limit her hospital duties to half days. This gave her opportunity to pursue another project that had intrigued her since early in the dictionary work—the compilation of a concordance in Pidgin. To the early morning and late night hours she could now add afternoons. Her normal daily schedule was six to seven hours in the hospital and about the same number of hours for translation. The work was all done on computer, and the copious manuscript was expected to be completed in 1986.

In addition to Dr. Ramsey's work, Bruce Blowers, himself a skilled linguist, was at work on a translation of the New Testament into Middle Wahgi. The Blowerses had already written the basic grammar and study lessons for this language.

In the meantime, in 1980 Dr. Ramsey had been appointed administrator of the hospital and mission director. She was thus involved in a $500,000 building expansion project largely financed by a West German philanthropic agency.

The building program was related to the nursing college facilities where 60 New Guinea students were enrolled in the Registered Nursing (RN) program directed by Virginia Stimer.

Finding an adequate staff of doctors was a continuing problem. Dr. Jack Patton and his wife came in 1973 and served until 1977, when they had to leave for health reasons. They did go back for the full year of 1980, however. Dr. and Mrs. Vernon Vore went to fill in on specialized assignment from 1978 to 1980. They returned to New Guinea in 1981 as career missionaries. Dr. and Mrs. James Radcliffe were appointed in 1985 and went to the field after the 1985 General Assembly. Drs. Charles Gray and Terry Hall also served in the hospital on specialized assignment.

Enhancing the outreach of the hospital, an airstrip was built nearby in 1968 under the direction of Daryl Schendel so that emergency cases could be brought in by helicopter and conventional aircraft virtually to the door of the hospital. The Maternal Child Health

Services program not only served over 10,000 children a year but was expanded to include family planning services and nutritional instruction.

Not forgetting that the fundamental purpose of the hospital program was to reach souls for Christ, an effective chaplaincy ministry was being carried on in the wards involving both missionaries and nationals. Rev. Mundua was appointed chaplain in 1985, the first national to occupy that post. Those who were won to the Lord in this way went back to their communities to witness to their own people. This meant many more open doors to the gospel. The Nazarene hospital had become an excellent medical facility that was serving both the physical and spiritual needs of its patients.

The Call of the Cities

In the early 1970s the Church of the Nazarene began to turn its attention to the cities of New Guinea. The first such venture was in October 1973, when Pastor Kawali Boi and his family were sent to the beautiful north coast city of Madang. They found a responsive community of Wakol people who invited them to hold services in their area. The meetings conducted in the open air soon attracted as many as 50 people. From April to August 1974 the Harold Fryes joined them and purchased a tent in which to hold the services. This violated some city building code, so the tent had to be taken down. Not only were the worshipers thus exposed to the frequent rains from above, the swampy area was subject to inundation when the tides were unusually high. The hordes of mosquitoes made for restless congregations as well.

Daryl Schendel took over supervision of the work, flying down from the Dusin airstrip as often as he could to give encouragement and guidance. He was able to secure the use of the local primary school for services. Early in 1975 the Don Walkers took up the challenge in Madang and launched several community projects such as religious education in the high school, home Bible studies, and recreational programs. Services were begun in several adjacent villages, and soon some significant conversions were taking place.

A choice tract of land was secured in the New Town area, the fastest-growing section of the city, and the first unit of a permanent church building was erected and dedicated in January 1977. During the course of construction the church was officially organized in September 1976.

The next step was the organization of the Madang District, which included the Kobon area. By 1985 there were 19 organized churches on the district with a total of 596 members.

In mid-1975 it was decided to move the headquarters of the New Guinea work to Mount Hagen, the key city of the highland area located at the western end of the Wahgi Valley. The Wallace Whites moved there and began regular services in the mission office building, ministering particularly to the Nazarene young people attending the local high school. Later a school for children of missionaries was built at Mount Hagen. Pastor Taime Dirye, graduate of the Bible school, was assigned to the work, and soon a good congregation was developed, consisting notably of young adults.

In 1980 property was purchased, and an attractive church seating 300 was erected. The building, which was dedicated in December of that year, also contained classroom and office space. A parsonage was also built beside it. The Mount Hagen congregation was soon averaging about 100 in attendance.

In 1975 Rev. Clive Burrows began making regular trips to the capital of Port Moresby to minister to Nazarene students in the university there. In March 1978, when the Wallace Whites returned from furlough, they were assigned to develop the work in the coastal towns and made Port Moresby their base of operation. They began holding regular services first in their home, then in a rented hall, and later a rented church building.

Two congregations were developed, one using New Guinea Pidgin and the other English. The latter group consisted first of the student group that Rev. Burrows had gathered, but soon began to attract businessmen, lawyers, doctors, and government office workers. With a major contribution from the Southern California District, construction began in 1981 on a church building, classrooms, and parsonage. Attendance was already averaging around 100.

In January 1981 services were begun in Lae, Papua New Guinea's second-largest city, by Rev. John Waka. As previously stated, he was the first New Guinean teacher in the Bible college.

This led to the organization of the Coastal District, which by 1985 reported three organized churches and a membership of 127. Its latest outreach was to Rabaul, on New Britain Island, where two congregations were organized to be added to their total.

National Leadership

A significant feature of the New Guinea field has been the development of national leadership. It was an important first when in 1966, the first district assembly was held and the New Guinea leaders gave their first reports. On that occasion the first two national pastors who had just graduated from the Bible college took up their pastorates. A District Council was formed that over the years evolved into a District Advisory Board.

It was not until 1977, however, that the first ordination took place. There were six candidates in the group including Taime Dirye, who at the same assembly was appointed the first national district superintendent. There was also Ap, who with Will Bromley pioneered the work in the Jimi Valley; Yekip, who was Daryl Schendel's assistant in opening the work in the Arami Valley; Kawali, first pastor of Madang; Waka, first national to teach in the Bible school; and Gandi Dama, leading evangelist on the district.

As time went by, more were ordained, and the 1985 figures showed 11 ordained and 24 licensed ministers.

The development of the national church moved on a parallel track with the movement of the nation itself toward political independence. On September 16, 1975, amid great celebration, Papua New Guinea became an independent nation. It is comprised of the eastern half of the island of New Guinea plus the adjacent islands to the northeast: New Britain, New Ireland, Bouganville, and the Admiralty Islands. Previously the area had been under the administration of the Australian government under a mandate following World War II. It is a tribute to the Australian leaders that they were able to bring the country peacefully to self-government in so short a time. "The land time forgot" had, in the words of Wallace White, "advanced 10,000 years in a lifetime."

The new national government is supportive of mission efforts. Its national song of independence speaks of "praising God and rejoicing" and exhorts:

> Give thanks to the good Lord above,
> This land of our fathers is free.

But not all the national traditions and celebrations are as supportive of the worship of God. The people of the highlands traditionally celebrate special occasions with great festivals called "sing sings." Here the warriors dress in their shells, bird-of-paradise feathers, and other paraphernalia and perform their tribal dances. A high-light of the event is a gigantic pig killing, roasting, and feasting. Sometimes there is actually a sacrificing of pigs to their ancestral spirits. Their religion is an animistic spiritism with a multitude of such spirits that they must appease and thus ward off sickness and catastrophe. They perceive that these spirits have an insatiable appetite for pork, and so the raising of pigs is a prime occupation.

The killing of a pig at one of these festivals accomplished several things. It involved one in a general tribal presentation to the ancestral spirits to appease them and gain favor. The meat of the pig could be used not only as food but perhaps as payment for a bride, for the resolving of a debt, or as a special gift. The missionaries themselves had been recipients of such gifts as the donor sought to find favor with the foreigners' God as well. To the Christians this presented a formidable dilemma. To what extent should they participate?

The year 1975 was the year of the great pig sacrifice in the area where the Kudjip and Pokorumb chuches are located. For a year preceding these ceremonies, pastors and missionaries, led by Rev. Bruce Blowers, had concentrated as never before on the scriptural teaching on this matter. The spiritual illumination began to bring results, and numbers of Christians firmly decided they would no longer become involved in the pig festival. Bible conferences in the churches were scheduled for the same time, and the Christians living near the festival grounds had an unusual opportunity to witness to their faith.

Many had predicted that this would be a very divisive issue in the church, but the result proved the opposite. The Spirit of God began to move in new and wonderful ways. Many who had bowed to tribal pressures and participted in the festival later repented. Those who stood firm had new inspiration and confidence. Best of all, the flow of new converts increased, and the following year there was an 18 percent net gain in full members and a 40 percent increase in new believers. It was a watershed event in the life of the New Guinea church.

In January 1984 seven churches and preaching points on the eastern side of the Highlands District were separated to form the Simbu Pioneer District with Missionary Neville Bartle as superintendent. Within two years there were 10 churches and 6 other preaching points with a membership of 101. At the time of the division, Rev.

Kawali Boi was elected superintendent of the Highlands District. He succeeded Rev. Taime Dirye, the first ever national superintendent.

By 1985 there were 72 organized churches and 8 other preaching points on the four New Guinea districts. Total membership stood at 2,599.

D. SAMOA

World War II brought to the attention of the world a huge mass of islands scattered over the southern Pacific Ocean that heretofore had been somewhat legendary and only vaguely known. Adventurers had visited them, and cruise ships had made such names as Tahiti, Fiji, and Pitcairn familiar yet remote. Then came the island-hopping Allied forces in their relentless march back toward Japan, and names like Guadalcanal, Tarawa, Kwajalein, Saipan, and Iwo Jima became household words.

Buried in this sea of islands, about 2,000 miles south of Hawaii and 1,500 miles north of New Zealand, was a small patch of territory known as Samoa, a chain of nine islands about 290 miles across. There was Western Samoa with its two main islands, Savaii and Upolu, and the much smaller American Samoa, whose main island was Tutuila, with about 125 miles separating the two. Western Samoa has been independent since January 1, 1962, but American Samoa is still under the administration of the United States, which pours millions of dollars each year into its development. The total population of the islands is less than 200,000, of which 90 percent are pure Polynesian. It is of interest to note that at least another 200,000-300,000 Samoans live in the United States and New Zealand.

The primitive religion of the people is animistic, which places great importance upon personified forces of nature and ancestral spirits. But in 1831 Rev. John Williams of the London Missionary Society arrived and with the help of eight Tahitian Christians virtually won the islands for Christ, including the Paramount Chief Malietoa. Today the islands are nominally Christian with roughly two-thirds Protestant and one-third Roman Catholic. Virtually every village has its high-steepled church, and reverence for the Sabbath is strong and pervasive.

The Church of the Nazarene

In 1958 the Church of the Nazarene was invited to come to American Samoa by one of its chiefs, Robert Manama, who had been converted in the Samoan Church of the Nazarene in Hawaii. In 1959 Dr. D. I. Vanderpool, general superintendent, was dispatched to investigate the situation and found a group of about 45 people who were holding services in the home of Chief Manama.

In a Crusade for Souls rally in Waco, Tex., that October, Dr. Vanderpool told of the profound effect that that Samoan worshiping group had upon him. One of his listeners was a young pastor, Rev. Jarrell Garsee, who responded to the challenge thus presented and in January 1960 was appointed by the General Board to open the work. He and his wife, Berniece, arrived in Samoa on April 28, 1960.

The Garsees settled in a third-story apartment in Pago Pago (pronounced "Pango Pango") and took stock of their situation. At the time there were only two miles of surfaced road on Tutuila Island, and one country store. Only one airplane a week came in to the airport, and one boat a month from the United States came by. A different lifestyle was in store for them.

There were 38 present for the first Sunday's service in the Manama home, and 66 at the service in Nu'uuli the following Sunday. But after a few weeks Mr. Manama began to have some second thoughts about the Nazarene way of doing things and decided to withdraw. About 35 of his group followed him, and the Garsees had to start up again with the 15 or 20 who remained faithful to them.

A Samoa-style 34' x 16' open-sided building with corrugated roof was built to hold services in. It would seat 60 people on mats on the floor, and 35 were present for the dedication service. Visits by Dr. and Mrs. Samuel Young in April 1961 and by Evangelist and Mrs. C. William Fisher in August were a great boost to the work, with crowds averaging over 100 in all the services.

In the meantime Rev. Garsee had arranged to have "Showers of Blessing" broadcast on a regular basis, which helped to introduce the Church of the Nazarene to the people. He also was diligently studying the difficult Samoan language so he could preach without an interpreter. His first solo effort was on September 24, 1961. Several visits to Western Samoa were opening the door to establishing a work over there, and while the Garsees were home on furlough in 1964, services were begun at Lefaga, near Apia, by Rev. John K. Abney, the interim missionary.

Returning in 1965, Rev. Garsee purchased land in Western Samoa's capital city, Apia. After the Jerry Applebys arrived, a church and parsonage were erected here and the work launched in 1971.

Meanwhile, a church and parsonage were built by Rev. Garsee at Nu'uuli, the project being completed in 1968, just before the Garsees returned permanently to the United States in May of that year.

Rev. and Mrs. John Stockett were scheduled to replace the Garsees, but both were killed in an airplane accident while on a deputation tour. A hurried call was sent to the Jerry Applebys, pastoring in Lubbock, Tex., and as soon as it could be arranged, they were sent off to Samoa. By the time they arrived in January 1969, the church had been without a leader for seven months.

Additional property was purchased in Western Samoa for expansion, and in 1971 the Applebys applied for residence permits there. Rev. and Mrs. Orville Swanson came to take charge of the work in American Samoa and continued there until 1974. It was while they were there that the Nu'uuli congregation became self-supporting. The earlier conversion of Chief Matai'a here while on a visit from Western Samoa was a great boon to the work when he returned to his own area.

In the beginning years, Samoan workers received their training in the Australian Nazarene Bible College, but the language and cultural differences created a severe problem. It was obvious that if a supply of national preachers were to be developed, it would have to be in their own school. This became a priority item for Rev. Appleby, who in 1974 released the superintendency to devote his full time to this task. A three-acre property was purchased in Ululoloa on the island of Upolu, basic buildings were constructed, and the school was opened that same year with 19 students. Within two years, classroom, library, dormitory, and faculty housing units were completed.

The Alvin V. Orchards arrived on the field in October 1975; and the following year when the Applebys were called to the pastorate of Honolulu First Church, Rev. Orchard was ready to take over direction of the school. By that time enrollment had reached 29. Unfortunately there came a precipitous decline in students, reaching an all-time low of 3 in 1980.

Rev. Conley Henderson, pastor of the Hanapepe Church in Hawaii, was appointed district superintendent of Samoa in 1974 when Rev. Appleby took on the school project. Under his leadership a general upgrading of church properties was done and a new church organized, bringing the total to seven. All were pastored by Samoans.

In August 1977 the Larry Duckworths were added to the missionary staff, and in 1980 Annette Taft from Australia served a year in the Bible college. Also the transfer of the Richard Reynoldses from Swaziland was approved in 1980. Rev. Vaimanino Pomele was appointed the first national district superintendent by Dr. Eugene Stowe at the 1983 District Assembly. In 1985 there were 10 organized churches with a total membership of 316, over double what it was in 1980.

E. INDONESIA

The work of the Church of the Nazarene in Indonesia is located on the island of Java, the fourth largest of the 13,677 islands in the archipelago. Here the capital city of Djakarta is located as well as the majority of the educational and cultural centers. It is also the most densely populated of the islands with 92 million of Indonesia's 171 million population crowded onto its 51,032 square miles of land.

When the Church of the Nazarene first turned its attention to Indonesia, the country had just come through a six- or seven-year period of far-reaching revival in which some 2 million were won to Christ. Though many of the stories concerning the revival were exaggerated, secondhand accounts, most of which originated in the remote island of Timor, the overall impact upon the islands was nonetheless profound. Not only had there been a great flood of converts, but a vast reservoir of goodwill and responsiveness to the gospel had been created.

This openness to the Christian message had some unique earlier roots. The established ancient religion of the islands is Islam, and even today 90 percent of the people are adherents of this faith. But with the coming of the Portuguese in 1497 to participate in the fabulously profitable spice trade came the Roman Catholic faith. Although the merchants had ulterior motives in using religion as a tool for their own ends, the missionaries they brought were sincere workers and won many converts from the Islamic faith. It is interesting to note that in those areas where they concentrated their efforts (the Moluccas, Flores, and Timor), the church is the strongest even today.

About the year 1600 the Dutch East India Company came onto the scene, driving out the Portuguese traders and even placing Dutch Reformed pastors in the Roman Catholic churches. Though the churches were operated only to serve the European immigrants, not to reach the populace, one of the notable achievements of the 350-year Dutch rule was the translation of the New Testament into the Malay language in 1733.

There was a brief interlude of about eight years (1811-19) in which the British ruled the area. They strongly encouraged missionary work, and by the time the Dutch were again in power, there was a strongly favorable attitude toward the gospel. In the period between then and the Japanese occupation, 1942-45, the church grew strong.

The Japanese ousted the Dutch and set up local governments under their own control. Out of this came a great surge of nationalism and a desire to be free. Sukarno gave inspired leadership to the movement that declared independence from the Netherlands on August 17, 1945. After the liberation he became president of the new republic. He was determined that Indonesia should not become an Islamic state, but at the same time he was misled by the Communists, which ultimately brought about his downfall in 1965. Through the years following independence there was much unrest as various factions in the far-flung republic struggled for supremacy, but the principles of government had been established by then.

Sukarno had based his republic on five principles, called the Pancasila, which became the official Indonesian national philosophy. The number one principle, "Belief in one God," made it possible for the Christian church to live and flourish. Also, the churches had participated fully in the revolution and so were recognized and accepted by the Muslim majority.

But godless Communism began to assert itself ever more strongly. Finally, in 1965 the party attempted to take over the government by the capture, torture, and murder of six generals of the Indonesian army. The people saw how ruthless and cruel Communism could be and joined General Suharto in his counterrevolution. The Muslims were fully behind him, and in the subsequent purge 300,000 to 500,000 Communist sympathizers were annihilated.

Because Communism was atheistic, the new government, in contrast, and following the Pancasila principles, decreed that all Indonesians must believe in God and accept one of the recognized religions. Hundreds of thousands chose to become Christians—in some cases whole villages. Though this did not constitute true evangelical conversion, it opened wide the door to the gospel. Central Java, inhabited by some 20 million people, proved to be the area most responsive to the Christian message, and it is there that the Church of the Nazarene chose to concentrate its initial efforts.

The Church of the Nazarene

In January 1967 I. Andrew Riise, a Nazarene strawberry farmer from California, visited the capital city of Djakarta. He was deeply moved by the spiritual need of the people but also challenged by the tremendous opportunity for gospel work that the revolution seemed to have opened up. Upon his return to the United States, he contacted the Department of World Mission and offered to give a substantial sum for the opening of work in Indonesia.

It was not until the General Board meeting in January 1971, however, that specific action was taken. The board voted to send Rev. and Mrs. George Rench, then missionaries in Taiwan, to this new area. They were to establish a base in Singapore and from there explore the possibilities in Indonesia.

Leaving his family in Taiwan, Rev. Rench went to Singapore to see about getting a visa and to find a place to live. He made numerous contacts, but at every turn he ran into insurmountable obstacles. The door to Singapore seemed closed.

Was God leading directly to Indonesia? the frustrated missionary wondered. He decided that before returning to Taiwan, he at least ought to look over the situation. So he flew to Djakarta. What he found captivated him. The sheer mass of humanity, the overpowering need both material and spiritual, but also the warm responsiveness of the people impressed him deeply.

One key obstacle stood in the way, however. In order for the Church of the Nazarene to begin work, it would be necessary to be sponsored by an already organized and government-recognized church. Nor could Rev. Rench be granted a visa without such sponsorship. But his five-week investigative tour of Java, Bali, and Kalimantan (Borneo) came to an end without his finding a solution to that problem.

On a return journey some months later, however, while looking specifically for a sponsoring organization, he miraculously came in touch with a struggling 20-member evangelical Chinese congregation. In fact, it was they who had searched him out. They told Rev. Rench that if he would become their missionary, they would sponsor his visa application and even might consider changing the name of their church to Church of the Nazarene. Cautiously, to be sure their motives were clear, the visitor investigated every phase of the church's operation. They showed him their government registration papers and the official letter of authorization from the Department of Religion.

Rev. Rench studied their legal charter, which specifically stated that the church is "based in Djakarta, with its branch offices in places where the Executive Board shall regard necessary." They could thus legally establish churches anywhere in Indonesia. What is more, the pastor, Rev. Chen Hung-Ying, was a graduate of a holiness Bible school in China, and the people were already instructed in the doctrine.

The General Board listened to Rev. Rench's enthusiastic recommendation and approved the arrangements. Finally, on May 30, 1973, the Renches arrived in Djakarta to begin working with the sponsoring group. They were ably supported by the pastor and three key laymen, Jacob Mandomo, Thomas Rahardjo, and Dr. Tjipto Tanuwidjaja.

The congregation was meeting Sunday afternoons in borrowed quarters, and it seemed imperative that a permanent church home be erected. With the help of an Alabaster gift of $17,000 coupled with the sacrificial gifts of the people themselves, the first floor of a projected three-story church plant was completed debt-free at a cost of $57,000.

After a year of service with the church, the congregation voted to officially unite with the Church of the Nazarene. Although the government at first refused the request to change the original name of the church, six months later, on January 18, 1975, the approval was granted. It was a major breakthrough. The Church of the Nazarene was now recognized throughout Indonesia.

In May of that year, Rev. and Mrs. Robert D. McCroskey, Jr., arrived to begin language study, and they were followed in January 1976 by Rev. and Mrs. Michael P. McCarty.

In January 1977 the three men made an intensive survey of the central Java region, particularly the university city of Yogyakarta and the cultural center of Surakarta. These two cities, nicknamed Yogya and Solo, are about an hour's drive from each other. The McCroskeys were assigned to the former, and the McCartys to the latter. In February 1979 further reinforcements arrived in the persons of Rev. and Mrs. Raymond L. Couey.

The Renches remained in Djakarta at the headquarters church, which continued a steady growth and was fully self-supporting. Soon plans were made to add the second and third stories to the building with the establishment of a Christian day school for 800 children in mind. Construction began in 1981.

In Gunung Krambil, a village near Yogya, 30 persons, most of them adult couples, were baptized the first year, and 1,500 people attended the Christmas program the second year. A church building was completed in 1980, the congregation providing the property and labor, and the Somerset, Ky., Church of the Nazarene paying for the materials.

The McCartys in Solo likewise saw gratifying progress where soon three preaching points besides the main church were in operation. A beautiful new church building was completed here in September 1981. When Ray and Donna Couey joined the missionary staff in 1979, they were sent to Semarang, the provincial capital of central Java. This became the fastest-growing area in the Indonesian field.

Particularly significant was the strong group of national leaders that had been secured to pastor the churches. These included Pastor and Mrs. Chen Hung-Ying in Djakarta, Pastor and Mrs. Stephanus Hartoyo in Yogya, Pastor and Mrs. Berhitu in Solo, and Pastor and Mrs. Thede Bungaa in Semarang.

Adding to the outreach of the church was the inauguration of an Indonesian version of the "Showers of Blessing" radio program. The response, even from distant areas of the island, was gratifying.

On October 5, 1981, a major step was taken when the Bible college (Sekolah Alkitab Nazarene Indonesia) was opened in Yogya under the leadership of Rev. Robert McCroskey, with eight full-time students enrolled. With the help of Alabaster funds a beautiful campus site was purchased at the foot of Mount Merapi in Yogyakarta. James Couchenour, church building consultant from Ohio, spent two weeks on the site helping to devise a master plan for campus development. Investments Eternal, a Nazarene family organization in Long Beach, Calif., made a significant contribution making possible the erection of the first building unit, which was dedicated in 1983. By 1985 there were 36 full-time students studying for the ministry.

In 1985 total church membership stood at 727. There were 8 organized churches and 30 preaching points. Twenty part-time pastors and lay evangelists were serving the church. Two of these pastors were ordained in 1984. Attendance in the Nazarene Elementary and Junior High School in the Djakarta church had reached 600.

When in late 1985 Rev. George Rench was named regional director of the Asia-Pacific Region, Rev. Robert McCroskey, Jr., became mission director for Indonesia.

F. MICRONESIA

The more than 30,000 islands that lie scattered across the Pacific Ocean, mostly on its western side, are the tips of mountain chains rising from the ocean floor. Some are mere mounds of windblown sand or reefs surrounding lagoons that are called atolls. Many islands are formed of volcanic lava and ash, some of the larger ones having several such peaks. Though many islands are small and uninhabited, large ones such as New Guinea and New Zealand are also included.

There are three major groups: (1) Melanesia, including New Guinea, the New Hebrides, and Fiji; (2) Polynesia, including New Zealand, Samoa, and the Hawaiian Islands; and (3) Micronesia, including the Caroline, Kiribati, Mariana, and Marshall islands groups. Micronesia consists of some 2,500 islands in the northwest section toward Japan and the Philippines. (Such groups as the Philippines, Taiwan, the Ryukyus, and Japan are not included among the so-called Pacific islands.) Among Micronesia's most famous single islands are Wake, Saipan, Iwo Jima, and Guam. The total population of the area in 1985 stood at 350,000.

On December 17, 1971, in the village of Dededo on the island of Guam, a Nazarene church was organized principally to serve the American servicemen who were stationed in this strategic outpost. Rev. Harold Dalrymple, then in the military service, was the moving force behind this organization. Over the years several pastors have served the church—Revs. Gaylord Rich, Keith Sears, Gene Giron, Donald Bard, and Joe Chastain. Membership was very fluid because of the constant turnover of military personnel, but the church continued to play an important ministering role.

Because of its nature, the Guam church had been launched under the auspices of the Department of Home Missions and was made a part of the Hawaii Pacific District. In 1984, upon the recommendation of the advisory board of the district, it was transferred to the jurisdiction of the World Mission Division and became the only church in the pioneer area of Micronesia in the South Pacific Region.

In 1985 the Guam church reported 23 members. But doors were opening for the Church of the Nazarene in the islands of Ponape, Truk, and Yap, and a viable pioneer district was an early possibility.

PART THREE

Appendixes

Introduction

Unless otherwise stated, the denominational statistics are taken from the *General Assembly Journals*. This appeared to be the most consistent source of numerical data, particularly in the first two decades, and probably the most reliable overall. Numerous discrepancies in the figures from various sources had to be reconciled, sometimes arbitrarily, but for purposes of comparison those given here present a fair indication of the situation.

Over the years the shift of districts from Home to Foreign (World) Missions and vice versa, plus the more recent adjustments occasioned by the regional restructure, have not been accounted for here except as noted. This produces some slight inaccuracies in comparisons but no major aberrations.

Note that nearly all the major intervals are quadrenniums (four years), except one triennium (1908-11) and two quinquenniums (1923-28 and 1980-85). Note also that figures reported at the General Assembly are usually those of the previous year.

A. STATISTICAL

1. General Statistics*

World Population

1900	1,619,886,800
1970	3,610,034,400
1980	4,373,917,500
1985	4,867,006,100
2000 (projected)	6,259,642,000

Distribution of Religions

	Christians**	% of Total	Muslims	Hindus	Buddhists
1900	558,056,300	34.5	200,102,200	203,033,300	127,159,000
1970	1,216,579,400	33.7	550,919,000	465,784,800	231,672,200
1980	1,432,686,500	32.8	722,956,500	582,749,900	273,715,600
1985	1,572,875,100	32.3	837,308,700	661,371,700	300,146,900
2000 (proj.)	2,019,921,400	32.3	1,200,653,000	859,252,300	359,092,100

Unevangelized Populations

	Total	% of World Pop.
1900	788,159,000	48.7
1970	1,391,956,000	38.6
1980	1,380,576,000	31.6
1985	1,326,319,700	27.3
2000 (proj.)	1,038,819,000	16.6

*These figures are reprinted by permission from the *International Bulletin of Missionary Research* (January 1986) of Ventnor, N.J. Copyright © 1986.

**Includes all Christendom (Protestant, Roman Catholic, etc.).

Note: A rapidly growing group are the nonreligious peoples, which in 1985 numbered 825,072,900 and by the year 2000 are expected to reach 1,071,888,400.

631

Number of Missionaries (expatriate)

1900	62,000
1970	240,000
1980	249,000
1985	250,200
2000 (proj.)	400,000

2. Nazarene Church Membership in World Mission Regions

(Totals include combined full and probationary members)

1908	n/a		1948	24,048
1911	n/a		1952	38,994
1915	n/a		1956	50,350
1919	n/a		1960	54,055
1920	1,594		1964	66,233
1923	2,913		1968	87,256
1928	6,330		1972	97,321
1932	13,879		1976	130,892
1936	15,238		1980	179,954*
1940	19,576		1985	247,244*
1944	14,182			

*From annual statistical reports (to harmonize with Chart 10).

Nazarene Church Membership
on World Mission Regions
(Full and Probationary)

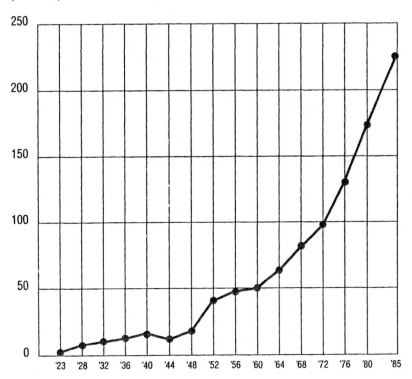

(Thousands)

3. *Regional Distribution of World Mission Membership*

(Data from annual statistical report)

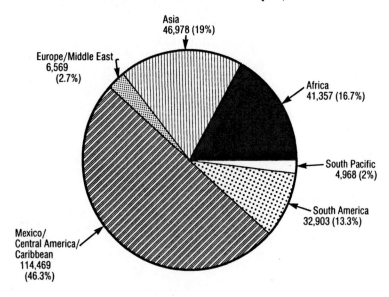

Asia
46,978 (19%)

Europe/Middle East
6,569
(2.7%)

Africa
41,357 (16.7%)

South Pacific
4,968 (2%)

South America
32,903 (13.3%)

Mexico/
Central America/
Caribbean
114,469
(46.3%)

4. *Chronology of Opening of World Mission Areas*

(Information provided by the World Mission Division)

Area	Date Work Opened	Area	Date Work Opened
India	1898	Mozambique	1922
Cape Verde	1901	Barbados	1926
Cuba	1902	Trinidad and Tobago	1926
Mexico	1903	Belize	1934
Guatemala	1904	Nicaragua	1937
Japan	1905	Puerto Rico	1944
Argentina	1909	Virgin Islands	1944
Great Britain	1909	Bolivia	1945
Swaziland	1911	Australia	1946
China	1913	Guyana	1946
Peru	1914	Philippines	1946
South Africa	1919	Italy	1948
(inc. Bophuthatswana, Venda)		Korea	1948
Syria	1920	Uruguay	1949
Israel	1921	Haiti	1950

Area	Date Work Opened	Area	Date Work Opened
Jordan	1950	Portugal	1973
Lebanon	1950	Antigua	1973
New Zealand	1952	Dominica	1974
Panama	1953	Dominican Republic	1974
Papua New Guinea	1955	Hong Kong	1974
Taiwan	1956	Colombia	1975
Malawi	1957	St. Vincent	1975
Brazil	1958	Martinique	1976
West Germany	1958	Grenada	1977
Denmark	1960	Namibia	1977
Samoa	1960	Nigeria	1977
Zambia	1961	France	1977
Chile	1962	Switzerland	1978
Zimbabwe	1963	Paraguay	1980
Costa Rica	1964	Spain	1981
El Salvador	1964	Venezuela	1982
Jamaica	1966	Ciskei	1983
Netherlands	1967	St. Kitts	1983
Bermuda	1970	Azores	1984
Honduras	1970	Botswana	1984
Bahamas	1971	Burma	1984
Guam (Micronesia)	1971	Kenya	1984
Ecuador	1972	Suriname	1984
St. Lucia	1972	Cyprus	1985
Indonesia	1973		

5. Number of Nazarene Missionaries

(Includes both career and specialized service or short term)

1908	19	1948	204
1911	35	1952	301
1915	38	1956	341
1919	56	1960	410
1923	112	1964	488
1928	83	1968	543
1932	71	1972	537
1936	69	1976	549
1940	94	1980	547
1944	78	1985	620

6. Distribution of World Mission Districts at Various Levels of Development

	Pioneer Area	Pioneer (Phase 1)	National-Mission (Phase 2)	Mission (Phase 3)	Regular (Phase 4)	Total
1973	0	32	29	6	0	67
1974	0	36	19	19	1	75
1975	14	18	14	32	1	79
1976	14	19	13	32	2	80
1977	15	23	18	37	2	95
1978	16	21	16	41	2	96
1979	12	21	25	41	2	101
1980	13	22	31	36	8	110
1981	8	27	32	35	9	111
1982	8	29	37	31	16	121
1983	3	32	39	35	19	128
1984	5	34	33	52	20	144
1985	13	27	63	35	21	159

7. Regular Mission Districts with Year They Were Opened

(Information provided by World Mission Division)

Field	Opened	Became Regular
Guatemala Las Verapaces	1915	1974
Peru North	1917	1976
Argentina Central	1919	1980
Japan	1905	1980
Mexico South	1903	1980
Puerto Rico	1944	1980
RSA European	1948	1980
Swaziland North	1910	1980
Korea Central	1948	1981
Barbados	1926	1982
Belize	1934	1982
British Isles North	1915	1982
British Isles South	1953	1982
Guyana	1946	1982
Mexico Central	1903	1982
Trinidad and Tobago	1926	1982
Mexico Northeast	1910	1983

Field	Opened	Became Regular
Mexico South Pacific	1903	1983
RSA Western Cape	1948	1983
Bolivia La Paz	1945	1985
Philippines Luzon Central	1946	1985

8. Representation from World Mission Districts at General Assembly Compared with Total Delegation

	Total	U.S.A./Canada	World Mission
1972	572	544	28 (5%)
1976	701	573	128 (18%)
1980	771	547	224 (29%)
1985	861	563	298* (35%)

*Includes addition of British Isles to Europe/Middle East Region.

9. Representation on the General Board from World Mission Regions Compared with Total

	Total	U.S.A./Canada	World Mission
1972	35	35	0
1976	40	34	6 (15%)
1980	54	40	14 (26%)
1985	58	40	18* (31%)

*Includes addition of British Isles to Europe/Middle East Region.

10. Comparison of World Mission Membership with Total (Worldwide) Membership (including probationary members)*

	Worldwide	World Mission	Percentage
1972	517,274	97,321	19%
1976	605,185	130,892	22%
1980	661,114	179,954	27%
1985	779,221	247,244	32%

*Probationary membership is almost exclusively in world mission areas and in 1985 amounted to 30% of that total.

11. *Nazarene World Mission Society Membership*

First reported membership (1921)   3,637

1923	5,329	Women's Missionary Society
1928	15,899	Women's Foreign Missionary Society
1932	24,880	
1936	41,604	
1940	51,797	
1944	60,214	
1948	74,518	
1952	90,095*	Nazarene Foreign Missionary Society
1956	120,470	
1960	173,825	
1964	227,532	Nazarene World Missionary Society
1968	272,219	
1972	299,488	
1976	385,900	
1980	430,056	Nazarene World Mission Society
1985	489,987	

*First inclusion of members on world mission fields in total.

(Figures are from official NWMS statistical records.)

12. *Alabaster Offering*

The first Alabaster Offering report was in 1950 when $46,603 was received.

1952	$ 57,469
1956	270,211
1960	398,515
1964	457,168
1968	630,414
1972	830,126
1976	1,243,981
1980	1,560,529
1985	2,157,660

(Figures are from official NWMS statistical records.)

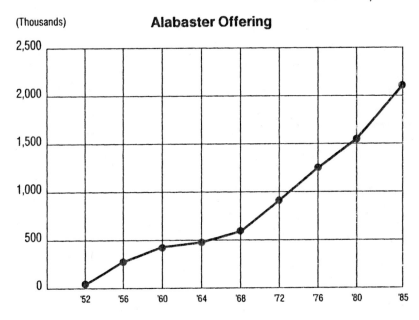

(Thousands)

Alabaster Offering

2,500
2,000
1,500
1,000
500
0

'52 '56 '60 '64 '68 72 76 '80 '85

13. *World Mission Educational Institutions*

as listed in *World Mission,* September 1985

Country	School	Director	Enrollment
Argentina	Instituto Biblico Nazareno	Rev. Rogelio Fernandez	22
Australia	Australasian Nazarene Bible College	Dr. Grady Cantrell	22
Bolivia	Seminario Nazareno Boliviano	Rev. Eduardo Aparicio	21
Brazil	Seminario e Instituto Biblico da Igreja do Nazareno	Rev. J. Elton Wood	38
Cape Verde	Seminario Nazareno	Rev. Paul Stroud	9
Chile	Seminario Biblico Nazareno	Rev. Ted Hughes	13
Costa Rica	Seminario Nazareno de las Americas	Rev. Jerry Porter	86
Cuba	Instituto Biblico Nazareno	Mr. Eliner Cobas	13
Guatemala	Indian Bible School	Rev. Julio Cuz	36
	Instituto Teologico Nazareno	Miss Mary Lou Riggle	38
Haiti	Institut Biblique Nazaréen	Miss Jeanine van Beek	44
India North	Nazarene Bible College	Rev. Padu Meshramkar	15
Indonesia	Nazarene Bible College	Rev. Bob McCroskey	33
Japan	Nazarene Theological Seminary	Rev. Masac Fujii	6
Korea	Nazarene Theological College	Rev. William Patch	71
Malawi	Nazarene Bible College	Rev. Tom Waltermire	36
Mexico	Seminario Nazareno Mexicano	Dr. H. T. Reza	85
Middle Europe	European Nazarene Bible College	Rev. Walter Crow	48
Mozambique	Maputo Nazarene Bible College	Rev. Simeon Mandlate	75
Papua New Guinea	Nazarene Bible College	Rev. Ray Bolerjack	57
Peru	Instituto Biblico Nazareno	Rev. Abiatar Sanchez	32
	Seminario Biblico Nazareno	Rev. Ernesto Lozano	46

Country	School	Director	Enrollment
Philippines	Asia-Pacific Nazarene Theological Seminary*	Dr. LeBron Fairbanks	38
	Luzon Nazarene Bible College	Rev. Ernesto Rulloda	83
	Visayan Nazarene Bible College	Rev. Roy Copelin	63
RSA European	Africa Nazarene Theological College	Dr. Ted Esselstyn	39
Samoa	Nazarene Bible College	Rev. James Johnson	14
South Africa	KwaZulu Nazarene Bible College	Rev. Philip Bedwell	
	Lula Schmelzenbach Memorial Theological College	Rev. E. Litswele	23
Swaziland	Nazarene Bible College	Mr. Ken Walker	44
Taiwan	Nazarene Theological College	Rev. Jim Williams	14
Trans South Africa	Nazarene Bible College	Rev. Ron Calhoun	35
Trinidad	Caribbean Nazarene Theological College	Rev. Farrell Chapman	57
Zambia	Nazarene Bible College	Dr. Glenn Kell	8
Zimbabwe	Nazarene Bible College	Rev. Jim Sage	8

*The only graduate seminary in the Church of the Nazarene outside of the Nazarene Theological Seminary in Kansas City.

B. PERSONNEL

1. The Board of General Superintendents

(Listed in order of first election)

Phineas F. Bresee	1908-15
H. F. Reynolds	1908-32
E. P. Ellyson	1908-11
E. F. Walker	1911-18
W. C. Wilson	1915
John W. Goodwin	1916-40
R. T. Williams	1916-46
James B. Chapman	1928-47
J. G. Morrison	1936-39
Orval J. Nease	1940-44, 1948-50
H. V. Miller	1940-48
Hardy C. Powers	1944-68
G. B. Williamson	1946-68
Samuel Young	1948-72
D. I. Vanderpool	1949-64
Hugh C. Benner	1952-68
V. H. Lewis	1960-85
George Coulter	1964-80
Edward Lawlor	1968-76
Orville W. Jenkins	1968-85
Eugene L. Stowe	1968—
Charles H. Strickland	1972—
William M. Greathouse	1976—
Jerald D. Johnson	1980—
John A. Knight	1985—
Raymond W. Hurn	1985—

2. Executive Secretaries/Directors of World Mission Division

H. F. Reynolds	1908-15,* 1926-28
E. G. Anderson	1915-26
J. G. Morrison	1928-36
C. Warren Jones	1936-48
Remiss Rehfeldt	1948-60
George Coulter	1960-64
Everette S. Phillips	1964-73
Jerald D. Johnson	1973-80
L. Guy Nees	1980-86
Robert L. Scott	1986—

*H. F. Reynolds had been serving in a similar capacity with the Association of Pentecostal Churches of America since 1896.

3. Missionaries Who Have Served in the Church of the Nazarene

The following is a complete roster of the 1,763 persons who have served on Nazarene world mission fields. It includes mostly career personnel, but there are a few who have been on specialized assignments. All those listed have been on the field at least one year. This being a computerized list, the names are given in strict alphabetical order, which means that in a number of cases husbands' and wives' names are not next to each other. Usually couples can be readily identified by comparing places and terms of service.

In the service records, credit is given for any years spent under the auspices of an organization that later became a part of the Church of the Nazarene. Besides the Bresee group in the West, this would include principally the Association of Pentecostal Churches of America in the East, the Holiness Church of Christ in the South, the Pentecostal Mission of Nashville, and the International Holiness Mission of Africa and Great Britain.

In cases where women began their missionary careers while single and later married, their service records appear after their married names. Their maiden names are also listed but cross-referenced to their married names.

This roster does not include those who began their missionary careers after 1985, but does make note of 1986 changes affecting those already in service.

Abla, Grace Evelyn, Swaziland, 1952-55
Abney, John Kyle, Samoa, 1964-65
Abney, Virginia, Samoa, 1964-65
Adams, Beryl, Brazil, 1981—
Adams, Brian, Brazil, 1981—
Adams, John Franklin, Papua New Guinea, 1971-83
Adams, Viola Jean, Papua New Guinea, 1971-83
Adkins, Betty Irene, Bolivia, 1959-67; Chile, 1970-77
Adkins, George Washington, Bolivia, 1959-67; Chile, 1970-77
Adragna, Mary Emma, Italy, 1962-64
Adragna, Vincent J., Italy, 1962-64
Ahleman, Dorothy Mable, Argentina, 1944-81
Ainscough, Albert Edward, India, 1973-79
Ainscough, Ramona, Argentina, 1947-75
Ainscough, Rosa Isabel, India, 1973-79
Ainscough, Thomas Albert, Argentina, 1947-76
Alexander, Douglas Robert, Swaziland, 1958-59; South Africa, 1959-68, 1975-76, 1978—; Mozambique, 1968-74; West Germany, 1976-78
Alexander, Marion Anne, Swaziland, 1958-59; South Africa, 1959-68, 1975-76, 1978—; Mozambique, 1968-74; West Germany, 1976-78
Alexander, Mayme Lee, Guatemala, 1946-60
Allen, Judy M., Swaziland, 1970-72
Allen, Michael H., Swaziland, 1970-72
Alstott, Charles Whiteman, Haiti, 1952-59, 1961-62
Alstott, Ida Alberta, Haiti, 1952-59, 1961-62
Andersen, Joan Elizabeth, Swaziland, 1972—
Anderson, Anna May Bursch, India, 1920-31
Anderson, Annie Maude, Guatemala, 1904-49
Anderson, Daniel Alan, Kenya, 1985—
Anderson, Doris Marie, India, 1966—
Anderson, F. Arthur, India, 1920-23, 1927-29
Anderson, Helen Harper, India, 1920-23, 1927-29
Anderson, John William, India, 1966—
Anderson, John Willis, India, 1936-70, 1978-79, 1981-82
Anderson, Mary Elizabeth, India, 1936-70, 1978-79
Anderson, Melody Ann, Kenya, 1985—

Anderson, Richard Simpson, Guatemala, 1904-45
Andrus, Bernice Elizabeth, Bolivia, 1965-75
Andrus, Paul Coulter, Bolivia, 1965-75
Appleby, Jerry, Samoa, 1969-76
Appleby, Polly, Samoa, 1969-76
Archer, Edmond, New Zealand, 1974-78
Archer, Jan, New Zealand, 1974-78
Armstrong, Glenda, Colombia, 1981-85; Venezuela, 1985—
Armstrong, Janet Beverly, Bolivia, 1950-54; Uruguay, 1955-82; Guyana, 1982-85
Armstrong, John Alfred (Jack), Bolivia, 1950-54; Uruguay, 1955-82; Guyana, 1982-85
Armstrong, John Harvey, Colombia, 1981-85; Venezuela, 1985—
Armstrong, Mack J., El Salvador, 1974-78
Armstrong, Martha Dawn, El Salvador, 1974-78
Armstrong, Norma June, Philippines, 1963-77
Ashley, Ina Lou, Belize, 1954-74; St. Lucia, 1975-82; Casa Robles Dir., 1984—
Ashley, Robert Lee, Belize, 1954-74; St. Lucia, 1975-82; Casa Robles Dir., 1984—
Ault, Donald Kingsley, Guyana, 1952-57
Ault, Elizabeth Mae, Guyana, 1952-57
Austin, Marilyn, Japan, 1980-81
Ayer, Elnora Louise, Japan, 1981-83
Ayer, Harold George, Japan, 1981-83
Ayuso, Betty Lou Zurcher, Nicaragua, 1974-75

Babcock, Kenneth Elwood, Mozambique, 1948-50
Babcock, Mildred Edith, Mozambique, 1948-50
Bach, Elizabeth, Swaziland, 1968-70
Bach, Tom, Swaziland, 1968-70
Bagley, Mary Violet, Swaziland, 1952-68
Baird, Linda Joyce, Ecuador, 1976-79
Baird, Stephen Kent, Ecuador, 1976-79
Bajoyo, Norma Felisa Palmejar, Swaziland, 1977—
Baker, Deborah Lynn Nelson, Peru, 1983—
Baker, Steven Rex, Peru, 1983—
Ball, D. C., Mexico, 1911-12
Ball, Mrs. D. C., Mexico, 1911-12
Barber, Marie, Panama, 1976-79
Barber, Paul, Panama, 1976-79
Bard, Donald, Zambia, 1986—

Bard, Paula Snellenberger, Philippines, 1979-80; Zambia, 1986—

Barnell, Emmor Holstein, Malawi, 1967-79

Barnell, Jack Merlin, Malawi, 1967-79

Barnes, Nellie, India, 1904-6

Bartle, Joyce Duncan Skea, Papua New Guinea, 1968—

Bartle, Neville Robert, Papua New Guinea, 1970—

Basford, Jessie, India, 1912-20

Bastian, Dick, Papua New Guinea, 1984-86

Bastian, Marge, Papua New Guinea, 1984-86

Bates, Elva Jane (see Morden)

Baty, Duane D., Philippines, 1984—

Baty, Susan K., Philippines, 1984—

Bauder, Kathleen Joan, Swaziland, 1972-78

Bauder, Linton Wayne, Swaziland, 1972-78

Beals, Bessie Littlejohn, India, 1920-52; Trinidad, 1955-56

Beals, Charlotte H., Barbados, 1959-61; Belize, 1961-70

Beals, Paul Wiley, Barbados, 1959-61; Belize, 1961-70

Beals, Prescott Loring, India, 1920-52; Barbados, 1954; Trinidad, 1955-57; Belize, 1959-63

Beckum, Florence Louise (Lorie), West Germany, 1978-81; France, 1986—

Beckum, Randell Edward, West Germany, 1978-81; France, 1986—

Bedwell, Howard Kenneth, South Africa, 1931-53, 1969-76; Swaziland, 1953-68

Bedwell, Karen Elaine, South Africa, 1970—

Bedwell, Margaret, South Africa, 1937-53, 1969-76; Swaziland, 1953-68

Bedwell, Philip, South Africa, 1970—

Beebe, Della MacLachlan, Papua New Guinea, 1971-75, 1977-82

Beech, Neva Jane, Philippines, 1962—

Beech, Ronald Ward, Philippines, 1962—

Bell, Don, Zimbabwe, 1979-83; Mexico, 1985—

Bell, Glenda Jean, Zimbabwe, 1979-83; Mexico, 1985—

Bellew, Leona McConnell (see Meek)

Benedict, Virginia Rose, Mozambique, 1957-76; South Africa, 1976-77

Bennett, Merril George Stanley, Japan, 1952-82

Bennett, Myrtlebelle, Japan, 1952-82

Bentley, David Connally, Australia, 1977-80

Bentley, Sheryl Marie, Australia, 1977-80

Berry, David Abbott, Japan, 1985—

Berry, Mary Ellen, Japan, 1985—

Best, Henry Charles, South Africa, 1919-22, 1945-55; Mozambique, 1922-45

Best, Lucy Latham, South Africa, 1919-22, 1945-55; Mozambique, 1922-45

Bevill, Dorothy Louise (see Eby)

Bicker, Clifford S., Peru, 1935-37

Bicker, Ruth Smith, Peru, 1935-37

Biddulph, Mary Ann Harper, India, 1952-59

Biggs, George August, Trinidad, 1967-79

Biggs, Marjorie Ellen, Trinidad, 1967-79

Birchard, Margaret Anderson, Guatemala, 1934-63; Nicaragua, 1963-74

Birchard, Russell Wagar, Guatemala, 1934-63; Nicaragua, 1963-73

Bishop, Ronald Carl, Jr., Belize, 1944-61

Bishop, Ruth Eileen Hower, Belize, 1944-61

Blachly, Ada Jones, South Africa, 1967-83

Blachly, David Hynd, South Africa, 1967-83

Black, Bessie Louise, No. Amer. Indian, 1974-76; San Antonio Sem., 1976-81; Papua New Guinea, 1981—

Black, Robert William, No. Amer. Indian, 1974-76; San Antonio Sem., 1976-81; Papua New Guinea, 1981—

Blackman, Frank, India, 1920-23

Blackman, Ruby May Elmore, India, 1920-25, 1944-54

Blair, Mary Joyce, Belize, 1943-76

Blamey, Cyril Ventnor, South Africa, 1938-68

Blish, Kenneth, Ecuador, 1980-86; Bolivia, 1986—

Blish, Susan, Ecuador, 1980-86; Bolivia, 1986—

Bloom, Byron Leon, Australia, 1979-83, 1986—

Bloom, Mary Ann, Australia, 1979-83, 1986—

Blowers, Bruce Lawrence, Papua New Guinea, 1965—

Blowers, Merna Mae, Papua New Guinea, 1964-76

Blowers, Ruth Evelyn, Papua New Guinea, 1965—

Boadway, Edwin Juhl, Papua New Guinea, 1973-82

Boadway, Rosemary, Papua New Guinea, 1973-82

Boesch, Alice Joan Bradshaw, South Africa, 1948-56

Boggs, Della Brown, Swaziland, 1944-79

Bolerjack, Helen Marie, Papua New Guinea, 1963—

Bolerjack, Patricia L., Australia, 1975-79

Bolerjack, Raymond Lee, Papua New Guinea, 1963—

Bolerjack, Roy T., Australia, 1975-79

Bomely, Ella Mae, San Antonio Sem., 1976-77

Bomely, Roger, San Antonio Sem., 1976-77

Bond, Jimmy Lee, Brazil, 1971-72

Bond, Sara I. (Sally), Brazil, 1971-72

Borden, Nancy Beth, Haiti, 1963-71

Bowling, Christina Joy, Venezuela, 1984—

Bowling, James Allen, Venezuela, 1984—

Bown, Eunice Camille, Swaziland, 1964-70

Boyles, Errol La Vaughn, Swaziland, 1974-79

Boyles, Janice Lynn, Swaziland, 1974-79

Bradbury, Merilyn Larmar, Papua New Guinea, 1971-73

Bradshaw, Alice Joan (see Boesch)

Brammer, Maxwell J., Papua New Guinea, 1980—

Brammer, Miriam Mellinger, Papua New Guinea, 1968-69, 1974-77, 1980—

Branstine, Bessie (see Guillermo)

Brewer, Carolyn Muriel Mary, Bolivia, 1968-86; Peru, 1986—

Brewer, Daniel Lee, Bolivia, 1968-86; Peru, 1986—

Brewington, Jane Ann, Swaziland, 1972-79

Brickman, Ruth E. (see Williamson)

Briles, Eula Horney, Bolivia, 1945-52

Briles, Ninevah Rush, Bolivia, 1945-52

Brocklebank, Eleanor, Papua New Guinea, 1974-76

Bromley, Margaret Joan Robson, Papua New Guinea, 1961-85

Bromley, William Ewart, Papua New Guinea, 1958-69

Brook, Robert, Papua New Guinea, 1983-84

Brook, Twyla, Papua New Guinea, 1983-84

Brough, Barbara, Nicaragua, 1966-68

Brough, Norlyn Eaton, Nicaragua, 1966-68

Brown, Annette F. Taft, Samoa, 1979-80

Brown, Barbara, South Africa, 1976-78

Brown, Bobby Ray, Haiti, 1966-71; Nicaragua, 1971-78; Guatemala, 1978-82

Brown, Doris Jessie, South Africa, 1926-67

Brown, Grace Kathleen Morley, Barbados, 1956-68; Guyana, 1969-80

Brown, Jerry, South Africa, 1976-78

Brown, Louise Jeannine, Haiti, 1966-71; Nicaragua, 1971-78; Guatemala, 1978-82

Brown, Phyllis Hartley (see Perkins)

Brown, Rhonda Ann, Philippines, 1985—

Brown, Richard Harold, South Africa, 1973-79

Brown, Robert, Barbados, 1956-68; Guyana, 1969-80

Brown, Vera Elizabeth, South Africa, 1973-79

Browning, David Franklin, Belize, 1944-55; Guyana, 1955-71; Philippines, 1971-82

Browning, Kay Frances Embick, Jordan, 1979-81; Israel, 1981—

Browning, Lindell Ray, Jordan, 1979-81; Israel, 1981—

Browning, Lucy Elizabeth Lumpkin, Belize, 1944-55; Guyana, 1955-71; Philippines, 1971-82

Broyles, Lucille Smith, Belize, 1947-52

Brunson, Norma Louise Hendrix, Peru, 1970-80; Costa Rica, 1981-83

Brunson, Robert Worth, Peru, 1970-80; Costa Rica, 1981-83

Brunt, Russell William, Trinidad, 1957—

Brunt, Thelma Jean (Tillie), Trinidad, 1957—

Bryant, Eunice Ruth, Guatemala, 1950-62; San Antonio Sem., 1962-64, 1979-81; El Salvador, 1964-77; Peru, 1977-79

Bryant, Richard Lawrence, Guatemala, 1950-62; San Antonio Sem., 1962-64; El Salvador, 1964-77; Peru, 1977-79

Buchanan, Arla Jean Pleyer, South Africa, 1985—

Buchanan, James, South Africa, 1985—

Buchanan, Julianne (see Dellepere)

Buell, Fannie May, Panama, 1963-77

Buell, Marvin Lee, Panama, 1963-77

Buess, Larry Duane, Lebanon, 1969-76; Jordan, 1977-79

Buess, Sharon Kay, Lebanon, 1969-76; Jordan, 1977-79

Buffett, Patricia Lou, Mozambique, 1967-78; Papua New Guinea, 1978-83

Bull, Ethel M., Papua New Guinea, 1981-85

Bunch, Gary Wayne, Portugal, 1974-79; Brazil, 1979—

Bunch, Harriet Fern Stanton, Portugal, 1974-79; Brazil, 1979—

Burchfield, Catharine Fay Anderson, Peru, 1940-54

Burchfield, Oscar Harrison, Peru, 1940-54

Burge, John Earl, Haiti, 1982-86; Suriname, 1986—

Burge, Martha Marie, Haiti, 1982-86; Suriname, 1986—

Burges, Geoffrey R., Australia, 1985—

Burges, Jeanne P., Australia, 1985—

Burgess, Elmer, India, 1904-5

Burgess, Patricia June, Taiwan, 1964-69

Burkhart, Alldeen L., Swaziland, 1962-67

Burkhart, Meryle Ilene, Guyana, 1962-72; Philippines, 1976—

Burkhart, Paul R., Swaziland, 1962-67

Burkhart, Peter Crosley, Guyana, 1962-72; Philippines, 1976—

Burnes, Donald, Japan, 1981-84

Burnes, Hilda, Japan, 1981-84

Burrows, Clive, Papua New Guinea, 1975-85; West Germany, 1985—

Burrows, Grace, Papua New Guinea, 1975-85; West Germany, 1985—

Bursch, Anna May (see Anderson)

Bustle, Louie Elvis, Virgin Islands, 1970-74; Dominican Republic, 1974-82; Peru, 1982-83; S. Amer. Reg. Dir., 1983—

Bustle, Sara Ellen, Virgin Islands, 1970-74; Dominican Republic, 1974-82; Peru, 1982-83; S. Amer. Reg. Off., 1983—

Butler, J. T., Guatemala, 1901-15

Butler, Mrs. J. T., Guatemala, 1901-2

Buttery, Pamela, Papua New Guinea, 1984—

Bynum, Kathleen Marie Miller, Bolivia, 1984—

Bynum, William Randolph, Bolivia, 1984—

Cairns, Edward, Belize, 1958-72

Cairns, Margaret Dowling, Belize, 1958-72

Calhoun, Ronald Clester, South Africa, 1965—

Calhoun, Shelva Jeanne, South Africa, 1965—

Campbell, Emma, India, 1908-15

Campbell, James Merritt, South Africa, 1980-84

Campbell, Lawrence, India, 1908-15

Campbell, Nancy Lou, South Africa, 1980-84

Carlsen, Bente Martha, Papua New Guinea, 1966-69

Carpenter, Dora Ann, Swaziland, 1922-48

Carpenter, Eva (see Roby)

Carson, Esther (see Winans)

Carson, F. W., Peru, 1927-29

Carson, Mrs. F. W., Peru, 1927-29

Carter, Clarence Lowell, India, 1950-62

Carter, Marjorie Lucile, India, 1950-62

Caudill, Bobby E., Trinidad, 1965-70

Caudill, Glendoris, Trinidad, 1965-70

Caudle, Cornie, India, 1918-22

Cerrato, Edna Cuff, Italy, 1960-64

Cerrato, Rocco James, Italy, 1960-64

Chalfant, Donald Morris, South Africa, 1947-52

Chalfant, Margaret Jane Atterbury, South Africa, 1947-52

Chandler, Leila Joyce, Belize, 1967-80

Chapman, Ida Louise Robinson, South Africa, 1920-42

Chappell, Geraldine Virginia, India, 1941-78, 1979-80

Chenault, J. A., Japan, 1910-12

Chenault, Minnie Upperman, Japan, 1905-12

Chiang, Bernadine Dringenberg, Taiwan, 1960-65

Childress, Charles Ray, Guatemala, 1963-75

Childress, Donnie Carolyn, Guatemala, 1963-75

Childs, Barbara, South Africa, 1983-85; Swaziland, 1985—

Childs, Bill R., South Africa, 1983-85; Swaziland, 1985—

Chism, Fairy Steele, Swaziland, 1928-49

Christensen, Clara, Denmark, 1965; West Germany, 1966

Christianson, Henrietta Hale, India, 1937-41

Chung, Mrs. Robert Namsooh, Korea, 1926-55

Chung, Robert Namsooh, Korea, 1926-55

Church, Cassandra Swinehoe, Mozambique, 1947-61

Church, Clifford Francis, Mozambique, 1947-61

Cintron, Mario A., Venezuela, 1984—

Cintron, Raquel R., Venezuela, 1984—

Clark, Agnes (see Graham)

Clark, Delores Darlene, Brazil, 1968-73

Clark, Elizabeth Anderson, Swaziland, 1946-53

Clark, Joseph Wendell, Swaziland, 1957-59

Clark, Larry Coleman, Brazil, 1968-73

Clark, Lloree Rose, Swaziland, 1957-59

Clark, Lowell Gene, Malawi, 1978-80; Zambia, 1985—

Clark, Marilyn Elaine, Malawi, 1978-80; Zambia, 1985—

Clayton, John Roy, Taiwan, 1966-72
Clayton, Natalie, Taiwan, 1966-72
Clegg, Eunice Manita, Swaziland, 1956-79
Clifton, Martha Waunita, Swaziland, 1961-67
Clinger, Maurice Edwin, Mexico, 1957-77
Clinger, Merilyn (see Manchester)
Clinkingbeard, Carolyn, Swaziland, 1981-83
Clyburn, James Michael, Australia, 1984-85
Clyburn, Sheila Jacqueline, Australia, 1984-85
Coats, Eugenia Alice Phillips, Guatemala, 1917-45
Coats, William Harvey, Guatemala, 1928-45
Cobb, Aubrey Brent, Korea, 1970-80
Cobb, Martha Weaver, Korea, 1970-80
Cochlin, Fairy Faith, Mozambique, 1948-57, 1964-75; South Africa, 1957-64
Cochran, Georgia Marie Goodson, Argentina, 1936-73
Cochran, John Aubrey, Argentina, 1936-73
Codding, Rosa Lowe, India, 1903-26
Codding, Roy G., India, 1903-26
Coetzer, Jacobus Christiaan B., South Africa, 1961-80
Coetzer, Susanna Carolina Olga, South Africa, 1961-80
Coffman, Marilyn Arlene, Papua New Guinea, 1973-84
Coil, Kenn R., Australia, 1985—
Coil, Marsha K., Australia, 1985—
Coldwell, Rhoda (see Restrick)
Cole, Elizabeth Marie, Swaziland, 1935-73
Cole, Lillian (see Short)
Collett, Christina Kay, South Africa, 1981—
Collett, Russell Allen, South Africa, 1981—
Collins, Frances Darlene, Brazil, 1962-68, 1969-84, 1986—
Collins, Helen, Papua New Guinea, 1971-72
Collins, Jeanne-Marie, Trinidad, 1980-82
Collins, Michelene (see Larrabee)
Collins, Robert Thomas, Brazil, 1962-68, 1969-84, 1986—
Conder, Mary Alice, Haiti, 1953-57; Papua New Guinea, 1957-61
Conder, Max A., Haiti, 1953-57; Papua New Guinea, 1957-61
Conrad, Maudie Modena, Cuba, 1957-61; Peru, 1961-68; Costa Rica, 1968-79
Conrad, William Howard, Cuba, 1957-61; Peru, 1961-68; Costa Rica, 1968-79
Cook, Dorothy Fay Davis, Swaziland, 1940-73

Cook, Orpha Charlotte Blackman, India, 1935-42, 1945-51; Trinidad, 1958-66; Jamaica, 1966-67
Cook, Ralph Alvin, India, 1935-42, 1945-51; Trinidad, 1958-66; Jamaica, 1966-73
Cook, Sharon Eldeana, Chile, 1977-81
Cook, Thomas L., Chile, 1977-81
Coolidge, Ardee Burr, Cuba, 1952-58; Argentina, 1958-75; Chile, 1975-77; Bolivia, 1977-82
Coolidge, Mary Faith Cochran, Cuba, 1952-58; Argentina, 1958-75; Chile, 1975-77; Bolivia, 1977-82
Cooper, Mary May, Mozambique, 1928-70
Copelin, Erna Kathryn, Philippines, 1954—
Copelin, Kathleen Joanne, Swaziland, 1981-84
Copelin, Roy Edward, Philippines, 1954—
Cornelius, Eleanor Ruth, Belize, 1965-71
Cornelius, Richard A., Belize, 1965-71
Cornett, Eldon, Korea, 1957-72
Cornett, Judith Elaine, Zimbabwe, 1983—
Cornett, Larry Edward, Zimbabwe, 1983—
Cornett, Marcella Eaton, Korea, 1957-72
Cory, Linda Marlene, Chile, 1975-80
Cory, Phillip Lee, Chile, 1975-80
Couey, Donna Marie, Indonesia, 1978—
Couey, Raymond Lee, Indonesia, 1978—
Courtney-Smith, Eric Albert, South Africa, 1947-55; Swaziland, 1955-73
Courtney-Smith, Frances Lilian, South Africa, 1967—
Courtney-Smith, Lilian Kate, South Africa, 1947-55; Swaziland, 1955-73
Cox, Anna Lee, Swaziland, 1928-48; No. Amer. Indian, 1948-49
Cox, Cheryl Lynn, Peru, 1975-77; Chile, 1977—
Cox, David Livingstone, Japan, 1972-79
Cox, Diana Louise, Japan, 1972-79
Cox, Donald Eugene, Peru, 1975-77; Chile, 1977—
Cox, Hilda Lee Oyler, India, 1952-73
Cox, Ira, Jr., India, 1952-73
Cox, Sarah Mai (see Marquis)
Crain, Esther Lois, Nicaragua, 1945-59
Crenshaw, Donald Eugene, Argentina, 1961-67; Dominican Republic, 1985—
Crenshaw, Lucy Ellen, Argentina, 1961-67; Dominican Republic, 1985—
Cretors, Maude, Swaziland, 1922-33
Crooks, Ruth Williams, India, 1920-25

Crouch, Evelyn Charlene (see Ovando)
Crouch, Rebecca L., South Africa, 1983—
Crow, Betty Lou, South Africa, 1981-86
Crow, Edythe Marie Wise, South Africa, 1965-73
Crow, Kenneth Eugene, South Africa, 1965-73
Crow, Linda Lavonne, Haiti, 1963-73, 1976-79; France, 1979-82; West Germany, 1982—
Crow, Richard, South Africa, 1981-86
Crow, Walter Edward, Haiti, 1963-73, 1976-79; France, 1979-82; West Germany, 1982—
Culbertson, Barbara Jo, Italy, 1974-83; Haiti, 1983—
Culbertson, Howard R., Italy, 1974-83; Haiti, 1983—
Culley, Olvette Louise, Nicaragua, 1952-61
Cummings, Betty Lou, Swaziland, 1960-72
Cunningham, Floyd, Philippines, 1983—
Cunningham, John Edwin, Ciskei, 1984—
Cunningham, Sandra Lee Schindler, Ciskei, 1984—

Daniels, Bert, New Zealand, 1985—
Daniels, Lola, New Zealand, 1985—
Danielson, Robert, Barbados, 1937-46
Danielson, Susan, Barbados, 1937-46
Danner, Marjorie Eithol Peel, South Africa, 1956-76
Darling, Priscilla Jean, India, 1945-85
Davidson, Ian, Papua New Guinea, 1984—
Davidson, James, India, 1904-5
Davidson, Jennie, India, 1904-5
Davidson, Jennifer, Papua New Guinea, 1984—
Davis, Bertha, India, 1908-15
Davis, Donald Harry, Argentina, 1958-81
Davis, Doris Kathryn Wagner, Japan, 1950-85
Davis, Dorothy Fay (see Cook)
Davis, Edward Young, Cuba, 1905-9, 1917-21; Mexico Border, 1921-23, 1924-26; Guatemala, 1923-24
Davis, Emma Elizabeth Zimmerman, Argentina, 1958-81
Davis, Harrison Ransom, Japan, 1950-85
Davis, Martha Mozelle Patterson, Cuba, 1905-9, 1917-21; Mexico Border, 1921-23, 1924-26; Guatemala, 1923-24

Dawson, Betty Jo, Swaziland, 1982-83, 1984—
Dawson, Charles William (Bill), Haiti, 1985—
Dawson, Martha Colleen Richesin, Haiti, 1985—
Dayhoff, Fannie, South Africa, 1919-60
Dayhoff, Irvin Earl, South Africa, 1919-60
Dayhoff, Margaret Lillian Stark, South Africa, 1954—
Dayhoff, Paul Stanley, South Africa, 1952—
Deale, Otis P., China, 1917-33
Deale, Zella Warner, China, 1917-33
Dean, Milton L. (Mickey), Belize, 1974-75; South Africa, 1980-82
Dean, Shirley J., Belize, 1974-75; South Africa, 1980-82
DeBow, Bethany (see Sibert)
Dech, Ruth Margaret, Belize, 1946-73; Costa Rica, 1973-85
Dellepere, Julianne Buchanan, Uruguay, 1974-78
Demetre, Betty Jo Oxner, Guyana, 1962-69; Barbados, 1969-70; Jamaica, 1970-78
Demetre, Jerry Larkin, Guyana, 1962-69; Barbados, 1969-70; Jamaica, 1970-78
Denbo, Pearl (see Schaffer)
Denniston, Reatha Adair, Swaziland, 1965-71
Denton, Sarah Ellen Byrd, Bolivia, 1947; Argentina, 1947; Uruguay, 1947-59, 1965-70; Brazil, 1959-64
Denton, William Ronald, Bolivia, 1947; Argentina, 1947; Uruguay, 1947-59, 1965-70; Brazil, 1959-64
Depasquale, Don, Syria, 1945-65; Lebanon, 1965-69
Depasquale, Frances Myrtle Daykin, Syria, 1945-65; Lebanon, 1965-69
Depasquale, James, Haiti, 1960-64; Greece, 1966-67
Depasquale, Mary, Haiti, 1960-64; Greece, 1966-67
Derby, E. G., Papua New Guinea, 1970-71
Derby, Mrs. E. G., Papua New Guinea, 1970-71
Devore, Elvin, Haiti, 1964-67, 1969-72; Barbados, 1967-69
Devore, Evelyn, Haiti, 1964-67, 1969-72; Barbados, 1967-69
Dias, Joana Lomba, Cape Verde, 1900-1938
Dias, John J., Cape Verde, 1900-1938

Diggs, Dorothy Prescott (Dorrie), Ciskei, 1984—
Dimbath, Carol Louise, Swaziland, 1959-71
Dipert, Myrna, Papua New Guinea, 1985—
Dipert, Robert H., Papua New Guinea, 1985—
Dixon, Kathyren Lititia, South Africa, 1936-71
Dobbs, Donald, West Germany, 1983-86
Dobbs, Patti, West Germany, 1983-86
Dodd, Carrie, Papua New Guinea, 1965-67, 1977-79
Dodd, Kenneth, Papua New Guinea, 1965-67, 1977-79
Dodds, Denzil Earl, South Africa, 1976—
Dodds, Kay Ann, South Africa, 1976—
Doerr, Jo L., Swaziland, 1981-83; Ciskei, 1983—
Doerr, Joan, Zambia, 1981—
Doerr, Stanley, Swaziland, 1981-83; Ciskei, 1983—
Doerr, Steve, Zambia, 1981—
Doll, Armand Millard, Mozambique, 1945-48, 1951-78; Caribbean, 1978-79; Jamaica, 1979-81
Doll, June Pauline Bower, Mozambique, 1945-48, 1951-78; Caribbean, 1978-79; Jamaica, 1979-81
Douglass, Elvin Malcolm, Peru, 1947-80
Douglass, Margaret Maria Major, Peru, 1947-80
Downing, Klawdia, Panama, 1972-77
Downing, Thomas Gwyn, Panama, 1972-77
Drake, Lois Jane, Swaziland, 1946-85
Drake, V. P., Casa Robles Dir., 1946-53
Dringenberg, Bernadine (see Chiang)
Drinkwater, Eleanor Adelaide, Swaziland, 1965-67; Zambia, 1967-70; Malawi, 1970-77, 1979-86; Zimbabwe, 1977-78
Drinkwater, Joseph Edward, Swaziland, 1965-67; Zambia, 1967-70; Malawi, 1970-77, 1979-86; Zimbabwe, 1977-78
Duckworth, Francine Ray Sapp, Samoa, 1977—
Duckworth, J. Larry, Samoa, 1977—
Dudney, Bennett Landers, West Germany, 1976-82
Dudney, Cathryn, West Germany, 1976-82
Duey, Carl, Swaziland, 1983—
Duey, Judi, Swaziland, 1983—

Dufriend, Diana Sue, Australia, 1981-86; Trinidad, 1986—
Dufriend, Jimmy Dale, Australia, 1981-86; Trinidad, 1986—
Dunton, Nancy Lee, Trinidad, 1976-77; Puerto Rico, 1984—
Dunton, Victor Henry, Trinidad, 1976-77; Puerto Rico, 1984—
Durham, Gary, Virgin Islands, 1981-83
Durham, Sheryl, Virgin Islands, 1981-83

Eades, Ernest Arthur David, Cape Verde, 1947-70
Eades, Jessie Munn, Cape Verde, 1947-70
Eaton, E. J., India, 1906-14
Eaton, Emma, India, 1906-14
Eby, Carol Anne, Papua New Guinea, 1963-82
Eby, Charles Lee, Papua New Guinea, 1963-82
Eby, Dorothy Louise Bevill, Swaziland, 1944-67
Eckel, Catherine Perry, Japan, 1953-65
Eckel, Florence Talbott, Japan, 1916-39, 1946-52
Eckel, William Andrew, Japan, 1916-39, 1946-65
Eddy, Evelyn (see Engstrom)
Edgerton, Anita Lynette Rudeen, Swaziland, 1975-81
Edgerton, Lawrence Wayne, Swaziland, 1975-81
Edlin, James Oliver, Philippines, 1985—
Edlin, Jo Elaine Goodman, Philippines, 1985—
Edwards, Beryl, Argentina, 1969-82; Paraguay, 1982-85; Spain, 1985—
Edwards, Victor, Argentina, 1969-82; Paraguay, 1982-85; Spain, 1985—
Elliott, Frank Charles, Chile, 1967-72
Elliott, Imogene, Chile, 1967-72
Ellison, Nellie (see Mayhew)
Elverd, Mary Elizabeth, Belize, 1956-59
Emslie, Beatrice Lilian (Betty), South Africa, 1947-78
Emslie, Rex Henry, South Africa, 1947-78
Engstrom, Evelyn Eddy, China, 1938-41
Esselstyn, Bessie L. Grose, Mozambique, 1936-62; South Africa, 1962-70
Esselstyn, Joan Kehm, South Africa, 1968—
Esselstyn, Margaret Eleanor Patin, Swaziland, 1928-38; South Africa, 1939-60

Esselstyn, Theodore Patin, South Africa, 1968—

Esselstyn, William Clayton, Swaziland, 1928-38; South Africa, 1939-70

Estes, Boonie, Mexico, 1907-12

Estes, John Howard, Mexico, 1907-12

Estey, John Stanley, South Africa, 1975-76; Swaziland, 1976-83; Ciskei, 1983—

Estey, Sandra Hetrick, South Africa, 1975-76; Swaziland, 1976-83; Ciskei, 1983—

Evans, Arthur Louis, Swaziland, 1964-77; Philippines, 1978-80; Div. Off. (HQ), 1980-81

Evans, Dorothy, Swaziland, 1964-77; Philippines, 1978-80

Evans, Miriam B., South Africa, 1947-55; Swaziland, 1955-74

Evans, Tabitha Ann, South Africa, 1928-67

Fahringer, David, Swaziland, 1979-86

Fahringer, Fonda, Swaziland, 1979-86

Fairbanks, E. Anne, West Germany, 1978-82; Philippines, 1984—

Fairbanks, E. LeBron, West Germany, 1978-82; Philippines, 1984—

Falk, David William, Swaziland, 1979-83, 1984-86; Ivory Coast, 1986—

Falk, Dawn Sandra Ann, Swaziland, 1979-83, 1984-86; Ivory Coast, 1986—

Farris, Anita Margaret Hoad, South Africa, 1981-82; Ivory Coast, 1986—

Farris, Ronnie Stewart, South Africa, 1981-82; Ivory Coast, 1986—

Faul, Betty Fay, Barbados, 1952-69; Guyana, 1969-70; Trinidad, 1970-74; Antigua, 1974-84; Jamaica, 1984—

Faul, Lawrence, Barbados, 1952-69; Guyana, 1969-70; Trinidad, 1970-74; Antigua, 1974-84; Jamaica, 1984—

Fell, Glenn Thomas, Ciskei, 1984—

Fell, Jeanne Ann, Ciskei, 1984—

Felts, Mary Lou King, Swaziland, 1984—

Felts, Melvin Dean, Swaziland, 1984—

Feree, Laura, Mozambique, 1925-43

Feree, Lawrence C., Mozambique, 1925-43

Ferguson, Bertie Haynes Karns, Japan, 1919-23, 1936-41; China, 1934-36; Mexico, 1947-50

Ferguson, Frank, Cuba, 1903-5, 1919-20; Peru, 1906-7, 1920-21; Bolivia, 1907-8; Argentina, 1909-18, 1921-39; Mexican Border, 1944-52

Ferguson, Lula Buford Hutcherson, Cuba, 1903-5, 1919-20; Peru, 1906-7, 1920-21; Bolivia, 1907-8; Argentina, 1909-18, 1921-39; Mexican Border, 1944

Fetter, Barbara, Papua New Guinea, 1970-73

Fetter, Merle Layne, Papua New Guinea, 1970-73

Fetters, Emma Lou, Swaziland, 1968-82, 1983—

Figge, Dorothy Eileen, Swaziland, 1962-69

Finger, James Ray, Swaziland, 1981-83

Finger, Lorene, Swaziland, 1981-83

Finkbeiner, A. J., West Germany, 1968-74; Panama, 1974; Israel, 1975-76

Finkbeiner, Ella Wilma, West Germany, 1968-74; Panama, 1974; Israel, 1975-76

Fitz, Doris I., South Africa, 1965-71; Swaziland, 1976

Fitz, Lura Katharine Witten, China, 1920-36, 1948-49

Fitz, Rudolph Guilford, Jr., South Africa, 1965-71; Swaziland, 1976

Fitz, Rudolph Guilford, Sr., China, 1920-36, 1948-49

Flagler, Catherine, China, 1903-10, 1912-27, 1929-37

Fletcher, Alberta Marie (see Smith)

Flinner, Genevieve Garney, Peru, 1954-65; Uruguay, 1970-74; Chile, 1974-77

Flinner, Harry G., Peru, 1954-65; Uruguay, 1970-74; Chile, 1974-77

Flitcroft, Eileen Mary, Swaziland, 1946-48

Flood, Neva Naomi, Nicaragua, 1947-69; Costa Rica, 1970-83

Fogo, Flora Linda Stark, South Africa, 1968-74

Ford, David Morrison, Haiti, 1968-78

Ford, Lois V. Rodeheaver, Haiti, 1964-78

Forster, Frederick James, Japan, 1963-85

Forster, June Florence, Japan, 1963-85

Fountain, Charles Acton, Panama, 1966-68; Barbados, 1968-71; Philippines, 1974

Fountain, Mary Louise Daugherty, Panama, 1966-68; Barbados, 1968-71; Philippines, 1974

Fowler, Nadia Gail, Belize, 1948-58, 1973-76; Guyana, 1958-63; Trinidad, 1963-73; Nicaragua, 1976-80; Philippines, 1980-86

Fowler, William Calvin, Jr., Belize, 1948-58, 1973-76; Guyana, 1958-63; Trinidad, 1963-73; Nicaragua, 1976-80; Philippines, 1980-86

Fox, J. Evelyn, Swaziland, 1932-47

Fraley, David Walter, France, 1979—

Fraley, Evelyn Carolita, France, 1979—

Frame, Mary Tanner, Swaziland, 1930-40

Franklin, Ethel Thomas, India, 1946-52

Franklin, George J., India, 1915-31

Franklin, George Weldon, India, 1946-52

Franklin, Hulda Grebe, India, 1913-31

Franklin, J. D., Mexico, 1908-12; Guatemala, 1917-22

Franklin, Mrs. J. D., Mexico, 1908-12; Guatemala, 1917-22

Fraser, Celeste Mary Johnson, New Zealand, 1980-81

Fraser, Mervyn Robert, New Zealand, 1980-81

Freeman, Ruth, India, 1945-52

Friberg, Evelyn Elaine, Mozambique, 1971-76; South Africa, 1977—

Friberg, Hughlon Ray, Mozambique, 1971-76; South Africa, 1977—

Friesen, Edelbert, Swaziland, 1982-85

Friesen, Marie, Swaziland, 1982-85

Fritzlan, Andrew David, India, 1907-32

Fritzlan, Daisy Skinner, India, 1912-32

Fritzlan, Ellen Gill, India, 1940-53

Fritzlan, Leslie Chapman, India, 1940-53

Frye, Harold Frederick, Papua New Guinea, 1968-74

Frye, Janice Irene Toone, Papua New Guinea, 1968-74

Fuller, James Roy, Italy, 1967-77

Fuller, Nina Sue, Italy, 1967-77

Fullom, Elizabeth Ann, South Africa, 1964-66, 1970-74

Gailey, Charles Robert, Swaziland, 1964-75, 1979-81

Gailey, Doris Eleanor, Swaziland, 1964-75, 1979-81

Galloway, Clint Dean, Nicaragua, 1953-71; Colombia, 1974-77

Galloway, Judy, Mexico, 1983-86

Galloway, Merle Gwendolyn, Nicaragua, 1953-71; Colombia, 1974-77; San Antonio Sem., 1978-79

Galloway, Ron, Mexico, 1983-86

Garde, Arlene B., Swaziland, 1983-85; Costa Rica, 1985—

Gardner, Agnes, India, 1919-25, 1937-42

Gardner, Juanita Irene, Swaziland, 1950-80; Papua New Guinea, 1980-82

Gardner, Leona, Cuba, 1902-27; Guatemala, 1927-34; Belize, 1934-38

Garman, Addie Pearl, Peru, 1964—

Garman, Larry Maurice, Peru, 1964—

Garner, E. Clayton, Barbados, 1961-66; Papua New Guinea, 1967-72

Garner, Erna Mae, Barbados, 1961-66; Papua New Guinea, 1967-72

Garrison, Gordon, West Germany, 1979-81

Garrison, Jeannette, West Germany, 1979-81

Garsee, Berniece, Samoa, 1960-68

Garsee, Jarrell, Samoa, 1960-68

Gastineau, Roger Allen, Zambia, 1971-85; Kenya, 1985—

Gastineau, Rowena Diane, Zambia, 1971-85; Kenya, 1985—

Gates, Charles Wise, Brazil, 1958-82; Div. Off. (HQ), 1982—

Gates, Ira Charles, South Africa, 1979—

Gates, Judy Ann, South Africa, 1979—

Gates, Roma Joanne, Brazil, 1958-82

Gay, Charlotte Adeline Munn, Cape Verde, 1955-72

Gay, Samuel Clifford, Cape Verde, 1936-72

German, C. Dale, Australia, 1985—

German, Emmalyn, Australia, 1985—

Gerritzen, Renate, Swaziland, 1980-81; South Africa, 1982-84

Gertson, Brenda Louise, Swaziland, 1979-80

Gibson, Gordon Garth, Sr., Philippines, 1983—

Gibson, Julia Roberts, India, 1904-10

Gibson, Mildred S., Philippines, 1983—

Gilbert, Dianna Bollinger, South Africa, 1985—

Gilbert, Ronnie, South Africa, 1985—

Glassco, Gary A., Papua New Guinea, 1981—

Glassco, Linda D., Papua New Guinea, 1981—

Goin, Marilyn Louise, South Africa, 1969-84

Golliher, Ira Leona, Peru, 1952-83

Golliher, William Clyde, Peru, 1952-83

Gonzalez, Beverly Jo Armstrong, Ecuador, 1985—

Gonzalez, R. Eduardo, Ecuador, 1985—

Goodwin, Mrs. Paul, Japan, 1920-22

Goodwin, Paul, Japan, 1920-22

Gordeuk, Victor Roland, South Africa, 1979-81

Gould, Brenda Kay, Haiti, 1971-78; Martinique, 1978—

Grabke, Martha L., Argentina, 1968-73

Grabke, Ronald K., Argentina, 1968-73

Graham, Agnes Clark, Swaziland, 1944-52; South Africa, 1952-57, 1977-81; Malawi, 1957-77; Zimbabwe, 1982-83

Graham, James Isaac, South Africa, 1948-57, 1977-81; Malawi, 1957-77; Zimbabwe, 1982-83

Graham, Olive, India, 1915-18

Grant, Pamela Denise, Philippines, 1983-86

Grantz, Howard, Peru, 1956-76

Grantz, Norine E. Roth, Peru, 1952-76

Gray, Carol L., Papua New Guinea, 1985-86

Gray, Cecial Maunette Hankins, Peru, 1958-83; Colombia, 1983—

Gray, Charles David, Papua New Guinea, 1985-86

Gray, Robert Louis, Peru, 1958-83; Colombia, 1983—

Grebe, Hulda (see Franklin)

Grebe, Leoda Voegelein, India, 1913-20

Green, Cora Lee, Guatemala, 1955-63; Belize, 1963-67

Green, Lewis Elward, Guatemala, 1955-63; Belize, 1963-67

Greene, Charlotte Ann, Nicaragua, 1967-79; Philippines, 1980—

Greene, Kyle Leon, Nicaragua, 1967-79; Philippines, 1980—

Greer, Bronell A., India, 1944—

Greer, Paula Whitener, India, 1944—

Gregory, Arthur, India, 1906-?

Gregory, Pearl, India, 1906-?

Griffith, Della Elizabeth, Nicaragua, 1962-73; Costa Rica, 1973-74; San Antonio Sem., 1974-81; Dominican Republic, 1981—

Griffith, Marshall G., Nicaragua, 1962-73; Costa Rica, 1973-74; San Antonio Sem., 1974-81; Dominican Republic, 1981—

Griffith, Mrs. R. E., New Zealand, 1952-58

Griffith, R. E., New Zealand, 1952-58

Grimm, Virginia Roush, India, 1914-17

Grose, Bessie L. (see Esselstyn)

Grose, Glenn Everett, Mozambique, 1936-41

Grube, Christopher J., Israel, 1985—

Grube, Susan K., Israel, 1985—

Guillermo, Bessie Branstine, Guatemala, 1925-31

Guillermo, Evelyn I. Ver Hoek, Guatemala, 1951-73

Gunter, Roxie Carr, Netherlands, 1974-76; West Germany, 1976-78

Gunter, William Stephen, Netherlands, 1974-76; West Germany, 1976-78

Hagens, Gloria Lucille, Malawi, 1961-63, 1965-67, 1976-79; Zambia, 1963-65, 1970-76; South Africa, 1979-80

Hagens, Leland Jesse (Pete), Malawi, 1961-63, 1965-67, 1976-79; Zambia, 1963-65, 1970-76; South Africa, 1979-80

Hale, Henrietta (see Christianson)

Hall, Bailey Maurice, South Africa, 1956; Swaziland, 1956-57; Malawi, 1957-63; Zimbabwe, 1963-75

Hall, Geraldine Ann, South Africa, 1956; Swaziland, 1956-57; Malawi, 1957-63; Zimbabwe, 1963-75

Hall, John Wesley, Jr., Ecuador, 1973-83; Costa Rica, 1983—

Hall, John Wesley, Sr., Cuba, 1947-60; Cuba Refugee Work, 1961-67

Hall, Patricia Irene Phillips, Cuba, 1947-60; Cuba Refugee Work, 1961-67

Hall, Sheila Carol, Ecuador, 1973-83; Costa Rica, 1983—

Hall, Susan Gail, Papua New Guinea, 1985—

Hall, Terry Glen, Papua New Guinea, 1985—

Hamlin, Howard, Swaziland, 1963-69; South Africa, 1969-73

Hamlin, Maxine, Swaziland, 1963-69; South Africa, 1969-73

Hampton, A. M., Mexico, 1910-12

Hampton, Gladys Jeannette, Guatemala, 1941-43; Belize, 1943-52; Puerto Rico, 1952-58; Eastern Spanish, 1958-71; Cent. Lat. Amer. Dist., 1971-75; Mexico—S. Amer. Evan., 1975-80

Hampton, Harold Louis, Guatemala, 1941-43; Belize, 1943-52; Puerto Rico, 1952-58; Eastern Spanish, 1958-71; Cent. Lat. Amer. Dist., 1971-75; Mexico—S. Amer. Evan., 1975-80

Hampton, Mrs. A. M., Mexico, 1910-12

Hance, Ray Lunn, Denmark, 1970-72

Hance, Vera, Denmark, 1970-72

Handloser, Rose Reed, South Africa, 1962—

Hannay, Abbie Carolyn Parsons, Papua New Guinea, 1969-78; Haiti, 1978-80

Hannay, Scott, Haiti, 1982-86

Hanson, Pearl Wiley, Japan, 1934-41

Hardesty, Karla Jane, Swaziland, 1982—

Harding, Dana Lantz, Swaziland, 1979—

Hargrove, Lela (see Hatfield)

Harmon, Iris Modell Robinson, Trinidad, 1952-74

Harmon, Wesley Lee, Trinidad, 1952-74

Harmon, William H., Mexico, 1911-12

Harper, Mary Ann (see Biddulph)

Harris, Aleta L., Bolivia, 1979-84; Paraguay, 1984—

Harris, Doris, Guyana, 1975-76; Windward Islands, 1976-77; India, 1977-78; Trinidad, 1978-83

Harris, Harold L., Guyana, 1975-76; Windward Islands, 1976-77; India, 1977-78; Trinidad, 1978-83

Harris, Lavonne, West Germany, 1980-85

Harris, Max III, West Germany, 1980-85

Harris, Wesley Edward, Bolivia, 1979-84; Paraguay, 1984—

Harrison, Donald O., Panama Canal Zone, 1973-74

Harrison, Patricia R., Panama Canal Zone, 1973-74

Hartley, Phyllis (see Perkins)

Harvey, John Austin, Bolivia, 1974-75

Harvey, Sharon Edith, Bolivia, 1974-75

Haselwood, Elsie, Peru, 1928-35

Hatch, Lou Jane, India, 1920-31

Hatfield, Lela Hargrove, India, 1912-22

Hawley, F. Lucille, India, 1919-24

Haworth, Diana Elizabeth, Uruguay, 1974-79

Haworth, William Royal, Uruguay, 1974-79

Hayne, Jemima Hester, China, 1921-26, 1934-41

Hayse, David Gerald, Ecuador, 1976-81; Mexico, 1981-85; Div. Off. (HQ), 1985—

Hayse, Gayle Louise Karker, South Africa, 1983—

Hayse, George Russell, South Africa, 1947-86

Hayse, Gerald Russell, South Africa, 1983—

Hayse, Jeanette Florence Vanderveen, South Africa, 1947-86

Hayse, Marcia Jean, Ecuador, 1976-81; Mexico, 1981-85

Heap, Brenda Lynne, Brazil, 1973—

Heap, Gwladys Elenud Jones, Colombia, 1940-56; Peru, 1956-62; Guatemala, 1962-71; Panama, 1971-75

Heap, Samuel Ewart, Colombia, 1940-56; Peru, 1956-62; Guatemala, 1962-71; Panama, 1971-75

Heap, Stephen Moffat, Brazil, 1973—

Heaps, Francis David, Swaziland, 1971-78

Heaps, Mary Kathryn, Swaziland, 1971-78

Hebets, Donna Lou, Swaziland, 1968-70, 1974-81; Lebanon, 1973-74

Hebets, Robert Louis, Swaziland, 1968-70, 1974-81; Lebanon, 1973-74

Heflin, Lesper Frances, Nicaragua, 1948-72

Hegstrom, H. E., Scandinavia, 1964-68

Hegstrom, Mrs. H. E., Scandinavia, 1964-68

Helling, Hubert William, Japan, 1952-80; U.S. Ethnic, 1980-85

Helling, Virginia Grace Hubbard, Japan, 1952-80; U.S. Ethnic, 1980-85

Helm, Phyllis Jean Louise Wunch, India, 1956-67

Helm, Wallace Rueben, India, 1956-67

Hemphill, Naomi Hazel, Swaziland, 1967-75

Hemphill, Robert Lee, Swaziland, 1967-75

Henck, Gloria Lea Crawford, Cape Verde, 1958—

Henck, Roy Malcolm, Cape Verde, 1958—

Henderson, Carolyn Sue, Samoa, 1974-80

Henderson, Conley Paul, Samoa, 1974-80

Henderson, Richard, New Zealand, 1980-82

Henderson, Ruby, New Zealand, 1980-82

Hendrick, Carolyn Lenora, Bolivia, 1968-77

Hendricks, Amelia H. Bailey, Trinidad, 1948-49; Barbados, 1949-52

Hendricks, Andrew Olivet, Trinidad, 1948-49; Barbados, 1949-52

Hendrix, Fae Litell Higgins, Argentina, 1941-55, 1962-69; Cuba, 1956-61; Chile, 1969-73; Uruguay, 1973-77

Hendrix, Spurgeon Lindsay, Argentina, 1941-55, 1962-69; Cuba, 1956-61; Chile, 1969-73; Uruguay, 1973-77

Herrick, Gayle, South Africa, 1964-65

Herrick, Robert S., South Africa, 1964-65

Hess, Harold Eber, Guatemala, 1942-56

Hess, Ruth Ursula Beebe, Guatemala, 1942-56

Hetrick, Glenda Burger, Swaziland, 1966-78

Hetrick, Mae Elizabeth Thompson, Swaziland, 1945-73; Mozambique, 1973-77; Leeward Islands, 1977-79

Hetrick, Paul Henry, Jr., Swaziland, 1966-78

Hetrick, Paul Henry, Sr., Swaziland, 1945-73; Mozambique, 1973-77; Leeward Islands, 1977-79

Hewson, Abigail, South Africa, 1947-78

Hickel, Jack, Swaziland, 1984—

Hickel, Jane, Swaziland, 1984—

Hicks, Marilyn Marie, Philippines, 1977-79

High, Carol June, Papua New Guinea, 1984—

Hill, James Ivy, Trinidad, 1926-28; Barbados, 1928-39

Hill, Nora M. Pulliam, Trinidad, 1926-28; Barbados, 1928-39

Hills, Darlene, Swaziland, 1974-76

Hills, Orrin E., Swaziland, 1974-76

Himes, Blanche, China, 1921-27

Hinds, Elizabeth, Cuba, 1917-19

Hinds, James Lorenzo, Cuba, 1917-19

Hitchens, Priscilla, India, 1904-11

Hofferbert, Deborah A., Brazil, 1985—

Hofferbert, Steven D., Brazil, 1985—

Holland, Julia Augustine, Guatemala, 1906-10, 1918-19; Bolivia, 1910-18; Peru, 1919-27; Belize, 1936-43

Hollenberg, Gregory, South Africa, 1983-85; Swaziland, 1985—

Hollenberg, Mary Beth, South Africa, 1983-85; Swaziland, 1985—

Hollis, Allen B., Jr., Israel, 1962-65

Hollis, Gloria June, Israel, 1962-65

Holstead, John Hiram, Taiwan, 1956-74; Hong Kong, 1974-86

Holstead, Natalie Grace Wheeler, Taiwan, 1956-74; Hong Kong, 1974-86

Hope, Minnie (see Singleton)

Hopkins, Marilyn Sue, El Salvador, 1971-76; Honduras, 1976-83; Guatemala, 1983—

Hopkins, Philip, El Salvador, 1971-76; Honduras, 1976-83; Guatemala, 1983—

Hopper, Ivis Marie (see Powell)

Houmes, Janet Ann, Australia, 1980-85

Houston, Dorothy Jane, Australia, 1979-80

Houston, Lowell Elton, Australia, 1979-80

Howard, Charles Albert, Swaziland, 1964-69, 1976-79

Howard, Esther Alice, India, 1952—

Howard, Everette Dewey, Cape Verde, 1935-51; Cent. Lat. Amer. Dist., 1951-71; Casa Robles Dir., 1971-75

Howard, Garnet Gray Sherman, Cape Verde, 1935-51; Cent. Lat. Amer. Dist., 1951-71; Casa Robles Dir., 1971-75

Howard, Lydia Alvena Wilke, Swaziland, 1940-49; Cape Verde, 1949-61

Howard, Margaret Goodnow, Swaziland, 1964-69, 1976-79

Howard, Margie Nell, Belize, 1954-56

Howard, Quentin E., Belize, 1954-56

Howerton, Joanna Lou Gault, Argentina, 1963—

Howerton, Norman Mason, Argentina, 1963—

Howes, Shirley Ann, Papua New Guinea, 1972-74, 1977-85

Howie, Frank, Mozambique, 1964-74; South Africa, 1974—

Howie, Heather Mary, Mozambique, 1964-74; South Africa, 1974—

Hudson, Ellison Catherine Kennedy, India, 1965-68

Hudson, James Harrison, India, 1965-68

Hudson, James Junior, Nicaragua, 1952-53; Guatemala, 1953-74; Div. Off. (HQ), 1974-81; Reg. Dir., 1981—

Hudson, Lucille Anne Gunter, Nicaragua, 1952-53; Guatemala, 1953-74

Hudson, Robert Dean, Nicaragua, 1969-78; El Salvador, 1978-83; Peru, 1983—

Hudson, Sheila, Nicaragua, 1969-78; El Salvador, 1978-83; Peru, 1983—

Huff, Dinah Kay Lee, New Zealand, 1979-85; South Africa, 1985—

Huff, Harold, Lebanon, 1963-66

Huff, James Frederick, New Zealand, 1979-85; South Africa, 1985—

Huff, Mrs. Harold, Lebanon, 1963-66

Huff, Robert, New Zealand, 1980-81

Hughes, Mima Jeanne, Cuba, 1959-61; Nicaragua, 1961-62; Cuban Work, Miami, 1962-63; Uruguay, 1963-80; Chile, 1980-86; Ecuador, 1986—

Hughes, Teddy Lee, Cuba, 1959-61; Nicaragua, 1961-62; Cuban Work, Miami, 1962-63; Uruguay, 1963-80; Chile, 1980-86; Ecuador, 1986—

Human, Russell Carol, Swaziland, 1963-72

Human, Ruth Ann, Swaziland, 1963-72

Humphrey, L. H., Japan, 1913-15

Humphrey, Mrs. L. H., Japan, 1913-15

Hunt, Carrie Lewis, Mexico, 1908-14

Hunt, Edwin, Mexico, 1905-14

Hunter, Alice Marie Jessee, Trinidad, 1966-75; Israel, 1976-81, 1983-84

Hunter, Earl Dean, Guatemala, 1946-52; Bolivia, 1952-60

Hunter, Eugene Merlin, Trinidad, 1966-75; Israel, 1976-81, 1983-84

Hunter, Mabel Irene Allen, Guatemala, 1946-52; Bolivia, 1952-60

Hunton, Carol Jeanne, Malawi, 1963-64; Zambia, 1964-69; Zimbabwe, 1969-72, 1975-77; Australia, 1977-82

Hunton, Jay Edgar, Malawi, 1963-64; Zambia, 1964-69; Zimbabwe, 1969-72, 1975-77; Australia, 1977-82

Hurst, George Allan, South Africa, 1974—

Hurst, Margaret Ellen Potter, South Africa, 1974—

Hutchens, Michael, Samoa, 1985-86

Hutchens, Patricia, Samoa, 1985-86

Hynd, Agnes Kanema Sharpe, Swaziland, 1925-62

Hynd, David, Swaziland, 1925-62

Hynd, Margaret Jane Sharpe, South Africa, 1963-69

Hynd, Phyllis J. McNeil, Swaziland, 1965-78

Hynd, Rosemarie S. C. Ballard, Swaziland, 1951-74

Hynd, Samuel Wilson, Swaziland, 1950-78

Ingle, Gordon Stahly, Philippines, 1970-72

Ingle, Irma Lou, Philippines, 1970-72

Ingram, Hannah Pearl Dixon, Guatemala, 1921-57

Ingram, Robert Clinton, Guatemala, 1921-57

Innis, Etta (see Shirley)

Irwin, Glenn Moore, Papua New Guinea, 1967-85

Irwin, Ruth Margaret, Papua New Guinea, 1967-85

Jackson, K. Hawley, India, 1919-24

Jackson, Lela Gertrude Olmsted, Argentina, 1943-46; Swaziland, 1946-52

Jackson, Robert Otis, Argentina, 1943-46; Swaziland, 1946-52

Jacobs, Barbara Gail, Swaziland, 1968-77

Jacques, V. J., India, 1906-13

Jakobitz, Arlen Wilfred, India, 1974—

Jakobitz, Kathryn Joyce Hester, India, 1974—

James, Clifton Cleve, India, 1951-65; Puerto Rico, 1965-74

James, Juanita Genevive Dennis, India, 1951-65; Puerto Rico, 1965-74

Janzen, F. B., Swaziland, 1920-27

Janzen, Katherine, Swaziland, 1920-27

Jay, Katherine Roberta, Swaziland, 1981—

Jenkins, Charles Somes, Swaziland, 1920-22; Mozambique, 1922-34, 1935-43, 1944-48; Cape Verde, 1934-35; Barbados, 1943-44; South Africa, 1948-64

Jenkins, Pearl Mae Kent, Swaziland, 1920-22; Mozambique, 1922-34, 1935-43, 1944-48; Cape Verde, 1934-35; Barbados, 1943-44; South Africa, 1948-64

Jerome, Jesse David, Swaziland, 1975-81, 1986—

Jerome, Marlene Sue, Swaziland, 1975-81, 1986—

Jester, Helen Irene, Swaziland, 1938-70

Jetter, Mary Eunice, Bahamas, 1976-77; Dominican Republic, 1977-81; Honduras, 1981—

Jetter, Paul Lawrence, Bahamas, 1976-77; Dominican Republic, 1977-81; Honduras, 1981—

Johnson, Alice Eva Schmidt, West Germany, 1958-69

Johnson, Bonnie Lou, Japan, 1984—

Johnson, James, Samoa, 1981—

Johnson, Jerald Dwight, West Germany, 1958-69; World Mission Dir., 1973-80

Johnson, Joy Anne Lanoue, Samoa, 1981—

Johnson, Kathryn Mae, South Africa, 1962-85; Swaziland, 1985—

Johnson, Levi Lloyd, Japan, 1984—

Johnston, Charles Lester, Argentina, 1945-59; Lat. Amer. Evan., 1962-68

Johnston, Gordon Keith, Lebanon, 1969-75; Jordan, 1976-81; Papua New Guinea, 1981—

Johnston, Mary Porteus, Haiti, 1984—

Johnston, Patricia Jean Stockett, Lebanon, 1969-75; Jordan, 1975-81; Papua New Guinea, 1981—

Johnston, Trevor Howard, West Germany, 1980-81; Haiti, 1984—

Johnston, Viola Veneta Maxey, Argentina, 1945-59; Lat. Amer. Evan., 1962-68

Jones, Ada Lillian, South Africa, 1937-56, 1960-77; Swaziland, 1956-60

Jones, Aletta Elizabeth, South Africa, 1939-79

Jones, Alfred Leslie, Australia, 1970-78

Jones, Barbara Jean Wright, Peru, 1969-81; Paraguay, 1983-86

Jones, C. Warren, Japan, 1920; World Mission Dir., 1937-48

Jones, Emily Maude, South Africa, 1911-54

Jones, Helen Ellen Emery, Barbados, 1944-50, 1952-59; Panama, 1959-63, 1967-72

Jones, James Henry, Barbados, 1944-50, 1952-59; Panama, 1959-63, 1967-72

Jones, Kenneth Dale, Peru, 1969-81; Paraguay, 1983-86

Jones, Kitty Catherine Ethyel, Australia, 1970-78

Jones, Neri, Japan, 1920

Jones, Reginald Ernest, South Africa, 1934-56, 1960-77; Swaziland, 1956-60

Jones, Rhoda V. (see Schurman)

Jones, Sharon E., Swaziland, 1972-85

Jones, Thomas Harold, South Africa, 1935-79

Julca, Rachel Snow, Peru, 1932-33

Kanis, Gezina Bertha (Ina), Mozambique, 1969-74; South Africa, 1974—

Kanis, Jakob, Mozambique, 1969-74; South Africa, 1974—

Karker, Louise Mae, Swaziland, 1952-62; South Africa, 1962-65, 1971-81; Lebanon, 1966-71

Karker, Oliver Gould, Swaziland, 1952-62; South Africa, 1962-65, 1971-81; Lebanon, 1966-71

Karns, Bertie Haynes (see Ferguson)

Kauffman, Alvin H., India, 1919-22; Palestine, 1922-39

Kauffman, J. Timothy, West Germany, 1974-86

Kauffman, Mary Esther, West Germany, 1974-86

Kauffman, Naomi Anderson, India, 1919-22; Palestine, 1922-39

Keeler, George H., Cape Verde, 1937-38

Keeler, Miriam Ruth, Cape Verde, 1937-38

Kell, Glenn Leroy, Zambia, 1984—

Kell, Peggy Linn Suelzle, Zambia, 1984—

Keller, Robert Steven, Ivory Coast, 1985—

Keller, Sherri, Ivory Coast, 1985—

Kellerman, Darlene Carol Broom, Taiwan, 1962-78

Kellerman, Phillip R., Taiwan, 1962-78

Kelly, Doris L., Swaziland, 1967-68

Kelvington, Emily Ruth Hinkley, Japan, 1966-78

Kelvington, William Herdman, Japan, 1966-78

Kennedy, David, Japan, 1981-84

Kennedy, Linda Crumley, Japan, 1981-84

Keoppel, Fern Elizabeth Fritch, Japan, 1971-80

Keoppel, Janell Edith (see Moore)

Keoppel, Kenneth Philip, Japan, 1971-80

Ketchum, Kathleen Ann, Martinique, 1981—

Ketchum, Linda Jean, Australia, 1981—

Ketchum, Ronald Clarence, Australia, 1981—

Ketchum, Teryl Ray, Martinique, 1981—

Kiehn, Anna Schmidt, China, 1906-11, 1913-38

Kiehn, Peter, China, 1906-11, 1913-38

King, Brenda Lee, Swaziland, 1971-75

King, Wesley Llewellyn, Swaziland, 1971-75

Kinne, C. J., China, 1923-30

Kitchen, Barbara Ann, New Zealand, 1976-80

Kitchen, Billy Joe, New Zealand, 1976-80

Kitsko, Mike, Ecuador, 1976-78

Kitsko, Sue, Ecuador, 1976-78

Klassen, George, Swaziland, 1982-85

Klassen, Nancy, Swaziland, 1982-85

Klein, Hilda F., Swaziland, 1982-85

Kleven, Mrs. Orville, Denmark, 1960-70

Kleven, Orville, Denmark, 1960-70

Knox, Elwanda Dawn, Guyana, 1957-68, 1976-79; Trinidad, 1968-76

Knox, Everette Wayne, Guyana, 1957-68, 1976-79; Trinidad, 1968-76

Knox, Sidney Cornell, Papua New Guinea, 1955-58

Knox, Wanda Mae Fulton, Papua New Guinea, 1955-58, 1960-75; Exec. Dir. NWMS, 1975-80; Israel, 1980-81; Trinidad, 1983-86

Koffel, Irma Viola, South Africa, 1945-85

Kranich, Irving Lowell, West Germany, 1976-80

Kranich, Wanda Mae, West Germany, 1976-80

Kratz, Carol Jeanne, Brazil, 1960—

Kratz, James Eldon, Jr., Brazil, 1981—

Kratz, James Eldon, Sr., Brazil, 1960—

Kratz, Lela Kay Neuenschwander, Brazil, 1981—

Krikorian, Hranoush Yardoumian, Palestine, 1921-49; Jordan, 1950-57

Krikorian, Samuel Coffing, Palestine, 1921-49; Jordan, 1950-57

Kristofferson, Mrs. Ulf, Denmark, 1967-68
Kristofferson, Ulf, Denmark, 1967-68

Labenski, Lois Santo, Belize, 1953-57
Lake, George Marvin, Papua New Guinea, 1977-80
Lake, Olive, Papua New Guinea, 1977-80
Lammerts Van Bueren, Agnes Barbara, India, 1985
Lane, Neva Pet, Guatemala, 1921-50, 1954-56; Peru, 1950-54
Lang, Gwendolyn, Papua New Guinea, 1970-72
Langford, Lynda Carolyn, Peru, 1979-84
Langford, Steven Ray, Peru, 1979-84
Larkin, Darrell Land, Peru, 1944-45; San Antonio Sem., 1949-51
Larkin, Esther, Peru, 1944-45; San Antonio Sem., 1949-51
Larrabee, Michelene Collins, Haiti, 1981-82; Malawi, 1986—
Larson, Joan Barbara, Swaziland, 1968-79; Papua New Guinea, 1979—
Larson, Wayne Alfred, Swaziland, 1968-79; Papua New Guinea, 1979—
Latham, Carolyn F., Philippines, 1963-70
Latham, Robert Wesley, Philippines, 1963-70
Lathrop, Ivan, Jordan, 1964-67, 1976-79; Lebanon, 1967-75; West Germany, 1975-76
Lathrop, Virginia Eleanor, Jordan, 1964-67, 1976-79; Lebanon, 1967-75; West Germany, 1975-76
Latta, Margaret, Swaziland, 1931-54
Laughbaum, Anna Belle, Korea, 1981-83
Laws, Melvin V., Philippines, 1975-78
Laws, Ruth K., Philippines, 1975-78
Lee, Earl Garfield, India, 1946-60
Lee, Hazel Crutcher, India, 1946-60
Leffel, Phyllis Marie, Panama Canal Zone, 1964-66
Leffel, Richard Harlon, Panama Canal Zone, 1964-66
Lehman, Alice, South Africa, 1922-25
Lehman, Isaac, South Africa, 1922-25
Leichtes, Fritz, Italy, 1966-67
Leichtes, Mrs. Fritz, Italy, 1966-67
Lesley, Anita Louise Long, Swaziland, 1947-52
Leth, Carl, West Germany, 1979-83
Leth, Nancy B., West Germany, 1979-83
Levens, Frances Lively, Swaziland, 1956-71

Lever, Maxa Lou, Papua New Guinea, 1985—
Lever, Samuel C., Papua New Guinea, 1985—
Lewis, Carrie (see Hunt)
Lewis, John Earl, Puerto Rico, 1971-73; Panama, 1973-78
Lewis, Naomi K., Puerto Rico, 1971-73; Panama, 1973-78
Lewis, Russell Edwin, Swaziland, 1946-51; Bahamas, 1979-82
Lewis, Ruth Naomi Dye, Swaziland, 1946-51; Bahamas, 1979-82
Lilienthal, Aileen, West Germany, 1975-77
Lilienthal, Alfred J., West Germany, 1975-77
Lindeman, Nada M., Japan, 1965-70
Lindeman, Richard W., Japan, 1965-70
Lively, Frances (see Levens)
Llanes, Eduardo G., Costa Rica, 1976-77
Llanes, Jill A., Costa Rica, 1976-77
Lloyd, Mary Lou Tiemann, Papua New Guinea, 1971-83
Lochner, Edna, Swaziland, 1953—
Lockwood, Florence Swartzlander, Argentina, 1938-45
Lockwood, Llewellyn Dewitt, Argentina, 1938-45
Long, Anita Louise (see Lesley)
Long, Barbara Pauline Holland, Italy, 1975-80; Spain, 1981—
Long, Thomas Joseph, Italy, 1975-80; Spain, 1981—
Lovelace, Ora (see West)
Lovett, Donna Sharon, Italy, 1977-81; France, 1981—
Lovett, Russell James, Italy, 1977-81; France, 1981—
Lowe, A. G., Mexico, 1906-12
Lowry, Ethel Joyce, Malawi, 1959-65
Lowry, Thomas Franklin, Malawi, 1959-65
Ludwig, B. Rex, Panama, 1970-73; Brazil, 1973—
Ludwig, Edith Louise, Panama, 1970-73; Brazil, 1973—

MacDonald, David, Australia, 1982-84
MacDonald, Estella D., Swaziland, 1934-53
MacDonald, Leatha, Australia, 1982-84
MacKenzie, Ada Constance, Belize, 1976-80; South Africa, 1980—
MacLachlan, Della (see Beebe)
MacMillan, Cora Coates Walker, Nicaragua, 1945-52

Main, Elaine, West Germany, 1985—
Main, James, West Germany, 1985—
Manaois, Lourdes, REAP Team, 1979-82; Nigeria, 1983-85
Manaois, Wilfredo, REAP Team, 1979-82; Nigeria, 1983-85
Manchester, Merilyn Clinger, Nicaragua, 1966-69; Mexico, 1970-76
Mander, Margaret Elizabeth, Papua New Guinea, 1975-85
Mangum, Lois, Papua New Guinea, 1979-80
Mangum, Myrtle (see White)
Mangum, Robert, Papua New Guinea, 1979-80
Marlin, Eunice N., Philippines, 1979-1981, 1982—
Marquis, Sarah Mai Cox, Guatemala, 1920-26
Marshall, Minerva, South Africa, 1920-25
Marshall, Paul Wesley, Malawi, 1964-73; South Africa, 1975-79
Marshall, Ruth Vadean, Malawi, 1964-73; South Africa, 1975-79
Martin, Judith M., Japan, 1972-86
Martin, Minnie Catherine, Swaziland, 1919-30; Mozambique, 1930-46
Matchett, Ruth Roberta, South Africa, 1947—
Mayhew, Nellie Ellison, India, 1921-29
Mayle, Emmagene, Swaziland, 1964
Mayo, Marjorie Jean, Peru, 1950-54
Maze, Mary Ann, Brazil, 1964-73
Maze, Roger Michael, Brazil, 1964-73
McCarty, Michael Patrick, Indonesia, 1976—
McCarty, Rachel, Indonesia, 1976—
McClelland, Mildred, China, 1924-27
McClintock, Elizabeth, South Africa, 1964-78; Namibia, 1978-83; Ciskei, 1983—
McClintock, Ralph R., South Africa, 1964-78; Namibia, 1978-83; Ciskei, 1983—
McConnell, Leona Bellew (see Meek)
McCormick, Kelley Steve, West Germany, 1984—
McCormick, Patricia Lynn, West Germany, 1984—
McCoy, Marsha L. Kinney, Swaziland, 1985—
McCoy, William K., Swaziland, 1985—
McCrory, Katherine, Swaziland, 1961
McCrory, Paul, Swaziland, 1961

McCroskey, Mathilda May, Philippines, 1956—
McCroskey, Robert Dwayne, Indonesia, 1974—
McCroskey, Rosa Nell Luginbyhl, Indonesia, 1974—
McCroskey, William Robert, Philippines, 1956—
McCulloch, David, Guatemala, 1976-85
McCulloch, Elizabeth, Guatemala, 1976-85
McDowell, Doris, Swaziland, 1981-85
McHenry, Guy C., Argentina, 1921-25; Peru, 1925-34
McHenry, Mrs. Guy, Argentina, 1921-25; Peru, 1925-34
McKay, Bartlett P., Japan, 1954-67
McKay, Grace Lucelia, Japan, 1954-67
McKay, John, India, 1926-64
McKay, Lula May Tidwell, India, 1920-35
McKay, Mary Estelle Hunter, India, 1937-64
McKinlay, Mary, Swaziland, 1947-77
McKinney, Mary Christene, Swaziland, 1982-86
McMahan, Cheryl, Philippines, 1983—
McMahan, Danny, Philippines, 1983—
McMurdock, Rhea Riitta Sanborg, Taiwan, 1984—
McMurdock, Robert Samuel, Taiwan, 1984—
McNabb, Mildred Avinell, Swaziland, 1952-86
McNeil, Phyllis J. (see Hynd)
McPherson, Flora Ethel, Japan, 1917-19
McRee, Mae Frances (Pansy), Philippines, 1982-85
Medcalf, Louise McKinley, West Germany, 1985-86
Meek, Billie Ann Jones, Swaziland, 1946-49; South Africa, 1949-51
Meek, Leona Bellew McConnell, Swaziland, 1924-28
Meek, Wesley Earl, Swaziland, 1946-49; South Africa, 1949-51
Meighan, Mary K., South Africa, 1967-82; Swaziland, 1982—
Mejia, Celia, Costa Rica, 1980—
Mejia, Miguel, Costa Rica, 1980—
Mellies, Amanda, India, 1928-35
Mellinger, Miriam (see Brammer)
Melton, Billie Jean, Japan, 1961-1966, 1986—
Melton, Charles, Japan, 1961-66
Mendell, Grace (see Santana)
Mercer, Mary L., Korea, 1979—

Mercer, Timothy J., Korea, 1979—
Merki, Elizabeth Jean Goodnow, South Africa, 1960-80
Merki, Robert Thomas, South Africa, 1960-80
Merritts, Marjorie Helen, Papua New Guinea, 1964—
Messer, Alfred Glenn, Papua New Guinea, 1975-80
Messer, Barbara, Malawi, 1975—
Messer, Carole, Taiwan, 1963-65
Messer, Donald Lee, Malawi, 1975—
Messer, Edra P., Papua New Guinea, 1975-80
Messer, Jack Taylor, Taiwan, 1963-65
Mewes, Evelyn Lenora, Mozambique, 1958-74
Miller, Charles H., Mexico, 1905-13; Argentina, 1919-26; Mexico Border, 1927-31
Miller, D. Allene, Swaziland, 1978-82
Miller, Donald Douglas, India, 1960-72
Miller, Hilbert Oscar, Swaziland, 1962-75; South Africa, 1975-83; Malawi, 1983—
Miller, Howard L., Swaziland, 1978-82
Miller, Leona Stallcup Turner, Mexico, 1910-13; Argentina, 1919-26; Mexico Border, 1927-31
Miller, Mary Moffat, Peru, 1954—
Miller, Norma Strickland, Swaziland, 1962-75; South Africa, 1975-83; Malawi, 1983—
Miller, Richard Raymond, Trinidad, 1949-56; Taiwan, 1956-63
Miller, Ruth Constance, Nicaragua, 1956-65; Argentina, 1966-71
Miller, Ruth Margaret Andrews, Trinidad, 1949-56; Taiwan, 1956-63
Miller, Willa Joyce, India, 1960-72
Mingledorff, Harry Warren, Peru, 1944-49
Mingledorff, Jean Elizabeth Stock, Peru, 1944-49
Mink, Nelson, Australia, 1968-69
Mischke, Carl Wilhelm, Swaziland, 1932-40, 1949, 1952-56; South Africa, 1940-48, 1950-51, 1957-62; Virgin Islands, 1966-67
Mischke, Velma, Swaziland, 1932-40, 1949, 1952-56; South Africa, 1940-48, 1950-51, 1957-62; Virgin Islands, 1966-67
Mishler, Susan Elizabeth, Swaziland, 1963-79
Moen, Hilda Pauline, India, 1956-82

Moon, Juanita Joyce Williams, Mozambique, 1956-63, 1986—; Swaziland, 1963-86
Moon, Perry William, Mozambique, 1956-63, 1986—; Swaziland, 1963-86
Moore, Benjamin Curt, Swaziland, 1971-73; Papua New Guinea, 1974-79
Moore, Gary William, Netherlands, 1975-77
Moore, Janell Edith Keoppel, Japan, 1970-74; Papua New Guinea, 1974-79
Moore, Laurie J., Papua New Guinea, 1982—
Moore, Lavonna, Netherlands, 1975-77
Moore, Ronald J., Papua New Guinea, 1982—
Morden, Elva Jane Bates, Swaziland, 1960-85
Morgan, Earl Lurraine, Italy, 1952-58, 1960-61; Lebanon, 1959-60, 1961-64; Israel, 1971—
Morgan, Norma Olive Weis, India, 1964-70; Israel, 1971—
Morgan, Thelma Arlene Dodd, Italy, 1952-58, 1960-61; Lebanon, 1959-60, 1961-64
Morrow, Charles Kendall, Haiti, 1972-81
Morrow, Joyce Ann, Haiti, 1972-81
Morse, Evelyn J. King, Swaziland, 1963-65; South Africa, 1965-68
Morse, Neil G., Swaziland, 1963-65; South Africa, 1965-68
Moses, Arthur, China, 1939-44
Moses, Blanche, China, 1939-44
Mosher, David, Swaziland, 1983—
Mosher, Marquita, Swaziland, 1983—
Mosteller, Earl Elwood, Cape Verde, 1946-58; Brazil, 1958-74; Portugal, 1974-83; Azores, 1983—
Mosteller, Gladys Marie Parker, Cape Verde, 1946-58; Brazil, 1958-74; Portugal, 1974-83; Azores, 1983—
Mowery, Linda Kay, South Africa, 1984—
Moyer, David Brooks, South Africa, 1972—
Moyer, Maryel Ruth, South Africa, 1972—
Mulder, Chester O., Australia, 1969-74; Japan, 1974-78
Mulder, Vivian, Australia, 1969-74; Japan, 1974-78
Munro, Sarah, Swaziland, 1927-31
Murray, Muriel, Papua New Guinea, 1969-73
Murray, Myron, Papua New Guinea, 1969-73
Murugan, Alice, Caribbean Reg. Off., 1984—

Murugan, Joseph P., Caribbean Reg. Off., 1984—

Muse, Eltie, India, 1919-30

Muth, Duane Erwin, West Germany, 1975-79

Muth, Florence M., West Germany, 1975-79

Myatt, Carolyn Beeler, India, 1965—

Myers, J. Leona Youngblood, Mozambique, 1945-66; Swaziland, 1966-72

Nacionales, Bienvenido D., Swaziland, 1977—

Nacionales, Maria A., Swaziland, 1977—

Najarian, Berge Samuel, Lebanon, 1950-61; Jordan, 1961-69; Israel, 1969-77; Antigua, 1978-84; Zambia, 1984-85

Najarian, Doris Mamie Roberts, Lebanon, 1950-61; Jordan, 1961-69; Israel, 1969-77; Antigua, 1978-84; Zambia, 1984-85

Naramor, Chester, Chile, 1964-70

Naramor, Doris, Chile, 1964-70

Neal, Janet, Papua New Guinea, 1979—

Neal, Warren, Papua New Guinea, 1979—

Needles, Margaret (see Williams)

Nelson, Dorothy Lorraine, Panama, 1955-76; Argentina, 1976-81; Dominican Republic, 1981-86; Paraguay, 1986—

Nelson, Elmer O., Panama, 1955-76; Argentina, 1976-81; Dominican Republic, 1981-86; Paraguay, 1986—

Nelson, Olive, India, 1907-15

Neuenschwander, Dwight, New Zealand, 1980-85

Neuenschwander, Evonne, New Zealand, 1980-85

Newlin, Kathaleen, South Africa, 1961-78

Nielson, Janice M., Denmark, 1975-80

Nielson, John B., West Germany, 1965-69; Trinidad, 1984

Nielson, John M., West Germany, 1966-67; Denmark, 1975-80

Nielson, Linda Jean Teague, Netherlands, 1975-79

Nielson, Merritt Joseph, Netherlands, 1975-79

Nielson, Mrs. John B., West Germany, 1965-69

Nielson, Peter, Swaziland, 1917-21

Noonan, Joan, Swaziland, 1969-74; Nicaragua, 1976-77; Ecuador, 1977-83; Peru, 1983—

Nothstine, Lauralee, Swaziland, 1975—

Nothstine, Thomas David, Swaziland, 1975—

Nyreen, Elizabeth Ann, Costa Rica, 1976-86; Dominican Republic, 1986—

Nyreen, Harry Charles, Costa Rica, 1976-86; Dominican Republic, 1986—

Oiness, Sylvia Marie, Swaziland, 1946-77

Onufrock, Richard, South Africa, 1981-84

Orchard, Alvin V., Samoa, 1975-80; Philippines, 1980—

Orchard, Bette J., Samoa, 1975-80; Philippines, 1980—

Orjala, Charlotte Jeanne, West Germany, 1979-81

Orjala, Mary Blanche, Haiti, 1950-64; West Germany, 1971-72; France, 1986—

Orjala, Paul Richard, Haiti, 1950-64; West Germany, 1971-72; France, 1986—

Osborn, Emma Doris Hammond, China, 1919-42; Taiwan, 1958-62

Osborn, Leon C., China, 1919-42; Taiwan, 1958-62

Otto, Donna, Swaziland, 1985—

Otto, Fred, Swaziland, 1985—

Ovando, Evelyn Charlene Crouch, Peru, 1965-68; Colombia, 1976-83; Mexico, 1983—

Ovando, Samuel, Colombia, 1976-83; Mexico, 1983—

Owen, Gladys Naomi (see Zahner)

Owens, Adeline Lois Preuss, Korea, 1954-66; Asia Reg. Off., 1981-85

Owens, Betty J. Cherry, Philippines, 1965-70, 1971-72, 1976-82

Owens, Denny G., Philippines, 1965-70, 1971-72, 1976-82

Owens, Donald Dean, Korea, 1954-66; Asia Reg. Dir., 1981-85

Page, Dorothy Christine, South Africa, 1977-80; Swaziland, 1982—

Page, Patrick Brown, South Africa, 1977-80; Swaziland, 1982—

Pallett, Clara, Northwest European, 1972-76

Pallett, Murray, Northwest European, 1972-76

Palmer, Alice Aurora, Colombia, 1977-79

Palmer, James Walter, Colombia, 1977-79

Palmquist, Frances P. Garst, New Zealand, 1958-70; Australia, 1970-81

Palmquist, Halvard Spencer, New Zealand, 1958-70; Australia, 1970-81

Pannell, Mary Elizabeth, China, 1925-32, 1935-41

Park, Mabel (see Winans)

Parker, Bertha Adeline, Swaziland, 1937-72

Parker, Maude Varnedoe, China, 1917-30

Parrish, Milton Blaine, South Africa, 1966-71

Parrish, Tommie Earleen Johnson, South Africa, 1966-71

Parsons, Abbie Carolyn (see Hannay)

Pass, Hazel Louie, South Africa, 1948—

Pass, Lois Myrtle, South Africa, 1953-77

Patch, Gail, Korea, 1973—

Patch, Patricia, West Germany, 1981-85

Patch, William Harold, Korea, 1973—

Pate, Juanita Lee, South Africa, 1955—

Pattee, John Willis, China, 1936-42, 1946-49; Philippines, 1950-72

Pattee, Lillian Kerr, China, 1936-42, 1946-49; Philippines, 1950-72

Patton, Jack Thomas, Papua New Guinea, 1973-78, 1979-81

Patton, Lynette Ann, Papua New Guinea, 1973-78, 1979-81

Pattrick, Meryl Hilary, South Africa, 1975-80; Swaziland, 1984—

Payne, Jalie, Mexico, 1908-12

Peacock, Mary Katherine, Swaziland, 1981-82

Pearsall, Kenneth, Korea, 1983-84; South Africa, 1986-87

Pearsall, Ruby, Korea, 1983-84; South Africa, 1986-87

Pearson, Gottfred Herman, No. Amer. Indian, 1954-75; Casa Robles Dir., 1975-83

Pearson, M. Gwendolyn, Swaziland, 1982-85

Pearson, Olive L., No. Amer. Indian, 1954-75; Casa Robles Dir., 1975-83

Pease, Lenora Mary Kaechele, India, 1954-74, 1975-83; Jamaica, 1974-75

Pease, William Jack, India, 1954-74, 1975-80; Jamaica, 1974-75

Peel, Marjorie Eithol (see Danner)

Pelley, Myrtle Adele (see Taylor)

Penn, Joseph Francis, Jr., Swaziland, 1945-61, 1969-74; Mozambique (Mines), 1962-68; South Africa, 1968-69, 1974-86

Penn, Joseph Francis Rowe, Swaziland, 1919-24, 1930-31; South Africa, 1924-30, 1931-39

Penn, Leta Ellen Pittenger, Swaziland, 1945-61, 1969-74; Mozambique (Mines), 1962-68; South Africa, 1968-69, 1974-86

Penn, Susan Powers Hall, Swaziland, 1919-24, 1930-31; South Africa, 1924-30, 1931-39

Penuel, Laura, Mexico, 1910-13

Perkins, Douglas Jerry, Argentina, 1979-82; Uruguay, 1982-86

Perkins, Elaine Marie Finkbeiner, Argentina, 1979-82; Uruguay, 1982-86

Perkins, Floyd Jerry, Mozambique, 1952-55, 1967-74; South Africa, 1955-67; Brazil, 1975

Perkins, Mary Elizabeth (Libby), Mozambique, 1952-55, 1967-74; South Africa, 1955-67; Brazil, 1975

Perkins, Phyllis Hartley Brown, Japan, 1962-68; Gen. NWMS Dir., 1980-85

Perkinson, Oather Kurtzy, Argentina, 1952-53, 1971-81; Uruguay, 1953-71; Puerto Rico, 1981-85

Perkinson, Ruth Dickson, Argentina, 1952-53, 1971-81; Uruguay, 1953-71; Puerto Rico, 1981-85

Perry, Ella Winslow, India, 1904-19

Perry, Gertrude Louise (see Tracy)

Perry, Peggy Joyce, Mozambique, 1964-70; Swaziland, 1970—

Perry, Robert Eugene, Mozambique, 1964-70; Swaziland, 1970—

Pettis, Sheila K. Hall, Bermuda, 1985; Portugal, 1986—

Pettis, Stephen J., Bermuda, 1985; Portugal, 1986—

Phillips, Eugenia Alice (see Coats)

Phillips, Jackson D., Jr., South Africa, 1964-71

Phillips, Janey L., South Africa, 1964-71

Pierson, Annette, West Germany, 1975-76; South Africa, 1976-77

Pierson, George, West Germany, 1975-76; South Africa, 1976-77

Pittam, Elsie Irene, Nicaragua, 1959-67; Panama, 1967-70, 1981-84

Pittam, Robert Earl, Nicaragua, 1959-67; Panama, 1967-70, 1981-84

Pitts, Joseph Staten, Philippines, 1948-58

Pitts, L. Pearl Jackson, Philippines, 1948-58

Pointer, Bessie L. Tallackson, Swaziland, 1921-39; Mozambique, 1939-48

Polley, Susan Margery (see Woodruff)

Poole, Lillian, Japan, 1905-10, 1914-15

Pope, George Henry, South Africa, 1928-35, 1953-65; Mozambique, 1935-53; Swaziland, 1965-71

Pope, Gladys Mary, South Africa, 1930-35, 1953-65; Mozambique, 1935-53; Swaziland, 1965-71

Pope, Marilla Wales, Guatemala, 1938-40

Porrill, Julie Anne, Swaziland, 1975-77

Porter, Chancey William, San Antonio Sem., 1951-54; Puerto Rico, 1954-76; New Zealand, 1976-80; Venezuela, 1980—

Porter, Jerry Duane, Dominican Republic, 1975-79; Costa Rica, 1979-86; MAC Reg. Off., 1986—

Porter, Mary Juanita, San Antonio Sem., 1951-54; Puerto Rico, 1954-76; New Zealand, 1976-80; Venezuela, 1980—

Porter, Toni Eloise, Dominican Republic, 1975-79; Costa Rica, 1979-86; MAC Reg. Off., 1986—

Poteet, Henry Theodore, Swaziland, 1946-50; South Africa, 1950-52

Poteet, Ruby Frances Dallas, Swaziland, 1946-50; South Africa, 1950-52

Pound, Sharon Elaine, Belize, 1973-80; Caribbean Reg., 1980-84

Pound, Thomas Bert, Belize, 1973-80; Caribbean Reg., 1980-84

Powell, Ivis Marie Hopper, Swaziland, 1945-62

Powers, Dudley, Papua New Guinea, 1965-68

Powers, Joan, Papua New Guinea, 1965-68

Prescott, Grace Irene Yoakum, Virgin Islands, 1944-45, 1961-70; Cuba, 1945-57; Puerto Rico, 1957-61

Prescott, Lyle Eldred, Virgin Islands, 1944-45, 1961-70; Cuba, 1945-57; Puerto Rico, 1957-61

Primrose, Margaret May, Bolivia, 1960-67

Prince, Evelyn, West Germany, 1970-76

Prince, William J., West Germany, 1970-76

Privat, Gertrude, Japan, 1919-22

Qandah, Jamil S. El-Mousa, Cyprus, 1985—

Qandah, Merja, Cyprus, 1985—

Quesenberry, Charles, Mexico, 1906-12

Quesenberry, Mrs. Charles, Mexico, 1906-12

Quiram, Nancy, West Germany, 1964-79; Switzerland, 1979—

Quiram, Rudy, West Germany, 1964-79; Switzerland, 1979—

Radcliffe, James Daniel, Papua New Guinea, 1985—

Radcliffe, Katherine Elaine Beam, Papua New Guinea, 1985—

Rademacher, E., Peru, 1920-24

Rademacher, Mrs. E., Peru, 1920-24

Ragains, Evelyn Elaine Hunt, Nicaragua, 1948-61, 1967-79; Colombia, 1979-84

Ragains, Louis Gorman, Nicaragua, 1948-61, 1967-79; Colombia, 1979-84

Ramsey, Evelyn Mae, Swaziland, 1957-70; Papua New Guinea, 1970—

Ratcliff, Alice Marie, Guyana, 1954-57; Trinidad, 1957-66, 1972-83; Puerto Rico, 1966-72; Dominican Republic, 1983-86; Bermuda, 1986—

Ratcliff, Herbert A., Guyana, 1954-57; Trinidad, 1957-66, 1972-83; Puerto Rico, 1966-72; Dominican Republic, 1983-86; Bermuda, 1986—

Ratlief, Judith, Puerto Rico, 1975-76; Australia, 1978-82

Ratlief, Steve R., Puerto Rico, 1975-76; Australia, 1978-82

Rawlings, Ruth Ellenora, Japan, 1964-76, 1979—; West Germany, 1978

Ray, Elva Emily Guillermo, Guatemala, 1966-68, 1974—; Argentina, 1969-74

Ray, Harold Cecil, Guatemala, 1966-68, 1974—; Argentina, 1969-74

Read, Donna Joan, Haiti, 1972-82; Brazil, 1982—

Read, Terence Bertram, Haiti, 1972-82; Brazil, 1982—

Reed, Donald Edward, Lebanon, 1954-67

Reed, Elva May, Lebanon, 1954-67

Reedy, Fred A., Texas-Mexican, 1946-50

Reedy, Lois R. Milligan, Texas-Mexican, 1946-50

Reid, Kathryn Jane, Swaziland, 1982—

Rench, George Everett, Taiwan, 1959-71; Indonesia, 1971-85; Asia Pac. Reg. Dir., 1985—

Rench, Vairadonna Faith Storey, Taiwan, 1959-71; Indonesia, 1971-85; Asia Pac. Reg. Off., 1985—

Rennie, Jessie Skinner, Swaziland, 1939-47; South Africa, 1947-71

Rensberry, Duane Vernell, Honduras, 1984—

Rensberry, Linda Kay Bradbury, Honduras, 1984—

Restrick, David W., South Africa, 1985—

Restrick, Rhoda Coldwell, Swaziland, 1977-78; South Africa, 1985—

Reynolds, Jane Ann, Swaziland, 1973-80; Samoa, 1980-82

Reynolds, Richard Paul, Swaziland, 1973-80; Samoa, 1980-82

Rhoden, Evelyn Jeanette Benton, Japan, 1956—

Rhoden, Maurice Marvin, Japan, 1956—

Ribeiro, Edgar A., Mozambique, 1938-40

Ribeiro, Mrs. Edgar A., Mozambique, 1938-40

Rich, Carolyn Frazier, Ecuador, 1984—

Rich, Dwight Daniel, Ecuador, 1984—

Rich, Harry Andrew, Haiti, 1957-71

Rich, Marion Lillian Kish, Haiti, 1957-71

Richards, Henryetta, Mexico, 1909-10

Richey, Donna Sue Suttles, Papua New Guinea, 1975-81

Rieder, Irene Bessie, Korea, 1967-72; Taiwan, 1973—

Rieder, Stephen John, Korea, 1967-72; Taiwan, 1973—

Riggle, Mary Lou, Belize, 1965-77; Guatemala, 1977—

Riggs, Dennis Edward, South Africa, 1982—

Riggs, Jacalyn Joyce, South Africa, 1982—

Riley, Jack Lee, South Africa, 1960-66, 1969-81; Zimbabwe, 1966-69; Ciskei, 1981-84

Riley, Loretta Faye, Swaziland, 1967-74, 1985—; South Africa, 1975-85

Riley, Martha, Swaziland, 1968-83

Riley, Mary Lou, South Africa, 1960-66, 1969-81, 1985—; Zimbabwe, 1966-69; Ciskei, 1981-84

Riley, Paul, Swaziland, 1968-83

Riley, Thomas Lowell, Swaziland, 1967-74, 1985—; South Africa, 1975-85

Rixse, Eva Elizabeth, Swaziland, 1919-23; Mozambique, 1923-32; South Africa, 1932-37

Roberts, Alice, Chile, 1971-77

Roberts, Charles David, Jr., Chile, 1971-77

Robinson, Ida Louise (see Chapman)

Robinson, Katherine G., Honduras, 1983—

Robinson, Michael L., Honduras, 1983—

Roby, Eva Carpenter, India, 1903-20

Rodeheaver, Lois V. (see Ford)

Rogers, Dennis, Mexico, 1910-12

Rogers, Kenneth Wayne, South Africa, 1963-83

Rogers, Lelan John, Trinidad, 1944-47; Guyana, 1947-52

Rogers, Mrs. Dennis, Mexico, 1910-12

Rogers, Mrs. W. J., India, 1906-8

Rogers, W. J., India, 1906-8

Rogers, Wanda Joyce, South Africa, 1963-83

Rogers, Wavy Estella Malone, Trinidad, 1944-47; Guyana, 1947-52

Romey, Carl Edwin, Brazil, 1978—

Romey, Shirley Jo, Brazil, 1978—

Ronnekamp, George B., New Zealand, 1977-80

Ronnekamp, Lois, New Zealand, 1977-80

Rosa, Adrian Wayne, Philippines, 1952-55

Rosa, Anna Willene Agee, Philippines, 1952-55

Rosbrugh, Lolis Marveen, Swaziland, 1969—

Roth, Norine E. (see Grantz)

Rotz, Carol J., South Africa, 1982—

Rotz, James H., South Africa, 1982—

Roush, Virginia (see Grimm)

Royall, Ann, China, 1934-41

Royall, Geoffrey, China, 1934-41

Rudeen, Cecil Gordon (Bill), Nicaragua, 1946-74; San Antonio Sem., 1974-81

Rudeen, Edna Ellen Keller, Nicaragua, 1946-74; San Antonio Sem., 1974-81

Rudeen, Evangeline Ruth Bolton, Peru, 1970-75; Panama, 1975-80; Costa Rica, 1981-84

Rudeen, Mark Antony, Peru, 1970-75; Panama, 1975-80; Costa Rica, 1981-84

Rudolph, Ruth Corbet, India, 1920-25, 1936-40

Rusling, Cora Snider, Japan, 1912-14

Russell, Grace Alice Keen, Jordan, 1947-57

Russell, William Alfred, Jordan, 1947-57

Ryan, Kristeen L., Colombia, 1985—

Ryan, Mark T., Colombia, 1985—

Ryding, Bonnie Rose, Zambia, 1978-82

Ryding, Richard Bruce (Rick), Zambia, 1978-82

Sage, Barbara Ann, Zimbabwe, 1977—

Sage, James Laverne, Zimbabwe, 1977—

Salgado, Jonathan, Guatemala, 1975-83; Costa Rica, 1983—

Salgado, Magda, Guatemala, 1975-83; Costa Rica, 1983—

Salmons, Joan Margaret, South Africa, 1952-54; Mozambique, 1954-70

Salmons, Norman, South Africa, 1949-54; Mozambique, 1954-70

Sanner, A. E., Casa Robles Dir., 1953-66

Santana, Grace Mendell, Cuba, 1917-19

Santee, Helen C., Japan, 1913-19

Santo, Lois (see Labenski)

Savage, Arthur Chester, South Africa, 1937-39; Swaziland, 1939-48

Savage, Kathryn Louise, Swaziland, 1968—

Savage, Martha Elizabeth Haselton, South Africa, 1937-39; Swaziland, 1939-48

Saxon, Ruth Ora, Trinidad, 1954—

Say, Leonard Paul, Argentina, 1961-77; Dominican Republic, 1977—

Say, Nancy Ann, Haiti, 1985—

Say, Robert Duane, Haiti, 1985—

Say, Thelma Arlowene, Argentina, 1961-77; Dominican Republic, 1977—

Sayes, Dorothy Kifer, Trinidad, 1953-65

Sayes, William Howard, Trinidad, 1953-65

Scarlett, Bonita Faye Quass, South Africa, 1962-78

Scarlett, Donald, South Africa, 1962-78

Schaffer, Pearl Denbo, China, 1917-22

Schendel, Daryl Arthur, Papua New Guinea, 1966-81

Schendel, Elizabeth P., Papua New Guinea, 1966-81

Schmelzenbach, Beverly Ann, South Africa, 1960-77; Namibia, 1977-84; Kenya, 1984—

Schmelzenbach, Dennis Ray, South Africa, 1970-80

Schmelzenbach, Elmer Faldiene, Swaziland, 1936-42; South Africa, 1943-73

Schmelzenbach, Harmon F., Swaziland, 1907-29

Schmelzenbach, Harmon Lee III, South Africa, 1960-77; Namibia, 1977-84; Kenya, 1984—

Schmelzenbach, Louise Lula Glatzel, Swaziland, 1908-53

Schmelzenbach, Mary Kate Wheeler, Swaziland, 1944-49

Schmelzenbach, Mary Louise Snyder, Swaziland, 1936-42; South Africa, 1943-73

Schmelzenbach, Maureen McClintock, South Africa, 1970-80

Schmelzenbach, Paul Julius, Swaziland, 1944-49

Schmidlin, Kurt, Chile, 1979—

Schmidlin, Susan, Chile, 1979—

Schofield, Marion, Europe/Mid. E. Reg. Off., 1983-86; Eurasia Reg. Off., 1986—

Schofield, Thomas William, Europe/Mid. E. Reg. Dir., 1983-86; Eurasia Reg. Dir., 1986—

Schortinghouse, Byron E. F., New Zealand, 1978-81; Australia, 1981-83; Philippines, 1983—

Schortinghouse, Leanna (Sunnie), New Zealand, 1978-81; Australia, 1981-83; Philippines, 1983—

Schriber, Sylvia Sue, Nicaragua, 1962-67

Schubert, Joanna Marie, Korea, 1974—

Schubert, Kenneth Charles, Korea, 1974—

Schultz, Lorraine Ogden, Swaziland, 1943-52; Mozambique, 1952-76

Schurman, Rhoda V. Jones, China, 1936-41

Scott, Edith, Mexico, 1910-12; Guatemala, 1920-25

Scott, J. D., Mexico, 1910-12; Guatemala, 1920-25

Scott, Jon Paul, Portugal, 1974-80, 1982—

Scott, Lois I., Australia, 1977-78

Scott, Mary Louise, China, 1940-49; Gen. NWMS Exec. Sec., 1950-75; Japan, 1976-78

Scott, Mary Margaret, Portugal, 1974-80, 1982—

Scott, Willis Royce, Australia, 1977-78

Scrivner, F. Charles, No. Amer. Indian, 1943-74

Scrivner, Fern G., No. Amer. Indian, 1943-74

Seale, Nancy Mary, Papua New Guinea, 1969—

Seaman, Constance Ellen Gregory, Swaziland, 1944-49

Seaman, Dolores, Trinidad, 1965-66; Japan, 1966-72

Seaman, John Earl, Martinique, 1976-86; Ivory Coast, 1986—

Seaman, Lauren Irving, Swaziland, 1944-49

Seaman, Lauriston, Trinidad, 1965-66; Japan, 1966-72

Seaman, Linda Sue Smith, Martinique, 1976-86; Ivory Coast, 1986—

Seay, Bessie, India, 1909-31; Swaziland, 1931-37

Sedat, Elizabeth Rusling (Betty), Guatemala, 1945-83

Sedat, William, Guatemala, 1945-71
Seely, Harvey Vincent, Bolivia, 1959-64
Seely, Orlea Burkley, Bolivia, 1959-64
Selvidge, Rebecca J., Hong Kong, 1979—
Selvidge, William Lynn, Hong Kong, 1979—
Semlar, Janie Lou, South Africa, 1975—
Sewell, W. J., Mexico, 1906-12
Sewell, Mrs. W. J., Mexico, 1906-12
Shalley, Julie Ann, South Africa, 1979-84;
　　Namibia, 1984—
Shalley, Michael Duane, South Africa,
　　1979-84; Namibia, 1984—
Sheffer, Jessica Vance, Papua New Guinea,
　　1981
Shelton, Ruthellen Lee, Trinidad, 1946-47
Shelton, Seabron Trueman, Trinidad,
　　1946-47
Shepherd, Doyle Mearle, Japan, 1948-67,
　　1979-81
Shepherd, Mattie Angeline Burton, Japan,
　　1948-67, 1979-81
Shipman, William, Guyana, 1966-70
Shipman, Zola, Guyana, 1966-70
Shirley, Edith Ann Winder, Swaziland,
　　1907-15
Shirley, Etta Innis, South Africa, 1907-10,
　　1920-25, 1929-46; Swaziland,
　　1910-20, 1925-29
Shirley, H. A., Swaziland, 1907-20, 1925-29,
　　1943-45; South Africa, 1920-25,
　　1929-43
Shmidt, Lynn Durwood, South Africa,
　　1981-86; Swaziland, 1986—
Shmidt, Shearon, South Africa, 1981-86;
　　Swaziland, 1986—
Short, Lillian Cole, Swaziland, 1916-26
Shroyer, Mina, India, 1898-99
Sibert, Bethany DeBow, Bolivia, 1963-77
Sievers, Dale Lewis, Bolivia, 1954-58; Nic-
　　aragua, 1958-64
Sievers, Mildred Irene, Bolivia, 1954-58; Nic-
　　aragua, 1958-64
Silvernail, Donald Keith, Swaziland, 1983—
Silvernail, Geneva Jane, Swaziland, 1983—
Simmons, Pearl, India, 1911-12
Sims, Glennie, China, 1914-27
Singleton, Kenneth Trevor, South Africa,
　　1952-71; Mozambique (Mines),
　　1971-83
Singleton, Minnie Hope, South Africa,
　　1946-71; Mozambique (Mines),
　　1971-83
Sinot, Lily D., Papua New Guinea, 1976-78

Sipes, John Ray, Zimbabwe, 1981-82
Sipes, Rosalie, Zimbabwe, 1981-82
Sisler, Claude, Chile, 1980—
Sisler, Sandra, Chile, 1980—
Skea, Irene Elizabeth, Papua New Guinea,
　　1975-77
Skea, Joyce Duncan (see Bartle)
Skinner, Boyd Conrad, Chile, 1953—
Skinner, Daisy (see Fritzlan)
Skinner, Mabel, Swaziland, 1920-54
Skinner, Marcia Lee Hayse, South Africa,
　　1968-82
Skinner, Neva Lucille, Chile, 1953—
Skinner, Robert Andrew, South Africa,
　　1968-82
Slater, Judith Ann, South Africa, 1964—
Slaughter, Margaret L., Swaziland, 1983—
Slaughter, Russell E., Swaziland, 1983—
Sluyter, John Curtis, Sr., Ecuador, 1974-80,
　　1984-86; Argentina, 1980-81; Uru-
　　guay, 1981-84
Sluyter, Laurel Faith, Ecuador, 1974-80,
　　1984-86; Argentina, 1980-81; Uru-
　　guay, 1981-84
Smee, John Milton, Jamaica, 1970-77; Div.
　　Off. (HQ), 1981—
Smee, Mary Alice McAllister, Jamaica,
　　1970-77; Div. Off. (HQ), 1984—
Smith, Aaron Jacob, China, 1920-27
Smith, Alberta Marie Fletcher, India, 1951-60
Smith, Catherine, China, 1916-23
Smith, Debbie, Swaziland, 1981-82
Smith, Gene Chester, Haiti, 1959-67,
　　1968-71, 1973-74; Trinidad,
　　1967-68; Bahamas, 1971-73; Barba-
　　dos, 1973; St. Lucia, 1974-75; Fr.
　　Antilles, 1975-82
Smith, George, South Africa, 1982-85
Smith, Ina Eilene, Belize, 1958-65
Smith, James Wilbur, South Africa, 1965—
Smith, Mary Catherine Hance, Haiti,
　　1959-67, 1968-71, 1973-74; Trin-
　　idad, 1967-68; Bahamas, 1971-73;
　　Barbados, 1973; St. Lucia, 1974-75;
　　Fr. Antilles, 1975-82
Smith, Mrs. Aaron Jacob, China, 1920-27
Smith, Patricia Stafford, South Africa,
　　1965—
Smith, Vesta, South Africa, 1982-85
Snellenberger, Paula (see Bard)
Snider, Cora (see Rusling)
Snow, Rachel (see Julca)

Spalding, Linda, Bolivia, 1962-79; Panama, 1979-84

Spalding, Tom, Bolivia, 1962-79; Panama, 1979-84

Speicher, Orpha Marie, India, 1936-77

Spencer, Dorsey Herman, South Africa, 1951-54, 1962-72; Swaziland, 1954-62, 1972-80

Spencer, Mary Elizabeth White, South Africa, 1951-54, 1962-72; Swaziland, 1954-62, 1972-80

Spijkman, Gijsbertha H. V. D. Leek, Netherlands, 1974-79

Spijkman, Jan, Netherlands, 1974-79

Spoon, Darrell Lee, Guatemala, 1959-70

Spoon, Reba Joan, Guatemala, 1959-70

Sprague, Lillian, India, 1898-1906

Srader, Duane E., Cape Verde, 1971-80; Portugal, 1980—

Srader, Linda Lee Triggs, Cape Verde, 1971-80; Portugal, 1980—

St. John, Kelvin, Guatemala, 1981—

St. John, Paula Skiles, Guatemala, 1981—

Stacy, Bern, Papua New Guinea, 1968-69

Stacy, Olive, Papua New Guinea, 1968-69

Stafford, Anne, Colombia, 1981—

Stafford, Ernest, Colombia, 1981—

Stafford, Samuel M., Mexico, 1903-10

Stamps, Don Larrel, Brazil, 1971-72

Stamps, Linda Sodowsky, Brazil, 1971-72

Stanfield, Evelyn Roxie Schumm, Nicaragua, 1943-59, 1972-75; Bolivia, 1959-72; Panama, 1976-77; Costa Rica, 1977-78; El Salvador, 1978; Guatemala, 1978-79; Chile, 1979-80

Stanfield, Harold William, Nicaragua, 1943-59, 1972-75; Bolivia, 1959-72; Panama, 1976-77; Costa Rica, 1977-78; El Salvador, 1978; Guatemala, 1978-79; Chile, 1979-80

Stanton, Daryll G., Zambia, 1982-84; South Africa, 1984—

Stanton, Verna M., Zambia, 1982-84; South Africa, 1984—

Staples, Isaac B., Japan, 1915-24

Staples, Minnie Frazier, Japan, 1915-24

Stark, Anne Mamie Scheel, Swaziland, 1949-73; India, 1981-82

Stark, Flora Linda (see Fogo)

Stark, Kenneth Alexander, Swaziland, 1949-73; India, 1981-82

Steigleder, Mary Lucile Graham, South Africa, 1952—

Steigleder, Philip Robert, South Africa, 1952—

Stephenson, Alberta Lucille, South Africa, 1972-85

Stephenson, David Van Buren, Jr., South Africa, 1972-85

Stevenson, Claudia Lucille, South Africa, 1969-79; Swaziland, 1979—

Stevenson, Grace, Bolivia, 1971-84; Spain, 1984—

Stevenson, Henry Alexander, Bolivia, 1971-84; Spain, 1984—

Stewart, Margaret, India, 1932-40

Stimer, Frances Virginia, Papua New Guinea, 1965—

Stocks, Jimmy, Swaziland, 1970-74

Stocks, Judith P., Swaziland, 1970-74

Stockwell, Eleanor Marjorie Whispel, Mozambique, 1945-75; South Africa, 1975-84

Stockwell, Oscar Marshall, Mozambique, 1945-75; South Africa, 1975-84

Storey, Nellie, South Africa, 1949-53, 1959-68; Swaziland, 1953-59, 1968-72

Storey, Norma Jeanne, Guatemala, 1956-65, 1982—; El Salvador, 1965-73; Honduras, 1973-82

Storey, Stanley Phillip, Guatemala, 1956-65, 1982—; El Salvador, 1965-73; Honduras, 1973-82

Stotler, Dale Wayne, South Africa, 1973—

Stotler, Patricia Irene, South Africa, 1973—

Strang, Barbara Joan, Papua New Guinea, 1985—

Strickland, Charles Hapgood, South Africa, 1921-27, 1930-32, 1935-55; Mozambique, 1927-30, 1932-35

Strickland, Charles Henry, Jr., South Africa, 1948-66

Strickland, Fannie Kate McManus, South Africa, 1948-66

Strickland, Irene Sophia Groom, South Africa, 1921-27, 1930-32, 1935-55; Mozambique, 1927-30, 1932-35

Stroud, Charles Lester, Korea, 1961-68

Stroud, Lois Alene, Korea, 1961-68

Stroud, Nettie Mae, Cape Verde, 1967-71, 1983—

Stroud, Paul Elvin, Cape Verde, 1967-71, 1983—

Stubbs, Barbara Ann, Korea, 1965-76

Stubbs, Paul Eugene, Korea, 1965-76

Studt, Linda Lee, South Africa, 1966-76

Studt, Robert Preston, South Africa, 1966-76

Stults, Donald Leroy, Korea, 1977—

Stults, Lucinda Sue, Korea, 1977—

Surbrook, George William, Barbados, 1930-34

Surbrook, Marion, Barbados, 1930-34

Sutherland, Ann Findlay Bowman, China, 1920-27, 1936-41

Sutherland, Anna Kachigian, Swaziland, 1960-72

Sutherland, Eunice Lucille, South Africa, 1955-68

Sutherland, Francis Campbell, China, 1920-27, 1936-41

Sutherland, John Campbell, South Africa, 1955-68

Sutherland, Paul William, Swaziland, 1960-72

Suttles, Donna Sue (see Richey)

Swain, Arlene Shannon, Peru, 1964-71; Costa Rica, 1971; Ecuador, 1972-82; Bolivia, 1982—

Swain, Robert Alfred, Peru, 1964-71; Costa Rica, 1971; Ecuador, 1972-82; Bolivia, 1982—

Swanson, Mona, Samoa, 1970-74

Swanson, Orville, Samoa, 1970-74

Swarth, Dowie, No. Amer. Indian, 1944-57

Swarth, Helen Elizabeth Kelsey, No. Amer. Indian, 1953-57

Swarth, Theressa Strikwerda, No. Amer. Indian, 1944-52

Swartz, Burton Earl, Belize, 1967-72

Swartz, Pat, Belize, 1967-72

Syvret, Ellen Mary Elizabeth, Papua New Guinea, 1969—

Taft, Annette F. (see Brown)

Tallackson, Bessie L. (see Pointer)

Tanner, Mary (see Frame)

Tarrant, Christine, Swaziland, 1971-74

Tarrant, Dorothy, West Germany, 1970-71

Tashjian, Donice Loriene, Taiwan, 1970-80

Tashjian, Jirair Samuel, Taiwan, 1970-80

Tate, Dean Albert, Swaziland, 1977-82

Tate, Elizabeth Lea, Swaziland, 1977-82

Taylor, Amy, Australia, 1952-60; Japan, 1965-66; West Germany, 1969-70

Taylor, Bruce Thomas, South Africa, 1971-74; Nigeria, 1986—

Taylor, Carolyn E. A., Swaziland, 1975-76

Taylor, David, Haiti, 1981—

Taylor, Ira Nelson, Peru, 1934-39, 1944-57; Bolivia, 1958-67

Taylor, Lois Eileen, Guyana, 1960-67; Trinidad, 1967-68; Barbados, 1968-74; Bahamas, 1974-79

Taylor, Lucille Logston, Peru, 1934-39, 1944-57; Bolivia, 1958-67

Taylor, Myrtle Adele Pelley, Swaziland, 1922-38; Mozambique, 1938-48

Taylor, Patricia, Haiti, 1981—

Taylor, Richard, Australia, 1952-60; Japan, 1965-66; West Germany, 1969-70

Taylor, Ruth Diana, South Africa, 1971-74; Nigeria, 1986—

Taylor, Samuel Miles, Guyana, 1960-67; Trinidad, 1967-68; Barbados, 1968-74; Bahamas, 1974-79

Taylor, Wesley A., Swaziland, 1975-76

Taylorson, Eldred Ladue, Japan, 1970-75

Taylorson, George, Japan, 1970-75

Teakell, Garnett, Belize, 1975-79; Costa Rica, 1979—

Teakell, Marilyn Skinner, Belize, 1975-79; Costa Rica, 1979—

Teare, Darrell B., New Zealand, 1970-76; Div. Off. (HQ), 1976-79; So. Pac. Reg. Dir., 1983-86

Teare, Dorothy J., New Zealand, 1970-76

Techau, Carol Anne Lane, Papua New Guinea, 1981-86

Techau, Joseph, Papua New Guinea, 1981-86

Terry, Dorothy Dell, Swaziland, 1964—

Terry, Douglas Wayne, Scandinavia, 1978-85

Terry, Peggy Elaine Smith, Scandinavia, 1978-85

Terry, Wanda Faye, Swaziland, 1961—

Thahabiyah, Emma, Syria, 1920-55

Thahabiyah, Laurice, Syria, 1947-50

Thahabiyah, Mulhim Abraham, Syria, 1920-55

Thatcher, Gertrude, Japan, 1917-19

Thatcher, Paul C., Japan, 1917-19

Thomas, Alfred, Papua New Guinea, 1978-79

Thomas, Betty-May, Swaziland, 1982-85

Thomas, Esther May, Swaziland, 1946-72

Thomas, Gordon James, Swaziland, 1982-85

Thomas, Lynn, Papua New Guinea, 1978-79

Thompson, Glen Dale, Australia, 1977-81

Thompson, J. W., Japan, 1910-13

Thompson, Mrs. J. W., Japan, 1910-13

Thompson, Myrl, China, 1930-35
Thompson, Wanda Lou, Australia, 1977-81
Thorpe, Raymond, South Africa, 1960-78,
    1981—
Thorpe, Shirley, South Africa, 1960-78,
    1981—
Tidwell, Lula May (see McKay)
Tiemann, Mary Lou (see Lloyd)
Timmer, E. H., No. Amer. Indian, 1945-65
Timmer, Esther, No. Amer. Indian, 1945-65
Tink, Fletcher Leroy, Bolivia, 1976-78
Tink, Frances Colleen Rogers, Bolivia,
    1976-78
Tipton, Mark C., South Africa, 1984—
Tipton, Regina M. Matlock, South Africa,
    1984—
Torgrimson, Mary Damaris Gunnoe, Peru,
    1947-77
Torgrimson, Phillip Albert, Peru, 1947-77
Torgrimson, Phillip Dee, Colombia, 1977-82
Torgrimson, Sharolyn Kay, Colombia,
    1977-82
Tracy, Gertrude Louise Perry, India, 1904-19,
    1929-34
Tracy, Leighton S., India, 1904-19, 1929-34
Tresham, Amber (see Wood)
Tressler, Veora Lee, Costa Rica, 1979-85;
    Guatemala, 1985—
Trim, Rodney Lee, South Africa, 1981-85;
    Malawi, 1986—
Trim, Susan Jane Elleman, South Africa,
    1981-85; Malawi, 1986—
True, Ira Llewellyn, Guatemala, 1921-24;
    Peru, 1924-26; West. Lat. Amer.,
    1942-63
True, Valora Mae, Guatemala, 1921-24; Peru,
    1924-26; West. Lat. Amer., 1942-63
Trumble, Margaret Mary L. (Peggy), Swazi-
    land, 1969—
Tryon, Charles, Philippines, 1961-67
Tryon, Lottie Jean, Philippines, 1961-67
Tubbs, Elisabeth Ann, Swaziland, 1973-81
Turner, Leona Stallcup (see Miller)
Turnock, Delma Jean, West Germany,
    1978-81
Turnock, John James, West Germany,
    1978-81
Tustin, Mabel Jane, Swaziland, 1960-80

Uerkvitz, Esther H., Costa Rica, 1969-71
Uerkvitz, T. David, Costa Rica, 1969-71
Ulmet, Peggy Ann, Japan, 1976-85
Undi, Alfred, Papua New Guinea, 1972-74

Undi, Olive, Papua New Guinea, 1972-74
Upperman, Minnie (see Chenault)

Van Beek, Jeanine Jacobe Marguerite, Haiti,
    1975—
Van Develder, Frank Radcliff, Bolivia,
    1955-57
Van Develder, Mary Beulah, Bolivia, 1955-57
Vanciel, Brian Wallace, Haiti, 1956-61
Vanciel, Evelyn May Kopp, Haiti, 1956-61
Varnedoe, Maude (see Parker)
Varro, Elizabeth Finnette Fitz, China,
    1947-49
Varro, Michael Franklin, China, 1947-49
Vaughters, Frances Laverne Boyd, Gua-
    temala, 1945-55; San Antonio Sem.,
    1955-74
Vaughters, William Clayton, Guatemala,
    1945-55; San Antonio Sem.,
    1955-74; Div. Off. (HQ), 1974-80
Vazquez Pla, Juan R., Costa Rica, 1979—
Vazquez Pla, Noemi Quintana Garcia, Costa
    Rica, 1979—
Vennum, Judith Pepper, Swaziland, 1977-78,
    1981-82
Vennum, Keith, Swaziland, 1977-78,
    1981-82
Ver Hoek, Evelyn I. (see Guillermo)
Vetter, Edith E., Swaziland, 1976-78
Vetter, James L., Swaziland, 1976-78
Vieg, Ida, China, 1914-37
Vine, Winnifred Frances, Philippines,
    1952-74, 1975-78
Vorce, Alicia Susanna, Costa Rica, 1984—
Vorce, Randy Lee, Costa Rica, 1984—
Vore, Roberta L., Papua New Guinea,
    1978—
Vore, Vernon W., Papua New Guinea, 1978—

Wachtel, Alexander, Israel, 1952-75
Wachtel, Hallie Irene, Israel, 1952-75
Wade, Carolyn June Whittington, South Af-
    rica, 1984-86; Botswana, 1986—
Wade, Kenneth Wayne, South Africa,
    1984-86; Botswana, 1986—
Wagner, Henry H., Japan, 1918-19
Wagner, Janet Elizabeth, Japan, 1985—
Wagner, Larry Eugene, Japan, 1985—
Wagner, Mary Ann, South Africa, 1965-71
Wagner, Mrs. Henry H., Japan, 1918-19
Wagner, Sherrill Lorraine, Swaziland,
    1977-81; South Africa, 1981—

Wagner, William Herman, Swaziland, 1977-81; South Africa, 1981—

Wales, Marilla (see Pope)

Walker, Cora Coates (see MacMillan)

Walker, Donald Richard, Papua New Guinea, 1974-82

Walker, Linda, Swaziland, 1972—

Walker, Mary Lou Goldman, Papua New Guinea, 1974-82

Walker, Peter Kenny, Swaziland, 1972—

Wall, Christopher, South Africa, 1980-81

Wallace, Florence Mary Loreen, Nicaragua, 1955-79; Chile, 1979—

Wallace, J. Eaton, Mexico, 1909-14

Wallace, Mrs. J. Eaton, Mexico, 1909-14

Walter, Myrtlebelle Elmore, India, 1918-23

Waltermire, Elizabeth May Stockwell, Malawi, 1970-85

Waltermire, Thomas Wayne, Malawi, 1970-85

Walworth, David Homer, Peru, 1921-38

Walworth, Edith Borbe, Peru, 1921-38

Ward, Natalie, Papua New Guinea, 1983—

Ward, Venus Joyce, Swaziland, 1976-84

Ward, Verne, Jr., Papua New Guinea, 1983—

Wardlaw, Donna Yeend, Swaziland, 1976-85

Wardlaw, E. David, South Africa, 1978-86

Wardlaw, Mabel Lena, South Africa, 1978-86

Wardlaw, Paul David, Swaziland, 1976-85

Watson, Janet Maxine, Papua New Guinea, 1973—

Webb, Larry Jo, Barbados, 1963-68; Bolivia, 1968-77

Webb, Mona Jean, Barbados, 1963-68; Bolivia, 1968-77

Weber, Linda Rae, Haiti, 1974-84

Weber, Steve Lynn, Haiti, 1974-84; Div. Off. (HQ), 1984—

Weis, Norma Olive (see Morgan)

Wellmon, Retha Idel Westmoreland, Nicaragua, 1945-61; Uruguay, 1961-65; El Salvador, 1976-78

Wellmon, Robert Childs, Nicaragua, 1945-61; Uruguay, 1961-65; El Salvador, 1976-78

Wesche, Henry C., China, 1926-41

Wesche, Mabel Katherine Arnold, China, 1926-41

Wessels, Mark Stephen, Swaziland, 1977-78

West, Charles Edward, Swaziland, 1921-25; China, 1925-28

West, Ora Lovelace, Swaziland, 1919-40; South Africa, 1940-44

Wheeler, Earl B., Trinidad, 1970-71; Jamaica, 1971-74

Wheeler, Eileen L., New Zealand, 1973-78

Wheeler, Faith A. Pallett, Trinidad, 1970-71; Jamaica, 1971-74

Wheeler, Raymond R., New Zealand, 1973-78

Whitaker, Paul Harrison, Swaziland, 1968-79; South Africa, 1979-82

Whitaker, Virginia Ellen, Swaziland, 1968-79; South Africa, 1979-82

White, Mona Rae, Papua New Guinea, 1959—

White, Myrtle Mangum, India, 1912-17

White, Wallace Filmore, Papua New Guinea, 1959—

Whited, James Edward, Swaziland, 1977—

Whited, Kathleen S., Swaziland, 1977—

Wiens, Evelyn Ruth, South Africa, 1972-81; Papua New Guinea, 1985—

Wiese, Harry Alvin, China, 1920-41, 1946-50; Philippines, 1957-63; Taiwan, 1963-66

Wiese, Katherine McAleer, China, 1920-41, 1946-50; Philippines, 1957-63; Taiwan, 1963-66

Wilcox, Galen Dale, Japan, 1983-86

Wilcox, Gwen, Japan, 1983-86

Wiley, Carrie Taylor, India, 1898-99

Wiley, Fred, India, 1898-99

Wiley, Pearl (see Hanson)

Wilke, Lydia Alvena (see Howard)

Wilkerson, Martha Gray, Taiwan, 1970-71

Wilkerson, Royce Dale, Taiwan, 1970-71

Wilkinson, Carol Evangeline Tooley, Argentina, 1956-61; Uruguay, 1961-68

Wilkinson, Melvin Leon, Argentina, 1956-61; Uruguay, 1961-68

Willard, Ronald Emery, Zambia, 1977-82; South Africa, 1982-84; Botswana, 1984—

Willard, Sara Jane, Zambia, 1977-82; South Africa, 1982-84; Botswana, 1984—

Williams, Florence, India, 1905-?

Williams, Huey Frederick, Haiti, 1980-83

Williams, James Edward, Taiwan, 1976—

Williams, James Kenneth, South Africa, 1981—

Williams, Janice Louise, Philippines, 1981—

Williams, Judi, Haiti, 1980-83

Williams, Julia Jean, Japan, 1961-70

Williams, Kaye Diana, Taiwan, 1976—

Williams, Lulu, Japan, 1905-19

Williams, Margaret Needles, China, 1924-28
Williams, Merrill Swain, Philippines, 1981—
Williams, Ramona Ruth Dautermann, South
 Africa, 1981—
Williams, Ruth (see Crooks)
Williamson, Ruth E. Brickman, China,
 1947-50; Swaziland, 1951-61
Willison, Viola, India, 1919-21
Willox, Agnes, India, 1946-59; Belize,
 1959-70
Wilson, Allen Dorothal, Guatemala, 1958-69;
 El Salvador, 1969-71; Costa Rica,
 1971-83; Colombia, 1983—
Wilson, Brenda Jean, Peru, 1966-77;
 Panama, 1977-79; Dominican Re-
 public, 1979-84
Wilson, Elizabeth Ann Watkins, Guatemala,
 1958-69; El Salvador, 1969-71;
 Costa Rica, 1971-83; Colombia,
 1983—
Wilson, Flora Beth Widger, Philippines,
 1958-85
Wilson, Jerry C., Peru, 1966-77; Panama,
 1977-79; Dominican Republic,
 1979-84
Wilson, Larry, Haiti, 1982—
Wilson, Martha, Haiti, 1982—
Wilson, Norma Ruth (see Wood)
Wilson, Stanley Eldon, Philippines, 1958—
Wiman, Charles Harris, Japan, 1920-22;
 Peru, 1935-43
Wiman, Maud W., Japan, 1920-22; Peru,
 1935-43
Winans, Esther Carson, Peru, 1918-28
Winans, Mabel Park, Peru, 1918-48
Winans, Mary Hunt, Peru, 1914-18
Winans, Roger Sherman, Peru, 1914-48
Winkle, Myrl Barie, Panama, 1974-76
Winkle, Sandie, Panama, 1974-76
Wire, Paul Wesley, Italy, 1964-69
Wire, Teddy K., Italy, 1964-69
Wise, John Harrison, Swaziland, 1946-53,
 1959-62, 1976-79; South Africa,
 1953-59, 1962-76
Wise, Marjorie Evangeline Stark, Swaziland,
 1946-53, 1959-62, 1976-79; South
 Africa, 1953-59, 1962-76
Wissbroeker, Edwin Kenneth, No. Amer. In-
 dian, 1955-57; Zambia, 1958-68
Wissbroeker, Phyllis Maurice, No. Amer.
 Indian, 1955-57; Zambia, 1958-68
Witthoff, Evelyn Martha, India, 1941-73
Wolcott, Connie, Papua New Guinea,
 1984-85

Wolcott, Randall, Papua New Guinea,
 1984-85
Wolstenholm, Bernice, Panama, 1983-86
Wolstenholm, James, Panama, 1983-86
Wood, Amber Tresham, India, 1920-24
Wood, George L., Swaziland, 1969-74
Wood, James Roy Elton, Cape Verde,
 1952-76; Brazil, 1976—
Wood, Jo Ann, Swaziland, 1985—
Wood, June, Swaziland, 1969-74
Wood, M. D., India, 1898-1906
Wood, Margaret Ethelyn Little, Cape Verde,
 1952-76; Brazil, 1976—
Wood, Mrs. M. D., India, 1898-1906
Wood, Norma Ruth Wilson, Swaziland,
 1970-79
Woodruff, Robert Leroy, Papua New Guinea,
 1973-74; Australia, 1977-86
Woodruff, Susan Margery Polley, Papua New
 Guinea, 1972-74; Australia, 1977-86
Woods, Twylla Joy, Japan, 1959—
Woods, Wendell Wardell, Japan, 1959—
Wright, Larry Verdell, Zimbabwe, 1972-82;
 South Africa, 1982—
Wright, Susan Rebecca Young, Zimbabwe,
 1972-82; South Africa, 1982—
Wuster, Charlotte Aileen, Philippines,
 1971-75
Wyman, Edward Grant, Peru, 1941-47; San
 Antonio Sem., 1947-50, 1952-55;
 Texas Mex. Dist., 1950-52; Lat. Amer.
 Evang., 1958-61, 1967-72; Belize,
 1961-64; Puerto Rico, 1964-67
Wyman, Ruth Boling, Peru, 1941-47; San
 Antonio Sem., 1947-50, 1952-55;
 Texas Mex. Dist., 1950-52; Lat. Amer.
 Evang., 1958-61, 1967-72; Belize,
 1961-64; Puerto Rico, 1964-67
Wynkoop, Mildred Bangs, Japan, 1964-67
Wynkoop, Ralph Carl, Japan, 1964-67

York, Leonard Frank, Belize, 1952-59
York, Miriam Esther Cummins, Belize,
 1952-59
Young, E. E., Australia, 1960-67
Young, James, Casa Robles Dir., 1966-71
Youngblood, J. Leona (see Myers)

Zachary, E. E., Australia, 1946-48
Zahner, Gladys Naomi Owen, Swaziland,
 1946-61
Zanner, Richard F., Africa Reg. Dir., 1980—
Zanner, Valerie, Africa Reg. Off., 1980—

Zickefoose, Craig Leon, Ecuador, 1984-85; Haiti, 1985—

Zickefoose, Gail Louise, Ecuador, 1984-85; Haiti, 1985—

Zimmerman, Dwain, Peru, 1980-85; Bolivia, 1985-86

Zimmerman, Gary Gifford, Costa Rica, 1974-79

Zimmerman, Jerri Louise, Costa Rica, 1974-79

Zimmerman, Rosalie, Peru, 1980-85; Bolivia, 1985-86

Zumwalt, Nancy Jane Zellmer, Taiwan, 1971—

Zumwalt, Willis Hosmer, Taiwan, 1971—

Zurcher, Betty Lou (see Ayuso)

Zurcher, Harry John, Peru, 1945-58; Puerto Rico, 1958-72

Zurcher, Helen Elvina, Peru, 1945-58; Puerto Rico, 1958-72

Zurcher, Marjorie J., South Africa, 1975-85

Zurcher, Nina Carol, South Africa, 1958—

Zurcher, Norman Dale, South Africa, 1958—

Zurcher, Theodore W., South Africa, 1975-85

Observations:

1. Thirty-three persons have served 40 or more years as missionaries. Furlough years, including terminal furlough, are counted as part of that service.

45 Years:

>Annie Maude Anderson (Guatemala)
>Lula Schmelzenbach (Africa)

44 Years:

>H. K. Bedwell (Africa)
>Charles S. Jenkins (Africa)
>Pearl Jenkins (Africa)
>T. Harold Jones (Africa)

43 Years:

>Emily Maude Jones (Africa)
>Reginald Jones (Africa)
>G. Henry Pope (Africa)

42 Years:

>Mary Cooper (Africa)
>W. A. Eckel (Japan)

41 Years:

>Richard Simpson Anderson (Guatemala)
>Margaret Anderson Birchard (Guatemala/Nicaragua)
>Doris Brown (Africa)
>Fanny Dayhoff (Africa)
>I. E. Dayhoff (Africa)
>W. C. Esselstyn (Africa)
>Frank Ferguson (Cuba/South America)
>Lula Ferguson (Cuba/South America)
>Ellen Penn (Africa)—ret. 1986
>Joseph Penn, Jr. (Africa)—ret. 1986
>Gladys Pope (Africa)
>Orpha Speicher (India)

40 Years:

> Jean Darling (India)
> Everette Howard (Cape Verde/Lat. Amer./Casa Robles)
> Garnet Howard (Cape Verde/Lat. Amer./Casa Robles)
> Aletta Elizabeth Jones (Africa)
> Lillian Jones (Africa)
> Irma Koffell (Africa)

Also in the 40-years-or-more group are two couples who are still (1986) on the active missionary list: Bronell and Paula Greer, who began their work in India in 1944; and Earl and Gladys Mosteller, who began their service in the Portuguese-speaking world beginning in the Cape Verde Islands in 1946. Numerous missionaries are in the 35-39 years bracket.

2. Reflecting great versatility, some missionaries have served on a number of different fields outside the United States. Harold and Evelyn Stanfield hold the record, having worked in seven countries during their 37-year careers: Nicaragua, Bolivia, Panama, Costa Rica, El Salvador, Guatemala, and Chile. Gene and Mary Catherine Smith served on six different Caribbean islands (including the Bahamas). Six couples served on five different fields outside the U.S.A.: Lawrence and Betty Faul, William and Nadia Fowler, Ted and Mima Hughes, Charles S. and Pearl Jenkins, Berge and Doris Najarian, and Herb and Alice Ratcliff. Fifteen couples and three other single missionaries served in four countries.

Reference Notes

PART ONE

CHAPTER 1: *The Worldwide Mission of the Church*

1. Stephen Neill, *A History of Christian Missions* (Grand Rapids: Wm. B. Eerdmans Publishing Co., 1965), 74.

2. Ruth A. Tucker, *From Jerusalem to Irian Jaya* (Grand Rapids: Academic Books [Zondervan], 1983), 22.

3. Quoted ibid.

4. Neill, *History of Christian Missions*, 237.

5. Kenneth Scott Latourette, *A History of the Expansion of Christianity* (Grand Rapids: Zondervan Publishing House, 1970 reprint), 6:443.

6. Charles Edwin Jones, *Perfectionist Persuasion: The Holiness Movement and American Methodism, 1867-1936* (Metuchen, N.J.: Scarecrow Press, 1974), 54.

CHAPTER 2: *The Development of Nazarene World Mission Administration*

1. Timothy L. Smith, *Called unto Holiness* (Kansas City: Beacon Hill Press of Kansas City, 1962), 1:250.

2. *Beulah Christian,* Apr. 2, 1902, 3.

3. Mendell Taylor, *Fifty Years of Nazarene Missions* (Kansas City: Beacon Hill Press, 1952), 1:12.

4. *Minutes of the Eighth Annual Assembly, Church of the Nazarene*, printed in the *Nazarene Messenger,* Nov. 12, 1903, 5.

5. Smith, *Called unto Holiness* 1:174.

6. Ibid., 198.

7. *Herald of Holiness*, Feb. 24, 1915, 10.

8. *General Assembly Journal,* 1911, 39.

CHAPTER 3: *The Executive Secretary of the Department of World Missions*

1. The story of the 1964 Nazarene Evangelistic Ambassadors is found in H. T. Reza's book, *Ambassadors to Latin Lands* (Kansas City: Nazarene Publishing House, 1965), and of the 1966 teams in Paul Orjala's *Ambassador Diary* (Kansas City: Nazarene Publishing House, 1967).

2. R. Franklin Cook, *Crucible of Concern* (Kansas City: Nazarene Publishing House, 1974), 8.

CHAPTER 4: *The Director of the World Mission Division*

1. *Proceedings of the General Board,* 1976, 17.

2. *Proceedings of the General Board,* 1977, 133.

3. *World Mission,* July 1980, 3.

4. *Journal of the 20th General Assembly, Church of the Nazarene,* 1980, 515.

5. *World Mission,* R. Franklin Cook, ed., March 1986, 1.

6. *Journal of the 20th General Assembly,* 11-12.

7. Ibid., 237-38.

8. Interview with David Hayse.

9. *World Mission,* January 1986, 10.

CHAPTER 5: *The Nazarene World Mission Society*

1. Report to the First General Assembly, 1907, by Mrs. C. P. Lanpher.

2. *Journal of the General Assembly,* 1907, 26.

3. *Journal of the General Assembly,* 1915, 60-61.

4. Ibid., 63.

5. James Hudson, *Work and Witness* (Kansas City: Nazarene Publishing House, 1983), 23.

6. *NWMS Handbook and Constitution,* 1985-89, 2.

7. *Other Sheep,* April 1924, 7.

8. *Handbook and Constitution,* 2.

CHAPTER 6: *Support Programs of World Mission*

1. Hudson, *Work and Witness,* 84.

2. *Work and Witness Handbook,* n.d., 10.

3. R. Franklin Cook and Steve Weber, *The Greening* (Kansas City: Nazarene Publishing House, 1986), 17.

PART TWO

I. AFRICA REGION

1. Correspondence in H. F. Reynolds' papers, Nazarene Archives, Kansas City. Actually there were probably 20 or more missionaries in the country, but that did not diminish the need or the opportunity.

2. Helpful details concerning the beginning of the work in Swaziland came from Mark Wessels, "A History of the Start of Nazarene Missions in Africa" (Master's thesis, University of Kansas, 1984).

3. Letter from Lula Schmelzenbach to H. F. Reynolds, Aug. 11, 1911, in Nazarene Archives.

4. *Other Sheep,* February 1926, 2.

5. Minutes of the African Field Council of the Church of the Nazarene, 1944, Committee Reports.

6. General Board of Foreign Missions Statistical Report, 1921-22.

II. ASIAN REGION

1. *Other Sheep,* April 1950, inside back cover.

IV. MEXICO, CENTRAL AMERICA, AND CARIBBEAN REGION

1. *Minutes of the General Board,* 1970, 45.

Index

This is a limited index in that not all the names and subjects appearing in the text are included. An effort has been made, however, to list at least all those who have occupied pioneer or leadership positions or have served on multiple fields. We beg the indulgence of those whose names should have been here but were inadvertently omitted. Note also that the appendixes are not indexed.

676 / Mission to the World

Printed in the United States
1545000004B/22-102